MW01156420

"Joe Sprinkle's commentary presents the best of evangelical scholarship on Daniel: an even-handed evaluation of the most recent thought on both individual passages and the theology of the book as a whole. While he strives to present his own view of the theological questions raised by Daniel, he also respectfully interacts with other scholars, allowing readers to grasp his method while also evaluating what others have to say."

Andrew Steinmann, *distinguished professor of theology and Hebrew, Concordia University Chicago*

"Dr. Sprinkle has produced a clear, well-researched commentary on a very difficult book. The introduction lays out the important issues necessary for understanding the book of Daniel, and the difficult issues are handled fairly while maintaining a conservative, evangelical perspective for the book. His attempt to provide a biblical-theological commentary that pulls together almost one hundred pages of biblical themes found in the book of Daniel may prove to be its greatest asset. Also, his discussion on Daniel 9:24–27 is even-handed and well-researched. I highly recommend this commentary from a very able scholar."

Paul D. Wegner, *distinguished professor of the Old Testament, Gateway Seminary*

DANIEL

DANIEL

Evangelical Biblical Theology Commentary

General Editors

T. Desmond Alexander, Thomas R. Schreiner,
Andreas J. Köstenberger

Assistant Editors

James M. Hamilton, Kenneth A. Mathews,
Terry L. Wilder

Joe M. Sprinkle

LEXHAM PRESS

Daniel
Evangelical Biblical Theology Commentary

Copyright 2020 Joe M. Sprinkle

Lexham Press, 1313 Commercial St., Bellingham, WA 98225
LexhamPress.com

Print ISBN 9781683594246
Library of Congress Control Number 2020941624

General Editors: T. Desmond Alexander, Thomas R. Schreiner,
    Andreas J. Köstenberger
Assistant Editors: James M. Hamilton, Kenneth A. Mathews, Terry L. Wilder
Lexham Editorial: Derek Brown, Josh Philpot, Danielle Thevenaz
Cover Design: Brittany Schrock

DEDICATION

In memory of my teachers,
Gleason Archer and Isaac Jerusalmi,
who taught me Aramaic and who in
their distinctive ways contributed
to my understanding of
the book of Daniel

CONTENTS

GENERAL EDITORS' PREFACE

I n recent years biblical theology has seen a remarkable resurgence. Whereas, in 1970, Brevard Childs wrote *Biblical Theology in Crisis*, the quest for the Bible's own theology has witnessed increasing vitality since Childs prematurely decried the demise of the movement. Nowhere has this been truer than in evangelical circles. It could be argued that evangelicals, with their commitment to biblical inerrancy and inspiration, are perfectly positioned to explore the Bible's unified message. At the same time, as D. A. Carson has aptly noted, perhaps the greatest challenge faced by biblical theologians is how to handle the Bible's manifest diversity and how to navigate the tension between its unity and diversity in a way that does justice to both.[1]

What is biblical theology? And how is biblical theology different from related disciplines such as systematic theology? These two exceedingly important questions must be answered by anyone who would make a significant contribution to the discipline. Regarding the first question, the most basic answer might assert that biblical theology, in essence, is *the theology of the Bible*, that is, the theology expressed by the respective writers of the various biblical books *on their own terms* and *in their own historical contexts*. Biblical theology is the attempt to understand and embrace *the interpretive perspective of the biblical authors*. What is more, biblical theology is the theology of the *entire* Bible, an exercise in *whole-Bible theology*. For this reason biblical theology is not just a modern academic discipline; its roots are found already in the use of earlier Old Testament portions in later Old Testament writings and in the use of the Old Testament in the New.

---

[1] D. A. Carson, "New Testament Theology," in *DLNT* 810.

Biblical theology thus involves a close study of *the use of the Old Testament in the Old Testament* (that is, the use of, say, Deuteronomy by Jeremiah, or of the Pentateuch by Isaiah). Biblical theology also entails the investigation of *the use of the Old Testament in the New*, both in terms of individual passages and in terms of larger christological or soteriological themes. Biblical theology may proceed *book by book*, trace *central themes* in Scripture, or seek to place the contributions of individual biblical writers within the framework of the Bible's larger overarching *metanarrative*, that is, the Bible's developing story from Genesis through Revelation at whose core is *salvation* or *redemptive history*, the account of God's dealings with humanity and his people Israel and the church from creation to new creation.

In this quest for the Bible's own theology, we will be helped by the inquiries of those who have gone before us in the *history of the church*. While we can profitably study the efforts of interpreters over the entire sweep of the history of biblical interpretation since patristic times, we can also benefit from the labors of scholars since J. P. Gabler, whose programmatic inaugural address at the University of Altdorf, Germany, in 1787 marks the inception of the discipline in modern times. Gabler's address bore the title "On the Correct Distinction between Dogmatic and Biblical Theology and the Right Definition of Their Goals."[2] While few (if any) within evangelicalism would fully identify with Gabler's program, the proper distinction between dogmatic and biblical theology (that is, between biblical and systematic theology) continues to be an important issue to be adjudicated by practitioners of both disciplines, and especially biblical theology. We have already defined biblical theology as whole-Bible theology, describing the theology of the various biblical books *on their own terms* and *in their own historical contexts*. Systematic theology, by contrast, is more topically oriented and focused on contemporary contextualization. While there are different ways in which the relationship between biblical and systematic theology can be construed, maintaining a proper distinction between the two disciplines arguably continues to be vital if both are to achieve their objectives.

---

[2] The original Latin title was *Oratio de iusto discrimine theologiae biblicae et dogmaticae regundisque recte utriusque finibus.*

The present set of volumes constitutes an ambitious project, seeking to explore the theology of the Bible in considerable depth, spanning both Testaments. Authors come from a variety of backgrounds and perspectives, though all affirm the inerrancy and inspiration of Scripture. United in their high view of Scripture and in their belief in the underlying unity of Scripture, which is ultimately grounded in the unity of God himself, each author explores the contribution of a given book or group of books to the theology of Scripture as a whole. While conceived as stand-alone volumes, each volume thus also makes a contribution to the larger whole. All volumes provide a discussion of introductory matters, including the historical setting and the literary structure of a given book of Scripture. Also included is an exegetical treatment of all the relevant passages in succinct commentary-style format. The biblical theology approach of the series will also inform and play a role in the commentary proper. The commentator permits a discussion between the commentary proper and the biblical theology it reflects by a series of cross-references.

The major contribution of each volume, however, is a thorough discussion of the most important themes of the biblical book in relation to the canon as a whole. This format allows each contributor to ground biblical theology, as is proper, in an appropriate appraisal of the relevant historical and literary features of a particular book in Scripture while at the same time focusing on its major theological contribution to the entire Christian canon in the context of the larger salvation-historical metanarrative of Scripture. Within this overall format, there will be room for each individual contributor to explore the major themes of his or her particular corpus in the way he or she sees most appropriate for the material under consideration. For some books of the Bible, it may be best to have these theological themes set out in advance of the exegetical commentary. For other books it may be better to explain the theological themes after the commentary. Consequently, each contributor has the freedom to order these sections as best suits the biblical material under consideration so that the discussion of biblical-theological themes may precede or follow the exegetical commentary.

This format, in itself, would already be a valuable contribution to biblical theology. But other series try to accomplish a survey of the Bible's theology as well. What distinguishes the present series is its orientation toward Christian proclamation. This is the Biblical Theology *for Christian Proclamation* commentary series! As a result, the ultimate purpose of this set of volumes is not exclusively, or even primarily, academic. Rather, we seek to relate biblical theology to our own lives and to the life of the church. Our desire is to equip those in Christian ministry who are called by God to preach and teach the precious truths of Scripture to their congregations, both in North America and in a global context.

The base translation for the Biblical Theology for Christian Proclamation commentary series is the Christian Standard Bible (CSB). The CSB places equal value on faithfulness to the original languages and readability for a modern audience. The contributors, however, have the liberty to differ with the CSB as they comment on the biblical text. Note that, in the CSB, OT passages that are quoted in the NT are set in boldface type.

We hope and pray that the forty volumes of this series, once completed, will bear witness to the unity in diversity of the canon of Scripture as they probe the individual contributions of each of its sixty-six books. The authors and editors are united in their desire that in so doing the series will magnify the name of Christ and bring glory to the triune God who revealed himself in Scripture so that everyone who calls on the name of the Lord will be saved—to the glory of God the Father and his Son, the Lord Jesus Christ, under the illumination of the Holy Spirit, and for the good of his church. To God alone be the glory: *soli Deo gloria.*

LIST OF ABBREVIATIONS

ABD	*Anchor Bible Dictionary*
AUSS	*Andrews University Seminary Studies*
BDAG	Bauer, W., F. W. Danker, W. F. Arndt, and F. W. Gingrich. *Greek-English Lexicon of the New Testament and Other Early Christian Literature*. 3rd ed. Chicago, 1999
BDB	Brown, F., S. R. Driver, and C. A. Briggs. *A Hebrew and English Lexicon of the Old Testament*. Oxford, 1907
BSac	*Bibliotheca Sacra*
CAD	*Chicago Assyrian Dictionary*
CBQ	*Catholic Biblical Quarterly*
CEB	Common English Bible (2011)
CEV	Contemporary English Version (1995)
COS	*Context of Scripture*. Ed. W. Hallo and K. Younger. 3 vols. Leiden, 1997–2002
CSB	Christian Standard Bible (2017)
D-stem	*pi'el* (Hebrew), *pa'el* (Aramaic), Semitic stems with similar meanings that double middle consonant of root (German *Doppelstamm*)
DSS	Dead Sea Scrolls
ESV	English Standard Version (2001)
EvQ	*Evangelical Quarterly*
EVV	English Versions
G-stem	the basic stem (German *Grundstamm*), *qal* (Hebrew), *pe'al* (Aramaic)
GNT	Good News Translation

GW	GOD'S WORD Translation (1995)
H-stem	*hiphʿil* (Hebrew), *haphʿel* (Aramaic), causative stems characterized by a prefect ה
HALOT	*The Hebrew and Aramaic Lexicon of the Old Testament.* L. Koehler, W. Baumgartner, and J. J. Stamm. Translated and edited under the supervision of M. E. J. Richardson. 5 vols. Leiden, 1994–2000
HB	Hebrew Bible (= MT Masoretic Text)
HNTC	Holman New Testament Commentary
HtD	*Hithpaʿel* (Hebrew), *Hithpaʿal* (Aramaic), the reflective/passive of the D-stem
HUCA	*Hebrew Union College Annual*
ICC	International Critical Commentary
IBHS	*An Introduction to Biblical Hebrew Syntax.* B. K. Waltke and M. O'Connor. Winona Lake, Indiana, 1990
JAOS	*Journal of the American Oriental Society*
JBL	*Journal of Biblical Literature*
JETS	*Journal of the Evangelical Theological Society*
JSOT	*Journal for the Study of the Old Testament*
KJV	King James Version (1611)
LCL	Loeb Classical Library
LEB	Lexham English Bible (2012)
LHBOTS	Library of Hebrew Bible/Old Testament Studies
LXX	Septuagint (early Greek translation of the Old Testament)
NABRE	New American Bible, Revised Edition
NAC	New American Commentary
NASB	New American Standard Bible (1995)
NBD	*New Bible Dictionary.* Edited by J. D. Douglas, N. Hillyer, D. Wood. 3rd ed. Downers Grove, 1996
NIDB	*New Interpreter's Dictionary of the Bible.* 5 volumes. Edited by K. Sakenfeld. Nashville. 2006–2009
NIV	New International Version (2011)

NJPS	Tanakh: The Holy Scriptures: The New Jewish Publication Society Translation according to the Traditional Hebrew Text (1985)
NKJV	New King James Version (1982)
NLT	New Living Translation (2015)
NRSV	New Revised Standard Version (1989)
NT	New Testament
OT	Old Testament
OTE	*Old Testament Essays*
OTL	Old Testament Library (series)
Š-stem	*Shaphel* (Aramaic causative stem)
Sanh.	Sanhedrin
TDOT	*Theological Dictionary of the Old Testament*. Edited by G. J. Botterweck and H. Ringgren. Translated by J. T. Willis, G. W. Bromiley, and D. E. Green. 15 vols. Grand Rapids, 1974–2006
TLOT	*Theological Lexicon of the Old Testament*. Edited by E. Jenni, with assistance from C. Westermann. Translated by M. E. Biddle. 3 vols. Peabody, Mass., 1997
TOTC	Tyndale Old Testament Commentaries
VT	*Vetus Testamentum*
VTSup	Supplements to Vetus Testamentum
WBC	Word Biblical Commentary
ZAW	*Zeitschrift für die alttestamentliche Wissenschaft*

INTRODUCTION

I. The Story of Daniel

The book of Daniel tells the story of a certain Jewish man named Daniel and his companions Hananiah, Mishael, and Azariah (later known as Shadrach, Meshach, and Abednego) who were taken to Babylon "in the third year of the reign of King Jehoiakim of Judah" (1:1; roughly 605 BC, see below). The exile of Daniel and his friends occurred some years before the exile of other Jews to Babylon. The exile of King Jehoiachin (Jehoiakim's son) and his entourage occurred in 597 BC, and the exile of many others occurred in c. 586 BC after the destruction of Jerusalem by Babylon.

The stories and prophecies of Daniel cover a period of time from Daniel's exile through the fall of Babylon to Darius the Mede and through the third year of King Cyrus of Persia (Dan 10:1). Thus, the story of Daniel covers a period of almost seventy years. These accounts depict Daniel and his Jewish friends remaining faithful to God despite a hostile environment. They were willing to die rather than disobey God. The book also indicates that Daniel had a God-given ability to interpret dreams and that he received revelations concerning the future of his people and of world empires, leading up to the end of history and the establishment of the kingdom of God.

II. Languages and Structure

Daniel begins and closes in the Hebrew language, but Dan 2:4b–7:28 is written in Aramaic, a Semitic language related to Hebrew but clearly distinguishable from it. Some scholars suggest that the

1

book was originally written in Aramaic and that the beginning and end were translated into Hebrew to give it a better reception among Jews.[1] But if that were the motive, why not translate all of it? Was the Aramaic portion originally a separate composition? Against this is the fact that the Aramaic of Daniel 7 crosses a genre boundary: In chapter 7 the book transitions from narrative to apocalyptic visions.

By genre the book divides as follows:

I. Court Narratives (Daniel 1–6)
   Daniel and friends in Nebuchadnezzar's court (Daniel 1)
   Daniel interprets Nebuchadnezzar's dream of a statue
      (Daniel 2)
   Shadrach, Meshach, and Abednego in the fiery furnace
      (Daniel 3)
   Daniel interprets Nebuchadnezzar's dream of a tree
      (Daniel 4)
   Daniel interprets the handwriting on the wall (Daniel 5)
   Daniel and the lion's den (Daniel 6)

II. Visions of Daniel (Daniel 7–12)
   First vision: Four beasts and the son of man figure (Daniel 7)
   Second vision: Ram and male goat (Daniel 8)
   Third vision: Seventy weeks (Daniel 9)
   Fourth vision: Kings of North/South, distress/resurrection
      (Daniel 10–12)

The Aramaic portion of the book has a striking chiastic structure that shows literary unity.

(A) A dream about four earthly kingdoms and God's kingdom (Daniel 2)
   (B) A story about Judeans who are faithful in the face of death (Daniel 3)
      (C) A story about royal pride that is humbled (Daniel 4)
      (C′) A story about royal pride that is humbled (Daniel 5)

---

[1] H. L. Ginsburg, "The Composition of the Book of Daniel," *VT* 4 (1954): 246–75.

(B′) A story about a Judean who is faithful in the face of death (Daniel 6)

(A′) A vision about four earthly kingdoms and God's kingdom (Daniel 7).[2]

This chiasm intertwines with another chiasm that together incorporate the whole book.[3] This shows that the final form of the book has a unified structure[4] that transcends genre and language divisions:

(A) Beginning of story (Dan 1:1–21)
- (B) Dream about four world kingdoms ended by the kingdom of God (Dan 2:1–49)
  - (C) Judeans faithful in the face of death (Dan 3:1–30)
    - (D) Royal pride humbled (Dan 4:1–37)
    - (D′) Royal pride humbled (Dan 5:1–31)
  - (C′) A Judean faithful in the face of death (Dan 6:1–28)
- (B′) Vision about four world kingdoms ended by the kingdom of God (Dan 7:1–28)
  - (E) Vision of Persian and Greek kingdoms to Antiochus (Dan 8:1–27)
    - (F) Vision of seventy weeks (Dan 9:1–27)
  - (E′) Vision of Persian and Greek kingdoms to Antiochus (Dan 10:1–11:35)
- (B″) World kingdoms ended and the righteous established (Dan 11:36–12:3)

(A′) End of story: Vision sealed until the end (Dan 12:4–13)

Why is there Aramaic in Daniel? Archer suggests that the Aramaic part of Daniel has to do with the "nations," and would be

---

[2] E. C. Lucas, "Daniel: Book of," in *Dictionary of the Old Testament: Prophets*, ed. M. J. Boda and G. J. McConville (Downers Grove: IVP Academic, 2012), 110.

[3] Compare the similar analysis of R. R. Lessing and A. E. Steinmann, *Prepare the Way of the Lord: An Introduction to the Old Testament* (St. Louis: Concordia, 2014), 438.

[4] Some critical scholars also argue for the unity of the book. E.g., H. H. Rowley, "The Unity of the Book of Daniel," *HUCA* 23 (1950): 233–73; cf. Rowley, *The Servant of the Lord and Other Essays on the Old Testament*, 2nd ed. (London: Oxford, 1965), 249–80. Rowley argued vigorously for the unity of Daniel based on the interrelatedness of the two parts of the book and the continuity of style.

of special interest to the "citizenry of the Babylonian and the Persian empires" for whom Imperial Aramaic was the international language of trade and diplomacy, whereas the rest of the book would be of more specific interest to the Jews.[5] This view can be supplemented with Snell's suggestion that Daniel's use of Aramaic (like Ezra's) serves to strive for authenticity when citing the speech of foreigners.[6]

III. A Bi-Genre Book: Narrative and Apocalyptic Visions

Daniel consists of two major genres: narrative and apocalyptic visions.

A. The Court Narratives (Daniel 1–6)

Daniel 1–6 is a third-person narrative account of Daniel and his companions in the court of the kings of Babylon. Daniel 4 is a first-person narrative by Nebuchadnezzar about his dealings with Daniel. Although there are prophecies within these narratives, including Nebuchadnezzar's apocalyptic dream of Daniel 2, the overall genre is clearly narrative. These narratives as a whole have a didactic function, teaching the people of God how to live in a hostile, gentile environment.

B. Autobiographical Apocalyptic Visions (Daniel 7–12)

Though introduced by the narrator (Dan 7:1–2a), the last six chapters of the book consist of a first-person account by Daniel, as if taken from a diary or an autobiography. The four visions of Daniel 7–12 do not match the chronological sequence of Daniel 1–6 but begin with the first year of Belshazzar and relate events at various points in time.

Daniel 7	First year of Belshazzar (c. 552 BC)
Daniel 8	Belshazzar's third year (c. 549 BC)
Daniel 9	First year of Darius (538 BC)
Daniel 10–12	Third year of Cyrus (536 BC)

---

[5] G. L. Archer, "Daniel," in *The Expositor's Bible Commentary*, ed. Frank E. Gaebelein, vol. 7 (Grand Rapids: Zondervan, 1985), 6; Archer, *Survey of Old Testament Introduction*, 3rd ed. (Chicago: Moody, 1994), 391.

[6] D. C. Snell, "Why is there Aramaic in the Bible?" *JSOT* 18 (1980): 83–100.

Apocalyptic[7] is a genre of biblical and extra-biblical writings. The term derives from *apokalupsis*, the Greek word used in the title and first sentence of the book of Revelation ("Apocalypse," meaning "the unveiling"). Daniel and Revelation are regarded as apocalyptic books. Other biblical books have apocalyptic elements: parts of Ezekiel, Isaiah 24–27, Zechariah, the Olivet Discourse (Matthew 24, Mark 13, Luke 21), and Paul's Thessalonian letters. Books outside the Bible labeled apocalyptic are *1 Enoch, Jubilees, Sibylline Oracles* (Books 3–5), *Testaments of the Twelve Patriarchs, Psalms of Solomon, Assumption of Moses, Martyrdom of Isaiah, Apocalypse of Moses, Apocalypse of Abraham, Testament of Abraham, 2 Enoch,* 2 Esdras (= *4 Ezra*), *2 Baruch,* and *3 Baruch.* Among the Dead Sea Scrolls are *War Scroll, Book of Mysteries, Prayer of Nabonidus,* and *Genesis Apocryphon.*

Typical features of apocalyptic include (1) esoteric revelations that emphasize the revealing of hidden mysteries, (2) highly symbolic visions, like an impressionistic painting in which much makes little sense but the whole is clear, and (3) a theology that expresses the belief that, though situations seem hopeless as far as human deliverance is concerned, God is transcendent and sovereign (see §3.4, §3.8).

These theological premises lead to many derived corollaries: Since circumstances are hopeless, one must look not to human strength for deliverance but to God. Events happen because of God's will, and everything is moving forward according to God's predetermined plan. Apocalyptic literature contains black-and-white contrasts without many shades of gray. Sharp dichotomies exist between good and evil, between God and the world, and between the present age and the age to come. Since God is transcendent, he does not have immediate contact with men. Accordingly, most apocalyptic writings speak of angels mediating revelation to men. Since God is sovereign, the kingdom of God will be ultimately victorious. The sun, moon, and stars are often involved in the final judgment and victory of God. Persecutors will not escape their oppression against the people of God. Instead God will condemn them at a last judgment.

---

[7] For more on apocalyptic, see D. S. Russell, *The Method and Message of Jewish Apocalyptic,* OTL (Philadelphia: Westminster, 1964). The present discussion draws heavily on Russell's work.

Most of these elements are seen in the apocalyptic portions of Daniel, which is a mixture of narrative and apocalyptic. Moreover, as will be seen below on authorship, critical scholars and conservative scholars typically have different understandings of how distinct apocalyptic as a genre is from the genre of biblical prophecy.

IV. Authorship and Historicity of Daniel

Probably in no book outside of the Pentateuch do traditional-conservative scholars and critical scholars differ as sharply as they do over the book of Daniel. Traditional conservatives say that the book portrays Daniel as a real, historical person of the sixth century BC and that the book contains his genuine prognostications. They believe that Daniel wrote the autobiographical part of the book (Daniel 7–12) and that the narratives about Daniel (Daniel 1–6), if not autobiographic, record what Daniel and his friends actually did in history. This assumes that Daniel was completed around the fifth century BC during the Achaemenid period of Persian history that begins with Cyrus and continues through the fall of the Persian Empire to Alexander the Great in 331 BC.

The most conservative view of Daniel's authorship is defended by Gleason Archer.[8] He argues that even the third person narratives about Daniel were written by Daniel in the sixth century BC following a literary convention seen also in the writings of Xenophon's *Anabasis* and arguably by John in John 21:24, in which one describes oneself in third-person narration. This kind of narration would be fitting for a book from the hand of a literary genius like Daniel, to whom God gave "knowledge and understanding in every kind of literature" (Dan 1:17). That said, it seems simpler to say that the third-person narration comes from a biographer and that only the autobiographical part (Daniel 7–12)—itself introduced by the narrator (7:1–2a)—comes directly from the hand of Daniel. The biographer then is an unknown disciple of Daniel,[9] perhaps writing in the late sixth or early fifth century. This unknown narrator organized the framework of the book and incorporated into it the autobiographic

---

[8] Archer, "Daniel," 4.

[9] A. E. Hill and J. H. Walton, *A Survey of the Old Testament*, 2nd ed. (Grand Rapids: Zondervan, 2000), 454. Similarly, T. Longman and R. Dillard, *An Introduction to the Old Testament*, 2nd ed. (Grand Rapids: Zondervan, 2006), 373.

writings of Nebuchadnezzar (Daniel 4) and the autobiographical visions of Daniel (Daniel 7–12).

What is essential for the traditional-conservative position is that the book records actual history and true, predictive prophecy. Traditional conservatives believe that by supernatural revelation Daniel prophetically anticipated many events known by us now to have occurred during the Persian, Greek, and Roman periods of Palestinian history. He also foresees matters related to the end times. To the traditional conservative, Daniel has some of the clearest, most-specifically fulfilled prophecy in the entire Bible, proving the supernatural nature of the revelation made to Daniel. This is in contrast with the anti-supernatural bias of most who affirm the critical view.

Most critical scholars, and some who self-identify as evangelicals or conservatives,[10] look at the book entirely differently. Typically, they see the book as fictional or, more precisely, historicized fiction. Since the book is fictional, Daniel is not a historically accurate description of events during the sixth century BC. Moreover, the autobiographical parts are pseudepigraphic or pseudonymous. In other words, the autobiographical sections in Daniel 4 and 7–12 were written and put into the mouth of Nebuchadnezzar and Daniel respectively by an unknown author or authors who actually wrote before 164 BC, the time of the Maccabean revolt against the Seleucid king Antiochus IV Epiphanes who tried to abolish the Jewish religion.[11] To these scholars, the book of Daniel as a whole is a "tract for hard times" to embolden Jews in the face of persecution by Antiochus IV to show courage and faith. John Hayes puts it this way: "The central figure of the book of Daniel probably does not reflect any historical personage but is instead to be associated with the legendary and wise Daniel [about which there is much folklore]."[12]

---

[10] E.g., George Beasley-Murray, "A Conservative Thinks Again about Daniel," *Baptist Quarterly* 12 (1948): 341–46, 366–71; J. E. Goldingay, *Daniel*, WBC 30 (Dallas: Word, 1989); E. C. Lucas, *Daniel*, Apollos Old Testament Commentary (Downers Grove: InterVarsity, 2002).

[11] E.g., W. Porteous, *Daniel: A Commentary*, OTL (Philadelphia: Westminster, 1965), 13.

[12] J. Hayes, *An Introduction to Old Testament Study* (Nashville: Abingdon, 1979), 368.

According to the critical view, what appears to be predictive prophecy in the book is actually apocalyptic rather than real prophecy (on apocalyptic, see discussion in previous section above). The predictions refer to things that already occurred before the book was completed. It is thus prophecy after the event (*vaticinium ex eventu*) or history in the guise of prophecy. Apocalyptic was a literary style of writing that became popular in the intertestamental period. Apocalyptic works outside of the Bible are typically pseudepigraphic, use wild imagery, and anticipate the end of the world. Porteous, speaking for the critical view, states,

> The only element of genuine prophecy relates to the anticipated death of Antiochus and the expected intervention of God in the establishment of his kingdom. Everything else that is "revealed" to Daniel is history viewed in retrospect either in symbol or as interpreted to Daniel, or in one case, by Daniel to a heathen king[13]

Moreover, this "genuine" prophecy about Antiochus' death is in fact inaccurate prophecy which did not occur as predicted. According to the typical critical view, one knows where prophecy after the fact ends and where true prediction begins at the very point where the prophecy fails. Thus the critical view sees virtually nothing supernatural about the predictions in Daniel.

I will now offer the arguments in favor of both views, first the critical view, followed by arguments for a traditional-conservative view of Daniel.

A. Case for a Maccabean Date and the Fictional Nature of Daniel

1. Daniel was not included among the Prophets but in the Writings in the Hebrew canon. According to a critical reconstruction of the development of the canon popularized by H. E. Ryle[14] and still followed by many critical scholars, canonization follows the three divisions of the Hebrew Bible. The law was made canonical first, perhaps around 400 BC, and next the Prophets around 200 BC. Then the Writings were made canonical in a process completed at the so-called Council of Jamnia (AD 90). According to scholars like

---

[13] Porteous, *Daniel*, 13.

[14] H. E. Ryle, *The Canon of the Old Testament*, 2nd ed. (London: Macmillan, 1909).

Ryle, Daniel was not included in the book of the Prophets because it was not yet completed in 200 BC when the canon of the Prophets was closed. This is consistent with the critical view that dates the completion of the book of Daniel to the time of the Maccabees.

2. The presence of Persian and Greek words proves Daniel was written late. Daniel is alleged to have lived in Babylon during the Neo-Babylonian Empire and shortly after its fall. It is therefore strange to find in the book not only many non-Semitic Persian words but also Greek words. How would these Persian and Greek words have found their way into the Semitic language of Daniel? Critical scholars typically say that Daniel was composed during and after the Persian Empire period, allowing the Persian language more than two centuries to influence the Hebrew and Aramaic language used in the book. Aramaic was especially influenced by Persian during the Persian period because Aramaic was the *lingua franca*, or international language of diplomacy and commerce. Greek words are found in the Aramaic of Daniel, according to critical scholars, because the book of Daniel was completed after the Persian Empire fell to Alexander the Great. Alexander took Tyre and Palestine c. 332, and by 331 had defeated Darius III to conquer the Persian Empire. Although Alexander's kingdom broke up, Greek culture remained under his generals who took over Egypt, Syria-Babylonia, Asia Minor, and Thrace. Daniel was completed, according to critical scholars, near the end of the reign of Antiochus IV (175–164 BC), who tried to Hellenize the Jews. If Daniel was completed shortly before 164 BC, it is understandable that Greek and Persian words would creep into its language.

3. Daniel contains alleged historical errors. Critical scholars typically argue that the author of Daniel betrays his second-century BC milieu by making a number of historical errors in his portrayal of the sixth century BC. This occurs, they say, because he had no first-hand knowledge of the sixth century BC. Among the alleged errors are the following.

a. Darius the Mede never existed. The book of Daniel attributes the conquest of Babylon to Darius the Mede, while historically it was accomplished by Cyrus of Persia. The Medes, whose empire was north and east of the Babylonian Empire, never conquered Babylon. Daniel arguably confuses a later emperor of Persia named Darius with the conqueror of Babylon. Cuneiform materials contemporaneous with the fall of Babylon that give an extra-biblical account of Babylon's fall and describe who governed Babylon mention no person by the name of Darius the Mede.

b. Belshazzar was not the last king of Babylon nor was he the son of Nebuchadnezzar. Daniel makes Belshazzar (cuneiform *Bēl-šar-uṣur*) the last king of Babylon, but the last king was actually Nabonidus. As far as we know from extra-biblical sources, Belshazzar was never more than the crown prince. Moreover, the writer of Daniel calls Nebuchadnezzar the father of Belshazzar (5:2, 11, 13, 18) when historically Belshazzar's father was Nabonidus, who did not have a blood relationship with Nebuchadnezzar.

Extra-biblical data indicates that the last king of Babylon was Nabonidus (*Nabu-nâid*), who ruled Babylon from 555–539 BC. But a strange thing happened during his reign: For some ten years Nabonidus left Babylon and went five hundred miles into the Arabian desert to Teima while his son Belshazzar was *de facto* ruler in Babylon (for details see comments at Dan 7:1). Nabonidus was a devotee of the moon god Sin, something he had learned from his mother Adad-guppi, who may have been a priestess of Sin at Harran. Nabonidus was the son of Nabu-balaṭsu-iqbi, not Nebuchadnezzar.

Belshazzar is never called king by Babylonian records even while Nabonidus was at Teima. Belshazzar may have ruled in Nabonidus' absence, but officially he was designated as the crown prince rather than king as Daniel calls him.

c. The siege of Jerusalem recorded in Dan 1:1 arguably never occurred, and its chronology contradicts Jeremiah. In Dan 1:1 Nebuchadnezar lays siege to Jerusalem in the "third year of the reign of King Jehoiakim." But Jeremiah 25 seems to imply that the Babylonian army had not yet entered Judah at this point. According to Jer 25:1, the *first* year of Nebuchadnezzar was the *fourth* year of Jehoiakim. In the fourth year of Jehoiakim, Nebuchadnezzar was still occupied with fighting the Egyptians at Carchemish (Jer 46:2), so it does not seem possible that he could have gone south to threaten Jerusalem as early as Jehoiakim's third year.

d. The prophecy about Antiochus IV in Daniel 11 is alleged to have failed. The first part of the Daniel 11 prophecy is reasonably accurate, according to critical scholars, because it is not real prediction but an example of *vaticinium ex eventu* ("prophecy after the event"). On the other hand, the prophecy concerning the end of the life of Antiochus IV Epiphanes is wrong, owing to its being real pre-diction rather than prediction after the fact. Hence, the "prophecy" can be dated to shortly before 164 BC, the point at which the proph-ecy goes astray.

Daniel 11:2–4 describes the period from Cyrus king of Persia to the period of the breakup of Alexander the Great's kingdom. Daniel 11:5–35 describes wars between the various kings of the South (the Ptolemaic Empire in Egypt founded in 323 by Ptolemy I) and various kings of the North (the Seleucid Empire founded in 312 by Seleucus I). This culminates in the life of Antiochus IV Epiphanes (175–164). These events can be correlated with known historical events during this period. But when Daniel 11:36–45 describes the reign and fall of Antiochus IV, critical scholars think the author betrays himself. The alleged final victorious war with Egypt, including the conquest of the Cyrenaics and Ethiopia, seems imaginary. Antiochus' demise was supposed to be between the Mediterranean Sea and Jerusalem in the holy land, but in fact he died at Tabea in Persia. At this point, according to critical scholars, the author goes from history in the guise of prophecy to genuine prediction, disclosing the date of his prediction by its failure.

e. Daniel misunderstands the history of world empires as shown in the identity of the four kingdoms of Daniel 2 and 7. In accordance with the late date for Daniel one common critical inter-pretation of the kingdoms of Daniel 2 and 7 can be described as follows:

TYPICAL CRITICAL UNDERSTANDING OF DANIEL'S FOUR KINGDOMS

	BABYLON	MEDIA	PERSIA	GREEKS
Daniel 2	Head of Gold	Breast of Silver	Belly of Brass	Legs of Iron/clay
Daniel 7	Lion	Bear	Leopard	Fourth Beast (Little horn = Antiochus IV)

Hence the author of Daniel follows events down to his own day, during the time of the Maccabees under the Greek rulers of Seleucid and Ptolemaic branches (cf. Daniel 11 described above). This scheme usually assumes that the author mistakenly thought that Media and

Persia successively conquered Babylonia and thus sees the book making yet another historical error.

Another view of the kingdoms in Daniel 2 and 7 that is consistent with the Maccabean dating of the book is as follows: (1) Babylon, (2) Medes/Persians, (3) Alexander, and (4) successors of Alexander (perhaps more specifically the Seleucid Empire).[15] According to Jerome, this was the view of the third/fourth-century anti-Christian, Neoplatonic philosopher Porphyry of Tyre.[16]

Lucas, Pierce, and Gurney[17] argue that one can identify Daniel's four kingdoms as Babylon, Medes, Persians, and Greeks without accusing Daniel of error. Perhaps the book of Daniel looks at things through the eyes of Jews in exile, some of whom were in captivity "in the cities of the Medes" (2 Kgs 17:6; 18:11). Judeans were interested in the plight of their northern kindred, as were the prophets (e.g., Jeremiah 30–31; Ezekiel 37; Micah 5). The prayer in Daniel 9 expresses distress for "all Israel—those who are near and those who are far, in all the countries where you have banished them" (Dan 9:7). If these four kingdoms are presented sequentially but allowed to overlap chronologically, then one need not say Daniel's portrayal is in error. Gurney even affirms that these are real predictive prophecies that go back to the historical Daniel. Without specifically endorsing the view, evangelical scholar John Walton suggests that the following interpretation should be seriously considered: (1) Assyria-Babylonia, (2) Media, (3) Media-Persia, (4) Alexander and successors.[18]

While some conservative scholars have adopted schemes along the lines of the critical view without concluding Daniel's description of the four kingdoms is erroneous historically, any identification of the fourth kingdom as Greece is consistent with the Maccabean dating and fictional character of the book. The traditional-conservative

---

[15] Cf. W. S. LaSor, D. A. Hubbard, F. W. Bush, *Old Testament Survey* (Grand Rapids: Eerdmans, 1982), 669; Archer, "Daniel," 48.

[16] St. Jerome, *Jerome's Commentary on Daniel*, trans. G. L. Archer (Grand Rapids: Baker, 1958), 77.

[17] Lucas, "Daniel," 116; R. Gurney, "The Four Kingdoms of Daniel 2 and 7," *Themelios* 2 (1977): 39–45; Gurney, *God in Control: An Exposition of the Prophecies of Daniel* (Worthing, England: Henry E. Walter, 1980), 19–21; R. W. Pierce, *Daniel* (Teach the Text; Grand Rapids, Baker, 2015), 46–47, 124–25, 130.

[18] J. H. Walton, "The Four Kingdoms of Daniel," *JETS* 29 (1986): 25–36.

view claims the four kingdoms are Babylon, Medo-Persia, Greece, and Rome. That view will be discussed below.

B. Case for the Early Date and Historicity of Daniel

This commentary affirms the traditional-conservative view that the book of Daniel is historically accurate and contains genuine, fulfilled predictive prophecies. The case for this view follows.

1. The book of Daniel appears to be making historical claims. The *prima facie* impression of the first half of Daniel is that it is historical narrative, not fiction. The second half of the book appears to be autobiography.

2. The critical view undermines Daniel's theological value. If Daniel was intended to be understood as history rather than fiction, then a second-century BC dating reduces the book to a "pious fraud" unworthy of inclusion in the Hebrew canon. It is sometimes claimed that pseudonymous writing was simply a literary convention, not dishonesty.[19] But this suffers several problems. First, the author failed to convey to his audience that his work was fictional since, as far as is known, nobody before Porphyry in the third century AD questioned the book's historicity (see below). Second, as Joyce Baldwin concludes in her survey of the topic, "There is no clear proof of pseudonymity in the Old Testament and much evidence against it."[20] Third, there is clear evidence that the early church did not look kindly on pseudonymity. Works discovered to be pseudonymous (*Epistle to the Laodiceans*; *Epistle to the Alexandrians*; *3 Corinthians*; *Gospel of Peter*) or fictional (*Acts of Paul*) were excluded from the canon, and their authors (if known) were removed from the ministry.[21] If the writer of Daniel took a figure from the past and put his words in his mouth in order to gain authority or notoriety for his work, then he acted unethically. Pseudonymity is undoubtedly among the reasons that extra-biblical apocalyptic works were not included in the canon. If one accepts a priori that Daniel deserves to be in the canon, then it cannot be pseudepigraphic. Or at least,

---

[19] D. S. Russell, *Prophecy and the Apocalyptic Dream* (Peabody, MA: Hendrickson, 1994), 35.

[20] J. G. Baldwin, "Is There Pseudonymity in the Old Testament?" *Themelios* 4.1 (1978): 6–12, esp. p. 12.

[21] B. Witherington III, *What's in the Word: Rethinking the Socio-Rhetorical Character of the New Testament* (Waco, TX: Baylor University Press, 2009), 27–28.

one cannot maintain that those who recognized it to be canonical believed it to be pseudepigraphic.

Whether Daniel is historical affects how one applies the book. If Daniel was not a historical figure, it is hard to see how he can be a model for how Jews or Christians should live. Fictional characters can serve as role models, but real flesh-and-blood human beings serve better. Moreover, if Daniel's prophecies are after the fact, then they cannot be used as the book itself uses them—as proof of God's supernatural foreknowledge and ability to reveal the future (e.g., Dan 2:27–28). Thus one of the central theological themes of the book is discredited (see §1; §3.5). Major theological problems ensue from the thesis that the book of Daniel is fictional and pseudonymous.

3. The earliest Jewish and Christian readers understood Daniel as historical. All Daniel's earliest interpreters received it at face value without seeing Daniel as a fictional character. Jesus said the "abomination of desolation" was "spoken of by the prophet Daniel." Moreover, he viewed it as predictive (Matt 24:15). For many conservative scholars, this statement alone is sufficient evidence to affirm Daniel's historicity. It also implies Daniel's authorship of the autobiographical section (Daniel 7–12). The three statements about the "abomination of desolation" are each spoken by an angel and not by the character Daniel (Dan 9:27; 11:31; 12:11), but Daniel did write the angel's message down.

No ancient Jewish or Christian tradition interpreted Daniel as fiction. Several early sources affirm its historicity.

Josephus. The late first-century AD Jewish historian Josephus affirms that the book of Daniel existed at the time of Alexander the Great (c. 332 BC) and that the prophecies were shown to him:

> when he [Alexander the Great] went up into the temple [of Jerusalem], he offered sacrifice to God, according to the high priest's direction, and magnificently treated both the high priest and the priests. And when the book of Daniel was showed him, wherein Daniel declared that one of the Greeks should destroy the empire of the Persians [see Dan

8; 11:1–4], he supposed that himself was the person intended. (*Antiquities* 11.8.5)[22]

Josephus believed that Daniel genuinely prophesied of Persia's overthrow by the Greeks, the coming of Antiochus Epiphanes, and the future overthrow of Rome by the kingdom of God (*Antiquities* 10.10.4; 10.11.7). He used the book as a legitimate source for reconstructing Israel's history rather than a fictional story (*Antiquities* 10.10–11).

1 Maccabees. In 1 Maccabees the dying Mattathias, father of Judas Maccabeus, refers to Daniel and his friends as real people: "Hananiah, Azariah, and Mishael believed and were saved from the flame. Daniel, because of his innocence, was delivered from the mouth of the lions" (1 Macc 2:59–60 NRSV). The author of 1 Maccabees writes in the second century BC, only a few decades after the Maccabean revolt and only a few decades from the time the book of Daniel was allegedly completed (in the 160s BC), according to the critical view. Yet the writer passes on a tradition that Mattathias, who died about the time the critical view claims Daniel was written, believed Daniel and his three friends were real persons. This is evidence against Daniel and his friends being fictional characters invented during the Maccabean revolt. First Maccabees 2 suggests, at least, that two episodes about Daniel and his friends (Daniel 3 and 6) within the larger court narratives (Daniel 1–6) predate the Maccabean period.

4 Maccabees. Dated as early as the first century BC, 4 Maccabees looks to Daniel and his friends as examples of faithful Jews who risked martyrdom for their faith and (like those at the time of the Maccabean crisis) are to be followed: "Brothers, let us die like brothers for the sake of the law; let us imitate the three youths in Assyria who despised the same ordeal of the furnace" (4 Macc 13:9 NRSV). "Daniel the righteous was thrown to the lions, and Hananiah, Azariah, and Mishael were hurled into the fiery furnace and endured it for the sake of God. You too must have the same faith in God and not be grieved" (4 Macc 16:21–22 NRSV). The author compares the

---

[22] Flavius Josephus, *The Works of Josephus: Complete and Unabridged*, trans. William Whiston (Peabody: Hendrickson, 1987).

fierceness of the lions that surrounded Daniel to the fierce love of the mother of martyrs (4 Macc 16:3).

Rabbinic Literature. The rabbis understood Daniel as a historical figure who fulfilled prophecy:

> According to rabbinical tradition Daniel was of royal descent; and his fate, together with that of his three friends, Hananiah, Mishael, and Azariah, was foretold by the prophet Isaiah to King Hezekiah in these words, 'and they shall be eunuchs in the palace of the king of Babylon' (Isa. xxxix. 7; compare Sanh. 93b; Pirḳe R. El. lii.; Origen, commentary to Matt. xv. 5; Jerome, commentary to Isaiah, l.c.). According to this view, Daniel and his friends were eunuchs, and were consequently able to prove the groundlessness of charges of immorality brought against them, which had almost caused their death at the hands of the king.[23]

Ezekiel 14:14, 20; 28:3. A good case can be made that Ezekiel refers to the Daniel of the book of Daniel as a historical figure.[24] Ezekiel speaks of a Daniel known for his wisdom (Ezek 28:3; cf. Dan 1:20; 2:13). He also mentions three men, "Noah, Daniel, and Job," who were known for their righteousness, but whose righteousness could only deliver themselves, not others (Ezek 14:14). Which Daniel does Ezekiel have in mind? Many scholars point to a certain heroic Danel from a second millennium BC Ugaritic legend, the Aqhat Epic, perhaps as garbled through Jewish folklore. However, this conclusion is doubtful. While it is true that Ugaritic Danel judged the cause of the widow and orphan, Ezekiel is unlikely to label someone "righteous" who was a worshiper of Baal and El. That this was softened in Jewish folklore is purely speculative since there is no evidence that the Danel of the Aqhat Epic was a figure in Jewish folklore. Ugarit Danel is also involved in vengeful curses, violent rage, drunkenness, and an assassination plot, none of which are marks of righteousness. Nor is Ugaritic Danel ever called wise. More likely Ezekiel, who lived in Babylonia and was called to ministry about 593 BC—a dozen years

---

[23] "Daniel" in *The Jewish Encyclopedia* (1906). Online http://jewishencyclopedia.com. Accessed 2 June 2014.

[24] T. E. Gaston, *Historical Issues in the Book of Daniel* (Oxford: Taanathshilo, 2009), 10–19.

after Daniel arrived in 605/604—is referring to his already famous contemporary prophet in exile.

The first person known to doubt Daniel's historicity is a neo-Platonic philosopher of the third century AD named Porphyry who wrote a now lost anti-Christian polemic, *Against the Christians* (originally twelve volumes). According to Jerome, whose commentary on Daniel cites this work, Porphyry argued that the book of Daniel was a forgery written by someone in Judea in the days of Antiochus IV Epiphanes. Porphyry used this argument to debunk the book of Daniel as a fraud with no real prophecy or history.[25] The critical view has essentially adopted Porphyry's anti-Christian, anti-supernatural position on date and historicity of Daniel, though not always Porphyry's anti-Christian conclusions.

4. Daniel claims to convey predictive prophecies. The book of Daniel affirms that it contains predictive prophecy (Dan 2:29–31; 4:24; 5:24–30; chapters 7–12). Daniel was told to write his visions down and seal them up (8:26; 12:4, 9), which seems designed to demonstrate that God was indeed speaking through the prophet. Daniel explicitly compares his work to that of Jeremiah (Dan 9:2–4).[26] Critical scholars draw a sharp distinction between apocalyptic and prophecy, saying the latter makes real predictions but the former does not. But this is not necessary. The earlier prophets had apocalyptic-like sections. Although extra-biblical apocalyptic wanders away from being genuine prophecy, biblical apocalyptic should be considered a subcategory of prophecy, "prophetic apocalyptic" (to quote George Ladd), and not an entirely distinct category.[27] Extra-biblical apocalyptic resembles the book of Daniel not because it is a work just like them but because some writers of extra-biblical apocalyptic were inspired by Daniel to imitate its style. Unlike extra-biblical apocalyptic, biblical prophetic apocalyptic arguably contains genuine, fulfilled prophetic predictions.

5. Daniel's placement in the third division of the Hebrew canon proves little. Although the Hebrew Bible places Daniel in its third division (the Writings), one ought not make too much of this. The LXX tradition, which divides the OT into four sections (Law,

---

[25] J. E. Smith, *The Major Prophets*, Old Testament Survey Series (Joplin, MO: College Press, 1992), 525.

[26] G. J. Wenham, "Daniel: The Basic Issues," *Themelios* 2.2 (1977): 50.

[27] G. E. Ladd, "Why Not Prophetic Apocalyptic?" *JBL* 76 (1957): 192–200.

History, Poetry, Prophets), places Daniel (with the Additions) among the Prophets after Ezekiel.[28] Similarly, in his work *Against Apion* 1.8.38–42,[29] Josephus seems to place Daniel among the Prophets rather than the Writings. The exact positioning of both Daniel and Esther in Prophets or Writings may have been a post-Christian development.[30]

A good case can be made that the OT canon was closed too early to have included any second-century work. Josephus, writing before Jamnia in *Against Apion* 1.8.38–42, lists the books of the Hebrew canon without any hint that the canon was still open. The view of Ryle cited above that the OT canon remained open until Jamnia in AD 90 has been thoroughly debunked by Jewish scholar Sid Leiman. Leiman observes that Jamnia was not a council or synod but only a gathering of some rabbis for discussions. Later rabbis rarely cited the opinions of those at Jamnia, and when they were cited they were not considered more authoritative that other rabbinic opinions. Moreover, the discussions on canon at Jamnia were limited to Ecclesiastes and perhaps Song of Songs, so they were not addressing the issue of canon generally. Leiman concludes, "The widespread view that the Council of Jamnia closed the biblical canon, or that it canonized any books at all, is not supported by the evidence and need no longer be seriously maintained."[31]

A better reconstruction places the canon much earlier:

> The same things are reported in the records and in the memoirs of Nehemiah, and also that he founded a library and collected the books about the kings and prophets, and the writings of David, and letters of kings about votive offerings. In the same way Judas also collected all the books that had been lost on account of the war that had come

---

[28] Daniel Scheetz, "Daniel's Position in the Tanach," *OTE* 23.1 (2010): 189.

[29] Flavius Josephus, *The Life*; *Against Apion*, Complete Works of Josephus Vol. I, LCL 186, trans. H. St. J. Thackeray (Cambridge, MA: Harvard University Press, 1926), 178–81.

[30] D. L. Christensen, "Josephus and the Twenty-Two-Book Canon of Sacred Scripture," *JETS* 29 (1986): 37–46.

[31] S. Z. Leiman, *The Canonization of Hebrew Scriptures: The Talmudic and Midrashic Evidence* (Hamden, CT: Archon, 1976), 124.

upon us, and they are in our possession (2 Macc 2:13–14 NRSV).

This text indicates that Nehemiah (in the late 400s BC) founded a library that included the various writings about kings and prophets and the writings of David. After the war with Antiochus IV, Judas Maccabeus regathered this collection that had been scattered during the period of anti-Judaism. Roger Beckwith argues that this is a true historical tradition. If so, then Nehemiah's collection included those works that ultimately came to be accepted as Scripture. It was necessary for Judas to establish a canon of Scripture to guide his reestablishment of the Jewish religion against the rampant Hellenism that had threatened it. Beckwith reasons from 2 Macc 2:13–14 that the closing of the OT canon can be dated to 164 BC when Judas established his library.[32]

If this plausible reconstruction is correct, a book written just before 164 BC would not have had time to earn canonical status. Moreover, 1 Macc 9:27 indicates the prophetic gift had already passed away by Judas' day, and it was believed that only prophets could write Scripture (Josephus, *Against Apion* 1.8.38–42). Thus a book written shortly before 164 BC could not have been considered for the Jewish canon. Regarding Daniel's placement in the Hebrew canon, there is a simpler explanation. Since much of Daniel is historical narrative, it seemed best to place it with the other post-exilic historical books.

6. The presence of Daniel manuscripts among the DSS and allusions to it in Tobit, Ecclesiasticus, and the Book of Watchers makes a second-century BC date unlikely. Daniel was a popular book at the Qumran community, as indicated by the presence of many fragments of its Hebrew text found among the Dead Sea Scrolls.[33] Only Isaiah, the Pentateuch, and the Psalms seem to be more popular in the Qumran library. The earliest Daniel texts appear

---

[32] R. T. Beckwith, *The Old Testament Canon of the New Testament Church* (Grand Rapids: Eerdmans, 1985), 150–53.

[33] Specifically, 1QDan^a, 1QDan^b, 4QDan^a, 4QDan^b, 4QDan^c, 4QDan^d, 4QDan^e, and pap3Dan, all of which are close to the Masoretic Text. Also present was the midrashic work 4QFlorilegium that cites Dan 11:32 and 12:10 as Scripture. For a translation of 4QFlorilegium, see G. Vermes, *The Dead Sea Scrolls in English*, rev. and extended 4th ed. (Sheffield: Sheffield Academic, 1995), 354.

to be 4QDan^c and 4QDan^e. They can be dated as early as 120 BC (late second or early first century BC)[34] on the basis of paleography. But if the critical view is correct that Dan 11:40–45 includes a failed prophecy, it seems unlikely that the Qumran community, established within a few decades of the so-called failed prophecy and in a position to evaluate it, would have held Daniel in such high esteem.[35]

Daniel was also known and appreciated in early Judaism outside of Qumran. Beckwith argues that Daniel is alluded to in Tobit, Ecclesiasticus, and the Book of Watchers in 1 Enoch 1–36.[36] Tobit, perhaps the earliest of the books of the Apocrypha, shows an awareness of "times and seasons" from Dan 9:2 (Tobit 14:4–5). First Enoch 1–36 makes frequent allusions to Daniel, specifically deriving its titles for angels as "watchers" and "holy ones" from Dan 4:13, 17, 23. First Enoch also reflects Daniel's description of the throne of God in Dan 7:9–10 (1 Enoch 14:8–23). Ecclesiasticus speaks of almsgiving atoning for sin (Sir 3:30), which may echo Daniel's advice to Nebuchadnezzar in Dan 4:27 [HB 4:24]. "Anointed time" in Sir 36:10 seems to allude to Dan 8:19; 11:27, 29, 35, and the prayer of Sir 36:22 seems to echo Daniel's prayer in Dan 9:17.[37] To this can be added the book of Baruch that also alludes to Daniel (compare the prayer of Baruch 1:15–22 with the prayer of Dan 9:7–14). All of these books may predate the Maccabean revolt, so their allusions to Daniel make the Maccabean hypothesis increasingly unlikely. Even if these books date somewhat after that revolt, their early allusions to the book of Daniel make a pre-Maccabean dating of Daniel more plausible than a Maccabean dating.

Daniel 11:33–35 (see commentary) speaks well of people like Judas Maccabeus who fought against Antiochus IV along with his brothers. But Judas' brothers began the Hasmonean Dynasty of priest-kings that the Qumran community rejected as wicked priests. So it would be odd for Daniel to have been popular in Qumran had it been written shortly before the sect began during the Hasmonean period. Daniel's wide acceptance both by the sectarians at Qumran

---

[34] C. A. Newsom, *Daniel*, OTL (Louisville: Westminster John Knox, 2014), 3.

[35] B. Waltke, "The Date of the Book of Daniel," *BSac* 133, no. 532 (1976): 321–23.

[36] R. T. Beckwith, "Early Traces of the Book of Daniel," *Tyndale Bulletin* 53.1 (2002): 75–82.

[37] A. E. Steinmann, *Daniel*, Concordia Commentary (Saint Louis: Concordia, 2008), 13–17.

and the rest of Judaism makes more sense if the book dates to long before the Maccabean period.[38]

7. The presence of Persian and Greek words can be explained without assuming a late date. Perhaps the most "damning" evidence, at first glance, against the early dating of Daniel is the existence of Persian and Greek words in the Aramaic text of Daniel. It seems to prove that what is written must be after the conquest of Palestine by Alexander the Great c. 332 BC. But on closer scrutiny, the evidence is not as convincing as it at first seems.

a. Persian Words in Daniel. The Persian words in the Aramaic of Daniel are primarily terms for officials and clothing. Daniel was an official in the Persian court (Daniel 6), so naturally by the end of his life he and his immediate disciples, such as the narrator of Daniel 1–6 writing during the Persian period, could have used Persian terminology for government officials and administrative terms. And given the close proximity of Persia (modern southern Iran) and Babylon (modern Iraq), it is not surprising to find imported goods retaining their Persian names and other loan words slipping into Babylonian Aramaic vocabulary. Indeed, the Chaldeans during the Assyrian period were known to have imported goods from places as far away as India or Southern Arabia.[39]

Among the Aramaic words of suspected Persian origin in Daniel are: אֲחַשְׁדַּרְפְּנַיָּא ("satraps") אֲדַרְגָּזְרַיָּא ("advisers"), הַדָּבְרַיָּא ("companions, high ranking officials"), סָרְכִין ("chief ministers"), גְדָבְרַיָּא ("treasurers"), תִּפְתָּיֵא ("police chiefs, magistrates"), דָּתָא ("law"), דְּתָבְרָא ("judge"), הַדָּמִין ("limbs," in the legal phrase "you shall be dismembered"), פִּתְגָם ("message"), and the idiom מֶלֶךְ מַלְכַיָּא ("king of kings"; though the words are Aramaic). Other terms are items of clothing, perhaps imports from Persia: הַמּוֹנְכָא ("necklace"), סַרְבָּלֵיהוֹן ("their trousers"), פַּטִּישֵׁיהוֹן ("their shirts"), כַּרְבְּלָתְהוֹן ("their hats, head coverings"). In addition, רָזָא ("secret") and אֲזְדָּא ("publically known")

---

[38] Beckwith, *Old Testament Canon*, 357–58; J. M. Hamilton, *With the Clouds of Heaven: The Book of Daniel in Biblical Theology*, New Studies in Biblical Theology 32 (Downers Grove: InterVarsity, 2014), 34–35.

[39] M. Liverani, *The Ancient Near East: History, Society and Economy*, trans. S. Tabatabai (New York: Routledge, 2013), 444.

are of Persian origin.[40] All of these terms could easily have been loan-words in the Aramaic of sixth/fifth-century BC Babylonia.

The Hebrew of Daniel also has Persian loanwords: פַּרְתְּמִים ("nobility"), פַּת־בַּג ("food, provisions"), and the proper name אַשְׁפְּנַז ("Ashpenaz"). But none of this is inconsistent with a Persian-period dating of the book.

b. Greek Words in Daniel. There are only three terms of Greek origin in Daniel, and all three are musical instruments: קִיתְרֹס, qay-thros = κιθάρα, kitharis ("zither"); פְּסַנְתֵּרִין, psanterin = ψαλτήριον, psalterion ("psaltery"); סוּמְפֹּנְיָה, sumphonya = συμφωνία, sumpho-nia ("bagpipe"? "harp"?). Does the presence of these Greek words prove that the Aramaic of Daniel was written after the conquests of Alexander the Great? Not at all. It may indicate instead that trade relations between Babylonia and Greece led to three exotic, Greek instruments being brought to Babylon.

Edwin Yamauchi[41] has shown that trade relationships between Babylonia and Greece existed long before the sixth century BC, indeed well before 1000 BC Mari tablets, discovered at a site near Babylon, show that Mari, conquered by Hammurabi, had relationships around 1700 BC with the original Philistine homeland Caphtor, usu-ally identified with Crete and/or the Aegean islands. Caphtor would be under the sphere of influence of pre-Greek culture. Between 1000 and 700 BC, Mesopotamian contact with Greeks came through the Phoenicians, from whom the Greeks borrowed their alphabet. The Phoenicians, in turn, brought Greek wares to Lebanon-Syria, and from there much of it found itself eastward. Greek-style geometric pottery in this period found its way to sites in Assyria, and Greek style "Nimrod ivories" were found in Nimrod of Assyria. The influ-ence of Mesopotamia on Greece was also significant, including items of trade as well as loan words from Akkadian into Greek. The bat-tle of Carchemish (605 BC) where Nebuchadnezzar fought Neco of Egypt took place in what is now near the southern border of Turkey. Archaeologist Leonard Wooley found at Carchemish arrowheads and a Greek shield in a house with Egyptian objects and seals of

---

[40] See F. Rosenthal, *A Grammar of Biblical Aramaic* (Wiesbaden: Harrassowitz, 1974), 58–59.

[41] E. M. Yamauchi, "The Greek Words in Daniel in the Light of Greek Influence in the Near East," in *New Perspectives on the Old Testament*, ed. J. B. Payne (Waco: Word, 1970), 170–200.

Neco, suggesting that Neco used Greek mercenaries to fight against Babylon. It is known that Nebuchadnezzar himself used Greek craftsmen, some seven being named in a cuneiform text.

In the context of this kind of significant cultural contact between Babylonia and Greece, it is not surprising that the "king of the world"—as Near Eastern kings called themselves—would choose to import exotic Greek instruments for his pleasure. Instruments so imported often keep their foreign names, as do the modern instruments "piano," "violin," and "trombone," all of which are derived from Italian. Accordingly, these three instruments of Greek origin retained their Greek names when imported to Nebuchadnezzar's court. This is a plausible alternative to the claim that these Greek terms prove a post-Alexander dating of the text.

8. The Aramaic and Hebrew linguistic evidence points to a pre-Maccabean dating. All languages change over time, and this is true of Aramaic. It is alleged that Daniel was completed c. 168–164 BC in Palestine. Particularly fortunate for comparison purposes, we have Jewish Aramaic works dated to two different time periods. Among the Dead Sea Scrolls was found a work called the *Genesis Apocryphon*, an Aramaic document from the second century BC—the time period consistent with a Maccabean dating of Daniel. In addition, we have Aramaic papyri found at a Jewish colony called Elephantine in Egypt that date to the fifth century BC, shortly after Daniel could have been written according to the traditional view. These Aramaic papyri preserve a Jewish Aramaic dialect at an earlier stage of the development of the language as compared with the Jewish Aramaic of the Genesis Apocryphon. When the Aramaic of Daniel is compared with the Aramaic of the second-century Genesis Apocryphon and the fifth-century Elephantine Papyri, Daniel's Aramaic exhibits more archaic features than does the Genesis Apocryphon, features it shares with the fifth-century BC Elephantine Papyri. More broadly, on the basis of linguistics the Aramaic of Daniel belongs to what is known as Official or Imperial Aramaic. The Aramaic of the Genesis Apocryphon, in contrast, belongs to Late Aramaic, the period after Imperial or Official Aramaic. Aside from Daniel (which is disputed), Imperial Aramaic is only known to have flourished from 700 BC to 300 BC, consistent with the assumption of a fifth-century BC Achaemenid dating of the book of Daniel rather than a second-century BC Seleucid period dating.[42]

Some details: As one goes from Imperial Aramaic to Late (Talmudic) Aramaic, several changes in the direction of simplification occurred. There was a tendency over time to drop the /h/ in certain words, as in Cockney English: "I 'ope you can 'elp 'em with 'is 'omework." Even standard English today pronounces "honor" as if there were no "h." In Aramaic there is a verbal tense called hophel. This form evolved from the shaphel form when /sh/ was simplified to /h/. By Talmudic Aramaic of the early Christian centuries, most hophels had evolved into aphels. That is, they had dropped their /h/. This is the natural tendency in Aramaic dialects over time.

The "causative" verbal forms in Daniel are almost always "hophels," not "aphels." The same is true of Elephantine Papyri (e.g., the hophel form ויהחיני, in "The Words of Ahikar," line 54).[43] But in the Genesis Apocryphon aphel forms occur. Likewise, hithpaels of Daniel and Elephantine are replaced with ithpaels in the Genesis Apocryphon. These and other differences between the Aramaic of Daniel/Elephantine and the Genesis Apocryphon are seen in the following chart.

	Daniel & Elephantine Papyri (Fifth Century BC)	Genesis Apocryphon (Second Century BC)
1	3fs suffix -ah ("her")	3fs suffix -ha (Targumic)
2	haphels and hitpaels	aphels and itpaels (Talmudic)
3	bet "house"	be "house" (Talmudic style abbreviation) Compare the Talmudic tendency to abbreviate words as in the case of the participle qayem ("being, standing"), which evolves as follows: qayem > qaye > qay > qa.

---

[42] G. L. Archer, "The Aramaic of the 'Genesis Apocryphon' Compared with the Aramaic of Daniel," in *New Perspectives on the Old Testament*, 160–69; K. A. Kitchen, "The Aramaic of Daniel," *Notes on Some Problems in the Book of Daniel*, ed. D. J. Wiseman et al. (London: Tyndale, 1965), 31–79; T. C. Mitchell, "Achaemenid History and the Book of Daniel," in *Mesopotamia and Iran in the Persian Period: Conquest and Imperialism 539–331 BC*, ed. J. Curtis (London: British Museum, 1997), 72–73.

[43] A. Cowley, *Aramaic Papyri of the Fifth Century B.C.* (1923; reprint, Osnabrück: Otto Zeller, 1967), 213.

	Daniel & Elephantine Papyri (Fifth Century BC)	**Genesis Apocryphon (Second Century BC)**
4	*dena* "this"	*den* (Talmudic style abbreviation)
5	vowel lengthener final *he*	vowel lengthener final *aleph* Biblical Aramaic occasionally uses final *aleph* as vowel lengthener, but the tendency in the history of the language was to replace *he* with *aleph*. Final *he* vowel lengtheners have all but completely disappeared in the Genesis Apocryphon.
6	occasional hophal passive	The hophal passive form is completely replaced by itpael type passive, as is true of Targumic and Talmudic Aramaic.

Differences in language could be based on geographical differences rather than chronological ones, but the Maccabean dating theory assumes Daniel was written in Palestine just like the Genesis Apocryphon. One would expect dialects of the same time, ethnic group, and region to be the same, but Daniel's Aramaic differs from Maccabean Aramaic in the Genesis Apocryphon.

In sum, the Aramaic of Daniel shows archaic features of language shared with the fifth-century BC Elephantine Papyri, but it differs from the Aramaic of the Targums, Talmud, and the second-century BC Aramaic of the Genesis Apocryphon that is much closer to later Talmudic and Targumic Aramaic in these features. A reasonable explanation for this is that the composition of Daniel was considerably earlier than the composition of the second-century BC Genesis Apocryphon and relatively close to the time of the fifth-century BC Jewish Aramaic papyri with which it is closer linguistically. Thus the Aramaic of Daniel supports an early date for the book.[44]

---

[44] Critical scholars treat this linguistic problem with their dating in various ways. In principle one might argue Daniel's Aramaic was written in an intentionally archaic style to make it seem older than it is. J. A. Montgomery, *Daniel*, ICC (Edinburgh: T&T Clark, 1927) argues that Daniel 1–6 came from Babylon of the third century BC, making it both earlier and from a different geographical locale than the rest of the book, which could explain the archaic Aramaic. Similarly, Russell (*Prophecy and the Apocalyptic Dream*, 35) states that Daniel 1–6 goes back to the sixth century but that Daniel 7–12 is Maccabean. J. J. Collins, *Daniel*, Hermenia (Minneapolis: Fortress, 1993), 13–18, argues that no firm line can be drawn between the Aramaic of Daniel

As for the Hebrew of Daniel, occasional loanwords from Persian are consistent with the book being finalized in the Achaemenid (Persian) period, but there is no indication that it dates later than the Hebrew of Ezra-Nehemiah or Esther, which are fifth-century BC works. A comparison of the Hebrew of Daniel with genuinely second-century BC sectarian documents among the Dead Sea Scrolls shows that the latter is markedly different than Daniel in areas of syntax, word order, morphology, and spelling. Here too dating the Hebrew of Daniel to the fifth century BC is quite plausible.[45]

9. The court narratives of Daniel 1–6 and the prayer of Daniel 9 do not fit the Maccabean hypothesis. Although Daniel 3, 6, and 7 encourage Jews to be faithful despite possible persecution for their religious beliefs, and Daniel 8 and 11 describe the crisis under Antiochus IV, much of the book does not work as a tract for the Maccabean crisis. Nebuchadnezzar pays homage to Daniel and appoints him and his religiously Jewish friends to positions of power (1:19–21; 2:46–49; 3:30). He shows some reluctance to punish Shadrach, Meshach, and Abednego when they defy his edict to worship the image he set up, giving them a second chance (3:14–15), and has an affectionate relationship with Daniel (4:19). Despite his flaws and the edict about the statue that inadvertently endangered Daniel's friends—he was encouraging a loyalty pledge, not trying to entrap Jews—Nebuchadnezzar is no Antiochus IV.

Similarly, Darius not only generously appointed pious Daniel to high office (6:1–3), but unlike Antiochus IV he was displeased when the stubbornly religious Jew Daniel was caught by the king's imprudent edict that was promoted by Daniel's jealous colleagues. Darius wanted to save Daniel, indirectly prayed for his salvation, rejoiced when God saved him, and punished those who had schemed against Daniel (6:14–16, 23–24). These narratives were clearly not written with the crisis of Antiochus IV in mind but instead assume a milieu in which it was still considered possible for Jews to work with a non-Israelite

---

and the Aramaic of Qumran and that late Imperial Aramaic simply had a variety of dialects that existed at the same time.

[45] Mitchell, "Achaemenid History and the Book of Daniel," 72; G. L. Archer, "The Hebrew of Daniel Compared with the Qumran Sectarian Documents," in *The Law and the Prophets: Old Testament Studies Prepared in Honor of Oswald Thompson Allis*, ed. J. H. Skilton, M. C. Fisher, and L. W. Sloat (Nutley, NJ: Presbyterian & Reformed, 1974), 470–81.

government.[46] Such considerations led Collins, among critical scholars, to date the court narratives to well before the Maccabean crisis.[47]

The prayer of Daniel 9 is also a problem for the Maccabean hypothesis. Daniel's prayer of confession seems inappropriate for the time of Antiochus IV. At that time the concern would have been less on the sins of Israel than the sins of Antiochus, for which reason critical scholars often dismiss the prayer as secondary.[48] But this prayer of national confession of sin does fit the context in the first year of Cyrus at the end of the exile as a response to Jeremiah's prophecy of the seventy years.

10. The alleged historical errors in Daniel can be resolved. Although Daniel is accused of many historical errors, there are plausible alternative explanations.[49]

a. Darius the Mede. Extra-biblical history knows nothing of Darius the Mede. But that does not necessarily mean there was no such person. Writing ancient history is like describing a room on the basis of what one can see though a small, old-fashioned key hole. Some things are clear, but many things are out of view, so there are many gaps in our knowledge.

The following is what we know from extra-biblical material related to the fall of Babylon. Belshazzar's father Nabonidus returned from Teima to Babylon before the invasion of Babylon by Cyrus of Persia in 539. According to a Harran inscription (perhaps propaganda) Nabonidus was received with kisses and presents, but his empire was soon to fall. The *Babylonian Chronicle* records that after an initial delay at Opis, Cyrus took Sippar and Babylon in 539 BC without a battle:

---

[46] Steinmann, *Daniel*, 319.

[47] J. J. Collins, "The Court-Tales in Daniel and the Development of Apocalyptic," *JBL* 94 (1975): 218–20.

[48] G. H. Wilson, "The Prayer of Daniel 9: Reflection on Jeremiah 29," *JSOT* 48 (1990) 92.

[49] Many of these problems are treated by A. R. Millard, "Daniel in Babylon: An Accurate Record," in *Do Historical Matters Matter to Faith*, ed. J. K. Hoffmeier and D. Magary (Wheaton: Crossway, 2012), 263–80); Millard, "Daniel 1–6 and History," *EvQ* 49.2 (1977): 67–73; D. J. Wiseman, "Some Historical Problems in the Book of Daniel," in *Notes on Some Problems in the Book of Daniel*, 9–18; T. E. Gaston, *Historical Issues in the Book of Daniel* (Oxford: Taanathshilo, 2009); G. L. Archer, "Modern Rationalism and the Book of Daniel," *BSac* 136, no. 542 (April–June 1979): 129–47; Mitchell, "Achaemenid History and the Book of Daniel," 68–78.

In Tishri [September/October] when Cyrus fought with the army of Babylon at Opis on the bank of the Tigris, the people of Babylon [Akkad] retreated. He took booty and killed people. On 14th Sippar was taken without battle. Nabonidus fled. On 16th Ugbaru, governor of Gutium, and the army of Cyrus entered Babylon without battle. Afterwards, after Nabonidus had retreated, he was taken in Babylon. … On 3rd Marcheswan [October/November] Cyrus entered Babylon.[50]

Cyrus is said to have entered the city on the third of Marcheswan, that is, 29 October 539. According to Cyrus' own account in the *Cyrus Cylinder*,[51] he was greeted as a liberator from the impious (to the national god Marduk) Nabonidus, and this may be more than just propaganda. These two cuneiform accounts of the fall of Babylon written by Cyrus and the Marduk priests are contemporary to the events described and appear relatively trustworthy.

There is no room for even a brief Median rule over Babylon preceding the rule of Cyrus, even though Dan 6:28 at first seems to imply that Darius preceded Cyrus as ruler: "So this Daniel enjoyed success in the reign of Darius and in the reign of Cyrus the Persian." So how can this be explained without assuming Daniel is in error?

There are three proposed conservative explanations for the identity of Darius in Daniel: Gubaru II, Gubaru I, and Cyrus. We will argue in favor of identifying Darius with Cyrus.

> *Gubaru II.* John Whitcomb[52] identified Darius the Mede with Gubaru II, a governor of Babylon under Cyrus, known from Greek sources as Gobryas, who ruled Babylon as the provincial governor not long after Babylon was conquered. Darius would then be a throne name, and his appointment a gesture of good will toward Cyrus' Median allies. Darius is called "the Mede" perhaps to distinguish him from the later Darius who ultimately succeeded Cyrus. Note the hophal passive form הָמְלַךְ in Dan 9:1 suggests that Darius

---

[50] *Babylonian Chronicle* 7 iii 12–16, 18. See *COS* 1.468.

[51] *COS* 2.314–316.

[52] J. C. Whitcomb, *Darius the Mede* (Grand Rapids: Eerdmans, 1959).

was "caused to be made king." Who is the agent of this passive verb? Perhaps Cyrus.

There are, however, serious problems with this proposal. There is no proof that Gubaru was a Mede, and he is nowhere called a son of Ahasuerus (Xerxes) (Dan 9:1). One must assume the Ugbaru who died shortly after Cyrus' conquest and Gubaru who ruled Babylon are different persons, but Ugbaru may simply be a variant spelling. In business documents dating from the fourth year of Cyrus to the fifth year of Cambyses, Gubaru is called as "satrap of Babylon and Ebir-nari," but he is never called a "king" in cuneiform sources. Indeed, there is no instance of a governor of Babylon ever calling himself king unless he were a usurper. It would thus be strange for Daniel to use that title for Darius/Gubaru. The agent of the passive verb in Dan 9:1 may well be God who sovereignly controls kings and nations. Grabbe argues that Gubaru II did not assume his office until the fourth year after Babylon's conquest, whereas before that time Cambyses the son of Cyrus was king (see below), thus ruling out Gubaru II from being the Darius of Daniel in Cyrus' first year (Dan 9:1).[53] Thus Whitcomb's proposal has problems and lacks corroboration.

Gubaru I. William Shea[54] proposes that Darius the Mede is a throne name for Ugbaru/Gubaru I. Shea makes a good case that Ugbaru and Gubaru are variations of the same name in cuneiform. Ugbaru was a former subject of Babylon who was governor of the Gutians in the Zagros (part of Iran). Ugbaru defected to the Persian side and led the Persian army "without battle" into Babylon on October 12, 539 (*Babylonian Chronicles* 7 iii 12–16). Gubaru appointed sub-officers in Babylon, as did Darius (*Babylonian Chronicle* 7 iii 20; Dan 6:1–2), though another reading of the cuneiform is that he was placed over them.[55] Daniel 5:28 refers to the kingdom being given to the Medes and the Persians and Darius receiving the kingdom at age 62, which Shea saw fulfilled when Gubaru I led the Medo-Persian army into Babylon. Shea also noted that in economic texts, Cyrus is called "king of lands" from the eighth month

---

[53] L. L. Grabbe, "Another Look at the *Gestalt* of Darius the Mede," *CBQ* 50 (1988): 205–07.

[54] W. Shea, "Darius the Mede: An Update," *AUSS* 20 (1982): 229–47.

[55] Grabbe, "*Gestalt* of Darius the Mede," 200.

of his ascension year till the tenth month of his next (first) year, but thereafter is also called "king of Babylon," suggesting someone else, that is, Gubaru I, held the title "king of Babylon" before that. Gubaru I, according to Shea's reconstruction, died after about a year. If this is correct, it could explain why Daniel switches from dating by the first year of Darius (Dan 9:1) to dating by the third year, not of Darius, but of Cyrus (Dan 10:1). This Darius was "made king" (hophal passive form) by Cyrus.

This reconstruction, however, has major difficulties. It is not known whether Gubaru I was of Median descent or was a son of Ahasuerus (Xerxes) (Dan 9:1). Whitcomb and others reject Ugbaru as candidate for Darius because the cuneiform text says Ugbaru died on the eleventh day of the ninth month of Arakshamna, that is, only a few days after conquering Babylon, not a year and a few days as Shea proposes. Moreover, there is a text dating to 538 BC that reads, "the first year of Cyrus, king of lands, and the first year of Cambyses, king of Babylon."[56] This suggests that Cambyses became king of Babylon under his father by 538, not in 530 as Shea (following an earlier scholar Dubberstein) thought. Grabbe argues that the missing "king of Babylon" from the economic texts cited above is Cambyses, not Gubaru.[57] Thus Shea's proposal has difficulties and lacks corroboration. Shea himself concludes that his own proposal and that of Whitcomb were no longer tenable in the light of Grabbe's critique, and so he adopted D. J. Wiseman's proposal and defended it against Grabbe's critique instead (see below).[58]

Cyrus. A third proposal made by Assyriologist D. J. Wiseman is that Darius the Mede is to be identified with Cyrus the Persian.[59] Theodotion and the Old Greek may have taken this view when in Dan 11:1 they translate Hebrew for Darius into Greek as Cyrus. The Median kingdom was larger and to the north of Cyrus' Persian kingdom, the latter being one of its vassals. Cyrus conquered the king of

---

[56] M. A. Dandamaev, *A Political History of the Achaemenid Empire* (Leiden: Brill, 1997), 58; Grabbe, "*Gestalt* of Darius the Mede," 203.

[57] Grabbe, "*Gestalt* of Darius the Mede," 204.

[58] W. H. Shea, "Darius the Mede in His Persian-Babylonian Setting," *AUSS* 29.3 (Autumn 1991): 235–57.

[59] Wiseman, "Some Historical Problems in the Book of Daniel," 9–18. Also B. E. Colless, "Cyrus the Persian as Darius the Mede in the Book of Daniel," *JSOT* 56 (1992) 113–26.

the Medes, Astyages—who happened to be Cyrus' grandfather, his mother's father—in 550/549 BC. At that point Cyrus assumed the Median throne. Upon taking a throne, kings often adopted a regnal name or throne name. Roman Catholic popes still do this when they become pope. A number of Israelite kings adopted throne names: Jehoiakim (Eliakim), Jehoahaz (Shallum), Uzziah (Azariah), Solomon (Jedidiah?), David (Elhanan?), and Jehoiachin (Jeconiah/Coniah). Tiglath-pileser III's other name Pul (1 Chr 5:26) might be a throne name.

> We know from Greek and Roman literary sources as well as from Late Babylonian chronicles and astronomical texts (i.e., from two traditions not related to each other) that the Achaemenid kings changed their (birth-)name upon accession to the throne and assumed a "royal name" expressing some religious-political program or motto.[60]

At time of his conquest of the larger Median kingdom, Cyrus may have taken a Median throne name of Darius (Old Persian *Dāraya-vauš,* "Holding firm (or: retaining) the good"[61]). Although later sources continued to use Cyrus' original name, Daniel for some reason prefers to call Cyrus by his Median regnal name, though on occasion he gives him his other name, "King Cyrus of Persia" (10:1).

A key verse for this interpretation is Dan 6:28: "So Daniel prospered during the reign of Darius *and* in the reign of Cyrus the Persian" (emphasis added). Grammatically the "and" (Aramaic/Hebrew *waw*) could be interpreted as epexegetic (explanatory) rather than conjunctive, and so be translated "So Daniel prospered during the reign of Darius, *even* in the reign of Cyrus the Persian" (CSB margin). Thus Dan 6:28 could be identifying Cyrus with Darius. Exactly this same use of epexegetic *waw* occurs in 1 Chr 5:26 to identify Pul with Tiglath-pileser, king of Assyria.

In favor this interpretation is that Cyrus would have been the right age. Darius was 62 years old when he conquered Babylon

---

[60] R. Schmitt, "Personal Names, Iranian III. Achaemenid Period," *Encyclopedia Iranica.* Online: http://www.iranicaonline.org/articles/personal-names-iranian-iii-achaemenid, accessed 7 June 2014.

[61] S.v. "Darius," *Eerdmans Bible Dictionary*, ed. A. C. Myers (Grand Rapids: Eerdmans, 1987), 260.

(Dan 5:32). Cyrus began his reign in Anshan of Persia c. 558, and he conquered the Medes in 550/549. If he were about 42 when he assumed the Persian throne of Anshan, then he would have been about 62 twenty years later when he conquered Babylon.

Cyrus held the title "King of the Medes" as well as "King of Persia," for in c. 546 Nabonidus himself declared that "the King of the Medes" welcomed his return from exile in Teima, and in c. 546 the King of the Medes could only refer to Cyrus.[62] Cyrus never used this title in extant inscription for himself, perhaps to keep harmony with his Median coalition.

Daniel 9:1 calls Darius "of the seed of the Medes," and this was true of Cyrus through his mother. Cyrus was the son of Mandane, a Median princess, the daughter of Astyages king of the Medes. His father Cambyses I of Anshan (a Persian vassal of Astyages) married Mandane. Herodotus 1.107–114 records a tradition that Astyages wanted to kill Cyrus because of two visions indicating that Cyrus would succeed him. So Mandane pretended that Cyrus had died at birth, claiming a stillborn child of a shepherd was the body of her child. She hid Cyrus among commoners for ten years under an assumed name. This is another factor that may explain why Cyrus ends up with two names. Subsequently, Cyrus defeated his grandfather Astyages in battle in 550/549. The fact that Astyages was Cyrus' grandfather would have made it easier for Cyrus to assume the throne of Media, since he was at least a member of the Median royal family.

As for Darius being "son of Ahasuerus [= Xerxes]" (Dan 9:1), Cyrus was not directly a son of any Ahasuerus, but Ahasuerus is plausibly an Achaemenid royal title. He might be the son (= descendant) of an earlier ancestor by that name through his father or mother. See commentary at 9:1 for more on this.

If Wiseman's proposal is true, why does Daniel use this rare name rather than Cyrus' common name? First, the book of Daniel likes to give dual names to its characters (Daniel/Belteshazzar, Hananiah/Shadrach, Mishael/Meshach, Azariah/Abednego; Dan 1:7). Second, Daniel was alive when Cyrus conquered the Medes and took the Median throne. The Medes had a mighty empire that rivaled Babylon's in its strength, extending all the way to Lydia, the

---

[62] Wiseman, "Some Historical Problems in the Book of Daniel," 13.

capital of Sardis in Asia Minor, with whom Cyaxares of the Medes fought on May 28, 585, at the battle of the Eclipse of the Sun, a battle that forced him to abandon his claim on Lydia. In the days after Nebuchadnezzar, before the Medes fell to Cyrus in 550/549, the Medes may have been even stronger than Babylon, its southern neighbor, though no war seems to have broken out between them. Meanwhile, Persia had been unimportant before Cyrus. After Cyrus defeated the Medes, he himself moved his capital from Anshan to the Median capital of Ecbatana to be the administrative head of the new empire.[63] Hence Daniel prefers to give Cyrus his Median title cognizant of the previous greatness of the Medes and the previous insignificance of Persia.

The major weakness of Wiseman's proposal is that it is specula-tive and cannot be proven.[64] But if it is seen as a working hypothesis rather than a proven fact, then Wiseman's proposal is unobjection-able and still viable.

The problem of Darius the Mede has not yet been solved satis-factorily. Someday, a discovery of cuneiform texts that refer to Darius the Mede and identify him more clearly could solve the difficulty, as the discovery of cuneiform texts in 1854 proved that Belshazzar was a real person and not a biblical myth as some skeptical scholars once asserted.[65] The Median capital of Ecbatana has never been thoroughly excavated. When it is, it could reveal a cache of texts that might help resolve this issue. In the meantime, Wiseman's proposal is the most promising one for those who wish to affirm Daniel's historicity.

b. Belshazzar and Nabonidus. What about the accusation that Belshazzar was not really king but only the crown prince, and that Belshazzar's father was Nabonidus and not Nebuchadnezzar? For practical purposes Belshazzar was king of Babylon for the ten years that Nabonidus was in Teima (discussed above and at Dan 7:1). Moreover, the semantic range of Hebrew/Aramaic מֶלֶךְ *melek* ("king") is broader than Akkadian *šarru* ("king"). In an Aramaic/ Akkadian inscription found at Tell Fakhariyeh Syria, the Akkadian

---

[63] Archer, "Daniel," 18.

[64] Grabbe, "*Gestalt* of Darius the Mede," 207.

[65] S.v. "Daniel," *New Schaff–Herzog Encyclopedia of Religious Knowledge*, ed. S. M. Jackson (New York: Funk & Wagnalls, 1908–1914), 3:350.

term *šakin* meaning "governor" is translated מֶלֶךְ.[66] In Jewish circles more than one person at a time could be a מֶלֶךְ, something not true of Akkadian *šarru*. Uzziah and Jotham are explicitly called co-kings (2 Kgs 15:5), and one can plausibly posit eight other coregencies (Omri/Tibni, Jehoash/Jeroboam II, Menahem/Pekah, Asa/Jehoshaphat, Jehoshaphat/Jehoram, Amaziah/Uzziah, Jotham/Ahaz, Hezekiah/Manasseh) in Israel's chronology.[67] Given that (1) Belshazzar was for practical purposes acting as king, (2) a cuneiform text says "kingship" was conferred to Belshazzar, [68] and (3) the idea of having more than one king (מֶלֶךְ) was not uncommon for Jews like Daniel, it is not surprising that Daniel would refer to Belshazzar as king (מֶלֶךְ).

There are also plausible solutions to the problem of Nebuchadnezzar being called the "father" of Belshazzar in Daniel. One solution takes "father" and "son" to mean contextually "predecessor" and "successor" (CSB, NLT, ESV margin). In the Aramaic Tel Dan inscription, Hazael calls his predecessor his "father" even though he was not biologically related, and Shalmaneser III in an Akkadian inscription calls Israel's King Jehu "the son of Omri," even though Jehu was a usurper and biologically unrelated to Omri.[69] The term "fathers" probably means Sennacherib's "predecessors" at 2 Kgs 19:12 (= Isa 37:12; cf. 2 Chr 32:14). See further in the commentary on Dan 5:2.

Alternatively, if "father" and "son" are to be taken as biological terms, Belshazzar could be related to Nebuchadnezzar through his mother. Hebrew/Aramaic אָב ("father") can denote an ancestor (cf. Dan 2:23; Ezra 4:15; 5:12), not only an immediate father. This is why Abraham, Isaac, and Jacob are called Israel's "fathers" (Exod 3:16). Belshazzar was the son of Nabonidus and Nabonidus was the son of *Nabu-balaṭsu-iqbi* on his father's side and Adad-guppi on his mother's

---

[66] Lucas, *Daniel*, 126; A. R. Millard and P. Bordreuil, "A Statue from Syria with Assyrian and Aramaic Inscriptions," *Biblical Archaeologist* 45 (Summer 1982): 135–41.

[67] E. R. Thiele, *The Mysterious Numbers of the Hebrew Kings* (Grand Rapids: Zondervan, 1983), 61–65.

[68] W. H. Shea, "Nabonidus, Belshazzar and the Book of Daniel," *AUSS* 20.2 (1982), 134; K. A. Kitchen, *On the Reliability of the Old Testament* (Grand Rapids: Eerdmans, 2003), 73–74; J. B. Pritchard, ed., *The Ancient Near Eastern Texts Relating to the Old Testament*, 3rd ed. with upplement (Princeton: Princeton University Press, 1969), 313.

[69] Gaston, *Historical Issues in the Book of Daniel*, 80–81 n. 229.

side. Nabonidus' mother was a worshiper of the moon god Sin in Harran who left behind an autobiographical inscription in Akkadian that tells her story and that of her son Nabonidus.[70] This at first seems to be bad news for the historical accuracy of Daniel. However, the name of Belshazzar's mother or her descent is not documented. One possibility, argued by H. C. Leupold,[71] is that Belshazzar's mother was a widow of Nebuchadnezzar who had already borne Belshazzar before the second marriage to Nabonidus, thus making Belshazzar a direct son of Nebuchadnezzar and making Nabonidus Belshazzar's stepfather.

Another, probably better, explanation is that one of Nebuchadnezzar's daughters married Nabonidus, so that Belshazzar was the grandson of Nebuchadnezzar.[72] This woman may be a certain legendary queen Nitocris, mentioned by Herodotus (1.185–88), though the reliability of Herodotus for this period is questionable. Nabonidus was already of high rank in the court of Nebuchadnezzar before he became king, being given the title "man of the king."[73] Nabonidus' kinship to Nebuchadnezzar, though indirect through marriage, would help him legitimize his throne. It should be noted that after Nebuchadnezzar's death there was a power struggle with Amel-Marduk, a true son of Nebuchadnezzar, reigning but two years (561–62), *Nergal-šarra-uṣur* (Neriglissar) his brother-in-law reigning three (559–56), and Labashi-Marduk son of Neriglissar reigning but three months (555), before Nabonidus was made king. In this climate, every claim to legitimacy would be used by both Nabonidus and his son Belshazzar. The problem with the biological explanations is that we lack the historical evidence presently to prove or disprove it.

Although Nabonidus is not mentioned explicitly in Daniel, his existence may be implied. The one who could interpret the "handwriting on the wall" was to be given "third highest position" or made "third ruler" in the kingdom (Dan 5:7, 16, 29). Why third? If

---

[70] *COS* 1.477–79.

[71] H. C. Leupold, *Exposition of Daniel* (Grand Rapids: Baker, 1949), 211–12.

[72] D. J. Wiseman, *Nebuchadrezzar and Babylon* (London: Oxford University Press, 1985), 11–12; R. P. Dougherty, *Nabonidus and Belshazzar*, Yale Oriental Series Researches 15 (New Haven, CT: Yale, 1929), 60–63.

[73] Sumerian, LU2.LUGAL; Wiseman, *Nebuchadnezzar and* , 11.

Belshazzar was but second rank after Nabonidus, he could only offer Daniel third rank. (Though see commentary at 5:7 for other views.)

c. Daniel 1:1 and history. Jeremiah 46:2 dates the battle of Carchemish that led to Nebuchadnezzar's taking control of Judah to the fourth year of Jehoiakim, which Jer 25:1 calls Nebuchadnezzar's first year. Dan 1:1 states that Nebuchadnezzar exiled Daniel and his friends in the third year of Jehoiakim. This seems impossibly early given Jer 46:2. How can this data be reconciled?

The best solution is that Daniel and Jeremiah follow different conventions in dating reigns.[74] The book of Daniel is following the Babylonian system of dating, which postdates reigns by starting year one at the beginning of the autumn new year (Tishri [September/October]). Whatever time a king reigns before the new year counts as year zero. This system means the total years of Babylonian kings add up correctly by simple addition of the number of years they reigned. Jeremiah follows a Palestinian way of counting in which year one begins immediately upon the king ascending to the throne. Moreover, Jeremiah follows a spring Nisan (March/April) dating system—unlike the book of Kings that uses an autumn system.[75] This makes for a more confusing chronology since the last year of the previous king is the first year of the new king, so adding up the number of years various kings reigned results in a number larger than reality. The chart below shows how, once these conventions are recognized, Jehoiakim's year four by Judean dating could overlap with year three by Babylonian dating.

	Tishri ↓	Tishri ↓	Tishri ↓	Tishri ↓	
BABYLONIAN SYSTEM (Daniel)	Year 0 609/608	Year 1 608/607	Year 2 607/606	Year 3 606/605	
JUDEAN SYSTEM (Jeremiah)	Year 1 609/608	Year 2 608/607	Year 3 607/606	Year 4 606/605	
	↑ Nisan	↑ Nisan	↑ Nisan	↑ Nisan	

---

[74] Following Millard, "Daniel in Babylon: An Accurate Record?" 264–65.

[75] The different dating system explains why Jehoiachin's capture can be dated to Nebuchadnezzar's seventh year in Jeremiah but to his eighth year by Kings (Jer 52:28; 2 Kgs 24:12).

Was there a besiegement in 605 as Dan 1:1 suggests? There could have been a short besiegement. As Wiseman points out, "besiegement" may be too strong a translation of צוּר in Dan 1:1, since it sometimes means no more than "threatening" or "showing hostility toward," or "treating as an enemy," in reference to actions preliminary to besiegement rather than being limited to actual besiegement.[76] Moreover, it is not impossible that a small band of Nebuchadnezzar's army was sent to demand tribute and could have begun a literal besiegement.

Neco's troops were defeated in 605 north of Palestine at Carchemish. Egypt's army fled and passed through Palestine on their way back toward Egypt, probably drawing some of the Babylonian army in pursuit—a plausible speculation. After Nebuchadnezzar's troops stopped pursuing Neco, they probably went to Jerusalem to demand allegiance. After all, Jehoiakim had been put on the throne by Pharaoh Neco (2 Kgs 23:34). The general may or may not have been there himself—at some point he must have returned home to be enthroned upon the death of his father—but he was the ultimate general who ordered these actions and so could be said to be responsible.

Baldwin[77] offers the following reconstruction of events in 605 based on a harmony of cuneiform and biblical accounts:[78]

DATE IN 605 BC	ACTION
January/February	Babylonian army returns from a campaign to Babylon.
April to August	Battle of Carchemish. Nebuchadnezzar (probably May/June) defeats Neco, pursues Egyptians south, and conquers whole Hatti land (Syria-Palestine). The "besiegement of Jerusalem" of Dan 1:1 occurs though it lasts but a short time.
August 15	Death of Nebuchadnezzar's father, Nabopolassar. Word sent quickly to Nebuchadnezzar who hastens home to Babylon. The rapid removal of Babylonians allows Jeremiah to speak as if the Babylonian threat had not yet arrived.
September 7	Nebuchadnezzar in Babylon ascends to be king.

---

[76] Wiseman (*Nebuchadrezzar and Babylon*, 23) points to 2 Kgs 24:10–11, Deut 20:12, 2 Kgs 16:5, Song 8:9, and Ps 139:5 for this interpretation of וַיָּצַר in Dan 1:1.

[77] Joyce G. Baldwin, *Daniel*, TOTC (Leicester: Inter-Varsity, 1978), 20.

[78] See also Wiseman, *Nebuchadrezzar and Babylon*, 16.

d. The so-called failed prophecy of Daniel 11. Although this passage is discussed fully in the commentary, the conclusion is as follows: The events recorded in Dan 11:36–45 do not find fulfillment in Antiochus IV. This does not mean Daniel has given a false prophecy. Rather, these verses describe the eschatological time of distress just before the resurrection of the just and the unjust described in the next several verses (12:1–3). In 2 Thessalonians 2 Paul describes a future figure by drawing from Daniel's language here and from the little horn of Daniel 7. Admittedly, there is an unforeseen time gap in the presentation of the kings of the North, because the text jumps from Antiochus IV to the end times. This is not unreasonable, however, because Antiochus IV in Daniel 8 and 11:21–35 serves to foreshadow this eschatological figure. Antiochus IV was a "type" of the antichrist. Thus Daniel 11–12 is a mixture of prophecy fulfilled in the past (from Babylon to Antiochus IV), and prophecy that is yet future (from the antichrist through the resurrection). This is a viewpoint that goes back to Jerome (d. AD 420), who offered it in contrast with Porphyry's accusation of failed Bible prophecy.[79]

e. The four kingdoms in Daniel. The theory that the author of Daniel mistakenly thought that the Medes conquered Babylon before the Persians, resulting in an erroneous order of the four kingdoms (Babylon-Media-Persia-Greece), is not supportable in the book. It is clear from usage that a single Medo-Persian Empire is envisioned in the visions, not two separate ones. Daniel 8:20 portrays Media and Persia as a single animal with two horns, whereas if Media and Persia were considered sequential, separate kingdoms, they should have been represented by two separate beasts. The prediction of the coming of the Persians (Aramaic *parsin*) is interpreted as the coming of the Medes-and-the-Persians as if a single entity (Dan 5:28). Darius the Mede was subject to the irrevocable law of the Medes and Persians (Dan 6:8, 12, 15). If the Medes were a kingdom separate from the Persians, there would be little reason for Darius to be subject to Persian law.[80] But this makes sense if Darius' kingdom is Medo-Persia, not just Media. Daniel served the Babylonian court until the first year of King Cyrus (Dan 1:21), which would not be true if a Median kingdom occurred before Cyrus. Hence Media is

---

[79] Jerome, *Daniel*, 138–43 and passim.
[80] Gaston, *Historical Issues in the Book of Daniel*, 107–08.

not viewed in Daniel as a separate kingdom that took Babylon before the Persians in the prophecies of Daniel. Rather, the Medes are one part of a single, Medo-Persian empire.

Symbol Dan 2 (Daniel 7)	Traditional Conservative	Old Critical View	Alternative Critical View
Head of Gold (First Beast)	Babylon	Babylon	Babylon
Breast of Silver (Second Beast)	Medo-Persia	Media	Medo-Persia
Belly of Brass (Third Beast)	Greek Empire	Persia	Alexander's Empire
Legs of Iron (Fourth Beast)	Roman Empire	Greek Empire	Successors of Alexander

The alternative view that the four kingdoms consist of Babylon, Medo-Persia, Alexander's empire, and the successors of Alexander (or perhaps more simply the Seleucid Empire) is also problematic. No unified empire existed after Alexander, but rather a whole series of broken ones grew out of Alexander's kingdom. There is not enough cultural or political distinction between Alexander's Greek kingdom and the Greek kingdoms that follow to justify representing them as separate kingdoms. The third kingdom of Alexander would be very short-lived (336–323) as compared with the span of the others (Babylon 605–539; Persian 539–331; Seleucid 312–63). The split up of Alexander's kingdom is seen as four horns coming out of the same beast that represents Alexander's Greek kingdom (Dan 8:8), not as a separate entity from a separate beast.

The traditional Christian view is that Daniel's four kingdoms are Babylon, Medo-Persia, Greece, and Rome. Out of the fourth kingdom of Rome comes the "little horn," or antichrist figure. Jerome (fourth/fifth century) calls this "the traditional interpretation of all the commentators of the Christian Church, that at the end of the world, when the Roman Empire is to be destroyed, there shall be ten kings who will partition the Roman world amongst themselves," one of whom Jerome identifies as the antichrist.[81] Both Paul and the book of Revelation apply the language of Daniel to the time of Rome (2 Thessalonians 2; Revelation 13). Thus, Daniel's prophecies are not

---

[81] Jerome, *Daniel*, 76–77.

erroneous, for the kingdom of God did not arrive at the downfall of Antiochus IV. Josephus (*Antiquities* 10.10.4; 10.11.7), writing in the first century, affirms that Daniel prophesies concerning Rome's desolation of Israel and concerning Rome itself being overthrown by the kingdom of God.

There are, nonetheless, a number of objections to this traditional view: The Roman Empire has come and gone, so how can the antichrist come out of it? Is the "spirit" of the Roman Empire somehow still alive? The little horn of Daniel 8 resembles the little horn of Daniel 7, but the little horn of chapter 8 is clearly Antiochus IV. Does this not imply that the little horn of Daniel 7 is Antiochus IV as well?[82] Not necessarily. The commentary below will argue that Antiochus IV foreshadows the antichrist typologically; thus they can be similarly described though they are not the same. As for the fourth kingdom of Daniel 7, perhaps it is not simply Rome which has come and gone but a still future, eschatological kingdom that is only Rome-like. Therefore, I call Daniel's fourth kingdom Rome-and-beyond. The commentary below will further defend this viewpoint.

C. Conclusion

The case against the historicity of Daniel turns out to be inconclusive, and a strong case can be made on linguistic grounds for an early dating. There is no persuasive reason, except for an anti-supernatural bias, to reject the *prima facie* meaning of the text which indicates that the first half of Daniel is intended to be taken as historical and that the second half is autobiographical. The commentary below accepts that Daniel contains real history and genuine predictive prophecies. I will also give further arguments in favor of its historicity.

V. The Additions to Daniel

Roman Catholic and Eastern Orthodox Bibles have longer versions of the book of Daniel that include verses not found in any extant copies of the Hebrew Bible. These verses are either not printed in Protestant Bibles or printed separately in the Apocrypha. The Additions to Daniel include Susanna (sixty-four verses in

---

[82] Lucas, "Daniel," 115–16.

Theodotion, forty-six verses in the Old Greek), the Prayer of Azariah and the Song of the Three Young Men (sixty-six verses), and Bel and the Snake (forty-two verses). Though found in the two ancient Greek versions of the Old Testament (the Old Greek and Theodotion), scholars debate whether these additions were originally written in Greek or whether they may have been translated from Hebrew or Aramaic. The fact that there are two different versions in Greek suggests they may have had Semitic originals. The least likely to have a Semitic original is Susanna, which has puns in Greek (vv. 54–55, σχῖνον/σχίσει; verses 58–59, πρῖνον/πρίσαι),[83] though even there frequent appearances of *kai* point to a translation of an original Semitic *waw*. Also, frequent instances of "and it happened" sounds like Hebrew וַיְהִי, further suggesting that there may have been a Semitic original.[84]

Susanna is the story of a pious Jewish woman falsely accused of committing adultery. She is saved by Daniel who by cleaver cross examination proves the charges to be false. This story appears as chapter 13 in the Septuagint Greek Bible and the Latin Vulgate, though in Theodotion, the version church fathers regularly quote, it appears as chapter 1. The Prayer of Azariah and Song of the Three Young Men are inserted between Dan 3:23 and 24, that is, after Shadrach, Meshach, and Abednego are cast into the furnace of fire.

Bel and the Snake consists of two stories added to Daniel 12 in the Greek but appears after Susanna as Daniel 14 in the Latin Vulgate. In the first story, Daniel proves that the large amount of food given to the god Bel was in fact eaten by the priests of Bel and their families. In the second story, Daniel kills a serpent that the Babylonians had worshiped, putting his own life at risk.

These stories are lacking in the Hebrew Bible and are only rarely acknowledged in ancient Judaism. They are absent from the library at Qumran (Dead Sea Scrolls). In particular, 1QDan[b] goes from Dan 3:22–23 to 24 without adding the Prayer of Azariah or the Song of the Three Young Men. The medieval midrash *Genesis Rabba* mentions the existence of Hebrew/Aramaic copies of "Bel and the

---

[83] E. Schürer, *The History of the Jewish People in the Age of Jesus Christ*, vol. 3.2; rev. and ed. G. Vermes, Fergus Millar, and Martin Goodman (Edinburgh: T&T Clark, 1986), 722–30.

[84] R. T. McLay, "Sousanna: To the Reader," in *A New Translation of the Septuagint*, ed. A. Pietersma and B. G. Wright (New York: Oxford, 2007), 986–87.

Snake" being in circulation among the Jews (68:16). Origen (Letter to Africanus 7) says he knew a learned Jew who accepted the story of Susanna as true Scripture, and even said the names of the elders were Ahab and Zedekiah—though modern scholars believe these names are actually a midrash from Jer 29:22–23 in which they are names of false prophets roasted in fire by Nebuchadnezzar. The same identification is made in two medieval copies of "Susanna" in Hebrew housed at Oxford University.

These Additions to Daniel were cited by a number of early church fathers as if they were authentic. For example, the longer version of Ignatius's Letter to the Magnesians alludes to Susanna: "For Daniel the wise, at twelve years of age, became possessed of the divine Spirit, and convicted the elders, who in vain carried their grey hairs, of being false accusers, and of lusting after the beauty of another man's wife" (3:1).[85] Irenaeus quotes Susanna v. 56 and ascribes it to Daniel (*Against Heresies* 4.26.3), and he quotes Bel and the Snake v. 3 as if it were real history (*Against Heresies* 4.5.2). Tertullian also quotes from both Susanna and Bel and the Snake. Hippolytus's commentary on Daniel includes the Additions. Cyprian refers to Song of the Three Young Men as a model of public oration.[86]

On the other hand, Africanus and Jerome rejected the Additions to Daniel as Scripture. Africanus writes to his teacher Origen to complain that part of Daniel, the story of Susanna, was "spurious" and "plainly a modern forgery," pointing to its containing word plays that work in Greek but not Hebrew/Aramaic, its absence from the Hebrew Bible, and stylistic difference between it and the rest of Daniel. Origen replied that since God provided the Greek Old Testament to the church, and because Susanna was widely accepted in the churches, it could not contain spurious additions. Origen writes, "Are we to suppose that that Providence which in the sacred Scriptures has ministered to the edification of all the Churches of Christ, had no thought for those bought with a price, for whom

---

[85] Ignatius of Antioch, "The Epistle of Ignatius to the Magnesians," in vol. 1, *The Apostolic Fathers with Justin Martyr and Irenaeus*, ed. A. Roberts et al., The Ante-Nicene Fathers (Buffalo, NY: Christian Literature Company, 1885), 60. It should be noted that there is a longer and shorter version of Ignatius's letter. The shorter version lacks this allusion to Susanna.

[86] See Schürer, *History of the Jewish People*, 726.

Christ died?" [87] Origen thought it unthinkable that God would allow spurious Scriptures to be in common use in the church. To explain why the additions are missing from the Hebrew Bible, Origen argued that the story of Susanna might be considered slanderous of the Jewish leaders, and this gave them a motive for removing it from the book. He also found Africanus's argument too rationalistic, saying that such reasoning might also eliminate the story of Solomon judging the dispute over a baby's ownership from the Scriptures. As for the word play in Greek, Origen supposed that this was perhaps poetic license by the translator, and he considered the argument from stylistic differences unconvincing.[88]

Jerome's commentary on Daniel includes comments on the Additions. But in the commentary prologue Jerome clearly rejects these apocryphal Additions as Scripture; therefore, he feels no obligation to defend them against Porphyry's attacks. He writes,

> The stories of Susanna and of Bel and the Dragon are not contained in the Hebrew. ... For this same reason when I was translating Daniel many years ago, I noted these visions with a critical symbol, showing that they were not included in the Hebrew. ... After all, both Origen, Eusebius and Appolinarius, and other outstanding churchmen and teachers of Greece acknowledge that, as I have said, these visions are not found amongst the Hebrew, and therefore they are not obliged to answer to Porphyry for these portions which exhibit no authority as Holy Scripture.[89]

The Additions are clearly intended to teach moral and spiritual lessons. Susanna is a charming morality tale that commends the virtue of chastity (as seen in Susanna) and condemns the sins of lust and religious hypocrisy (the elders). The Prayer of Azariah and Song of the Three Young Men assert that God is transcendent over his creation, works in human history, and delivers those who trust him. Bel

---

[87] "A Letter to Origen from Africanus about the History of Suzanna" and "A Letter from Origen to Africanus," trans. F. Crombie, in vol. 4, *Fathers of the Third Century: Tertullian, Part Fourth; Minucius Felix; Commodian; Origen, Parts First and Second*, ed. A. Roberts et al.; The Ante-Nicene Fathers, 385–92. The quotation is from p. 387.

[88] Schürer, *History of the Jewish People,* 726–29.

[89] Jerome, *Daniel,* Prologue, 15–18.

and the Snake mocks idolatry, reminding us that the true God does not eat and cannot die. These are all valid theological truths.

Protestants accept as OT Scripture only what is found in the Hebrew Bible; therefore, they reject the Additions to Daniel. So, although the Additions have value as devotional literature, they are not Scripture and will not be treated in the commentary below.

EXPOSITION

Throughout the exposition, each pericope will include two outlines: one with a simple structure and one that reflects the book's
intertwining chiastic structure.

I. Court Narratives (Daniel 1–6)
  **A. Daniel and friends in Nebuchadnezzar's court
(Daniel 1)**
  B. Daniel interprets Nebuchadnezzar's dream of a statue
(Daniel 2)
  C. Shadrach, Meshach, and Abednego in the fiery furnace
(Daniel 3)
  D. Daniel interprets Nebuchadnezzar's dream of a tree
(Daniel 4)
  E. Daniel interprets the handwriting on the wall (Daniel 5)
  F. Daniel and the lion's den (Daniel 6)

II. Visions of Daniel (Daniel 7–12)

  (A) Beginning of story (1:1–21)
    (B) Dream about four world kingdoms ended by the
kingdom of God (2:1–49)
      (C) Judeans faithful in the face of death (3:1–30)
        (D) Royal pride humbled (4:1–37)
        (D′) Royal pride humbled (5:1–31)
      (C′) A Judean faithful in the face of death (6:1–28)
    (B′) Vision about four world kingdoms ended by the
kingdom of God (7:1–28)

[1] In the third year of the reign of King Jehoiakim of Judah, King Nebuchadnezzar of Babylon came to Jerusalem and laid siege to it. [2] The Lord handed King Jehoiakim of Judah over to him, along with some of the vessels from the house of God. Nebuchadnezzar carried them to the land of Babylon, to the house of his god, and put the vessels in the treasury of his god.

[3] The king ordered Ashpenaz, his chief eunuch, to bring some of the Israelites from the royal family and from the nobility— [4] young men without any physical defect, good-looking, suitable for instruction in all wisdom, knowledgeable, perceptive, and capable of serving in the king's palace. He was to teach them the Chaldean language and literature. [5] The king assigned them daily provisions from the royal food and from the wine that he drank. They were to be trained for three years, and at the end of that time they were to attend the king. [6] Among them, from the Judahites, were Daniel, Hananiah, Mishael, and Azariah. [7] The chief eunuch gave them names; he gave the name Belteshazzar to Daniel, Shadrach to Hananiah, Meshach to Mishael, and Abednego to Azariah.

[8] Daniel determined that he would not defile himself with the king's food or with the wine he drank. So he asked permission from the chief eunuch not to defile himself. [9] God had granted Daniel kindness and compassion from the chief eunuch, [10] yet he said to Daniel, "I fear my lord the king, who assigned your food and drink. What if he sees your faces looking thinner than the other young men your age? You would endanger my life with the king."

[11] So Daniel said to the guard whom the chief eunuch had assigned to Daniel, Hananiah, Mishael, and Azariah, [12] "Please test your servants for ten days. Let us be given vegetables to eat and water to drink. [13] Then examine our appearance and the appearance of the young men who are eating the king's food, and deal with your servants based on what you see." [14] He agreed with them about this and tested them for ten days. [15] At the end of ten days they looked better and healthier than all the young men who were eating the

king's food. [16] So the guard continued to remove their food and the wine they were to drink and gave them vegetables.

[17] God gave these four young men knowledge and understanding in every kind of literature and wisdom. Daniel also understood visions and dreams of every kind. [18] At the end of the time that the king had said to present them, the chief eunuch presented them to Nebuchadnezzar. [19] The king interviewed them, and among all of them, no one was found equal to Daniel, Hananiah, Mishael, and Azariah. So they began to attend the king. [20] In every matter of wisdom and understanding that the king consulted them about, he found them ten times better than all the magicians and mediums in his entire kingdom. [21] Daniel remained there until the first year of King Cyrus.

Context

Daniel 1–6 constitutes the court narratives of Daniel. Ancient Near Eastern court narrative is a genre of stories recounting the wisdom, abilities, intrigues, and adventures of royal courtiers. This includes tales of foreign courtiers who demonstrate superior wisdom to that of the king's staff and are rewarded accordingly.

This genre fits well with an early date for Daniel, as opposed to a Maccabean date during the reign of Antiochus IV (see discussion of authorship and historicity in the Introduction). Court tales do not particularly fit the context of Antiochus IV in Palestine in the 160s BC, where there was no royal court and where working in a non-Israelite king's court would have been considered treasonous among pious Jews. Collins argues that court narratives can "most plausibly be located in a milieu where such a court existed and was a focus of attention," and so he takes these court tales in Daniel to contain materials that are older than the rest of the book, though in Collins's view they were then re-edited in the Maccabean period to fit with Daniel 7–12.[1] Patterson pushes the argument in the other direction. For him, evidence for the literary unity of the book of Daniel combined with the probable pre-Maccabean milieu for the court narratives is an argument for the pre-Maccabean date and Babylonian/Persian milieu for the whole book.[2]

---

[1] J. J. Collins, "The Court-Tales in Daniel and the Development of Apocalyptic," *JBL* 94 (1975): 218–20.

[2] R. D. Patterson, "Daniel in the Critics' Court," *JETS* (1993): 444–54.

Daniel 1–6 has sometimes also been categorized as wisdom literature. The stories of Daniel and his friends exercising godly wisdom to navigate successfully though life's difficulties provide examples that readers were expected to imitate.[3]

This first court narrative is a salvation story of sorts.[4] Here God delivers Daniel and his friends not from death but from a situation in which they might be required to compromise their moral and religious ideals. God does not deliver them by overt miracle, although the healthiness of the young men after being on a vegetarian diet as opposed to eating the royal food might be thought a covert one. Rather than by overt miracle, Daniel and his friends are saved from this situation by the wisdom God gave Daniel (1:17).

The passage follows a chiastic structure (after Goldingay[5]).

> A   Babylonians defeat Judah (1:1–2)
>   B   Jewish young men taken for training (1:3–7)
>   C   Daniel seeks to avoid defilement (1:8–10)
>   C' Daniel succeeds in avoiding defilement (1:11–16)
>   B' Jewish young men successfully complete training (1:17–20)
> A' Daniel (the Jew) outlasts Babylon (1:21)

1:1 Jehoiakim, who reigned over Judah from 609 to 598 BC, began as a vassal appointed by Neco king of Egypt and was regarded by the Bible as an evil king (2 Kgs 23:34, 37). He changed his allegiance from Egypt to Babylon after Nebuchadnezzar took control of Judah following the battle of Carchemish (2 Kgs 24:1; Jer 46:2). Daniel's chronology appears to follow the Babylonian regnal year dating system that counts the time between a king's assumption of the throne and the start of the new year on the first day of the month of Tishri (Sep/Oct) as year zero. Jeremiah dates Babylon's control of Judah to the fourth year of Jehoiakim rather than the third (Jer 46:2), but this can be reconciled with Daniel on the assumption that Jeremiah follows a Jewish, non-regnal year dating system that puts

---

[3] T. Longman III, *Daniel*, NIV Application Commentary (Grand Rapids: Zondervan, 1999), 58.

[4] Collins, "The Court-Tales in Daniel," 227.

[5] J. E. Goldingay, *Daniel*, WBC 30 (Dallas: Word, 1998), 8.

the new year at Nisan (Mar/Apr). Thus Jehoiakim's fourth year in Jer 46:2 overlaps the third year of Jehoiakim in Dan 1:1, both referring to an event in 605 BC. See the discussion of authorship and historicity in the Introduction for more details.

There are two spellings for Nebuchadnezzar in the Hebrew Bible. The more common is Nebuchadnezzar (נְבוּכַדְנֶאצַּר). The less common, found in Jeremiah and Ezekiel, is spelled with an /r/ instead of an /n/ as Nebuchadrezzar (נְבוּכַדְרֶאצַּר; cf. Jer 21:2; Ezek 26:7). The latter is closer to the Akkadian *Nabu-kudurri-uṣṣur* that probably means "Nabu, protect my offspring." An earlier but less likely interpretation of the Akkadian takes it to mean, "Nabu, protect the boundary." The letters /r/ and /n/ are often interchanged between Semitic languages, so not much should be made of the spelling variation. However, it is tempting to see the more common spelling as based on a derogatory mispronunciation of the name as *Nabu-kudanu-uṣṣur* "may Nabu protect the mule."[6] By defeating Pharaoh Neco at the battle of Carchemish (Jer 46:2–12), the soon-to-be king Nebuchadnezzar was able to drive Egypt out of the Levant and take control of Palestine around May or June 605 BC. See further in the Introduction.

The words "laid siege" refer to a very short besiegement before Jerusalem surrendered. It is likely that the reference in 2 Chr 36:6 to Nebuchadnezzar's attacking Jehoiakim and bounding him in shackles to take him to Babylon occurs at this time (see comments on v. 2). Although this besiegement was minor enough that the historical books of the Bible fail to mention it explicitly, it is important for Daniel and his friends personally since it led to their deportations. It is also important for the book of Daniel since this event in 605 BC begins the period of seventy years that Daniel will mull over in Dan 9:2. See further in the Introduction.

1:2 Note the theology of God's sovereign, providential workings in and molding of human events: "The Lord handed King Jehoiakim ... over." Hebrew נתן ("give, put, set") is used similarly in 1:9 and 17 to express God's sovereign work (see §3.8). Whereas the Babylonians would likely attribute the plundering of the temple of Yahweh to the superiority of their god Marduk, Daniel attributes

---

[6] D. J. Wiseman, *Nebuchadrezzar and Babylon* (Oxford: Oxford University, 1985), 2–5.

these events to the sovereign will of Yahweh (see Dan 9:11–14). In judging Israel as a nation, God allows the innocent to suffer along with the wicked,[7] including the exile of Daniel and his friends. The narrator likely derives from Jeremiah the idea that God handed his people over to Nebuchadnezzar (cf. Jer 21:7; 25:9). On "Lord" rather than "LORD" (Yahweh), see comments at 9:3.

A plundering of Judah by Babylon was predicted by the prophets (Isa 39:6; Jer 20:5). Second Chronicles 36:7 ("Also Nebuchadnezzar took some of the articles of the LORD's temple to Babylon and put them in his temple in Babylon") may draw on Daniel's language here or vice versa. Though Daniel could be telescoping two plunderings of the temple, a minor plundering in 605 and a more significant plundering at the end of Jehoiakim's reign in 598/7, 2 Chronicles is better taken as referring to a plundering in 605. Jehoiakim was placed on the throne by Pharaoh Neco in 609 BC (2 Kgs 23:34). According to 2 Chr 36:6–7, using language similar to Dan 1:2, Nebuchadnezzar shackled Jehoiakim for exile and took items from the temple to Babylon. This does not fit the end of Jehoiakim's reign in 598/7 BC since at that time Jehoiakim died and was buried in Jerusalem after his corpse was cast outside the walls of the city (2 Kgs 24:6; Jer 22:18–19; 36:30), but this could refer to a brief exile after Nebuchadnezzar took control of Jerusalem or perhaps a threat of exile that was annulled when Jehoiakim swore allegiance to Nebuchadnezzar.[8]

The "vessels from the house of God" play a role in Dan 5:2. They are considered holy, derived from God's holiness (see §3.6). The theological theme of desecration and/or restoration of God's holy temple recurs a number of times in Daniel (1:2; 5:2; 8:11–14; 9:26–27; 11:31; 12:11). That God's temple was plundered would have raised questions in the minds of Jews as to whether God was really sovereign (see §3.8).[9] In fact God, as an expression of his sovereignty, was himself responsible for allowing the sanctuary to be destroyed (9:16; cf. Lam 2:7).

"Babylon" in Hebrew is "Shinar" (CSB note; NASB). It is often rendered "Babylon" in the Old Greek LXX, as is the case here, though

---

[7] R. W. Pierce, *Daniel*, Teach the Text (Grand Rapids: Baker, 2015), 14.

[8] T. E. Gaston, *Historical Issues in the Book of Daniel* (Oxford: Taanathshilo, 2009), 22–29.

[9] G. Goswell, "The Temple Theme in the Book of Daniel," *JETS* 55/3 (2012): 514.

Theodotion transliterates as a proper noun in Greek. The plain of Shinar is first mentioned in conjunction with the great hunter and king Nimrod and with the tower of Babel story, which makes Babylon a symbol of sinful pride and disobedience to God (Gen 10:8–11; 11:2). Nebuchadnezzar's sacking of the temple is another example of this (see Daniel 4). Shinar included the cities Babylon, Erech (or Uruk), and Accad (or Akkad) in central Mesopotamia, a region that includes the modern city of Baghdad some fifty miles north of Babylon. On the biblical-theological theme of Babylon as a proud nation in rebellion against God, see §7.

The expression "house of his god" or "house of his gods" (CSB note) is lacking in the Old Greek, leading some translators (e.g., NRSV) to think it not original and omit it as dittography. Assuming the expression is original, "house of his god" is probably a reference to the Esagila temple of Marduk, patron god of the city of Babylon, suggesting the singular translation "god." That said, Mesopotamian temples dedicated to one god could be "visited" by other gods, as when the image of Nabu, son of Marduk in the mythology, was brought from his own temple in Borsippa about ten miles away to Esagila in Babylon on the New Year's Akitu festival to visit his "father."[10]

1:3 Josephus cites the Greek historian Berosus to the effect that immediately upon learning of the death of his father (Nabopolassar) Nebuchadnezzar dealt with "captive Jews, and Phoenicians, and Syrians, and those of the Egyptian nations" before hastening to Babylon to be crowned (*Antiquities* 10.11.1). Daniel and his friends may have been among the Jews captured at this time as Nebuchadnezzar came to Judah to consolidate his territories captured from Egypt. From a theological perspective, their exile fulfills God's warnings that covenant violations would lead to exile (Lev 26:33, 38; Deut 28:64; see §4.3).

Ashpenaz's job was to direct the education of foreigners in Babylonian language, literature, and customs. Judging from his name, Ashpenaz appears to be non-Babylonian, probably Persian.[11] He presumably had a Babylonian court name, as did officials in

---

[10] H. W. F. Saggs, *The Greatness That Was Babylon*, rev. ed. (London: Sidgwick & Jackson, 1988), 310.

[11] P. W. Coxon, "Ashpenaz," *ABD* 1:490–91.

Nebuchadnezzar's so-called Court List.[12] Daniel and his friends had Babylonian court names as well.

"His chief eunuch" (literally, "chief of his eunuchs") is a rendering based on the Old Greek and Theodotion that takes סָרִיס to mean eunuch, though it is better taken to mean "[court] official" (NASB; NIV). Hebrew סָרִיס is derived from Akkadian *ša rēši (šarri)* "the one of the (king's) head."[13] Potipher, who had a wife, is called a סָרִיס (Gen 39:1; cf. v. 7). Any association with eunuchs is secondary, going back to the common practice of employing eunuchs in positions of intimate contact with the court, especially in caring for wives (e.g., Hegai and Shaashgaz in Esth 2:3, 14). There is little reason contextually to assume that either Ashpenaz or the Hebrew young men were eunuchs. That the Hebrews were "without any physical defect" (v. 4a) probably precludes their being eunuchs at that time since Lev 21:17–20 identifies "crushed testicle" as a "defect" (cf. Deut 23:1). The cognate expression in Akkadian does not typically mean eunuch.[14]

Though the young men are called "Israelites," that is, descendants of the patriarch Jacob (renamed Israel), more specifically they are Jews (3:8, 12), people from the country and tribe of Judah. The northern kingdom of Israel had long ago ceased to exist (722 BC).

"Royal family" is literally "seed of kingship." This fulfills the prophecy of Isaiah that descendants of Hezekiah would go into exile as eunuchs/court officials (סָרִיסִים; Isa 39:7). The Jewish young men may have been brought into exile in conjunction with Judah's King Jehoiakim's exile (see comments on v. 2). That Daniel and his friends had to be of royal descent suggests they were intended from the beginning to play some political role, perhaps as liaisons between Babylon and its vassal nation of Judah. It turns out instead that Daniel serves as an adviser of kings, giving advice based on his insights into the supernatural, a role also played by Nebuchadnezzar's diviners (see v. 20). "Nobility" (פַּרְתְּמִים) is a loanword from Old Persian *fratama*[15] used only here and Esth 1:3; 6:9. On loanwords, see Introduction.

1:4 Daniel and his friends were probably in their early teens at their exile. They lack "defect" (מְאוּם; without "blemish," ESV)—that is, they are "handsome" (NIV), like Joseph whom Daniel resembles

---

[12] Wiseman, *Nabuchadrezzar and Babylon*, 84–85.

[13] R. D. Patterson, "סָרִיס," *TWOT* 634–35.

[14] Wiseman, *Nabuchadrezzar and Babylon*, 85.

[15] "פַּרְתְּמִים," *HALOT* 3:979.

(Gen 38:6). This not only suggests that they are not eunuchs (see v. 3) but alludes to the sacrificial system. They are like animal sacrifices and priests, dedicated to God and without physical defect/blemish (Lev 22:20–25; 21:17–21). They are also intellectually gifted. Specifically, they had to be "suitable for instruction" (or alternatively "having insight/success"). The Hebrew root שָׂכַל means "to have success, insight, be clever." It is unclear whether this is a statement of "aptitude" (NIV) or accomplishment ("versed," NRSV). It likely implies both. On this root's theological connections, see v. 17 below.

"Chaldean" was originally a term for Babylon's ruling ethnic group. The Chaldeans entered southern Babylonia about 850 BC, and by the mid-700s took over the throne. Merodach-Baladan (2 Kgs 20:12; Isa 39:1) was Chaldean of the Bit Yakini tribe. The Chaldeans quickly assimilated to Babylonian culture and over time "Chaldean" came to mean "Babylonian." In Dan 2:2 it is a term for diviners of Chaldean-Babylonian descent. The language spoken at court was in fact Aramaic (Dan 2:4), so Aramaic was presumably part of their studies.

The scholarly Babylonian language in Daniel's day was Akkadian (Late or Neo-Babylonian dialect), and Daniel and his friends were given new personal names in Akkadian (see comments on vv. 6–7 below). So they presumably also studied the Akkadian literature that includes a whole range of historical, religious, magical, economic, and legal texts in Akkadian—much of which remains extant today: Laws of Hammurabi (widely copied in Neo-Babylonian times[16]), the Gilgamesh Epic (which contains a version of the flood story), Enuma Elish (Babylonian creation story of how Marduk, the god of Babylon, became king of the gods), the Babylonian Chronicle (gives historical data concerning activities of Babylonian kings), and the like. The curriculum perhaps included the omen literature with the expectation that Daniel would serve as a *baru* ("seer") or expert in divination, and could have included various writings about the magical arts (dream books, celestial omen collections, extispicy manuals, etc.).[17] Since knowledge of Sumerian is helpful in the study of Akkadian, it too was probably part of the curriculum.

---

[16] Wiseman, *Nabuchadrezzar and Babylon*, 88.

[17] J. H. Walton, *Ancient Near Eastern Thought and the Old Testament: Introducing the Conceptual World of the Hebrew Bible* (Grand Rapids: Baker Academic, 2006), 243.

1:5 "Food" is Hebrew פַּת־בַּג (also vv. 8, 13, 15–16), a loanword from Old Persian *patibaga*,[18] or Elamite *batibaziš*,[19] referring to food for the royal court, which would be of finest quality. Daniel and his friends were to be "trained [better, "educated"] for three years." Hebrew גָּדַל is also used of raising children. Babylon of the Neo-Babylonian period considered itself the "city of learning/wisdom" (Akkadian *al nemeqi*), a title once claimed by Assur, the capital of Assyria.[20] This would prepare them to "attend the king," literally "stand before the king" (CSB note).

1:6–7 Only four young men from Judah are named. There could have been others who, unlike these, did not maintain their Jewish distinctives. "Chief," used in vv. 7–11 and 18, is a different Hebrew word than "chief" in v. 3 (שַׂר rather than רַב), though contextually they are synonyms for the man in charge. Daniel and his companions are each given Akkadian-Babylonian names, not only to make their names easier for Babylonians to pronounce but also to enculturate them. Babylon became a cosmopolitan home to various ethnic groups, and the Aramaic language was probably more widely spoken than Babylonian by this time. But Babylonian civilization remained the cultural norm, which is why the Chaldeans (of whom Nebuchadnezzar was one) who had migrated to Babylonia themselves adopted Babylonian names in the process of acculturation, as did other ethnic groups besides the Jews who found themselves living in Babylon.[21] The intent is religious indoctrination as well as education. Each Hebrew name refers to the God of Israel, whereas the new Babylonian names, though there are uncertainties in the exact etymologies, refer to Babylonian gods, as Nebuchadnezzar himself explains for Belteshazzar (4:8). The Babylonians sought to assimilate these Jews into their polytheistic culture and wean them from their own religion. This was an affront to God's call for his people to be holy and distinct from the nations (see §4.1).

The names of Daniel and his friends teach about God (see §3.2). Daniel is derived from דִּין ("to judge") and אֵל ("God") and means "God judges," "God is judge," "God is my judge" (see §4.2). There is

---

[18] "פַּת־בַּג," *HALOT* 3:984.

[19] Wiseman, *Nebuchadrezzar and Babylon*, 85.

[20] Ibid., 86.

[21] P.-Al. Beaulieu, "Nebuchadnezzar's Babylon as World Capital," *Journal of the Canadian Society for Mesopotamian Studies* 3 (2008): 5–12, esp. p. 6.

broader debate as to whether î in personal names is usually a case vowel or the first-person singular pronoun "my."[22] While the /î/ element in *Dan-i-el* could mean "my," the alternative spelling in Ezek 14:14, 20; 28:3 (taken in the Introduction as a reference to the Daniel of the book of Daniel) suggests that it might not mean "my" since that spelling of the name lacks the letter yod (ʾ) denoting "my." His Babylonian name Belteshazzar is probably derived from Akkadian *beletsharuṣṣur*, which means "may the lady [goddess Ishtar] protect the king" or, possibly, *Balaṭsu-uṣṣur*, "May he [Marduk? Nabu?] protect his life"[23] A less likely possibility is that Belteshazzar is an intentionally garbled form of Belshazzar ("May Bel protect the king"; see comments at 5:1). In other words, Daniel's Babylonian name is the same name as that of a subsequent king, though the book garbles Daniel's Babylonian name to distinguish the two men and to obscure the association of Daniel's name with a false god.[24]

Hananiah means "Yahweh is gracious" (see §3.6). He is renamed Shadrach, which may be an intentionally garbled pronunciation of Marduk the god of Babylon[25] or derived from *šaduraku* (or *šuduraku*) meaning, "I am very much afraid."[26] A Persian derivation has also been proposed, though it seems less likely since the other names appear to be Babylonian.[27] The older proposal that takes Shadrach from *šudur-Aku* ("command of Aku")[28] appears generally abandoned since neither šudur or *Aku* can be confirmed.[29]

Mishael in Hebrew is a rhetorical question that implies the greatness of God: "Who is what God is?" (see §3.7). He is renamed Meshach. The meaning is uncertain, but the name could be derived from Akkadian *mešaku*, "I am insignificant," or *mešahu*, "I am

---

[22] *IBHS*, 127.

[23] Wiseman, *Nebuchadrezzar and Babylon*, 85; Stephen R. Miller, *Daniel*, NAC 18 (Nashville: Broadman & Holman, 1994), 65.

[24] William Shea, "Bel(te)shazzar meets Belshazzar," *AUSS* 26.1 (Spring 1988), 67–81.

[25] S.v. "Shadrach," *ABD* 5:1150.

[26] Wiseman, *Nebuchadrezzar and Babylon*, 85; "שַׁדְרַךְ," *HALOT* 4:1423.

[27] "שַׁדְרַךְ," *HALOT* 4:1423.

[28] "שַׁדְרַךְ," BDB 995.1; Miller, *Daniel*, 65.

[29] No deity by the name of Aku is known in the Babylonian pantheon, though it could be a garbled form of Anu. *Aku* as a common noun means "cripple" or spelled *akku* "owl" (W. von Sodon, *Akkadisches Handwörterbuch* [Weisbaden: Harrassowitz, 1965], 1:29, 30). The Akkadian noun šudur does not exist, and the meaning of the rare word *šudduru* (*šunduru*) is unknown (*CAD*, s.v. *šunduru*).

forgiven."[30] The older proposal that derives it from *mi-sha-Aku* ("who is what Aku is?")[31] lacks support.

Azariah means, "Yahweh helps" (see §4.8). Abednego appears to be derived from *abdi nabu*, "servant of Nabu [son of Marduk]," in which the divine name Nabu is intentionally garbled to Nego by replacing the letter ב with the next letter of the Hebrew alphabet ג,[32] perhaps influenced by an Aramaic wordplay on Nabu: *Ebed (Arad)-negu* "Servant of the Shining One [= Nabu]."[33]

Subsequently in the narratives, the Babylonian names of these four young men tend to be used in overtly Babylonian contexts (Dan 2:49 3:12–30; 4:9, 18–19; 5:12), while in other settings, and when mentioned by the narrator, their Hebrew names tend to be used (2:13–14, 17; etc.).[34]

1:8 Up until now Daniel and his companions are portrayed as pawns under the control of the Babylonians. Then Daniel, showing himself a leader,[35] asserted himself to maintain his religious heritage (see §4.8). The problem with the king's food (see v. 5) is not spelled out. Was the food initially offered to idols before being served? This is also a matter of concern in the New Testament (1 Cor 10:28; Rev 2:14, 20). Oppenheim gives evidence that after being symbolically set before the image of deity, food would then be taken to the king—in one case brought to Belshazzar as the crown prince—for consumption. The idea was that offering it first to a deity transferred a blessing on the one who ate it.[36] To eat food offered to an idol could be considered acknowledging the deity to whom it had been offered, something a pious Jew like Daniel could not do.

Or was the food non-kosher, including pork which is forbidden by the Jewish food laws (Lev 11:7)? Or was the problem that the meat did not have its blood properly drained (cf. Gen 9:4)? The request to substitute vegetables (v. 12) suggests the problem is especially with

---

[30] Wiseman, *Nebuchadrezzar and Babylon*, 85.

[31] "מֵישַׁךְ," BDB 568.2; Miller, *Daniel*, 65.

[32] "עֲבֵד נְגוֹ," *HALOT* 2:776.

[33] Wiseman, *Nebuchadrezzar and Babylon*, 86.

[34] Shea, "Bel(te)shazzar Meets Belshazzar," 73; A. E. Steinmann, *Daniel*, Concordia Commentary (Saint Louis: Concordia, 2008), 89.

[35] Steinmann, *Daniel*, 99.

[36] A. L. Oppenheim, *Ancient Mesopotamia*, rev. ed. E. Reiner (Chicago: University of Chicago Press, 1964), 188–89.

the meat. Yet Daniel objects also to the wine, which is not inherently forbidden to Jews by the Torah, though gentile wine is forbidden in later Judaism by the Mishnah (*Avodah Zarah* 2:3), perhaps based on this passage. More than one explanation may apply.

Here is the driving theological issue: Israel's food laws were meant to separate Israel from the gentiles (see Lev 20:25–26) to maintain Israel as a holy people separated to God (see §4.1). Daniel knew that to compromise even in the area of diet was spiritually detrimental.

1:9–10 That "God had granted [נתן] Daniel kindness" (v. 9) affirms God's sovereign providential working in the affairs of his people (see §3.8; cf. 1:2 and 1:17 for more on this theme). Two attributes associated with God are "kindness" and "compassion" (see §3.6). "Kindness" (Hebrew חֶסֶד) is a covenant term (see §4.3) with a broad range of meanings, referring to the love, grace, favor, mercy, loyalty, faithfulness, or kindness shown to someone with whom one has a relationship.[37] God's granting Daniel חֶסֶד thus implies he was in good standing with God. "Compassion" (רַחֲמִים, always plural) is an emotion frequently attributed to God in prayers (Dan 9:9 and comments there). It is cognate with the mother's womb (רֶחֶם), suggesting this is a deep-seated, mother-like emotion of love or pity.

There is a strong contrast between Ashpenaz's wanting to help Daniel and the official's fears. As subsequent narratives show, Nebuchadnezzar was someone to be feared (2:5; 3:6, 29; 5:19). This is followed by a question, "What if he see your faces looking thinner … ?" "Thinner" (זעֵף), which could also be rendered "poorer" (cf. NRSV; NIV "worse"; NASB "more haggard"), is only used elsewhere in Gen 40:6, where EVV render it "distraught, troubled, dejected, sad" rather than thin. The Old Greek uses διατρέπω ("changed for the worst") and Theodotion renders with σκυθρωπός ("sad, sullen"). "Your age" (גִּיל, "age-group, circle") is a word that only occurs here in the Hebrew Bible. The meaning is based on the Greek (Theodotion, συνῆλιξ, "of like or equal age"; Old Greek, συντρέφω, "grow up together") and cognates in later Hebrew and Arabic. "Endanger my life" is more literally "You would make my head guilty" (CSB note)— that is, subject to decapitation.

---

[37] K. D. Sakenfeld, *The Meaning of Ḥesed in the Hebrew Bible: A New Inquiry* (Missoula, MT: Scholars, 1978); Sakenfeld, "Love (OT)," *ABD* 4:377–381.

1:11–14 "Guard" or "guardian" (NABRE) (v. 11; מֶלְצַר) is a person whose job was to protect. It is a loanword from Akkadian *manṣāru/ maṣṣāru.[38] Daniel showed his practical wisdom (vv. 17, 20) by persistence in trying to maintain his Jewish scruples after being refused by Ashpenaz. Rather than give up, he attempted to work with a lesser official, the guard, who proved more amenable. Daniel proposed a "scientific" experiment, which the guard accepted. Though the verb "test" is an imperative, the term "servants" shows humility and subordination to Babylonian authority. "Ten days" is a lengthy period of verification to show any detrimental effects of their diet of vegetables and water in comparison with the "control group" of young men eating the royal food and wine. Revelation 2:10 seems to allude to this ten days of testing for Daniel and his three friends when it speaks of Smyrna being similarly tested ten days.[39] John appears to mean for his audience to think of themselves in a position similar to that of Daniel and his friends—ruled by a hostile, demanding foreign power but committed to faithfulness to God. The faithfulness of Daniel and his friends thus typifies—both in the book of Daniel and more broadly in biblical theology—how the people of God must remain faithful under pressure.

The guard may have exchanged his own food for the royal rations issued to the young men.[40] "Vegetables" (זֵרְעִים) is actually a term broader than vegetables, denoting "a class of food that is not meat but including grains,"[41] like a modern vegetarian diet. The root זרע is related to to "seeds" and "sowing."

1:15–16 "Better and healthier" is literally "better and fatter (בְּרִיא) of flesh." In a world where starvation and malnutrition were greater dangers than obesity, fatter (well-fed) was healthier. In Pharaoh's dream the skinny (= unhealthy) cows and grain are contrasted with the fat (= healthy) cows and grain (Gen 41:3–7). In addition, Ps 73:4 describes the wealthy as "fat" in the sense of well-fed and healthy (Ps

---

[38] "מֶלְצַר," HALOT 2:594.

[39] G. K. Beale and S. M. McDonough, "Revelation," in Commentary on the New Testament Use of the Old Testament, ed. G. K. Beale and D. A. Carson (Grand Rapids: Baker Academic, 2007), 1093.

[40] J. G. Baldwin, Daniel, TOTC (Leicester: Inter-Varsity, 1978), 84.

[41] J. Swanson, "זרעים (zē·rō·ʿîm)," Dictionary of Biblical Languages with Semantic Domains: Hebrew (Old Testament), electronic ed. (Oak Harbor: Logos Research Systems, 1997).

73:4). It is known today that vegetarian diets, so long as they include items with enough protein, vitamins, and minerals, can be as healthy as any non-vegetarian diet. On the other hand, the author probably intends the reader to understand the healthier appearance of the young men as a miracle.

1:17 Theologically, intellect and academic success are among blessings given (נתן) by God (see §4.4; see Jas 1:17; 1 Cor 4:7). The intelligence of Daniel is repeated later (5:11, 14). Thus Daniel affirms that fervent faith and intelligence are entirely compatible with each other.[42] This is the third time נתן is used to express God's sovereign work (1:2, 9; see §3.8). "Understanding" (from שׂכל; see 1:4 above) includes qualities of success and insight. Thus "skill" (ESV, NKJV) and "understanding" (CSB, NIV) are both correct renderings, but neither is complete. Those whom God is with find שׂכל (1 Sam 18:14; 2 Kgs 18:7). Studying God's word—an activity in which Daniel engages (Dan 9:1–2)—is a source of שׂכל (Josh 1:8–9; 1 Kgs 2:1–4). It is associated with obeying God's covenant (Deut 29:9), turning to God (Jer 10:21), and trusting God (Prov 16:20). The serpent tempted Eve with a type of שׂכל apart from and in contradiction with God's revelation, a שׂכל that led to death (Gen 3:6). On "literature" see v. 4.

As seen in Proverbs, "wisdom" (Hebrew/Aramaic חָכְמָה) has to do with skillfulness in living. The root can refer to skills such as craftsmanship and navigating rough seas (Exod 36:1–2, "skilled/wisdom"; Ps 107:27, "skill" CSB). It thus goes beyond mere knowledge to proper use of knowledge in practical situations. Only God knows where true wisdom lies (Job 28:23). Godliness and obeying God's instructions in Scripture—both exhibited by Daniel—are the first steps in attaining wisdom (Ps 111:10; Prov 1:9; 9:10).

"Daniel also understood" does not bring out the pending case syntax with its emphatic subject suggesting contrast with his friends: "But as for Daniel, he understood visions and dreams." In terms of biblical theology, this statement invites the reader to associate Daniel with others who have had revelatory dreams and visions: Abraham, Jacob, Joseph, Moses, and the prophets. Visions and dreams are not infrequently mentioned together (Num 12:6; Job 33:15; Dan 2:28; 4:5; 7:1; Joel 2:28) to describe how God conveys revelation (see §2) both to prophets and other individuals. The person received

---

[42] Baldwin, *Daniel*, 167.

messages and/or symbolic imagery while dreaming or in some sort of trance. Such visions/dreams were given to Nebuchadnezzar (Dan 2:3; 4:5) and to Daniel himself (Dan 2:19; 7:1; 8:1–2; 9:23; 10:1). That Daniel understood "dreams of every kind" may imply a superiority to divination priests who specialized in certain kinds of dreams.[43]

1:18–19 The "chief eunuch" (better "chief official"; see comments at v. 3) is Ashpenaz, who presented Daniel and his comrades to the king to interview them and commission them for public service in accordance with their abilities. "They began to attend the king" is literally, "they stood before the king," a phrase probably metaphorical for entering the king's service. However, another interpretation is possible. The expression may refer to how Nebuchadnezzar confirmed that these young men were so gifted. They stood before him, he asked them questions, and their answers proved that their abilities surpassed all others.

1:20–21 On "wisdom," see v. 17. "Wisdom and understanding" is literally "wisdom *of* understanding." That is, they showed insight and balanced, professional judgment in all their responses. "Understanding" (בִּינָה, "insight, understanding"), often used as a synonym for wisdom, is derived from the verb בִּין, used in v. 4. Like wisdom, בִּינָה and its cognates can refer to professional skills (see 1 Chr 15:22 [music]; 27:32 [counselor]: Exod 31:3 [craftsman/artisan]) as well as intellectual ability. "Ten times better" is a hyperbole to indicate they were decisively better. The Hebrew reads "ten hands" (CSB note). "Hands" meaning "times" occurs also in Gen 43:34. Daniel's superiority finds confirmation in Daniel 2 during Nebuchadnezzar's second year (Dan 2:1–49) while Daniel was still in his three years of training (see 1:5). Only Daniel (not Babylon's wise men) could interpret Nebuchadnezzar's dream. On "magicians and mediums" see 2:2. From the Babylonian perspective, Daniel with his prophetic gift was regarded as a diviner.

"The first year of King Cyrus" takes us to near the end of Daniel's career (cf. 6:28; 10:1) and the end of Jeremiah's prophecy of a seventy-year Babylonian exile (see comments at 9:2), which began with Daniel's own exile in 605/604 (1:1–5). Thus this verse forms an

---

[43] A. L. Oppenheim, *The Interpretation of Dreams in the Ancient Near East with a Translation of an Assyrian Dream Book*, Transactions of the American Philosophical Society 46.3 (Philadelphia: American Philosophical Society, 1956), 239.

inclusio with the beginning of the chapter. Daniel finished his training around 602 BC. He remained in the employ of the Babylonian court until the Persians replaced them. Cyrus conquered Babylon in 539 BC, roughly six and a half decades after Daniel first came to Babylonia. No mention is made of any Median rule between Babylon and Cyrus of Persia, contrary to a common critical view of Daniel's four kingdoms (see Introduction).

Bridge

Daniel 1 fits into the biblical-theological motifs of the need for God's people to be holy (see §4.1), to remain faithful to God even at personal risk (see §4.8), and to use their God-given practical wisdom (one of God's blessings, see §4.4) within a hostile environment. God allowed the exile in accord with his covenant threats (Dan 1:1–3; see §4.3). Though he is given the title "Lord" (Dan 1:2; see §3.2), at issue is whether God would remain Lord in the lives of these exiles. Would loyalty to their new lord Nebuchadnezzar—and his attempt to indoctrinate them in Babylonian culture—take precedence over their submission to God?

Daniel and his friends were keen not to violate God's laws concerning forbidden foods (Lev 11; Deut 14:3–21; cp. the forbidden fruit in Gen 2:16–17), even though this was not without danger (cf. Dan 1:10). A major purpose of Israel's food laws was to help make Israel separate from the nations (Lev 11:44–45; 20:25–26). In the context of exile it was not possible for Jews like Daniel to be totally separated from gentiles, but this was not essential. Nor was it necessary to remain ignorant of Babylonian ways. That Daniel and his friends became experts in the Babylonian language and literature, and excelled in its educational system, is to be celebrated. They even became officials in the Babylonian government despite the idolatrous elements. What was essential was to resist the pressure to assimilate to the culture morally and spiritually—something Israel at the time of the judges failed to do (Judg 2:11–13).

Christians today are likewise pressured to conform to the world's values, and we too must remain holy (1 Pet 1:15–16). This holiness does not require a special diet, for Israel's food laws were abolished (Mark 7:19; Acts 10:9–16; 11:9; Rom 14:14). Even meat possibly sacrificed to idols can in most cases be eaten by a Christian with a clear conscience (1 Cor 10:25-30). This abolition of the food laws conveys deep theological symbolism, namely a breaking down of the barrier between Jews and gentiles in the church, as God taught Peter (Acts 11:4-9). Under the new covenant, we are sent into a world that is hostile to our God and his Word, but we are not to be "of the world" morally or religiously (John 17:14-19).

In such situations we must be "as shrewd as serpents and as harmless as doves" (Matt 10:16), just as Daniel wisely found ways to remain faithful despite his environment. Other court narratives contain overt supernaturalism, but here God expresses his sovereignty (see §3.8) and blesses his faithful servants (see §4.4) in more subtle, providential ways without obvious miracles: in history (1:2), in working unseen to create good results (1:9), and in granting his servants practical wisdom (1:17). This narrative is an example of what Paul states in Rom 8:28: "We know that all things work together for the good of those who love God." Daniel and his friends show God's people that living holy in an environment not supportive of our religion is not only possible but that we might even thrive in that kind of environment—with faith, commitment, wisdom, and God's help.

I. Court Narratives (Daniel 1–6)

A. Daniel and friends in Nebuchadnezzar's court (Daniel 1)

B. Daniel interprets Nebuchadnezzar's dream of a statue (Daniel 2)

C. Shadrach, Meshach, and Abednego in the fiery furnace (Daniel 3)

D. Daniel interprets Nebuchadnezzar's dream of a tree (Daniel 4)

E. Daniel interprets the handwriting on the wall (Daniel 5)

F. Daniel and the lion's den (Daniel 6)

II. Visions of Daniel (Daniel 7–12)

(A) Beginning of story (1:1–21)

 (B) Dream about four world kingdoms ended by the kingdom of God (2:1–49)

  (C) Judeans faithful in the face of death (3:1–30)

   (D) Royal pride humbled (4:1–37)

   (D′) Royal pride humbled (5:1–31)

  (C′) A Judean faithful in the face of death (6:1–28)

 (B′) Vision about four world kingdoms ended by the kingdom of God (7:1–28)

  (E) Vision of Persian and Greek kingdoms to Antiochus (8:1–27)

   (F) Vision of seventy weeks (9:1–27)

  (E′) Vision of Persian and Greek kingdoms to Antiochus (10:1–11:35)

 (B″) World kingdoms ended and the righteous established (11:36–12:3)

(A′) End of story: Vision sealed until the end (12:4–13)

¹ In the second year of his reign, Nebuchadnezzar had dreams that troubled him, and sleep deserted him. ² So the king gave orders to summon the magicians, mediums, sorcerers, and Chaldeans to tell the king his dreams. When they came and stood before the king, ³ he said to them, "I have had a dream and am anxious to understand it."

⁴ The Chaldeans spoke to the king (Aramaic begins here): "May the king live forever. Tell your servants the dream, and we will give the interpretation."

⁵ The king replied to the Chaldeans, "My word is final: If you don't tell me the dream and its interpretation, you will be torn limb from limb, and your houses will be made a garbage dump. ⁶ But if you make the dream and its interpretation known to me, you'll receive gifts, a reward, and great honor from me. So make the dream and its interpretation known to me."

⁷ They answered a second time, "May the king tell the dream to his servants, and we will make known the interpretation."

⁸ The king replied, "I know for certain you are trying to gain some time, because you see that my word is final. ⁹ If you don't tell me the dream, there is one decree for you. You have conspired to tell me something false or fraudulent until the situation changes. So tell me the dream and I will know you can give me its interpretation."

¹⁰ The Chaldeans answered the king, "No one on earth can make known what the king requests. Consequently, no king, however great and powerful, has ever asked anything like this of any magician, medium, or Chaldean. ¹¹ What the king is asking is so difficult that no one can make it known to him except the gods, whose dwelling is not with mortals." ¹² Because of this, the king became violently angry and gave orders to destroy all the wise men of Babylon. ¹³ The decree was issued that the wise men were to be executed, and they searched for Daniel and his friends, to execute them.

¹⁴ Then Daniel responded with tact and discretion to Arioch, the captain of the king's guard, who had gone out to execute the wise men of Babylon. ¹⁵ He asked Arioch, the king's officer, "Why is the decree from the king so harsh?" Then Arioch explained the situation to Daniel. ¹⁶ So Daniel went and asked the king to give him some time, so that he could give the king the interpretation.

¹⁷ Then Daniel went to his house and told his friends Hananiah, Mishael, and Azariah about the matter, ¹⁸ urging them to ask the God of the heavens for mercy concerning this mystery, so Daniel and his friends would not be destroyed with the rest of Babylon's wise men. ¹⁹ The mystery was then revealed to Daniel in a vision at night, and Daniel praised the God of the heavens ²⁰ and declared:

> May the name of God
> be praised forever and ever,
> for wisdom and power belong to him.
> ²¹ He changes the times and seasons;
> he removes kings and establishes kings.
> He gives wisdom to the wise

and knowledge to those
who have understanding.
²² He reveals the deep and hidden things;
he knows what is in the darkness,
and light dwells with him.
²³ I offer thanks and praise to you,
God of my fathers,
because you have given me
wisdom and power.
And now you have let me know
what we asked of you,
for you have let us know
the king's mystery.

²⁴ Therefore Daniel went to Arioch, whom the king had assigned to destroy the wise men of Babylon. He came and said to
him, "Don't destroy the wise men of Babylon! Bring me before the
king, and I will give him the interpretation."
²⁵ Then Arioch quickly brought Daniel before the king and
said to him, "I have found a man among the Judean exiles who can
let the king know the interpretation."
²⁶ The king said in reply to Daniel, whose name was Belteshazzar, "Are you able to tell me the dream I had and its interpretation?"
²⁷ Daniel answered the king: "No wise man, medium, magician, or diviner is able to make known to the king the mystery he
asked about. ²⁸ But there is a God in heaven who reveals mysteries,
and he has let King Nebuchadnezzar know what will happen in the
last days. Your dream and the visions that came into your mind
as you lay in bed were these: ²⁹ Your Majesty, while you were in
your bed, thoughts came to your mind about what will happen in
the future. The revealer of mysteries has let you know what will
happen. ³⁰ As for me, this mystery has been revealed to me, not
because I have more wisdom than anyone living, but in order that
the interpretation might be made known to the king, and that you
may understand the thoughts of your mind.
³¹ "Your Majesty, as you were watching, suddenly a colossal
statue appeared. That statue, tall and dazzling, was standing in front
of you, and its appearance was terrifying. ³² The head of the statue
was pure gold, its chest and arms were silver, its stomach and thighs
were bronze, ³³ its legs were iron, and its feet were partly iron and
partly fired clay. ³⁴ As you were watching, a stone broke off without a
hand touching it, struck the statue on its feet of iron and fired clay,

and crushed them. ³⁵ Then the iron, the fired clay, the bronze, the silver, and the gold were shattered and became like chaff from the summer threshing floors. The wind carried them away, and not a trace of them could be found. But the stone that struck the statue became a great mountain and filled the whole earth.

³⁶ "This was the dream; now we will tell the king its interpretation. ³⁷ Your Majesty, you are king of kings. The God of the heavens has given you sovereignty, power, strength, and glory. ³⁸ Wherever people live—or wild animals, or birds of the sky—he has handed them over to you and made you ruler over them all. You are the head of gold.

³⁹ "After you, there will arise another kingdom, inferior to yours, and then another, a third kingdom, of bronze, which will rule the whole earth. ⁴⁰ A fourth kingdom will be as strong as iron; for iron crushes and shatters everything, and like iron that smashes, it will crush and smash all the others. ⁴¹ You saw the feet and toes, partly of a potter's fired clay and partly of iron—it will be a divided kingdom, though some of the strength of iron will be in it. You saw the iron mixed with clay, ⁴² and that the toes of the feet were partly iron and partly fired clay—part of the kingdom will be strong, and part will be brittle. ⁴³ You saw the iron mixed with clay—the peoples will mix with one another but will not hold together, just as iron does not mix with fired clay.

⁴⁴ "In the days of those kings, the God of the heavens will set up a kingdom that will never be destroyed, and this kingdom will not be left to another people. It will crush all these kingdoms and bring them to an end, but will itself endure forever. ⁴⁵ You saw a stone break off from the mountain without a hand touching it, and it crushed the iron, bronze, fired clay, silver, and gold. The great God has told the king what will happen in the future. The dream is certain, and its interpretation reliable."

⁴⁶ Then King Nebuchadnezzar fell facedown, worshiped Daniel, and gave orders to present an offering and incense to him. ⁴⁷ The king said to Daniel, "Your God is indeed God of gods, Lord of kings, and a revealer of mysteries, since you were able to reveal this mystery." ⁴⁸ Then the king promoted Daniel and gave him many generous gifts. He made him ruler over the entire province of Babylon and chief governor over all the wise men of Babylon. ⁴⁹ At Daniel's request, the king appointed Shadrach, Meshach, and Abednego to manage the province of Babylon. But Daniel remained at the king's court.

Context

In Daniel 1 we saw one side of Daniel—namely, his determination to be faithful to God and not to assimilate to the Babylonian culture. In this chapter we see another side of Daniel: his role as a prophet of God that shows the superiority of God in revealing mysteries as compared with Babylonian diviners (see §2). This passage is closely related to Daniel 7, which describes the coming of four kingdoms followed by the kingdom of God (see chiastic outline above). This requires that the two passages be read in conversation with each other.

Daniel 2 follows a chiastic structure (after Greidanus[1]):

A King's throne room: failure of Babylon's wise men to explain the dream (2:1–13)
  B King's palace: Daniel requests more time (2:14–16)
    C Daniel's home: God reveals the dream (2:17–23)
  B′ King's palace: Daniel requests to see the king (2:24–25)
A′ King's throne room: success of Daniel in explaining the dream (2:26–49)

This structure suggests that the heart of the message is found at the center of this chiasm: Daniel's prayer extolling God's sovereign control over history and his ability to reveal future mysteries. The revelation given to Daniel has great significance for our view of history, for it tells us that history is indeed going somewhere. God sovereignly controls history, and it will culminate in the establishment of God's kingdom.

2:1 Nebuchadnezzar's "second year" dates to 603/602 BC. This is probably a flashback during the time Daniel and his friends were still in their three years of training (1:5). The plural "had dreams" may imply that he dreamed the same dream repeatedly,[2] or perhaps more likely "dreams" is a plural of majesty or respect for the king's one really important, complex nightmare, in which case it can be translated as a singular ("had a dream" GNT, NABRE; Steinmann, "a

---

[1] S. Greidanus, *Preaching Christ from Daniel: Foundations for Expository Sermons* (Grand Rapids: Eerdmans, 2012), 58.

[2] R. W. Pierce, *Daniel*, Teach the Text (Grand Rapids: Baker, 2015), 29.

single dream that had many detailed parts and extended for a long time"[3]). In vv. 2-3 plural "dreams" (v. 2) is used, followed by singular "a dream" (v. 3). The singular is used in the rest of the chapter.

Not many prophetic dreams are described in OT narratives. There are Joseph's dreams about ruling over his brothers (Gen 37:5-11), the dreams of the cupbearer and the baker in prison foreshadowing their fates (Gen 40:8-22), and Pharaoh's dreams about the coming famine that Joseph interpreted (Gen 41:1-36). Scholars often compare dream interpretation in the Joseph story with dream interpretation in Daniel, seeing similar motifs (e.g., a captive becoming an official and dream interpreter in a foreign land; the failure of idolatrous magicians but success of God's spokesman; Gen 41:8, 24). In the millennium between Joseph and Daniel only a few other dreams are recorded.[4]

2:2-3 Among many Mesopotamian divination techniques is dream interpretation.[5] Divination, though broadly condemned in the Bible as contrary to Israelite religion (Deut 18:9-14; Lev 19:26; Isa 2:6), played a central role in Babylonian religion. Incantations were used to drive away evil demons, sickness, or bad luck. Amulets (e.g., an image of a god) were used to keep demons away. A whole variety of divination techniques were used to divine the future: liver omens, lecanomancy (oil in water), oneiromancy (interpretation of dreams), astrology, libanomancy (smoke from incense), psephomancy (casting lots), cledonomancy (chance remarks of strangers), necromancy, and *dagilissuri* (movements of birds).

A work known as the Assyrian Dream Book has survived in Neo-Babylonian script, suggesting it was studied and used at the time of Nebuchadnezzar. Daniel himself may have studied it along with the rest of Babylonian literature (cf. Dan 1:4). By this method Mesopotamian kings could bring in divination priests to (a) report

---

[3] A .E. Steinmann, *Daniel*, Concordia Commentary (Saint Louis: Concordia, 2008), 113.

[4] These include the dream that assured Gideon of God's victory over the Midianites (Jdgs 7:13-15) and Solomon's dream of God that prompted the king to ask for wisdom (1 Kgs 3:5-15). It's also possible that Balaam's conversation with his donkey was part of a prophet dream (Num 22:20-36). See J. M. Sprinkle, *Leviticus and Numbers*, Teach the Text (Grand Rapids: Baker, 2015), 342-43.

[5] J. H. Walton, *Ancient Near Eastern Thought and the Old Testament: Introducing the Conceptual World of the Hebrew Bible* (Grand Rapids: Baker Academic, 2006), 241-44.

one's dream to another person, or (b) to interpret the meaning of an enigmatic dream, or (c) to ward off by means of magic the ill effects that the dream portends.[6] In the seventh year of one of Nebuchadnezzar's successors, Nabonidus, an astrologer reported a dream about the Great Star (Jupiter?), Venus, Siris, the sun, and the moon. The dream was taken to foretell a favorable omen for Nabonidus and his son Belshazzar. Nabonidus himself has a dream in which he saw Nebuchadnezzar and an attendant standing on a chariot. The attendant told Nebuchadnezzar, "Do speak to Nabonidus so that he can report to you the dream he has seen." Nebuchadnezzar then asked Nabonidus, "Tell me what good (signs) you have seen," followed by Nabonidus, within his dream, describing a dream concerning the Great Star and the moon, with Jupiter (Marduk) calling him by name.[7]

"Magicians" is Hebrew/Aramaic חַרְטֹם. This term was originally an Egyptian word for soothsaying, magic-practicing priests (ḥrytp) meaning in Egyptian, "chief bearer of the ritual scrolls." Familiarity with sacred documents made one an expert in magic and healing.[8] Probably among the ritual scrolls were Egyptian books on dream interpretation that go back to the second millennium BC. Dream interpretation seems to have played a somewhat greater role in Egypt than in Mesopotamia. The Chester Beatty "Dream Book" is an Egyptian work. The extant copy dates to the Nineteenth Dynasty of Egypt, but its original composition may go back to the Twelvth Dynasty. It is currently the oldest surviving manual of dream interpretation.[9] In NeoAssyrian times ḥrytp appears as a loan word in Akkadian (ḥartibi) taken to mean "interpreter of dreams."[10] Mantics in Mesopotamia bearing this title and having Egyptian names were consulted during or before the time of Assurbanipal (668 to c. 627 BC), and one is listed as a prisoner brought from Egypt at

---

[6] A. L. Oppenheim, *The Interpretation of Dreams in the Ancient Near East with a Translation of an Assyrian Dream Book*, Transactions of the American Philosophical Society 46.3 (Philadelphia: American Philosophical Society, 1956), 219.

[7] D. J. Wiseman, *Nebuchadrezzar and Babylon* (Oxford: Oxford University Press, 1985), 92.

[8] H.P. Müller, "חַרְטֹם ḥarṭōm," *TDOT* 5:177.

[9] *COS* 1:52.

[10] "ḥartibi," *CAD* 6:116.

the time of Esarhaddon (681–669 BC).[11] Nebuchadnezzar invaded Egypt, so the חַרְטֹם of Daniel could be magicians captured in war. In the Bible חַרְטֹם is used for Egyptian dream interpreters (Gen 41:8, 24) who, unlike Joseph (whom Daniel resembles), try in vain to interpret Pharaoh's dream. They also were "magicians" (so rendered in Exod 7:11, 22; 8:3–4). The חַרְטֹם tried to imitate Moses' miracles by their magical arts. Hence, these are probably Egyptian "wise men" brought to Nebuchadnezzar from the far reaches of his empire or else those who had learned Egyptian magical lore, including the art of dream interpretation.

"Mediums" is Hebrew אַשָּׁף (= Aramaic participle אָשַׁף in 2:10) related to Akkadian *ašipu* "exorcist."[12] In Akkadian, the *ašipu* sometimes is a "diagnostician," almost a "physician" in connection with medical practice though by modern standards more like an exorcist or "witch doctor." The *ašipu* drove away demons, worms, or bad luck that caused illness or other calamities, or else divined the outcome of the illnesses.[13] They received portions from the food offered to deities, indicating they were considered priestly personnel.[14] Such a priest could be summoned to cure nightmares.

"Sorcerer" is a D-stem participle מְכַשֵּׁף (from the root כשף) that means "to practice sorcery." The sorcerer is condemned in the Bible (Deut 18:10), and the feminine form is used of the "witch" or "sorceress," who is also condemned (Exod 22:18). The Akkadian cognate verb *kašapu* means "to bewitch, cast an evil spell." *Kaššapu* is the most common Akkadian term for sorcerers, known for casting evil spells. It occurs more frequently in the feminine form *kaššaptu*. Laws of Hammurabi §2 makes one accused of sorcery (*kišpu*) subject to a river ordeal. Sorcery was not condemned as such in Mesopotamia but only in so far as it was used for harm.

"Chaldeans" is Hebrew כַּשְׂדִּים (= Aramaic כַּשְׂדָּי in 2:10), a cognate of Akkadian *kaldu* (Kaldu region or Chaldea). The pronunciations differ through a linguistic shift between /ld/ and /śd/. Kaldu was a region in southern Babylonia/Mesopotamia, around Nippur,

---

[11] Müller, *TDOT* 5:177.

[12] S.v. "*ašipu*," *CAD* 1.2:431

[13] H. W. F. Saggs, *The Might that Was Assyria* (London: Sidgwick & Jackson, 1984), 217. Saggs identifies the "fish men" and "lion men" of Assyrian reliefs (showing men wearing fish or lion costumes) as portrayals of the *ašipu*.

[14] Walton, *Ancient Near Eastern Thought and the Old Testament*, 266.

Ur, and Uruk bordering on Elam. The English "Chaldean" is based on the LXX that, like the Akkadian, reads with a /d/ (Χαλδαῖος). Chaldean is a term for a tribal ethnic group that appeared historically in southern Babylonia in the mid-ninth century BC. We know of five powerful, early Chaldean tribes (Bit Yakini, Bit Dakkuri, Bit Ammukani, Bit Shaalli, and Bit Shilani). Chaldeans were affiliated with (though clearly distinct from) Aramean tribes.[15] The names of Chaldean kings of Babylon are in Akkadian, not Aramaic. By the mid 700s Chaldeans were taking leadership roles politically (e.g., King Merodoch-baladan of the Bit Yakini tribe). Over time the term Chaldean came to mean "Babylonian" (e.g., Dan 1:4; Hab 1:6), but here it has become by synecdoche a term for diviners of Chaldean descent. Another meaning may occur in v. 4.

2:4 "Chaldeans" may now take on a more general meaning in which one category of diviner (Chaldean) stands for all the diviners. Or Chaldean diviners as the "natives" (see v. 2) perhaps serve as spokesmen for the others.

The text switches to the Aramaic language from 2:4b through 7:28 to add realism to the narrative and to make this part of Daniel accessible to non-Israelites (see Introduction). Aramaic, like Hebrew, is a Northwest Semitic language. It became the international language of diplomacy as early as Sennacherib of Assyria (701 BC; 2 Kgs 18:26) and was used for correspondences between officials in Judah and Persia during the Persian period, as seen in the Aramaic section of Ezra 4:8–6:18; 7:12–26. Aramaic was the *lingua franca* of the western Achaemenid Empire until the conquests of Alexander in the fourth century BC. Jews who returned from Babylonian exile often spoke Aramaic better than Hebrew, and so needed the Bible to be translated into Aramaic (see Neh 8:8). Jesus in Mark's Gospel often speaks in Aramaic (e.g., Mark 5:41; 7:34; 15:34).

The royal greeting, "May the king live forever," is used in addressing King David (1 Kgs 1:31) as well as non-Israelite kings Nebuchadnezzar, Belshazzar, Darius, and Artaxerxes (Dan 3:9; 5:10; 6:6; Neh 2:3). It is meant to exclude any treasonous hint that a speaker might want the king dead. Using language of humble subservience

---

[15] M. Liverani, *The Ancient Near East: History, Society and Economy*, trans. S. Tabatabai (New York: Routledge, 2013), 444.

("tell your servants the dream"), the diviners indicate that they need to know the content of the dream to interpret it.

2:5–6 The king's word was "final." "Final" translates Aramaic אַזְדָּא, a Persian loanword meaning a "notice," but in Daniel it means something "publicly known." From an authority figure, it implies something is "decided"[16] or "irrevocable."[17] "Tell me" here and in v. 9a is literally "cause me to know" (KJV, ESV "make known"). This might suggest that the king was not able to remember the dream fully himself, so he wanted them to jog his memory ("cause me to know") by making the details known first. Alternatively, it may have been a test of their abilities, in which case "tell me" means that, though he remembered the dream, he wanted them to tell it to him as a demonstration of their supernatural abilities. Either way, Nebuchadnezzar rightly (see §2) came to distrust his counselors who practiced divination (see v. 9). This test, unreasonable as it is, sought to confirm whether these diviners had genuine insight into the mysterious powers of the universe. If so, then they could tell him the content of the dream and thus give credence to their interpretation of it.

If they failed to do this they would be "torn limb to limb," an excessive punishment characterizing the king as an unjustly cruel despot, one of many sins for which God holds people accountable (see §4.2). "Limbs" is Aramaic הַדָּמִין, probably a Persian loanword from Old Persian *handāman ("limb, body part"), and the whole expression (literally "made into limbs") may be an Old Persian idiom for mutilation followed by execution. Makujina cites a parallel on the Persian part of the trilingual Bihistan Rock Inscription (2:70–78) in which Darius I boasts of executing Phraortes, who claimed to be a king in Media and who had fought Darius. Darius had Phraortes' nose, ears, and tongue cut off, and he had one eye struck out before he was executed by impalement.[18] Theodotion softens the language to "destroyed," and Old Greek LXX softens further to "you will be made an example, publicly disgraced" (παραδειγματισθήσεσθε), both

---

[16] F. Rosenthal, *A Grammar of Biblical Aramaic* (Weisbaden: Harrassowitz, 1974), 41, 76.

[17] "אַזְדָּא," *HALOT* 5:1808.

[18] J. Makujina, "Dismemberment in Dan 2:5 and 3:29 as an Old Persian Idiom, 'To Be Made into Parts,'" *JAOS* 119.2 (April–July 1999): 309–12. For the text, see R. G. Kent, *Old Persian: Grammar, Text, Lexicon*, 2nd ed. (New Haven, CT: American Oriental Society, 1953), 124.

perhaps finding the literal rendering too offensive, or in the case of the Old Greek possibly misunderstanding the Aramaic. That their "houses will be made a garbage dump" (or "piles of rubble" NIV) would affect their wives and children.

On the other hand, "gifts and a reward and great honor" would come if they successfully described and explained the dream. The exact nuance of "reward" (Aramaic נְבִזְבָּה) is uncertain, though it strengthens the idea of "gifts." Royal honoring could result in a person being paraded with public proclamations of royal appreciation (cf. Esth 6:9-11).

2:7-9 The dialogue becomes ever more agitated. Dream interpreters were typically told the dreams they were asked to interpret. To ask for a dream interpretation without describing the dream seemed unfair to the diviners. Nebuchadnezzar correctly surmised that they were "trying to gain some time," literally, "buying time." They understood perfectly well what the king meant. But they were stalling in hopes that he would relent, or until the "situation [עִדָּן; literally "time"] changes" (v. 9), perhaps a reference to the end of the king's reign, which he fears the dream portends.[19] The king in turn is suspicious of the honesty of his diviner-counsellors. Skepticism about revelations from divination in fact has merit (see §2). "Fraudulent" could be rendered "corrupted, spoiled," metaphorical here for dishonest words. A few others in Mesopotamian history have shown doubts about diviners. Oppenheim[20] mentions a legend concerning the doubts of Naram-Sin, and there is an account of Sennacherib in which he divided his diviners into groups in order to compare their predictions after divining independently. Such expressions of doubt are rare in extant ancient Near Eastern accounts, however.

2:10-11 "Chaldean," "magician," and "medium" are Aramaic cognates of terms discussed at vv. 2 and 4. Nebuchadnezzar's request is unprecedented and impossible. Based on Targumic Aramaic, "difficult" (Aramaic יַקִּיר) means literally "heavy" but (like Hebrew כָּבֵד) metaphorically can mean "precious" or, as here, "difficult." The diviners correctly believed that this request required the insight of a deity (actually of the true God, v. 28) to fulfill. "Mortals" is literally

---

[19] C. A. Newsom, *Daniel*, OTL (Louisville: Westminster John Knox, 2014), 69-70.

[20] A. L. Oppenheim, *Ancient Mesopotamia*, rev. ed. E. Reiner (Chicago: University of Chicago Press, 1964), 227.

"flesh" (KJV, ESV). In their theology, the abode of the gods is remote in heaven. Unlike Daniel's God (see §4), these deities do not deal directly with men, which may be why the diviners do not bother to pray to these gods to save them.[21] Divination in Mesopotamian religion was an indirect means of mediating a message from the gods as revealed through the fates (Akkadian *šimtu*), though divination did not necessarily involve consulting gods because the fates could be more important than gods: even the gods were subject to the fates.[22] Contrast the true God (see §3.7).

2:12–13 The diviners are considered "wise men" though they lacked the qualities of true, biblical wisdom that comes from God (see comments at 1:17). Their response reinforces Nebuchadnezzar's suspicions that they are frauds taking his money without providing any genuine insights. In general he was right. A "decree" is Aramaic (and Hebrew) דָּת ("decree, law"), a loanword from Persian denoting a written command that has the effect of law. It is used in Daniel, Ezra, and Esther for decrees/laws both of God (Dan 6:5) and of human monarchs.

The HtD participle מִתְקַטְּלִין rendered "were to be executed" multiplies the action, makes it passive, and indicates an impending event: "the wise men were *about to* [in the immediate future] be massacred [or possibly "killed one by one"].[23] The order to execute the wise men telescopes a process whose implementation would take some time, first arresting them and eventually publicly executing them.

Daniel was superior in wisdom to the wise men of Babylon (1:20). True prophets do not use divination techniques (see Deut 18:10–14), but because of Daniel's prophetic and dream-interpretation gifts the Babylonians categorize him as a "wise man" along with various diviners (cf. v. 18). "Wise men" (חַכִּימַיָּא) is a broad category that includes various kinds of wise men: mediums, Chaldeans, and diviners (5:7; see comments at 5:15).

---

[21] Pierce, *Daniel*, 31.

[22] J. N. Lawson, *The Concept of Fate in Ancient Mesopotomia of the First Millennium: Towards an Understanding of "Shimtu,"* Orientalia Biblica et Christiana 7 (Weisbaden: Harrassowitz, 1994), 38, 49.

[23] I. Jerusalmi, *The Aramaic Sections of Ezra and Daniel: A Philological Commentary* (Cincinnati: Hebrew Union College-Jewish Institute of Religion, 1982), 55.

"Friends" (Aramaic חֲבַר) or "comrades, companions," like its Hebrew cognate חָבֵר, indicates a close relationship through a common bond. These friends, Hananiah, Mishael, and Azariah (1:6; 2:17), are "wise men" by training (1:3–7, 17–20) and may have had prophetic gifts like Daniel's (see 3:17).

2:14 Here Daniel displays his God-given practical wisdom (see §4.4 and comments at 1:17). "Tact and discretion" reads more literally "counsel and taste," idiomatic for "with wise and prudent words"[24] or "tactful counsel" as in v. 15. Aramaic טְעֵם (rendered "discretion") is from a root evidently meaning in the basic stem "to taste,"[25] though the noun has a wide semantic range: "judgment, discretion,"[26] "understanding,"[27] and "order, decree, information, attention, influence [of wine]."[28]

The name "Arioch," also used of a king of Ellasar (Gen 14:1), may be derived from Hurrian *Arriyuk* (*Arriwuk* in Mari; *Ariukki* in Nuzi)[29] or less likely from Persian. Empires were inclined to draw many foreigners to their capitals both as captives and for business or diplomacy.

"Guard" (טַבָּחַיָּא) in "captain of the king's guard" has a cognate in Hebrew used of "butchers," specifically of cooks who butcher meat (1 Sam 9:23–24). Here it could mean "executioners" (CSB note; NRSV), though this is probably too strong a rendering. The Hebrew cognate טַבָּח is used of non-executioners: Potiphar was "captain of the *guard* [טַבָּחִים]" (Gen 37:36), but these were probably not executioners. In an expression virtually identical to the Aramaic in Dan 2:14, Nebuzaradan was "captain of the *guards* [רַב־טַבָּחִים]" (2 Kgs 25:8) who burned Jerusalem, tore down its walls, and deported the population as soldiers. That a term that can mean "butcher" is applied to guards or a group of soldiers is probably a way of emphasizing their fierceness in fighting.

"Execute the wise men" reads in Aramaic more literally as "*massacre* the wise men*"—that is, kill repeatedly or one by one (D-stem

---

[24] Ibid., 56.

[25] "טעם," in *Comprehensive Aramaic Lexicon, Targum Lexicon*, ed. S. A. Kaufman (Cincinnati: Hebrew Union College Press, 2004), electronic edition, n.p.

[26] "טְעֵם," BDB 1094.2.

[27] "טְעֵם," *HALOT* 5:1885–1886.

[28] Rosenthal, *A Grammar of Biblical Aramaic*, 85.

[29] "אַרְיוֹךְ," *HALOT* 5:1824–1825.

קְטַל, "kill"). This telescopes the process. The immediate job of the guard would be to arrest the wise men in preparation for their execution, which allows Daniel time to save them since none have been executed yet (cf. 2:24).

2:15–16 Here Daniel's "tact and discretion" (v. 14) is seen in his calm and shrewd response despite the current terrorizing crisis. "Officer" is Aramaic שַׁלִּיט ("mighty/powerful one"), a synonym of "captain" (v. 14), denoting the one in charge. On "decree" see comments at v. 13. "Harsh" (H-stem participle of חצף) can also be rendered "urgent" (CSB note) or "rash" (CEB at 3:22). This root is only used here and at 3:22 in the HB. In other Aramaic/Syriac literature the Haphel of חצף can mean "bold," "daring," or "severe,"[30] and in late Aramaic "bare-faced," "imprudent," "arrogant," "energetic," or "strong."[31] The Old Greek takes it to mean "bitter, harsh" (πικρῶς), while Theodotion takes it to mean "shameless, bold" (ἀναιδής).[32] The best contextual meaning here in Daniel is hard to determine. "Harsh" is slightly more in keeping with the semantic range of this root than "urgent," though perhaps "rash" (CEB in 3:22) catches the meaning best.

The diviners who tried to "buy time" previously were not granted it (2:8), but Daniel was given time. Acceptance of Daniel's request may relate to the high esteem in which Nebuchadnezzar held him in comparison with the other so-called wise men (1:20) and reflects God's providential protection (see §3.8; §4.5).

2:17–19 On "friends," see comments at 1:6 and 2:13. The use of their Hebrew names is appropriate for this context of prayer to the Hebrew God.[33] This passage underscores the importance of petitionary prayer (see §4.7), especially asking God for wisdom (Jas 1:5), and praying as a group.

The expression "the God of the heavens" or "the God of heaven" (most EVV) is one of many names and titles of God in Daniel (see §3.2) and is used to show God above and beyond this world (see

---

[30] "חצף," *Comprehensive Aramaic Lexicon, Targum Lexicon*, n.p.

[31] "חצף," Marcus Jastrow, *A Dictionary of the Targumim, the Talmud Babli and Jerushalmi, and the Midrashic Literature* (1903; reprint, Brooklyn: P. Shalom, 1967), electronic eed., 495–96.

[32] A. Pietersma and B. G. Wright, eds., *A New Translation of the Septuagint* (New York: Oxford, 2007), 996.

[33] J. G. Baldwin, *Daniel*, TOTC (Leicester: Inter-Varsity, 1978), 89.

§3.4). It is used in Genesis (Gen 24:3, 7) and in the NT (Rev 11:13; 16:11), and it is not unknown in the biblical world outside the Bible. A title for the god Baal, "Baal of heaven" (Baalšamēm), is attested in the tenth century BC in a Phoenician inscription from Byblos.[34] But more relevant for Daniel is the expression's echoing of a title used for Ahura-Mazda, a celestial deity portrayed as a sun-disk in the heavens, who was the main god of Persian kings. Cyrus' use of this expression for Yahweh in Ezra 1:2 (= 2 Chr 36:23) may be his way of identifying Yahweh with his own god. The use of "God of heaven" in Jewish circles in a book (Daniel) completed during the Achaemenid period may reflect influence from Persian usage, being a way of identifying Yahweh rather than Ahura-Mazda as the true God of heaven. As a title for Yahweh it emphasizes his superiority over and power to control the world (Dan 2:37; 44), like the parallel title "King of the heavens" (4:37). Relevant here, the title suggests that, though he is above and beyond this world, he nonetheless looks from there upon his people on earth, concerned and willing to answer their petitions.

"Mercy" (Aramaic רַחֲמִין = Hebrew רַחֲמִים, "mercy, compassion") is an attribute related to God's goodness (see §3.6). It is cognate with רֶחֶם *rehem* "mother's womb" and thus probably has a hint of motherly compassion (compare 1 Kgs 3:26), though רַחֲמִים is applied most often to God.

"Mystery" or "secret" (KJV) is Aramaic רָז, a Persian loanword related to modern Persian *rāz*.[35] The Old Greek and Theodotion render it with μυστήριον ("mystery, secret [teachings]"). A characterstic of Daniel according to Ezek 28:3 ("Yes, you are wiser than Daniel; no secret is hidden from you!") is that he knows every "secret" (Hebrew סָתוּם), literally something sealed or shut up and hence hidden and secret. A passive participle of the same root occurs at Dan 12:9 denoting the "secret" of when Daniel's vision would be fulfilled. Targum Jonathan of Ezek 28:3 uses רָז to render Hebrew סָתוּם, suggesting these two words are roughly synonymous. In Daniel רָז takes on a special sense, referring to the "concealed intimation of future events that will be disclosed or interpreted only by God or by those whom he inspires (2:28–29; 4:9)."[36] That God alone reveals such mysteries

---

[34] J. A. Soggin, "שָׁמַיִם šāmayim," in *TLOT* 3:1371.

[35] Rosenthal, *A Grammar of Biblical Aramaic*, 59.

[36] G. Bornkamm, "μυστήριον" in *Theological Dictionary of the New Testament*, abridged ed., ed. Gerhard Kittel et al. (Grand Rapids: Eerdmans, 1985), 616.

illustrates his supernatural knowledge (see §3.5). On "Babylon's wise men" see comments at v. 13.

Daniel here received the first of a number of visions recorded in the book, though this one is given as a summary rather than spelled out. "Vision" (Aramaic חֵזְוָא = Hebrew חָזוֹן) is from the Hebrew/Aramaic root חזה meaning "to see," usually connoting revelation from God through visions (see §2). The participle of the same root means "seer" (one who sees), a synonym for prophet. Gad and Amos, among others, are called seers (2 Sam 24:11; Amos 7:12), and the Hebrew equivalent חָזוֹן, "vision," is used of Daniel's visions in Dan 8:1–2 and of the prophetic writings of Isaiah, Obadiah, Nahum, and Habakkuk (Isa 1:1; Obad 1:1; Nah 1:1; Hab 2:2).

On "praised" (or "blessed" KJV, ESV; Aramaic/Hebrew root ברך) see §4.6. When people like Daniel bless God in worship, they "praise" him, proclaiming good things about him (Dan 2:20–23).

2:20–23 God receives and answers prayers (see §4.7). Daniel's hymn of praise is a natural and appropriate response to answered prayer. His prayer emphasizes how God governs human history (see §7) and grants wisdom to his people (see §4.4). Arguably this prayer, at the heart of the chapter's chiastic structure (see Context discussion above), is the theological center of this chapter, more central than the dream and its interpretation.[37] As a hymn it is naturally poetic, which adds emphasis to the content. The "name of God" in the OT is Yahweh (usually rendered in English translations as LORD), alluded to here even though Yahweh does not occur in the Aramaic portion of Daniel. On "praised" see comments at v. 19. The remainder of the prayer praises God for who he is and what he does, as shown either in the revelation of the meaning of the dream that will follow, or in the content of that revelation (see table).

---

[37] Steinmann, *Daniel*, 109; D. R. Davis, *The Message of Daniel: His Kingdom Cannot Fail*, The Bible Speaks Today (Downers Grove: InterVarsity, 2013), 40.

Who God Is:	What God Does:
Eternal ("forever and ever") Wise Omnipotent ("power") Omniscient ("he knows what is in the darkness")	God shows his power establishing epochs and eras ("times and seasons," see comments) for kingdoms, raising up and deposing kings. God shows his own wisdom and knowledge by giving people wisdom and knowledge, specifically by revelation of truth.
Enlightened ("light dwells with him")	God demonstrates his omniscience by revealing unfathomable and hidden truths as seen by his revealing the secret of Nebuchadnezzar's dream.

"Wisdom and power" (vv. 20, 23) could be stating two distinct attributes of God (see §3.5, §3.7), both seen in creation (Pss 65:7; 104:24). Alternatively, they could be taken together as a hendiadys meaning "powerful wisdom" and/or "wise power." "Power" (also v. 23; Aramaic/Hebrew גְּבוּרָה, "strength") refers to the ability to do or accomplish something, though strength requires wisdom to be effective. "Times" and "seasons" (v. 21) are synonym plurals for "time" in Aramaic (עִדָּן and זְמַן). The first term can mean "years" (Dan 7:25, "time, times, and half a time" = three and one-half years), while זְמַן in the plural can refer to "religious festivals" (7:25 CSB). But given the following statement about removing / establishing kings, as well as the content of the dream about the rise and fall of kingdoms, the reference is more likely to God's changing "epochs and eras" (Moffatt Bible). God in his sovereignty fixes periods of time for nations and kings to dominate (see §7.2).

"Deep ... things" (v. 22; Aramaic עַמִּיק) refers to "unfathomable" things[38] showing God's omniscience (see §3.5). The Aramaic verbs in v. 23, "thanks" and "praise" (H-stem participle ידה and D-stem participle שבח), are here synonyms and represent the proper human response to God for his blessings (see §4.6). In Hebrew/Aramaic no word means "to thank," but thanks is expressed by praising a person, as here. "Praise" (Aramaic/Hebrew שבח) can be rendered "honor," "laud," "praise," or "commend." The phrase "God of my fathers" (v. 23) alludes to Israel's patriarchal ancestors, namely Abraham, Isaac, and Jacob (Exod 3:15–16), through whom God made a covenant with

---

[38] "עַמִּיק," *HALOT* 5:1950–51.

Israel. Some of God's "wisdom and power" (v. 20) is bestowed to Daniel, allowing him to interpret the dream (v. 23).

2:24-25 The story hastens to a climax, with urgency conveyed by the word "quickly" (v. 25a). This word (Aramaic בְּהִתְבְּהָלָה) is based on a root (בהל) associated with fear, alarm, and terror, as well as haste (cf. Dan 4:5, 19; 5:6, 9–10; 7:15, 28), so there may be a hint of fear in this urgency. Arioch emphasizes his own role ("I have found") and minimizes the qualifications of Daniel (merely "a man among the Judean exiles").[39]

2:26-27 On "Belteshazzar," see comments at 1:7. Daniel was asked to do what the king requested of the diviners (2:3–5). Unlike Arioch's self-promoting statement of v. 25, Daniel's response (v. 27) shows humility in order to exalt God. Daniel echoes the truth proclaimed by Joseph, who also interpreted prophetic dreams: God and God alone, not human wise men, can interpret dreams (Gen 40:8; 41:16; see §2). "Wise man" (literally "wise men"; the other diviner terms are plural too) can be generic for all diviners (see v. 12). So the list of four terms in v. 27 could be understood as three types under a general category of wise men (not four types of wise men) and render: "no wise men who were, specifically, mediums, magicians, or diviners, were able to make known to the king the mystery" (after Steinmann).[40] For "medium" and "magician," see comments at vv. 2–3 and 10. The word rendered "diviner" (Aramaic גָּזְרִין) is an Aramaic participle of גזר, meaning "ones who cut/decree/determine." The Old Greek and Theodotion may not have known how to translate the word, so they transliterated the Aramaic into Greek. If a specific divination is in mind, it is more likely extispicy, divination by cutting open and examining the remains of sacrificed animals, especially their livers (hepatomancy). Compare the early Greek rendering of Symmachus as θυτάς, "sacrificers."[41] Extispicy was considered one of the most reliable forms of divination throughout ancient Near Eastern times.[42]

2:28-29 The key theological point of the chapter is that Daniel's God, the true God, "reveals mysteries" (v. 28), meaning in this case he knows and reveals the future as portended in the dream (see

---

[39] Baldwin, *Daniel*, 91.
[40] Steinmann, *Daniel*, 111.
[41] J. A. Montgomery, *Daniel*, ICC (Edinburgh: T&T Clark, 1927), 163.
[42] Walton, *Ancient Near Eastern Thought and the Old Testament*, 255–56.

§2, §3.5). That God alone reveals secrets and gives wisdom echos a theme found in Isaiah (Isa 42:9; 45:19, 21).[43] Indeed, God is given the title, "revealer of mysteries" (v. 29), denoting him as the source of true revelation. On "heaven" and "mystery," see comments at v. 18. "Visions" (v. 28c) is another term for "your dream" and (like "dreams" in 2:1) is probably a plural of majesty for the single complex vision. "Last days" (v. 28) is an idiom that can mean little more than "the future" (see comments on the Hebrew equivalent at 10:14), like the similar expression rendered "future" in v. 29 (CSB note, "after this"). However, in this instance the interpretation of the dream that follows does refer to eschatological events. The Aramaic of "Your Majesty" reads "You, O King" (also v. 37).

2:30 Though Daniel is inherently wiser than the diviners (1:20), the wisdom to explain Nebuchadnezzar's dream is God's, not Daniel's (see §3.5). Daniel wishes to give all the credit to God, not his own cleverness.

2:31 Daniel complies with Nebuchadnezzar's demand to describe the dream before giving an interpretation. "Standing in front of you" implies that Nebuchadnezzar was a participant within the dream.[44] The Aramaic "dazzling" reads, "its splendor exceeding." Aramaic זִיו ("splendor, countenance [of face]") is cognate with Akkadian *zimu(m)* ("appearance, looks, countenance, luster").[45] This could be especially an allusion to the dazzlingly bright luster of the golden countenance of the head (v. 32). "Terrifying" or "frightening" (ESV) (passive participle דְּחִיל) employs the same Aramaic root used to describe the terrifying fourth beast in the parallel vision of Dan 7:7, 19.

2:32-33 The materials from top to bottom of the statue (gold, silver, bronze, iron, fired clay) generally go from most valuable to least valuable (but see comments at vv. 39-40), though with increasing strength. In fifth-century BC Persian times according to Herodotus, gold was about thirteen times more valuable than silver.[46] Bronze

---

[43] G. B. Lester, *Daniel Evokes Isaiah: Allusive Characterization of Foreign Rule in the Hebrew-Aramaic Book of Daniel*, LHBOTS 606 (London: Bloombury T&T Clark, 2015), 33.

[44] Newsom, *Daniel*, 75.

[45] "*zīmu(m)*," *CAD* 21:119.

[46] Herodotus, *Histories* 3.95.2. Silver is relatively less valuable today: A quick online check showed the ratio of gold to silver prices in July 2014 was about 60:1, and the

is an alloy of copper hardened by small quantities of tin and hence stronger, though cheaper, than gold or silver. Iron is the strongest of the metals mentioned. At the feet the iron was mixed with cheap baked clay (terracotta), which was used for common household pottery and bricks, though it could also be used in artwork. A smaller statue with these characteristics could be made from a cast of iron with gold, silver, and bronze plating added over the iron along with terracotta over the feet. Perhaps such a statute provided the idea for this imagery. The classical writer Hesiod (eighth or seventh century BC) in his poem "Works and Days" (lines 110–200) uses similar imagery for five ages of mankind: a golden race, a second generation of silver ("less noble by far"), a third generation (a "brazen race") sprung of ash wood (?), a fourth generation of god-like heroes (no material), and a fifth generation called a race of iron.[47] Parallels with Hesiod indicate that this kind of imagery predates Daniel in 603/602 BC, though there is no conclusive evidence that Hesiod's writing, which gives no higher goal for history but only points to degeneration, has influenced Daniel's imagery. If it has, the imagery in Daniel represents a creative reworking of the scheme for a different message.

2:34–35 The image of the stone crushing the statue may have been the reason Nebuchadnezzar was terrorized by the vision. The king rightly (v. 38) suspected that the statue represented him and/or his kingdom, and so the vision of its destruction might foretell his own demise. For "stone" the Old Greek and Theodotion imply a longer text, "stone from a mountain" (cp. v. 45), a text followed by some versions (CEV, NABRE, NLT). The Aramaic "broke off" (Aramaic גזר) is better rendered "was cut" (most EVV; cf. v. 27). "Without hands" implies supernaturally.

The simplest interpretation of the stone is that it refers to the kingdom of God that supplants the kingdoms of the world (see §7.4.3). A more complex view found in early Christian commentators like Jerome, Hippolytus, and Theodoret is that this stone refers to Jesus Christ, the king of the kingdom of God, who came into being supernaturally by the virginal conception of Mary without the

---

ratio of silver to copper about 100:1, and scrap copper to scrap iron over 20:1.

[47] Hesiod, *The Homeric Hymns and Homerica with an English Translation by Hugh G. Evelyn-White, Works and Days* (Cambridge, MA: Harvard University Press; London, William Heinemann, 1914).

human "hands" of a father being involved (see §6.2).[48] Matthew and Luke refer to Christ as a stone that is both a foundation and something that pulverizes all opposition (Matt 21:42, 44; Luke 20:17–18). Though the first half of these texts quotes Ps 118:22, the second half (Matt 21:44; Luke 20:18) is probably an allusion to Daniel 2, in which case it provides NT support for the messianic interpretation of the stone. The parallel of the son of man figure in Daniel 7 who supplants the fourth kingdom supplies further support for this messianic view within Daniel. More comments on this at v. 44 and §6.2.

The stone "struck the statue on its feet of iron and fired clay" (v. 34) because clay is vulnerable to shattering and so represents the weakest part of the statue. "Crushed them" (v. 34) and "were shattered" (v. 35) could be rendered "pulverized them" and "were pulverized." Both verbs are of the same Aramaic root (דקק) that refers to crushing into small, fine pieces. "Like chaff" employs an agricultural simile. Chaff refers to husks and other materials separated from the kernels of grain during the threshing process. The wheat/chaff mixture would be tossed in the air, allowing the light, worthless chaff to blow away in the wind (Hos 13:3), while the heavy, edible kernels would drop near where they were tossed. That the dust of the pulverized statue blew away like chaff without trace indicates that it ultimately lacks substance. The imagery may build on Isa 41:15–16, where God's people are told they will thresh and pulverize mountains (representing problems and/or foreign nations) and turn them into chaff that the wind blows away.[49] It may also allude to Ps 1:4, in which the wicked are blow away like chaff.[50] As the stone became a great mountain, it surpassed the size of the original statue and displaced it.

2:36–38 Nebuchadnezzar was "king of kings" (also used of him in Ezek 26:7) in that he and his empire ruled over other kings.

---

[48] St. Jerome, *Jerome's Commentary on Daniel*, trans. G. L. Archer (Grand Rapids: Baker, 1958), 32; Theodoret of Cyrus, *Commentary on Daniel*, Writings from the Greco-Roman World, trans. R. C. Hill (Atlanta: Society of Biblical Literature, 2006), 51, 53; Hippolytus of Rome, "Treatise on Christ and Antichrist," in *Fathers of the Third Century: Hippolytus, Cyprian, Novatian, Appendix*, ed. A. Roberts, J. Donaldson, and A. C. Coxe, trans. S. D. F. Salmond, vol. 5 of The Ante-Nicene Fathers (Buffalo, NY: Christian Literature Company, 1886), 5209.

[49] Lester, *Daniel Evokes Isaiah*, 110.

[50] J. M. Hamilton, *With the Clouds of Heaven: The Book of Daniel in Biblical Theology*, New Studies in Biblical Theology 32 (Downers Grove: InterVarsity, 2014), 88.

This was a title used by Nebuchadnezzar's successors according to cuneiform sources.[51] But Babylon's greatness was only possible because "the God of the heavens" had granted him all the fruit of kingship ("sovereignty, power, strength, and glory"; see §3.8). The "head of gold" stands for Nebuchadnezzar, or more specifically to his Babylonian kingdom, since the other parts of the statue are called kingdoms rather than kings (vv. 39–42).

"Wherever" (most EVV) in v. 38a misses the admittedly awkward syntax of the original in which the ב of בְכָל־דִּי is probably governed by the verb "rule" (שׁלט) that follows.[52] It should be rendered instead, "*Over* [ב] everything that lives—whether humans, wild animals, or birds of the sky—he has put [them] in your power and caused you to rule *over* (ב) them all." What seems emphasized here (as in Dan 4:12, 21) is the array of creatures over which Nebuchadnezzar has dominion rather than the breadth of his territory. This language ascribes to Nebuchadnezzar dominion over creation that is elsewhere ascribed to mankind (Gen 1:28; Ps 8:6–8), as if he were humanity itself.[53] In the sweep of biblical theology, though, only Jesus as the true archtypical man ultimately fulfills this language (Heb 2:5–9; cf. Dan 7:14).

2:39–40 For "crushes" (Aramaic דקק) see comments at vv. 34–35. "Inferior to" means "lower than," literally "toward the earth" (אַרְעָא, Ketiv), using the old accusative ending (-ā).[54] It could simply mean "closer to the ground" (lower on the statue in the vision), though it is usually read in conjunction with the decreasing value of the materials of the statue (gold-silver-bronze-iron-clay). The Qere, which lacks the -ā, is a less likely reading.

The identity of the four kingdoms of Daniel 2 and 7 is discussed in the Introduction and will be treated further in Daniel 7. Historically, Babylon was conquered by the Medo-Persian Empire under Cyrus, which then fell to the Macedonian Greek Empire of Alexander. It is not clear how Medo-Persia is "inferior" to Babylon. Judging from Daniel 7, the fourth kingdom is the most powerful, so it is superior in that sense. The fourth kingdom is Rome, though it

[51] Wiseman, *Nebuchadrezzar and Babylon*, 41.

[52] Jerusalmi, *The Aramaic Sections of Ezra and Daniel*, 72.

[53] J. Goldingay, "Daniel in the Context of Old Testament Theology" in *The Book of Daniel Composition and Reception*, ed. J. Collins and P. Flint, VTSup 83, (Leiden: Brill, 2001), 2:644.

[54] Jerusalmi, *The Aramaic Sections of Ezra and Daniel*, 73.

is better taken as "Rome-and-Beyond," extending to the coming of God's kingdom.

2:41–43 Some interpreters relate the "toes" (vv. 41, 42), that are presumably ten in number, to the ten horns on the fourth beast that represent ten kings (7:7, 20, 24), though nothing is made of their number here. The reading "toes" is probably correct, though the fact that the Old Greek lacks the term "toes" raises some doubt as to whether that reading is original. "Brittle" is more literally "breakable," hence "fragile." "The peoples will mix with one another" reads in the Aramaic, "The peoples will mix with one another in the seed of men" [CSB note]. This may mean people groups will intermarry (NRSV) or that different ethnic groups will be thrown together. In any case the fourth kingdom, though strong like iron, has inherent weaknesses represented by the fragile clay.

2:44–45 "In the days of those kings" is curious since the kingdoms appear consecutively (vv. 39–40). Perhaps the reference is to the kings of the fourth kingdom, or alternatively that the earlier human kingdoms in some sense live on in the fourth kingdom. The kingdom of God is inaugurated by Jesus Christ during the Roman Empire (see §7.4.3), suggesting that the fourth kingdom is related to Rome. Dempster suggests that collectively the four kingdoms of the "gigantic figure made by human hands represents hubris, the original sin" that, like the wicked, generally gets blown away like chaff (Ps 1:4). He sees an intentional parallel between the small stone that destroys the giant statue and David's small stone that felled the giant Goliath.[55] This parallel is consistent with the view (defended in comments at v. 34 and §6.2) that Daniel's stone is a Davidic stone that represents the Messiah. (On "the God of the heavens" see comments at v. 18.) This last kingdom is the kingdom of God, which will displace the kingdoms of the world and last forever, just as the kingdom of David endures forever (2 Sam 7:13, 16). The enduring nature of both God's kingdom and David's dynasty (2 Sam 7:13, 16) gives further support to the view that the stone represents the Messiah and his kingdom. On "break off" (better, "cut") and "crushed" (better, "pulverized"), see comments at v. 34. On the relationship of this mountain with the temple and Jesus, see §7.4.3.

---

[55] S. G. Dempster, *Dominion and Dynasty: A Biblical Theology of the Hebrew Bible*, New Studies in Biblical Theology 15 (Downers Grove: InterVarsity, 2003), 214.

Greatness ("the great God") is an attribute of God (see §3.7). The adjective "great" (Aramaic רַב) is used often in this chapter. In contrast to the "great" king Nebuchadnezzar (v. 10) and the "great image" of human kingdoms (v. 31 ESV), there is the "great mountain" of the kingdom of God (v. 35), which is greater than the kingdoms of the world and will be established by "the great God" (v. 45). "The dream is certain, and its interpretation reliable" reflects the broader truth that all genuine revelation from God is true and certain (see §2).

2:46 Nebuchadnezzar may have been relieved to learn that the destruction of the statue relates to the distant rather than the immediate future. The king's responses to Daniel—falling facedown, worshiping (or doing "homage" ESV, NASB), presenting an offering, burning incense—are acts of veneration often given to gods. By Hellenistic times they were also done for benefactors whose help was thought to merit god-like veneration,[56] though each could be done for kings as early as Babylonian times in a non-worship sense of honor offered by an inferior to a superior (obeisance, offering a gift, burning incense/perfume).[57]

The verb (Aramaic סְגִד) rendered "worshiped" is used for the "worship" of Nebuchadnezzar's statue eleven times in Daniel 3. Falling prostrate is a way of showing respect to kings and gods. For Nebuchadnezzar the king to do this before his subject Daniel was most ironic, though the real purpose may be to pay homage to Israel's God by honoring his servant Daniel. This appears blasphemous from a Jewish perspective—compare Paul's and Barnabas' reaction in Acts 14:8–18 to the attempt by the natives to sacrifice to them at Lystra. Daniel did not overtly object to the king's actions, perhaps being too flabbergasted to know how to respond or, more likely, because he saw it as giving him not divine status but (temporary) quasi-royal status. In paganism, images were a sign of divine presence and could be a means of revelation.[58] Because Nebuchadnezzar had no image of Yahweh to worship—and worshiping Yahweh is appropriate (see §4.6)—he worshiped Yahweh indirectly through honoring his mouthpiece, Daniel.

---

[56] B. A. Martin, "Daniel 2:46 and the Hellenistic World," *ZAW* 85.1 (1973): 80–93.

[57] A. Millard, "Incense—the Ancient Room Freshener: The Exegesis of Daniel 2:46," in *On Stone and Scroll: Essays in Honor of Graham Ivor Davies*, ed. James K. Aitken, et al., BZAW 420 (Berlin: de Gruyter, 2011), 111–22.

[58] Walton, *Ancient Near Eastern Thought and the Old Testament*, 116–18.

"Offering" is a Hebrew loanword (מִנְחָה) that can specifically denote a "grain offering" (NRSV; NJPS; cf. Lev 2:1; Ezra 7:17), though more generally means a "gift, present" or sometimes even "tribute" (Judg 3:15). It could be used for the non-grain gifts to people (Jacob's gifts to Esau, Gen 32:21–22) as well as both animal and vegetable offerings to God (Gen 4:3–5; 1 Sam 2:17). "Incense" (Aramaic/Hebrew נִיחוֹחַ) refers to "the smell of appeasement"[59] and is used of "soothing" or "tranquilizing"[60] or "pleasing" things that placate God's anger (see Gen 8:21) and make him favorably disposed. Offering this to Daniel was an indirect way of seeking to appease Daniel's God, who holds people accountable for sin (see §4.2). Incense was also burned before Persian and Mesopotamian kings though these kings were not worshiped as gods.[61]

2:47 On the lips of an idolatrous king, "God of gods" meant "the greatest of the gods." Nebuchadnezzar, though extolling Yahweh, is still polytheistic. On the lips of Israelites, however, "God of gods" (Dan 11:36; Deut 10:17; Ps 136:2) meant "the most divine One" or "the God without peer" (see §3.2). "Lord of kings" trumps Nebuchadnezzar's own title "king of kings" (2:36), acknowledging Daniel's God as his "lord." "Revealer of mysteries" echoes Daniel's words in vv. 28–29. On "mystery," see comments at v. 18.

2:48–49 "Made him ruler" may be rendered less strongly, "gave him authority," specifically over other "wise men." The expression "over the entire province of Babylon" could possibly mean "over all the district of Babylon." The province of Babylon extended at least to the "plain of Dura" (Dan 3:1), though the meaning of that expression is problematic (see comments at 3:1). In Persian times it included other places beyond the city where Jews lived and sent gifts supporting Jerusalem (Ezra 7:16). The sense is that Daniel was "head of all the royal advisers" (GNT) and later is called "head of the magicians" (4:9, Hebrew/Aramaic חַרְטֹם). On "wise men," see comment at 2:12. Mesopotamian kings often consulted with groups of experts, sages,

---

[59] "נִיחוֹחַ," *HALOT* 5:1930.

[60] "נִיחוֹחַ," BDB 1102.2.

[61] Martin, "Daniel 2:46 and the Hellenistic World," 93; A. T. Olmstead, *History of the Persian Empire* (Chicago: University of Chicago Press, 1948), 217, suggests Persian kings were worshiped. But Millard, "Incense—the ancient Room Freshener," 111–22, argues that incense burners before Mesopotamian and Persian kings were used as perfume air fresheners (as in Prov 27:9), not to worship.

and scholars (Akkadian *enqūtu* and *ummânu*), some of whom were diviners, each led by a "chief" (רַב).[62]

It is remarkable that Daniel, despite the call of God's people to radical holiness and faithfulness (see §4.1, §4.8), agreed to be an administrator over Babylon's wise men. Why Daniel as a pious Jew was willing to administrate diviners condemned by the law (Deut 18:7–12) is a question difficult to answer, though he no doubt did his duties faithfully. Like Daniel, Christians working in non–Christian settings must sometimes balance their religious and moral integrity with duties employers may ask of them. Note that Daniel was able to obtain jobs for his friends in Nebuchadnezzar's administration. Daniel's duties were in "the king's court," or more literally at "the gate of the king" (KJV).

Bridge

The overall message of the Bible and a major theme in Daniel is that God is in control of history and has a plan for it (see §3.8 and §7.1), what Rev 5:7–9 symbolizes as a sealed scroll of destiny and Dan 10:21 calls "the book of truth." This divine plan was hidden from reputed wise men like Nebuchadnezzar's diviners. Only God can foreknow the future (see §3.5), and God alone predetermines the plan for history. Only he can reveal the mystery of history's destiny, in this case to a polytheistic king, and do so supernaturally though prophets like Daniel (2:19, 45). Idolatrous sages are unreliable guides (see §2).

When Daniel's life was threatened along with the diviners of Babylon because of their failure to interpret the king's dream (2:13), Daniel did not panic. Instead he employed his God-given wisdom (2:14; cf. 1:17), relied on God's circumstantial providence (2:16; see comments there), and prayed with his friends for divine revelation (2:17–18; see §2), knowing that God answers prayer (see §4.7) and is the "revealer of mysteries" (2:29). Just as Daniel appropriately responded to God's revelatory answer (2:19), so should we respond with thanksgiving when God answers our prayers. Daniel praised

---

[62] T. E. Gaston, *Historical Issues in the Book of Daniel* (Oxford: Taanathshilo, 2009), 41; K. van der Toorn, "Scholars at the Oriental Court: The Figure of Daniel against its Mesopotamian Background," in *The Book of Daniel: Composition and Reception*, ed. J. J. Collins and P. W. Flint, VTSup 83 (Leiden: Brill, 2001), 1:37–54.

him as "the great God" (2:45) who is eternal, wise, omnipotent, omniscient, and enlightened (2:20–23; see §3.3, §3.5).

The bookends of history are Genesis 2–3 with paradise and its tree of life lost, and Rev 22:2 with paradise and the tree of life restored. In between, God allows empires to rise and flourish. He fixes epochs and eras, establishes kings, and controls their destinies (Dan 2:21–22, 37). Paul's statement about civil authority in Rom 13:1 ("for there is no authority except from God, and those that exist are instituted by God"; cf. 1 Pet 2:13–14) arguably is derived from Daniel's statements about God establishing kings and kingdoms (Dan 2:21, 37–38; 4:17).[63] Among these kingdoms are the ones symbolized by the statue in Nebuchadnezzar's dream: Babylon, Medo-Persia, the Macedonian Greeks, and Rome. Whereas human kingdoms are temporary and prone to break apart like the statue's feet (2:33–35, 41–43), God's great kingdom will supplant all others and never end (see §7.4.3). When first-century Jews heard Jesus' announcement that the kingdom of God was at hand (Mark 1:16), they would have understood him in light of passages such as Daniel 2, which anticipates the coming of God's kingdom.

God's plan involves displacing the kingdoms of the world with the kingdom of God, the great mountain of Nebuchadnezzar's dream (2:44; see §7.3, §7.4). That kingdom starts small (a stone) but will eventually grow immense (a great mountain). Compare the parable of the mustard seed (Matt 13:31–32; Mark 4:30–32). Great kings like Nebuchadnezzar ("king of kings" 2:37) will be displaced by the kingdom of God whose king, the "Lord of kings," is sovereign over Nebuchadnezzar (2:47; see §3.8), language echoed in John's description of the Messiah as "King of kings and Lord of lords" (Rev 17:14; 19:16). God's right to kingship (see §3.8) is based on the fact that he created the world (Genesis 1)—a truth celebrated in Israel's worship ("The Lord reigns," Pss 93:1; 96:10; 97:1; 99:1; 146:10). The stone made without hands probably symbolizes the Messiah (see comments vv. 34, 44–45 and §6.2). Believers should live in light of the coming, eternal kingdom of God and not for the kingdoms of this world that will come to an end (see §7.5).

---

[63] K. Boa and W. Kruidenier, *Romans*, HNTC 6 (Nashville: Broadman & Holman, 2000), 392.

I. Court Narratives (Daniel 1–6)

A. Daniel and friends in Nebuchadnezzar's court (Daniel 1)

B. Daniel interprets Nebuchadnezzar's dream of a statue (Daniel 2)

C. Shadrach, Meshach, and Abednego in the fiery furnace (Daniel 3)

D. Daniel interprets Nebuchadnezzar's dream of a tree (Daniel 4)

E. Daniel interprets the handwriting on the wall (Daniel 5)

F. Daniel and the lion's den (Daniel 6)

II. Visions of Daniel (Daniel 7–12)

(A) Beginning of story (1:1–21)

   (B) Dream about four world kingdoms ended by the kingdom of God (2:1–49)

      (C) Judeans faithful in the face of death (3:1–30)

         (D) Royal pride humbled (4:1–37)

         (D') Royal pride humbled (5:1–31)

      (C') A Judean faithful in the face of death (6:1–28)

   (B') Vision about four world kingdoms ended by the kingdom of God (7:1–28)

      (E) Vision of Persian and Greek kingdoms to Antiochus (8:1–27)

         (F) Vision of seventy weeks (9:1–27)

      (E') Vision of Persian and Greek kingdoms to Antiochus (10:1–11:35)

   (B'') World kingdoms ended and the righteous established (11:36–12:3)

(A') End of story: Vision sealed until the end (12:4–13)

[1] King Nebuchadnezzar made a gold statue, ninety feet high and nine feet wide. He set it up on the plain of Dura in the province of Babylon. [2] King Nebuchadnezzar sent word to assemble the satraps, prefects, governors, advisers, treasurers, judges, magistrates, and all the rulers of the provinces to attend the dedication of the statue King Nebuchadnezzar had set up. [3] So the satraps, prefects, governors, advisers, treasurers, judges, magistrates, and all the rulers of the provinces assembled for the dedication of the statue

the king had set up. Then they stood before the statue Nebuchadnezzar had set up.

⁴ A herald loudly proclaimed, "People of every nation and language, you are commanded: ⁵ When you hear the sound of the horn, flute, zither, lyre, harp, drum, and every kind of music, you are to fall facedown and worship the gold statue that King Nebuchadnezzar has set up. ⁶ But whoever does not fall down and worship will immediately be thrown into a furnace of blazing fire."

⁷ Therefore, when all the people heard the sound of the horn, flute, zither, lyre, harp, and every kind of music, people of every nation and language fell down and worshiped the gold statue that King Nebuchadnezzar had set up.

⁸ Some Chaldeans took this occasion to come forward and maliciously accuse the Jews. ⁹ They said to King Nebuchadnezzar, "May the king live forever. ¹⁰ You as king have issued a decree that everyone who hears the sound of the horn, flute, zither, lyre, harp, drum, and every kind of music must fall down and worship the gold statue. ¹¹ Whoever does not fall down and worship will be thrown into a furnace of blazing fire. ¹² There are some Jews you have appointed to manage the province of Babylon: Shadrach, Meshach, and Abednego. These men have ignored you, the king; they do not serve your gods or worship the gold statue you have set up."

¹³ Then in a furious rage Nebuchadnezzar gave orders to bring in Shadrach, Meshach, and Abednego. So these men were brought before the king. ¹⁴ Nebuchadnezzar asked them, "Shadrach, Meshach, and Abednego, is it true that you don't serve my gods or worship the gold statue I have set up? ¹⁵ Now if you're ready, when you hear the sound of the horn, flute, zither, lyre, harp, drum, and every kind of music, fall down and worship the statue I made. But if you don't worship it, you will immediately be thrown into a furnace of blazing fire — and who is the god who can rescue you from my power?"

¹⁶ Shadrach, Meshach, and Abednego replied to the king, "Nebuchadnezzar, we don't need to give you an answer to this question. ¹⁷ If the God we serve exists, then he can rescue us from the furnace of blazing fire, and he can rescue us from the power of you, the king. ¹⁸ But even if he does not rescue us, we want you as king to know that we will not serve your gods or worship the gold statue you set up."

¹⁹ Then Nebuchadnezzar was filled with rage, and the expression on his face changed toward Shadrach, Meshach, and Abednego. He gave orders to heat the furnace seven times more than was customary, ²⁰ and he commanded some of the best soldiers in his

army to tie up Shadrach, Meshach, and Abednego and throw them into the furnace of blazing fire. ²¹ So these men, in their trousers, robes, head coverings, and other clothes, were tied up and thrown into the furnace of blazing fire. ²² Since the king's command was so urgent and the furnace extremely hot, the raging flames killed those men who carried Shadrach, Meshach, and Abednego up. ²³ And these three men, Shadrach, Meshach, and Abednego fell, bound, into the furnace of blazing fire.

²⁴ Then King Nebuchadnezzar jumped up in alarm. He said to his advisers, "Didn't we throw three men, bound, into the fire?"

"Yes, of course, Your Majesty," they replied to the king.

²⁵ He exclaimed, "Look! I see four men, not tied, walking around in the fire unharmed; and the fourth looks like a son of the gods."

²⁶ Nebuchadnezzar then approached the door of the furnace of blazing fire and called: "Shadrach, Meshach, and Abednego, you servants of the Most High God — come out!" So Shadrach, Meshach, and Abednego came out of the fire. ²⁷ When the satraps, prefects, governors, and the king's advisers gathered around, they saw that the fire had no effect on the bodies of these men: not a hair of their heads was singed, their robes were unaffected, and there was no smell of fire on them. ²⁸ Nebuchadnezzar exclaimed, "Praise to the God of Shadrach, Meshach, and Abednego! He sent his angel and rescued his servants who trusted in him. They violated the king's command and risked their lives rather than serve or worship any god except their own God. ²⁹ Therefore I issue a decree that anyone of any people, nation, or language who says anything offensive against the God of Shadrach, Meshach, and Abednego will be torn limb from limb and his house made a garbage dump. For there is no other god who is able to deliver like this." ³⁰ Then the king rewarded Shadrach, Meshach, and Abednego in the province of Babylon.

Context

The story of the statue in Nebuchadnezzar's dream (Daniel 2) transitions to a court narrative in which Nebuchadnezzar erects a statue and God saves Daniel's friends from a fiery furnace. Worshiping this statue symbolized loyalty to the king, who may have had reason to doubt the loyalty of some of his officials (see comments at v. 1). Nebuchadnezzar's earlier recognition that Daniel's God is "the God of gods" (Dan 2:47) did not preclude, in his mind, the need to worship other gods as represented by his statue.

Lucas[1] proposes the following chiastic structure for this passage:

A   Nebuchadnezzar's decree to worship the golden image (3:1–7)
   B   The Jews accused (3:8–12)
      C   The Jews threatened (3:13–15)
         D   The Jews confess their faith (3:16–18)
      C′   The Jews punished (3:19–23)
   B′   The Jews vindicated (3:24–27)
A′   Nebuchadnezzar's decree honoring the Jews and their God (3:28–30)

This structure suggests that the central message is the Jews' confession of faith at the center of the chiasm. In the broader outline of the book, this story is parallel with Daniel 6, the account of Daniel and the lions' den, which echos themes found here. This story also echoes the theme of resisting assimilation into paganism found in Daniel 1.

This chapter raises important questions. To what extent should we allow ourselves to be coerced by the power of the state in our religious practices? In Daniel 3 Shadrach, Meshach, and Abednego, now court officials, were commanded by the state to bow before an image created by King Nebuchadnezzar. This was further complicated by the existence of enemies in the royal court who sought to bring these Jews down. The refusal of these men to comply with the king's orders provided such an opportunity. This raises a more general issue: Whose law are we to follow when laws conflict? Will we follow God's law or the state's law? Whose kingdom wins our first loyalty, the kingdom of the world or the kingdom of God? Will we obey God even if it puts our lives at risk? And what can we expect from God in such circumstances?

3:1 There is no chronological indication provided, so we do not know whether this is shortly after the dream of Daniel 2 or years later. Regardless, the gold statue is reminiscent of the one with a head of gold from the previous chapter. Nebuchadnezzar may have been inspired by his earlier dream to build this statue. "Gold" refers to gold plating or leaf rather than a statue of pure gold that would

---

[1] E. C. Lucas, *Daniel*, Apollos Old Testament Commentary (Downers Grove: InterVarsity, 2002), 86.

have been prohibitively expensive even for Nebuchadnezzar. He was also involved in other religious building projects. One was the restoration of the Emah temple in Babylon for which an inscription has been discovered.[2] The dimensions, "ninety feet high and nine feet wide," approximate the Aramaic "sixty cubits by six cubits," a cubit being about one and a half feet. The statue seems tall but skinny (like a totem pole), though perhaps the overall height included a large base like the Statue of Liberty, whose base is about the same height as the statue. Mentioning these grotesque dimensions may be a way of mocking idolatry (see §3.1).[3]

What does the statue represent? One suggestion is that it represents a deified Nebuchadnezzar, just as the head of gold in Daniel 2 represents Nebuchadnezzar and his kingdom (Dan 2:32, 38). The Assyrians set up images of themselves as conquerors in vanquished regions to symbolize their control and to intimidate. Various tyrants in modern times (such as Mao and Sadam Hussein) have done the same, plastering their images everywhere. The objection to this suggestion is that while kings elsewhere sometimes claimed to be gods (Sumerian, Egyptian, Seleucid, Roman), Babylonian kings were never (as far as is known) deified and worshiped as gods. Another view is that the statue represents Marduk, the national god of Babylon. Or it could represent the king's personal god or some other god (e.g., Nabu, Shamash, etc.). Marduk seems the most likely explanation.

Whether the statue is the king or a god, it symbolizes the deification of the state, either through its national deity, gods, or royal leader. Kings demand absolute loyalty. Worshiping this statue was in effect a loyalty oath. Historically, Nebuchadnezzar had to put down a political rebellion in December/January 595/4 in which many leading officials, including a certain Babu-aha-iddina, were executed.[4] Steinmann thinks that putting down that rebellion may constitute

---

[2] P.-A Beaulieu, "A New Inscription of Nebuchadnezzar II Commemorating the Restoration of Emaḫ in Babylon," *Iraq* 59 (1997): 93–96.

[3] Lucas, *Daniel*, 89.

[4] D. J. Wiseman, *Nebuchadrezzar and Babylon* (Oxford: Oxford University Press, 1985), 34–35.

the motive for Nebuchadnezzar's demand that his provincial officials worship his image as an expression of loyalty.[5]

The "plain of Dura in the province of Babylon" could also be rendered "plain of the wall in the city of Babylon" (cp. "recessed area in the wall," GW). The exact meaning of Dura (דּוּרָא) is uncertain. Dura derives from Akkadian *duru*, "city wall, fortification wall, fortress," so the text could thus mean: "in the plain of (the town of) Dura" or "in the plain of the wall/fortress."[6] No town called Dura is known to exist near Babylon, though Dur- is often part of a longer name, such as Dur-Kurigalzu. Baldwin suggests Dura is a suburb of Babylon Duru-Sha-Karrabi.[7] Dura might also be Tell Dēr, seventeen miles southwest of Baghdad, or structures found southeast of Babylon at Doura.[8] Alternatively and perhaps more likely, *dur* could be a common noun borrowed from Akkadian into Aramaic with the article (אָ) and mean "the wall/enclosure." The Old Greek (but not Theodotion) interpreted it this way rendering with περίβολος ("walled place, enclosure"). If this is true, then מְדִינָה ("province") might instead be rendered "city, district" and thus be rendered in Dan 3:1, "in the plain of the wall of the city-district of Babylon."[9] Aramaic מְדִינָה can mean "city" in later Palmyrene (Middle Aramaic), Palestinian Aramaic, Syriac, and Jewish Babylonian Aramaic.[10] The likely location of the "plain of the wall," if that is the correct rendering, is the Processional Way between the Esagila temple of Marduk and the Akitu temple to the north of the city, the latter technically outside the outer wall in the vicinity of the great outer fortification wall and moat.[11]

---

[5] A. E. Steinmann, *Daniel*, Concordia Commentary (St. Louis: Concordia, 2008), 167.

[6] D. Vanderhooft, "Dura," *NIDB*, 2:167; E. M. Cook, "In the Plain of the Wall (Dan 3:1)," *JBL* 108.1 (Spring 1989): 115–16.

[7] J. G. Baldwin, *Daniel*, TOTC (Leicester: Inter-Varsity, 1978), 101, citing E. G. Kraeling, *Rand McNally Bible Atlas* (London: Collins, 1956), 322–23; D. Asheri, A. Lloyd, A. Corcella, *A Commentary on Herodotus Books 1–4*, ed. O. Murray and A. Moreno (Oxford: Oxford University Press, 2007), 200.

[8] D. J. Wiseman, "Dura," *NBD*, 284.

[9] Cook, "In the Plain of the Wall (Dan 3:1)," 116.

[10] "מדינה," in S. A. Kaufman, ed., *Comprehensive Aramaic Lexicon, Targum Lexicon* (Cincinnati: Hebrew Union College Press, 2004; electronic ed.), n.p.

[11] Vanderhooft, "Dura," *NIDB*, 2:167.

3:2–3 This long list indicates that every provincial official of any importance was present. The exact distinctions between these officials are uncertain, though judging from the syntax it may go from a group of more important officials (satraps, prefects, governors) to a group of less important officials.[12] Several of these terms are Persian in derivation. This dates the final form of this biographical section (Daniel 1–6) to the Persian period. (On Persian words in Daniel see the Introduction.)

"Satrap" (אֲחַשְׁדַּרְפַּן) is derived from Old Persian *Xšaθrapāvan* ("protector of the empire")[13] and is also found in Neo-Babylonian cuneiform.[14] They were powerful officials who ruled over large areas. During the reign of Darius I of Persia there were only twenty satraps ruling the empire.[15] "Prefect" (Aramaic סְגַן) appears to be a loanword from Neo-Babylonian Akkadian *sagānu* which is often used of provincial governors,[16] though its cognate in Hebrew means simply "official, state functionary." "Governor" (פֶּחָה) is a Neo-Assyrian/Neo-Babylonian Akkadian loanword shortened from *bēl pīḫati* referring to a governor or in Babylonia a (minor) provincial official.[17] "Adviser" (אֲדַרְגָּזַר) is related to Old Persian *handarža* ("advice"). "Treasurer" (גְּדָבַר) is a loanword from Persian *ganzabara*.[18] "Judge" (דְּתָבַר) is a Persian loanword from *dātabara* ("lawyer, someone versed in the law") and is related to Aramaic דָּת ("law"), also a Persian loanword. "Magistrate" (תִּפְתָּי) is derived from Persian *tāyupātā*.[19] If מְדִינָה ("province") actually means "city" in v. 1 (as discussed above), then these could be "rulers of the cities"—that is, regional mayors.

"Dedication" (Hebrew/Aramaic חֲנֻכָּה) is a word used for the dedication of altars (Num 7:10–11; 2 Chr 7:9), Nehemiah's wall (Neh 12:27), and the rebuilt temple (Ezra 6:16–17). The Jewish festival Hanukkah celebrates the rededication of the temple in 164 BC.

---

[12] C. A. Newsom, *Daniel*, OTL (Louisville: Westminster John Knox, 2014), 104.

[13] R. G. Kent, *Old Persian: Grammar, Text, Lexicon*, 2nd ed. (New Haven, CT: American Oriental Society, 1953), §78.

[14] "*Aḫšadrapannu*," *CAD* 1A:195.

[15] Herodotus, *Histories* 3.89–94.

[16] "סְגַן," *HALOT* 5:1937.

[17] "*Pīḫatu*," *CAD* 12:367–69.

[18] F. Rosenthal, *A Grammar of Biblical Aramaic* (Weisbaden: Harrassowitz, 1974), 41, 58 (§189).

[19] Rosenthal, *A Grammar of Biblical Aramaic*, 58 (§189).

Dedication means an "initiation" or "inauguration" of something for its first use.[20] The statue is meant to be an object of worship subsequently.

3:4–7 Three of the instruments listed are of Greek derivation, probably import items that kept their original names (see Introduction). Assyrian art from the period just before Nebuchadnezzar shows instruments that might be similar to the ones described here, though the the instruments are unnamed.[21] While there are uncertainties as to the exact identification of these instruments, collectively they portray Nebuchadnezzar's royal splendor and wealth.

- "Horn" (Aramaic/Hebrew קֶרֶן) is used of animal horns (Dan 7:7), which can be hollowed out and used as wind instruments, as with the ram's horn used at Jericho (Josh 6:5).
- "Flute" (מַשְׁרוֹקִי), or "pipe" (ESV), is perhaps derived from שׁרק "whistle, hiss"[22] and so refers to some sort of wind instrument with a tube-like cylinder shape, made of wood, reed, or even bone which produced a coarse, shrill whistling sound,[23] perhaps like the double pipes in Assyrian art.
- "Zither" (קִיתָרוֹס [Qere קַתְרֹס]), or "lyre" (ESV) or "harp" (CEV), is derived from Greek κίθαρις, itself derived from κιθάρα, which is the rendering of the Old Greek and Theodotion. The English words zither and guitar are etymologically derived from κιθάρα. The term refers to some sort of harp or lyre-like stringed instrument either imported from Greece or following the Greek design.
- "Lyre" (שַׂבְּכָא; LXX σαμβύκη) is probably a similar stringed instrument, perhaps a "trigon"[24] (NRSV), a triangular, four-stringed harp. Pre-Babylonian Assyrian art shows two types of "harps," one vertical and one horizontal.

---

[20] V. P. Hamilton, "חנך," *TWOT* 1:301–02.

[21] T. C. Mitchell and R. J., "The Musical Instruments in Nebuchadnezzar's Orchestra," in *Notes on Some Problems in the Book of Daniel*, ed. D. J. Wiseman (London: Tyndale, 1965), 19–27, esp. pp. 22, 25.

[22] Mitchell and J., "Musical Instruments," 23.

[23] "מַשְׁרוֹקִי (măš·rô·qî)," in *Dictionary of Biblical Languages with Semantic Domains: Aramaic (Old Testament)*, ed. J. Swanson, electronic ed. (Oak Harbor: Logos Research Systems, 1997).

[24] "שַׂבְּכָא," BDB 1113.2.

- "Harp" (פְּסַנְטֵרִין) is derived from Greek ψαλτήριον ("psaltery") and is related to English "psalm." It is a harp or lyre type of stringed instrument of Greek origin or design.
- "Drum" (סוּמְפֹּנְיָה) is derived from Greek συμφωνία (from which the English word "symphony" is derived), but its meaning is variously interpreted.[25] Drum (CSB, LEB) makes musical sense as a complement to the wind and stringed instruments just mentioned. Other suggestions include a wind instrument like a "bagpipe" (ESV) or "flute" (CEB), or another kind of stringed instrument like a "dulcimer" (KJV). Most likely, it does not refer to an individual instrument at all but rather to the previous instruments playing together: "*playing at the same time* with all other kinds of instruments" (GW).
- By metonymy, "music" may mean "musical instrument,"[26] and thus the phrase may mean "all other types of instruments" (NJPS) or more simply the "entire musical ensemble" (NRSV).

The term "furnace" (אַתּוּן) is derived from Akkadian *utūnu* ("oven, kiln, furnace," *CAD*), which typically refers to brick furnaces used for burning, glass making, pottery, and smelting. Nebuchadnezzar's extensive building projects required massive kilns.[27] Executions by fire are not unknown in the Bible (Gen 38:24; Lev 20:14; Judg 14:15; including cremation after execution [Dan 7:11]), in Mesopotamian laws (Laws of Hammurabi §25, §110, §157), or among the Persians. Cyrus ordered the execution of King Croesus of Sardis by fire on a pyre of wood, wanting to see if the gods would save him in view of Croesus' piety.[28] But execution by being cast into a furnace is unusual. A couple of Akkadian texts indicate that kilns or ovens could be used for horrific punishments.[29] An Old Babylonian letter records how a king (Rim-Sin) decreed a talionic punishment for a murderer to be thrown into a brick kiln (*utunu*) just as he had killed his victim by throwing

---

[25] "Συμφωνία," BDAG, 961.

[26] "זְמָר," HALOT 5:1866.

[27] Wiseman, *Nebuchadrezzar and Babylon*, 112. On the possible design of this kiln, see C. E. Baukal Jr., "The Fiery Furnace," *BSac* 171 (April–June 2014): 148–71.

[28] Herodotus, *Histories* 1.86–87.

[29] "*Utūnu*," *CAD* 20:347. For a discussion, see P.-A. Beaulieu, "The Babylonian Background of the Motif of the Fiery Furnace in Daniel 3," *JBL* 128.2 (2009): 273–90.

him into an oven (*tinuru*). Edict 19 from the time of Assur-resa-isi (ca. 1132–1115 BC) threatens witnesses who fail to inform on those who are breaking the rules of the harem with being thrown into an oven.[30] Egyptian literary and religious texts, though not historical texts, envision the binding and throwing of a few men together into a large furnace for execution.[31] Jeremiah mentions that false prophets named Zedekiah and Ahab, who fomented rebellion among the Jewish exiles, would be punished by Nebuchadnezzar by being roasted (Jer 29:21–23), suggesting that Nebuchadnezzar had a propensity toward horrific punishments involving fire.

3:8–11 Previously in Daniel, "Chaldeans" were diviner-advisers (cf. NIV "some astrologers"; see comments at 1:4 and 2:3–4). Here it is instead an ethnic term in contrast with "some Jews" (v. 12). These Chaldeans appear jealous of Daniel's friends, who are rival advisers. "Maliciously accuse" renders an Aramaic idiom that does not necessarily denote maliciousness and so could be rendered a little less pejoratively, "take legal proceedings against."[32] However, in this particular case the accusers certainly have malicious intent. Literally, the Aramaic reads, "eat the pieces of" (CSB note; אכל + קַרְצִין), an idiom derived from Akkadian *karṣi akālu* referring to "calumny; (unfounded) accusation."[33] The same idiom occurs in Dan 6:24 (HB 6:25). The accusations, though malicious and self-serving, are true, though Nebuchadnezzar's original decree was inherently unjust. Had the accusation not been made, Daniel's friends might have gotten away with their non-observance of the king's command.

"The Jews" are people from the country of Judah, whether or not they are from the tribe of Judah; hence, Levites from Judah were also Jews. While the specific reference is to Shadrach, Meshach and Abednego (v. 12), this statement may reflect a broad anti-Jewish bias against all Jews (e.g., Daniel). On "live forever," see comments at 2:4. On טְעֵם ("decree"), see comments at 2:14.

3:12 These Jews were appointed to public service at Daniel's request (Dan 2:49). Nonetheless, as an act of civil disobedience, they

---

[30] T. L. Holm, "The Fiery Furnace in the Book of Daniel and the Ancient Near East," *JAOS* 128.1 (Jan/Mar 2008): 85–104.

[31] Beaulieu, "The Babylonian Background of the Motif of the Fiery Furnace," 287.

[32] "קְרַץ," *HALOT* 5:1974.

[33] "*Karṣu (qarṣu)*," *CAD* 8:222–23.

refused to comply with the king's command to bow to his image (cp. Dan 1:8–16; 6:10). From the king's perspective this implied ingratitude toward him for having appointed them.[34] From their persective, they were obeying the Jewish law against idolatry (Exod 20:3–6; cp. Dan 3:16–18, 28). On the Babylonian names Shadrach, Meshach, and Abednego, see comments at 1:7. Using their Babylonian names rather than their Jewish names (Hananiah, Mishael, and Azariah) may have been a rhetorical way of separating them from their Jewishness.[35]

Where is Daniel? We can only speculate why he does not appear in this story. Perhaps he is away. Daniel sometimes traveled outside of Babylon as far away as Susa (cf. 8:2). Perhaps, as a member of the king's court, Daniel was not required to attend, while his friends (rulers of the province of Babylon) were required (cf. 2:47–48; 3:2–3).[36] Or perhaps Daniel was ill.

"Ignored you" is the first of several interrelated accusations. Not only were they called ungrateful for their appointments, they were accused of disrespect toward royal authority. The Aramaic employs an idiom, "they do not place upon you influence/deference/attention [טְעֵם]," an expression that means they did not show appropriate concern or regard for the king.[37] "The king" is better rendered as a vocative, "O king" (most EVV). Another accusation relates to their Jewish monotheism ("they do not serve your gods"), which is at odds with Babylonian polytheism. Aramaic פלח ("serve") functions like Hebrew עבד ("serve") as a term for worship (on which see §4.6). Semitic worship is active: One serves a god by bringing gifts, offerings, and homage. But faithful Jews would not do this for an idol (see §3.1). A final accusation ("or worship the gold statue") confirms the others (ingratitude, disrespect of royal authority, failure to worship Babylon's gods). This specific violation of the king's edict made these Jews subject to the death penalty (vv. 4–6; 10–11). On "worship" (סגד), see comments at 2:46.

3:13–15 The Aramaic rendered "in furious rage" reads more literally, "in anger and wrath." The first term for anger (רְגַז) is from a root meaning to "tremble" and the second (חֲמָה) is thought to be

---

[34] Lucas, *Daniel*, 94.

[35] R. W. Pierce, *Daniel*, Teach the Text (Grand Rapids: Baker, 2015), 51–52.

[36] Steinmann, *Daniel*, 143.

[37] "שׂים" and "טְעֵם," *HALOT* 5:1986, 5:1885–86.

from a root (יחם) meaning to "be hot" (so BDB).[38] The imagery is of the king visibly showing "hot" rage. The king's question, "is it true?" (v. 14), portrays him as a good judge in court who starts by establishing the facts. Nebuchadnezzar was not willing to condemn these Jewish men on hearsay alone.

Having confirmed that they failed to comply, Nebuchadnezzar gave them a second chance to obey, perhaps because he liked them. "Who is the god who can rescue you from my power?" denigrates Yahweh. To Nebuchadnezzar's mind, Yahweh is at best inferior to the great patron god he was asking them to worship. But, in fact, Yahweh is the only God, infinite in power, who alone can save (see §3.1, §3.7, §4.5). This is one of several instances in which pagan leaders challenged whether Israel's God could stop them. Other examples include Pharaoh (Exod 5:2) and Rabshakeh (2 Kgs 18:32–35; Isa 36:18–20). Compare also the similar mocking of Christ's faith that God could save him (Matt 27:43).[39] In contrast, the parallel story in Daniel 6 has a king (Darius) who knows himself powerless to save Daniel from the lions and who instead hopes and prays that Daniel's God would. Each of these stories ends with God vindicated. "Rescue" שֵׁיזִב is an archaic Shaphel (Š-stem) form of עזב that suggests the Aramaic of Daniel is pre-second century BC. See Introduction.

3:16–18 The three Jews answered as one, giving moral support to each other in the decision to defy the king in this matter. Their confession forms the center of this passage structurally and theologically (see discussion of context above). They considered Nebuchadnezzar's challenge arrogant and absurd. If their God actually existed, a God who unlike finite pagan gods is infinitely great, then of course he could rescue them from death (see §3.7, §4.5). On "serve," see comments at v. 12.

"He can rescue us from the power of you" can also be rendered as a wish, "may he rescue us from your hand" (cp. NRSV "let him deliver us"). Rendering these verbs as expressing ability ("can" CSB) or wish ("let him" NRSV) is preferable to most EVV that read, "he will deliver us" (ESV, KJV, NASB, NIV) or similar, as if the text were a prophetic prediction. The Aramaic verb יְשֵׁיזִב (v. 17) is an imperfect that is capable in context of various nuances, among which are

---

[38] "יחם," BDB 1095.2, 404.1.
[39] Ibid., 185.

simple future ("*he will* rescue us"), modal with emphasis on ability ("*he can* rescue us"), or jussive expressing wish ("*may he* rescue us"). But the first reading contradicts v. 18 ("but even if he does not"). It is clear that the three men have no certainty that God *will* save them even if they are confident that he *can*.

Supporting the CSB rendering is the parallel with the first half of the verse, where "can" is expressed explicitly by the verb יכל ("to be able"). This contextually could sway a reader to take the subsequent imperfect verb יְשֵׁיזִב as a modal of ability ("can rescue"). So the verse affirms that God "can" rescue from both furnace and the king's power. But the rendering "may he rescue us" also makes good sense as an indirect, brief prayer to God in a crisis. Both CSB and the alternative are plausible, though I slightly prefer the alternative: "may he deliver us from your hand." In any case, they would rather die than commit idolatry.

"Gods" (v. 18) may be a plural of majesty for Nebuchadnezzar's "god" (NJPS, GNT, NABRE), since presumably the statue represented a single god. Alternatively, the men may have been affirming that they would not serve it or any other of Babylon's many gods.

3:19–20 On "rage" (חֱמָא), see comments at vv. 13–15. The "expression on his face changed" in Aramaic reads the "image of his face changed." Image (צְלֵם) is the same word as "statue" (see comments at 2:31). No longer did the king look favorably on these Jewish men. Nebuchadnezzar dreamed about one image (2:31), had another erected (3:1) and changed another (his face). The furnace was heated "seven times more than customary." "Seven times" is hyperbole indicating the furnace was heated as much as possible. "Customary" is literally "seen" (חֲזֵה). This could mean it was heated more than normally or previously done ("seen"), though it probably means beyond what was "fit" or "appropriate."[40]

"Some of the best soldiers in his army" paraphrases an awkward text. The superlative "best" or "strongest" (NIV) is not explicit. EVV regularly do not reproduce a wordplay using חַיִל. The Aramaic reads "men of חַיִל who are in his חַיִל." The word can mean "strength" or "army." The expression "man of חַיִל" can simply mean a soldier ("a man of the army"), though sometimes it is used of particularly brave

---

[40] I. Jerusalmi, *The Aramaic Sections of Ezra and Daniel: A Philological Commentary* (Cincinnati: Hebrew Union College-Jewish Institute of Religion, 1982), 86.

or noble soldiers ("man of valor"). The wordplay could be brought out literally, if awkwardly, here by rendering as "certain men of force [i.e., soldiers] who were in his forces." The work of soldiers is limited to stronger, youthful men. In this case bravery may be more important than strength in approaching an over-heated furnace.

3:21 The term rendered by CSB as "trousers" (Aramaic סַרְבָּל) is identified by Rosenthal as a Persian loanword,[41] though others think it may be Scythian in origin.[42] It denotes an item of clothing whose precise meaning is uncertain. The Old Greek simply translated generally with ἱματισμός ("clothing"). Theodotion chooses to translate/transliterate סַרְבָּל with the foreign loanword σαραβάρα. Used only rarely outside the Bible, it is taken by Liddell and Scott to mean *"loose trousers* worn by Scythians,"[43] specifically oriental style "loose trousers" prone to being set aflame near a furnace. Translating as "trousers" goes back to the Latin Vulgate. But it might instead mean "coat" (KJV, ESV "cloaks") or "robes" (NIV), perhaps even a garment that could do double duty as a mantle. Yet another proposal is "head covering," used to protect from the sun,[44] based on סַרְבָּל which has a similar meaning in Talmudic Aramaic[45] and in Arabic (*sirbal*).[46] Translations of סַרְבָּל are thus little more than reasonable guesses.

The second term rendered "their robes" (Ketiv פַּטִּישֵׁיהוֹן or Qere פַּטְּשֵׁיהוֹן) is also problematic. Rosenthal glosses פטיש "shirt (?)"[47] (so NJPS; cp. RSV "tunic"; NASB "coats"). Jastrow thinks it means in Rabbinic Hebrew/Aramaic "undergarment, breeches"[48] (cp. NIV "trousers"). The Syriac cognate *petsha* means "leggings"[49] or possibly "head covering"[50] (cf. NLT "turbans").

The third term rendered by CSB as "head covering" (כַּרְבְּלָה) has cognates in both Persian and Akkadian (*karballatu*), but seems

---

[41] Rosenthal, *A Grammar of Biblical Aramaic*, 59 (§189).

[42] "סַרְבָּל," *HALOT* 5:1940.

[43] "Σαράβαρα," in H. G. Liddell and R. Scott, *A Greek-English Lexicon*, rev. and augmented by Henry Stuart Jones (Oxford: Clarendon, 1968), 1583.

[44] S. R. Driver, *The Book of Daniel With Introduction and Notes* (Cambridge: Cambridge University Press, 1900), 42–43.

[45] "סרבל," Kaufman, *Comprehensive Aramaic Lexicon, Targum Lexicon*, n.p.

[46] "סַרְבָּל," *HALOT* 5:1940.

[47] Rosenthal, *A Grammar of Biblical Aramaic*, 93.

[48] "פטיש," in Jastrow, *A Dictionary of the Targumim*, 1155.

[49] J. P. Smith, ed., *A Compendious Syriac Dictionary* (Oxford: Clarendon, 1903), 443.

[50] "פטיש," *HALOT* 5:1956.

to be a part of Persian dress.[51] In Akkadian it refers to a piece of linen headgear for soldiers.[52] Thus it is something like a "hat" (ESV; NRSV) or, better, "turban" (NIV).

Though exact identifications are uncertain, these items of clothing are mentioned to indicate that the Jewish men were cast into the furnace fully dressed in flammable garb. This prepares for v. 27 where none of these materials were affected by the fire, thus emphasizing the extent of God's miracle.

3:22–23 On "Urgent" or, better, "rash" (CEB), see comments at 2:15. "Hot" is literally "heated" (passive participle of אזה, "set light to, heat up"). The verb rendered "killed" is in the D-stem of קטל, which implies repeated action: "killed *one by one*."[53]

The Greek versions insert the "The Prayer of Azariah" and "The Song of the Three Young Men" at this point (see Introduction). The oldest copy of the Aramaic text of 3:23 is DSS 1Q Dan[b] that proceeds to v. 24 without these insertions.

3:24–25 "In alarm" (or "in a start"; Aramaic בְּהִתְבְּהָלָה) mixes the ideas of haste and fear. "Advisers" (Aramaic הַדָּבַר) is likely another Persian loanword.[54] The large furnace either did not have a door or was left hanging open so that Nebuchadnezzar, who stayed to witness the execution, could see inside. "Walking around" (מְהַלְכִין) reflects an H-stem of הלך that would be expected to mean "cause [self?] to walk," though the form should probably be revocalized to a D-stem מְהַלְּכִין that indicates multiplied action ("walking a lot, walking back and forth, walking about").

A key interpretive issue is the identity of the "fourth man" in the furnace. Jewish tradition identifies the figure as an angel (on angels, see §5). The Babylonian Talmud regards him as the angel Gabriel (*Pesahim* 118a–b).[55] Taking the fourth figure as an angel is consistent with what Nebuchadnezzar says at 3:28: "he sent his angel and rescued his servants." Later Daniel says God sent his angel to save him from the lions (6:22).

---

[51] Rosenthal, *A Grammar of Biblical Aramaic,* 59 (§189).

[52] "*Karballatu,*"*CAD* 8:215.

[53] Jerusalmi, *The Aramaic Sections of Ezra and Daniel,* 89.

[54] "הַדָּבַר," *HALOT* 5:1856.

[55] J. Neusner, *The Babylonian Talmud: A Translation and Commentary,* vol. 4 (Peabody, MA: Hendrickson, 2011), 547–48.

The alternative view is that the fourth figure is a theophany, perhaps a preincarnate manifestation of Christ (see §6.5). The KJV rendering of v. 25 supports this interpretation by saying the fourth figure is "like the Son of God." While "like the Son of God" is a grammatically possible rendering of the Aramaic, it is unlikely. There is no article ("the") in the Aramaic. Also, the form אֱלָהִין is the plural of the Aramaic word for God (אֱלָה), which (in the plural) does not usually designate the one true God, even though its plural cognate in Hebrew (אֱלֹהַּ) usually does. (See comments at 4:8 for a possible exception.) Moreover, it is far more likely that a pagan, Babylonian king would refer to "a son of the gods" than that he would refer to "the Son of God." The KJV rendering appears anachronistic. That said, "a son of the gods" on Nebuchadnezzar's lips means a "divine being" ("looks like a god" NLT, CEV; similarly NRSV).

The original Jewish readers might be expected to interpret this "angel" or "divine being" as "the angel of Yahweh," that is, a theophany.[56] The "angel of Yahweh" in the OT appears to be, in most cases, a theophany (M. F. Rooker;[57] *pace* W. G. MacDonald[58]). When God appears in the burning bush, he appears in the form of his "angel" (Exod 3:2). The angel of Yahweh is identified as God (Gen 16:7–13; 18:2, 10, 13; 22:10–18; Exod 3:2–6, 14, 18; Judg 2:1, 5; 6:11–16, 22–24), calls himself "God" (Gen 31:11, 13; Exod 3:6), and receives worship as God (Josh 5:14; Judg 2:1–5). The KJV rendering of v. 25 supports a specifically christological interpretation when it says the fourth figure is "like the Son of God" (contrast CSB "like a son of the gods"). The KJV thus identifies this figure with Jesus Christ, though "the Son of God" here appears anachronistic. Even if "like a son of the gods" is the correct translation, "a son of the gods" to Nebuchadnezzar would be a "divine being." The original Jewish readers might well have interpreted Nebuchadnezzar's "divine being" as the divine "angel of Yahweh,"[59] the way Theodotion's version in the Additions does. On

---

[56] Newsom, *Daniel*, 112.

[57] M. F. Rooker, s.v. "Theophany," pp. 863–864 in *Dictionary of the Old Testament: Pentateuch*, es. T. D. Alexander and D. Baker (Downers Grove: InterVarsity, 2003).

[58] W. G. MacDonald, "Christology and the 'Angel of the Lord,' " in *Current Issues in Biblical and Patristic Interpretation*, Feststchrift Merrill Tenney, ed. G. Harthone (Grand Rapids: Eerdmans, 1975), pp. 324–35. MacDonald argues that *malak YHWH* does not refer to God or Christ, but to an angel that serves as God's spokesman.

[59] Newsom, *Daniel*, 112.

the basis of such reasoning, Christians have often taken this angel as a reference to the pre-incarnate Christ (Jerome mentions this view, though he rejects the direct messianic interpretation).[60] If one accepts that the angel of Daniel 3 is a theophany, it follows that the parallel story in which God's angel saves Daniel from the lions (Dan 6:22) may be a theophany (the angel of Yahweh) as well.

It is thus possible, though by no means certain, that the "angel" in the furnace is in fact the angel of the Lord, that is, God. This seems to be how Theodotion in the Additions understood this fourth figure, calling him "the angel of the Lord" (ὁ ... ἄγγελος κυρίου, 3:49). It is similarly possible that the angel who saved Daniel in 6:22 is also a theophany, though the evidence there is weaker. Whether an angel or a theophany, this fourth figure affirms for the king that the Jewish God "exists" (see §3.1; cf. v. 17a).

3:26 "Door" is better rendered "opening" (NIV) or "mouth" (KJV). The basic meaning of תְּרַע is "gate." Since the king can see people inside, the door (if present) is hanging open. The term "servants" (from Aramaic עֲבַד) means "worshiper" (more at 3:12; see §4.6). "Most High God" (Dan 3:26; 4:2, 17; 5:18, 21) is one of many titles of God in Daniel (see §3.2). This title goes back to Genesis (Gen 4:18–22) and indicates that the true God is exalted above all, even other so-called gods (Ps 97:9), with authority over all the earth (Ps 47:2). The Babylonian king of Isa 14:14 tried to make himself as exalted as the Most High. But Nebuchadnezzar began to recognize that the Most High God is a sovereign superior to him (see §3.8).

3:27 Previously some of these officials served as accusers of the Jewish men, but now they served as witnesses of a stupendous miracle showing the greatness of God (see §3.7). "The fire had no effect on the bodies" can be rendered, "The fire had not had any power over" (NRSV). Their hair and clothing and smell were unaffected except that the cords binding them were gone. It is as if nothing had happened. Hebrews 11:34 (similarly 1 Macc 2:59) alludes to Shadrach, Meshach, and Abednego as exemplary heroes of faithfulness (see §4.8) who by faith "quenched the raging of fire." On "robes," see comments at v. 21. In the parallel story in Daniel 6:23, Daniel likewise emerges from the den completely unharmed by the lions, again emphasizing the enormity of God's miracle.

---

[60] Jerome, *Daniel*, 43–44.

3:28 "Praise to" can be rendered "blessed be" (בְּרִךְ) and constitutes worship (see §4.6); see comments at 2:19. The theme of God as Savior and rewarder of his faithful people is important in Daniel (see §4.4 and §4.5). The Aramaic of "risked their lives" reads they "yielded up their bodies" (ESV)—that is, they put their bodies at risk of cremation. Theodotion's expanded rendering of this verse ("yielded up their bodies to the fire") is probably alluded to in some manuscripts of 1 Cor 13:3 that read "give up ... body to be burned" (KJV, NASB, ESV), using these Jewish men as an example of extreme sacrifice for God. "Rather than serve or worship any god" could be more accurately rendered, "that they not serve." The construction should be understood as expressing purpose: "in order not to serve or worship." On "serve," see comments at v. 12. On "worship," see 2:46 and §4.6. "Except their own God" describes Jewish monotheism (see §3.1). In practice it does not matter whether these Jews believed that other gods existed. Regardless, Yahweh alone was to be worshiped.

3:29-30 On the distinctions between the terms "people, nation, or language," see comments at v. 4. Previously, "peoples, nations, and tongues" are called upon to worship Nebuchadnezzar's image (vv. 4, 7), but now ironically they are commanded not to disrespect the Jewish God who demanded that such images not be worshiped (see §3.1, §4.6). "Anything offensive" (שֵׁלָה) is usually thought to be an error for שָׁלוּ ("negligence"; so the Qere), though S. Paul cogently argues that the word here should instead be vocalized שֵׁלָה and taken as a cognate of Akkadian šillatu, which means "blasphemy, sacrilege, insult" (cf. NRSV "utters blasphemy").[61] On "torn limb to limb" and "house made a garbage dump," see comments at 2:5.

Nebuchadnezzar's statement about "no other god" still assumes the existence of other gods (contrast §3.1). His edict makes Judaism a legal, state-recognized and protected religion despite its monotheism.[62] Later Julius Caesar similarly recognized Judaism as a legitimate religion in the Roman Empire.[63] This decree, while not fully monotheistic, expressed a reversal of the king's previous opinion (see v. 15) by acknowledging God's unique ability to save among gods (see §4.5). This acknowledgement echoes a periodic OT theme

---

[61] S. M. Paul, "Daniel 3:29—A Case Study of 'Neglected' Blasphemy," *Journal of Near Eastern Studies* 42.4 (1983): 291–94. See "*šillatu*," *CAD* 17.2:445–47.

[62] Baldwin, *Daniel*, 106.

[63] Josephus, *Antiquities* 14.190–95.

that Yahweh is superior to the gods (Exod 15:11; 18:11; 1 Chr 16:25; 2 Chr 2:5; Pss 86:8; 95:3; 96:4; 135:5).

This story parallels (see outline) Daniel 6, where God again shows his unsurpassed ability to save. It also begins the process of God's humbling of royal pride, a theme emphasized in Daniel 4 and 5 (see outline). "The king awarded" more literally reads "the king caused [them] to prosper" (H-stem of צלח; cp. NASB and the similar outcome at 6:28), whether by promoting the three men or by rewarding them in some way. The ultimate cause of their prospering is the intervention of God who regularly intercedes to protect and bless his people (see §4.4).

Bridge

Daniel 3 fits into the biblical-theological motif of the need for God's people to be holy (see §4.1) and to remain faithful to him even at personal risk (see §4.8). What are we to do when our loyalty to God and to the state conflict? Romans 13, perhaps alluding to Daniel's teaching about how God establishes kings (Dan 2:21, 37–38; 4:17), indicates that in general governments have been instituted by God to maintain order. Thus rebellion against governments constitutes rebellion against God (Rom 13:1–7). In Daniel 1, Daniel tried to work with his Babylonian overlords to avoid compromising his faith rather than simply defying them. But what about when authorities command us to do things that directly contradict the teaching of God's Word? Peter and the apostles conclude that in such cases, "We must obey God rather than men" (Acts 5:29). This is exactly what Shadrach, Meshach, and Abednego decided, as highlighted in their confession at the center of the chiastic structure of this passage (3:16–18; see discussion of context above). Unlike Daniel 1, here compromise was not possible. Rather than buckle to the pressure to conform and to obey the king's demand to commit idolatry (see §3.1), they chose instead to resist, risking their lives. For this reason they become known as examples to be followed (4 Macc 13:9) and as heroes who by faith "quenched the raging fire" (Heb 11:34).

A recurring theme in Daniel is that God may expect his people to sacrifice their lives rather than disobey his commands (see §4.8). Jesus too warned of the possibility of martyrdom among his followers (Matt 10:21; 24:9; John 16:2). But he exhorted his disciples not to fear people, who can only kill their bodies. Instead they are to fear God who can destroy soul and body in hell (Matt 10:28). John the Baptist was martyred during Jesus' earthly ministry (Matt 14:1–12). In the early church both Stephen and James were martyred (Acts 7:57–60; 12:2), and Revelation speaks of Antipas and many other martyrs (Rev 2:12–13; 6:9–11; 11:7–8; 20:4). In some parts of the world Christians are still being martyred for their faith.

In the case of Shadrach, Meshach, and Abednego, God saved them from death and allowed them to prosper, but this is not a general promise. They knew that God exists (see §3.1) and that he is infinitely powerful and able to save (see §3.7). Although they believed that he could sovereignly reverse the decrees of kings (see §3.8), they did not know if he would do so (see comments at vv. 17–18). Peter may have had Daniel 3 in mind when he warned Christians that they too can expect at times to go through "fiery trials" (1 Pet 4:12).[64] But the fourth figure in the furnace—whether an angel or a theophany (see comments at v. 25)—reminds us that God is with us in our fiery trials and often works to save his people from distress (see §4.5).[65]

---

[64] Lucas, *Daniel*, 96.
[65] S. R. Miller, *Daniel*, NAC 18 (Nashville: Broadman & Holman, 1994), 124.

I. Court Narratives (Daniel 1–6)
   A. Daniel and friends in Nebuchadnezzar's court (Daniel 1)
   B. Daniel interprets Nebuchadnezzar's dream of a statue
      (Daniel 2)
   C. Shadrach, Meshach, and Abednego in the fiery furnace
      (Daniel 3)
   **D. Daniel interprets Nebuchadnezzar's dream of a tree
      (Daniel 4)**
   E. Daniel interprets the handwriting on the wall (Daniel 5)
   F. Daniel and the lion's den (Daniel 6)

II. Visions of Daniel (Daniel 7–12)

   (A) Beginning of story (1:1–21)
      (B) Dream about four world kingdoms ended by the
         kingdom of God (2:1–49)
      (C) Judeans faithful in the face of death (3:1–30)
         (D) Royal pride humbled (4:1–37)
         (D') Royal pride humbled (5:1–31)
      (C') A Judean faithful in the face of death (6:1–28)
   (B') Vision about four world kingdoms ended by the
      kingdom of God (7:1–28)
      (E) Vision of Persian and Greek kingdoms to
         Antiochus (8:1–27)
         (F) Vision of seventy weeks (9:1–27)
      (E') Vision of Persian and Greek kingdoms to
         Antiochus (10:1–11:35)
   (B")World kingdoms ended and the righteous estab-
      lished (11:36–12:3)
   (A') End of story: Vision sealed until the end (12:4–13)

   [1]King Nebuchadnezzar,

To those of every people, nation, and language, who live on the
whole earth:

May your prosperity increase. [2] I am pleased to tell you about the
miracles and wonders the Most High God has done for me.

[3]   How great are his miracles,
      and how mighty his wonders!

His kingdom is an eternal kingdom,
and his dominion is from generation to generation.

⁴ I, Nebuchadnezzar, was at ease in my house and flourishing in my palace. ⁵ I had a dream, and it frightened me; while in my bed, the images and visions in my mind alarmed me. ⁶ So I issued a decree to bring all the wise men of Babylon to me in order that they might make the dream's interpretation known to me. ⁷ When the magicians, mediums, Chaldeans, and diviners came in, I told them the dream, but they could not make its interpretation known to me.

⁸ Finally Daniel, named Belteshazzar after the name of my god—and a spirit of the holy gods is in him—came before me. I told him the dream: ⁹ "Belteshazzar, head of the magicians, because I know that you have the spirit of the holy gods and that no mystery puzzles you, explain to me the visions of my dream that I saw, and its interpretation. ¹⁰ In the visions of my mind as I was lying in bed, I saw this:

There was a tree in the middle of the earth,
and it was very tall.
¹¹ The tree grew large and strong;
its top reached to the sky,
and it was visible to the ends of the earth.
¹² Its leaves were beautiful, its fruit was abundant,
and on it was food for all.
Wild animals found shelter under it,
the birds of the sky lived in its branches,
and every creature was fed from it.

¹³ "As I was lying in my bed, I also saw in the visions of my mind a watcher, a holy one, coming down from heaven. ¹⁴ He called out loudly:

Cut down the tree and chop off its branches;
strip off its leaves and scatter its fruit.
Let the animals flee from under it,
and the birds from its branches.
¹⁵ But leave the stump with its roots in the ground
and with a band of iron and bronze around it
in the tender grass of the field.
Let him be drenched with dew from the sky
and share the plants of the earth
with the animals.

¹⁶ Let his mind be changed from that of a human,
and let him be given the mind
of an animal
for seven periods of time.
¹⁷ This word is by decree of the watchers,
and the decision is by command from the holy ones.
This is so that the living will know
that the Most High is ruler
over human kingdoms.
He gives them to anyone he wants
and sets the lowliest of people over them.

¹⁸ This is the dream that I, King Nebuchadnezzar, had. Now, Belteshazzar, tell me the interpretation, because none of the wise men of my kingdom can make the interpretation known to me. But you can, because you have a spirit of the holy gods."

¹⁹ Then Daniel, whose name is Belteshazzar, was stunned for a moment, and his thoughts alarmed him. The king said, "Belteshazzar, don't let the dream or its interpretation alarm you."

Belteshazzar answered, "My lord, may the dream apply to those who hate you, and its interpretation to your enemies! ²⁰ The tree you saw, which grew large and strong, whose top reached to the sky and was visible to the whole earth, ²¹ and whose leaves were beautiful and its fruit abundant—and on it was food for all, under it the wild animals lived, and in its branches the birds of the sky lived— ²² that tree is you, Your Majesty. For you have become great and strong: your greatness has grown and even reaches the sky, and your dominion extends to the ends of the earth.

²³ "The king saw a watcher, a holy one, coming down from heaven and saying, 'Cut down the tree and destroy it, but leave the stump with its roots in the ground and with a band of iron and bronze around it in the tender grass of the field. Let him be drenched with dew from the sky and share food with the wild animals for seven periods of time.' ²⁴ This is the interpretation, Your Majesty, and this is the decree of the Most High that has been issued against my lord the king: ²⁵ You will be driven away from people to live with the wild animals. You will feed on grass like cattle and be drenched with dew from the sky for seven periods of time, until you acknowledge that the Most High is ruler over human kingdoms, and he gives them to anyone he wants. ²⁶ As for the command to leave the tree's stump with its roots, your kingdom will be restored to you as soon as you acknowledge that Heaven rules. ²⁷ Therefore, may my advice seem good to you my king. Separate yourself from your sins

by doing what is right, and from your injustices by showing mercy to the needy. Perhaps there will be an extension of your prosperity." [28] All this happened to King Nebuchadnezzar. [29] At the end of twelve months, as he was walking on the roof of the royal palace in Babylon, [30] the king exclaimed, "Is this not Babylon the Great that I have built to be a royal residence by my vast power and for my majestic glory?"

[31] While the words were still in the king's mouth, a voice came from heaven: "King Nebuchadnezzar, to you it is declared that the kingdom has departed from you. [32] You will be driven away from people to live with the wild animals, and you will feed on grass like cattle for seven periods of time, until you acknowledge that the Most High is ruler over human kingdoms, and he gives them to anyone he wants."

[33] At that moment the message against Nebuchadnezzar was fulfilled. He was driven away from people. He ate grass like cattle, and his body was drenched with dew from the sky, until his hair grew like eagles' feathers and his nails like birds' claws.

[34] But at the end of those days, I, Nebuchadnezzar, looked up to heaven, and my sanity returned to me. Then I praised the Most High and honored and glorified him who lives forever:

> For his dominion is an everlasting dominion,
>   and his kingdom is from generation to generation.
> [35] All the inhabitants of the earth are counted as nothing,
>   and he does what he wants with the army of heaven
>   and the inhabitants of the earth.
> There is no one who can block his hand
>   or say to him, "What have you done?"

[36] At that time my sanity returned to me, and my majesty and splendor returned to me for the glory of my kingdom. My advisers and my nobles sought me out, I was reestablished over my kingdom, and even more greatness came to me. [37] Now I, Nebuchadnezzar, praise, exalt, and glorify the King of the heavens, because all his works are true and his ways are just. He is able to humble those who walk in pride.

Context

The account of God's deliverance of his servants in Daniel 3 is followed by two chapters that tell of the divine humbling of royal pride: Nebuchadnezzar in Daniel 4 and Belshazzar in Daniel 5.

Another account of deliverance then follows in Daniel 6 (Daniel and the lions) that parallels Daniel 3 (see outline). Combined, the two stories of divine deliverance surrounding accounts of divine humbling of gentile kings provides motivation to readers to remain faithful despite arrogant royal opposition. God can humble such kings and save his people. Daniel 4 is the last of the chapters featuring Nebuchadnezzar, quoting the king's own autobiographic testimony of his experiences with Daniel's God. Like Daniel 2, this chapter centers on a prophetic dream of Nebuchadnezzar for which he sought interpretation, though this time without threats of punishment. The dream portends that Nebuchadnezzar's pride will be humbled by a period of madness. In the process, Nebuchadnezzar not only learns humility before God but even comes to confess the sovereign superiority of Daniel's God who rules over the affairs of men (4:17b, 25c, 32c).

This unit follows a simple chiastic structure:

A   Nebuchadnezzar's testimony and proclamation of praise (4:1–3)
    B   Nebuchadnezzar's dream described (4:4–18)
        C   Daniel interprets Nebuchadnezzar's dream (4:19–27)
    B′   Nebuchadnezzar's dream executed (4:28–35)
A′   Nebuchadnezzar's testimony and proclamation of praise (4:36–37)

4:1–3 [HB 3:31–33] There is a difference in the tradition as to whether Nebuchnezzar's testimony and praise serve to conclude the story of Shadrach, Meshach, and Abednego (so the HB, which places it in chapter 3), or whether it serves to introduce the new section on Nebuchadnezzar's pride in chapter 4. Arguably it does both: the mention of God's miracles (vv. 2–3) is a fitting conclusion to the story of the fiery furnace, while the mention of miracles God has done for King Nebuchadnezzar anticipates what follows. However, it seems more like an introduction than a conclusion. The chapter in English opens and closes with Nebuchadnezzar's autobiographical statements addressed to all his subjects. "Who live in all the earth" is synecdoche-hyperbole for throughout his large empire. "Those of every people, nation, and language" (v. 1b) is hyperbole for the various ethnic groups in Nebuchadnezzar's extensive empire covering Syro-Palestine and Mesopotamia.

"Prosperity" (v. 1c) is Aramaic שְׁלָם (cognate with Hebrew שָׁלוֹם) that is normally glossed "peace" (cf. "Peace be multiplied to you!" ESV), though it often refers more broadly to "welfare, health" or "well-being" (so NJPS; similarly CSB's "prosperity"). In addition, it can be part of greetings: "How are you?" in Hebrew is literally, "What is your peace?" Here "May your prosperity increase" serves as a greeting that in effect means, "May you be increasingly well!"

"Miracles and wonders" can be rendered "signs and wonders" (ESV). The two words for miracles (אָת and תְּמַה) occur together in Aramaic here and at 6:28. This combination is the functional equivalent of the frequent Hebrew expression "signs and wonders" (e.g., Exod 7:3; Deut 6:22; 26:8; Neh 9:10) that uses אוֹת (cognate with Aramaic אָת) and מוֹפֵת. The expression first occurs to describe the power God unleashed in his contest with Pharaoh in Egypt. Such miracles are used by God as a means of revelation (see §2) and as a demonstration of his greatness (see §3.7) so that witnesses could come to know him (cf. Exod 7:5), as Nebuchadnezzar apparently did here.

On "Most High" see comments at 3:26 and §3.2. Verse 3 breaks into poetry with two pairs of lines in synonymous parallelism (great/mighty, miracles/wonders, kingdom/dominion, eternal/generation-to-generation).

4:4 [HB 4:1] This continues the autobiographical narration from 4:1 [HB 3:31]. "At ease" (Aramaic שְׁלֵה = Hebrew שָׁלֵו) is used of the ease Job enjoyed before his troubles came (Job 16:12) and that Jerusalem enjoyed before Babylon destroyed and depopulated it (Zech 7:7). It can refer to the ease associated with fertile and peaceful pastures (1 Chr 4:40) and the ease of the prosperous wicked (Ps 73:12). Reference to Nebuchadnezzar's ease serves as a contrast with his subsequent madness. It is the nature of life that times of ease are always temporary. "Flourishing" (Aramaic/Hebrew רַעֲנַן) is used of healthy, leafy, green trees (e.g., Deut 12:2; 1 Kgs 14:23; Jer 11:16); "fresh" oil (Ps 92:10 ESV [HB 92:11]); and (by analogy here) prospering/healthy people.

In the excavations of Tell Babil extensive remains of what appears to be Nebuchadnezzar's palace were discovered, the structure having several large courts around which were grouped myriad halls and rooms.[1] This would have contributed to the king's "ease" and "flourishing." More on this at v. 30.

4:5-7 [HB 4:2-4] These verses echo the account of Nebuchadnezzar's dream in Daniel 2. In both instances although diviners were unable to interpret his dream, Daniel could. This account differs in that this time Nebuchadnezzar volunteered to describe the dream. CSB's "decree" (v. 6) which implies a law is too strong here. "I commanded" (CEV) or "I gave an order" (NJPS) is better. On "decree" (טְעֵם) see comments at 2:14. "Magicians, mediums, and Chaldeans" are explained at 2:2, "diviners" at 2:27. The theme of the failure of diviners to interpret dreams or revelations occurs at 4:6–7, previously at 2:2–11, and in 5:7–8. In contrast God through his prophet Daniel in each case successfully explained these mysteries, showing the superiority of God and true religion (see §2, §3.1).

4:8 [HB 4:5] On how "Belteshazzar" relates to the "name of [Nebuchadnezzar's] god," see comments at 1:6–7. The king said that "a spirit of the holy gods" was in Daniel (vv. 8, 9; 5:11). Nebuchadnezzar recognized Daniel's divine spirit as the source of his interpretative ability. Previously, Daniel gave God credit for revealing dreams (2:27–28). Like Daniel, Joseph affirmed that God alone could interpret prophetic dreams (Gen 40:8; 41:16), and Pharaoh recognized that God's Spirit was in Joseph (41:38).

Though Yahweh is holy (Lev 11:44–45; 19:2; 20:26; 21:8), the idea of the gods being holy—that is, "set apart" ethically and ritually (Aramaic/Hebrew קדש)—is unusual in Mesopotamia and may reflect Daniel's influence on Nebuchadnezzar. E. Jan Wilson notes, "Although one might expect the gods to be called holy that does not occur with any great frequency." She adds that, even where a god is called holy, as with the goddess Inanna, the goddess shows no attribute of ethical holiness.[2] Mesopotamian terms for "holy" only rarely are applied to humans.[3] Mesopotamian gods were often not

---

[1] "Babylon (City of); Babylonians," *The Archaeological Encyclopedia of the Holy Land*, ed. Avraham Negev (New York: Prentice Hall, 1990; electronic ed., Logos Research Systems), n.p.

[2] E. J. Wilson, *"Holiness" and "Purity" in Mesopotamia* (Neukirchen-Vluyn: Neukirchener Verlag, 1994), 30.

[3] Ibid., 31.

even considered "pure," much less "holy."[4] Wilson concludes that the Hebrew concept of holiness and the concept of holiness in ancient Mesopotamian religions are markedly different. Holiness is not usually expected of the gods in the ancient world.

Unlike Hebrew, the plural of majesty for God is very rare in Aramaic (though see the plural of majesty, עֶלְיוֹנִין ["Most High"], at 7:18). Nonetheless, it is likely that "gods" (אֱלָהִין) is a plural of majesty in reference to the one true God here, and hence "spirit of the holy gods" should be rendered, "the divine Holy Spirit" (*The Message*), referring to Israel's holy God (see §3.6), or "a holy spirit of God [or a god]" (πνεῦμα θεοῦ ἅγιον; Theodotion). This is likely how the original readers of Daniel would have interpreted Nebuchadnezzar's words, whether or not that is precisely what the king himself means. The paucity of references to the gods as holy in Mesopotamia, in contrast with the common attribution of holiness to Israel's God, lends support to this interpretation, as does the parallel with Joseph, whom Pharaoh called, "a man who has God's spirit in him" (Gen 41:38). While Nebuchadnezzar was a polytheist, he could have had Daniel's God in mind. Even if "a spirit of the holy gods" is correct, it shows that Nebuchadnezzar recognized a divine holy spirit in Daniel, which is consistent with with the biblical-theological affirmation that prophets speak by God's Holy Spirit (2 Pet 1:21; see §2).

4:9 [HB 4:6] Daniel is "head of the magicians," meaning a government administrator of diviners. "Magician" (Hebrew/Aramaic חַרְטֹם) denotes an Egyptian-style diviner (see comments at 2:2–3), though here it is a synecdoche in which a specific kind of "magician" (Egyptian-style diviners) stands for all the "wise men" (v. 6). Nebuchadnezzar in fact appointed Daniel as "chief governor over all the wise men of Babylon" (Dan 2:48) not just the חַרְטֹם-diviners. Daniel was considered one of the "wise men of Babylon" (2:12), but v. 9 need not mean that Daniel was considered a חַרְטֹם. It need only mean that he served as their administrator. On "a spirit of the holy gods," see comments at v. 8. "No mystery puzzles you" reads in the Aramaic "no mystery oppresses [participle אֲנַס] you." This means "no mystery is too difficult for you."[5] Ezekiel 28:3 echoes this statement, saying of the ruler of Tyre, "Yes, you are wiser than Daniel; no

---

4 Ibid., 76.
5 "אנס," *HALOT* 5:1818.

secret [סְתוּם] is hidden from you!" On "mystery, secret" (Aramaic
רָז) see comments at 2:18. "Explain to me" in Aramaic more simply
reads, "say." Theodotion uses a text with a second verb, namely שְׁמַע
"hear," a reading followed by the CEV ("*listen* to what I dreamed and
tell me what it means") and the NRSV ("*Hear* the dream that I saw;
tell me its interpretation"). On "visions" see comments at 2:17–19.

4:10–12 [HB 4:7–9] Verses 10b–12 break into poetry with the
distinctive feature of Hebrew parallelism. "Was visible to the ends of
the earth" reads literally "its appearance was to the end of the earth,"
assuming Aramaic חֲזוֹת is from חזה "to see." There is, however, some
controversy among lexicographers concerning the meaning of this
word. An alternative interpretation proposed by Gesenius is that
חֲזוֹת instead means the "span/canopy" that reached to the end of
the earth.[6] This is supported by Theodotion's rendering of חֲזוֹת with
κύτος "crown, extent (of tree)." This alternative rendering fits the
context better than the traditional view, though it leaves the etymology of חֲזוֹת, presumably a loanword, unexplained.

The tree symbolizes Nebuchadnezzar and his empire (vv. 20–
21), which provided a degree of prosperity and protection for his
people (wild animals, birds, creatures; cf. Rom 13:1–7), though he
will be (temporarily) cut down. That it is large and has a top in the
sky echoes Babel (Babylon) in Gen 11:4. Daniel's imagery is also
similar to imagery used by his contempory Ezekiel. Ezekiel 31:3–15
(c. 587 BC) describes Assyria as a great cedar tree where birds nested
and under whose branches animals gave birth (31:6) but which God
determined to cut down (31:10–14). Similarly, in Daniel 4 God
cuts down the tree symbolizing Nebuchadnezzar and his kingdom,
which succeeded Assyria. The imagery is also similar to an undated
prophecy in Ezek 17:1–24 in which a cedar tree represents Israel
with focus on its royal lineage. Though the royal line is exiled, God
will transplant it so it will grow into a great tree where birds nest
and find shelter (17:23). There the ultimate plan of God is to bring
down great trees (empires) and establish his lowly tree of messianic
heritage (17:24).

All this is picked up by Jesus in Matt 13:31–32 [= Mark 4:30–
32], where the kingdom of heaven/God, rather than great kingdoms of the world, provides protection ("the birds of the sky nest

---

[6] "חֲזוֹת," *HALOT* 5:1873.

in its branches"). Thus the dream of Daniel 4 fits into a larger biblical-theological motif that great kingdoms like Assyria and Babylon will ultimately be cut down by God and replaced by the kingdom of God under its Davidic, messianic king, as Daniel teaches (Daniel 2, 7; see §7.4, §7.4.3). In yet broader biblical-theological terms, the humanistic tree of death that ruined Adam and Eve (Genesis 2–3) is ultimately to be replaced by the purely divine tree of life (Revelation 22).

4:13–14a [HB 4:10–11a] "Watcher" (Aramaic עִיר) could be rendered "a wakeful one" (from עִיר, "to wake up"). The reference is to an angel (CSB note; Old Greek). Angels are mentioned often in Daniel (see §5) and are called "holy ones" elsewhere in the Bible (Deut 33:2–3; Job 15:15; Ps 89:7; Zech 14:5; Jude 1:14). They are holy in that they are set apart for divine service. They come down from heaven (also v. 23) since they come from the abode of God. "Loudly" is literally "in strength," which suggests something of the power of this creature. He will bark out orders mightily in what follows.

4:14b–17 [HB 11b–14] Verses 14b–17 are poetic with corresponding parallelism. The language, "Cut down ... chop off ... strip off ... scatter. Let the animals flee ... and the birds," emphasizes that the greatness of the tree and the habitat it provided are destroyed. Aramaic אֱסוּר, "band," (v. 15a) is from an Aramaic/Hebrew root used of tying, shackling, or imprisoning captives. This hints at the symbolism that Nebuchadnezzar's madness is like being bound as a prisoner. "Tender grass" in v. 15b (Aramaic דְּתֵא = Hebrew דֶּשֶׁה) refers to "sproutings," whether vegetation or grass, though "sproutings of the field" refers primarily to grass. "Tender" over-translates.

Reference to the "mind of a human" (v. 16) show that the tree symbolizes a man. The Hebrew cognate of "plants" (עֵשֶׂב) is used of the food given to animals and man at creation (Gen 1:11–12, 29–30). The dream finds fulfillment when Nebuchadnezzar eats grass (עֵשֶׂב) like cattle (v. 25). "Mind" (Aramaic לְבַב = Hebrew לֵבָב) also means "heart," though in Hebrew/Aramaic, the heart is considered the seat of the intellect. This story seems to describe a case of zoanthropy or lycanthropy, a rare mental disorder in which a person thinks himself a beast.

"Seven periods of time" is usually taken as seven years (cf. CSB note; compare "time, times, and half a time," in 7:24). That timescale fits with the fulfillment beginning twelve months later (v. 29).

Some see a parallel with Joseph's dream where seven years of plenty is followed by seven years of famine (Gen 41:25–36). This parallel is supportive of the seven periods of time being years. But it is important to note that Daniel never calls these periods "years." One problem is fitting a seven-year madness into what we know historically of Nebuchadnezzar. Little is known of the last thirty years of Nebuchadnezzar's forty-three-year reign (605–562 BC). So presumably his madness, if seven years, took place during these thirty. Steinmann reasons that it must be after Nebuchadnezzar's thirteen-year besiegement of Tyre (586–573 BC), but not during his campaign against Egypt (568/7 BC), suggesting 573–569 BC as a plausible time for his madness.[7] If "seven periods of time" refers to seven weeks or months, or symbolically to the "complete time" decreed, it would be possible to fit it in earlier in his reign.

Critical scholarship often sees the book of Daniel as confusing Nebuchadnezzar with his successor Nabonidus who had a ten-year absence from Babylon. This leads some to speculate without substantiation that Nabonidus' absence was due to madness. Found among the Dead Sea Scrolls in Qumran was a text called the "Prayer of Nabonidus," which is used to support the critical view. In it Nabonidus supposedly states, "I was stricken for seven years, and ever since [that time] I became comparable [with the beasts. Then I prayed before God], and (as for) my offense—he forgave it."[8] Items in brackets are not fully preserved but have been reconstructed by the translator. There are two significant differences between the "Prayer of Nabonidus" and Daniel 4. First, Nabonidus may suffer a physical illness, whereas Nebuchadnezzar suffers mental illness. Second, the locale of the "Prayer of Nabonidus" is Teima in Arabia, not Babylon. Complicating matters, the text of the "Prayer of Nabonidus" is fragmentary, so various interpretations are possible depending on how one fills the gaps. Alternatively, rather than Daniel confusing Nebuchadnezzar's madness with Nabonidus', the Prayer of Nabonidus may be a garbled retelling of Daniel 4, which attributes to Nabonidus what actually happened to Nebuchadnezzar, or spins a story about Nabonidus that draws motifs from Daniel 4.

---

[7] A. E. Steinmann, *Daniel*, Concordia Commentary (St. Louis: Concordia, 2008), 208.

[8] *COS* 1.286.

Although there is no unambiguous extrabiblical corroboration of Nebuchadnezzar's madness, there is a broken Babylonian cuneiform text describing events near the end of Nebuchadnezzar's reign that might refer to it. It states, "Nebuchadnezzar pondered ... his life was of no value to him. ... To Amel-Marduk he speaks what was not ... he does not heed the mention of his name (or pronouncement) ... he does not have in mind (any concern) for son or daughter, for him there is no family and clan does not exist ... he prays to the lord of lords, his hands raised (in supplication). He weeps bitterly to his god."[9] A. K. Grayson, who published this text, took the language as mostly applying to Amel-Marduk, Nebuchadnezzar's son and unpopular successor whom the text mentions. Wiseman, however, argues that it more likely applies to Nebuchadnezzar. The broken nature of the text precludes certainty, though if it does apply to Nebuchadnezzar it may well be describing further symptoms of his madness.

On "decree" (v. 17a), see v. 24. On "watchers" and "holy ones" (v. 17a), see comments at vv. 13–14a. These watchers may be part of the heavenly council who sometimes propose that God take certain actions and then carry out those actions. In 1 Kgs 22:19–22 an angel, called a "spirit," volunteered before God to become a lying spirit in the mouth of the prophets, a request God granted. Similarly, in Job 1–2 Satan proposed actions against Job. The pronouncements of watchers are authoritative and powerful, though behind them—something Nebuchadnezzar does not mention and may not know—is the authority and power of God, who sent them. The ultimate purpose of all divine revelation (see §2) is "so the living will know" (v. 17b). This broader, general principle to the "living" is applied specifically to Nebuchadnezzar in vv. 25–26, 32. On "Most High" see comments at 3:26. God's ruling over the kingdoms of the world and giving kingship to the humblest of people underscores God's supreme sovereignty and serves as a poke at Nebuchadnezzar's excessive self-esteem.

4:18 [HB 4:15] This verse recapitulates the episode introduction in vv. 7–9. See comments there.

---

[9] D. J. Wiseman, *Nebuchadrezzar and Babylon* (Oxford: Oxford University Press, 1985), 102–03; A. K. Grayson, *Babylonian Historical-Literary Texts* (Toronto: University of Toronto Press, 1975), 87–91; T. E. Gaston, *Historical Issues in the Book of Daniel* (Oxford: Taanathshilo, 2009), 63–66.

4:19–23 [HB 4:16–20] The account of Nebuchadnezzar's madness in vv. 19–23 switches to third person narration rather than the first person autobiographic narration of the rest of the chapter. The change may be because the king was in no condition to record what he experienced during his period of madness, so the narrator does it for him.[10]

4:19 [HB 4:16] Aramaic/Hebrew שְׁמַם, "stunned," used psychologically, has to do with being devastated, startled, made to shutter, frightened, appalled,[11] or "stiff (with fear)."[12] Daniel may have been stunned by the shocking message, afraid of how the king will react, taken aback while he considers how to break the bad news, or some combination of these. "For a moment" is in the Aramaic "for an hour," an idiom meaning, "for a while." "Alarmed him" can be rendered "terrified him" (NIV). The Aramaic/Hebrew root בהל, "alarm," includes a sense of fear. The king perceived Daniel's anxiety, so he tried to reassure Daniel. The expression, "may the dream apply to those who hate you," means, "I wish the dream were for those who hate you (though it is not)." Cf. NASB, NIV: "if only the dream applied."

4:20–22 [HB 4:17–19] Now in his role as prophet rather than court adviser (see §2), Daniel identified Nebuchadnezzar as the tree of the dream (v. 22a) using imagery similar to Jeremiah (Jer 27:5–7), whom Daniel read (see Dan 9:2). On details, see comments at vv. 10–12. Nebuchadnezzar's vast, wealthy empire is like the tree of the vision. The tree symbolizes the sky-high greatness that was Babylon. That it "extends to the ends of the earth" is hyperbole, like the common title of Mesopotamian kings, "king of the four corners/quarters." This title is used, for example, by Nebuchadnezzar's successor Nabonidus who called himself, "the king of Babylon, the king of the four corners,"[13] and by his Persian successor Cyrus who similarly called himself, "king of Babylon, king of Sumer and Akkad, king of the four quarters [*šar kib-ra-a-ti ir-bit-tim*]."[14] Babylon was a large

---

[10] J. A. Montgomery, *Daniel*, ICC (Edinburgh: T&T Clark, 1927), 223, who notes that a similar change of person for dramatic effect occurs in Tobit 3:7.

[11] "שׁמם," *HALOT* 5:1998

[12] F. Stolz, "שׁמם," in *TLOT* 3:1372.

[13] "The Sippar Cylinder of Nabonidus (2.123A)," trans. b P.-A. Beaulieu in *COS* 2.310.

[14] "Cyrus Cylinder (2.124)," trans. M. Cogan in *COS* 2.315.

empire that controlled Mesopotamia to Cilicia, Pirindu and Lydia to the northwest, and the Levant including Palestine all the way to the border of Egypt to the west.[15]

4:23–24 [HB 4:20–21] On v. 23 see comments at vv. 13–16. God's "decree" (v. 24) is called the decree of the watchers in v. 17. The word גְּזֵרָה, "decree," is from a root meaning to "cut, determine." On "Most High" see comments at 3:26. "Issued against my lord" is better and more simply rendered as "has come upon my lord" (NRSV).

4:25–26 [HB 4:22–23] By whom was Nebuchadnezzar "driven away" (v. 25a)? The answer: he was driven away by God or by the watchers as an expression of the sovereignty of God, a key theme of this book (see §3.8). "Grass" (v. 25b) is Aramaic עֲשַׂב that in v. 15 was rendered "plants" (see comments there). "Drenched with dew from the sky" means, among other things, being exposed to the rain. "Heaven" is a metonym in which abode (heaven) stands for inhabitant (God). So "Heaven rules" (note the capitalization in CSB) is equivalent to "the Most High is ruler" used elsewhere in this chapter (vv. 17, 25, 32) and further expresses God's sovereignty. "As soon as you acknowledge" (v. 26b) implies, despite God's sovereignty, the king can influence his destiny.

4:27 [HB 4:23] Speaking further as a prophet (see §2), Daniel called the king to repentance and works worthy of repentance (compare Paul's similar message in Acts 26:20). This assumes that God expects goodness and as judge holds him accountable even though he is a gentile (cf. Rom 2:12, 15–16). Yet God may show mercy in view of repentance (see §4.1, §4.2). "Separate yourself from your sins by doing what is right" reads more literally, "redeem/remove (Aramaic/Hebrew פרק) your sins with righteousness." Aramaic צִדְקָה ("righteousness") rendered here, "what is right," may have the meaning contextually of "benevolence, alms,"[16] though rendering "justice" or "righteousness" seems more appropriate for a king.[17] "Your injustices" can also be rendered "your misdeeds" (traditionally, "your iniquities"). The rendering "injustices" suggests that offenses of the king in conducting his governing duties is in view, things that often negatively affect the needy to whom he ought to show mercy. A more

---

[15] Wiseman, *Nebuchadrezzar and Babylon*, 41.

[16] K. Koch, "צדק," in *TLOT* 2:1061.

[17] E. C. Lucas, *Daniel*, Apollos Old Testament Commentary (Downers Grove: InterVarsity, 2002), 101.

general rendering like "misdeeds/iniquities" adds all other sins into consideration. Repentance involves not only turning away from sin but also doing what is right, in this case "showing mercy to the needy." "Perhaps there will be" could instead be rendered "If there would be." In other words, a lengthening of the king's prosperity is conditional on repentance. God's sovereignty does not necessarily preclude human ability to influence one's fate (see §7.1).

4:28–30 [HB 4:25–27] This records the fulfillment of the decree a year later, an extension of time that gave Nebuchadnezzar opportunity to repent (cf. 2 Pet 3:9), though in fact the king ignored Daniel's advice by continuing to display a proud self-centeredness that constituted an idolatrous self-worship. The phrase "the roof of" (v. 29) is not in the text, though it is a reasonable deduction. "My vast power" in the Aramaic reads "in the strength of my might." "My majestic glory" is literally, "the honor of my glory."

The biblical-theological theme of the arrogant greatness of Babylon as a place opposed to God runs throughout the Bible (see §7). It starts with the tower of Babel (Gen 11:1–9), whose top, like the tree in the proud king's dream, was in the sky (Gen 9:4).[18] This theme continues through the prophets who see Babylon as the instrument of God's wrath against sinful Judah and the place of their exile (Ps 137:1; Jer 20:4–5; Dan 1:1–2), but who also look forward to Babylon's downfall under God's judgment (Isa 13:19–23; 14:22–23; 47:1). The New Testament uses Babylon as a metaphor for Rome that similarly opposes God (1 Pet 5:13) and as the label for the immoral capital of the beast that is destined for destruction by God's wrath in the last days (Rev 14:8; 16:19; 17:5; 18:2–24).

A good case can be made that these words about Nebuchadnezzar's power and achievements are substantially true. It was Nebuchadnezzar who as general and crown prince conducted military operations against the remnant of the Assyrians and who defeated their allies led by Pharaoh Neco at the battle of Carchemish in 605 BC (2 Kgs 23:29; 2 Chr 35:20; Jer 46:2). These victories by Nebuchadnezzar allowed Babylon to become an empire that extended through Syria and Palestine to Egypt. That in turn allowed Babylon's wealth to grow and be put on public display in the capital.

---

[18] Steinmann, *Daniel*, 234.

Even today some of Babylon's ruins are magnificent. The Ishtar Gate was colossal, forty-seven feet high and one hundred feet wide. The gate and walls were painted in bright blues and gold, decorated with a flower design. It was covered with representations of lions, mythological dragons, and ancient (now extinct) wild cattle called aurochs. Magnificent architecture was everywhere. The Esagila temple (dedicated to Marduk), whose name means the "temple whose top is in heaven," is fabulous. Beside it was the ziggurat temple Etemenanki, whose name means the "temple of the foundation of heaven and earth." Daniel 3:1 indicates Nebuchadnezzar built a magnificent idol-statue some ninety feet high. Besides these were thirteen other temples dedicated to various gods.[19]

Berossus (c. 270 BC) is the first writer to mention the so-called Hanging Gardens of Babylon which came to be considered one of the seven wonders of the ancient world. He claims Nebuchadnezzar was responsible for creating these gardens to please his queen of Median descent.[20] S. Dalley thinks these ancient sources mistakenly apply to Babylon gardens created by Sennacherib of Assyria in Nineveh[21] because to date no sources contemporary with Nebuchadnezzar have been discovered mentioning these gardens. That said, Nebuchadnezzar would surely have wanted gardens no less magnificent than those of the Assyrian kings whose kingdom he had finally snuffed out,[22] so the tradition of magnificent gardens in Babylon should not be quickly dismissed. In any case, there is no doubt that Babylon's cultural might was readily apparent.

4:31–33 [HB 4:28–30] No sooner had Nebuchadnezzar uttered his words of pride and arrogance ("my vast power"; "my majestic glory") than the sentence was carried out. This illustrates the proverbial truth that pride comes before destruction (Prov 16:18) and invites God's judgment against human sin (see §4.2). The king's claims in verse 30 are in effect a denial of God's sovereignty (see §3.8)—the Most High ultimately rules over the affairs of humans. The "voice … from heaven" is probably the voice of a "watcher" (vv.

---

[19] Wiseman, *Nebuchadrezzar and Babylon*, 54–55.

[20] J. R. McIntosh, *Ancient Mesopotamia: New Perspectives* (Santa Barbara: ABC-CLIO, 2005), 311.

[21] S. Dalley, *The Mystery of the Hanging Garden of Babylon: An Elusive World Wonder Traced* (Oxford: Oxford University Press, 2013).

[22] Wiseman, *Nebuchadrezzar and Babylon*, 56–60.

13, 23), though it might be God's voice. On "driven away" see comments v. 25. "Feathers" and "claws" (v. 33c) are not in the Aramaic but are deduced from context. His hair is eagle-like—that is, unkempt, matted, and perhaps long like tail feathers.[23] His nails are long, curling, and unclipped like bird claws. These similes contribute to portraying the king as an animal. Compare the eagle wings of the first beast of Dan 7:4.

4:34–35 [HB 4:31–32] Looking "to heaven" (v. 34a) is a gesture of prayer (cf. Ps 123:1; Luke 18:13; John 17:1; see §4.7) that looks toward the abode of God, and thus to God himself. "My sanity" (v. 34b) in Aramaic reads "my knowledge/understanding" (מַנְדַּע from יְדַע "to know"). "Praised [בָּרֵךְ] ... honored [שְׁבַח] ... glorified [הָדַר]" (v. 34b) are synonyms for worship combined for poetic emphasis, which befits God as king. On the meanings of these terms see §4.6. On "Most High" (v. 34b) see comments at 3:26.

Verses 34c–35 are poetic. On "his dominion is an everlasting dominion ... his kingdom is from generation to generation" (v. 34b), see v. 3. That Nebuchadnezzar associated himself with "all the inhabitants of the earth" whom God counts as nothing (v. 35a) shows that the king had learned some humility and saw the superior sovereignty of God. "Army of heaven" (v. 35b) might be rendered the "*strength* of heaven" (Aramaic/Hebrew חַיִל; cf. NIV "powers"). The reference is probably to the angelic "heavenly army" (1 Kgs 22:19) related to the "watchers" in this chapter (see §5), though it could refer to God's inherent heavenly omnipotence (see §3.7). "Hold back" (v. 35c) is literally "strike" (מְחָא) with the imagery of striking the hand so as to hinder it.[24]

4:36–37 [HB 4:33–34] Pride leads to divine retribution and Nebuchadnezzar's insanity. But when Nebuchadnezzar acknowledges God's superior sovereignty, God restores him to his throne (cf. 5:20–21). This divine-judgment / royal-repentance / divine-grace pattern is similar to the story of Jonah in which, after the king of Nineveh repented, God relented of the threatened disaster (Jonah 3:7–10).[25] This reflects the broader biblical-theological theme of judgment-repentance-redemption (e.g., Judg 2:11–19; see §4.5).

---

[23] A. Hill, "Daniel," in *The Expositor's Bible Commentary*, ed. T. Longman and D. E. Garland (Grand Rapids: Zondervan, 2008), 8:98.

[24] "מְחָא," *HALOT* 5:1913.

[25] Steinmann, *Daniel*, 204.

On "my sanity" (v. 36a) see comments at v. 34. On "my majesty and splendor" (v. 36a), see comments at v. 30. "Advisers" (v. 36b) is from Aramaic הַדָּבַר, also used in 3:24. It is probably a Persian loanword.[26] "Nobles" (or "lords, magistrates"[27] is from Aramaic רַבְרְבָנִין, derived from רבב ("be great") and thus implies the meaning, "great ones," though its exact connotation is uncertain. "Even more greatness" (v. 36b) might be hyperbole for a complete restoration, though compare what happens in the more than complete restoration of Job (Job 42:10).

"Praise" (שׁבח) in v. 37a is rendered "honor" in v. 34. "Exalt" (v. 37a) is a polel of Aramaic רום ("be high, rise") that means more literally, "declare the highness of." On "glorify" in v. 37a (Aramaic הדר) and these other terms for worship, see §4.6. "King of the heavens" (v. 37b) is a title used only here in the Bible (though see 1 Esdras 4:46). It is similar to the title "God of the heavens" (comments at 2:17; cf. 2:19, 21, 37, 44) and emphasizes God's transcendence beyond this world (see §3.4) and his superiority over the kings of the earth like Nebuchadnezzar. "His works are true" (v. 37c), literally "his works are truth [קְשֹׁט]," employs a noun that can include the notions of justice and privilege.[28] "His ways are just" is literally "his ways are justice [דִּין]." "Walk" is an H-stem of הלך, though like 3:25 it should probably be revocalized to a D-stem. If it is a D-stem, it multiplies the action to "walk about, do a lot of walking" as opposed to a one-time event. If an H-stem, it is probably an internal passive: "causing [themselves] to walk/live." Either way, "walk" here has the sense of "live." "Pride" (גֵּוָה) is from the Hebrew/Aramaic root גאה meaning "to be high" and metaphorically denoting arrogance or presumption.

The last line of v. 37 ("He is able to humble those who walk in pride") gives the moral of the whole story of Nebuchadnezzar's madness and is the apex of God's dealings with King Nebuchadnezzar. The king saw the greatness of God's wisdom in Daniel 2 when God gave Daniel the interpretation of his dream, and he learned of the greatness of God's power to save in Daniel 3. He praised the Jewish God in both incidents, and yet he continued in idolatry and pride, mixing praise of God with threats of oppression (3:29). Now,

---

26 "הַדָּבַר," HALOT 5:1856.
27 "רַבְרְבָנִין," HALOT 5:1978.
28 "קְשֹׁט," HALOT 5:1974.

however, there seemed to be a change in him. This time he was content merely to influence others by his testimony with no threats.[29] Whether Nebuchadnezzar is truly repentant and converted to exclusive Yahweh worship is an open question, though there is reason to hope that the king at last truly understood and humbly acknowledged God.

Bridge

God is a judge who holds people accountable for their sins (see §4.2). In Daniel 4 Nebuchadnezzar's genuine accomplishments led him to display sinful pride, an inflated, excessive self-esteem, what John calls the "pride of one's lifestyle" (1 John 2:16). That kind of pride is condemned throughout the Bible, from the pride of Adam and Eve who wanted to be their own gods (Gen 3:5 CSB note), to the pride of the ruler of Tyre (taken by some interpreters as reflecting the pride of Satan; see Ezek 28:2), to the apostle Paul who lists pride among other sins (Rom 1:30; 1 Cor 8:1; 2 Tim 3:2). In Nebuchadnezzar's case, pride led him to act unjustly, specifically toward the poor (Dan 4:27), and to kill anyone he wanted (Dan 5:19). Because of his pride, God gave him a dream warning him of coming judgment, a revelation that only God's prophet could explain (see §2). When Nebuchadnezzar failed to respond rightly, the dream came true, executed by angelic watchers (see §5), displaying a promise-warning / fulfillment motif.

God's humbling of Nebuchadnezzar's pride illustrates the proverb, "Pride comes before destruction, and an arrogant spirit before a fall" (Prov 16:18). As Mary's Magnificat observes, God scatters the proud (Luke 1:51–52). James and Peter state that "God resists the proud, but gives grace to the humble" (Jas 4:6; 1 Pet 5:5; cf. Prov 3:34). Gerald Cowen observes, "Pride is rebellion against God because it attributes to oneself the honor and glory due to God alone."[30] Historically, the nation of Babylon as a whole often displayed such pride (see §7). Instead, one should exalt and set one's hope on God (Isa 2:11, 17; 1 Tim 6:17), as Nebuchadnezzar eventually did (Dan 4:37). This meant acknowledging God's sovereignty (see §3.8):

---

[29] Lucas, *Daniel*, 114.

[30] G. Cowen, "Pride," in *Holman Illustrated Bible Dictionary*, ed. Chad Brand et al. (Nashville: B&H, 2003), 1327.

"The Most High is ruler over human kingdoms, and he gives them to anyone he wants" (4:25). That sovereignty is sometimes, as here, expressed through angelic intermediaries, the "watchers."

But God mixes grace with his judgment (see §3.6). When Nebuchadnezzar acknowledged that God can do what he wants and that no person can hold back his actions or question his judgments (4:35), he shows that anyone, even a proud king, can be humbled, repent, and find redemption (see §4.5).

The theme of God's judgment over sins like the pride of kings (see §4.2) continues in the next chapter with the story of Belshazzar (Daniel 5), and it will continue with the arrogance of the little horns of Dan 7:8 and 8:10–11 and with the kings of the North in Dan 11:12, 18, 36. The example of God's humbling Nebuchadnezzar's pride in Daniel 4 (and Belshazzar in Daniel 5) in juxtaposition with the preservation of his faithful servants (Daniel and his friends, and the holy ones) in Daniel 2–3, 6–7 provides encouragement for God's people to remain faithful when they confront proud leaders who are hostile to their religion. Daniel's empathy toward the king and his horrible fate despite Nebuchadnezzar's sins (Dan 4:19) is paradigmatic of how we should treat unbelievers, even proud ones, with dignity and humanity.

I. Court Narratives (Daniel 1–6)

A. Daniel and friends in Nebuchadnezzar's court (Daniel 1)

B. Daniel interprets Nebuchadnezzar's dream of a statue (Daniel 2)

C. Shadrach, Meshach, and Abednego in the fiery furnace (Daniel 3)

D. Daniel interprets Nebuchadnezzar's dream of a tree (Daniel 4)

E. Daniel interprets the handwriting on the wall (Daniel 5)

F. Daniel and the lion's den (Daniel 6)

II. Visions of Daniel (Daniel 7–12)

(A) Beginning of story (1:1–21)

   (B) Dream about four world kingdoms ended by the kingdom of God (2:1–49)

      (C) Judeans faithful in the face of death (3:1–30)

         (D) Royal pride humbled (4:1–37)

         (D′) Royal pride humbled (5:1–31)

      (C′) A Judean faithful in the face of death (6:1–28)

   (B′) Vision about four world kingdoms ended by the kingdom of God (7:1–28)

      (E) Vision of Persian and Greek kingdoms to Antiochus (8:1–27)

         (F) Vision of seventy weeks (9:1–27)

      (E′) Vision of Persian and Greek kingdoms to Antiochus (10:1–11:35)

   (B″) World kingdoms ended and the righteous established (11:36–12:3)

(A′) End of story: Vision sealed until the end (12:4–13)

[1] King Belshazzar held a great feast for a thousand of his nobles and drank wine in their presence. [2] Under the influence of the wine, Belshazzar gave orders to bring in the gold and silver vessels that his predecessor Nebuchadnezzar had taken from the temple in Jerusalem, so that the king and his nobles, wives, and concubines could drink from them. [3] So they brought in the gold vessels that had been taken from the temple, the house of God in Jerusalem, and the king and his nobles, wives, and concubines drank from

them. ⁴ They drank the wine and praised their gods made of gold and silver, bronze, iron, wood, and stone.

⁵ At that moment the fingers of a man's hand appeared and began writing on the plaster of the king's palace wall next to the lampstand. As the king watched the hand that was writing, ⁶ his face turned pale, and his thoughts so terrified him that he soiled himself and his knees knocked together. ⁷ The king shouted to bring in the mediums, Chaldeans, and diviners. He said to these wise men of Babylon, "Whoever reads this inscription and gives me its interpretation will be clothed in purple, have a gold chain around his neck, and have the third highest position in the kingdom." ⁸ So all the king's wise men came in, but none could read the inscription or make its interpretation known to him. ⁹ Then King Belshazzar became even more terrified, his face turned pale, and his nobles were bewildered.

¹⁰ Because of the outcry of the king and his nobles, the queen came to the banquet hall. "May the king live forever," she said. "Don't let your thoughts terrify you or your face be pale. ¹¹ There is a man in your kingdom who has a spirit of the holy gods in him. In the days of your predecessor he was found to have insight, intelligence, and wisdom like the wisdom of the gods. Your predecessor, King Nebuchadnezzar, appointed him chief of the magicians, mediums, Chaldeans, and diviners. Your own predecessor, the king, ¹² did this because Daniel, the one the king named Belteshazzar, was found to have an extraordinary spirit, knowledge and intelligence, and the ability to interpret dreams, explain riddles, and solve problems. Therefore, summon Daniel, and he will give the interpretation."

¹³ Then Daniel was brought before the king. The king said to him, "Are you Daniel, one of the Judean exiles that my predecessor the king brought from Judah? ¹⁴ I've heard that you have a spirit of the gods in you, and that insight, intelligence, and extraordinary wisdom are found in you. ¹⁵ Now the wise men and mediums were brought before me to read this inscription and make its interpretation known to me, but they could not give its interpretation. ¹⁶ However, I have heard about you that you can give interpretations and solve problems. Therefore, if you can read this inscription and give me its interpretation, you will be clothed in purple, have a gold chain around your neck, and have the third highest position in the kingdom."

¹⁷ Then Daniel answered the king, "You may keep your gifts and give your rewards to someone else; however, I will read the inscription for the king and make the interpretation known to him.

¹⁸ Your Majesty, the Most High God gave sovereignty, greatness, glory, and majesty to your predecessor Nebuchadnezzar. ¹⁹ Because of the greatness he gave him, all peoples, nations, and languages were terrified and fearful of him. He killed anyone he wanted and kept alive anyone he wanted; he exalted anyone he wanted and humbled anyone he wanted. ²⁰ But when his heart was exalted and his spirit became arrogant, he was deposed from his royal throne and his glory was taken from him. ²¹ He was driven away from people, his mind was like an animal's, he lived with the wild donkeys, he was fed grass like cattle, and his body was drenched with dew from the sky until he acknowledged that the Most High God is ruler over human kingdoms and sets anyone he wants over them.

²² "But you his successor, Belshazzar, have not humbled your heart, even though you knew all this. ²³ Instead, you have exalted yourself against the Lord of the heavens. The vessels from his house were brought to you, and as you and your nobles, wives, and concubines drank wine from them, you praised the gods made of silver and gold, bronze, iron, wood, and stone, which do not see or hear or understand. But you have not glorified the God who holds your life-breath in his hand and who controls the whole course of your life. ²⁴ Therefore, he sent the hand, and this writing was inscribed.

²⁵ "This is the writing that was inscribed: MENE, MENE, TEKEL, and PARSIN. ²⁶ This is the interpretation of the message:

'Mene' means that God has numbered the days of your kingdom and brought it to an end.
²⁷ 'Tekel' means that you have been weighed on the balance and found deficient.
²⁸ 'Peres' means that your kingdom has been divided and given to the Medes and Persians."

²⁹ Then Belshazzar gave an order, and they clothed Daniel in purple, placed a gold chain around his neck, and issued a proclamation concerning him that he should be the third ruler in the kingdom.

³⁰ That very night Belshazzar the king of the Chaldeans was killed, ³¹ and Darius the Mede received the kingdom at the age of sixty-two.

Context

The humbling of Nebuchadnezzar in Daniel 4 is followed by the humbling of Belshazzar in Daniel 5. Belshazzar is like his prideful father/predecessor Nebuchadnezzar. Daniel 5 refers back to the story of Daniel 4 (5:18–21) and picks up on themes from the earlier chapter: a troubling supernatural revelation (4:5; 5:5–6), the failure of diviners to explain it (4:6–7; 5:7–8; cf. 2:10–11), the calling in of Daniel with his special holy spirit (4:8–9; 5:11), who explains the negative portent of the message (4:19–27; 5:25–28), and the fulfillment of the revelation (4:33; 5:30–31). The difference is that Nebuchadnezzar repents and is restored to power (4:34–37), whereas Belshazzar is killed.

The chapter broadly follows a chiastic structure that goes from promised threat to fulfillment:

A   Belshazzar's insolence leads to a terrifying revelation (5:1–6)
   B   Pagan diviners cannot explain the revelation despite promised gifts (5:7–9)
      C   Queen mother recommends Daniel (5:10–12)
      C′   Belshazzar calls Daniel (5:13–16)
   B′   Daniel succeeds in explaining the revelation regardless of promised gifts (5:17–29)
A′   Belshazzar's insolence leads to deadly fulfillment of the revelation (5:30–31)

The events of this chapter date to October of 539 BC, the year Babylon fell to Cyrus of Persia and his armies. The war was going badly for Babylon. Cyrus defeated the Babylonians at Opis in the north on the Tigris and took the city. A few days later (Oct 10, 539), Cyrus took Sippar without opposition. The Persians led by Gubaru/Ugbaru, governor of Gutium, ultimately took Babylon on October 12, 539.

5:1 Nebuchadnezzar died in 562. A period of short reigns followed (Amel-Marduk 562–560, Neriglissar 560–556, Labashi-Marduk 556), with political intrigues involved. Amel-Marduk was assassinated. Neriglissar mysteriously died. Labashi-Marduk was deposed by the chief offices of the state who installed Nabonidus

(555–539), not a biological descendant of Nebuchadnezzar, as king. Belshazzar was Nabonidus' son.

Some nineteenth-century liberal scholars doubted that Belshazzar (Akkadian Bēl-šar-uṣur, "May Bel protect the king") actually existed since he is not mentioned by the Greek historians. But when Akkadian was deciphered, his name was discovered in cuneiform texts that refer to him as Nabonidus' eldest son and crown prince.[1] Nabonidus served as acting king for about ten years of his father's seventeen-year reign. He is called "king" by the book of Daniel though in cuneiform sources he is only mentioned as crown prince. Daniel may have superimposed over Babylonian practice the Jewish custom of co-regencies in which a crown prince who acts as king can be called king (see Introduction).

Probably for some combination of religious and economic reasons, Nabonidus, Belshazzar's father, chose to leave Babylon for ten years and go into the desert roughly 500 miles away to Teima in what is now Tayma (or Tema) in Saudi Arabia. During that time Belshazzar, the crown prince, was de facto king in Babylon. Belshazzar is treated as co-king with his father by contemporary local documents dating to the twelfth year of Nabonidus recording unusual oaths sworn in the names of both men[2] and the statement that the father "had entrusted the kingship into his hands."[3] Nabonidus returned to Babylon around October of 540 BC when Cyrus was preparing to make war against Babylon, and he led the armies against Cyrus while Belshazzar apparently continued to rule over Babylon itself, perhaps having just returned there from the theater of war.

On "nobles" see comments at 4:36. "A thousand of his nobles and drank wine in their presence" could be rendered "A thousand of his nobles all the while drinking wine before the thousand." The Aramaic repeats reference to the thousand (cf. KJV, ESV), and the

---

[1] E.g., "Nabonidus' Rebuilding of E-lugal-galga-sisa, The Ziggurat of Ur (2.123B)," in *COS*, 2.313.

[2] R. P. Dougherty, *Nabonidus and Belshazzar*, Yale Oriental Series 15 (New Haven, CT: Yale University Press, 1929), 96–97.

[3] W. H. Shea, "Nabonidus, Belshazzar and the Book of Daniel," *A.s University Seminary Studies* 20.2 (1982): 134; K. A. Kitchen, *On the Reliability of the Old Testament* (Grand Rapids: Eerdmans, 2003), 73–74; J. B. Pritchard, ed., *The Ancient Near Eastern Texts Relating to the Old Testament*, 3rd ed. with supplement (Princeton: Princeton University Press, 1969), 313.

waw clause with the participle שָׁתָה ("drinking") implies simultaneous action with the main clause. "Thousand" is a round number for all the leading officials left in Belshazzar's kingdom, the number having been reduced by recent military defeats.

That there is a drunken orgy just before Babylon fell to Persia is confirmed by the classical historian Xenophon (*Cyropaedia* 7.5.15). But why does Belshazzar throw this party? There are several hypotheses, more than one of which could be true simultaneously.

- *Hypothesis #1—Last bash before doom arrives.* This drunken orgy occurs just before the fall of Babylon. It is quite possible that they got drunk knowing that "the handwriting was on the wall" metaphorically before it was there literally! Cyrus had already defeated Nabonidus one or two days earlier fifty miles away at Sippar, and so perhaps these men knew the end was near. Thus they lived up to the saying: "Let us eat and drink, for tomorrow we die!" (Isa 22:13; cf. 1 Cor 15:32).

- *Hypothesis #2—To rally and encourage the leaders for the battle to come.* According to this hypothesis the banquet was meant to rally the troops (that is, their leaders) before the coming battle. Belshazzar felt confident given Babylon's well-fortified wall that he could hold out. The temple vessels were reminders of previous victories, in this case the one at Jerusalem. This reminder served to encourage his officials.

- *Hypothesis #3—To declare Belshazzar sole king.* Belshazzar may have also used this occasion to declare himself sole king upon the defeat of his father.[4] If that were the case, then calling him king in this chapter naturally follows. This view, however, does not explain why Belshazzar is called king years earlier in Dan 7:1.

- *Hypothesis #4—A religious festivity.* Another reconstruction leans on the traditions given by Greek historians Herodotus and Xenophon. Herodotus (1.191.6) says Babylon was taken by surprise while rejoicing during religious festivities when "they were dancing and celebrating a holiday which happened to fall then."[5] According to Xenophon (*Cyropaedia* 7.5.15),

---

[4] Shea, "Nabonidus, Belshazzar and the Book of Daniel,"146.

[5] Herodotus, *Herodotus, with an English Translation by A. D. Godley*, ed. A. D. Godley (Medford, MA: Harvard University Press, 1920), 1.191.6.

this was "a certain festival [that] had come round in Babylon, during which all Babylon was accustomed to drink and revel all night long."[6] This could explain Belshazzar's drunken party in Daniel 5.

Babylon was taken on the sixteenth of Tishri. In Harran, where Belshazzar's grandmother Adad-guppi had been a worshiper and perhaps priestess of the moon god Sin, the Akitu festival of the moon god Sin began on the seventeenth of Tishri. Thus this could be a religious celebration of Sin's Akitu festival a few days early. However, there are problems with this view. It assumes without solid evidence that Nabonidus imposed elements of Harran Sin worship in Babylon in accord with the tradition of his mother since Babylon itself did not have a festivity on this date. There are other problems in reconciling the Greek historians with the contemporary cuneiform accounts. Herodotus (1.191.3–5) and Xenophon (7.5.16) say Cyrus laid siege to Babylon, draining the river to capture the city. However, this may be legend, since contemporary cuneiform accounts explicitly say no battle occurred and is silent on draining the river. Draining the river would have been a major engineering feat that Cyrus would be expected to boast about. P.-A. Beaulieu, in *The Reign of Nabonidus*, gives a full discussion of the problems of reconciling sources here.[7]

5:2–4 In biblical teaching "wine" (v. 2a) can be a symbol of joy (Ps 104:15) and as such was provided by Jesus at a wedding (John 2:3–10). In diluted form ("mixed wine"), wine is even served by Lady Wisdom (Prov 9:5). But excessive wine drinking is unwise, leading to inappropriate actions, words, and outcomes (Prov 20:1; 21:17; 23:33–34; 31:4–5), which is why the NT condemns drunkenness from wine (Eph 5:18). In Belshazzar's case, "influence" (טְעֵם) might refer to a mere "tasting" of wine without drunkenness.[8] But two things make this less likely: the lascivious behavior to be expected in

---

[6] Xenophon, *Xenophon in Seven Volumes, 5 and 6*, trans. W. Miller (London: W. Heinemann, 1914), 7.5.15.

[7] P.-A. Beaulieu, *The Reign of Nabonidus, King of Babylon, 556–539 B.C.*, Yale Near Eastern Researches 10 (New Haven, CT: Yale University Press, 1989), 225–32.

[8] R. W. Pierce, *Daniel*, Teach the Text Commentary (Grand Rapids: Baker, 2015), 85–86.

drunken men implied by the presence of women at the party (v. 2c) and the way the king emptied his bladder at the appearance of the hand (v. 6b with comments below). Aramaic טְעֵם elsewhere refers to the commands or decrees of kings (Dan 3:10; 4:6; 6:26; Ezra 4:9; 6:1), so the text implies an irony: even monarchs who think themselves absolute and whose word is law can put themselves under the "command" (טְעֵם) of something outside themselves (wine). This serves to diminish human sovereignty in preparation for exalting divine sovereignty (see §3.8).

Nebuchadnezzar had stolen temple treasures (v. 2b) during the reign of Jehoiakim, probably in 605 (2 Chr 36:7; see comments at Dan 1:2), and again at the beginning of the reign of his son Jehoiachin (2 Kgs 24:13). He further looted and destroyed the temple around 587/6 when Jerusalem fell (2 Kgs 25:8, 13–16; 2 Chr 36:18–19; Jer 52:19). Nebuchadnezzar treated these items as holy and placed them in a temple. Belshazzar arrogantly used them profanely.[9] In the Mosaic law, sacrilege involving profaning a holy thing requires a guilt offering (Lev 5:14–16).

"Predecessor" (v. 2b) is Aramaic אַב, normally rendered "father." Calling Nebuchadnezzar Belshazzar's "father" is something critical scholars consider an error (see Introduction). One way to resolve this problem is rendering אַב as Belshazzar's "predecessor" (CSB; NLT; ESV margin; Steinmann;[10] most EVVs use "father"). See Introduction for the evidence supporting this view. That said, the emphasis on their father-son relationship (5:18, 22) seems too much to sustain a metaphoric meaning like "predecessor" here. Nebuchadnezzar could be Belshazzar's father if Belshazzar's mother is Nebuchadnezzar's widow whom his (step)father Nabonidus married after his father's death. However, if that were the case, it is strange that Belshazzar was not named as king instead of Nabonidus. More probably "his father" means "his ancestor," or more specifically "his grandfather" (CSB note), assuming his mother was both Nabonidus' wife and a daughter of Nebuchadnezzar (see Introduction). See further on this at v. 10.

---

[9] E. C. Lucas, *Daniel,* Apollos Old Testament Commentary (Downers Grove: InterVarsity, 2002), 138.

[10] A. E. Steinmann, *Daniel,* Concordia Commentary (St. Louis: Concordia, 2008), 261.

Theodotion interpreted the rare Aramaic words rendered "wives" (v. 2c; from שֵׁגַל) and "concubines" (v. 3c; from לְחֵנָה) as "concubines" (παλλακαί) and "consorts/mistresses" (παράκοιτοι), suggesting pure moral decadence of the king partying with women used solely for pleasure. It was sometimes the practice subsequently in the Near East to bring in the concubines and wedded wives to sit by the men after the giving of a great banquet, though in more modest societies men and women were kept separate at banquets. Where wives and concubines sat with their husbands at banquets, this could be the occasion of sexual orgies (Herodotus, *Histories* 5.18.2–5; 5.20.1).

"Gold vessels" (v. 3) may originally have read "gold and silver vessels" (CSB note; NRSV; cf. v. 2) based on Theodotion and the Vulgate. The temple utensils were holy by virtue of being dedicated to Israel's holy God (see §3.6). Desecration of holy things produced guilt according to Mosaic law (Lev 5:14–16). The use of the sacred temple objects for a drunken party and idolatry while implicitly boasting of the superiority of their gods over Yahweh constitutes the sin of sacrilege for which Belshazzar is held accountable (see §4.2).

From the profane use of the holy utensils, the story moves to treating idols as holy (v. 4). The emphasis on the various materials of their idols ("gold and silver, bronze, iron, wood, and stone") suggests these gods have no existence beyond their physical images (cf. Isa 44:12–20; 46:6–7; see §3.1). Israel's law prohibited the use of idols (Exod 20:2–5a).

5:5–6 Belshazzar's sacrilegious worship of dead gods provoked a miraculous revelation from the living God. The "fingers of a man's hand" appear out of nowhere to write on the wall. The walls of Babylon, according to excavations, were covered with "plaster" created from white gypsum.[11] The handwriting on this white material would stand out clearly, especially since "the lampstand" (נֶבְרַשְׁתָּא, probably a Persian loanword[12] also found in Syriac and Targumic Aramaic[13]) shone on the wall. This light highlighted the hand while the hand's owner remained invisible in the shadows, or perhaps was

---

[11] R. Koldewey, *The Excavations at Babylon*, trans. Agnes S. Johns (London: McMillan, 1914), 89, 103–4, 291, 299.

[12] "נֶבְרְשָׁה," *HALOT* 5:1925.

[13] "נברשה," in *Comprehensive Aramaic Lexicon, Targum Lexicon*, ed. S. A. Kaufman (Cincinnati: Hebrew Union College Press, 2004; electronic edition Logos Research Systems), n.p.; "נֶבְרַשְׁתָּא," in M. Jastrow, *A Dictionary of the Targumim, the Talmud*

actually invisible. The hand may be that of an angelic messenger or a theophany in which God himself wrote on the wall (compare the tablets of the law written by the "finger of God" in Exod 31:18). Regardless, the message is from God.

Only the king is explicitly said to see the hand and his fearful reaction is the only one described. It may be that only he saw the hand, or even that only he saw the writing at all, making this account parallel with Nebuchadnezzar's hidden dream seen only by the king (Daniel 2).[14] Against this latter suggestion is that there is no indication that the writing was invisible. "Hand" (v. 5a) consists of two Aramaic words, פַּס יְדָה. The element יְדָה means "the hand," but the precise meaning of פַּס is not certain. Traditionally the expression is understood to mean "palm of the hand," but it could mean "back of the hand" or refer to large, prominent "knuckles of the hand."[15] The last of these interpretations of פַּס is found in Theodotion (ἀστραγάλους). The Aramaic of "his face turned pale" (v. 6a) reads, "his זִיו changed," in which Aramaic זִיו (also used in 2:31) has a range of possible glosses: "face, countenance, brightness, complexion" (cf. CSB note, "the King's brightness changed"). Here it refers to the bright radiance characteristic of kings.[16] This apparition "terrified" (from בהל) Belshazzar as the dream previously terrified Nebuchadnezzar (4:5), and later Daniel's vision terrifies Daniel himself (8:15).

"That he soiled himself" (v. 6b) reads literally, "the knots of his loins were loosed." Al Wolters argues convincingly that this idiom actually means he involuntarily emptied his bladder (and perhaps colon) out of fear.[17] Heavy drinking (v. 4) would have contributed to this outcome. Direct contact with the supernatural (and probable anxiety over the present war circumstances; see comments v. 1) produced such utter terror so that "his knees knocked together" involuntarily.

Babli and Jerushalmi, and the Midrashic Literature (1886; reprint, Brooklyn: P. Shalom, 1967), 871.

[14] M. Segal, *Dreams, Riddles, and Visions: Textual, Contextual, and Intertextual Approaches to the Book of Daniel*, BZAW 455 (Berlin: de Gruyter, 2016), 59–61.

[15] "פַּס," *HALOT* 5:1958.

[16] "זִיו," *HALOT* 5:1864.

[17] Al Wolters, "Untying the King's Knots: Physiology and Wordplay in Daniel 5," *JBL* 110 (1991): 117–22.

5:7 "Shouted" more literally reads, "called with strength"—that is, he "shouted for" (GNT, NLT, NABRE) or "screamed for" (GW) his diviner-advisers. On "mediums" and "Chaldeans," see comments at 2:2. On "diviners" see comments at 2:27. "Purple" (אַרְגְּוָנָא) is more precisely a reddish purple.[18] In OT times purple dye was expensive so it was largely limited to kings and those associated with kings (see Judg 8:26 and Esth 8:15 where the Hebrew cognate is used) and the rich (Luke 16:19). The same applies to a "gold chain," something also used by Pharaoh to reward Joseph for interpreting his dream (Gen 41:42). Both here are signs of respect and honor.

Why offer the interpreter of the inscription specifically "the third highest position" (Aramaic תַּלְתִּי, literally "third") in the kingdom? If Belshazzar had not yet declared himself sole ruler (see comments at v. 1 above), then he himself would only be second in rank to his father Nabonidus and thus could not grant a higher rank without forfeiting his own. Thus this offer may hint that the writer of Daniel was aware of Nabonidus' existence (see Introduction). Alternatively, if Belshazzar was declaring himself sole king at this party, then he may have been saving second rank for his own son. Or possibly "third position" is an otherwise unknown office in the Babylonian administration, perhaps a third member of some triumvirate.[19] Under Darius, Daniel did become part of a triumvirate (Dan 6:2).

5:8–12 The futility of diviners (v. 8) is a recurring theme in Daniel (2:4–11, 27; 4:6–7; 5:8). While the king was terrorized (v. 9a), as Nebuchadnezzar had been troubled and frightened by his dreams (2:1; 4:5), the nobles were merely "perplexed" (ESV) or "bewildered" (CSB) by what had happened (v. 9b), though "bewildered" (Hithpa'al of שבש) in context may also imply some degree of terror or anxiety on the nobles' part.[20] On "nobles" (vv. 9, 10), see comments at 4:36.

The "outcry of the king" (v. 10a) (Aramaic, "the words of the king"; so ESV) led "the queen" (v. 10b) to make a dramatic entrance. While she could have been Belshazzar's full, legitimate wife as opposed to the secondary consorts of v. 2, that she did not go to the

---

[18] "אַרְגְּוָן," HALOT 5:1823.

[19] L. F. Hartman and A. A. Di Lella, *The Book of Daniel*, Anchor Bible 23 (New Haven, CT: Yale University Press, 2008), 184. Akkadian cognate šalšu, "third," is at least once used of "a ruler equal to us" (literally, "our third one"), which lends some support to the triumvir interpretation; see "šalšu," CAD 17.1:265.

[20] "שבש," HALOT 5:1991.

banquet and appeared with such assurance and authority, and that she comforted the terrorized Belshazzar like a mother, suggests that she was the queen mother, Nabonidus' wife. See comments at v. 2 and the Introduction where her possible identity with queen Nitocris is discussed. She was old enough to be acquainted with Daniel's dream interpretations for Nebuchadnezzar. On "May the king live forever" (v. 10c), see comments at 2:4.

The expression "a man ... who has a spirit of the holy gods" (v. 11a) could mean he has "the divine Holy Spirit" (*The Message*) or "a holy spirit of God" (also used at 4:8–9, 18; see comments at 4:8). "Your predecessor" (v. 11b–c), or "your father," refers to Nebuchadnezzar (see comments at 5:2). "Insight" (v. 11b) is Aramaic נְהִירוּ related to נְהִיר ("light") and so refers to someone who is "enlightened" or has a clear light on things. "Intelligence" (שָׂכְלְתָנוּ) is from the same root (Hebrew/Aramaic שׂכל, "to have success, insight, be clever") as "suitable for instruction" in Dan 1:4. "Wisdom" (Hebrew/Aramaic חָכְמָה) has to do with skillfulness in living. The root can refer to skills such as craftsmanship and navigating rough seas (Exod 36:1–2, "skilled/wisdom"; Ps 107:27, "skill" [CSB]). It thus goes beyond mere knowledge to proper use of knowledge to practical situations. "Wisdom of the gods" (or possibly the wisdom of a god) goes back to Daniel's special "spirit" (v. 11a). "Appointed him chief of the magicians" (v. 11c) refers to 2:48. On various diviners, see comments at 2:2 and 2:27.

On "Belteshazzar" (v. 12a) see comments at 1:7. Daniel was an old man now, having arrived in Babylon in 605/604, nearly sixty-six years earlier. He did not originally appear among the king's advisers, perhaps because at roughly eighty years of age he may have been in semi-retirement. Daniel's "extraordinary spirit" (v. 12b) refers to Daniel's human spirit enhanced by the divine Spirit that he possessed (5:11; cf. 4:8). On "knowledge" see comments at 1:17 and 2:21. On "ability to interpret dreams" see Dan 2:31–45 and 4:19–27. "Riddles" is from the Aramaic noun אֲחִידָה that means "something that is closed up tightly," hence a "puzzle, riddle."[21] "Solve problems" is literally, "loosen knots," echoing the expression in v. 6 where it ironically refers to something very different ("soiled himself"; see comments there).

---

[21] "אֲחִידָה," *HALOT* 5:1809.

5:13–16 "My predecessor" probably means, "my (grand)father" (see comments at v. 2). On vv. 14–15 see comments at vv. 7–8, 11–12. "Wise men and mediums" lacks in Aramaic the word "and." It may actually denote one class of diviner "the wise men, namely the diviners." The Syriac and Arabic versions along with a few Hebrew manuscripts add "holy" to "spirit of the gods," a reading adopted by the RSV ("spirit of the *holy* gods") as at 5:11 (cf. 4:8–9, 18). "Solve problems" (v. 16a) is literally "loosen knots," echoing the language of v. 6 where "the knots of his loins were loosed," arguably a reference to the incontinence of the terrorized king (see comments). On "clothe with purple" and "third highest position" (v. 16b), see comments at v. 7.

5:17 Daniel's refusal to accept gifts may be partly because gifts can influence one's message or be perceived to do so (cf. Exod 23:8), and partly because the kingdom is about to fall, so the offer is of no real value and indeed could be dangerous to Daniel. Belshazzar may be subconsciously trying to "buy" a favorable interpretation of the inscription. False prophets change their message depending on how they are paid (Mic 3:5), though Daniel as a true prophet refuses to give Belshazzar a false (favorable) interpretation.[22]

5:18–21 On "the Most High God" (v. 18), see comments at Dan 3:26. On "gave sovereignty … glory," compare 2:37–38. "Terrified and fearful" is a hendiadys meaning, "shook with fear" (CEV)—literally "were trembling [זוע] and afraid [דחל]." On דחל ("be afraid"), see comments at 2:31.

"Killed … kept alive" (v. 19b) is seen when Nebuchadnezzar ordered the death of the wise men of Babylon, ordered the death of Shadrach, Meshach, and Abednego, and threatened to kill any who spoke against the Jewish God (2:13; 3:6, 20, 29). "Exalted anyone he wanted" (v. 19c) is seen in Nebuchadnezzar's promoting Daniel and his friends (2:48–49; 3:30). "Humbled anyone he wanted" (v. 19c) is ironic since he who humbled others got humbled by God (4:37; 5:20–21). Unlike Belshazzar, Nebuchadnezzar had actual accomplishments to be arrogant about since he "built" his kingdom (4:30). Belshazzar merely inherited the greatness he had, putting on a pretense of accomplishment by show. Accordingly, people supported Nebuchadnezzar due to the greatness of his splendor and raw power,

---

[22] Pierce, *Daniel*, 93.

whereas Belshazzar had to buy support by lavish parties and was only a pretender in terms of greatness.[23]

Verses 20–21 describe the events of Dan 4:28–36. "Heart" (לְבַב) and spirit (רוּחַ) are here synonyms for the mind, the former translated "mind" by CSB in v. 21 and at 4:16. "Was exalted" (v. 20) is literally "became high"—that is, conceited, as explained by "his spirit became arrogant." "Became arrogant" is more literally, "became strong [תִּקְפַת] to act presumptuously/impiously [H-stem זִיד]." God as judge held Nebuchadnezzar accountable for this arrogance (see §4.2), punishing him with a madness that forced him to relinquish his throne. "Wild donkeys" (v. 21) refers to "onagers," an Asiatic/Syrian wild ass (*Equus hemionus*) that is intermediate between the true horse and the true ass.[24] This is a new detail. Daniel 4:25, 32 says Nebuchadnezzar dwelt among wild animals but does not specifically refer to wild donkeys.

5:22–24 "Lord of the heavens" (v. 23) as an expression for God occurs only here in the OT, though the NT refers to God as "Lord of heaven and earth" (Matt 11:25; Luke 10:21; Acts 17:24). It is similar to the title "king of the heavens" in Dan 4:37. Like "king of the heavens," "Lord of the heavens" emphasizes God's superiority (see §3.7) and his being above and beyond this world (see §3.4). It also implies his lordship over the lords of this world, something that Belshazzar by his sacrilegious abuse of God's temple utensils and praising of lifeless idols had disregarded. Belshazzar's defiance of the lordship of the true God brings on the miracle of the handwriting on the wall. Reference to God's "hand" (v. 23c) implies that God sovereignly holds and controls the king's life (see §3.8). This is related to the "hand" (v. 24) that writes on the wall, perhaps being the same hand (cf. comments at v. 5).

5:25 Theodotion reflects a shorter text consisting of three words and nine letters: מנא תקל פרס. Wolters,[25] Montgomery, *The Message*, and the NABRE take the shorter reading to be the original, based in part on the fact that these shorter forms are the basis of Daniel's comments in vv. 26–28. The shorter text is easier to reconcile with

---

[23] Lucas, *Daniel*, 138, citing D. N. Fewell, *Circle of Sovereignty* (Nashville: Abingdon, 1991), 81–83.

[24] "Animals" in *Baker Encyclopedia of the Bible*, ed. W. A. Elwell and B. J. Beitzel (Grand Rapids: Baker, 1988), 94.

[25] A. Wolters, "The Riddle of the Scales in Daniel 5," *HUCA* 62 (1991): 155–77.

the interpretation that follows, but no major difference in interpretation hinges on the decision as to the original text. I will work with the more difficult longer text.

David I. Brewer fascinatingly proposes that the writing on the wall was scratches on the plaster made by a left hand with four verticals by the four fingers, and one horizontal made by the thumb crossing the vertical made by the index finger. This is as if the hand scratches the wall while making a fist. In cuneiform the resulting strokes with three vertical strokes and a cross | | |+ can represent the numbers 60, 60, 1, and ½ respectively, the vertical stroke having a double meaning of 60 and 1 depending on the context. According to Brewer, these cuneiform symbols for numbers are converted by Daniel into the Aramaic for mina (מנא; 60 shekels), mina (מנא; 60 shekels), tekel (תקל; one shekel), and a half (פרס). This could explain why Darius' experts, who presumably know well the *lingua franca* of the day (Aramaic), still could not make heads or tails of the writing on the wall.[26]

Even if the inscription was written in Aramaic script, there would still be ambiguity. Aramaic, like Hebrew, was written without vowels, so the same form can have different meanings depending on which vowels are supplied. The most obvious meaning of the Aramaic words, at first glance, is a message about money: "Is weighed out a mina, a shekel, and two half shekels." But surely a supernatural message would have greater purpose than to count money. The absurdity of the most obvious reading of the text may be why the court officials were unable to interpret it satisfactorily. There are several options of interpretation for each word, depending on what vowels are supplied to the consonants. There are even more possibilities if, as some suggest, there were no divisions between the letters to distinguish words.

---

[26] D. I. Brewer, "*MENE, MENE, TEQEL UPARSIN*: Daniel 5:28 in Cuneiform," *Tyndale Bulletin* 42.2 (Nov 1991): 310–16.

Aramaic	Possible Transliteration	Possible Meanings
מנא	1. *māneʾ*	1. "A mina," a weight equivalent to sixty shekels.
	2. *měniʾ*	2. Passive participle or perfect passive meaning "[it is] weighed" (of silver), or "[it is] numbered" (of days), or "it is reckoned" [often used as a weight of silver] (of life).
	3. *měnāʾ*	3. Perfect verb meaning "he weighed; he counted; he numbered [days]."
	4. *mānē*	4. Active participle meaning "weighing, counting."
	5. *mānʾē*	5. "Vessels" as a biform of מָאנֵי in Dan 5:2–3.
		The double מנא could be repetition for emphasis or be vocalized as different words.
תקל	1. *těqēl*	1. Noun for a weight (often of silver). A "shekel" (its Hebrew cognate). Hebrew שׁ (*š*) sometimes becomes ת (*t*) when words go from Hebrew to Aramaic.
	2. *těqal*	2. Perfect verb of תקל meaning "he weighed."
	3. *těqil*	3. Perfect passive or a passive participle of תקל meaning "[he/it] is weighted."
	4. *tāqēl*	4. Verb in the imperfect from קלל meaning "you are light."
	5. *těqal*	5. Verb meaning "he fell, stumbled."
פרסין	1. *parsîn/parsayin*	1. "Half-shekels" or, better, dual "two half shekels."
	2. *pěrisîn*	2. Passive participle, "divided, separated [ones]."
	3. *pārěsîn*	3. Active participle, "[they] divide," or, with an impersonal "they," equivalent to the passive "is divided."
	4. *parsîn*	4. Persians.

Michael Segal[27] solves the riddle by looking to the earlier context: "He counted the vessels [see v. 3], he stumbled [Belshazzar's idolatry/sacrilege concerning the vessels, v. 4], and (so) Persians (are coming)." Segal's interpretation of the riddle is initially plausible, and possible as yet-another level of meaning (see below). But against it is

---

[27] Ibid., 78.

the fact that Daniel's authoritative interpretation (vv. 26–28) makes no mention of vessels or stumbling. Al Wolters gives three other possible interpretations of the riddle in terms of money, assessment, and results:

(i) Money. "Is counted a mina, a shekel, and two half shekels [of silver]."

(ii) Assessment. "He has reckoned an account [Aramaic 'counted mina' as a merchant would do in calculating a bill]. He has assigned the bill [Aramaic 'he weighed']. And they assessed the value of payment [Aramaic 'they divided']."

(iii) Results. "It is weighed out twice. You are light [that is, 'short' and unable to pay the bill]. And (consequently), Persians." This takes the *waw* (ו) as a *waw* of consequence.[28]

With the first possibility, the weight adds up to the equivalent of 62 shekels of silver. The second possibility simply states in three ways that the bill has been assessed. The third of these possibilities builds on the fact that there are not yet silver coins, but silver grain or nuggets would be weighed on a scale or the balance (v. 27) against a standard weight to determine value. If one's silver weighs too little to pay the bill, it will show up as light on the scale, for which there would be negative consequences, in this case involving Persians.

5:26–28 Daniel's interpretation draws on various options listed above. Daniel vocalizes מנא "Mene" as Aramaic מְנָה, rendered by CSB as "numbered" (v. 26b). This could mean with most EVVs that God "has numbered [the days of] your kingdom," but the words in brackets are lacking in the Aramaic. Perhaps it is better taken to mean, "God has reckoned/evaluated your reign," which is why he will end it. "Brought it to an end" (v. 26c) could be rendered "brought it to completion" (H-stem of שלם). This is a perfect of future reference (popularly called a "prophetic perfect") referring to what would actually take place that evening (vv. 30–31) as if it had already happened.

Daniel initially vocalizes "Tekel" as a perfect passive of *tql* rendered "you have been weighed" (תְּקִילְתָּה; v. 27a). But then he

---

[28] Wolters, "The Riddle of the Scales in Daniel 5," 155–77.

apparently sees a double entendre since the interpretation "found wanting" (הִשְׁתְּכַחַתְּ חַסִּיר) suggests he also vocalizes it to mean "you are light" (from *qll*) in the sense of you cannot pay the bill owed. The agent of this passive verb is God who as judge finds Belshazzar coming up short morally (see §4.2).

Daniel simplifies the plural form "Parsin" (v. 25) to a singular "Peres" in the interpretation (v. 28) and again sees a double entendre. Thus it can be understood as a passive participle indicating the kingdom is "divided" or perhaps better (following Wolters) "assessed." The root פרס (Aramaic פורסן) is used in the Targum Onqelos of Lev 27:2, 8 in the sense of "assessment"[29] ("If one is too poor to pay the *assessment*"). The singular passive participle of פרס is equivalent to the plural active form in v. 25: "they assess/divide." Such plurals with an impersonal "they" are passive in sense. Because in that assessment they are found wanting, the double meaning is that Babylon will be punished by פְּרַס, a proper noun meaning "Persia," another vocalization. As a singular, it can be a collective for Persia's people, an equivalent of the plural form in v. 25. Note that Persians are interpreted as "Medes and Persians," that is, the combined "Medo-Persian" empire. This is contrary to the critical view of Daniel's four kingdoms in Daniel 2 and 7 that sees a separate Median kingdom arriving before Persia. Compare 8:20, which symbolizes Medes and Persians with one beast, a ram. It is true that the Medes once had an empire north of Babylon's, but the Medes were conquered by Cyrus so that, when Babylon fell, it fell to a Persian-Median combined empire (see Introduction).

In the light of Daniel's interpretation, *MN*ʾ, *MN*ʾ, *TQL*, *UPRYN* means: *MN*ʾ—It [your reign] is thoroughly (that is, twice) evaluated. *TQL*—(double meaning): It is both weighed [appraised] (one meaning) and falls short of the standard (second meaning). *UPRYN*—(double meaning): And they have assessed it (one meaning), but since it is lacking in that assessment there will be consequential punishment from the Persians (the other meaning). Yet a third meaning is hinted at in v. 31 (see comments below).

5:29-31 [HB 5:29-6:1] Belshazzar found Daniel's explanation convincing and carried out his promises (cf. v. 7), foisting on Daniel the gifts he earlier indicated he did not want. Belshazzar's dressing

---

[29] "פורסן," in Jastrow, *Dictionary of the Targumim*.

Daniel in fine clothing, putting a gold chain around his neck, and giving him a high rank unknowingly reenacts what Pharaoh did for Joseph when Joseph interpreted Pharaoh's revelation (Gen 41:42–43). One might have expected Belshazzar to be angry and want to kill the messenger since the message was unfavorable, though to his credit he did not.

Belshazzar's death (v. 30) was an act of divine judgment for the king's sins (see §4.2). He died in conjunction with Persia's entrance into Babylon (cf. v. 28). Belshazzar may have been assassinated since, according to cuneiform sources (Cyrus Cylinder, Babylonian Chronicle), Babylon fell without a battle. The Cyrus Cylinder states, "He [Marduk] made him [Cyrus] enter his city Babylon without fighting or battle; he saved Babylon from hardship."[30] The Babylonian Chronicle states, "On 14th Sippar was taken without battle. Nabonidus fled. On the 16th Ugbaru, governor of Gutium, and the army of Cyrus entered Babylon without battle."[31] Alternatively, Greek historian Xenophon says upon entering Babylon a group of soldiers led by Gadatas and Gobryas came to the palace against limited resistance and killed the king and those around him (*Cyropaedia* 7.5.29).

"Darius the Mede" (v. 31) took over in accord with the divine prophecy and God's sovereign right to remove and install kings (Dan 2:21; §3.8). Darius the Mede is probably another name for Cyrus the Persian (see comments at 6:28; see also Introduction). "At the age of sixty-two" is the approximate age of Cyrus at the time of Persia's invasion of Babylon. Cyrus came to the Persian throne around 559, conquered the Medes in 550/549, and then conquered Babylon in 539.[32] If he were forty-two when he first took Persia's throne, then he would be sixty-two at the conquest of Babylon twenty years later.

The number sixty-two seems to be another application of the riddle of the writing on the wall. Taken as money, "Is counted a mina, a shekel, and two half shekels" (v. 25), the total weight is sixty-two shekels (1 mina = sixty shekels). Thus the weight of the money symbolizes the age of the coming invader, giving the riddle a triple (if not quadruple) entendre at points.

---

[30] *COS* 2.315.
[31] *COS* 1.468.
[32] "Cyrus" in *NBD*.

Bridge

Like Nebuchadnezzar in Daniel 4, Belshazzar displays a sinful pride for which God as judge holds him accountable (see §4.2). Comparison between the two kings is made explicit (v. 20), but Belshazzar's offense is worse. Nebuchadnezzar had real accomplishments—building an empire—of which to be proud, while Belshazzar did not. In Belshazzar's case, arrogance led him to desecrate the holy utensils by using them in a drunken and idolatrous orgy (vv. 2–5), an act in which Belshazzar in effect "exalted [himself] against the Lord of the heavens" (v. 23). When holy things are profaned it brings God's judgment (cf. 1 Cor 3:17; 11:29; cf. §4.2). A hand wrote a supernatural revelation on a wall that portends God's judgment. Belshazzar's sacrilege is compounded by the king's looking to idolatrous diviners for wisdom to reveal supernatural mysteries that only God through his prophets can reveal (see §2) (vv. 7–8). Pride today also leads to ungodliness and looking to wisdom from inadequate human sources rather than God's revelation.

Though Nebuchadnezzar and Belshazzar are alike in their pride, there are also differences. Nebuchadnezzar at least treated sacred temple objects with respect rather than putting them to profane use, and at the end he humbled himself by acknowledging the superior kingship of God. Belshazzar on the other hand failed to learn from his predecessor's example (vv. 21–22). Thus Nebuchadnezzar was restored while Belshazzar's pride led to his death and replacement (vv. 30–31). This is an example of a prophecy/fulfillment motif, since God's revelation quickly comes true. God's "hand" writing the inscription portends the future, and God's "hand" reflects God's sovereign control of the fate of people like Belshazzar (v. 23; see §3.8). In Belshazzar's case the king is "weighed in the balance and found deficient" (v. 27). Moreover the inscription shows Daniel's God to be the God of history who foreknows (see §3.5) and can sovereignly determine what will happen (see §7.1, §7.2), numbering a kingdom's days, bringing kingdoms to an end, and handing a kingdom over to others (vv. 26–28).

More broadly, the author of Daniel wants his audience to remain faithful in the face of overwhelming opposition from the kingdoms of the world. He encourages them by examples. Just as God rescued Daniel and his friends (Daniel 3, 6) and humbled worldly kings

(Nebuchadnezzar and Belshazzar, Daniel 4–5), so Daniel's readers can look for God to rescue the faithful and suppress wicked kings, whether Belshazzar, Antiochus Epiphanes (Daniel 8, 11), or the antichrist (Daniel 7, 11).

I. Court Narratives (Daniel 1–6)

A. Daniel and friends in Nebuchadnezzar's court (Daniel 1)
B. Daniel interprets Nebuchadnezzar's dream of a statue (Daniel 2)
C. Shadrach, Meshach, and Abednego in the fiery furnace (Daniel 3)
D. Daniel interprets Nebuchadnezzar's dream of a tree (Daniel 4)
E. Daniel interprets the handwriting on the wall (Daniel 5)
F. **Daniel and the lion's den (Daniel 6)**

II. Visions of Daniel (Daniel 7–12)

(A) Beginning of story (1:1–21)
  (B) Dream about four world kingdoms ended by the kingdom of God (2:1–49)
    (C) Judeans faithful in the face of death (3:1–30)
      (D) Royal pride humbled (4:1–37)
      (D') Royal pride humbled (5:1–31)
    (C') A Judean faithful in the face of death (6:1–28)
  (B') Vision about four world kingdoms ended by the kingdom of God (7:1–28)
    (E) Vision of Persian and Greek kingdoms to Antiochus (8:1–27)
      (F) Vision of seventy weeks (9:1–27)
    (E') Vision of Persian and Greek kingdoms to Antiochus (10:1–11:35)
  (B″)World kingdoms ended and the righteous established (11:36–12:3)
(A') End of story: Vision sealed until the end (12:4–13)

¹ Darius decided to appoint 120 satraps over the kingdom, stationed throughout the realm, ² and over them three administrators, including Daniel. These satraps would be accountable to them so that the king would not be defrauded. ³ Daniel distinguished himself above the administrators and satraps because he had an extraordinary spirit, so the king planned to set him over the whole realm. ⁴ The administrators and satraps, therefore, kept trying to find a charge against Daniel regarding the kingdom. But they could find no charge or corruption, for he was trustworthy, and no

negligence or corruption was found in him. ⁵ Then these men said, "We will never find any charge against this Daniel unless we find something against him concerning the law of his God."

⁶ So the administrators and satraps went together to the king and said to him, "May King Darius live forever. ⁷ All the administrators of the kingdom, the prefects, satraps, advisers, and governors have agreed that the king should establish an ordinance and enforce an edict that for thirty days, anyone who petitions any god or man except you, the king, will be thrown into the lions' den. ⁸ Therefore, Your Majesty, establish the edict and sign the document so that, as a law of the Medes and Persians, it is irrevocable and cannot be changed." ⁹ So King Darius signed the written edict.

¹⁰ When Daniel learned that the document had been signed, he went into his house. The windows in its upstairs room opened toward Jerusalem, and three times a day he got down on his knees, prayed, and gave thanks to his God, just as he had done before. ¹¹ Then these men went as a group and found Daniel petitioning and imploring his God. ¹² So they approached the king and asked about his edict: "Didn't you sign an edict that for thirty days any person who petitions any god or man except you, the king, will be thrown into the lions' den?"

The king answered, "As a law of the Medes and Persians, the order stands and is irrevocable."

¹³ Then they replied to the king, "Daniel, one of the Judean exiles, has ignored you, the king, and the edict you signed, for he prays three times a day." ¹⁴ As soon as the king heard this, he was very displeased; he set his mind on rescuing Daniel and made every effort until sundown to deliver him.

¹⁵ Then these men went together to the king and said to him, "You know, Your Majesty, that it is a law of the Medes and Persians that no edict or ordinance the king establishes can be changed."

¹⁶ So the king gave the order, and they brought Daniel and threw him into the lions' den. The king said to Daniel, "May your God, whom you continually serve, rescue you!" ¹⁷ A stone was brought and placed over the mouth of the den. The king sealed it with his own signet ring and with the signet rings of his nobles, so that nothing in regard to Daniel could be changed. ¹⁸ Then the king went to his palace and spent the night fasting. No diversions were brought to him, and he could not sleep.

¹⁹ At the first light of dawn the king got up and hurried to the lions' den. ²⁰ When he reached the den, he cried out in anguish to Daniel. "Daniel, servant of the living God," the king said, "has

your God, whom you continually serve, been able to rescue you from the lions?"

²¹ Then Daniel spoke with the king: "May the king live forever. ²² My God sent his angel and shut the lions' mouths; and they haven't harmed me, for I was found innocent before him. And also before you, Your Majesty, I have not done harm."

²³ The king was overjoyed and gave orders to take Daniel out of the den. When Daniel was brought up from the den, he was found to be unharmed, for he trusted in his God. ²⁴ The king then gave the command, and those men who had maliciously accused Daniel were brought and thrown into the lions' den—they, their children, and their wives. They had not reached the bottom of the den before the lions overpowered them and crushed all their bones.

²⁵ Then King Darius wrote to those of every people, nation, and language who live on the whole earth: "May your prosperity abound. ²⁶ I issue a decree that in all my royal dominion, people must tremble in fear before the God of Daniel:

> For he is the living God,
> and he endures forever;
> his kingdom will never be destroyed,
> and his dominion has no end.
>
> ²⁷ He rescues and delivers;
> he performs signs and wonders
> in the heavens and on the earth,
> for he has rescued Daniel
> from the power of the lions."

²⁸ So Daniel prospered during the reign of Darius and the reign of Cyrus the Persian.

Context

In the broad structure of this book, Daniel 6 is the last of the court narratives. In the intertwined chiastic structure of the book it is in parallel with the narrative of Daniel 3, the story of the fiery furnace. Both stories involve unjust royal edicts that faithful Jews would find impossible to obey. In both stories there are conspiracies by government officials who are jealous of Jewish fellow government officials whom they accuse of ignoring the king and his decrees (3:12; 6:13). In this case, the restructuring of the government after the fall of Belshazzar to Cyrus in 539 BC created the conditions for court intrigues that led to Daniel in his old age (about eighty years old) being thrown into a lion's den. The conspirators in both stories use faithfulness to the Jewish religion against their rivals. There is a difference between the two stories: in Daniel 3 Daniel's friends are faulted for refusing to do what God prohibits (idolatry), while in Daniel 6 Daniel is faulted for doing what God expects (regular prayer, see §4.7). Daniel in chapter 6, like his friends in chapter 3, chooses faithful commitment to God over personal safety, being willing to accept martyrdom if necessary rather than compromise his Jewish faith (see §4.8). In both accounts God intervenes to save his faithful servants and thwart their enemies (see §4.5 and §4.2).

This passage has a chiastic structure that has deliverance at its heart (after Goldingay[1]):

A   Introduction: Daniel's success (6:1-3)
    B   Darius issues an edict against prayer to God, but Daniel takes his stand (6:4-10)
       C   Daniel's colleagues seek Daniel's death (6:11-15)
          D   Darius hopes for Daniel's deliverance (6:16-18)
          D'   Darius witnesses Daniel's deliverance (6:19-23)
       C'   Daniel's colleagues receive the death they sought for Daniel (6:24)
    B'   Darius issues an edict to worship God and takes his stand (6:25-27)
A'   Conclusion: Daniel's success (6:28)

6:1-5 [HB 6:2-6] On "satrap" see comments at 3:2. Later under emperor Darius I, Persia had but twenty satraps (Herodotus, *Histories* 3.89-94). The "120 satraps" (v. 1) might represent an earlier organization of the empire, but more likely this includes governors (compare Esther 1:1 and 8:9, "127 provinces").[2] "Administrators" (v. 2) is from Aramaic סְרַךְ, a loanword from Persian *sāraka*, "to stand at the ready,"[3] meaning a "high official." If the historical setting of this chapter follows the death of the first Persian governor of

---

[1] J. E. Goldingay, *Daniel*, WBC 30 (Dallas: Word, 1989), 124.

[2] J. D. Wineland, "Satrap, Satrapy," *NIDB*, 5:116.

[3] "סְרַךְ," *HALOT* 5:1940.

Babylon, Gubaru, this triumvirate may be a temporary measure of Darius (= Cyrus) until he could choose a permanent governor over Babylon.[4] That Daniel was one of three top administrators is reminiscent of Belshazzar's making Daniel third-highest ruler (5:29).

Evidently word reached Darius of Daniel's great competence and integrity, qualities that overcame any reluctance to appoint an octogenarian and a Jew. Daniel's integrity came from his living out the goodness and holiness that God expected of his people (see §4.1). He "distinguished himself" (v. 3a; literally, "was successful above" [the administrators]) due to his "extraordinary spirit" (v. 3b), probably a reference to his human spirit enhanced by the Holy Spirit (see comments at Dan 4:8; 5:12, 14; 9:23), an example of God's blessings on his faithful servant (see §4.4). The fact that the king considered appointing Daniel produces the same kind of jealousy in his fellow administrators as the fellow officials show against Shadrach, Meshach, and Abednego because Nebuchadnezzar had "appointed [them] to manage the province of Babylon" (Dan 3:12).

The "charge" (v. 4) made against Daniel translates Aramaic עִלָּה that denotes "a cause, a pretext" (thus Theodotion πρόφασις). It was irrelevant to these officials whether the "charge" were true so long as it successfully discredited Daniel. "The kingdom" refers to the realm of Daniel's duties as a governmental official. Daniel is an unusual character being an honest politician, an outcome of his religious devotion (see §4.1).

"Law" in the expression "law of God" (v. 5) is Aramaic (and Persian loanword) דָּת. Artaxerxes' letter to Ezra in Aramaic called Ezra an "expert in the דָּת of the God of the heavens" (Ezra 7:12, 21). Ezra is similarly called a scribe skilled in the תּוֹרָה ("law") of Moses and a student of the תּוֹרָה of Yahweh (Ezra 7:6, 10). Aramaic דָּת ("law") is the equivalent of Hebrew תּוֹרָה ("law, instruction"), though here it may take the broader sense attested in later Aramaic of "religion" (cf. CEB "his religious practice" and CEV, GNT "his religion"). It was Daniel's devotion to the "law of his God" as divine revelation (see §2) that made him a man of integrity, though it also made him vulnerable to attack by his enemies.

---

[4] A. E. Steinmann, *Daniel*, Concordia Commentary (St. Louis: Concordia, 2008), 313.

6:6–7 [HB 6:7–8] "Went together" (v. 6) is the Aramaic H-stem of רגשׁ that can be more precisely rendered, "came thronging" (NJPS; cf. NKJV) or "entered as a crowd." "Have agreed" could be rendered "advise after much deliberation" (itpaal of יעט [= Hebrew יעץ] "advise, counsel"). The itpaal form makes the root reflective and multiplies the action. That "all" agreed is misleading since Daniel did not agree to this advice. Thirty days is roughly the length of a lunar month—new moon sighting to new moon sighting—used by both Israel and ancient Babylon. Lunar months are either twenty-nine or thirty days (approximately 29.5 days on average).

Kings of Persia historically were not considered gods, so this proposed decree to pray to Darius, while it flatters his ego, is probably not meant to deify Darius. Instead the thrust of this law was probably to have Darius serve as the mediator or priest between the people and the Persian god Ahura-Mazda. This would encourage them to accept Persian piety by adding the Persian god to their pantheon.[5] But the real purpose behind getting Darius to forbid prayer to "any god or man" is to entrap Daniel.

"Lion's den" (v. 7c) could be rendered "lion's pit" (cf. CEV; LEB). Aramaic גֹּב, "den" (= Hebrew גֵּב), denotes a man-made, dug-out area such as trenches (2 Kings 3:16) or cisterns for catching water (Jer 14:3), or here a pit for holding lions. Reliefs from the time of Ashurbanipal (600s BC) now in the British Museum show lions being released from cages so the king could hunt them for pleasure from his chariot.

6:8–9 [HB 6:9–10] Rendering כְּעַן as "therefore" (v. 8) makes very good sense here and may be right, though the only fully established meaning of כְּעַן is "now" (so most EVVs). The Aramaic of "your Majesty" reads "O King." "Establish" and "sign" are better rendered as wishes: "may you establish … sign." The imperfects express urging but are not commands here. "Sign" translates Aramaic רשׁם that means to "mark, inscribe." Inscribing could mean "sign" in order to put the edict into effect, but perhaps more likely means to write the edict down ("put it in writing," NJPS) to make it irrevocable (see following discussion).

---

[5] J. H. Walton, "The Decree of Darius the Mede in Daniel 6," *JETS* 31/3 (1988): 279–86.

The Persian and Median laws that were irrevocable are not statutory laws, but decrees or verdicts. The unchanging nature of Medo-Persian edicts is also affirmed in Esther (1:19; 8:8). This custom goes along with Mesopotamian legal tradition that indicates a judge must not reverse a verdict once written down; if he does he should be removed from office (Laws of Hammurabi §5). The unchangeable nature of Persian decrees may be illustrated by Diodorus (*History* 17.30.1–7), who indicates that Darius III in anger issued an edict of death on a certain Charidemus, but, "Once the king's passion had cooled he promptly regretted his act and reproached himself for having made a serious mistake, but all his royal power was not able to undo what was done."[6] This doctrine of the irrevocable nature of decrees or verdicts may be based on an assumption that kings make such decisions by divine inspiration (cf. Prov 16:10; 21:1), which (in theory) cannot be wrong.[7]

"Signed the written edict" (v. 9) more likely means "put the ban in writing" (NJPS) as was discussed in v. 8. The Aramaic says Darius "inscribed the document and the edict." On "edict" see comment at v. 7. "The document and the edict" is a hendiadys for "the interdiction document."

6:10 [HB 6:11] Prayer is an important religious obligation (see §4.7). Daniel in v. 10 was confronted with a stark choice: obey the "law of his God" (v. 6) or the irrevocable and unchangeable law of the Medes and Persians (v. 9). In other words, obey God or man. If he chooses the former, it puts his life at risk, but if he chooses the latter, he betrays his God and his own spiritual integrity. The need to show faithfulness despite putting oneself at risk is an important theme in Daniel (see §4.8). Daniel chose God and made no attempt to hide his violation of the decree in an act of civil disobedience. The Aramaic uses pending case word order that could be brought out, "As for Daniel, when he learned." On "signed" or "put in writing" (NJPS) see comments at v. 8. "Upper room" renders Aramaic עֲלִי that

---

[6] Translation from Diodorus Siculus, *Diodorus of Sicily in Twelve Volumes with an English Translation*, trans. C. H. Oldfather (Cambridge, MA: Harvard University Press, 1989), 17.30.6, accessed online through http://www.perseus.tufts.edu. An alternative reading is that Darius could not undo the order because the execution had already been carried out.

[7] M. Lefebvre, *Collections, Codes, and Torah: The Re-characterization of Israel's Written Law*, LHBOTS 451 (London: Bloombury T&T Clark, 2008), 99–100.

could be rendered "roof chamber" (NASB),[8] that is, a room on or below the roof area. Some houses at this time had a second story over all or part of the house that provided additional family space, access to which was provided by stone or wooden stairs or ladders.[9]

Daniel's practice was to pray "toward Jerusalem" (v. 10b), the temple site, as Solomon recommended for those outside the land (1 Kgs 8:48–49). On the theological importance of the temple, see §3.6 and §7.4.3. This practice of praying toward Jerusalem continued subsequently in Jewish circles (1 Esdras 4:58). It corresponds with and provides precedence for the traditional Jewish practice of praying toward Jerusalem and having doors and windows of synagogues face Jerusalem so that Jews can pray toward it, a practice codified in the Halakha, *Shulhan Arukh* (Orah Hayyim, Hilkot Tefillah, 90:4), and the Code of Maimonides.[10]

The Jewish temple had been destroyed, but its site was still considered by Daniel to be the place of God's special Presence. Daniel prayed "three times a day." Rabbinic tradition subsequently made morning, afternoon, and evening prayers obligatory (Mishnah Berakoth 4:1; Talmud Berakoth 26b). "Kneeling" (G-stem participle of ברך) is a homonym with "he praised, blessed" (D-stem of ברך) and in this context hints at a double-entendre ("he blessed/kneeling on his knees"). "Prayed" (D-stem of צלה) perhaps implies a posture of "leaning" or "bending" (the meaning of צלה in Qal), but certainly denotes "beseeching" and "imploring." This is also true of the Akkadian cognate ṣallû, as in praying "for the life of the king and his sons" (Ezra 6:10), though here the prayer may also be for himself in his act of defiance of an unjust decree. "Gave thanks to" is the H-stem of ידה, used previously of giving thanks for answered prayer (Dan 2:23), but here means "praised" (NRSV) or "lauded" as an act of worship (see §4.6). By praying "just as he had done before" (v. 10d), Daniel was in conscious, direct violation of the king's interdict.

6:11–13 [HB 6:12–14] "Went as a group" (v. 11) more precisely means "came thronging in" (NJPS; cf. comments at v. 6 above). They "found Daniel petitioning and imploring" in direct violation of Darius' interdict (see v. 7). "Imploring" (HtD of חנן) has to do

---

[8] "עֲלִי," *HALOT* 5:1948; "עֲלִי," BDB 1106.1.

[9] J. F. Drinkard Jr., s.v. "Architecture, OT," *NIDB*, 1:255.

[10] S. Spero, "Turning To Jerusalem In Prayer," *JBQ* 31.1 (April/June 2003): 97–100.

with making "supplication" (KJV; NJPS) or "seeking mercy before" (NRSV). This triggers the trap set on Daniel and gives them a basis of accusing him (vv. 12–13). See comments at vv. 7–8 for details in v. 12. On the idiom behind "ignored you," see comments at 3:12. Thus this accusation is similar to the one made against Shadrach, Meshach, and Abednego. On "edict" see v. 7. On "signed" (better, "put into writing"), see comments at v. 8. On "prays three times a day," see v. 10.

6:14–15 [HB 6:15–16] Darius was trapped by his own decree. "Was very displeased" is an acceptable rendering of a stative verb באש whose general meaning is clear but whose exact nuance is hard to pin down. A possible, more precise nuance comes from Imperial Aramaic and biblical Hebrew where באש means "to stink" (see Exod 7:18 and 8:10 of rotting fish and frogs), suggesting the matter is "repugnant" or "odious" to him. Another possibility notes that באש is the opposite of being "overjoyed" in v. 23 (HB 6:24) and can mean "be sad" (Syriac),[11] which is similar to Theodotion's rendering ἐλυπήθη (aorist passive of λυπέω), which means Darius "became sad, sorrowful, distressed"[12] (compare Douay-Rheims "was very much grieved"). Darius sought to come up with a plan consistent with Persia's rigid rules concerning decrees (see comments at v. 8) to save Daniel. He obviously thought well of Daniel, whom he intended to appoint above the other officials (v. 3). The wicked motives of the officials who persuaded him to adopt the edict had become clear. He "labored" (ESV, KJV) or "made every effort" to deliver him, employing the HtD of שׁדר that can mean to "struggle" or "strive."[13] In other words, with intensity Darius racked his brain all day long to come up with a way of saving Daniel, though without success. Darius, whom the edict seemed to exalt to a semi-divine status, found himself powerless to save Daniel.

---

[11] "באשׁ," in Comprehensive Aramaic Lexicon, Targum Lexicon, ed. S. A. Kaufman (Cincinnati: Hebrew Union College Press, 2004; electronic edition Logos Research Systems), n.p. Also I. Jerusalmi, The Aramaic Sections of Ezra and Daniel: A Philological Commentary (Cincinnati: Hebrew Union College-Jewish Institute of Religion, 1982), 130, renders the verb "it grieved him."

[12] "Λυπέω," in W. Arndt, F. W. Danker, and W. Bauer, A Greek-English Lexicon of the New Testament and Other Early Christian Literature (Chicago: University of Chicago Press, 2000), 604. A. Pietersma and B. G. Wright, eds., A New Translation of the Septuagint (New York: Oxford, 2007), render it "grieved."

[13] "שְׁדַר," TWOT 1079.

The officials, perhaps having heard of the king's desire to save Daniel, "went to the king" (v. 15) to intervene and dissuade him. They reminded him of the law: "no edict or ordinance the king establishes can be changed" (see comments at v. 8). Were the king to violate Medo-Persian legal tradition, it would invite a coup.

6:16 [HB 6:17] The king feels trapped by his own edict and Medo-Persian legal tradition that prohibited edicts from being reversed. On "lion's den/pit," see comments at v. 7. "May your God, whom you serve continually, rescue you!" (v. 16b) is in contrast with Nebuchadnezzar. Nebuchadnezzar boasted that not even a god could "rescue" the Hebrew youths from the furnace (3:15). But Darius knew that only the Jewish God could "rescue" Daniel from the lions. The verb "rescue" in both verses is a shaphel imperfect of עזב (lexical entry שֵׁיזִב) that grammatically can be rendered as prediction of what God will do (KJV, NASB). But given that Darius is no prophet, the imperfect is best taken contextually as a modal wish—that is, an indirect prayer expressing the king's affection for Daniel and reflecting the theology that Daniel's God is a God of salvation (see §4.5). "Serve" (Aramaic פלח) here means to worship or venerate as a religious obligation (see §4.6), a meaning Hebrew עבד ("to serve") can also convey. Compare the Akkadian cognate palāḫu "fear, respect, venerate." "Continually" (literally, "with duration") may refer to Daniel's unwillingness to abstain from prayer for a month until Darius' edict expires and/or to his lifelong service to God.

6:17 [HB 6:18] "Signet ring" (עִזְקָה) (v. 17) is a ring with a seal engraved with a unique reverse design that could be stamped onto clay (or other material) to mark an item as sent from and approved by the official or belonging to that official. The pit's stone, mortared on its edges with clay or plaster with the seal impressions of the king and the other officials, would prove that the stone could not have been moved subsequent to the officials' sealing it. The stone was placed "over the mouth of the den" (v. 17). "Over" (Aramaic/Hebrew עַל) is consistent with an opening in the ceiling of the pit or cave. Verse 24 ("not reached the bottom of the den") further suggests victims would be cast in from above. Baldwin[14] suggests that there were two entrances: a ramp for bringing lions in or out and an opening above for feeding lions and throwing in victims.

---

[14] J. G. Baldwin, *Daniel*, TOTC (Leichester: InterVarsity, 1978), 130.

6:18 [HB 6:19] Jews fasting is often associated with prayer (Neh 1:4; Ps 35:13; Dan 9:3). Prayer could be implied here too, though alternatively perhaps Darius was simply too upset to eat. For more on the religious significance of fasting, see comments at 9:3 and §4.7. Fasts occurring with prayer could be partial (cf. Dan 10:2–3).

The term rendered "diversions" (Aramaic דַּחֲוָן) from which Darius abstained is obscure. Guesses (see *HALOT*[15]) include concubines [to sleep with] (Darby translation; compare Arabic *dahay*, an outstretched mat, in an obscene sense), food/delicacies (Theodotion ἐδέσματα; NRSV), musical instruments (Ibn Ezra; KJV), female dancers or jesters (Jastrow;[16] Amplified Bible, "dancing girls"), perfume (from Arabic *duhān*, "smell"), and dining board (portable table) (Rashi).[17] BDB and others suggest emending the text from דַּחֲוָה to לְחֵנָן, "concubines, consorts" (see comments at 5:2), though this assumes the corruption of two different consonants which is not likely. Though uncertain, in favor of the "food" interpretation (either food/delicacies or dining board/table that by metonymy means food) is the context of the previous phrase and Theodotion's translation.

6:19–20 [HB 6:20–21] On "the king got up," EVVs and Theodotion render the imperfect verbal form יְקוּם as simple past, though it might instead mean, "The king wished to arise at dawn at daybreak"—that is, he instructed his servants to wake him at that hour. "Hurried" or "went in haste" (בְּהִתְבְּהָלָה) is based on a root (בהל) that mixes the ideas of haste and fear. It echoes 3:24, futher underscoring similarities between this incident and the story of the fiery furnace.

"In anguish" (v. 20) reads in Aramaic, "in an anguished voice." The passive participle עֲצִיב can denote both grief and pain, and perhaps both are implied here, along with feelings of regret. EVVs differ as to which nuance they think is most emphasized: "in a tone of anguish" (ESV); "in an anxious voice" (NIV; cf. NRSV); "with a lamentable voice" (KJV); "in a mournful voice" (NJPS); "sorrowfully" (NABRE); "with a troubled voice" (NASB). Theodotion's rendering, "loud voice," seems to miss the mark. On "servant" in v. 20

---

[15] "דְּחֵוָה," *HALOT* 5:1849–1850.

[16] "דַּחֲוָא," in M. Jastrow, *A Dictionary of the Targumim, the Talmud Babli and Jerushalmi, and the Midrashic Literature* (1903; reprint, Brooklyn: P. Shalom, 1967), 291.

[17] Ibid., 291.

(עֲבֵד) meaning "worshiper," and "serve" (פלח) meaning "worship," see comments at 3:12 and 3:26.

Addressing Daniel as "servant of living God" echoes Nebuchadnezzar's words to Daniel's friends in 3:26, another point of parallel between Daniel 3 and Daniel 6. The expression "living God" is used thirteen times elsewhere in the OT. On Israelite lips, "living God" contrasts with dead idols (Jer 10:9–10; cf. Lev 26:30). It is doubtful that this is what Darius means. On the lips of a gentile king it probably means "undying, immortal," as Darius later stated, "For [Daniel's God] is the living God, and he endures forever" (6:26). Perhaps the king heard Daniel speak of God as "the living God" and was echoing Daniel's words. Regardless, the story does prove that God is alive. "Able to rescue you" reflects one purpose of this story, which is to teach God's power to save (see §4.5).

6:21–22 [HB 6:22–23] On "live forever" (v. 21), see comments at 2:4. "God sent his angel" (v. 22a) might refer to a theophany, the "angel of the Lord," as a visible manifestation of God's presence (see comments at 3:24–25 and §5, §6.5). Alternatively, it may simply be an angel. Later two angels, Gabriel (8:16; 9:21) and Michael (10:13, 21; 12:1), are mentioned by name. "God … shut the lions' mouths" (v. 22a) is alluded to in Heb 11:33, which speaks of those who "by faith … shut the mouths of lions." God as judge (see §4.2) found Daniel "innocent" (v. 22b). Aramaic זָכוּ ("innocence") is a loanword from Akkadian or Canaanite[18] that denotes purity before God. The implication is that God is more likely to intervene to help the innocent than the guilty (cf. Jas 5:16).

6:23–24 [HB 6:24–25] "Overjoyed" (v. 23a) means the king's feelings of v. 14 are now reversed. "Taken out" (v. 23b) probably implies either the use of a rope (the way Jeremiah was removed from a cistern, Jer 38:11–13) or a ladder from the ceiling entrance. "Uninjured" (v. 23c) parallels the similar result for Daniel's friends in the furnace (3:27). Just as God is inclined to rescue the innocent (v. 22), so also the narrator adds that God is inclined to rescue believers who trust in him (v. 23c; see §4.4, §4.5). By implication he is less inclined to save unbelievers.

On "maliciously accused" (v. 24), see comments at 3:8. "They, their children, and their wives" reflects an unjust practice of executing

---

[18] "זָכוּ," *HALOT* 5:1865.

children (and wives) for the offenses of their fathers (or husbands). Darius' execution of children for what their fathers did violates the Mosaic law (Deut 24:16), but such was the nature of crude Persian justice. For the men themselves, this punishment is an appropriate expression of God's judgment though human government (cf. Rom 13:1–7) and is poetic justice: they receive what they sought to inflict on Daniel (see §4.2). "Bottom" is Aramaic אַרְעִי that is cognate with אֲרַע (= Hebrew אֶרֶץ), "earth." Thus, the sense is "before they hit the ground" (cf. NIV "floor of the den"). This again suggests they are thrown in from a ceiling opening (cf. comment v. 17).

6:25–27 [HB 6:26–28] This proclamation of Darius to various peoples echoes the earlier proclamations of Nebuchadnezzar (3:28–4:3). Both Nebuchadnezzar and Darius addressed every people, nation, and language (4:1; 6:25). Nebuchadnezzar's decree provokes fear by threatening to destroy the family of anyone who speaks against the God of Shadrach, Meshach, and Abednego (3:29), while Darius destroyed the families of Daniel's enemies (6:24) and exhorts people to fear and tremble before the God of Daniel (6:26a). Both Nebuchadnezzar and Darius praise the eternality of God and his kingdom (4:3b; 6:26b), God's miracles (4:2–3a; 6:27b), and God's ability to save (3:28b, 29b; 6:27). In the end Nebuchadnezzar rewards the three young men (3:30), while Daniel prospers in the reign of Darius (6:28).

On the terms "people, nation, and language" (v. 25), see comments at 3:4. "All the earth" is hyperbole for "throughout the Persian Empire." "On "prosperity" (or "peace"), see comments at 4:1. "Tremble in fear" (v. 24) reflects a hendiadys that literally reads, "tremble and fear," meaning they should worship Daniel's God and out of respect obey him (see §4.6).

Verses 26b–27 break into poetry with the distinctive feature of Hebrew poetry: parallelism. On "living God" and "endures forever," see comments at 6:20. "His kingdom will never be destroyed" is a concept repeated in 2:44 and 7:14. "His dominion has no end" reads in Aramaic, "His dominion is unto the end"—that is, temporally to the end of time. "Rescues" (the š-stem of עזב) and "delivers" (H-stem of נצל) are synonyms piled up to emphasize God's propensity to save (see §4.5). For more on עזב, see comments at 3:15, 17. On "signs and wonders" (v. 27b), see comments at 4:2 and §2. God's miracles are "in the heavens and on the earth"—that is, throughout the world (cp. Acts 2:19, "I will display wonders in the heaven above and signs on the earth below"; Joel 2:30). Rescuing Daniel from the lions was a miracle on earth, but God also displayed wonders in the sky such as the Egyptian plagues of hail and darkness (Exod 9:22–26; 10:21–23) and at the second coming (Matt 24:30; cf. Dan 7:13). That God miraculously "rescued Daniel from the power of the lions" (v. 27c) fully convinced Darius of the true greatness of Daniel's God.

6:28 [HB 6:29] "Prospered" ("fared well," NJPS) is the H-stem of Hebrew/Aramaic צלח that can mean "prosper," "succeed," or "fare well." The same outcome occurs with Daniel's friends at the fiery furnace in 3:30 ("the king *rewarded* Shadrach, Meshach, and Abednego") where the H-stem of צלח also occurs. This is yet another parallel between Daniel 3 and 6. "The reign of Darius *and* the reign of Cyrus the Persian" probably employs an epexegetic *waw* and should be rendered "the reign of Darius, *even* the reign of Cyrus the Persian" (CSB note). Such a rendering identifies Darius the Mede with Cyrus the Persian emperor, a view proposed by D. J. Wiseman (see Introduction).

Bridge

Daniel 6 picks up on many of the same themes as Daniel 3, the story of the fiery furnace with which it is in parallel in the book's outline. In both stories jealous colleague-officials used the religiosity of Jews to maliciously accuse them in order to remove them as rivals (3:8; 6:24). These Jews, however, refused to compromise their religious faith and practice, even though it put their lives at risk. In both cases God sent his "angel" to save them (3:28; 6:22). As a result, gentile kings praise, promote, and honor the Jewish God (3:28–29; 6:25–27), worshiping him as all people should (see §4.6). In both stories these faithful Jews prosper (H-stem צלח) (3:30; 6:28).

Among the theological themes in Daniel 6 is the truth that God's people are to maintain a special consecration him and not hide their faith (see §4.1). They should remain faithful to God and his covenant even if this puts their lives at risk (see §4.8). Just as Daniel's rivals hate him for his godliness, we should not be surprised when the world hates us (John 15:19).[19] God allows his people to endure times of trial, though he is present with them and often works to save his people (see §4.5). On the presence of God's "angel" as a possible theophany, see §5, §6.5. God can miraculously save people from seemingly impossible situations (6:27), which shows God's greatness (see §3.7). It is also a means of revelation (see §2). It shows how God ultimately blesses those who remain faithful to him (see §4.4).

Daniel 1, 3, and 6 address the question of what we are to do when our loyalty to God and our loyalty to the state come into conflict. This has always been an issue for Christians in authoritarian states, though increasingly it is an issue in the West too. Sometimes resisting the state is done more or less privately (Daniel 1), while at other times believers may have to openly resist (Daniel 3, 6). In Daniel 3 the state commanded what God forbids. In Daniel 6 the state forbade what God expects (prayer). Prayer is an important part of piety (see §4.7), so Daniel prayed despite the king's decree. Daniel 6 put the matter in terms of whose law we are to follow: the law of God (v. 5) or the law of man (v. 8).

Believers are called to remain faithful to God and obey him rather than people (Acts 5:29), even if it puts us in danger. Faithfully following God may sometimes open us to suffering and persecution (see §4.8), but the reward is eternal life (Dan 12:2; Matt 10:29–30). Behind the question of whose law is to be followed is a higher question: Who is sovereign? The narrative mocks the pretentions of kings like Darius who think themselves absolute demigods. Even they can be manipulated by lower officials and by rules to which they must be subject. But God also works in the life of this king. In the end Darius acknowledged God as the true supreme sovereign (v. 26; see §3.8). God answered Darius' prayer (6:16b), and presumably also Daniel's unquoted prayer from the den (see §4.7). Daniel is presented as a model for believers to follow (see §4.1), showing exemplary competence (v. 3), integrity (vv. 4, 22), courage (v. 10a), and religious devotion (vv. 10b, 13). The writer of Hebrews alludes to Daniel who by faith "shut the mouths of lions" (Heb 11:33).

---

[19] D. R. Davis, *The Message of Daniel: His Kingdom Cannot Fail*, The Bible Speaks Today (Downers Grove: InterVarsity, 2013), 85.

I. Court Narratives (Daniel 1–6)

II. Visions of Daniel (Daniel 7–12)
First vision: Four beasts and son of man figure (Daniel 7)
Second vision: Ram and male goat (Daniel 8)
Third vision: Seventy weeks (Daniel 9)
Fourth vision: Kings of North/South, distress/resurrection (Daniel 10–12)

(A) Beginning of story (1:1–21)
  (B) Dream about four world kingdoms ended by the kingdom of God (2:1–49)
    (C) Judeans faithful in the face of death (3:1–30)
      (D) Royal pride humbled (4:1–37)
      (D′) Royal pride humbled (5:1–31)
    (C′) A Judean faithful in the face of death (6:1–28)
  (B′) Vision about four world kingdoms ended by the kingdom of God (7:1–28)
    (E) Vision of Persian and Greek kingdoms to Antiochus (8:1–27)
      (F) Vision of seventy weeks (9:1–27)
    (E′) Vision of Persian and Greek kingdoms to Antiochus (10:1–11:35)
  (B″) World kingdoms ended and the righteous established (11:36–12:3)
(A′) End of story: Vision sealed until the end (12:4–13)

[1] In the first year of King Belshazzar of Babylon, Daniel had a dream with visions in his mind as he was lying in his bed. He wrote down the dream, and here is the summary of his account. [2] Daniel said, "In my vision at night I was watching, and suddenly the four winds of heaven stirred up the great sea. [3] Four huge beasts came up from the sea, each different from the other.

[4] "The first was like a lion but had eagle's wings. I continued watching until its wings were torn off. It was lifted up from the ground, set on its feet like a man, and given a human mind.

[5] "Suddenly, another beast appeared, a second one, that looked like a bear. It was raised up on one side, with three ribs in its mouth between its teeth. It was told, 'Get up! Gorge yourself on flesh.'

⁶"After this, while I was watching, suddenly another beast appeared. It was like a leopard with four wings of a bird on its back. It had four heads, and it was given dominion.

⁷"After this, while I was watching in the night visions, suddenly a fourth beast appeared, frightening and dreadful, and incredibly strong, with large iron teeth. It devoured and crushed, and it trampled with its feet whatever was left. It was different from all the beasts before it, and it had ten horns.

⁸"While I was considering the horns, suddenly another horn, a little one, came up among them, and three of the first horns were uprooted before it. And suddenly in this horn there were eyes like the eyes of a human and a mouth that was speaking arrogantly.

⁹"As I kept watching,
thrones were set in place,
and the Ancient of Days took his seat.
His clothing was white like snow,
and the hair of his head like whitest wool.
His throne was flaming fire;
its wheels were blazing fire.
¹⁰ A river of fire was flowing,
coming out from his presence.
Thousands upon thousands served him;
ten thousand times ten thousand stood before him.
The court was convened,
and the books were opened.

¹¹"I watched, then, because of the sound of the arrogant words the horn was speaking. As I continued watching, the beast was killed and its body destroyed and given over to the burning fire. ¹² As for the rest of the beasts, their dominion was removed, but an extension of life was granted to them for a certain period of time. ¹³ I continued watching in the night visions,

and suddenly one like a son of man
was coming with the clouds of heaven.
He approached the Ancient of Days
and was escorted before him.
¹⁴ He was given dominion,
and glory, and a kingdom;
so that those of every people,
nation, and language

should serve him.
His dominion is an everlasting dominion
that will not pass away,
and his kingdom is one
that will not be destroyed.

[15] "As for me, Daniel, my spirit was deeply distressed within me, and the visions in my mind terrified me. [16] I approached one of those who were standing by and asked him to clarify all this. So he let me know the interpretation of these things: [17] 'These huge beasts, four in number, are four kings who will rise from the earth.

[18] But the holy ones of the Most High will receive the kingdom and possess it forever, yes, forever and ever.'

[19] "Then I wanted to be clear about the fourth beast, the one different from all the others, extremely terrifying, with iron teeth and bronze claws, devouring, crushing, and trampling with its feet whatever was left. [20] I also wanted to know about the ten horns on its head and about the other horn that came up, before which three fell—the horn that had eyes, and a mouth that spoke arrogantly, and that looked bigger than the others. [21] As I was watching, this horn waged war against the holy ones and was prevailing over them [22] until the Ancient of Days arrived and a judgment was given in favor of the holy ones of the Most High, for the time had come, and the holy ones took possession of the kingdom.

[23] "This is what he said: 'The fourth beast will be a fourth kingdom on the earth, different from all the other kingdoms. It will devour the whole earth, trample it down, and crush it. [24] The ten horns are ten kings who will rise from this kingdom. Another king, different from the previous ones, will rise after them and subdue three kings. [25] He will speak words against the Most High and oppress the holy ones of the Most High. He will intend to change religious festivals and laws, and the holy ones will be handed over to him for a time, times, and half a time. [26] But the court will convene, and his dominion will be taken away, to be completely destroyed forever. [27] The kingdom, dominion, and greatness of the kingdoms under all of heaven will be given to the people, the holy ones of the Most High. His kingdom will be an everlasting kingdom, and all rulers will serve and obey him.'

[28] "This is the end of the account. As for me, Daniel, my thoughts terrified me greatly, and my face turned pale, but I kept the matter to myself."

Context

Daniel 7–12 constitutes the visions of Daniel. Although the language of Daniel 7 continues to be in Aramaic, and there are affinities between this chapter and Daniel 2 (see outline above), the content transitions from the biography or history of Daniel to his autobiography and prophecies in which he describes his own visions. This part of Daniel is more apocalyptic in genre.

Daniel 7   Vision of the four beasts and the son of man figure

Daniel 8   Vision of ram and male goat

Daniel 9   Daniel's prayer and the seventy weeks

Daniel 10–12   Vision of kings of North/South, distress/resurrection

While the visions of Daniel 7–12 are in chronological sequence with each other, they are not in chronological sequence with Daniel 1–6. The visions of Daniel 7 and 8 came to Daniel during the Babylonian period, when Belshazzar was still in power, while Daniel 6 dates to the reign of Darius after the fall of Belshazzar.

This is summarized in the chart below:

Chapter	Content	Date
Daniel 7	Vision of the four beasts and the son of man figure	First year of Belshazzar (c. 552 BC, when Nabonidus left for Teima)
Daniel 8	Vision of ram and male goat	Belshazzar's third year (c. 549)
Daniel 9	Daniel's prayer and the seventy weeks	First year of Darius (538)
Daniel 10–12	Vision of kings of North/South, distress/resurrection	Third year of Cyrus (536)

While there is considerable discontinuity between Daniel 1–6 and Daniel 7, Daniel 7 elaborates on Nebuchadnezzar's vision of the statue in Daniel 2, which predicts the coming of four kingdoms beginning with Babylon followed by the coming of the kingdom of God. N. T. Wright adds several interesting areas of continuity between Daniel 6 and Daniel 7.[1] In Daniel 6 Daniel is threatened by beasts (lions); in Daniel 7 one of the threatening beasts is like a lion. In Daniel 6 King Darius is a royal judge; in Daniel 7 the Ancient of Days is a royal judge. In both stories the human figure (Daniel in chapter 6; the son of man in chapter 7) is vindicated and lifted up, and the enemies of God's people are destroyed.

Daniel 7 itself divides into two parts: the symbolic vision of vv. 1–14 followed by the interpretation of vv. 15–28. The vision proper has two venues: one on earth where beasts come out of the sea (vv. 1–8, 11–12) and another in heaven where God sits in judgment and the son of man appears (vv. 9–10, 13–14).

    I. The Vision (7:1–14)
        Earth: The four beasts (vv. 2–7) and the little horn (v. 8)
           Heaven: Ancient of Days, court convened (vv. 9–10)
        Earth: Fourth beast, little horn burned (v. 11), other
        beasts' life extended (v. 12)
           Heaven: Son of man figure appears in clouds (v. 13),
           receives kingdom (v. 14)

    II. The Interpretation (7:15–28)
        Daniel's reaction (v. 15)
           Interpreting angel approached (v. 16)
               Summary interpretation: Four kingdoms followed
               by kingdom of holy ones (vv. 17–18)
               Inquiry about fourth beast and the little horn
               (vv. 19–22)
           Interpretation of fourth beast and the little horn
           (vv. 23–27)
         Daniel's reaction (v. 28)

The interpretation of this passage hinges on several cruxes: the identity of the four kingdoms represented by the beasts, the identity of the little horn on the fourth beast, the identity of the son of man figure, and the identity of the holy ones. The commentary that

---

[1] N. T. Wright, *The New Testament and the People of God*, Christian Origins and the Question of God, vol. 1 (London: Society for Promoting Christian Knowledge, 1992), 295.

follows will argue that (1) the four beasts represent Babylon, Medo-Persia, Greece, and Rome-and-beyond, (2) the little horn represents the end-time antichrist who will persecute believers, (3) the son of man figure is the Messiah, whose coming in the clouds is a vivid vision of his second coming, and (4) the holy ones are God's people for whom the Messiah will bring to an end the kingdoms of the world to establish the kingdom of God. Daniel 7 is the most important chapter in the book theologically.

7:1 The "first year of Belshazzar" occurs over fifty years after Daniel first went into exile in 605/604 BC. When Belshazzar's father Nabonidus departed for Teima (or Tema) in Arabia, roughly 552 BC, he left his son in charge of the kingdom, at which time Belshazzar's "reign" began. His "first year" probably began at the New Year (Tishri) following Nabonidus' departure, the time previous to that counting as year 0. See discussion in Introduction.

The *Verse Account of Nabonidus* 2.20 states,

> He [Nabonidus] entrusted the "Camp" to his oldest (son), the first-born,
> The troops everywhere in the country he ordered under his (command).
> He let (everything) go, entrusted the kingship to him
> And, himself, he started out for a long journey.[2]

According to a Harran Inscription of Nabonidus, Nabonidus remained in Teima for ten years, roughly 552–542 BC: "For ten years I was moving around among these (cities) [Teima, Dadanu, Padakku, Hibra, Jadihu even as far as Jatribu] and did not enter my own city Babylon."[3] During this time the Marduk priests complained repeatedly in the so-called Nabonidus Chronicle that they were not able to conduct the Akitu festival since the king was not present to participate in the ceremony:

> Nabonidus, the king, (stayed) in Tema; the crown prince, the officials and the army (were) in Akkad. The king did not come to Babylon for the (ceremony of the) month of

---

[2] J. B. Pritchard, ed., *The Ancient Near Eastern Texts Relating to the Old Testament*, 3rd ed. with supplement (Princeton: Princeton University Press, 1969), 313.

[3] Ibid., 562.

Nisanu; the god Nebo did not come to Babylon, the god Bel did not go out (of Esagila in procession), the festival of the New Year was omitted.[4]

Nabonidus' ten-year absence allowed Belshazzar to function as *de facto* king (see Introduction).

"Visions" is used as a synonym for this "dream," both being means of divine revelation (see §2). The Aramaic terms "vision" (חֱזוּ) and "saw" (חזה) are from the same root that in Hebrew often refers to prophetic visions (Obad 1:1; Nah 1:1; Hab 2:2–3). As a participle it is rendered "seer" (that is, one who sees), a term for a prophet (2 Sam 24:11; Amos 7:12). These terms identify Daniel as a prophet.

"Summary of his account" should read "beginning" (cf. CSB note) rather than "summary." The Aramaic reads, "head of words [Aramaic מִלִּין] he said." This can be paraphrased, "[This marks the] beginning of [the] words [that] he said [in that account]." Theodotion lacks this phrase, which along with its awkwardness in Aramaic raises doubts about its authenticity, but it should be seen as complementing v. 28 that speaks of the "end of the account."

7:2–3 Verses 1 and 2a are still in third-person narration about Daniel. Verse 2b switches to first-person narration, which continues through the end of the book. The narrator appears to cite from Daniel's autobiographical account of his visions. "At night I was watching" rightly catches the dynamic sense of the participle חָזֵה with the perfect of הוה ("I was"). On "vision" and "saw," see comments at v. 1. "And suddenly" (or "and behold"; also vv. 5, 6, 7, 8, 13, 31) employs Aramaic אֲרוּ ("behold!" "lo!") that like Hebrew הִנֵּה can denote vivid immediacy, describing the dream as if it were still happening.

The "four winds of heaven" appears to mean winds from all four compass directions (cf. Jer 49:36; Dan 8:8; 11:4; Zech 2:6; Rev 7:1). The "great sea" often refers to the Mediterranean Sea (Num 34:6 ESV; Josh 1:4 ESV, CSB), though even if that is the meaning here, it is symbolic. It might refer to the wicked throng of humanity whom Isaiah likens to a churning sea (Isa 57:20). "Stirred up" (H-stem גוח) probably refers to "churning" (NIV) the sea (marked by the lamed direct object marker), though others have taken it as intransitive of

---

[4] Ibid., 306.

winds "breaking forth upon [ל] the great sea" or similar (KJV, Darby, LXX [Old Greek]). H-stem forms are more likely transitive than intransitive.

The "four huge beasts" (v. 3) represent four kings who arise "from the earth" (v. 17), also called kingdoms (v. 23). That the empires are symbolized by ravenous beasts coming out of a churning sea is clearly derogatory, warning God's people that they are dangerous. The imagery (vv. 4–7) of lion, a bear, a leopard, and an unidentified vicious beast may be derived from Hos 13:7–8, where God warns that he would attack Israel like a lion, a leopard, a bear robbed of her cubs, and a wild beast.[5] In Hos 13:7–8 the kingdoms are used as implements of God's judgment of his people, which may be the implication here too.

7:4–6 This section shows God's workings throughout history (see §7.3). The first three beasts are treated more briefly than the fourth beast and are less directly opposed to God than the fourth. The key to interpreting the four beasts is the statue of four materials in Daniel 2. On the assumption that the first beast (v. 4) symbolizes the same king/kingdom as the first part of the statue (the head of gold), then the lion/eagle-like beast must represent the Babylonian Empire of Nebuchadnezzar (Dan 2:37–38). Lions play a prominent role in Neo-Babylonian iconography. Lions along Babylon's Processional Way are often taken as a symbol of the goddess Ishtar, but since the lions are male they may instead be a symbol of the king[6] and speak of his predatory fierceness.

Its "eagle's wings" (v. 4) are consistent with the view that the lion represents Nebuchadnezzar. Jeremiah also compares Babylon to both a lion (Jer 49:19) and an eagle (Jer 49:22). Eagles symbolize swift conquest (Deut 28:49; 2 Sam 1:23; Jer 4:13; Lam 4:19; Hab 1:8). Aramaic נְשַׁר (= Hebrew נֶשֶׁר) rendered "eagle" probably includes several species of birds. It sometimes refers to the griffon vulture with its bald head (Mic 1:16 NIV),[7] though some species of eagle fits the swift, predatory imagery here better than a scavenger vulture.

---

[5] E. C. Lucas, *Daniel*, Apollos Old Testament Commentary (Downers Grove: InterVarsity, 2002), 178.

[6] J. Marzahn and B. Sass, *Aramaic and Figural Stamp Impressions on Bricks of the Sixth Century B.C. from Babylon* (Weisbaden, Germany: Harrassowitz, 2010), 178–82.

[7] G. Eidevall, "Eagle," in *NIDB*, 2:171.

Nebuchadnezzar's eagle-like conquests include his routing of the Egyptian army at Carchemish (605 BC) just before he was declared king. This led immediately to Babylon's seizing the region of Hamath, Riblah, and the conquest of Syro-Palestine,[8] an event that resulted in Daniel and his companions going into exile (1:1–6). Nebuchadnezzar also besieged Tyre for thirteen years, the exact dates being uncertain, though it may have begun as early as 603. By Nebuchadnezzar's fortieth year, Tyre had a Babylonian governor.[9] Nebuchadnezzar besieged Jerusalem two more times, once in 598/7 BC, at which time Judah's King Jehoiachin was taken into Babylonian exile (2 Kgs 24:16),[10] and again in 588 BC (2 Kgs 25:1), leading to the destruction of Jerusalem and the end of its monarchy in August of either 586 or 587 BC.[11] Nebuchadnezzar also controlled Que (Cilicia) by 585 BC.[12] Jeremiah 43:8–13 predicted that Nebuchadnezzar would strike Egypt, and there is a fragmentary cuneiform text (BM 33041) that perhaps indicates he did around 568 BC.[13] Nebuchadnezzar thus carved out a kingdom that "stretched from Egypt in the south-west through Syro-Palestine to Cilicia, Pirindu, and Lydia in the north-west" and extended southeast to Elam.[14]

"I continued watching" (v. 4b; also vv. 11, 13) catches the dynamic sense of the perfect verb "I was" (הֲוֵית) combined with the participle "watching" (חָזֵה). What follows shows God's judgment on Nebuchadnezzar, God's sovereign working in Babylonian history (see §3.8, §4.2, §7.2), and his grace in view of the king's repentance (see §3.6). The wings being plucked off symbolizes Nebuchadnezzar's humiliation and falling into madness ("given the mind of an animal," 4:16). At this time his hair grew like eagle's feathers and his nails grew like bird's claws (4:33, see comments there). Being set on its

---

[8] D. J. Wiseman, *Nebuchadrezzar and Babylon* (Oxford: Oxford University Press, 1985), 12–17.

[9] Ibid., 27–28.

[10] Ibid., 32–33.

[11] Ibid., 36–37.

[12] Ibid., 28.

[13] Ibid., 39–40. The fragmentary nature of the text means conclusions must be tentative. Wiseman believes BM 33041 does refer to Babylon's invasion of Egypt, but he cites A. Malamat ("Josiah's Bid for Armageddon," *JANES* 5 [1973]: 278), who argues that BM 33041 speaks of foreign mercenaries and has nothing to do with an invasion of Egypt in 568 BC.

[14] Wiseman, *Nebuchadrezzar and Babylon*, 41.

feet and given a human mind (KJV "heart") refers to the restoration of Nebuchadnezzar's sanity by God after the period of madness and his subsequent praising of Daniel's God (Dan 4:34–37). These things "humanized" him and perhaps even religiously converted him, so that he was no longer a beast. Since the prophecy dates to after Nebuchadnezzar's death (Dan 7:1), this part of the vision portrays history rather than predicts the future.

Verse 5 moves on to a bear-like creature. The "bear" (דֹּב) refers to the Syrian brown bear.[15] Most critical scholars argue that Daniel's second beast symbolizes the Medes as distinct from the Persians (see Introduction), but historically the Medes did not conquer Babylon or in any sense succeed Babylon. The book of Daniel elsewhere treats Medo-Persia as a single entity. Instead the bear symbolizes the strength and fierceness of Medo-Persia that under Cyrus conquered Babylon in 539 BC and took over its kingdom. "Raised up on one side" (v. 5b), while possibly merely a threatening posture,[16] is probably like the two-horned ram in which one horn was longer than the other (see 8:3). In both cases the united Media and Persia empire (8:20) is portrayed in a way showing Persia as the more prominent partner over Media.

"Gorge yourself on flesh" indicates the predatory nature of this beast. The "three ribs" could represent no more than the various victims of Persia's insatiable appetite for conquest, though some interpreters look for three specific conquests. Church father Hippolytus took this as a reference to Cyrus conquering the Persians, the Medes, and the Babylonians.[17] Theodoret understood it as Persia (east), Egypt by Cambyses (south), and the Scythians (north).[18] Archer argues the three specific conquests in mind are Lydia, Babylon, and Egypt.[19] (1) Cyrus' conquest of Lydia and its wealthy king Croesus in Asia Minor (546 BC) was an event that "sent a shockwave throughout

---

[15] O. Borowski, "Bear," *NIDB*, 1:411.

[16] C. A. Newsom, *Daniel*, OTL (Louisville: Westminster Knox, 2014), 224.

[17] Hippolytus of Rome, "Treatise on Christ and Antichrist," in *Fathers of the Third Century: Hippolytus, Cyprian, Novatian, Appendix*, ed. A. Roberts, J. Donaldson, and A. C. Coxe, trans. S. D. F. Salmond, The Ante-Nicene Fathers 5 (Buffalo, NY: Christian Literature Company, 1886), 5209.

[18] Theodoret of Cyrus, *Commentary on Daniel*, trans., introduction, and notes by R. C. Hill (Atlanta: Society of Biblical Literature, 2006), 179.

[19] G. L. Archer, "Daniel," in *The Expositor's Bible Commentary*, ed. Frank E. Gaebelein (Grand Rapids: Zondervan, 1985), 7:86.

the Near East nearly as great as that which had attended the fall of Nineveh in 614."[20] (2) Cyrus' conquest of Babylon (539 BC) is a key event for the Jewish people. (3) Cambyses' conquest of Egypt (525–522 BC) was the last of Persia's major conquests.[21]

"It was told" employs an impersonal participial formulation, "they say to it" (cf. NASB), conveying a passive sense in which the "they" is no one in particular (as in English, "They say it is going to rain tomorrow"). If the "they" were specific, it presumably would be angels speaking on behalf of God, showing this beast is subject to God's control (see §3.8). "Gorge yourself on flesh" paraphrases the Aramaic that says, "eat much flesh." Flesh (בְּשַׂר = Hebrew בְּשָׂר) can refer either to animals (Dan 4:12) or to mankind ("mortals" [Dan 2:11 CSB]; "humanity" [Isa 40:5 CSB]), so eating "flesh" may symbolize Medo-Persia's swallowing up various peoples. Persia is given divine permission at least for its conquest of Babylon (Isa 13:17–19; 43:1–3; Jer 51:11, 28). Unlike the fourth beast, this second beast is, to some degree, under the control of God.

The third beast is like a "leopard" (v. 6; נְמַר = Hebrew נָמֵר) or perhaps more broadly a "panther."[22] The leopard is known for its spots (Jer 13:23), hill country/mountainous habitat (Song 4:8), predatory stalking and ripping of its prey (Hos 13:7; Jer 5:6), and quickness (Hab 1:8). The third beast stands for the Greek kingdom of Alexander the Great, labeled by Theodoret "the Macedonians."[23] Alexander conquered the Medo-Persian Empire from 334 to 331 BC. "Four wings" stands for Alexander's extremely rapid speed of conquest. Between 335 and 323 BC, Alexander conquered Greece, Asia Minor, Egypt, and Persia, and invaded India.

As early as church father Jerome the "four heads" has been taken to refer to the breakup of Alexander's kingdom among his generals, their sons, and/or other colleagues of Alexander (the *diadochoi/ diadochi* or "successors"). There is more than one interpretation of exactly how to apply this approach. Jerome took the four divisions to be among Ptolemy, Selecus, Philip Arridaeusan (the illegitimate brother of Alexander who was proclaimed king upon Alexander's

---

[20] P. Briant, *From Cyrus to Alexander: A History of the Persian Empire*, trans. P. T. Daniels (Winona Lake, IN: Eisenbrauns, 2002), 36.

[21] Ibid., 50–52.

[22] "נָמֵר," *HALOT* 5:1931.

[23] Theodoret, *Daniel*, 181.

death but never exercised genuine power), and Antigonus, who preceded Selucus in ruling the eastern part of Alexander's empire.[24] More convincing is to see the four as the eventual division of Alexander's kingdom into roughly four parts after a complicated period of civil war: (1) Ptolemy I Soter took over Egypt upon Alexander's death (323 BC). (2) Seleucus I Nicator took control over the eastern part of Alexander's empire, including Babylon and extending into Persia to the east and Asia Minor to the west (312 BC). (3) Cassander (son of General Antipater) eventually gained undisputed control over Greece and Macedonia (301 BC). (4) After the battle of Ipsus, Lysimachus came to rule Thrace, Lydia, Ionia, Phrygia, and the north coast of Asia Minor (301 BC).[25] Others take "four heads" less specifically as a symbol of totality or universal activity,[26] or as looking in all four directions to attack.[27] The passive "given dominion" (שְׁלִטָן) implies God allows this beast's sovereignty for a time (see §3.8).

7:7–8 The most prominent and dreadful "beast" is the fourth one. On "night visions" and "suddenly," see comments at v. 2. Since Rome succeeded Greece as the power over Palestine, Rome is the preliminary identification of this fourth beast. That is the view of church fathers Hippolytus and Jerome.[28] Some critical scholars have attempted to make the fourth kingdom the successors of Alexander (the *diadochoi*), but their kingdoms are merely fragmented continuations of Alexander's Greek kingdom and cannot count as a new kingdom on par with those of Babylon, Medo-Persia, or Alexander.

Nevertheless, the identification with Rome is also problematic since the destruction of this fourth beast seems to be in the eschatological future (see comments at v. 13). Yet the Roman Empire in any meaningful sense has long since ceased to exist. It will not do to say that Roman culture lives in Western Culture or continued in the Austrian Hapsburg's Holy Roman Empire (which was neither holy

---

[24] St. Jerome, *Jerome's Commentary on Daniel*, trans. G. L. Archer (Grand Rapids: Baker, 1958), 75.

[25] F. W. Walbank, A. E. Astin, M. W. Frederiksen, R. M. Ogilvie, eds., *The Hellenistic World*, vol. VII in *The Cambridge Ancient History* (London: Cambridge University, 1984), 60, 119, 211, 426.

[26] J. E. Goldingay, *Daniel*, WBC 30 (Dallas: Word, 1989), 163.

[27] J. G. Baldwin, *Daniel*, TOTC (Downers Grove: IVP Academic, 1978), 141.

[28] Hippolytus of Rome, "Treatise on Christ and Antichrist," 5209; Jerome, *Daniel*, 75.

nor Roman!). John in Revelation does use Roman imagery in conjunction with the kingdom of the Daniel-like "beast" (e.g., "seven hills," Rev 17:9), but this may mostly reflect his cultural setting and audience. To speak of a future "revived Roman Empire" seems special pleading. But perhaps this problem can be resolved by understanding the beast to be something more than Rome. It may be a future, eschatological kingdom that resembles Rome—enough so that the book of Revelation can use Roman imagery for it. Rome is at most a prototype of what this terrifying kingdom will be like. For this reason, I choose to call this kingdom "Rome-and-beyond."

"Frightening and dreadful" are two synonyms for fear used together to reinforce the degree to which this fourth beast terrorizes. "Incredibly strong" is more specific than the original which means "exceedingly strong" (ESV). "Teeth" (שִׁנַּיִן) is a dual form, probably meaning two rows of teeth. Large, iron teeth emphasizes that this beast is both powerful and extremely vicious. This mention of iron connects the fourth beast of Daniel 7 with the fourth kingdom in Nebuchadnezzar's dream represented by iron legs with feet of iron mixed with clay (2:33, 40–43). There iron symbolizes strength and destructive power ("strong as iron … like iron that smashes, it will crush and smash all the others," Dan 2:40). Iron-teeth imagery suggests fierce, predatory behavior, as seen, for example, in Rome's conquests, gladiator fights, and practice of crucifixion. Ancient Rome was, to be sure, a dominant power that ripped, pulverized, and smashed the world. "Trampled" is Aramaic רפס. Its cognate in Hebrew occurs in a case of trampling a person to death (2 Kgs 7:17).

While each beast is unique (v. 3), the fourth beast is "different" in that it is not likened to a known beast (lion, bear, leopard). It is beyond earthly analogy, incomparably fiercer than the previous beasts, and less subject to God's control than they are. That it is so "different" is one reason not to identify the fourth beast as historical Rome. Rome was not significantly different from previous empires to justify putting it in a category of its own. Rather, it is best to see it as Rome-and-beyond, culminating in the last human kingdom in the eschatological future and its leader the "little horn" antichrist (see §7.4, §7.4.1).[29]

---

[29] Similarly, D. R. Davis, *The Message of Daniel: His Kingdom Cannot Fail*, The Bible Speaks Today (Downers Grove: InterVarsity, 2013), 95–96.

The "ten horns" is sometimes compared with the toes of the fourth kingdom (2:41–42), though note the textual issue there and its lack of reference to the number of the toes. These horns are later called kings (7:24a). Horns on animals are often used aggressively against perceived enemies. Horns metaphorically represent power and conquest (Deut 33:17; Zech 1:19). Broken-off horns represent weakness and defeat (Jer 48:25; Dan 8:7).

The "little horn" is identified as another king who will subdue three of the ten previous kings (7:24b). It is called "little" perhaps to denigrate this king. On the identity of this little horn, see below. Its "eyes" and "mouth" hint that it symbolizes a human being. Both eyes and mouth are means of expressing hubris. "Speaking arrogantly" reads in the Aramaic, "spoke great things" (ESV). A ruler speaking arrogantly against God with proud, lifted eyes continues a motif found in Isa 10:12 and 37:23 concerning Sennacherib of Assyria.[30] Revelation 13:5 echoes this language concerning "the beast" ("A mouth was given to him to speak boasts and blasphemies").

7:9–14 At vv. 9–10 and vv. 13–14, the scene changes from earth to heaven. This change shows God's transcendence and superiority (see §3.4, §3.7). These verses also transition to poetry to emphasize the description of God in a worshipful tone (see §4.6), in contrast with the description of the four beasts, and to emphasize the importance of the one like a son of man.

7:9 That "thrones were set in place" implies a judgment scene. Cf. Dan 7:22. The "Ancient of Days" is God whose title and "hair ... like whitest wool" (v. 9b) stress his eternality and wisdom associated with advanced age (Job 15:10; see §3.3, §3.5). His throne symbolizes his kingship and role as chief judge (see §3.8, §4.2). White clothing (v. 9b) symbolizes God's splendor (cf. Lam 4:7; Matt 17:2) and pure righteousness (cf. Ps 51:7; see §3.6, §3.7). "Whitest wool" can be rendered "pure" or "clean" wool (נְקֵא). It is unclear if "clean wool" is only meant to convey color or also its coarser or clumpier consistency than human hair.

The identity of the enthroned judges in v. 9 is not the multitude of v. 10 who are not seated. It may refer to specially appointed angels in the divine assembly among whom God judges (Ps 82:1), or it may

---

[30] G. B. Lester, *Daniel Evokes Isaiah: Allusive Characterization of Foreign Rule in the Hebrew-Aramaic Book of Daniel* (London: Bloombury T&T Clark, 2015), 85–89.

be a plural of majesty for God's one throne. Probably there are two thrones, one for the Ancient of Days and one for the son of man.[31] The son of man figure would naturally be enthroned as king after he receives God's eternal kingdom (7:14).[32] This was the view of Rabbi Aqiba in the Talmud, who identified the one like a son of man as the Messiah, "one [throne] for Him [the Ancient of Days], and one for David" (b. Hagigah 14a; see §6.1).

God's "throne" of "flaming fire" is spectacularly glorious. A throne of wood covered with gold is glorious. But a throne of fire shows God's glory to be greater than that of earthly kings. The fire provokes fear and awe ("I fell facedown," Ezek 1:28; cf. 1 Enoch 14:14). The "wheels" are "blazing fire" or more simply "burning fire" (ESV). Compare Ezekiel's vision of a divine throne with wheels (Ezek 1:15–21, 26) that Sirach 49:8 rightly identifies as a chariot. Daniel may be alluding to Ezekiel's imagery of a chariot-throne with fiery wheels that allow it to move rapidly as required. First Enoch 14:8–23 combines the chariot-throne imagery of Daniel and Ezekiel.

7:10 "A river of fire was flowing, coming out from His presence" employs two participles (flowing, coming out) expressing vivid immediacy of the vision and could be rendered as present tenses. The fire-river adds to the awesomeness of this scene and conveys a feeling of fear appropriate before the divine judge. The judgment of the fourth beast involves burning with fire (v. 11), so fire may be a symbol of judgment. "Thousands upon thousands served him; ten thousand times ten thousand stood before him" employs verbs in the imperfect emphasizing continuous action and could be rendered as a vivid present tense: "thousands ... are serving him ... ten thousand ... are standing before him." "Ten thousand" (Aramaic רִבּוֹ) may imply an indefinitely large number ("myriad upon myriads," NASB). Presumably these are angels (so Rev 5:11), though it might possibly include the souls of the righteous dead (cf. Rev 7:9).

"The court was convened" paraphrases the Aramaic that reads, "the court was seated" (NIV), meaning it was in session. The verbs return to perfects, conveying simple narrative past. Jerusalmi

---

[31] M. Zehnder, "Why the Danielic 'Son of Man' is a Divine Being," *BBR* 24.3 (2014): 343.

[32] A. E. Steinmann, *Daniel*, Concordia Commentary (St. Louis: Concordia, 2008), 351.

suggests an alternative rendering, "He sat in judgment,"[33] in reference to God. While Aramaic דִּין can mean "judgment," Theodotion and the Old Greek render it with κριτήριον "lawcourt, tribunal." Virtually all English versions take דִּין to refer here to a judicial assembly or court. "Books" uses Aramaic סְפַר (= Hebrew סֵפֶר) that does not mean "book" in the modern sense. It can denote a scroll wound on a stick, but it can refer to written documents in whatever format including collections of laws and legal certificates (Exod 24:7; Deut 24:1). Here the reference is to legal writings of some sort, whether a ledger of accusations or the documentation of evidence. "Books" are used by the court to condemn the fourth beast and its little horn. In Dan 12:1 a similar book allows God's people (whose names are included in it) to escape the terrible distress.

7:11–12 Back on earth, the little horn speaks "arrogant words" (v. 11a), or more literally, "great words" (ESV), as anticipated in v. 8. This beast with the little horn will be "killed" and completely "destroyed" (v. 11b; cf. 7:26) with "burning fire" as judgment, unlike the other three for whom "an extension of life" is given (v. 12). Here God is portrayed as infinitely powerful (see §3.7), effortlessly bringing order out of chaos just as he effortlessly creates in Genesis 1, acting judicially (see §4.2) rather than militarily.[34] Revelation picks up on this imagery, describing how "the beast" will be cast into the lake of fire (Rev 19:20). How can an extension of life be given to already defunct kingdoms in contrast to the fourth kingdom God destroys and burns? Perhaps the other kingdoms—Babylon, Persia, and Greece—continued to exist in some form culturally and politically after their heyday of power, but this fourth kingdom will cease to exist once God removes its authority to rule. This apparently rules out Imperial Rome as identical to the fourth kingdom since it continued on long after its heyday, though in a sense Rome also lives on in this fourth, Rome-and-beyond kingdom. Revelation 13:1–2 portrays aspects of the first three beasts as living on in the fourth. "For a certain period of time" (v. 12) employs an idiom in Aramaic using two synonyms for time: "until a time [זְמַן] and a time [עִדָּן]."

---

[33] I. Jerusalmi, *The Aramaic Sections of Ezra and Daniel: A Philological Commentary* (Cincinnati: Hebrew Union College-Jewish Institute of Religion, 1982), 141.

[34] Lester, *Daniel Evokes Isaiah*, 46–47.

7:13–14 Verses 13–14, like verses 9–10, are poetic and return the scene to heaven. Here the poetry underscores the importance of the son of man figure. On "I continued watching" (v. 13a), see v. 4. "Son of man" (v. 13b) at minimum implies a human being as opposed to the four beasts. The identity of this figure is a major crux in the interpretation of the prophecy. See the excursus below where we argue in favor of the view that this is the divine Messiah. This "one like a son of man" approaches the throne "escorted" (v. 13c). The Aramaic literally reads, "they brought him near" (KJV), though the sense is passive: "he was brought near" (perhaps accompanied by an angelic entourage; see §5).

This son of man is given "dominion" (v. 14a; Aramaic שָׁלְטָן), a term that typically refers to governmental power (4:22; 7:6). Having been escorted before the divine tribunal, the son of man emerges as the true king, supplanting the earthly kings (beasts) who strove for dominion.[35] It is the son of man, not the earthly beasts, to whom dominion rightly belongs. "Glory" in the same verse (or "honor," NLT) is Aramaic יְקָר that is from a Hebrew/Aramaic root meaning to "be of worth, precious, esteemed."[36] It is used of rewards granted by authorities (2:6) and of the glory/dignity/honor associated with kingship (4:27; 5:18). Both apply here as the son of man is rewarded with kingship by the Ancient of Days.

"A kingdom" can be rendered "rulership." This again underscores that the one like a son of man is a king. That "those of every people, nation, and language should serve him" (v. 14b) describes a worldwide, multiethnic dominion. On "people, nation and language," see comments at 3:4. "Serve" (פלח) in the Bible is primarily used of worshiping gods (3:12, 14, 17–18, 28; 6:16, 21), an important point for identifying the "one like a son of man" as divine (see excursus). On the other hand, פלח is also used of "serving" people and nations (Words of Ahiqar line 17; –[37] Targum O. Lev 25:39; Targum O. Gen 15:14). The dominion of the one like a son of man is not only worldwide but "everlasting" (v. 14c). This shows that he is more than a mortal man; he is a supernatural being. This contrasts with

---

[35] L. Wade, " 'Son of Man' Comes to the Judgment in Daniel 7:13," *Journal of the Adventist Theological Society* 11 (2000): 277–81.

[36] "יקר," *HALOT* 2:431–432, 5:1893.

[37] A. Cowley, ed., *Aramaic Papyri of the Fifth Century B.C.* (Oxford: Clarendon, 1923), 212.

the temporary dominions of the four kingdoms and especially the fourth beast, which comes to an abrupt and complete end (v. 11).

Excursus: Who Is the "One Like a Son of Man" in Dan 7:13–14?

There are three common interpretations of the "one like a son of man" in 7:13–14 to whom the Ancient of Days presents the kingdom.
1. *The "one like a son of man" is an angel.* Some rabbinic and modern commentators (e.g., J. J. Collins[38]) argue that this "one like a son of man" is an angel, perhaps Michael or Gabriel, and that the "saints" or "holy ones" mentioned later (7:18, 21–22) are also angels.

In favor of the "holy ones" being angels is 4:17, in which angels/watchers are called "holy ones." This "son of man" figure appears in the court of God, as do angels (Job 1:6; 2:1; 1 Kgs 22:18–23; Isa 6:1–3; Rev 4:4–11). In Dan 10:13, 21; 12:1, the angel Michael is called "your [= Israel's] prince" and "the protector of your people." So this "one like a son of man" could be Michael, the leader of the angelic "holy ones" who is the angelic protector, defender, and representative of Israel. While "son of man" means "member of the human race," this figure is not said to be a human being but only "like" a human being. An angel is "like" a human (cf. 8:15; 10:16, 18). Verse 27 could be rendered, "the people of the holy ones" (NRSV), rather than "the people, the holy ones" (CSB). Thus the people (Israel) may be distinguished from the "holy ones" (angelic protectors led by Michael).

There are strong arguments against this view. The "one like a son of man" is said to be "served," a term often used of worship (see comments v. 14). But the Hebrew Bible does not condone the worship of angels and the New Testament explicitly condemns it (Col 2:18; Rev 22:8–9). Even if "serve" does not imply worship, the idea of humans serving an angel seems odd. Michael watches over Israel (Dan 12:1), but Israel does not serve him. Also, as far as is known elsewhere, Michael's jurisdiction is over Israel, not the nations. Gabriel serves Daniel by explaining visions and giving God's message to him (8:16; 9:21–22), but Daniel does not serve him. Nowhere else in the Hebrew Bible do angels appear in the clouds as does the son of man figure (see below).[39] The idea of an angel having a world-

---

[38] J. J. Collins, *Daniel*, Hermeneia (Minneapolis: Fortress, 1993), 304–10.
[39] Zehnder, "Why the Danielic 'Son of Man' is a Divine Being," 337–39.

wide, everlasting dominion (v. 14) is without support elsewhere in Scripture. The "holy ones" are defeated by the little horn (vv. 21, 25), but how can God's angels be defeated by a human king? This makes more sense if the "holy ones" are God's people, who at times are overcome. In v. 27 the Masoretes marked the word for "people" with a disjunctive accent, separating it from "the holy ones of the Most High" along the lines of the CSB punctuation. Even if it is rendered "the people of the holy ones," this does not require "holy ones" to be angels (see comments at v. 27). Furthermore, if the "one like a son of man" is either Michael or Gabriel, why is he not named or referred to later in the explanation?

2. *The "one like a son of man" is Israel.* Another view contends that the "one like a son of man" is a symbol for Israel, to be identified with "the holy ones of the Most High" (v. 18).

The main argument in support of this view is that the "holy ones of the Most High" receive the eternal kingdom (vv. 18, 27) just as the "one like a son of man" receives it (vv. 13–14). This suggests that the son of man figure is a symbol of Israel, the way "Uncle Sam" is a symbol of the United States. The "son of man" is distinct from the nations that come to pay him (Israel) homage.

Against this view, however, is that the holy ones are defeated (vv. 21, 25), but the son of man figure is exclusively triumphant. The son of man appears after the beasts in contrast to them and on the same level as the Ancient of Days, who is clearly an individual (i.e., God) and not symbolic. Accordingly, this son of man may be an individual rather than a symbol.[40] The holy ones, like the beasts, are on earth, but the son of man is in the clouds of heaven (v. 13). This suggests the son of man and the saints are not the same. Moreover, the one like a son of man is served, which typically (but not always) means worshiped (see comments at v. 14), something inappropriate to do for a nation.

3. *The "one like a son of man" is the divine Messiah.* The final view, which might be called the traditional Christian view, takes the figure to be a messianic king who also exhibits characteristics of divinity. Some Jewish interpreters (b. Sanhedrin 98a; b. Hagigah 14a) understood vv. 13–14 to refer to the Messiah, so a messianic view is

---

[40] M. B. Shepherd, "Daniel 7:13 and the New Testament Son of Man," *WTJ* 68.1 (2006): 101.

not exclusively a Christian one, though regarding this personage as divine is unique to Christian interpretation.

In favor of this position is the fact that the figure is described in royal terms and has authority to rule. He is "given dominion, and glory, and a kingdom" in what resembles a coronation ceremony (vv. 13–14). The relationship between this son of man and the "holy ones" is then the relationship between a king and his subjects. Kings serve and represent their people; thus it is natural to speak of the kingdom as belonging to both the king (vv. 13–14) and to his people (vv. 18, 27). The four beasts are clearly kingdoms, and yet in v. 17 they are called "kings." Kings and their kingdoms are both represented in these images, so the language is fluid. The son of man then emerges from his presentation before the Ancient of Days as the king who permanently supplants all the previous beast-kings.

The New Testament applies this language to Jesus as an individual using the imagery of Dan 7:13–14: "Behold, he is coming with the clouds" (Rev 1:7); " 'They will see the Son of Man coming on the clouds of heaven' with power and great glory" (Matt 24:30 [cf. Mark 13:26, Luke 21:27]); "You will see the Son of Man seated on the right hand of power and coming on the clouds of heaven" (Matt 26:64 [cf. Mark 14:62]). This suggests that they identified Jesus with the "son of man" in Daniel 7.

Zehnder cogently argues for the divine nature of the son of man figure.[41] Although it may be that the son of man comes to earth to destroy the little horn, this is not stated. Instead his abode is portrayed exclusively in the heavenly sphere, suggesting that he is a divine being. This figure is given "god–like" characteristics. He is worshiped/served by "every people, nation, and language" (v. 14) just as the Most High is to be worshiped/served by "all rulers" (v. 27) using a verb (פלח) frequently used of worshiping pagan gods (3:12, 14, 17–18, 28; 6:16, 21) and used a few verses later of worshiping the true God (v. 27). Thus the son of man, while distinguishable from the Most High, is identified with him.[42] Moreover, this son of man has an everlasting dominion (v. 14), something consistent with his being an eternal, divine being and echoing God's eternal kingship

---

[41] Zehnder, "Why the Danielic 'Son of Man' is a Divine Being," 331–47.

[42] J. M. Hamilton, *With the Clouds of Heaven: The Book of Daniel in Biblical Theology*, New Studies in Biblical Theology (Downers Grove: InterVarsity, 2014), 152–53.

(Ps 145:13; Dan 6:26). His worldwide dominion picks up on language used elsewhere of God's universal kingship (Ps 103:19). The figure is "like" a son of man, just as God in theophanies appears "like a man" (Ezek 1:26–28). The word "like" contrasts the cloud-borne human figure with the beasts that are "like" animals. It does not deny that he may in fact be human as are the beastly figures, though perhaps there is a hint in this language that he is more than human (that is, a divine man).

His elevated role before the Ancient of Days sets him apart from angelic heavenly beings. Indeed this "son" appears before the white-haired father-like figure on the throne, suggesting a father-son relationship. The son of man appears on the clouds, but elsewhere in the Hebrew Bible it is God who appears on the clouds (Isa 19:1; Nah 1:3; Pss 18:10; 97:2; 104:3). Angels never do. Similarly, in the ancient Near East, it is gods who appear in the clouds: the storm god Adad of Mesopotamia (Atrahasis ii:49; Gilgamesh xi:97)[43] and Ugaritic Baal "rider of the clouds" with Anath "spray of the rider of clouds" (Anath iii AB A; II AB iii 10; B 36; D; iv AB iii 33; Aqht C i 43).[44] The background of cloud imagery in OT times suggests that portraying the son of man on the clouds is to portray him as divine.

Viewing the figure as both messianic and divine is supported by comparing this scene with Psalm 110 and Isaiah 9 on which Daniel may well be drawing. In Psalm 110 David's messianic "Lord" (cf. Matt 22:41–45) sits enthroned at the right hand of Yahweh's (heavenly) throne in a father-son type imagery (cp. Ps 2:7 and Ps 45:6 which associate the Davidic king's throne with Yahweh's throne[45]). In a similar way, the "son" in Daniel appears, and is probably "enthroned" (see comments at Dan 7:9), with the Ancient of Days father figure in heaven. In Psalm 110 the enemies of David's "Lord" are subdued, and he is given a worldwide kingdom. So also the little horn is subdued and the son of man receives a worldwide kingdom in Daniel 7. Note also that Isa 9:6–7 describes the Messiah as "Mighty God, Eternal Father" and as having an eternal reign. Perhaps Daniel's vision intentionally draws on imagery from Psalm 110 and Isaiah 9 to identify its

---

[43] COS 1:451, 459; Pritchard, *Ancient Near Eastern Texts,* 94.

[44] Pritchard, *Ancient Near Eastern Texts,* 130, 132, 136, 137, 138, 142.

[45] Hamilton, *With the Clouds of Heaven,* 149.

son of man with the Davidic Messiah and to suggest that he is more than a mere man.

Against this view, the text of Daniel does not explicitly identify the figure as a human king or as a divine (non-angelic) being. The subordinate status of the son of man, who is passively presented to and receives his dominion from the Ancient of Days, could argue against his divinity. Nevertheless, in the NT Jesus is portrayed as sent by, submitting to, and being exalted by the Father; yet he is called God (John 1:1). Those who reject the divine-Messiah view think it represents a reading of the Christian view of the Messiah back into Daniel. But the evidence presented above shows that the divine-Messiah view is in fact plausible in the OT context, compatible with a close exegesis of the text, and presents fewer weaknesses and more strengths than the alternative views. This view is adopted in this commentary.

7:15–18 In vv. 15–28, an angel explains the visions of the four beasts and the heavenly courtroom scene to Daniel. "Deeply distressed" (v. 15a) is Aramaic כרה, only used here in the Hebrew Bible. Therefore, one must look to early translations and cognates to determine its meaning. Theodotion says Daniel "shuddered" (φρίσσω), and the Old Greek says he was "exhausted" or "anguished" (ἀκηδιάω).[46] In Syriac and Targumic Aramaic, כרה means to "be sick."[47] Its cognate in Akkadian (karû) means to be "short," used (among other things) of shortness of breath, sometimes of someone near death.[48] Since רוּחַ ("spirit") can also mean "breath," the Akkadian meaning might work here. In other words, Daniel showed shortness of breath like a person near death.

On "terrified" (v. 15b), Aramaic בהל is used when Nebuchadnezzar's tree dream "alarmed" both him and Daniel (4:5, 19), and it occurs when Belshazzar was terrified by the handwriting on the

---

[46] "Φρίσσω," in BDAG, 1065; "φρίττω [= φρίσσω]" and "ἀκηδιάω," in J. Lust, E. Eynikel, and K. Hauspie, *A Greek–English Lexicon of the Septuagint*, rev. ed. (Stuttgart: Deutsche Bibelgesellschaft, 2003; electronic edition, Logos Research Systems), n.p.

[47] "כרה," in *Comprehensive Aramaic Lexicon, Targum Lexicon*, ed. S. A. Kaufman (Cincinnati: Hebrew Union College Press, 2004; electronic edition, Logos Research Systems), n.p.; "כְּרָה," in M. Jastrow, *A Dictionary of the Targumim, the Talmud Babli and Jerushalmi, and the Midrashic Literature* (reprint, Brooklyn: P. Shalom, 1967), 664.

[48] "Karû," in *CAD* 8:229–230.

wall (Dan 5:6, 9–10). "Within me" is apparently "in the middle of its sheath" (cf. CSB note; assumes revocalization of נִדְנֶה to נִדְנַהּ with a feminine suffix at the end). The Hebrew cognate for Aramaic נִדְנֶה means "sheath" (for a sword) at 1 Chr 21:27, but here it is probably metaphoric for Daniel's body. In sum, though the precise meaning of these words is uncertain, the general meaning is clear. Daniel's vision leaves him feeling shaken, exhausted, sick, and/or gasping for breath.

Verse 16 introduces an interpretative angel. On angels in Daniel see §5. Interpretative angels often appear in late prophetic and apocalyptic writings (Ezek 40:1–3; Dan 8:16; 9:21–22; 10:10–14; 12:7–9; Zech 1:9; 2:1–3; 4:1–7; 5:2, 5; 6:4; Rev 1:1; 7:13–14; 10:1–10; 17:1, 7; 18:1–3; 19:9; 22:8–11; 1 Enoch 17–36; 72–82; 4 Ezra; 2 Baruch; Hermes; Apocalypse of Peter; Apocalypse of Paul). Mediating revelation indirectly through angels emphasizes God's transcendence (see §3.4). Later in Daniel, Gabriel serves as the interpretative angel (Dan 8:16; 9:21–22). The unnamed angel here may be Gabriel too. "Asked him to clarify all this" reads literally "and asked him the truth concerning all this" (ESV, NRSV). Aramaic יַצִּיבָא ("the truth") could also be rendered, "what is certain, reliable."

These "beasts" are identified as "four kings" (v. 17), but later the fourth is called a kingdom (v. 23). The Old Greek and Theodotion, followed by some modern translations (CEV, GW, NLT), render "kingdoms" rather than "kings," reflecting a change of one Hebrew letter (מלכון versus מלכין). But in Nebuchadnezzar's dream of four materials in Daniel 2 (which Daniel 7 resembles), the materials can be labeled either a king (2:37) or kingdoms (2:39–40). The interchangeable labeling in both chapters probably reflects the fluid nature of apocalyptic imagery.

"Most High" (v. 18; also vv. 22, 25b, 27; see comments at 3:26) renders עֶלְיוֹנִין. This term is different from but cognate with the other term used for "Most High": עִלָּי (3:26; 4:2; 5:18; 7:25a). The former utilizes a plural of majesty or respect, being plural in form but denoting the one true God, as does the term אֱלֹהִים ("God") in Hebrew. On a distinction between the two forms, see comments at 7:25 below. On "possess" see v. 22 below.

"Holy ones" or "saints" (ESV, KJV) is Aramaic קַדִּישִׁין (= Hebrew קְדוֹשִׁים). The word קַדִּישׁ refers to persons or things set apart to God or for divine service. In biblical Aramaic it can refer to angels (4:13, 23), though its cognate in Hebrew can refer to all Israel (Lev 20:7) or "saints" in the sense of pious ones (Pss 16:3; 34:9), as well as holy priests (Lev 21:6). The interpretation of "holy ones" hinges on one's interpretation of the "one like a son of man" in v. 13 (see excursus above for more details). Those who see the son of man figure as an angel will interpret the holy ones as angels too, though how the little horn can make war against angels is not convincingly explained (v. 21). Others see the "holy ones" as referring to faithful Israel. In the vision, the one like a son of man received the kingdom while here it is the holy ones who receive it. Thus this verse may be meant to identify the son of man figure as a symbol of Israel, though differences between the son of man and the holy ones—his heavenly venue versus their earthly one, his being utterly victorious versus their temporary oppression—argues against that identification. Yet another view, proposed by Segal, takes "holy ones" (קַדִּישֵׁי) to be a plural of majesty for the divine son of man. He takes קַדִּישֵׁי עֶלְיוֹנִין to mean "the Most High Holy One,"[49] a view that explains why in v. 14 the kingdom is given to the son of man while in v. 27 it goes to קַדִּישֵׁי עֶלְיוֹנִין ("the people of the Most High Holy One"). While Segal's view has merit, it runs into trouble in vv. 21 and 25 (see comments).

The view adopted here (and defended in the excursus) is that the son of man figure is the divine Messiah and that the holy ones are his people who are set apart for him (see §4.1) and for whom he acts. So the relationship between him and the holy ones is like the relationship of kings and kingdoms among the beasts (see comments at v. 17). If "holy ones" here means Israel, it does not preclude a parallel struggle in the heavenly realm involving angels and demonic forces that corresponds to events on earth, as will be seen in 8:10 and 10:1–21. Ultimately, "all of God's 'holy ones' (saints and angels) will share his kingdom (Matt 25:31–46)."[50]

7:19–22 For the description of the "fourth beast" (v. 19) see v. 7 and comments there. Verse 19 adds that it has terrorizing bronze claws. On the "ten horns," etc. (v. 20), see comments at v. 9. That three horns are "uprooted" in v. 9 is here explained as "fell," a term whose cognate in Hebrew can mean to be defeated or killed in battle (1 Sam 4:10). "Looked bigger" (v. 20c) reads in Aramaic "its appearance was

---

[49] M. Segal, *Dreams, Riddles, and Visions: Textual, Contextual, and Intertextual Approaches to the Book of Daniel*, BZAW 455 (Berlin: de Gruyter, 2016), 139–43.

[50] R.W. Pierce, *Daniel*, Teach the Text (Grand Rapids: Baker, 2015), 129.

greater than its companions" (cp. NKJV). This has been variously interpreted as "more stout" (ASV), "larger" (NASB), "more conspicuous" (NJPS), "more important" (CEB), "more imposing" (NIV), or "more formidable" (NET). "Others" is more specifically "its companions," in which "its" and "companions" are feminine forms because "horn" (Aramaic קֶרֶן) is a feminine noun.

In verse 21 "war" (קְרָב) may be a Neo-Assyrian Akkadian loan-word from *qarābu*.[51] "Waged war" is literally "made war." Compare the similar idiom in Hebrew (עָשׂוּ מִלְחָמָה אֶת, Gen 14:2). Revelation 13:7 echoes Dan 7:21, saying "the beast" is permitted to "wage war" (ποιῆσαι πόλεμον) against the saints. This echo speaks against Segal's view mentioned above that "holy ones" means "the Holy One" in reference to the son of man. That said, if Segal's view were adopted, the only way the little horn could wage warn against the son of man would be to wage war against his holy people. The verb יכל ("be able") in the sense of "prevail" occurs also in its Hebrew cognate when Jacob wrestled with the angel of Yahweh and "prevailed" over him (Gen 32:28; Hos 12:5). Though this could be used to support the view that the "holy ones" are angels, it is difficult to see how a king can wage war with a group of angels. "Holy ones" in this verse fits best with the interpretation that they are the "saints" (KJV, ESV), the "holy people" (NIV) of God.

Verse 22 expands on vv. 13–14. On "Most High" see comments at vv. 18 and 25. In the interpretation the son of man figure disappears from view, and the holy ones appear—a fact used by some interpreters to identify the son of man as a symbol of the holy people of God (see excursus above). But as was noted in v. 9, the divine Messiah son of man figure is likely seated on one of the thrones beside (at the right hand of) the Ancient of Days and thus included in the rendering of a "judgment" in favor of his people, the holy ones. "For the time had come" presumes that God predetermines set times for future events, in this case the establishment of the kingdom of God.

"The holy ones took possession of the kingdom" repeats v. 18. The root חסן here in the H-stem verb and rendered "take possession" means in the Qal "to be strong." An alternative interpretation of this

---

[51] "קְרָב," *HALOT* 5:1973.

H-stem is that the saints "exercised royal authority over, ruled"[52] the kingdom (cf. Rev 5:10). Although these are future events, the verbs speak of these events as if they were past ("took possession"). Verbs in Hebrew/Aramaic, strictly speaking, lack tenses. Even though perfects usually refer to past actions, they can also refer to present or future actions, depending on the verb and its context. Prophetic books often employ the perfect of future reference (popularly called the "prophetic perfect") in predictions of the future. This may be to express the certainty of future events, speaking of them as if they have already occurred. Or it may be used here in Daniel specifically because Daniel's vision of the future is now in the past.

7:23–26 Translators disagree over whether vv. 23–27 are prose (CSB, NASB, NIV) or poetry (ESV, NRSV, NABRE). A good case can be made for either interpretation. If poetry, this underscores what is otherwise clear: that the emphasis of the prophecy is on the fourth beast and its little horn to be supplanted by the kingdom of God.

On the identity of this dreadful, eschatological "fourth kingdom" and other details of v. 23, see comments at v. 7. "Trample" here (דּושׁ) is a synonym for "trampled" in verse 7 (רפס). Aramaic דּושׁ can be used of trampling a person to death (Targum Jonathan 2 Kgs 7:17).

Just as the fourth kingdom is more terrible than the earlier ones, so the last of its kings will be "different" (v. 24)—that is, more formidable and fiercer. Previously, the verbs "uprooted" (v. 8) and "fell" (v. 20) were used for the defeating of three of the ten horns. Now it is interpreted as "subdue" (CSB) or "put down" (ESV; literally "bring low," NJPS). This verb (H-stem of שׁפל, "be low") is earlier rendered, "humble" (4:37; 5:19, 22; cf. NET "humiliate three kings"). Here the kings are humiliated in defeat. How can he subdue three other kings of the same kingdom? Perhaps they reign simultaneously with the little horn becoming preeminent. How literally is one to take the "ten" here? Is it a precise number or a reference to a multitude of kings? If the latter, it is symbolic for completeness.[53] It is hard to decide these questions.

---

[52] "חֲסַן (ḥăsăn)," in J. Swanson, *Dictionary of Biblical Languages with Semantic Domains: Aramaic and Hebrew (Old Testament)*, electronic ed. (Oak Harbor: Logos Research Systems, 1997), #10277.

[53] S. R. Miller, *Daniel*, NAC 18 (Nashville: Broadman & Holman, 1994), 203.

The little horn speaks ill of God, "the Most High," and persecutes God's people, "the holy ones of the Most High" (v. 25). Two
terms for "Most High" occur in v. 25. The first is an Aramaic form
in the singular meaning "the Most High" (עִלָּיָא). The second is a
cognate form in the plural used as a plural of majesty (עֶלְיוֹנִין) that
is an Aramaicized form of the Hebrew for "Most High." This plural form occurs in the expression "the holy ones of the Most High,"
קַדִּישֵׁי עֶלְיוֹנִין, in v. 25 (also vv. 18, 22, 27). A good case can be made
that two different terms for Most High are used here because they
refer to different persons. As Hamilton notes, the singular form עִלָּיָא
may refer to the Ancient of Days while the second, plural term refers
to the son of man figure (vv. 13–14) as a divine being.[54] Segal agrees
with this but takes the expression קַדִּישֵׁי עֶלְיוֹנִין to mean not "the holy
ones of the Most High" but "the Most High Holy One"[55] in reference
to the son of man, taking קַדִּישֵׁי also as a plural of majesty. Segal's
view leaves unexplained how the little horn can oppress (v. 25) and
make war against (v. 21) a divine being, though perhaps he does so
through oppressing his people (see v. 27).

"Oppress" (D-stem of בלה) could also be rendered "wear out"
(ESV, NRSV; cf. NASB "wear down"; Theodotion, παλαιώσει, "wear
out, make old"; Old Greek, κατατρίψει, "wear out, rub down/away").
Its Hebrew cognate is used of wearing out clothes (Deut 8:4; 29:5).
This metaphor is variously interpreted as "harass" (NJPS), "persecute" (NKJV), or "torment" (NJB). This expands on the statement in
v. 21 that the little horn waged war against them.

"He will intend to change" could be rendered "He will think
of changing" (NJPS), or "hope to change" (סבר, "hope, intend,
think"[56]). The Aramaic of "religious festivals and laws" (v. 25b) reads,
"times [זִמְנִין] and law/decree [דָּת]," which could be a hendiadys for
legally established dates for religious (cultic) activities. The juxtaposition of this statement with the persecution of the holy ones suggests that "law" here refers to the law of God (Dan 6:5; Ezra 7:12)
and hence the religious activities relate to the people of God (though

---

[54] Hamilton, *With the Clouds of Heaven*, 151–53, citing C. Caragounis, *The Son of Man: Vision and Interpretation* (Tübingen: J.C.B. Mohr, 1986) and P. J. Gentry, "The Son of Man in Daniel 7: Individual or Corporate," in *Acorns and Oaks: The Primacy and Practice of Biblical Theology*, ed. M. Haykin (Tornonto: Joshua Press, 2003).

[55] Segal, *Dreams, Riddles, and Visions*, 139–43.

[56] "סבר," in Kaufman, *Comprehensive Aramaic Lexicon, Targum Lexicon*, n.p.

דָּת is also used of non-Israelite laws and decrees in Dan 6:8, 12, 15). Alternatively and probably better, one may look to 2:21 for guidance on the meaning of "times." There God establishes "times and seasons" (זִמְנִין; or "epochs and eras") by providentially removing and establishing kings. So perhaps the little horn wrongly thinks he can change "times and law/decree" in the sense of changing God's decree (דָּת) of judgment against him (v. 26), a decree that will bring his "time" to an end (v. 22).[57]

"Time, times, and half a time" (v. 25c; also Dan 12:7; Rev 12:7) during which the holy ones are handed over to the little horn probably means three and one-half years (one year + two years + one-half year). John in Revelation apparently takes this to mean forty-two months (Rev 13:5; cf. Rev 11:2). On "the court will convene" (v. 26), see 7:9–10, and on "his dominion … taken away, completely destroyed forever," see 7:11, 22.

Excursus: Who is the "Little Horn" in Daniel 7?

Interpreters are divided as to the identity of the "little horn" of Daniel 7. Critical scholars generally identify him with the Syrian-Greek Seleucid king Antiochus IV Epiphanes, while most traditional/conservative scholars identify him with an end-time antichrist figure.

1. *Antiochus IV.* Critical scholars, as well as some who self-identify as theologically conservative,[58] equate the little horn with Antiochus IV Epiphanes who attempted to abolish the Jewish religion in Palestine in 167–164 BC. In favor of this view, Dan 8:9–14 describes a ruler who comes out of the Greeks as a "little horn," just as the figure in 7:8 is called a "little horn." Both arguably disrupt Jewish worship (7:25 [by one interpretation]; 8:11). This supports their identification. Conservative and critical scholars generally agree that the little horn of Daniel 8 is referring to Antiochus IV (as is 11:21–35). Thus, if Antiochus is a prominent figure in chapters 8 and 11, it is reasonable to see him in chapter 7 as well.

---

[57] D. S. Russell, *Daniel*, Daily Study Bible (Louisville: Westminster John Knox, 1981), 135.

[58] E.g., G. Beasley-Murray, "A Conservative Thinks Again about Daniel," *Baptist Quarterly* 12 (1948): 341–46, 366–71; Goldingay, *Daniel*, 170, 174–81; Lucas, *Daniel*, 190–94, 197–98; Pierce, *Daniel*, 46–47, 129–30.

Moreover, Antiochus IV fits the character of the little horn in Daniel 7. Antiochus tried to abolish the Jewish religion: he prohibited Sabbath keeping and Jewish religious festivals, made the temple into a temple of Zeus, and made practicing circumcision a capital offense (2 Macc 6:1–11). Also after a revolt over who should be high priest, Antiochus slaughtered thousands of Jews (2 Macc 5:11–14). He thus persecuted the "holy ones" (pious Jews as opposed to Hellenistic Jews adopting Greek religion), and by decree he attempted to "change religious festivals and laws" (Dan 7:25), arguably a reference to abolishing the Jewish festivals. Though it is disputed whether his title "Epiphanes" is an actual claim to deity—it is sometimes taken to mean something like "illustrious"[59]—in Jewish ears it was taken to mean "manifest [appearing of a god]," just as his predecessor Antiochus II had taken the title *Theos* ("god"). That interpretation makes this title a blasphemous claim to demigod status.

On the other hand, there are problems with identifying the little horn as Antiochus. There is nothing historically in Antiochus' life that corresponds with the ten horns nor the uprooting of the three horns. He did not participate in a ten-king confederation, and he was eighth (not tenth) in the Seleucid line. Nor did he uproot three of his predecessors. Goldingay, who adopts the critical view, acknowledges, "We cannot with certainty identify the ten kings arising from the fourth kingship, or the three who are overthrown."[60]

Moreover, the identification of the little horn with Antiochus depends on the identification of Daniel's fourth kingdom as either Alexander's kingdom or as that of Alexander's successors. But as argued in the Introduction, the view that Daniel's four successive kingdoms are Babylon, Medes, Persia, and Greeks is not only inaccurate history, it is also contradicted by the book of Daniel itself, which makes Medes-and-Persians one kingdom with one set of laws, not two (5:28; 6:8, 12, 15; 8:20). The view that Daniel's four kingdoms are Babylon, Medo-Persia, Alexander, and Alexander's successors (the *diadochoi*) falls on the fact that Alexander and his successors (called four horns) are treated as one kingdom in 8:8, 21–22, not two.

---

[59] F. L. Cross and E. A. Livingstone, eds., *The Oxford Dictionary of the Christian Church* (New York: Oxford University Press, 2005), 79.

[60] Goldingay, *Daniel*, 179. On page 180, Goldingay lists four attempts to reconcile the ten kings with Antiochus IV as the little horn, but all seem forced.

If one accepts the view adopted in the excursus above that the son of man is the Messiah, then the Messiah appearing on the clouds to judge the fourth beast and its little horn looks like future eschatology rather than ancient history. Pierce[61] is a conservative who takes the little horn of Daniel 7 to be Antiochus IV. Yet he interprets the son of man in a messianic way, apparently seeing the text as jumping from the demise of Antiochus' kingdom (and all earthly kingdoms) to the establishment of the ultimate kingdom of God, though this is awkward.

A good case can be made that the little horn of Daniel 7 is different from the little horn of Daniel 8. The tyrant of Daniel 8 is clearly from Greece, arguably the third kingdom of Daniel 7, whereas the tyrant of Daniel 7 is from the fourth kingdom. The beast of Daniel 7 has ten horns, three of which are uprooted by the little horn, whereas the beast from which the little horn of chapter 8 arises has only four horns and none are uprooted (8:8–9). The little horn of Daniel 7 is destroyed in conjunction with the arrival of the heavenly son of man figure, whereas the horn of chapter 8 is merely broken and nothing is said about his kingdom going to the son of man or the holy ones (8:25c).[62] These differences suggest that the two little horns are different individuals.[63] We will argue later, however, that there is a typological relationship between the little horns. Indeed, Antiochus in chapters 8 and 11 foreshadows the end-time antichrist (see Bridge for Daniel 8 and §7.4.1).

2. *The antichrist.* Traditional conservatives generally identify this little horn with an end-time figure, the antichrist. Neither Daniel nor Revelation uses the term "antichrist." This Greek word meaning both "against" Christ and "instead of" Christ is used by John in his epistles (1 John 2:18, 22; 4:3; 2 John 7). A reasonable deduction can be made that eschatological, evil figures in the book of Revelation, Paul (2 Thess 2:3–12), John's epistles, and Daniel (Daniel 7; 11:36–45) all refer to the same entity whom John calls the antichrist.

Revelation 13:1–5 picks up on Daniel's imagery. It refers to a beast that emerges from the sea like the four kingdoms in Daniel 7, with features of all four: a beast like a leopard (Daniel's third beast),

---

[61] Pierce, *Daniel,* 124–26, 129.

[62] Baldwin, *Daniel,* 162n1.

[63] For other arguments, see A. E. Steinmann, "Is the Antichrist in Daniel 11?" *BSac* 162.646 (April 2005): 204.

with ten horns (Daniel's fourth beast), feet like a bear (Daniel's second beast), and a lion's mouth (Daniel's first beast), speaking boastful and blasphemous words (like the little horn of Daniel's fourth beast). The little horn persecutes the holy ones for "a time, times, and half a time" (Dan 7:25c; cf. 12:7), an expression that seems to mean three and one-half years, whereas the book of Revelation speaks of the woman (symbolizing God's people) being persecuted for "a time, times, and half a time" (Rev 12:14), and the beast being given authority to act for forty-two months = three and one-half years (Rev 13:5). The little horn makes war on the holy ones in Dan 7:21 while the beast makes war on the "saints" in Rev 13:7. In Daniel the fourth beast is destroyed, burned with fire in conjunction with the coming of the son of man (Dan 7:11, 13–14). In Revelation the beast is thrown into the lake of fire at the coming of Christ (Rev 19:11–13, 19–20).

Daniel 7 Fourth Beast, Little Horn	Revelation 13 Beast from the Sea
"He will speak words against the Most High" (Dan 7:25a)	"a mouth to utter boasts and blasphemies" (Rev 13:5a)
"and oppress the saints" (Dan 7:25b)	"to wage war against the saints and to conquer them" (Rev 13:7; cf. Rev 11:7)
"handed over to him for a time, times, and half a time" = 3½ years (Dan 7:25d)	"allowed to exercise authority for forty-two months" = 3½ years (Rev 13:5b)
"the beast was killed and its body destroyed and given over to be burned with fire" (Dan 7:11)	"The beast was ... thrown alive into lake of fire" (Rev 19:20)

Clearly Revelation is closely associating its beast with the imagery of Daniel 7. It is possible that Revelation is employing this imagery for a different purpose. The interpretation of Revelation itself is, of course, controversial. But it is not unreasonable to suppose that these similarities were intended by John to identify his "beast" with Daniel's four kingdoms, three of which have an extension of life in the fourth kingdom (cf. Dan 7:12) whose sovereignty will come to a complete end at the Christ's second coming. That in turn suggests that Daniel 7 should be interpreted in light of Revelation 13 and 19.

Another factor favors the end-time interpretation of the fourth beast and its little horn. This view seems to most easily allow Daniel's prophecy to be true. The Greek Seleucid kingdom does not come to a complete and abrupt end at the demise of Antiochus IV, for Judah remained nominally under Greek Seleucid control through the governorship of Judas Maccabeus' brother Jonathan (160–143/2 BC). It was only in the first year in the reign of Judas' brother Simeon (142–134 BC) that Judah gained full freedom from the Seleucids (1 Macc 13:41–42). This is over two decades after Antiochus' demise in 164. Moreover, Antiochus' kingdom was not displaced by the establishment of the eternal kingdom of God at the coming of a heavenly son of man. For the prophecy to be true, the little horn should probably not be identified with Antiochus IV but rather understood as the antichrist.

7:27 On "Most High" see comments at v. 18. At issue in this verse is its punctuation. It could be punctuated "a people, the holy ones" or alternatively "the people *of* the holy ones" in a construct relationship (cf. "the people of the saints" ESV, KJV, NASB). The latter interpretation is necessary (though not sufficient) to support the view that the "holy ones" are angels (see excursus on the one like a son of man). In favor of the CSB punctuation, the Masoretes punctuated "people" with a *tiphhah* disjunctive accent, which implies a comma. Additionally, in Aramaic the "of" relationship is often indicated by the particle *di* (דִּי) as occurs earlier in this verse ("greatness of [דִּי] the kingdoms"). Accordingly, Aramaic expresses an "of" relationship using mere juxtaposition of words (construct) less often than does Hebrew. To be unambiguously an "of" relationship, the particle *di* should have been used. Thus, this favors the Masoretic punctuation. In favor of this being a construct relationship ("the people *of* the holy ones") is the lack of the article "the" on "people," suggesting the meaning "a people" even though contextually the sense feels definite (cf. CSB "the people"). If in construct with "Most High," it would be definite.

Even if the correct rendering is "the people of the holy ones," this need not mean "the holy ones" are angels. "The people of the holy ones" could refer to the larger group (people) to whom the smaller group (the holy/pious ones) belong. Or the relationship could be appositional, "the people *who are* the holy ones" just as "land of Egypt" means the "land *which is* Egypt." A third alternative is that "people of the holy ones" has an adjectival sense, "the holy people" (NIV, Old Greek), just as a "kingdom of priests" (Exod 19:6) probably means a "priestly kingdom." Segal[64] suggests another option, taking "holy ones" (קַדִּישֵׁי) as a plural of majesty for Yahweh, just as "Most High" (עֶלְיוֹנִין) is a plural of majesty for God. He thus renders it as, "the people of the Most High Holy One," understanding it as refering to the divine son of man figure. Thus the angel interpretation of "the holy ones" is hardly a necessary conclusion from v. 27, whatever its punctuation. For further arguments against the angel view of "holy ones" see the excursus on one like a son of man above.

On v. 27b ("His kingdom will be an everlasting kingdom and all rulers will serve and obey him"), cf. Dan 4:34; 7:14. "Rulers" (Aramaic שָׁלְטָן) is elsewhere in the CSB, including earlier in this same verse, rendered "dominion" (3:3; 7:14, 27a). So the CSB takes "dominions" by synecdoche to mean "rulers," though it seems simplest and best to translate the plural as "dominions" here (ESV, NJPS, KJV, NASB, NRSV). The "him" appears to allude to the divine son of man figure of v. 14, the language of which this verse echoes. This is consistent with taking "Most High" (עֶלְיוֹנִין) as a reference to the divine son of man as discussed above. The same word for "dominion" and "serve" (meaning "worship") there is also used here. The "holy ones" receive the kingdom, dominion, and greatness under this son of man's authority. Note statements elsewhere that one day the nations will serve God's people Israel (Isa 14:1–2; 49:22–23; 60:10–12).[65]

7:28 "Account" (Aramaic מִלָּה) means "word, matter, affair" (like Hebrew דָּבָר). It could signify "the end of the matter" (ESV, NIV), or better "the end of the word [of revelation]" (cf. NASB, "the revelation ended"), referring back to v. 1, which introduces a "summary of his account" (more literally, "head/beginning of words").

"My face turned pale" is literally "my countenance/brightness/complexion changed." Aramaic זִיו (also used in 2:31 of the splendor of Nebuchadnezzar's dream-statue) can denote the bright radiance characteristic of kings (4:36), which is lost when something terror-izes them and their "countenance changes." Nebuchadnezzar and Belshazzar both were terrorized by their dreams/visions, the latter also having his face turn pale (Dan 4:5; 5:6, 12). "I kept the mat-ter to myself" is literally, "I kept the matter in my heart" (ESV). A

---

[64] Segal, *Dreams, Riddles, and Visions*, 139–43.
[65] Lucas, *Daniel*, 183.

similar idiom occurs in Luke 2:19, where Mary treasured words "in her heart."

Bridge

Daniel 7 shares many themes with Daniel 2, its parallel in the book's chiastic outline. Both chapters describe God's plan for history (see §7.1), in which he directs events toward the replacement of all worldly kingdoms by the kingdom of God (see §7.4). What Daniel 7 adds is depth of detail. God's people can expect to confront dangerous and sometimes hostile gentile powers. God grants sovereignty even to beastly kingdoms for a time, directing them for his sovereign purposes yet working to restrain them (see §7.3; cf. Rom 13:1–7; 2 Thess 2:6–8). The fourth kingdom rebels against God and his people, though God incorporates this in his sovereign plan (see §3.8, §7.4). "In Dan 7, these frightful and rebellious nations are not defeated so much as judged and dismissed."[66] That these nations, even the worst of them, stand under God's all-powerful judgment encourages God's suffering people to believe that God will ultimately deliver them.

There is a dual focus in Daniel 7 on the son of man figure and the little horn. In light of the New Testament (see the above excurses), it becomes clear that the "son of man" is Christ, and "the little horn" is the antichrist. Thus Daniel 7 is a useful starting point for expounding the nature of Jesus Christ (see §6.1). He is the divine Son to be worshiped, a judge to be feared, and our king to be obeyed. He will destroy evil and establish the eternal kingdom of God (see §7.4.3). Daniel 7 also warns God's people of the coming antichrist (see §7.4.1), an arrogant blasphemer who will depose other political leaders and persecute God's people. Therefore, believers must brace themselves for this time of suffering and persecution (see §7.4.2) as they await the return of Jesus Christ. This warning is not merely for the final days of history. John warns us that many antichrists will come into the world before the ultimate antichrist (1 John 2:18; Antiochus IV is a good example). Christians today should be prepared for persecutions and trials as brutish kingdoms come and go. We must purpose to remain faithful despite such persecutions (see

---

[66] Lester, *Daniel Evokes Isaiah*, 47.

§4.5, §4.8, §7.5; cf. 1 Thess 3:3–4; 2 Tim 3:12). Those who remain faithful and holy will receive Christ's kingdom (see §7.4.3).

I. Court Narratives (Daniel 1–6)

II. Visions of Daniel (Daniel 7–12)
First vision: Four beasts and son of man figure (Daniel 7)
Second vision: Ram and male goat (Daniel 8)
Third vision: Seventy weeks (Daniel 9)
Fourth vision: Kings of North/South, distress/resurrection (Daniel 10–12)

  (A) Beginning of story (1:1–21)
    (B) Dream about four world kingdoms ended by the kingdom of God (2:1–49)
      (C) Judeans faithful in the face of death (3:1–30)
        (D) Royal pride humbled (4:1–37)
        (D') Royal pride humbled (5:1–31)
      (C') A Judean faithful in the face of death (6:1–28)
    (B') Vision about four world kingdoms ended by the kingdom of God (7:1–28)
      (E) Vision of Persian and Greek kingdoms to Antiochus (8:1–27)
        (F) Vision of seventy weeks (9:1–27)
      (E') Vision of Persian and Greek kingdoms to Antiochus (10:1–11:35)
    (B'')World kingdoms ended and the righteous established (11:36–12:3)
  (A') End of story: Vision sealed until the end (12:4–13)

¹In the third year of King Belshazzar's reign, a vision appeared to me, Daniel, after the one that had appeared to me earlier. ² I saw the vision, and as I watched, I was in the fortress city of Susa, in the province of Elam. I saw in the vision that I was beside the Ulai Canal. ³ I looked up, and there was a ram standing beside the canal. He had two horns. The two horns were long, but one was longer than the other, and the longer one came up last. ⁴ I saw the ram charging to the west, the north, and the south. No animal could stand against him, and there was no rescue from his power. He did whatever he wanted and became great.

⁵ As I was observing, a male goat appeared, coming from the west across the surface of the entire earth without touching the ground. The goat had a conspicuous horn between his eyes. ⁶ He

came toward the two-horned ram I had seen standing beside the canal and rushed at him with savage fury. ⁷ I saw him approaching the ram, and infuriated with him, he struck the ram, breaking his two horns, and the ram was not strong enough to stand against him. The goat threw him to the ground and trampled him, and there was no one to rescue the ram from his power. ⁸ Then the male goat acted even more arrogantly, but when he became powerful, the large horn was broken. Four conspicuous horns came up in its place, pointing toward the four winds of heaven.

⁹ From one of them a little horn emerged and grew extensively toward the south and the east and toward the beautiful land. ¹⁰ It grew as high as the heavenly army, made some of the army and some of the stars fall to the earth, and trampled them. ¹¹ It acted arrogantly even against the Prince of the heavenly army; it revoked his regular sacrifice and overthrew the place of his sanctuary. ¹² In the rebellion, the army was given up, together with the regular sacrifice. The horn threw truth to the ground and was successful in what it did.

¹³ Then I heard a holy one speaking, and another holy one said to the speaker, "How long will the events of this vision last—the regular sacrifice, the rebellion that makes desolate, and the giving over of the sanctuary and of the army to be trampled?"

¹⁴ He said to me, "For 2,300 evenings and mornings; then the sanctuary will be restored."

¹⁵ While I, Daniel, was watching the vision and trying to understand it, there stood before me someone who appeared to be a man. ¹⁶ I heard a human voice calling from the middle of the Ulai: "Gabriel, explain the vision to this man."

¹⁷ So he approached where I was standing; when he came near, I was terrified and fell facedown. "Son of man," he said to me, "understand that the vision refers to the time of the end." ¹⁸ While he was speaking to me, I fell into a deep sleep, with my face to the ground. Then he touched me, made me stand up, ¹⁹ and said, "I am here to tell you what will happen at the conclusion of the time of wrath, because it refers to the appointed time of the end. ²⁰ The two-horned ram that you saw represents the kings of Media and Persia. ²¹ The shaggy goat represents the king of Greece, and the large horn between his eyes represents the first king. ²² The four horns that took the place of the broken horn represent four kingdoms. They will rise from that nation, but without its power.

²³   Near the end of their kingdoms,
        when the rebels have reached

the full measure of their sin,
a ruthless king, skilled in intrigue,
will come to the throne.

24 His power will be great,
but it will not be his own.
He will cause outrageous destruction
and succeed in whatever he does.
He will destroy the powerful
along with the holy people.

25 He will cause deceit to prosper
through his cunning and by his influence,
and in his own mind he will
exalt himself.
He will destroy many in a time of peace;
he will even stand against the Prince of princes.
Yet he will be broken—not by human hands.

26 The vision of the evenings and the mornings
that has been told is true.
Now you are to seal up the vision
because it refers to many days in the future."

27 I, Daniel, was overcome and lay sick for days. Then I got up
and went about the king's business. I was greatly disturbed by the
vision and could not understand it.

Context

The vision of Daniel 8 occurs two years after that of Daniel 7
and elaborates on it. Daniel 7 indicates God in his sovereignty allows
great kingdoms to come and go. Daniel 8 reiterates that truth by indicating that though Medo-Persia would be a great empire, it will suddenly fall to the Greek kingdom. The vision of Daniel 7 indicates that
a "little horn" of the fourth kingdom (understood in this commentary as Rome-and-beyond) will come just before the establishment
of the kingdom of God to persecute God's people. Daniel 8 indicates
that another "little horn" comes earlier during the Greek kingdom,
well before the arrival of God's kingdom, to persecute God's people.
But both visions together assure God's people he will preserve them.

Daniel 2:4b–7:28 is written in Aramaic. Chapter 8 through the
end of the book, like Dan 1:1–2:4b, uses the Hebrew language. The
passage can be outlined as follows:

I. The vision of a ram and a male goat (8:1–14)
Introduction (vv. 1–2)
The ram (vv. 3–4)
The male goat (vv. 5–7)
The conspicuous horn replaced by four horns (v. 8)
The little horn (vv. 9–12)
The 2,300 evenings and mornings (vv. 13–14)

II. Gabriel's interpretation (8:15–27)
Gabriel comes to interpret (vv. 15–19)
The ram explained (v. 20)
The male goat and conspicuous horn explained (v. 21)
The four horns explained (v. 22)
The little horn explained (vv. 23–25)
The 2,300 evenings and mornings affirmed (v. 26)
Daniel's reaction to the vision (v. 27)

8:1–2 Belshazzar's "third year" is approximately 549 BC, assuming Nabonidus departs for Teima in 552. Around 550/549 Cyrus defeated his grandfather Astyages to become king of both the Medes and Persians, assuming the titles "king of the Medes" and "king of Elam."[1] Daniel here sees himself in Susa in a vision. He may have actually come to Susa of Elam as part of a diplomatic mission to Persia on the occasion of Cyrus' victory over the Medes that made Medo-Persia the rising power east and north of Babylonia. The "third year" of Belshazzar is two years after the vision of 7:1. "Earlier" (v. 1b) is more literally "at the first" (KJV, ESV), referring to the vision of Daniel 7.

"Fortress city" (v. 2b) is Hebrew בִּירָה, a loanword from Akkadian *birtu* referring to a place protected by fortified outposts. Elam was once its own country in what is now southern Iran with Susa as its capital in the western part of the country toward Babylon. The Assyrian king Ashurbanipal sacked Susa in 640 BC and defeated Elam. Later Elam was incorporated into the Persian (Achaemenid) Empire,[2] Susa becoming one of its capitals. Cyrus, along with his

[1] D. J. Wiseman, "Cyrus," *NBD,* 250.
[2] J. J. M. Roberts, "Elam, Elamites," *NIDB,* 2:229.

great-grandfather Teispes, claimed the title "king of Anshan" (another Elamite city to the east toward Persia).

A Persian settlement had lived in Susa since the end of the seventh century,[3] so Cyrus probably already controlled Susa as an early acquisition of the Achaemenid Empire.

"Province" is Hebrew מְדִינָה. See discussion of the Aramaic cognate at Dan 3:1. "Province of Elam" suggests that Susa along with Anshan are already in a province of the Persian Empire, though it could possibly mean Susa is in the "jurisdiction" (another meaning of מְדִינָה) or "country" of Elam. Others think Cyrus did not take control of Susa until just before his conquest of Babylon in 539 BC.[4] In a cuneiform text known as the Cyrus Cylinder dating to shortly after Cyrus' conquest of Babylon, Cyrus claims to have restored to Susa images plundered by the Babylonians, showing that Cyrus certainly controlled Susa by then. Whether or not Cyrus controlled Susa at the time of this prophecy (as seems likely), Cyrus would soon control it. Alexander the Great captured Susa in 331 without resistance and it remained an important city. Alexander's successors the Seleucids made Susa a full-fledged Greek *polis* and renamed it "Seleucia-on-the-Eulaios."[5] Susa's importance to Persia and later to the Greeks makes this an appropriate site for a vision concerning Persian and Greek conflicts that follow.

"Ulai" (v. 2c) denotes a canal that flowed on the northern side of Susa, connecting the Choaspes (present-day Kerkha) and Coprates (present-day Abdizful) Rivers.[6] The Old Greek (LXX) translates the Hebrew rendered "canal" (אוּבַל) with πύλη "gate," leading some interpreters (e.g., Jerome) to suppose Ulai is a city gate of Susa. Against this view is the fact that at the time of Alexander the Great the Ulai (classical sources, Eulaeus/Eulaios [Εὐλαῖος]) is used by Nearchus the commander of Alexander's fleet to reach Susa by water and by Alexander to leave Susa heading toward the Tigris.[7]

---

[3] E. M. Yamauchi, *Persia and the Bible* (Grand Rapids: Baker, 1990), 293.

[4] E. Carter, Matthew Stolper, *Elam: Surveys of Political History and Archaeology* (Berkeley: University of California Press, 1984), 55.

[5] Yamauchi, *Persia and the Bible,* 302; R. N. Frye, *The History of Ancient Iran* (Germany: C. H. Beck, 1984), 157.

[6] D. E. Wittman, "Ulai," *NIDB,* 5:706.

[7] P. Briant, *From Cyrus to Alexander: A History of the Persian Empire,* trans. P. T. Daniels (Winona Lake, IN: Eisenbrauns, 2002), 381.

8:3–4 The ram symbolizes the kings of Media and Persia (v. 20). "Long … longer" concerning the horns could be rendered "high … higher" (NJPS, ESV). Persia is ultimately the more prominent part of the Medo-Persian Empire, though Media had been more prominent until Cyrus defeated his grandfather Astyages in battle in 550/549 BC and took over his grandfather's Median Empire. According to the Sippar Cylinder of Nabonidus, Cyrus "scattered the vast Median hordes with his small army. He captured Astyages, the king of the Medes, and took him to his country as captive."[8]

"Charging" (v. 4a) is a D-stem participle from נגח that is better rendered "butting" (NASB, NJPS, GNT). This root in the G-stem is used of a "goring" ox (Exod 21:28, 31–32; cp. CEB). However, while some sheep varieties have horns that might gore, most sheep, like the ones shown on the reliefs at Achaemenid-period Persepolis, have curved horns more suitable for butting than goring (cf. Ezek 34:21). The D-stem denotes multiplied/repeated action, so the verb more precisely means the ram is "butting again and again" or "butting repeatedly." "West … north … south" describes various military campaigns of Medo-Persia, though apparently not in chronological sequence. To the west Cyrus conquered Babylon (539 BC), which led to Persia's taking over Babylon's vassals, including Syria and Judah. Earlier Cyrus moved north and west into Asia Minor, where he defeated Croesus king of Lydia at his capital of Sardis in 547, leading to the Achaemenid annexing of Lydia into the empire. His son Cambyses moved south to conquer Egypt (525 BC).

"He did whatever he wanted" (v. 4b) is hyperbole. Cambyses, for example, made plans to move into North Africa to conquer Carthage (in modern Tunisia), and while the Libyans west of Egypt did send him tribute, according to Herodotus, Cambyses abandoned plans to take Carthage when his Phoenician sailors balked at joining in a campaign against Carthage because it was a Phoenician city (Herodotus 3.17, 19). A military campaign to Siwa four hundred miles west of the Nile got frustrated by a sandstorm, and he was forced temporarily to abandon Persia's campaign against Ethiopia or Nubia (modern Sudan; Herodotus 3.25–26).[9] Nonetheless, overall Medo-Persia was remarkably successful in quickly building its empire.

---

[8] *COS* 2:311.

[9] Yamauchi, *Persia and the Bible*, 110–13.

"Became great" is the H-stem of גדל. The Qal can mean "become great," so to translate the more dynamic (causative) H-stem as if it were a Qal is too weak. Slightly better is to render it "grew great" (NJPS) or "did great things" (BDB), though perhaps it is best to render it "magnified himself" (NASB, RSV) in the sense that the grammatical subject causes itself to be regarded as great by "talking big," declaring itself great by boasting.[10] The same applies to this form at Dan 8:8, 11, and 25.

8:5 "Observing" (v. 5a) is better rendered "considering" (ESV, KJV) or "thinking about this" (NIV). This root (Hebrew בין) in the Qal means "to understand," and in the H-stem can mean to "make understand." Here it seems to mean "making [oneself] understand"—that is, Daniel is mulling over and trying to make sense of what he has just seen. "Appeared" is not in the Hebrew but is supplied contextually. "Male goat" is literally "a billygoat of the goats." Perhaps something like the fierce-looking Persian wild goat (ibex) is behind this imagery. The domestic goat is probably descended from the ibex. Hebrew מַעֲרָב, "west" (v. 5b), can also mean the "place of sunset," here used for that direction. The goat in v. 21 is identified as Greece, beginning with Alexander the Great who came generally from the west to conquer the Persian Empire from 334 to 331 BC. "Earth" and "land" (v. 5b) are the same word in Hebrew (אֶרֶץ). The fact that this goat seems to fly over the ground speaks of Alexander's speed of conquest. The goat begins with a unicorn-like "conspicuous horn." Single-horned goats have been produced for circuses in modern times by transplanting horn buds on kid-goats so a single horn results. It is not known whether this technique was used in OT times, though an occasional unicorn goat could have occurred and form the basis of the unicorn legends. "Conspicuous horn" (Hebrew, "horn of appearance/vision") indicates it appeared "prominent" (NIV) or "very large" (NLT). This stands for the Greek kingdom's first king (v. 21 below), Alexander the Great.

8:6–7 The two-horned ram (v. 6) represents Medo-Persia (v. 20). On "canal" see comments at v. 2. "Rushed at him" can be rendered more simply "ran at him" (ESV). The Hebrew of "with savage fury" reads, "in the heat/rage of his strength," meaning "in his powerful wrath" (ESV).

---

[10] "גדל," *HALOT* 1:179; *IBHS*, 439–40 (§27.2.f); see note 16.

Verse 7 describes Greece's conquest of Medo-Persia under Alexander. "Infuriated with him" (v. 7) reads in the Hebrew, "and he embittered himself toward him," like a bull preparing itself to charge. "Breaking" (v. 7) translates D-stem יְשַׁבֵּר as if it were a Qal (יִשְׁבֹּר). Indeed, the consonants could be revocalized that way (compare the N-stem [passive of Qal] for שבר in v. 8). The D-stem multiplies the action, and thus the MT implies "breaking to pieces, shattering" (NIV; cf. NASB), or at least, contextually, "breaking one followed by the other." "Trampled" (Hebrew רמס) can be used of trampling a person to death (2 Kgs 7:17, 20).

8:8 The goat "acted even more arrogantly" (v. 8a) is the H-stem of גדל plus a phrase meaning "exceedingly" (עַד־מְאֹד) that in combination is more literally rendered "magnified himself exceedingly" (NASB, RSV, ESV) in the sense of very great boasting. See further comments at 8:4.

The "four *conspicuous* horns" (v. 8b)[11] symbolize Alexander's successors (see vv. 21–22 below). Four-horned goats do occasionally occur in nature. The successors (*diadochoi*) are also represented by the four heads in Daniel's third beast (see comments at 7:6). One analysis takes the "four" horns specifically as the eventual division of Alexander's kingdom into roughly four parts scattered in all four directions—"the four winds of heaven" (see comments at 7:2)—after a complicated period of civil war. Jerome takes the four divisions to be among Ptolemy, Seleucus, Philip Arridaeusan, and Antigonus, who preceeds Seleucus in ruling the eastern part of Alexander's empire.[12] Another alternative takes the four as: (1) To the south, Ptolemy I Soter took over Egypt upon Alexander's death (323 BC) and founded the Ptolemaic Kingdom. (2) To the east, Seleucus I Nicator took control from Asia Minor through Babylon extending into Persia (312 BC) and founded the Seleucid Empire. (3) To the west, Cassander (son of General Antipater) gained undisputed

---

[11] "Four *conspicuous* [חזות] horns" reads in the Old Greek "four *other* horns," reflecting a presumed Hebrew *Vorlage* of אחרות with an additional aleph [א] and a change from zayin [ז] to a similar-looking resh [ר] as compared with the Masoretic Text, a reading followed by NABRE. No great difference in meaning hinges on which reading is adopted.

[12] St. Jerome, *Jerome's Commentary on Daniel*, trans. G. L. Archer (Grand Rapids: Baker, 1958), 75. Similarly C. A. Newsom, *Daniel*, OTL (Louisville: Westminster John Knox, 2014), 262.

control over Greece and Macedonia (301 BC). (4) To the north, after the battle of Ipsus, Lysimachus came to rule Thrace, Lydia, Ionia, Phrygia, and the north coast of Asia Minor (301 BC).[13] A different analysis takes the four horns pointing in four directions less specifically, merely indicating that Alexander's kingdom breaks up in every which way in a disorderly manner.

8:9 Though occasionally a commentator will understand vv. 9–12 to be about the antichrist (e.g., M. Hassler),[14] most commentators, conservative and critical, believe these verses describe Antiochus IV Epiphanes (175–164 BC), who came out of the Seleucid branch of Alexander's kingdom.

"A little horn" could be rendered "a single, very small horn" (CEB) or "a rather small horn" (NASB), or "another horn which started small" (NIV). The word "little" is from מִצְּעִירָה "from small" or "from/of smallness," perhaps meaning "smallish" or "starting small." The little horn is Antiochus IV Epiphanes who emerged "from one of" the four horns mentioned in v. 8, namely from the Seleucid branch. He was "little" in that he was not the legitimate heir to the throne (cf. comments at Dan 11:21). Antiochus was held hostage in Rome for twelve years until 175 when his nephew Demetrius went to Rome to serve as Antiochus' substitute. Antiochus' brother and Demetrius' father King Seleucus IV was assassinated. With the rightful heir Demetrius still being held hostage in Rome, and his brother (also named Antiochus) too young to rule, Antiochus IV assumed the throne (Polybius, *Histories* 31.12). On differences between this "little horn" and the "little horn" on the fourth beast (Dan 7:8), see the above excursus, "Who is the 'Little Horn' in Daniel 7?"

That Antiochus IV grows "toward the south and the east and toward the beautiful land" represents Epiphanes' military activities. Toward the south Antiochus IV conducted two campaigns against Egypt beginning in 169 BC (1 Macc 1:16–19; 2 Macc 5:1). To the east (מִזְרָח; a term that can mean, "the dawn"; cp. "west" in v. 5) were his campaigns against Persia and Media in 165–164 BC (1 Macc 3:31–37;

---

[13] F. W. Walbank, A. E. Astin, M. W. Frederiksen, R. M. Ogilvie, eds., *The Hellenistic World*, vol. VII in *The Cambridge Ancient History* (London: Cambridge University, 1984), 60, 119, 211, 426.

[14] M. A. Hassler, "The Identity of the Little Horn in Daniel 8: Antiochus IV Epiphanes, Rome, or The Antichrist?" *Master's Seminary Journal* 27.1 (2016): 33–44.

2 Macc 9:1–3). The "beautiful land" [v. 9c] is from צְבִי "splendor, glory, beautifulness" (compare ESV, NKJV, "the glorious land"). The Hebrew reads literally "the beautifulness" (הַצֶּבִי), which lacks the word "land." That "the beautifulness" means "the beautiful land" is based on Dan 11:16, 41, which speak of "the *land* of beautifulness [אֶרֶץ־הַצֶּבִי]." The "beautiful land" refers to Israel, the most beautiful of all lands (Ezek 20:6, 15), because it is the land promised by God to Israel (see §4.3). Over this land the "king of the south" (Ptolemies of Egypt) and the king of the north (the Seleucids of Syria) fought, but it ultimately fell into the hands of the Seleucids around 198 BC when the Seleucid king Antiochus III defeated the Ptolemies at the battle of Panium and entered Jerusalem. Antiochus IV passed through his tributary Judah on the way to and from fighting in Egypt.

8:10 "Grew" (v. 10a) continues the thought of v. 9, that the little horn does not remain little for long. "Heavenly army" reads in Hebrew "the host of heaven." "Army" (צָבָא) can refer to a heavenly, angelic army that stands in God's presence and worships him (1 Kgs 22:19; Neh 9:6; cf. the expression "Yahweh of hosts"). It can also refer to "stars" and other heavenly bodies like the sun and moon (Deut 4:19 where CSB's "the stars in the sky" is the "צְבָא [host] of heaven"). Host and stars may be identified here: "some of the army and some of the stars" is probably better rendered "some of the army, that is, some of the stars" (CSB note). The imagery is literally of the heavenly bodies (e.g., "stars"), but based on this dual usage of צָבָא, these stars represent angels (Ps 103:20–21 where CSB "armies" [צְבָא] may refer to the stars; cf. Rev 1:20; 9:1). This is confirmed in v. 11 where God is called "Prince of the heavenly army/host."

Antiochus IV exalts himself to the angelic abode of God. This evokes language ("heavens," "stars," "earth," "fall") used in Isa 14:13–15 of the king of Babylon, who says, "I will ascend to the heavens" like a god and who seeks to "sit on the mount of the gods' assembly." Contrary to the the king of Babylon who is immediately cast down in Isaiah, Antiochus is surprisingly successful and even throws down some of the "stars." Yet in the end the downfall of royal hubris is the same.[15] Making "some of the army … fall" may refer to spiritual warfare in the heavenly realm pertaining to Antiochus. What happens in the heavenly realm corresponds with what happens

---

[15] Lester, *Daniel Evokes Isaiah*, 79–84.

in the earthly realm, namely, the fall of stars, and some of the host corresponds with Antiochus' persecuting God's holy people on earth who will one day shine like stars (Dan 12:3). Compare the similar case in Rev 12:7–12 where the war of Michael and other angels with the devil and his angels in heaven corresponds with the persecution of the saints on earth. On spiritual warfare cf. Dan 10:1–21 and §5.

8:11 "Acted arrogantly" represents the H-stem of גדל, which probably means it causes itself to be regarded as great by "talking big," declaring itself great by boasting (see comments on v. 4). "Acted arrogantly even against the Prince" more likely means "even exalted himself as high as the Prince" (NKJV). Antiochus claimed divine status in his title "Epiphanes," meaning "Manifest" (appearing of a god). Though some scholars think "Epiphanes" means little more than "Illustrious," to Jews it seems to have expressed Antiochus' pretensions of deity. Compare this with "as high as the heavenly army" in v. 10, which seems to refer to the same thing.

"The Prince of the heavenly army" (שַׂר־הַצָּבָא) uses שַׂר, whose plural is reasonably rendered "leaders" in Dan 9:6, 8. The word שַׂר is better rendered here "commander" (NASB, NIV). Compare Deut 20:9 שָׂרֵי צְבָאוֹת, "military commanders" (CSB), which more literally reads "commanders (שָׂרֵי) of armies" (NASB), and Josh 5:14–15, "the commander of the Lord's army" (שַׂר־צְבָא־יְהוָה). In Dan 11:5 שַׂר is used of one of the military commanders under the king of the South, namely Alexander's general Seleucus I who was given refuge in Egypt by Ptolemy I. The term שַׂר refers to various leaders: royal rulers like the messianic "prince of peace" (Isa 9:6), military commanders (1 Sam 18:30), government officials (Gen 12:15; Jer 26:10), and even angelic and demonic "princes" (10:13, 20–21). The "Prince of the heavenly army" here refers to God, as in Josh 5:13–15 (cp. God on the chariot throne in Dan 7:9). God is also the "Prince of princes" (v. 25), making this one of many titles for God in Daniel (see §3.2). Some commentators see this "Prince" as the preincarnate Christ (see §6.6).[16]

"His regular sacrifice" (מִמֶּנּוּ ... הַתָּמִיד) refers to the daily offerings at the temple instituted by God (see §3.6, §4.5), so abolition of this would be horrifying to Jews. Daily (or "regular" or "continual")

---

[16] E.g., A. E. Steinmann, *Daniel*, Concordia Commentary (St. Louis: Concordia, 2008), 401–3.

burnt offerings would occur every morning and evening along with accompanying grain offerings, both of which were always to be burning on the altar (Exod 28:38–41; Num 28:3–6). "Revoked" could also be more precisely rendered "suspended" (NJPS), reflecting the H-stem of רום ("be high"), nominally meaning to "lift up." The Qere (marginal reading in the Masoretic Hebrew text) takes the form as a Hophal passive verb (הורם) that can be rendered "his regular sacrifice was removed/suspended" (cf. KJV, ESV) in parallel with the following verb (see below). This reading is supported by some Hebrew manuscripts and the text of Daniel as found at Qumran. The Ketiv (what is written) reads the verb as a Hiphil active (הרים; "it removed/suspended," NIV, NRSV) that places more emphasis on the actions of the little horn. This seems contextually more appropriate and is probably the correct text.

"It overthrew the place of his sanctuary" should be rendered as passive, "the place of his sanctuary was overthrown" (ESV). At the time of this prophecy, the third year of Belshazzar (8:1), roughly 549 BC, the temple sanctuary lay desolate from its Babylonian destruction in 586, so mention of it implies that it will be rebuilt and yet will suffer further desolations.

In 167 BC Antiochus IV became frustrated with Jewish rebellion over his meddling in their religion. In 175 BC he deposed the high priest Onias III, appointing Onias' brother Jason instead after Jason promised him a bribe of at least 440 talents of silver (2 Macc 4:7–10, 23). Three years later Antiochus replaced Jason with a certain Menelaus as high priest, the latter having outbid Jason by promising Antiochus an additional 300 talents for the honor (2 Macc 4:24–25). When Jason fomented a riot attempting to depose Menelaus, Antiochus intervened and decided to abolish Judaism (1 Macc 1:41–50; 2 Macc 5:1–14). In an act of sacrilege (see §3.6), Antiochus desecrated the temple in Jerusalem by plundering it (1 Macc 1:20–40; 2 Macc 5:15–16, 21) and then turning it into a temple of the Greek god Zeus (2 Macc 6:1–2). He prohibited Jews from making offerings to God in the sanctuary (1 Macc 1:45). Antiochus' desecration of the sanctuary rendered it unfit for sacrifice in the minds of pious Jews. Thus the regular offerings to the God of Israel ceased.

8:12 Verse 12 has exegetical problems. One issue is whose פֶּשַׁע—"rebellion," "transgression" (ESV), or crime (see comments at v. 13)—is in view here and in v. 13. Is it the transgression of the Jews against God, or the rebellion of the Jews against Antiochus IV, or the transgression/crime of Antiochus IV against God and the Jews? It is probably the last of these.

There is also a textual issue since the Old Greek and Theodotion suggest the reading may have been "the rebellion" (הַפֶּשַׁע) rather than "In [the] rebellion" (בְּפָשַׁע)," and the term "host" is missing from these Greek versions.

Another issue is the syntax of v. 12a. Some EVVs understand the syntax in a way similar to the CSB, saying that an army and the regular offering are given over presumably to Antiochus (ESV, NRSV, KJV, NASB, NIV). An alternative rendering is, "An army was arrayed iniquitously against the regular offering" (NJPS; similarly CEB, GW).

Not unrelated is the question of which "host/army" (צָבָא) is in mind (assuming the MT reading is correct, see above). The possibilities include the following: (1) The angelic army of heaven, as in v. 10. (2) The army of Antiochus that took over the temple (NJPS, CEB, GW). (3) The army of Judah, the host on earth corresponding with the angelic host of v. 10, which was initially put down by Antiochus. (4) The Jewish people more generally ("the Lord's people," NIV). View (1) is unlikely since the context is earth, not heaven. View (4) is also unlikely because צָבָא is regularly used for an army or stars but not for a group of people. View (2) makes good sense in itself and corresponds with the historical reality that Antiochus used his army to take the temple and end regular sacrifice. View (3) seems best because it fits with vv. 10–11 by making what happens with the host/army of heaven correspond with what happens to God's host/army on earth. Antiochus not only took the temple and ended regular sacrifice (see comments at v. 11), he also slaughtered God's "host/army," namely the men of Judah who refused to fight back on the Sabbath (1 Macc 2:29–38; 2 Macc 5:24–26).

The host of heaven falling to the ground (v. 10) is now said to represent "truth" being thrown down. Antiochus IV replaced Yahweh worship and biblical religion (truth) with idolatry (falsehood) and was successful for a time. Any discovered copies of the books of the law (truth) were shredded and burned, and their owners were executed (1 Macc 1:56–57).

8:13–14 A "holy one" here is an angel, as in Dan 4:13, 17–18, 23 (on angels, see §5). "To the speaker" (פַּלְמֹנִי) means more precisely, "to the certain (but unknown) one who was speaking." On "regular sacrifice" (v. 13b) see comments at v. 11. The Old Greek and Theodotion expand to "the daily offering that has been removed," which implies the text they were translating had the Hophal participle מורם. "Rebellion" (פֶּשַׁע) could also be rendered "transgression" (ESV) or even "crime,"[17] a word also used in v. 12. Its root can refer to rebellion against authority (2 Kgs 8:20–22) but more basically denotes criminal acts like defrauding someone, theft, slave-trading, atrocities of war, and perverting justice by accepting bribes (Gen 31:36; Exod 22:9; Prov 28:24; Amos 1:6, 13; 2:6). The participle "makes desolate" (שֹׁמֵם) combines the ideas of desertion and destruction. It seems likely that the פֶּשַׁע in v. 12 is the same פֶּשַׁע as verse 13. If the "host" in v. 12 refers to military men of Israel, then this could be the rebellion of the Jews against Antiochus led by Judas Maccabeus, though it seems doubtful that the text would emphasize the negative results of Judas' actions ("desolation, desertion"). More likely it refers to the transgression/crime of Antiochus against God (and his people), which led to the slaughter of many Jewish men and made the temple/Jerusalem desolate, devoid of legitimate priests, and trampled by gentiles. Compare the similar expression, "the abomination of desolation" (9:27; 11:31; 12:11).

"He said to me" may originally have read, "He said to him" (Theodotion, Old Greek, Syriac), which represents an addition of the letter waw ו in Hebrew (אליו rather than אלי). There is debate as to whether "2,300 evenings and mornings" (v. 14) means 2,300 days or 1,150 days. The latter fits the historical context in which for about three years the temple was "desolate" (devoid of legitimate sacrifice) from 15 Kislev (Dec 6) 167 BC to 25 Kislev (Dec 14) 164 (1 Macc 1:54; 4:52–53). Steinmann calculates this as precisely 1,106 days, though he suggests that the ban on sacrifice may have begun a little earlier (to reach 1,150 days) or that 1,150 is a round number rather than exact.[18] The 2,300-day interpretation would refer to years of trouble following the deposing and murder of Onias III as high priest. Specifically, this period begins some time after 172 BC when the non-Zadokite Menelaus bought the right to become high priest. In the midst of this period, Antiochus IV turned the temple into a

---

[17] R. Knierim, "פֶּשַׁע pešaʿ," in *TLOT* 2:1033–37.
[18] Steinmann, *Daniel*, 405–6.

temple of Zeus. The 2,300-day period ends with the rededication and restoration of the temple as a temple of Yahweh under Judas in 164. The rededication of the temple by Judas Maccabeus is the basis of the Jewish festival of Hanukkah.

8:15–16 Verse 15a, "While I, Daniel, was watching the vision and trying to understand it," is better rendered, "When I, Daniel, had seen the vision, I sought understanding [of it]" (cf. ESV, KJV, NASB). Daniel often does not immediately understand the meaning of his visions (7:15–16; 8:15; 9:22–23; see §2). "Stood" (v. 15b) is the participle עֹמֵד ("[was] standing"), implying action simultaneous with Daniel's seeking understanding. "Appeared to be a man" (v. 15c) reads in Hebrew "like a man" (cp. "like a son of man," 7:13). In this case the "man" is actually an angel (see below) whose mediation of God's revelation underscores God's transcendence (see §3.4). "Man" (גֶּבֶר) is from a root that emphasizes might or strength. It connotes a vigorous, strong-looking man and is used in the name Gabriel (see below).

"Human voice" (v. 16a) reads in Hebrew "a voice of a man [אָדָם]" (cf. NASB). Hebrew אָדָם denotes "man, mankind." The voice is actually that of God or of another angel, perhaps the chief prince Michael (Dan 10:13; cf. Jude 1:9), who would have authority to command Gabriel. On Ulai see comments at v. 2. "Middle of the Ulai" could be rendered "between the Ulai," perhaps in the sense of "between [the banks of] the Ulai" (ESV, NASB, KJV), or it may more simply mean from above the middle of the canal.[19]

"Gabriel" (v. 16b) in Hebrew probably means "man [גֶּבֶר] of God" in accord with the use of גֶּבֶר in the previous verse, though others propose that it means "strength of God"[20] or "God is my mighty one."[21] Gabriel is mentioned twice in Daniel (8:16; 9:21) and is presumably the same angel who appears in Luke 1:19, 26. Gabriel and the angel Michael (Dan 10:13, 21; 12:1; Jude 9; Rev 12:7) are the only two angels named in Scripture. Raphael is named in the Apocrypha (e.g., Tobit 3:1; 5:4, 11), and others are named in the Pseudepigrapha and other early Jewish writings. In the Pseudepigrapha Gabriel is

---

[19] "בֵּין," *HALOT* 1:123.
[20] R. J. Bauckham, "Gabriel," *NBD*, 389.
[21] R. B. Vinson, "Gabriel," *NIDB*, 2:501.

called an "archangel" (Apocalypsis of Moses 40:1; 2 Enoch 21:3; cf. 1 Enoch 40:9–10) but is not designated an archangel in the Bible.

"Explain the vision to this man" (v. 16b) can be rendered "make this man understand [H-stem imperative of בִּין] the vision" (ESV, NKJV). On "vision" (מַרְאֶה) see v. 26 below. The pronoun "this" (הַלָּז) is rare, used only seven times in the Hebrew Bible. It may have a "strengthened demonstrative force"[22] as compared with the regular demonstrative pronoun: "that man over there/this man over here." Gabriel's explanation is an essential element in completing the process of revelation to Daniel of the message of the vision.

8:17–19 Daniel was gripped with fear or "terrified" (v. 17a) when the angel Gabriel approached him, so that he fell upon his face. "Son of man" (v. 17b) or "son of Adam/mankind" (Hebrew בֶּן־אָדָם) is an expression used ninety-three times in Ezekiel to designate the prophet. It broadly means "human being" (NCB; cf. CEB), but in this context suggests human frailty (NRSV, "O mortal"; similarly GNT) in contrast with angelic power and immortality.

"Understand" (H-stem imperative of בִּין) is the same form as "explain" in v. 16 and represents its fulfillment. "Time of the end" (v. 17c) here does not mean the "end times" in the eschatological sense, but a distant future "time of judgment" (cf. v. 19),[23] though a case can be made that Antiochus IV's actions foreshadow the end times. Daniel also calls end-time events "the time of the end" (11:40; 12:4; see §7.4). From Daniel's perspective the time of Antiochus IV and eschatological events are both distant future times of judgment.

"Fell into a deep sleep" (v. 18a) is the N-stem of רדם, a root that refers to a state of being "dazed" or "stunned," or perhaps with later Hebrew to "lie in a drugged sleep"[24] or "be overcome with sleep."[25] The sense may be that Daniel fell into a "trance" (CEB, LEB, NET) or simply "fainted" (GW, NLT). The cognate noun תַּרְדֵּמָה is used of Adam's God-induced "deep sleep" (Gen 2:21), so that Adam's rib could be made into Eve. Here this root relates, as at Dan 10:9, to

---

[22] W. Gesenius, *Gesenius' Hebrew Grammar*, 2nd ed., ed. E. Kautzsch, trans. A. E. Cowley (Oxford: Clarendon, 1910), 110, §34.f.

[23] "עֵת," *HALOT* 2:901.

[24] "רדם," *HALOT* 3:1191.

[25] "רדם," in M. Jastrow, *A Dictionary of the Targumim, the Talmud Babli and Jerushalmi, and the Midrashic Literature* (1886–1903; repr., Brooklyn: P. Shalom, 1967), 1453.

states where visions are received. The Hebrew of "made me stand up" (v. 18b) reads, "caused me to stand at the place I was standing" (cf. v. 17). In other words, the angel stands him up where he had been standing before.

"Tell you" (v. 19a) is the H-stem of יָדַע that is more precisely rendered "make known to you" (ESV) and is equivalent with Aramaic הוֹדַע (also an H-stem of יָדַע), used as a term for divine revelation (see §2). Whose "wrath" or "indignation" (זַעַם) is in view? Is it God's or that of Antiochus IV? In Daniel 11:30 the cognate verb is used of Antiochus IV's "rage against the holy covenant" of the Jews, suggesting that it is Antiochus' rage here. Even though two terms for "end" are used (אַחֲרִית and קֵץ), neither refers here to "end times" in the eschatological sense but to the time of Antiochus IV. "Conclusion of the time of wrath" (or "when the wrath is at an end," NJPS) may instead mean "at the future [time of] wrath/indignation." "Conclusion" (אַחֲרִית) often means the "end" in the sense of the indefinite future (Isa 46:10; Jer 29:11; Prov 23:18) and arguably means that here ("future time of wrath"), though אַחֲרִית is used more specifically of the "end" of the Greek kingdoms (v. 23 below) in the distant future from Daniel's perspective.

"Appointed time" (מוֹעֵד) here seems to mean "the time fixed for the end,"[26] an expression of God's sovereignty over history (see §3.8; §7.3). Habbakuk 2:3 similarly refers to a vision for the "appointed time" of Babylon's invasion of Judah.

8:20–22 Gabriel explains the meaning of what Daniel saw in vv. 3–4. It is highly significant for the identification of the four kingdoms of Daniel 2 and 7 that Media and Persia are represented here by a single animal, not two. Critical scholars in Daniel 2 and 7 typically see Daniel's second kingdom as the Medes and his third kingdom as the Persians, but the representation of the kings of Media and Persia as a single ram in Daniel 8 suggests Daniel considers Medo-Persia to be one kingdom (see Introduction).

Next Gabriel explains vv. 5–7. The goat's prominent horn represents "the king of Greece," particularly its "first king," Alexander the Great (356–323 BC), who conquered the Persian Empire from 334 to 331. "Greece" is Hebrew יָוָן, a loanword cognate with Greek "Ionia" (ἰωνιά). The Ionians were one of four major Greek tribes

---

[26] "מוֹעֵד," HALOT 2:558.

whose homeland was the Aegean Sea coastlands and its islands at the western end of Asia Minor. Their prominent cities included Ephesus, Priene, Miletus, and Didyma.[27] The Hebrew term derived from this Greek tribe/region and came by synecdoche to be used for all Greek-speaking peoples, including Alexander who was actually from Macedonia, not Ionia.

CSB simplifies the awkward Hebrew syntax of v. 22 that begins with a pending case substantive participle. The ESV/NRSV rendering is close to the original's syntax: "As for the horn that was broken, in place of which four others arose, four kingdoms shall arise from his nation, but not with his power." Gabriel here explains v. 8, describing the *diadochoi*, or "successors" of Alexander whose Greek kingdoms were individually weaker than his. See comments at v. 8 for historical details and an attempt to identify the four kingdoms.

8:23–26 CSB and some other versions (NKJV, NASB) see this section as poetry. The NRSV sees poetry through v. 25. Since these verses lack overt parallelism, the distinctive feature of Hebrew poetry, perhaps the genre should be considered at most elevated prose rather than poetry.

8:23 "Near the end of their kingdoms" (CSB) reads more precisely in Hebrew, "When their kingship nears its end," that is, the latter stage of the rule of the Greek kings. "When the rebels have reached the full measure of their sin" plausibly paraphrases the Hebrew that more simply, if ambiguously, reads something like, "when the rebels reach perfection/completion." "Rebels" (פֹּשְׁעִים) or "transgressors" (ESV, NASB) or, best, "those behaving criminally"[28] echoes the "rebellion/crime" (פֶּשַׁע) in v. 13. As in v. 13, it seems to refer to crimes against God and his people under Antiochus IV. The ambiguity of 8:23 leads some versions to substitute "rebels, transgressors, criminals" with "rebellions, transgression(s), sins" or similar (CEB, GW, LEB, NLT, NRSV, NJPS, Old Greek, Theodotion), perhaps assuming that פֹּשְׁעִים "rebels/criminals" in the MT should be revocalized to פְּשָׁעִים "rebellions/crimes."

"Ruthless" in the expression "a ruthless king" (v. 23c) reflects a Hebrew idiom, "strong of face" (עַז־פָּנִים). The exact nuance of this

---

[27] D. DeWitt Lowery, "Anatolia," in *Lexham Bible Dictionary*, ed. John D. Barry et al. (Bellingham, WA: Lexham, 2012–2014).

[28] Knierim, "פֶּשַׁע *pešaʿ*," 2.1035.

idiom is uncertain, as reflected in the range of translations among the versions and lexicons: "insolent" (NASB); "bold" (NRSV, ESV); "imprudent" (NJPS); "fierce" (NLT, NKJV, NIV, KJV); "ruthless" (CSB); "defiant, cheeky, grim-faced";[29] "fierce of countenance, (perhaps) imprudent";[30] "intense, harsh";[31] "bold, stern, hard, or insolent countenance."[32] But it clearly denotes a derogative quality. The same idiom occurs in Deut 28:50 where CSB renders it "ruthless" (of a nation).

"Skilled in intrigue" (v. 23c) or more literally one "who understands riddles" (ESV) uses חִידָה, which refers to difficult speech requiring interpretation such as Samson's riddles (Judg 14:12–20), the difficult questions that the queen of Sheba posed to Solomon (1 Kgs 10:1; 2 Chr 9:1), proverbs or parables whose meanings are not immediately obvious (Ps 49:5; Ezek 17:2), and "mysteries" from the past (Ps 78:2). Here the sense needs to be pejorative, hence CSB's (and NRSV's) rendering, "skilled in intrigue" or "skilled in misinformation."[33]

Antiochus IV lived up to these negative characteristics by falsely claiming to be divine. On the meaning of the title "Epiphanes," see comments at v. 11. Of course, not everyone was fooled. According to Polybius, some mocked Antiochus' claim to deity by calling him Epimanes, "madman," because of his erratic behavior (Polybius, *Histories* 26.1). He demonstrated intrigue when his brother Seleucus IV was murdered. With Seleucus' son Demetrius still a hostage in Rome, Antiochus assumed the throne supposedly as co-regent until an infant son of Seleucus IV, also named Antiochus, could reach maturity. Coins from the period show images of both Epiphanes and the infant Antiochus, and cuneiform documents speak of "Antiochus and Antiochus kings."[34] But, according

---

[29] "עַז," *HALOT* 2:804 and "עֹז," *HALOT* 3:939.

[30] "עַז," BDB 738.2.

[31] "עַז ('ăz)," in J. Swanson, *Dictionary of Biblical Languages with Semantic Domains: Aramaic and Hebrew (Old Testament)*, electronic ed. (Oak Harbor: Logos Research Systems, 1997), #6434.

[32] R. Wakely, "עָזַז," in *New International Dictionary of Old Testament Theology and Exegesis*, ed. W. VanGemeren (Grand Rapids: Zondervan, 1997), 3:371.

[33] G. Wilson, "חִידָה," in *New International Dictionary of Old Testament Theology and Exegesis*, 107.

[34] B. K. Waltke, "Antiochus IV Epiphanes," in *International Standard Bible Encyclopedia*, ed. G. W. Bromiley (Grand Rapids: Eerdmans, 1975), 1:145–46.

to Diodorus, a few years later the child Antiochus was murdered by Andronicus, one of Epiphanes' officials who was executed for this crime (Diodorus, *History* 30.7.2). This was probably the same Andronicus who was executed for allegedly having Onias III the high priest killed (2 Macc 4:36–44). Epiphanes likely ordered both the child and the priest murdered and then treacherously blamed his agent Andronicus for both crimes to exonerate himself.[35]

Another shrewd action by Antiochus occurred after he first invaded Egypt and captured its boy king Ptolemy VI Philometor (1 Macc 1:17–19), who happened to be Antiochus' nephew though his sister Cleopatra I. The Egyptian throne was then assumed by Ptolemy VIII Euergetes. Epiphanes invaded Egypt under the guise of returning Ptolemy VI to his rightful throne. Since Ptolemy VI was still a minor, Antiochus as his patron could have used this ruse to assume the throne through co-regency, so his nephew would have been at most a puppet king or at worst suffer a fate similar to the child Antiochus, son of Seleucus IV. This ruse was also meant to avoid triggering the mutual defense pact Egypt made with Rome since Epiphanes had Egypt's legitimate king on his side and so arguably was not really a foreign invader.

8:24 The power of Antiochus IV "will not be his own" (v. 24a). There is some doubt whether this phrase is original since Theodotion and the Old Greek lack it, thus some versions omit it (RSV, NRSV, NEB). If original, this statement may imply God's permissive will that allowed Antiochus to act, or hint at the "spiritual forces of evil" that lie behind Antiochus' rule.[36] More likely it refers to historical circumstances. Antiochus took the throne that rightly belonged first to his nephew Demetrius the son of Seleucus IV who was detained in Rome as a hostage (Polybius, *Histories* 31.12, 19; Appian, *Syriaca* 46–47) and second to Seleucus' infant son Antiochus with whom Epiphanes was co-regent for a time (see comments at v. 23).

---

[35] D. Gera, *Judaea and Mediterranean Politics: 219 to 161 B.C.E.* (Leiden: Brill, 1997), 129–30. Gera thinks the story of Onias III's murder by Andronicus is unhistorical because Josephus (*Antiquities* 12.237) seems to imply Onias III died from natural causes. But the story conflates Andronicus' murder of Onias with his murder of the co-regent child Antiochus. Alternatively, he was used by Epiphanes to kill both.

[36] R. W. Pierce, *Daniel*, Teach the Text Commentary (Grand Rapids: Baker, 2015), 143.

"Terrible destruction" (v. 24b) is better rendered, "astounding destruction" (GW). The verb (N-stem of פלא) rendered "outrageous" is from a root that refers to things beyond ordinary human ability that produce astonishment, like miraculous acts of God. His acts of destruction included his conquest and plundering of Egypt (1 Macc 1:19), his fleet's temporary conquest of Cyprus, and his devastation of Judah. Compare Dan 11:36 in which the same N-stem root is used of the things the king (the antichrist?) says about God. The statement that he would "succeed in whatever he does" (v. 24b) is hyperbole, but the thrust of it is true: early on Antiochus was very successful. Until Rome intervened it appeared that he would successfully take Egypt and occupy Cyprus. Egyptian inscriptions show that his army occupied Thebes until at least August/September 169 BC, though he never captured Alexandria.[37] After his first campaign to Egypt he returned to plunder the temple (1 Macc 1:20–24), and after the second he attempted to abolish Judaism (see comments at v. 11). Until the rise of Judas Maccabeus, Antiochus IV was able to impose his will on Judah.

"He will destroy the powerful along with the holy people" (v. 24c) finds fulfillment in the life of Antiochus IV. He was arguably responsible for the death of at least three politically "powerful" people: the high priest Onias III, his co-regent nephew Antiochus, and his official Andronicus, who was blamed for murdering the first two (see comments at v. 23). Also after his second campaign Antiochus slaughtered, according to 2 Macc 5:11–14, as many as 80,000 Jews, "young and old … boys, women, and children … young girls and infants" (2 Macc 5:13 NRSV).

8:25a "Deceit" (מִרְמָה) regularly refers to "betrayal, deceit, or treachery carried out by various parties against another party,"[38] including such things as dishonest scales (Prov 11:1), misleading and deceptive responses (Gen 34:13), dishonest words/lips (Ps 17:1), swearing falsely (Ps 24:4), false witness (Prov 12:17), and plotting evil (Prov 12:20). Such things follow from his throwing truth to the ground (cf. 8:12). "Cunning" (שֵׂכֶל) is an intellectual quality that can be either positive or negative. As a positive quality it can be

---

[37] Gera, *Judaea and Mediterranean Politics*, 138.

[38] E. Carpenter and M. A. Grisanti, "רָמה," in *New International Dictionary of Old Testament Theology and Exegesis*, 1122.

translated "insight, understanding, success," but here (and only here in the Hebrew Bible) it seems to be the negative quality of "cunning, craft."[39] On historical details of Antiochus' deceit and cunning, see comments at 11:21 and 11:23. "By his influence" reflects a Hebrew idiom, "by his hand" (cf. ESV "under his hand"). Hand can be metaphorical for power (Ps 31:15) or authority (Gen 41:35), so here may mean something like "by his authority."

Text Critical Note on 8:24–25a

The Hebrew of Dan 8:25a is awkward, suggesting that there may be a problem with the Masoretic Text. Theodotion vocalizes MT's עַל (translated "through" by the CSB) as עֹל ("yoke") instead and renders the next word as "his collar" rather than "his cunning." This perhaps reflects a confusion in the Hebrew text between the MT's שֵׂכֶל ("cunning") and כֶּבֶל ("collar") used by Theodotion's *Vorlage* Hebrew text. Theodotion's "yoke of his collar" evidently refers to oppression. Plugged into the MT this phrase could be rendered something like, "And as for his oppression, it will cause deceit to prosper," though this reading is itself somewhat awkward.

The Old Greek LXX also differs from the MT, reading "his thought [= cunning] will be against the holy ones," which suggests קְדֹשִׁים ("holy ones")—which also occurs in v. 24—originally occurred in v. 25 but was accidentally omitted by the MT textual tradition. Some scholars build on the LXX rendering and propose that "holy people" of v. 24 (עַם־קְדֹשִׁים) is misplaced and should go after עַל in v. 25a. This would result in a translation similar to NABRE, "his cunning shall be against the holy one, his treacherous conduct shall succeed." The NABRE also omits "along with the holy people" in v. 24.

Of the alternatives to the MT mentioned above, the simplest and therefore the most likely is to follow the Old Greek and merely add "holy ones" after the MT's עַל without omitting anything in verse 24. But even though the MT is awkward, and adding "holy ones" to v. 25a to solve the problem is attractive, the evidence for this emendation is hardly conclusive. Theodotion's

---

[39] "שֵׂכֶל," BDB 968.2.

Greek version reflects a corruption of the MT reading and provides no support for the Old Greek's adding of "holy ones." Accordingly, modern translations have been reluctant to adopt the emendation. My commentary on v. 25a is based on the CSB's rendering of the MT as the most likely text, but the possibility that the Old Greek more accurately preserves the original reading cannot be ruled out.

8:25b–c On "he will exalt himself" (v. 25b), the H-stem of גדל, see comments at vv. 4, 11. "In a time of peace" (v. 25c; also 11:21, 24) is Hebrew בְּ ("in, during") and שַׁלְוָה, whose glosses includes "ease, rest, tranquility, security." Perhaps the sense is "without warning" (ESV), "when they feel secure" (NIV), "when they don't expect it" (GW; cp. Old Greek, ἐξάπινα), or even "in deceit/treachery, unscrupulously" (Theodotion, δόλῳ). According to 2 Macc 5:24–26, Antiochus sent Apollonius with 22,000 troops who "pretended to be peaceably disposed and waited until the holy Sabbath day" (NRSV) before putting to the sword all those who came out to see them, killing a great number of Jews.

On "the Prince of princes" (v. 25c), compare the similar title "Prince of the host" in v. 11 and the comments at vv. 10–11. "Prince of princes" is a title for God, like "King of kings" (Rev 17:14), meaning the greatest of princes, the prince to whom other princes submit. In attacking God's people and claiming the blasphemous title "Epiphanes," Antiochus IV stood against God and failed to understand that his own kingship depended on divine allowance.

"Not by human hands" is an idiom: "by nothingness [אֶפֶס] of hand." It probably means he will be shattered "not by human power" (NIV), reflecting the metaphoric use of hand for "power" (cf. "influence" earlier in v. 25). Antiochus died by a divine act. There are several versions of his death. According to 2 Maccabees, during a military campaign into Persia when he attempted to plunder the temples of Persepolis, the people of the city rose up and attacked Antiochus and his men for the impiety of temple robbery. While he was in retreat, his bowels were struck with pain and he fell out of his racing chariot and eventually died of his injuries with worms and stench of decay (2 Macc 9:1–12). Another version in the same book says the priests and followers of the goddess Nanea in Persia killed and dismembered him (2 Macc 1:11–17). The latter account may have confused

Antiochus IV with Antiochus III, who died while raiding a temple of Bel in Elymais (see comments at Daniel 11:17–19).[40]

Other sources say that Antiochus IV attempted to take temple treasures in the region of Elymais (Elam) in Persia. He failed because of resistance by the natives and died of a disease (1 Macc 6:1–13; Appian, *Syriaca* 66; Polybius, Histories 31.11; Josephus, *Antiquities* 12.9.357–60). Jewish writers (Josephus, *Antiquities* 12.9.358; 1 Macc 6:12–13; 2 Macc 1:17; 9:18) see Antiochus' death as God's punishment for his sacrilegious plundering of Jerusalem and its temple (among other crimes). Some non-Jews also blame Antiochus' death on divine retribution, not for his defiling of Jerusalem's temple but for his plundering of the temple of the goddess Nanea (Polybius, *Histories* 31.11). While various versions of Antiochus' death are compatible with the language of Dan 8:25 ("not by human hands"), death by disease best fits Daniel's description of an act of God.

8:26 On "the evenings and mornings," see comments at vv. 13–14. "Vision" (מַרְאֶה) is a term for God's revelation (see §2) and is used here and elsewhere interchangeably with the more common word for prophetic vision, חָזוֹן (8:16–17, 26–27). God's prophetic revelations are necessarily "true" (literally, "truth," אֱמֶת). To say that a vision is אֱמֶת means that what it portends will happen, for God who reveals it is true (4:37) and knows the secrets of the future (2:27–29). Elsewhere God's word, law, and commands are also אֱמֶת (Pss 119:43, 142, 151, 160).

"Now you are to seal up the vision" (v. 26b) misses the emphasis of the Hebrew in which "you" is emphatic. Cf. NRSV, "As for you, seal up the vision." Three times Daniel is told to "seal up" (סתם) his vision (8:26; 12:4, 9). This verb is used of stopping up wells (Gen 26:15; 2 Kings 3:19, 25) and closing breaches in walls (Neh 4:7). The passive participle, "a sealed thing," can denote the hidden, inner person, the thought life that can receive wisdom (Ps 51:6). It can also denote a hidden secret that only an extraordinarily wise person like Daniel can know (Ezek 28:3). Here "sealing up" the vision means to keep it hidden or "secret" as the CSB renders the verb in 12:4, 9. In these verses the verb is parallel with חתם, which means "to seal [a document with a seal]." Since this vision was subsequently published

---

[40] J. R. Bartlett, *The First and Second Book of Maccabees*, Cambridge Bible Commentaries on the Apocrypha (Cambridge: Cambridge University, 1973), 82.

in the book of Daniel, it was not kept secret. Perhaps the sense here is that Daniel should not inquire further of Gabriel about the exact details of the meaning of the vision but should allow elements of it to remain obscure until its fulfillment.

8:27 "I, Daniel, was overcome and lay sick for days." While the general sense of this sentence is clear (the effect on Daniel is similar to other visions, 7:15; 10:17), the meaning of the Hebrew verb נִהְיֵיתִי ("I was overcome") is uncertain. The form is a rare N-stem of the verb היה that in Qal means "to be, become." The N-stem sense may indicate a "change of state,"[41] perhaps in the sense that he turned pale (cf. Dan 7:28) or that his change of state led to sickness. Theodotion may reflect this reading of the verbs by combining them to read, "having been weak/sick" (ἀσθενήσας). The Old Greek renders the first verb as "I slept" (ἐκοιμήθην), perhaps implying that Daniel fainted (KJV). However, these are not well-established meanings of the N-stem of היה. BDB takes it to mean Daniel is "finished, at an end" (a usage attested in Dan 2:1) and hence "exhausted."[42] Another possibility is that נִהְיֵיתִי should be emended to נֶהֱוֵיתִי from a different verb, הוה, that means "fell." In that case the sense is that Daniel fell down, or fell ill, hence is "stricken" (NJPS). The rest of the sentence that Daniel "lay ill for days" (or more literally "was ill for days") is clear enough and establishes overall sense.

That Daniel "got up and went about the king's business" shows Daniel was disabled by the vision only a short time before he resumed his official, governmental duties (Dan 1:5; 2:48). "Greatly disturbed" can be rendered "appalled" (ESV). Even after recovering from the initial shock, the vision continued to affect Daniel. The Qal of שמם often refers to physical devastation or desolation (Ezra 6:4; Ezek 36:35) or being psychologically "appalled" (Job 18:20). The Hitpolel of שמם is used here of being emotionally devastated or "dismayed" (NRSV). "Could not understand it" is better rendered, "there was none to explain it" (NASB; similarly NJPS). Gabriel already "explained" (8:16; H-stem of בין as here) the vision in part, but now that he was gone Daniel was left with many unanswered questions and no interpreter.

---

[41] "הָיָה (hā·yā(h))," in Swanson, *Dictionary of Biblical Languages with Semantic Domains,* #2118.

[42] "היה," BDB 227.2.

Bridge

Like Daniel 7, Daniel 8 portrays gentile empires as aggressive beasts, this time as a ram (Medo-Persia) and a wild goat (Greeks). Yet God directs history by allowing kingdoms like Persia (the ram) to flourish and fall (see §7, §7.3). This illustrates a general truth that even great and powerful empires like Persia are eventually humbled.[43] Specifically, Persia was humbled by its defeat at the hands of Alexander.

God periodically allows his people to suffer trials and persecution (8:11–14, 24–25; see §4.5). The vision does not refer to the attempt to destroy the Jewish people by Haman during the Persian period (Esther 3:6–11) but focuses instead on troubles under the Greeks (the male goat), who threatened to destroy the Jewish religion. The primary purpose of Daniel 8 was to prepare God's faithful people for a horrible persecution coming under the "little horn," Antiochus IV. Similarly, Jesus warned his disciples of persecutions that they would experience (John 16:1–4). The vision is a reminder that God remains in control (see §3.8). The evil ruler will flourish only until God's predetermined "appointed time" (8:19), after which he will be shattered (8:35c). His desecration of God's sanctuary is limited by God to "2,300 evenings and mornings" (8:14).

This prophecy about Antiochus IV illustrates a biblical-theological redemptive pattern in which kings and kingdoms exalt themselves against God and persecute his people, followed by God's deliverance of his people.[44] That pattern will culminate in God delivering his people from the antichrist (Rev 19:19–20). Antiochus in our view is like, though different from, the antichrist "little horn" of Daniel 7 (see §7.4.1). In Daniel 7 and 8 both the antichrist and Antiochus are called little horns because the latter foreshadows the former typologically. Antiochus is a prototype of the end-time antichrist, illustrating something of what that figure will be like. This is also the case in Daniel 11, in which a description of Antiochus IV (11:21–35) is followed by a description of the antichrist (11:36–45). The apostle John may well have had Antiochus IV in mind when he states that though the antichrist is coming, "even now many

---

[43] Davis, *Daniel*, 108–9.

[44] J. M. Hamilton, *With the Clouds of Heaven: The Book of Daniel in Biblical Theology*, New Studies in Biblical Theology 32 (Downers Grove: InterVarsity, 2014), 52.

antichrists have come" and that "the spirit of the antichrist ... is already in the world" (1 John 2:18; 4:3). Other figures throughout history have fit John's antichrist description, such as Pharaoh during the days of Moses, some Caesars of Rome in John's own day (cf. Rev 17:10–11), and ruthless rulers of our modern era (e.g., Mao, Hitler, and Stalin). Daniel 8 affirms the truth of Acts 14:22: "It is necessary to go through many hardships to enter the kingdom of God" (see §7.5).

Taken as genuine prophetic prediction, Daniel 8 highlights the greatness of God who foreknows and reveals the future to his prophet Daniel (see §3.5). Like all of God's revelation (see §2), biblical prophecy always proves "true" (8:26a) and gives us assurance that yet-to-be-fulfilled prophecies will also come true.

I. Court Narratives (Daniel 1–6)

II. Visions of Daniel (Daniel 7–12)
    First vision: Four beasts and son of man figure (Daniel 7)
    Second vision: Ram and male goat (Daniel 8)
    Third vision: Seventy weeks (Daniel 9)
    Daniel's prayer of confession (9:1–19)
    Gabriel's answer and seventy week prophecy (9:20–27)
    Fourth vision: Kings of North/South, distress/resurrection
    (Daniel 10–12)

  (A) Beginning of story (1:1–21)
      (B) Dream about four world kingdoms ended by the
           kingdom of God (2:1–49)
          (C) Judeans faithful in the face of death (3:1–30)
             (D) Royal pride humbled (4:1–37)
             (D') Royal pride humbled (5:1–31)
          (C') A Judean faithful in the face of death (6:1–28)
      (B') Vision about four world kingdoms ended by the
           kingdom of God (7:1–28)
          (E) Vision of Persian and Greek kingdoms to
             Antiochus (8:1–27)
          (F) Vision of seventy weeks (9:1–27)
             Part 1: Daniel's prayer of confession
             (9:1–19)
             Part 2: Gabriel's answer and seventy-
             week prophecy (9:20–27)
          (E') Vision of Persian and Greek kingdoms to
             Antiochus (10:1–11:35)
      (B'')World kingdoms ended and the righteous estab-
           lished (11:36–12:3)
  (A') End of story: Vision sealed until the end (12:4–13)

¹In the first year of Darius, the son of Ahasuerus, a Mede by birth, who was made king over the Chaldean kingdom— ² in the first year of his reign, I, Daniel, understood from the books according to the word of the Lᴏʀᴅ to the prophet Jeremiah that the number of years for the desolation of Jerusalem would be seventy. ³ So I turned my attention to the Lord God to seek him by prayer and petitions, with fasting, sackcloth, and ashes.

⁴I prayed to the Lord my God and confessed:

Ah, Lord—the great and awe-inspiring God who keeps his gracious covenant with those who love him and keep his commands— ⁵we have sinned, done wrong, acted wickedly, rebelled, and turned away from your commands and ordinances. ⁶We have not listened to your servants the prophets, who spoke in your name to our kings, leaders, fathers, and all the people of the land.

⁷Lord, righteousness belongs to you, but this day public shame belongs to us: the men of Judah, the residents of Jerusalem, and all Israel—those who are near and those who are far, in all the countries where you have banished them because of the disloyalty they have shown toward you. ⁸Lord, public shame belongs to us, our kings, our leaders, and our fathers, because we have sinned against you. ⁹Compassion and forgiveness belong to the Lord our God, though we have rebelled against him ¹⁰and have not obeyed the Lord our God by following his instructions that he set before us through his servants the prophets.

¹¹All Israel has broken your law and turned away, refusing to obey you. The promised curse written in the law of Moses, the servant of God, has been poured out on us because we have sinned against him. ¹²He has carried out his words that he spoke against us and against our rulers by bringing on us a disaster that is so great that nothing like what has been done to Jerusalem has ever been done under all of heaven. ¹³Just as it is written in the law of Moses, all this disaster has come on us, yet we have not sought the favor of the Lord our God by turning from our iniquities and paying attention to your truth. ¹⁴So the Lord kept the disaster in mind and brought it on us, for the Lord our God is righteous in all he has done. But we have not obeyed him.

¹⁵Now, Lord our God, who brought your people out of the land of Egypt with a strong hand and made your name renowned as it is this day, we have sinned, we have acted wickedly. ¹⁶Lord, in keeping with all your righteous acts, may your anger and wrath turn away from your city Jerusalem, your holy mountain; for because of our sins and the iniquities of our fathers, Jerusalem and your people have become an object of ridicule to all those around us.

[17] Therefore, our God, hear the prayer and the petitions of your servant. Make your face shine on your desolate sanctuary for the Lord's sake. [18] Listen closely, my God, and hear. Open your eyes and see our desolations and the city that bears your name. For we are not presenting our petitions before you based on our righteous acts, but based on your abundant compassion. [19] Lord, hear! Lord, forgive! Lord, listen and act! My God, for your own sake, do not delay, because your city and your people bear your name.

Context

Daniel 9:1–19 includes the prophet's earnest prayer of confession for Israel's sins. It reflects his desire for the nearly seventy-year-long Babylonian captivity, punishment for Israel's covenant violations (see §4.3), to come to an end. Following the prayer is a response by the angel Gabriel (9:20–27), who reveals that not only seventy years but also seventy weeks (of years) pertain to Israel's future. Together these two sections constitute Daniel's third vision, though the commentary will treat them separately. The prayer represents Daniel's response to the writings of Jeremiah (Dan 9:2), both his prophecy of a seventy-year captivity and his directions for what Israel in exile could do to be restored to God (Jer 29:10–14).[1]

Daniel is a man of prayer, and prayer is an important theme in the book (see §4.7). In 2:17–18 he prays to discover the mystery of Nebuchadnezzar's dream. In chapter 6 he chooses to accept a death sentence rather than cease to pray to God. Now, in 9:1–19, Daniel prays on behalf of the Jewish people, confessing their sins and interceding for them. Behind Daniel's prayer and Jeremiah's prophecy of restoration lies God's promise to restore his people whom he scattered once they confess their sin and repent (Lev 26:40–45; Deut 4:27–31; 30:2–3). His prayer is an attempt to claim this promise (see §4.3).

The whole chapter can be outlined as follows with an A-B-A structure, though further outlines of sections will be provided in the exegesis:

---

[1] G. H. Wilson, "The Prayer of Daniel 9: Reflection on Jeremiah 29," *JSOT* 48 (1990): 91–99.

A   Jeremiah's Prophecy of Seventy Years (vv. 1–3)
　　B   Daniel's Prayer of Confession and Supplication (vv.
　　　　4–19)
　　　　　　Invocation (v. 4)
　　　　　　Confession of sin (vv. 5–11b)
　　　　　　Punishment list (vv. 11c–14)
　　　　　　Supplication for forgiveness and restoration
　　　　　　(vv. 15–19)
　A′   Daniel's Prophecy of Seventy Weeks of Years (vv. 20–27)

9:1 On identifying Darius the Mede as Cyrus of Persia, see Dan 6:28 and the Introduction. In any case Darius' first year would be identical with Cyrus' first year. Babylon was taken by Medo-Persia on October 12, 539, which in the Babylonian calendar would start the regnal year—namely, year 0. Year 1 would then begin after the regnal on 1 Nisan, which was 24 March 538 BC.[2] Daniel's prayer occurs after the dust of Babylon's fall has settled a bit. He meditated on Jeremiah's prophecy of the seventy-year Babylonian captivity (v. 2; cf. Jer 25:9–11). Jeremiah predicted that God would eventually punish Babylon and its king (Jer 25:12–13), a predication fulfilled in Dan 5:30.

"Ahasuerus" reflects the Hebrew spelling of the Greek "Xerxes," both a garbling of Old Persian "Khshayarsha." The Old Greek (LXX) and the NIV render "Ahasuerus" as "Xerxes." If Darius the son of Ahasuerus is another name for Cyrus the Persian (cf. 6:28), Ahasuerus may here refer to the Median king Cyaxares, Cyrus' maternal great-grandfather whose Median name Uvakhšatara possibly can also be rendered "Ahasuerus" in Hebrew.[3] In support of this is Tobit 14:15 in which Cyaxares the father of Astyages—who, allied with Nebuchadnezzar, took Nineveh in 612—is called "Ahasuerus" in some LXX manuscripts. Alternatively, "Ahasuerus" may refer to a distant ancestor of the Achaemenid line. Wiseman suggests

---

[2] A. E. Steinmann, *Daniel*, Concordia Commentary (St. Louis: Concordia, 2008), 434.

[3] R. W. Pierce, *Daniel*, Teach the Text (Grand Rapids: Baker, 2015), 146; L. F. Hartman and A. A. Di Lella, *The Book of Daniel*, Anchor Bible (New Haven, CT: Yale University Press, 2008), 240; G. Law, *Identification of Darius the Mede* (Pfafftown, NC: Ready Scribe Press, 2010), 94–95.

that "Ahasuerus" may be an ancient Achaemenid royal title that all Achaemenid kings could claim.[4]

"Was made king" (v. 1b) is הָמְלַךְ, a Hophal (causative-passive) of מלך ("to rule"). This is the only occurrence in the Hebrew Bible of the H-passive of this root. By form it would be expected to mean, "was caused to reign" (cf. ESV, KJV, NIV, NJPS). This rendering has come into play in the discussion of the identity of Darius. By whom was Darius "caused to reign"? This could mean Darius is another name for Babylon's governor Gubaru I or Gubaru II who was made king by Cyrus. If, as seems likely, Darius is another name for Cyrus, the Hophal could mean he was made king by God as an expression of God's sovereignty (see §3.8) or made king by the army that took the city of Babylon. Alternatively, this passive form might not actually be passive in sense. Though the Masoretes vocalize the verb as a passive, neither Theodotion nor the Old Greek renders it as a passive. Some lexicographers think the H-passive could simply mean that Darius "was installed as king" in the sense that he "became king"[5] by the usual ceremony with no emphasis on the agent. Revocalized as an H-stem perfect הִמְלִךְ instead of הָמְלַךְ, it could be an internal causative, "caused himself to reign, assumed the throne," just as the H-stem of גדל ("be great") probably means, "magnified himself, caused himself to be regarded as great" (Dan 8:4, 8, 11, 25; see comments at 8:4). Given the ambiguities, one should not make too much of this Hophal passive verb. For "Chaldeans" see comments at 1:4 and 2:3–4.

9:2 "The books" are the Scriptures as a written revelation, including Jeremiah and the law of Moses (cf. v. 11). Minimally, Daniel regarded these books as authoritative writings of God's prophets. The reliability and authority of divine revelation, including predictive prophecy, are important themes in Daniel (see §2). "For the desolation" (v. 2b) is more literally plural "to fulfill/complete the desolations" (לְמַלֹּאות לְחָרְבוֹת) in which "fulfill/complete" (D-stem מלא) means either to complete a period of time (so *HALOT*;[6] NASB) or to fulfill a promise or prophecy (so NRSV). Daniel's words echo the

---

[4] D. J. Wiseman, "Some Historical Problems in the Book of Daniel," in *Notes on Some Problems in the Book of Daniel*, ed. D. J. Wiseman (London: Tyndale, 1965), 15; citing R. N. Frye, *The Heritage of Persia* (London: Weidenfeld, 1962), 97, cf. 95.

[5] "מלך," *HALOT* 2:591.

[6] "מלא," *HALOT* 2:583.

prophecy of Jer 25:11 ("desolate ruin … for seventy years"). Hebrew חָרְבָּה refers to a "site of ruins"[7]—what Nebuchadnezzar made of Jerusalem in 586 (cf. Jer 7:34; 22:5).

Daniel mulled over Jer 25:11 and 29:10, which predicted a desolation of Judah and a seventy-year exile of Jews to Babylon.[8] There are several ways of reading Jeremiah's prophecy of the seventy years. These are not mutually exclusive since Jews went into exile at various times—605/604 BC, Daniel and his friends (Dan 1:1); 597 BC, King Jehoiachin and thousands of others (2 Kgs 24:12–14); 586 BC, after the fall of Jerusalem (2 Kgs 25:21; Jer 52:25)—and later Jews returned at various times. One way of looking at Jeremiah's prophecy is to see seventy as a round number for a lifetime (Ps 90:10), essentially saying those who go into exile will never return. A second way is to see Jeremiah's seventy years as beginning from the destruction of the temple in 586 BC and ending with the rebuilding of the temple in 516 BC under Zerubbabel (Ezra 6:13–16). This may be the interpretation of Zech 1:12. A third way takes the seventy years as beginning in 605 BC after the battle of Carchemish when Babylon took control of Judah (Dan 1:1, see comments there). About sixty-six years later in 538 BC ("first year of Darius"), Daniel calculated that the seventy years of Jeremiah's prophecy must be nearly over. He may have assumed with Jeremiah that such prophecies could be shortened or lengthened depending on the presence or lack of repentance (see Jer 18:7–10). The Chronicler (2 Chr 36:20–21) agrees that Jeremiah's seventy years lasted "until the rise of the Persian kingdom," making it approximately seventy years.

9:3 "I turned my attention" conveys the Hebrew idiom, "I set my face" (KJV). Elsewhere in Daniel the prophet faces Jerusalem in prayer (6:10). "Lord" (אֲדֹנָי), or "my Lord" (CEB), occurs here and at vv. 2, 4, 7, 9, 17, and 19. Daniel often portrays God's character using titles (see §3.2). This title denotes God as one to whom his people submit as servants or subjects. Hebrew אֲדֹנָי is the word that the Masoretes regularly substituted for the divine name, leaving the consonants of "Yahweh" (YHWH, יהוה) but adding the vowels of אֲדֹנָי to indicate that the word was to be read "Adonai" instead of "Yahweh."

---

[7] "חָרְבָּה," *HALOT* 1:350.

[8] Perhaps there is also an allusion to Moses' warning of sevenfold punishment upon disobedience (Lev 26:18, 21, 24, 28). See Lester, *Daniel Evokes Isaiah*, 38.

"Yahweh" occurs in seven verses in Daniel 9 (vv. 2, 4, 8, 10, 13–14, 20) but not elsewhere in the book. Substituting אֲדֹנָי for "Yahweh" becomes customary sometime after the Babylonian exile, and the practice is reflected in the LXX, which usually translates it with Greek κύριος ("Lord"). In Dan 9:3 one might be tempted to speculate that "Lord [אֲדֹנָי] God" originally read "Yahweh God" (as in Gen 2:4). But this fails to explain why, in the same chapter, five other verses use אֲדֹנָי while יהוה remains in seven verses. More likely Daniel already reflects the postexilic custom of using אֲדֹנָי as a designation for God interchangeable with, and increasingly used in place of, "Yahweh."

"Seek" (D-stem בקש) represents Daniel's appropriation of the promise that God had plans for the welfare of his exiled people (Jer 29:11). Daniel did what Jeremiah exhorted Israel to do: He called on God in prayer from the exile so that God would listen (Jer 29:12). Jeremiah directed Israel to "search [Qal בקש] for [God] with all your heart" (Jer 29:13). "Prayer" (תְּפִלָּה) is a way to "seek" God—to find him personally (Deut 4:29; Isa 65:1; Jer 29:13), request his favor or protection (Zech 8:22; Ezra 8:21), or express remorse in repentance (Jer 50:4). The Hebrew word can mean a plea for help (Pss 39:12; 55:1), an intercession (2 Kgs 19:4; Pss 35:13; 109:4; Jer 7:16), an act of worship (Ps 141:2), a pouring out of feelings to God (Hab 3:1 [cp. rest of chapter]), a priestly blessing (2 Chr 30:27), or a curse against the wicked (Ps 141:5). Some of the psalms of lament are labeled in their superscripts as a תְּפִלָּה (Psalms 17, 86, 90, 102, 142). The prayer that follows expresses confession and repentance of sin on behalf of Daniel's people. "Petitions" (תַּחֲנוּנִין; always plural; also vv. 17, 18, 23) is a synonym for prayer (cf. Ps 147:1) and related to the root חנן ("show grace, favor"). It seems to connote a "pleading for grace/favor/mercy," like a cry for help (Ps 31:22), a begging for money (Prov 18:23), or a plea for mercy (Job 40:27).

"Fasting" (צוֹם) often accompanies earnest prayer in the Bible. Moses, Elijah, and Jesus all experienced forty-day fasts (Exod 34:28; 1 Kgs 19:8; Matt 4:2; Luke 4:2). Daniel fasted in preparation for prayer (Dan 9:3; see also 10:3). By fasting, worshipers seek to avert or end a calamity by eliciting God's compassion, displaying their humility, sorrow, and (if necessary) repentance. David sought (but failed) to avert the death of Bathsheba's baby by fasting and prayer (2 Sam 12:16–23). Ahab mitigated his punishment because he fasted and humbled himself (1 Kgs 21:27–29). The king of Nineveh declared a fast for man and beast, and God relented of his announced judgment (Jonah 3:5–10). Fasting humbles human pride and psychologically represents dedication of oneself to God. There are various types of fasts, from a complete fast to a partial fast, such as abstaining from choice foods (Dan 10:2–3), or like Muslims at Ramadan fasting only during daylight hours. The only fast day recorded in the Pentateuch was the Day of Atonement (Lev 16:29, 31; 23:27–32; "practice self-denial" ["afflict yourselves," ESV] means fasting). After the exile Zechariah speaks of fast days of the fourth, fifth, seventh, and tenth months (Zech 5; 7:3; 8:19) that may relate to stages in the Babylonian capture of Jerusalem and the destruction of the temple. Other fasts, as here in Daniel, are spontaneous.

"Sackcloth and ashes" accompany fasting and prayer as outward signs of humiliation, mourning, and/or repentance. Compare Psalm 35:13: "Yet when they were sick, my clothing was sackcloth; I humbled myself with fasting, and my prayer was genuine." "Sackcloth" (שַׂק) is a cheap, coarse cloth usually made from goat's hair (*Sifra* 53a) or camel's hair.[9] It was typically black in color (Rev 6:12) and worn during times of mourning (2 Sam 3:31) or in conjunction with earnest prayer (2 Kgs 19:1–2). The humiliation could be more pronounced by sprinkling ashes and/or dust on the head (2 Sam 13:19; Esth 4:1; Ezek 27:30; 1 Macc 3:47).

9:4a The etymology of the verb "to pray" (HtD of פלל) is disputed. Traditionally it has been related to the noun פָּלִיל, "judge, assessment" (whose meaning is also disputed), and taken to mean "to seek a favorable judgment/assessment for oneself." Whatever its etymology, it is often used of intercessory prayer, as here. Daniel prays on the basis of his personal, covenant relationship with God ("my God"; also vv. 18–20; see §4.3). "Confessed" (HtD ידה), though sometimes used of praise (2 Chr 30:22), is more often used of confession of sin (Lev 5:5; Dan 9:20; Neh 1:6). Identifying with his people, Daniel confessed Israel's sins and may have been intentionally following the directions of Lev 26:40–45. If Israel acted unfaithfully toward the Lord and incurred his wrath, he promised to remember his covenant, provided that they confess their sin and the sin of their fathers (see §4.3).

---

[9] B. B. Schmidt, "Sackcloth," *NIDB*, 5:16.

9:4b While CSB prints 9:4b–19 as poetry, it is best viewed as elevated prose. The prayer includes an invocation (4b), a confession of sin (vv. 5–11a), the effects of sin (vv. 11b–14), and an appeal for mercy (vv. 15–19).[10] McLain proposes[11] that 9:5–11b and 11c–14 each have a chiastic structure:

A   Sin list (v. 5)
   B   Failure to listen (v. 6)
      C   God's character (v. 7a)
         D   Israel's character (v. 7b)
            E   Vocative address "O YHWH!" (v. 8a)
         D′   Israel's character (v. 8b)
      C′   God's character (v. 9)
   B′   Failure to listen (v. 10)
A′   Sin list (v. 11a–b)

A   The punishment is poured out on Israel (v. 11c)
   B   God confirms the punishment (vv. 12–13a)
      C   Israel is guilty before God (v. 13c)
   B′   YHWH watches the punishment (v. 14a)
A′   God brought the punishment on Israel (v. 14b)

"Ah" is אָנָּא. Like English "Oh!" it is a sigh that precedes a statement.[12] On "Lord" see comments at v. 3. "God" is not אֱלֹהִים but אֵל, a Semitic term for deity with cognates in Ugaritic, Akkadian, and Arabic. It occurs 238 times in the Hebrew Bible.[13] It is found in unusual designations for God during the time of the patriarchs: אֵל עֶלְיוֹן, "God Most High" (Gen 14:18), אֵל שַׁדַּי, "God Almighty" (17:1), אֵל עוֹלָם, "the Everlasting God" (21:33), and הָאֵל בֵּית־אֵל, "the God of Bethel" (31:13). It also occurs in proper names (Bethel, "House of *El*"; Ishmael, "*El* hears"; Immanuel, "*El* is with us"; Daniel, "*El* is [my] judge"). Daniel may have used אֵל rather than אֱלֹהִים because, though there are exceptions (e.g., Neh 8:6), the former

---

[10] C. E. McLain, "Daniel's Prayer in Chapter 9," *Detroit Baptist Seminary Journal* 9 (2004): 276.

[11] Ibid., 304.

[12] "אָנָּא," *HALOT* 1:70.

[13] W. H. Schmidt, "אֵל *ʾēl*," in *TLOT* 1:108.

more readily lends itself to adjectives of divine attributes ("great, awe-inspiring").[14]

To say God is "great" incorporates all his wonderful attributes and deeds. He shows his greatness by his mighty acts, delivering Israel from Egypt, forgiving them, and listening to their prayers (Deut 3:24; 9:26; Num 14:19; Ps 79:11). He demonstrates greatness in his role as king (1 Chr 29:11; Mal 1:14) and in his revelations to his people (2 Sam 7:21). He is great because there is no one like him and no God besides him (2 Sam 7:22–23; 2 Chr 2:5).[15] In this context "great and awe-inspiring" may be a hendiadys meaning simultaneously "greatly awe-inspiring" and "awe-inspiringly great." "Awe-inspiring" (נוֹרָא) is an N-stem participle from a root meaning to "be afraid." Formally, נוֹרָא would mean someone/something "feared" or "fearsome." While God produces cringing fear in his enemies when he is angry (Pss 66:3; 76:7), fear of God is not meant to produce terror in his people but a respect that results in obedience, trust, and worship (Exod 20:18; 1 Sam 12:14, 24; Job 1:8; 28:28; Pss 15:4; 33:18; 128:1; Prov 3:7; 8:13). It is the fear or respect a subject should show to a great king (Ps 47:3). The same root denotes God's works that are "awe-inspiring" (Exod 34:10) so that he should be "revered" (נוֹרָא) in his people's praises (Exod 15:11).

"Who keeps his gracious covenant with those who love him and keep his commands" underscores the important theme of God's good, gracious character (see §3.6), as well as the theme of covenant in this chapter (see §4.3), echoing Deut 7:9 and 1 Kgs 8:23 (cf. Neh 1:5; 9:32). The phrase more literally reads "who keeps the covenant and grace," which CSB takes to be a hendiadys for "his gracious covenant." The word rendered "gracious" (חֶסֶד) is notoriously difficult to translate precisely. Nelson Glueck argues that it primarily means "merited obligations, rights, and duties" rather than "grace."[16] But scholarship subsequent to Glueck, while accept-

---

[14] The expression, "great [גָּדוֹל] and awe-inspiring [נוֹרָא] God [אֵל]," also occurs at Deut 7:21 and Neh 1:5 (cp. Neh 9:32, which adds "mighty"). The same modifiers (גָּדוֹל and נוֹרָא) are used of Yahweh in 2 Chr 16:25 and of אֲדֹנָי in Neh 4:14. In Ps 47:3 Yahweh is "awe-inspiring" and a "great" king. In Ps 89:7 אֵל is called "awe-inspiring," and אֱלֹהִים is awe-inspiring in Ps 68:35.

[15] E. Jenni, "גָּדוֹל gādôl," in *TLOT* 1:304.

[16] N. Glueck, *Ḥesed in the Bible*, trans. A. Gottschalk (Cincinnati: Hebrew Union College Press, 1967), 7–55.

ing his view that חֶסֶד is a term related to covenants or relationships, has tended to back away from his emphasis on merit, rights, and mutual obligation.[17] Spieckermann argues cogently that the semantic range of חֶסֶד includes grace, mercy, compassion, kindness, and love. "God's self-determination towards love" is the foundation not only of NT theology (as one might expect), but also of OT theology (cf. Exod 34:6–7).[18] John 1:14, 17 seems to echo חֶסֶד וֶאֱמֶת of Exodus 34:6 ("faithful love and truth" CSB), rendering חֶסֶד with Greek χάρις, "grace."[19] Thus the CSB's emphasis in Dan 9:4 on grace in its rendering of חֶסֶד here is defensible, though as with all renderings of חֶסֶד it does not quite catch the whole breadth of its nuances.

God's people are "those who love him and keep his commandments." This implies that he keeps the related covenant promise of land to the descendants of Abram/Abraham (Gen 15:18; Exod 6:4). Daniel and his people were now separated from that land but were looking for God to restore that promise.

9:5 "Sinned, done wrong, acted wickedly" reflects the theological theme that God holds people accountable for their sins (see §4.2). Daniel's wording clearly echoes Solomon's prayer during the temple dedication, when he spoke of Israel's future repentance in exile for sinning against God (1 Kgs 8:47).[20] In contrast with God who had been faithful (v. 4), Daniel's people had sinned greatly in degree and kind. "Sinned" (חטא; also vv. 8, 11, 15) has to do with missing God's standard or deviating from his norms. "Done wrong" (עוה) is a verb cognate with the noun "iniquities" in v. 13 (see comments there). "Acted wickedly" (H-stem of רשע; also v. 15 in Qal "be guilty, wicked") is a verb whose cognate noun refers to people who commit violence and oppression (Pss 71:4; 94:4–6; Prov 10:6, 11; 12:10;

---

[17] K. Sakenfeld, "Love (OT)," *ABD* 4:377; R. L. Harris, "חֶסֶד, *Ḥesed*," in *TWOT* 1:305–7. S. Romerowski, "Que signifie le mot *ḥesed*?" *VT* 40 (1990): 89–103, argues that the word means "kindness, benevolence, affection, friendship, love, favor, grace, mercy or piety" rather than loyalty or mutual obligations. On the other hand, H. –J. Zobel, "חֶסֶד, *Ḥesed*," in *TDOT* 5:44–64, argues, "The one who receives an act of חֶסֶד *ḥesed* is justified in expecting an equivalent act in return" (47).

[18] H. Spieckermann, "God's Steadfast Love: Towards a New Conception of Old Testament Theology," *Biblica* 81 (2000): 305–27.

[19] See J. M. Sprinkle, *Biblical Law and Its Relevance* (Langdon, MD: University Press of America, 2006), 32–36.

[20] J. M. Hamilton, *With the Clouds of Heaven: The Book of Daniel in Biblical Theology*, New Studies in Biblical Theology 32 (Downers Grove: InterVarsity, 2014), 107.

21:7). "Wicked" (רשע) is the most important OT antonym to being righteous (צדק).[21] "Rebelled" (מרד; also v. 9) can be used of political revolts (Neh 6:6; 2 Kgs 18:7; 24:1) but here refers to rebelling against God's authority.

To "turn away" (סור; also v. 11) from God's commandments is to turn away from God (Ezek 6:9) and is the opposite of turning away from evil (Prov 3:7). Turning away from God's commands can refer specifically to apostasy/idolatry (Exod 32:8; Deut 9:12; 11:16), an offense that brought on the exile (2 Kgs 22:17; 2 Chr 34:25; Jer 41:23) and that tempted Jews during the exile (cf. Dan 3:14–15). God's "ordinances" (מִשְׁפָּטֶי) is a term found in Exod 21:1 to describe the norms of God's law, whether moral, civil, or cultic-ceremonial.[22] "Turned away from your commands and ordinances" may echo Lev 26:15–16, which indicates such things would lead to judgment and exile.

9:6 Not listening to God's prophets (v. 6) underscores the theological importance of God's revealed word (see §2) and our acountability to it (see §4.2). Ignoring God's spokesmen helped bring on the exile (2 Chr 36:15–19; Jer 44:4–5), for it was committed by "kings, leaders, fathers, and all the people of the land" (language that echoes Jer 37:2 and 44:21). The kings of Israel and Judah were not faithful to God, with a few exceptions (Asa, Jehoshaphat, Hezekiah, Josiah), nor were others of the aristocratic class (cf. Jer 5:1–5). On "leaders" or "officers" (NJPS), the plural of שַׂר, see comments at 8:11. "Fathers" (אָבֹת) in this context means "ancestors" (NIV). "The people of the land" might refer to "common people," as CSB sometimes renders the expression (e.g., Lev 4:27), but more probably refers here to landed, wealthy classes who during the monarchy could depose or install kings or make covenants to free all slaves (2 Kgs 21:24; 23:30; Jer 34:19). This seems to be the meaning the expression has in Jer 37:2 and 44:21, which Daniel (meditating on Jeremiah, Dan 9:2) echoes.

9:7 Part of God's goodness (see §3.6) is his attribute of "righteousness." Righteousness (צְדָקָה) or "what is right" (NJPS) is a characteristic of a "righteous" (צַדִּיק) person. In legal contexts, the צַדִּיק is the one who is acquitted, the one declared "innocent"

---

[21] C. van Leeuwen, "רשע rš‘," in *TLOT* 3:1262.

[22] J. M. Sprinkle, *'The Book of the Covenant': A Literary Approach*; JSOTSup 174 (Sheffield: JSOT Press, 1994), 204.

(Deut 25:1 CSB). A righteous man "does what is just [מִשְׁפָּט] and right [צְדָקָה]" (Ezek 18:5) and walks in the ways of the Lord (Hos 14:9). Righteousness thus stands for moral norms that reflect God's character, including God's mercy and compassion (see comments at vv. 16 and 18 below). God credited "righteousness" to Abram for his faith even before he obeyed (Gen 15:6; cf. Hab 2:4; Rom 4:1–4). A righteous person meets the claims another has upon him, resulting in a right, harmonious relationship. The relationship aspect of "righteousness"[23] is seen in Genesis 15 when, in conjunction with declaring Abram righteous, God established a formal covenant with him. A harmonious relationship is possible with God when he declares a person righteous in the forensic sense of "declared not guilty."

There is a sharp contrast between God and his people: "righteousness belongs" to him, but "public shame [בֹּשֶׁת] belongs" to them. "Public shame" reflects the Hebrew idiom "shame of face." This probably means that Daniel and his people have a visible "face filled with shame."[24] The righteous person evades shame by dispensing justice instead of doing what is wrong. The unrighteous know no shame (Zeph 3:5). Israel's sins, including shameful idolatry (Hos 9:10), brought the shame of exile upon them (Ezra 9:7; Dan 9:8).

This guilt applied to all of Daniel's people, both those still in the land of Israel ("those who are near") and those in exile like Daniel ("those who are far"). Jewish exiles were not only in Babylonia but also in Egypt (Jer 44:1). "Disloyalty they have shown" uses the noun מַעַל and its cognate verb מעל in a typical Hebrew style of redundancy: "in their disloyalty in which they have shown disloyalty against you." What "disloyalty," "unfaithfulness" (NIV, NASV), or "treachery" (NRSV) is in mind? In ritual texts מעל regularly means "to commit sacrilege" against God through illicit offerings, idolatry, defiling consecrated things, defiling the temple, or swearing falsely in an exculpatory oath (2 Chr 26:16–18; 28:19, 22–24; 29:19; 36:14; Lev 5:14–16; 6:1–7).[25] A secular instance of מעל is a wife being sexually unfaithful to her husband (Num 5:12), though this may also be sacrilege since adultery is a violation of the marriage vow made before God. Other examples of מעל include deceptive or treacherous

---

[23] B. Johnson, "צדק ṣdq," in *TDOT* 12:244, 259–60.

[24] "בֹּשֶׁת," *HALOT* 1:165.

[25] J. Milgrom, *Leviticus*, AB 3, 3A, 3B, 3 vols. (New York: Doubleday, 1991–2000), 1:345–56, 2:1327.

words (Job 21:34), a king rendering an unjust verdict (Prov 16:10), and Jews marrying foreign wives (Neh 13:27). These examples illustrate the sort of מַעַל that Daniel had in mind.

9:8–10 "Lord" (v. 8a) is the divine name "Yahweh," which in this chapter alternates with the title "Lord." See comments at v. 4. On "public shame" see comments at v. 7. On "kings/leaders/fathers" see comments at v. 6. Israel's sin included the people in general ("us"), but its leaders were especially guilty since they could have used their influence and authority to stop Israel's sin and idolatry. Instead they participated in it. Compare v. 6.

"Compassion" (v. 9a) or "mercy" (ESV) (רַחֲמִים, always plural; see §3.6) is frequently attributed to God in prayers (e.g., Pss 25:6; 40:11; 51:1; Lam 3:22; Neh 9:19). When Solomon threatened to cut the child in half and divide it between two prostitutes, the true mother expressed רַחֲמִים (1 Kgs 3:26). Joseph showed רַחֲמִים when he was overcome with emotion over seeing his brother Benjamin after many years (Gen 43:30). Feelings of רַחֲמִים in the sense of pity or mercy might lead someone to release a prisoner (Gen 43:14) or to avert one's anger (Deut 13:17). God's compassion could result in forgiving his people's sins and allowing them to return from exile to the land (1 Kgs 8:50).

"Forgiveness" סְלִחוֹת (v. 9a) is one aspect of God's saving his people (see §4.5). The verb סלח ("forgive, pardon") occurs in v. 19. The noun is plural in its three occurrences in the Hebrew Bible, being a plural of abstraction ("forgivenesses," meaning "forgiveness"), though the singular does occur in Rabbinic Hebrew. The plural in Rabbinic Hebrew and the cognate of סלח in both Akkadian and Aramaic can mean to "sprinkle, pour out" in rituals that convey purification. The meaning "forgive" may have developed out of this usage.[26] In the Hebrew Bible the root סלח expresses divine forgiveness; it is not used of human forgiveness. Combined with רַחֲמִים, the pair forms a hendiadys that describes God as one who forgives on the basis of pity/mercy rather than human merit (cf. v. 18 below). He also forgives on the basis of his covenant relationship with Israel (also vv. 10, 13, 14, 15, 17, 18), their repentance (v. 13), and atoning sacrifice (v. 27).

---

[26] J. J. Stamm, "סלח slḥ," in *TLOT* 3:797.

On "rebel" (v. 9b) see comments at v. 5. "Obeyed," שָׁמַע (v. 9b), has to do with "hearing" or "listening to" and often means heeding what God says. On "following" or "walking in" (ESV), see comment at v. 11. "Instructions" (v. 10) is plural of תּוֹרָה, traditionally rendered "law" (cf. KJV, ESV). This term denotes the totality of God's regulations which were mediated through the prophets. This verse echoes the book of Jeremiah, which says repeatedly that not obeying God through his "servants the prophets" leads to disaster and exile (Jer 7:25–26; 25:3–7; 29:19; 32:23; 35:15; 44:2–6). In the eighth century the northern tribes went into Assyrian exile for much the same reasons (2 Kgs 17:13–20; 18:11–12).

9:11–12 "Broken" (v. 11a) is עבר, traditionally rendered "transgressed." It is a verb of motion that conveys the imagery of "passing by, crossing." To transgress God's law is to violate it. It is the opposite of "following" or "walking in" (ESV) God's law (v. 10), and is parallel in imagery with "turned away" in the same verse. "Law" is the same word rendered in v. 10 "instruction." On "turned away" see v. 5. The Hebrew of "refusing to obey you" reads "not heeding your voice," the same idiom as v. 10. "Promised curse" (v. 11b) is more literally "the curse and the oath" (CSB note).

"Curse, oath" (אָלָה) and "oath, swearing" (שְׁבֻעָה) are near synonyms. Here אָלָה places more emphasis on God's solemn promises and warnings closely associated with his covenant (Deut 29:12, 14), while שְׁבֻעָה places more emphasis on the process of swearing an oath. Together these terms form a hendiadys meaning "the sworn curse."[27] God in the Mosaic law swore that he would bless Israel if they obeyed the covenant commands (Lev 26:3–12; Deut 28:9, 11), but he correspondingly warned of various curses for disobedience, culminating in expulsion from the land (Lev 26:14–33, esp. v. 33; Deut 28:15–68, esp. vv. 63–64). This curse would allow the land to make up for neglected years of Sabbath rest; it would lie desolate for the corresponding number of years (Lev 26:34–35, 43). Sadly, God's sworn curses were fulfilled after good King Josiah died. Judah's sins and idolatry (2 Chr 34:24–28) brought seventy years of desolation.

The Hebrew for "our rulers" (v. 12) reads more redundantly, "our rulers/judges who judged/ruled us" (cf. CSB note). The verb שׁפט can refer to settling disputes (Exod 18:13). As a participle, it

---

[27] "שְׁבֻעָה, שְׁבוּעָה," *HALOT* 4:1385.

can describe court judges (Deut 25:1) and leaders like those of the book of Judges who delivered Israel (Judg 2:16). Like its Akkadian cognate *šapīṭu*, the Hebrew participle שֹׁפֵט can, and here does, refer to other high administrative officials ("rulers"). In Isaiah 39:6–7 the ruler Hezekiah is told that his treasures and his descendants would someday be taken to Babylon.

"Disaster" is Hebrew רָעָה ("evil, misfortune, calamity"). It is used to speak of such things as the devastation of a city (Gen 19:19; Jonah 3:10 [cf. v. 4]; Judg 20:40–41), the death of a son (Gen 44:29), or the destruction of a people (Exod 32:14). God warned Judah and Jerusalem through the prophet Jeremiah of the coming "disaster" (רָעָה) due to their covenant violations (Jer 11:10–12, 17; 19:3, 15; 35:17). This disaster was unlike ("nothing like what has been done") any previous calamity in Jerusalem (perhaps alluding to Ezek 5:9). It was fulfilled when Nebuchadnezzar invaded Judah and burned Jerusalem in August of either 587 or 586 BC[28] (Jer 21:11; 44:2). That nothing like this had ever been done "under heaven" previously is hyperbole, but the truth is that Babylon's destruction of Jerusalem was horrific (2 Kgs 25:8–10; 2 Chr 36:18–19). Although not every place in Jerusalem or the surrounding country was devastated, clear archaeological evidence, specifically in the hill country (Jerusalem, Tell Beit Mirsim, Beth Shemesh, Lachish, Ramat Raḥel, Tell el-Fûl), reflects Nebuchadnezzar's terrible destructions.[29]

9:13–14 On "as it is written in the law of Moses" (v. 13a) see comments at v. 11. The Hebrew of "sought the favor of the Lord" (v. 13b) is an idiom meaning something like "softened/weakened [D-stem חלה] the face of" in the metaphorical sense of soothing God's angry face. Hezekiah did this and averted disaster from God (Jer 26:19), as did his wicked son Manasseh at the end of his life (2 Chr 33:12). Jehoiakim and Zedekiah did not.

"Turning" (v. 13c; שׁוב) is the verb commonly used to describe repentance (often in Jeremiah: e.g., 3:12, 14; 4:1; 5:3; 8:5; 15:19). Hence NJPS renders it, "repent of our iniquity." Genuine repentance

---

[28] D. J. Wiseman, *Nebuchadrezzar and Babylon* (Oxford: Oxford University Press, 1985), 36–37.

[29] Hans M. Barstad, "After the 'Myth of the Empty Land': Major Challenges in the Study of Neo-Babylonian Judah," in *Judah and the Judeans in the Neo-Babylonian Period*, ed. O. Lipschitz and J. Blenkinsopp (Winona Lake, IN: Eisenbrauns, 2003), 3–20, esp. p. 6.

requires a change of direction, turning from sin and to God. "Iniquities" is the plural of עָוֹן, a common word (231 times) for sin in the Bible. It is derived from the verb עוה ("do wrong") used in v. 5. The noun is thus an act of עוה. The verb is used in the N-stem to mean "to be bent" (Ps 38:7) and in the D-stem and HtD of twisting or making crooked or perverse (Isa 24:1; Lam 3:9; Job 33:27).

"Paying attention to your truth" is better rendered, "gaining insight by your truth" (ESV). "Paying attention" weakly renders the H-stem of שׂכל that has to do with having insight or gaining understanding, something Daniel excelled at (cf. comments at 1:4, 17). Instead of sinning, Israel should have attended to and learned from God's "truth" (אֱמֶת), found in his word, law, and commands (Ps 119:43, 142, 151, 160). On אֱמֶת see comments at 8:26.

On "disaster" (רָעָה; v. 14a) see comments at v. 12. "Kept ... in mind" is from שקד which is probably more accurately rendered "kept watch [over the disaster]" (NRSV; cf. Job 21:32). As often in his prayer, Daniel draws on the language of Jeremiah which in turn clarifies the meaning here. In Jeremiah God says, "I watch [שקד] over my word to accomplish it. ... Disaster [רָעָה] will be poured out from the north" (Jer 1:12, 14). Again, "I watched [שקד] over them to uproot and to tear them down, to demolish and to destroy, and to cause disaster [H-stem of רעה which is cognate with רָעָה]" (Jer 31:28), and "I am watching over them for disaster [רָעָה] and not for good" (Jer 44:27). God "watches over the disaster" in the sense that he pays attention to his curse of disaster for covenant violations (cf. v. 11 above). On "righteous" (v. 14b) see comments at v. 7. "Not obeyed him" can be rendered "not heeded his voice" as in vv. 10–11.

9:15–16 The prayer in vv. 15–19 finally gets to the request Daniel is making of God: that God turn away his anger and allow his people to return and restore the desolate temple sanctuary. That this forgiveness is possible is promised in Scripture (Lev 26:40–45; Deut 30:1–10; 1 Kgs 8:46–53), including the prophecy of Jeremiah (29:12–14) on which Daniel has meditated. On "Lord" and "our God" (v. 15a), see comments at vv. 3 and 9a.

The exodus was God's great saving act and is a major theological motif in the OT, portraying God as savior of his people (see §4.5). In conjunction with the exodus, God established a covenant relationship with Israel (Exod 24:7–8; see §4.3) wherein he was their God and they were his people (Exod 6:7; Lev 26:12–13). "Strong hand" (also Exod 13:9; Deut 5:15) refers to God's use of extraordinary measures (signs and wonders) as a means of revelation (see §2). These were necessary to force stubborn Pharaoh to let Israel go (Exod 3:19–20; Jer 32:21). The exodus established God's reputation ("made your name renowned") as Israel's mighty Savior.

On "sinned" (v. 15c) see comments at v. 5. "Acted wickedly" renders the Qal of רשׁע, used in the H-stem in v. 5, though the change of stem suggests the meaning may be somewhat different. It seems best to render the Qal here with a stative meaning: "have been wicked" (NASB) or "are guilty" (NABRE). On the root רשׁע see comments at v. 5. Israel's special relationship as God's people was contingent on obedience to the covenant (Exod 19:5; Lev 26:3, 11–13; Jer 11:4). All Israel could do now was confess their sins and beg for God's mercy.

"Righteous acts" (v. 16a) renders the plural of צְדָקָה ("righteousness"), though the meaning is unusual since a righteous judge is normally constrained to condemn the wicked (1 Kgs 8:32). Daniel appeals to God's righteousness in the sense of God's divine mercy (so Theodotion's rendering, ἐλεεμοσύνη, "[acts of] mercy, benevolence"). A truly righteous person out of compassion, sympathy, or loyalty will at times show mercy, as Joseph "being a righteous man" decided to divorce Mary secretly when he discovered she was pregnant (Matt 1:19). In addition, it is righteous to keep one's promises. God through Jeremiah seems to limit Jerusalem's desolation to seventy years (9:2). So in keeping with God's righteous acts he should keep that word.

"Anger and wrath" (v. 16b) is a hendiadys for "raging anger" (CEB, NET; cf. NJPS "wrathful fury"). The sins of the ancestors bringing "anger and wrath" against Jerusalem echoes Jer 32:31–32a, which uses the same terms for God's rage (אַף and חֵמָה). Daniel in effect asks for a reversal of Jer 32:31–32. There is an emphatic, even begging tone to this request for God's wrath to "turn away" (יָשָׁב־נָא) in that it is strengthened with the emphatic particle נָא־. Most EVVs leave it untranslated, but some render it "please" (CEB, LEB, NET). "Your holy mountain" is Mount Zion (Pss 2:6; 48:1–2). Specifically it refers to the temple mount, though by synecdoche it often (as here) refers to the whole city of Jerusalem. The expression emphasizes that Jerusalem is the site of God's temple abode. Jeremiah also prophesies of the restoring of the fortunes of God's "holy mountain" (Jer

31:23). On "sins" see comments at v. 5. On "iniquities" see comments at v. 13. On "fathers" or "ancestors" (NIV), see vv. 6 and 8.

9:17 On "prayer" and "petitions" (v. 17a), see comments at v. 3. "Hear" is an anthropomorphism; see comments at v. 18 below. Daniel speaks of himself as God's "servant." Since he also speaks of prophets and Moses as servants of God (vv. 6, 10, 11), his statement here may include himself in their rank. It's more likely though that he focuses on himself as God's servant in that his righteousness might make the prayer more effective (Ps 145:19; John 9:31; Jas 5:16). The anthropomorphic metaphor, "make your face to shine on," is also used in the Aaronic blessing (Num 6:25) and means, in effect, "look with favor on" (NIV). When someone's face "lights up" to see you, that means he or she is favorably disposed toward you. God's shining face can result in deliverance or salvation (Pss 31:16; 80:3, 7, 19). "Desolate" (שָׁמֵם) can mean to be uninhabited or deserted. The temple area was so desolated after its destruction by Nebuchadnezzar that no one came to it and wild beasts began to inhabit it (Lam 1:4; 5:18).

"For the Lord's sake" (v. 17c) is literally, "for the sake of *my* Lord [אֲדֹנָי]" (cf. comments v. 3) in which "my Lord" contextually can mean "you." This probably means God should act "for *your* own sake." Theodotion and the Old Greek read, "for your sake, O Lord" which could be a paraphrase of what the MT reads or reflect a text that has an additional kaph, לְמַעֲנָךְ, as compared with the MT's לְמַעַן. This alternative text is adopted by some versions (ESV, NASB, RSV). An alternative interpretation of the MT is that Hebrew לְמַעַן "for the sake of, because of" connects the sanctuary's destruction to God as causal agent: "[look favorably on your] sanctuary that is made desolate, *by* the Lord" (Jubilee Bible, italics mine), rather than the showing of favor "for the sake of my Lord." Against this alternative view is that at this stage of the prayer, a reason for grace seems more fitting than an explanation of the destruction. As to why restoring his people and sanctuary are for God's own sake, see v. 19.

9:18 "Listen closely ... hear. ... Open your eyes ... see" (v. 18a) are further anthropomorphisms (see v. 17). "Desolations" (v. 18b) is a Qal participle of שמם (also 9:26). Similar to v. 17, this may refer to the desolations of the land of Judah and Jerusalem (Dan 9:26; cf. Isa 64:10). Alternatively, שמם may be used in the psychological sense of being horrified, appalled, or stiff with fear (Lev 26:32; Jer 18:16; Job

18:20). So "our desolations" may refer to the emotional devastation experienced by God's people. The expression "city that bears your name" (v. 18c) echoes Jer 25:29 which follows the prophecy of a seventy-year Babylonian captivity on which Daniel has been meditating (Jer 25:11; cf. Dan 9:2). Anything called by God's name belongs to him. Zion-Jerusalem was called the "city of God" because God's dwelling place was there (1 Kgs 8:43; Pss 46:4; 48:1–2; Jer 7:11). Moreover, it was the capital of the people of Israel who were also called by God's name (cf. v. 19 below; Deut 28:10; 2 Chr 7:14; Jer 14:9). Israel lacked sufficient "righteous acts" (v. 18c) to merit God's forgiveness (cf. vv. 5–11, 13–15). This is in contrast with God's "righteous acts" (v. 16; see comments there), which include his mercy and "compassion."

9:19 Daniel piles up synonyms for hearing in vv. 18–19: "Listen closely" (v. 18), "hear" (vv. 17, 18, 19; שמע), and "listen" (v. 19; H-stem קשב). He asks God to act for his "own sake" to bring the exile to an end, since God's "name" (v. 19c), and hence his reputation, was associated with the people, city, and temple (see comments at v. 18). Their humiliation humiliates God. Moreover, allowing his people to continue to suffer and his city to remain in ruins runs contrary to his promise limiting this desolation to seventy years (Jer 25:11; 29:10; cf. Dan 9:2). If God failed to keep this promise it would sully his reputation even further. Daniel therefore urges God to act immediately to remedy the suffering of his people and the desolation of his holy city.

Bridge

Prayer is an important theme in Daniel (see §4.7), as is the fact that God holds people accountable for sin (see §4.2). Daniel in prayer confessed the sins of his people, trusting in God's forgiving and compassionate nature, faithfulness to his covenant, and promises to his people (see §3.6, §4.3). He acted in accordance with the directions God gave Israel (see Lev 26:40–45; Jer 29:12–14): if the people repent in exile, he would restore them (see §4.5). Prayers of confession seek God's mercy despite sin. These occur at various points in Scripture. Moses interceded for Israel more than once (Exod 32:11–14; Num 14:13–19; 16:22). David confessed his own sins (Ps 51). Both Ezra and Nehemiah confessed their people's sins (Ezra 9; Neh 1). The NT also encourages prayers of confession, both through example and instruction. The tax collector confesses his sin to God (Luke 18:13), the Lord's Prayer includes an element of confession (Matt 6:12; Luke 11:4), and John encourages believers to confess their sins to God (1 John 1:9).

Daniel provides an example of how we might confess to God in prayer: (i) Pray in accord with the promises of God's word (vv. 2, 11b–13). God's word is true (see §2) and gives direction and enlightenment in times of uncertainty. (ii) Pray with humility (v. 2) and passion (e.g., vv. 4 ["Ah, Lord"], 8, 16, 19a). (iii) Pray in the light of God's covenant and saving relationship, which make him "our God" (vv. 4, 13–15, 17, 19c; see §4.3). (iv) Pray in view of God's righteous yet merciful character toward his people (vv. 4, 7, 9, 14b, 16, 18; see §3.6, §4.1, §4.3). (v) Pray for the promotion of God's honor and reputation, which are tied to his people (vv. 16–19). (vi) Confess specific sins (vv. 5–6, 10–11, 13). (vii) Commit to repentance (vv. 13b; see §4.2).

I. Court Narratives (Daniel 1–6)

II. Visions of Daniel (Daniel 7–12)
First vision: Four beasts and son of man figure (Daniel 7)
Second vision: Ram and male goat (Daniel 8)
Third vision: Seventy weeks (Daniel 9)
Daniel's prayer of confession (9:1–19)
Gabriel's answer and seventy week prophecy (9:20–27)
Fourth vision: Kings of North/South, distress/resurrection
(Daniel 10–12)

(A) Beginning of story (1:1–21)
(B) Dream about four world kingdoms ended by the
kingdom of God (2:1–49)
(C) Judeans faithful in the face of death (3:1–30)
(D) Royal pride humbled (4:1–37)
(D') Royal pride humbled (5:1–31)
(C') A Judean faithful in the face of death (6:1–28)
(B') Vision about four world kingdoms ended by the
kingdom of God (7:1–28)
(E) Vision of Persian and Greek kingdoms to
Antiochus (8:1–27)
(F) Vision of seventy weeks (9:1–27)
Part 1: Daniel's prayer of confes-
sion (9:1–19)
**Part 2: Gabriel's answer and
seventy-week prophecy (9:20–27)**
(E') Vision of Persian and Greek kingdoms to
Antiochus (10:1–11:35)
(B'')World kingdoms ended and the righteous estab-
lished (11:36–12:3)
(A') End of story: Vision sealed until the end (12:4–13)

[20] While I was speaking, praying, confessing my sin and the sin
of my people Israel, and presenting my petition before the LORD
my God concerning the holy mountain of my God— [21] while I was
praying, Gabriel, the man I had seen in the first vision, reached me
in my extreme weariness, about the time of the evening offering.
[22] He gave me this explanation: "Daniel, I've come now to give you
understanding. [23] At the beginning of your petitions an answer

went out, and I have come to give it, for you are treasured by God. So consider the message and understand the vision:

²⁴ Seventy weeks are decreed
about your people
    and your holy city—
to bring the rebellion to an end,
to put a stop to sin,
to atone for iniquity,
to bring in everlasting righteousness,
to seal up vision and prophecy,
and to anoint the most holy place.
²⁵ Know and understand this:
From the issuing of the decree
to restore and rebuild Jerusalem
until an Anointed One, the ruler,
will be seven weeks and sixty-two weeks.
It will be rebuilt with a plaza and a moat,
but in difficult times.
²⁶ After those sixty-two weeks
the Anointed One will be cut off
and will have nothing.
The people of the coming ruler
will destroy the city and the sanctuary.
The end will come with a flood,
and until the end there will be war;
desolations are decreed.
²⁷ He will make a firm covenant
with many for one week,
but in the middle of the week
he will put a stop to sacrifice
    and offering.
And the abomination of desolation
will be on a wing of the temple
until the decreed destruction
is poured out on the desolator."

Context

Daniel 9:20–27 completes the account of Daniel's third vision that begins in 9:1–19. There Daniel prayed after meditating on Jeremiah's prophecy of a seventy-year Babylonian captivity (9:2; Jer 25:12; 29:10).

Jeremiah's prophecy applies the pattern of sevens from Leviticus 26 that says Israel would be punished "seven times" for their sins (vv. 18, 21, 24, 28) and that the land would enjoy its neglected seventh-year Sabbatical years by laying fallow many years (vv. 34–35, 43). Jeremiah's seventy-year prophecy represents an application of this warning in Leviticus 26 (cf. 2 Chr 36:20–21). Then God sent Daniel a prophecy through the angel Gabriel. Though the fulfillment of Jeremiah's prophecy of seventy years provided a timetable for the end of Jerusalem's desolations (9:2) and Judah's exile, the pattern of sevens (from Leviticus 26) does not end there, nor does Jeremiah's seventy-year prophecy give the full timetable for Israel's restoration. The timespan for full restoration of Daniel's people involves not just seventy years, but another pattern of sevens—namely, seventy times seven.[1]

Chapter 9 outlines as follows:

A   Jeremiah's prophecy of seventy years (9:1–3)
   B   Prayer of confession and supplication (9:4–19)
A′   Daniel's prophecy of seventy weeks (9:20–27)

A simple outline of 9:20–27 is:

I. Gabriel comes in response to Daniel's prayer (9:20–23)

II. The prophecy of the seventy weeks (9:24–27)

A further outline of 9:25–27 is provided below under the explanation of the Roman view in the excursus.

9:20–21 On v. 20 and its various terms, see commentary at 9:1–19. God sometimes answers us before we finish calling on him (cf. Isa 65:24). "Presenting" in Hebrew uses the imagery of "casting down, laying down" (H-stem causative of נפל, "to fall"; Theodotion, ῥιπτέω, "hurl, lay down"; cp. Rev 4:10). The "holy mountain of my God" (v. 20b) is Jerusalem (9:16) made holy because it was the site of the temple (see comments at v. 24). On Gabriel (v. 21a), see comments

---

[1] D. R. Davis, *The Message of Daniel: His Kingdom Cannot Fail*, The Bible Speaks Today (Downers Grove: InterVarsity, 2013), 26; J. M. Hamilton Jr., *With the Clouds of Heaven: The Book of Daniel in Biblical Biblical Theology*, New Studies in Biblical Theology 32 (Downers Grove: InterVarsity, 2014), 43–44.

at 8:16. God's revelation mediated by an angel shows God's transcendence (see §3.4). "Came to me in my extreme weariness" (v. 21b) is ambiguous in the Hebrew. It could instead mean, "He [= Gabriel] was weary with exhaustion" (CEB) or "[Gabriel] came [to me] in swift flight" (NRSV, ESV; cf. KJV, NJPS, ASV). There is debate over the root יעף used as a verb and a noun here. In Jewish tradition the root יעף is taken to mean "to be weary" and can be rendered literally, "being made weary [Hophal participle] in weariness [noun]." If that is the meaning, there is still a question as to the subject, whether it is Daniel exhausted by prayer and fasting or Gabriel exhausted by the journey to see Daniel (see 10:12–14, in which it took an angel twenty-one days to arrive). The former seems more probable. The Old Greek LXX ("the man whom I had seen at first in my sleep"[2]) relates this weariness to the sleep Daniel experienced in the vision of Gabriel in 8:18. Alternatively, יעף may be from a different root known from Arabic *wǧf* meaning to "run, hurry," and/or it may be a bi-form with the root עוף meaning "to fly."[3] Theodotion understood it to mean that Gabriel came "flying" (πετόμενος). This meaning is the view adopted by the KJV, NRSV, ESV, and NJPS.

The "evening offering" was conducted at twilight, the second of the daily morning and evening burnt offerings (Exod 29:38–41; Lev 6:20). This statement may be poignant: the temple was destroyed in 586, so there may not be any regular burnt offerings in Daniel's day (though see Jer 41:5). They were only restored by Zerubbabel and Joshua after the first return from exile (Ezra 3:1–3). The evening offering is among the atoning sacrifices that allowed God to forgive his people's sins (see further §4.5). Therefore, it is no coincidence that Gabriel arrived in response to Daniel's prayer for forgiveness at the time of the regular evening sacrifice, an activity that facilitated forgiveness.

9:22 The rendering "He gave me this explanation" (v. 22a) simplifies the Hebrew that reads, "He gave understanding (H-stem of בין) and spoke with me and said." The Old Greek reads instead "He came," reflecting a different original text (adopted by the RSV,

---

[2] A. Pietersma and B. G. Wright, eds., *A New Translation of the Septuagint* (New York: Oxford University Press, 2007), 1017.

[3] "יעף II" and "עוף," *HALOT* 1:421, 2:801.

NRSV) with an aleph rather than a nun (ויבא versus ויבן). Assuming the MT is original, "gave understanding" anticipates the cognate noun "understanding" (בִּינָה) later in the verse. "I've come" (יצא) is more precisely "come forth" (NASB, NJPS), presumably from the heavenly realms. "To give you understanding" reads in the Hebrew closer to the NASB's "give you insight with understanding." Give insight (or "instruct, make wise") is the H-stem of שׂכל, a verb used of Daniel's intellectual abilities or accomplishments at 1:4 and 17. On "understanding" (בִּינָה *binah*), compare 8:16, in which Gabriel was told to "explain" (literally, "give understanding regarding [H-stem of בין]") the vision of that chapter.

9:23 "At the beginning of your petitions" corresponds with Daniel's request for God to "act … and not delay" (9:19). On "petitions" see comments at v. 3. "Answer" (דָּבָר) is literally "a word" (NRSV, NJPS) in the sense of "message" (so CSB later in this verse), though contextually the message is the answer to Daniel's petitions. The alternative rendering of דָּבָר as a "command" (NASB; KJV; NLT), that is, a command for Gabriel to go, seems less likely. "To give it" is more precisely "to tell" (ESV, NJPS, NIV, NASB), though it could mean to tell "you" (NASB, NIV) rather than to tell "it" (ESV, NJPS).

The term "treasured" (חֲמוּדוֹת) is odd since here it is a feminine plural passive participle used as a noun that means, "precious things, desirable things." This may be a plural of abstraction meaning a "treasure," in which case the text might be rendered, "you are a treasure." This same word is used in 10:11 where the expression is אִישׁ־חֲמֻדוֹת—literally, "a man of treasure(s)," meaning "a treasured/ precious/loved man." It is possible that חֲמוּדוֹת here is short for אִישׁ־חֲמֻדוֹת. The Hebrew lacks the phrase "by God," though it is implied by the context. God is favorably disposed to bless faithful people (see §4.4).

"Message" (Hebrew דָּבָר) was rendered "answer" earlier in this verse, as it should be here. "Consider" is the Qal of בין, while "understand" is the H-stem of that same verb. Since both the Qal and the H-stem of בין can mean "to understand," the distinction between the two is not immediately obvious. The Qal may mean to "pay attention to, consider"[4] as with the CSB, rather than "understand" here. The

---

4 "בין," *HALOT* 1:122.

H-stem, though it can mean "make understand," probably means to "make [oneself] understand" as in 8:5.

9:24–27 CSB and some other versions (NET, NKJV, NABRE) take this unit to be poetry, though other translations render it as prose (NJPS, NRSV, NIV, ESV). This unit is among the most difficult prophecies in the Bible to interpret.

Because of the difficulty and complexity of this passage, the method here will be to lay out various exegetical possibilities line by line and then follow that by comparing three possible holistic interpretations of the passage.

9:24 "Weeks" (שָׁבֻעִים) has been rendered "sevens" (NIV) related to the fact that the Hebrew word "week" (שָׁבוּעַ) is cognate with the number seven (שֶׁבַע). The word formally means a period of seven, though elsewhere in the Hebrew Bible, even in Dan 10:2–3, it means a period of seven days. Some take it as indefinite periods of time consisting of a relatively restricted time (seven weeks), followed by a more extensive time (sixty-two weeks), followed by a climactic time (one week).[5] Given that Jeremiah's prophecy on which Daniel had been meditating (see 9:2) concerned seventy "years," this prophecy is often taken to mean seventy weeks of years—that is, 7 x 70 years (RSV, NJPS margin), though the text never explicitly states this. See further in the excursus below.

Jeremiah's seventy years represents ten Sabbatical year periods (cf. Lev 25:1–7). The seventy made up for Israel's lack of keeping Sabbatical years (Lev 26:34–35; 2 Chr 36:21). A Jubilee is seven times seven years (Lev 25:8) and is, in effect, a super-Sabbatical year.[6] Dean Ulrich argues[7] that four hundred ninety years (seventy times seventy weeks of years) represents ten Jubilees (cf. Lev 25:8–11). The Jubilee occurred every forty-nine years (thus, once a lifetime) to forgive people's debts and servitude and restore their lost inheritances. God warned that the land would be forced to "rest" for neglected Sabbatical and Jubilee years, but he promised that after Israel repented he would forgive and restore his people (Lev 26:34–35, 40–45).

---

[5] D. R. Davis, *The Message of Daniel: His Kingdom Cannot Fail*, The Bible Speaks Today (Downers Grove: InterVarsity, 2013), 134.

[6] J. M. Sprinkle, *Leviticus and Numbers*, Teach the Text (Grand Rapids: Baker, 2015), 166–71.

[7] D. R. Ulrich, *The Antiochene Crisis and Jubilee Theology in Daniel's Seventy Sevens*, OTS 66 (Leiden: Brill, 2015), 131.

Daniel 9:1–19 represents Daniel's obedience to that call for repentance. The Jubilee pattern of the seventy weeks, in answer to Daniel's expression of repentance, anticipates an ultimate Jubilee of Jubilees (cf. Isa 61:1).[8] This, according to Ulrich, gives the prophecy a hopeful tone of ultimate restoration of lost inheritance and forgiveness of covenantal violations.[9]

"Decreed" (N-stem חתך) is a verb that only occurs in v. 24. It might have the nuance of "determined" (KJV, NKJV) rather than "decreed." "Your people" means Daniel's Jewish/Israelite people. "Your holy city" is Jerusalem (earlier called God's "holy mountain," 9:16, 20), symbolizing Israel's covenant relationship with their holy God (see §3.6, §4.3), who set Israel apart and in the temple symbolically dwells among his people (Exod 15:17; 19:16; 1 Kgs 8:12–13).

Six infinitive clauses are used to describe what occurs in conjunction with these seventy weeks of years: (1) "bring the rebellion to an end," (2) "put a stop to sin," (3) "atone for iniquity," (4) "bring in everlasting righteousness," (5) "seal up vision and prophecy," and (6) "anoint the most holy place." The first three have to do with the problem of sin (rebellion, sin, iniquity), for which God holds people accountable (see §4.2). Nevertheless, through atoning sacrifices he saves and forgives (see §4.5). The fourth speaks of righteousness, which God wants people to display (see §4.1). The last two are more problematic to interpret.

On "rebellion" (also NLT; or "transgression," ESV, NASB, NIV, NRSV), see comments at 8:13. Most versions take the verb (D-stem of כלה) to mean "complete" in the sense of "finish, bring to an end," but the NJPS gives another possible rendering, "until the measure of transgression is filled"—that is, transgression is brought to its apex.

The Masoretic tradition has two readings for the phrase "to put a stop to sin." One (the Ketiv) in the main text is "to seal up sins [plural]." The verb in the Ketiv is the Qal of חתם, also used of sealing vision later in this verse. The Qere in the margin reads, "to complete/reach the full measure of sin [singular]." The verb of the Qere is the H-stem of תמם. Theodotion follows the Ketiv. The LEB among modern translations follows the Ketiv verb and the Qere noun, and the

[8] Ibid., 13, 89, 131.
[9] Ibid., 13.

NKJV and CEB follows the Ketiv plural noun "sins," though most versions follow both Qere readings.

KETIV	QERE	QERE + KETIV	KETIV + QERE
לְחָתֵם חַטָּאוֹת "to seal up sins" "seal up the sins" (Geneva Bible)	לְהָתֵם חַטָּאת "to complete/ reach the full measure of sin" "to put a stop to sin" (CSB; cf. NIV)	לְהָתֵם חַטָּאוֹת "to complete/ reach the full measure of sins" "To make an end of sins" (NKJV)	לְחָתֵם חַטָּאת "to seal up sin" "to seal up sin" (LEB)

The verb of the Ketiv (חתם) was probably inadvertently copied from later in this verse, thus Qere is most likely the original reading. Assuming the verb is the H-stem of תמם, there is still more than one possible interpretation of its meaning: (1) It could mean to "stop" sin (CSB, GW), (2) suffer the price of sin (CEV), (3) put an end to sin (ESV), or (4) complete sin (NJPS) in the sense of bringing it to full measure.

"To atone for iniquity" employs "iniquity, wickedness" (see comments at v. 13) and "atone." The exact meaning and derivation of the D-stem of כפר "to make atonement" is disputed, but there is no question that the term was used in the sacrificial system for making atonement for people in a way that allows God's forgiveness of their sins (Lev 4:20, 26, 31, 35; 5:10, 13; see §4.5). In a secular context it can be used of placating, mollifying, satisfying, or appeasing an offended party by a gift (Gen 32:20–21). This is part of the meaning in the ritual laws in which God is appeased by sacrifice. In addition, this verb takes on the secondary connotation of "cleansing, purging." Ritual purity occurs through the application of blood (Ezek 43:20; cf. Lev. 4:7). In 9:24 it is iniquity that is cleansed or purged.

"Righteousness" (צֶדֶק) is cognate with צְדָקָה (see v. 7) and has a meaning more or less the same as this term, though the sense here may be "eternal justice" (NABRE). "Everlasting righteousness" reads in the Hebrew "righteousness/justice of eternities [עֹלָמִים]." Eternity or distant time (עוֹלָם) can refer to the distant past or the distant future. Here "righteousness of eternities" may refer to the justice of the eschatological ages to come.

The Hebrew of "to seal up vision and prophecy" reads "to seal vision and prophet" (LEB; cf. ESV). "Vision and prophet" is likely a hendiadys for "prophetic vision" (CEB, NET, NLT). To "seal" (Qal of חתם) can mean to seal a document with a seal or signet ring on clay to mark ownership or to prove authenticity (Esth 8:8; Jer 32:10–11). To seal can also mean to block something (a locked garden, a sealed spring) to which only the owner has access, or to block off light (Song 4:12; Job 9:7). Metaphorically, to seal a prophecy can mean to make a prophecy hidden (Isa 29:11; Dan 12:4, 9). At issue is whether the text means "seal up" vision and prophecy in the sense of making it hidden or no longer available (CSB, NASB, NIV), or whether it instead means "to seal" vision in the sense of confirming it (NLT), ratifying it (NJPS, NABRE), or making it come true (CEV, GNT).

"The most holy place" could be changed to "a most holy place" with the ESV since the Hebrew (קֹדֶשׁ קָדָשִׁים) lacks the article "the." It also lacks the term "place." Some versions render "most holy" without adding the interpretive paraphrase "place" (KJV, NKJV). Formally, קֹדֶשׁ קָדָשִׁים denotes something extremely holy. The expression without the article can refer to the most holy altar of burnt offering (Exod 29:37; 40:10), the incense altar (Exod 30:10), all the utensils associated with the tabernacle (Exod 30:29), the tabernacle incense (Exod 30:36), most holy offerings eaten by priests (Lev 2:3, 10; 6:17, 25, 27; 7:1, 10; 10:12, 17; 24:9), and even the land around God's temple (Ezek 43:12; 48:12). The expression with the article ("*the* most holy," קֹדֶשׁ הַקֳּדָשִׁים) can refer to the innermost sanctum of the tabernacle/ temple, the holy of holies where the ark of the covenant was stored (Exod 26:33; 1 Kgs 8:6; Ezek 41:4; 2 Chr 3:8; 5:7). This is not the meaning elsewhere when the article is lacking. The temple's inner sanctuary might be the meaning in Daniel, though the lack of the article here is a strike against this identification.

"Anoint" (משח) is used of people consecrated to an office— prophets (1 Kgs 19:16), priests (Exod 28:41), and kings (1 Sam 15:1). It is also used of holy things such as the tabernacle consecrated to divine service (Exod 30:26; 40:9–11; Lev 8:10–11), though there is no record of anointing of a sanctuary after its use has been initiated. Some take the meaning here as "anoint the Holy One" (GW)—that is, the Messiah (see excursus below). Others take it metaphorically for "inaugurating Yahweh-ordained worship."[10] Thus, there are several

---

[10] Davis, *Daniel*, 131.

possible objects of the anointing: a (or the) most holy place, a most holy thing (or things), most holy worship, or a most holy person.

9:25 The second verb, "understand this," is the H-stem of שָׂכַל, which relates to having insight or gaining understanding. "The decree" could be rendered indefinitely "a decree" (NASB) since דָּבָר lacks the definite article. The word דָּבָר more often means "word" (ESV) than a decree, though contextually it could refer to a decree or a word of "command" (NKJV, NLT). Alternatively, it could be a prophetic word.

The specific command or prophetic word in mind is disputed. Among the proposed identifications are the following: (1) Jeremiah's prophetic "word" of a seventy-year Babylonian desolation first given in 605 BC, a "word" on which Daniel had been meditating (Jer 25:11; 29:10; cf. Dan 9:2). (2) Cyrus' "decree" in 538 to restore the temple (Ezra 1:1–4) or Daniel's "word" in the same year asking God to restore Jerusalem (9:16–19).[11] (3) One of the command-decrees of Artaxerxes I to Ezra in 458 or Nehemiah in 445 or 444 BC (Ezra 7:11–28; Neh 2:7–8). See excursus below.

"To restore and rebuild Jerusalem" could be rendered, "to cause the building of Jerusalem again." "Restore" (H-stem of שׁוּב, "return") in the Qal before another verb can mean to do something again,[12] as is the case later in this same verse where "it will be rebuilt" literally says, "it will return [Qal of שׁוּב] and be built." Arguably, the H-stem functions here in the same way except adding a causative element.

The phrase "an Anointed One, the ruler" could instead be rendered, "Messiah the Prince" (NASB, NKJV), or "an anointed leader" (NJPS). Neither "Anointed One" nor "ruler" has the article, though this may not matter (see comment at v. 26). Anointed one (מָשִׁיחַ) is the word from which the English "Messiah" is derived. It could be a proper noun ("Messiah"), though this is not clear. As noted in v. 24, kings, prophets, and priests could be "anointed ones." The term "prince, leader, ruler" (נָגִיד) is "applied to leaders in several fields—governmental, military, and religious."[13] It is used, for example, of the king of Tyre (Ezek 28:2) and as a synonym for kings (Ps 76:12, note parallelism), but it is also a title for the high priest (Jer 20:1;

---

[11] C. A. Newsom, *Daniel*, OTL (Louisville: Westminster John Knox, 2014), 304.

[12] P. Joüon, *Grammar of Biblical Hebrew*, trans. and rev. T. Muraoka, 2 vols. (Rome: Pontificio Intituto Biblico, 1991), §177b.

[13] L. L. J. Coppes, "נָגַד," in *Theological Wordbook of the Old Testament*, 550.

Neh 11:11). It is not used of prophets in the Hebrew Bible. Thus, it is unclear whether "an anointed one, a ruler" refers to a king (the Messiah) or a priest.

If weeks are weeks of strict years, then "seven weeks and sixty-two weeks" would be 49 years followed by 434 years, for a total of 483 years, though see comments at v. 24. "Will be rebuilt" uses a similar idiom as "restore and rebuild" in the same verse (see comments above), except that שׁוּב (denotes repeated action) is in the Qal.

"Plaza" (רְחוֹב) can refer to a courtyard such as the one in the temple compound (Ezra 10:9), or a square adjacent to city gates (Jer 5:1). The form is probably a collective, so it could be translated as a plural (ESV, NABRE "squares"). Some translators think it means "streets" (NIV, NRSV, Theodotion). "Moat" (חָרוּץ) occurs only here in the Hebrew Bible. This rendering is derived from its cognate in Akkadian that means a town-moat or trench.[14] However, since a moat with water (as the "moat" usually implies) seems unsuitable for the geography of hilly Jerusalem and the root חרץ can mean, "to cut, sharpen," it is probably best to render it a "trench" (CEV, NIV) for a fortified city.

The Hebrew of "in difficult times" reads "in distress of times." The noun "distress" (צוֹק) only occurs here in the Hebrew Bible, but based on its root (צוק) meaning of "compel, oppress," it seems to denote something like a state of hardship, trouble, oppression, or affliction. Theodotion instead took this noun to be from צוק meaning "to pour out" and thus rendered it, "the seasons will be emptied out."[15]

9:26 "The Anointed One will be cut off" uses the same term (מָשִׁיחַ) without the article as in v. 25. If it is a proper noun (Messiah), then both would refer to the same person. If a common noun ("an anointed one"), verses 25 and 26 might refer to two separate anointed ones. If they refer to the same person, one would expect the first indefinite reference ("an anointed one") to be followed by a definite "the [aforementioned] anointed one" in v. 26. However, if CSB is right in seeing this section as poetry, then there would be considerable poetic license in the use or non-use of the article. This is seen

---

[14] "ḫarīṣu," in *CAD* 6:103.
[15] Pietersma and Wright, *A New Translation of the Septuagint*, 1017.

later in the verse where עַם נָגִיד "the people of the ... ruler" lacks the article in Hebrew, but the participle הַבָּא "coming" that modifies עַם נָגִיד has the article and so treats נָגִיד as definite. "Cut off" (N-stem of כרת) might mean to be put to death (NIV; cp. Isa 53:8, "cut off from the land of the living," though this uses a different verb), punished by being banished or excluded from the community (cf. Exod 12:15), or "disappear."[16] In Leviticus to be "cut off from one's people" probably refers to a divine punishment—namely, exclusion from one's relatives in the afterlife.[17]

The Hebrew behind "will have nothing" is quite ambiguous. It reads "and there is not to him" (וְאֵין לוֹ). If "cut off" means the anointed one is killed, then the rendering "will have nothing" seems gratuitous since, of course, the dead have nothing. Other attempts to make sense of this phrase include, "no one will support him" (CEB; cf. NABRE), "[cut off] but not for himself" (KJV, NKJV), "appearing to have accomplished nothing" (NLT), "he will be gone" (ERV), or combined with "cut off" mean "will disappear and vanish" (NJPS). Given the ambiguity, little can be deduced from this phrase.

The word "ruler" is נָגִיד as in v. 25 (see comments there). It lacks the article, though the participle "coming" has the article and so treats נָגִיד as if it were definite, justifying the rendering "the coming ruler." Various interpreters have taken this "coming prince" as Antiochus IV (171–164 BC), Titus of Rome (AD 70), and the antichrist. The "city" is Jerusalem (v. 25). "The sanctuary" or "the [sphere of] holiness" can denote the tabernacle (Exod 35:19) or the temple (Ps 150:1), though the expression "the city and the holiness" could possibly be a hendiadys meaning "the holy city" (cf. Dan 9:16 and comments).

The CSB avoids ambiguity by rendering קִצּוֹ generally as "the end." The CSB note cites the literal renderings, "its end" (so ESV, NASB, NRSV) or "his end" (so CEB, GW, NABRE). Since "its/his" is a masculine pronoun, it cannot have "city" (feminine עִיר) as its antecedent. However, it could refer to the ruler or the sanctuary.

"Flood" (שֶׁטֶף) can mean a deluge of water by overflow of a river or rain (Job 38:25; Ps 32:6; Nah 1:8). Here it might mean the end comes through a flood of water. But the root שׁטף can be used

---

[16] "כרת," *HALOT* 2:501, as an alternative interpretation.

[17] Sprinkle, *Leviticus and Numbers*, 50–51.

metaphorically of anger or military invasion (Prov 27:4; Isa 8:8). Perhaps here it is metaphoric of an abrupt end, like one caused by a flash flood.

On "war" until the end, compare the similar statement by Jesus (Matt 24:6; Mark 13:7; Luke 21:9). It could mean, "until the end of [the] war, desolations are decreed," or something similar (NJPS; NKJV, KJV). "Decreed" (N-stem of חרץ; see comments at v. 25 on "moat") can also be rendered "decided" (CEV) or "determined" (NASB, NKJV). Presumably this is determined or decreed by God, and thus this verse is an expression of God's sovereign directing of history. On "desolations" (Qal participle feminine plural of שמם) see comments at 8:13 and especially 9:18.

9:27 Again there is ambiguity. The "he" of "he will make" could also be rendered "it" or "one." The last of these would make the sense passive ("A firm covenant will be made"). "Will make firm a covenant" is an H-stem [causative] of גבר ("be strong"). This form could also be rendered, "will enforce a covenant," "will confirm a covenant" (NIV), or possibly even "will make difficult a covenant" in the sense of "will cause a violation of a covenant."[18] A covenant (בְּרִית) is an agreement between parties, which could be rendered here "alliance" or "treaty" (NLT; cf. 1 Kgs 20:34). "Many" seems to have the more inclusive meaning of "everyone" (see comments at Dan 12:2). "For one week" lacks the Hebrew word "for," but it is supplied by most EVVs. Alternatively, it could means "*in* one week" (Douay-Rheims) or "*during* one week" (NJPS). Some take this covenant to refer to one Antiochus IV made with Hellenizing Jews (1 Macc 1:11). Others think it refers to the new covenant established by Jesus (Luke 22:20). Still others see it as a covenant made by the antichrist during the great tribulation.

"He will put a stop to sacrifice and offering" could possibly mean "one will stop" in a passive sense for "sacrifice and offering will stop." "Desolation" is a Polel participle from שמם meaning, "makes desolate," which combines the ideas of desertion and destruction. James Hamilton[19] understands the participle, "one that/who desolates," to mean that the "abomination" is a person, as (arguably)

---

[18] "גבר," *HALOT* 1:175.
[19] Hamilton, *With the Clouds of Heaven*, 122, 132, 137.

does Mark 13:14 ("the abomination of desolation standing where *he* ought not," ASV, ESV; similarly GNT, NABRE, NLT).

Expressions similar to "abomination of desolation" occur three times in Daniel, though each is slightly different, even though they seem to mean more or less the same thing. To make them read exactly the same requires emendations. Daniel 9:27 reads, שִׁקּוּצִים מְשֹׁמֵם, "abominations [plural], one that desolates [polel]." Daniel 11:31 reads, הַשִּׁקּוּץ מְשׁוֹמֵם, "the abomination [singular with article], one that desolates." Daniel 12:11 reads, שִׁקּוּץ שֹׁמֵם, "an abomination [singular without article] that is desolate [Qal]." The first two instances are grammatically problematic and the third contextually problematic. Contrary to usual grammar, the participle, "one that desolates," in v. 27 does not agree with "abominations" in number, though "abominations" (if a plural of abstraction as seems likely) can be treated as a singular. *BHS* emends "abominations" to the singular supported by the early versions of Theodotion and the Old Greek (LXX) to solve the grammatical problem, though those same versions make "desolation" plural. In 11:31 "one that desolates" does not agree with "the abomination" in terms of definiteness, which leads BHS to emend the text by adding the article (see comment there).

Only 12:11 follows the usual rules of grammar, though the verb is a Qal with a stative meaning rather than a Polel that produces that state, thus making the meaning different than the other two cases. To be consistent, a mem (מ) should be added to the consonants שמם to turn the Qal participle into a polel participle as in the other two verses. I tentatively adopt all three emendations, resulting in the translations "an abomination that makes desolate" or similar (9:27; 12:11), and "the abomination that makes desolate" (11:31). This is also similar to the NT quote of this phrase from the Old Greek of 12:11.

"Abomination of Desolation" in the Masoretic Text, Theodotion, Old Greek (LXX), and the Gospels			
	Masoretic Text	**Theodotion**	**Old Greek (LXX)**
Dan 9:27	שִׁקּוּצִים מְשֹׁמֵם	βδέλυγμα τῶν ἐρημώσεων	βδέλυγμα τῶν ἐρημώσεων
	"abominations, one that desolates"	"abomination of the desolations"	"abomination of the desolations"
	Suggested emendation, removing plural ending: "an abomination that desolates" שִׁקּוּץ מְשֹׁמֵם		
Dan 11:31	הַשִּׁקּוּץ מְשׁוֹמֵם	βδέλυγμα ἠφανισμένον	βδέλυγμα ἐρημώσεως
	"the abomination, one that desolates"	"an obliterated abomination"	"an abomination of desolation"
	Suggested emendation, adding article: "the abomination that desolates" הַשִּׁקּוּץ הַמְשׁוֹמֵם		
Dan 12:11	שִׁקּוּץ שֹׁמֵם	βδέλυγμα ἐρημώσεως	τὸ βδέλυγμα τῆς ἐρημώσεως
	"an abomination that is desolate"	"an abomination of desolation"	"the abomination of desolation"
	Suggested emendation, adding mem: "an abomination that desolates" שִׁקּוּץ מְשֹׁמֵם		
Matt 24:15 Mark 13:14	Greek NT (after Old Greek [LXX] Dan 12:11) τὸ βδέλυγμα τῆς ἐρημώσεως		

"Abomination" (שִׁקּוּצִים) is one of many offenses people can commit against God for which he holds them accountable (see §4.2).

It is from a root that means to "spurn, scorn"[20] and thus implies something to be scorned, something detestable or abhorrent (cf. CEV "Horrible Thing"). It is often used of idols (Deut 29:17; 1 Kgs 11:5; 2 Kgs 23:13; Jer 4:1), suggesting that the meaning here might be something like "sacrileges." That is especially defensible for the same noun in the singular at Dan 11:31 in reference to the actions of Antiochus IV, who makes the temple into an idolatrous temple of Zeus and sacrifices a ceremonially unclean animal, a pig, on its altar (see comments at 11:31). The NT applies this language to the destruction of Jerusalem by Titus of Rome (Matt 24:15; Mark 13:14).

The expression "of the temple" is lacking in the Hebrew, though both the Old Greek and Theodotion see a reference to the temple here. "Wing" could refer to the "pinnacle" or "summit" of the temple mentioned in Matt 4:5 and Luke 4:9. The Greek for pinnacle (πτερύγιον) in those verses means literally "winglet," a diminutive of "wing"; thus, a part of the temple complex may be in mind.

On "decreed" (חרץ) see comments at v. 26. The Hebrew reads, "until complete destruction and what is decreed will pour out on one who [or "something that"] is desolate." "Complete destruction and what is decreed [N-stem participle of חרץ]" forms a hendiadys meaning "the decreed destruction" (CSB) or "a decided annihilation."[21] The agent who "decreed" this destruction is probably God who intervenes to direct history. "One who [or "something that"] is desolated" fits better with the meaning of the Qal participle שֹׁמֵם, unless the text is emended to מְשֹׁמֵם ("one who makes desolate"), a form used earlier in this verse.

Excursus: The Meaning and Fulfillment of Daniel 9:24–27 (The "Seventy Weeks")

As seen above, there are a bewildering range of possible meanings of the phrases and expressions in 9:24–27. This ambiguity has led to a variety of interpretations of the passage as a whole and its fulfillment.

For the overall interpretation the key questions are these: When does the seventy weeks begin? When does the first seven weeks end?

---

[20] "שקץ," in *HALOT* 4:1646.
[21] "כְּלָה,"in *HALOT* 2:477.

When do the sixty-nine weeks end? What happens in the middle of the seventieth week? Related questions include these: Are the weeks literally weeks of years, or are they just periods of time? Are there any time gaps within or events beyond the seventy weeks? How one answers these questions will determine one's overall interpretation of the passage.

Although there are other views,[22] the following discussion will lay out three commonly adopted approaches—the Antiochus view, the classical dispensationalism view, and the Roman view—and evaluate their strengths and weaknesses.

Antiochus view. One view sees this prophecy as building on Daniel's interest in Antiochus IV in Daniel 8. In this approach the seventy weeks go from the time of Jeremiah to Antiochus IV Epiphanes, though it assumes that the numbers are "wrong-headed arithmetical calculations"[23] since they do not work out exactly. The first seven weeks could be calculated from Jeremiah's prophecy in 605 (Jer 25:11–14) to the rise of Cyrus who was the first anointed prince in c. 558, roughly forty-nine years. The book of Isaiah refers to Cyrus as God's "anointed" (Isa 45:1). The sixty-two weeks (nominally 434 years) go from Jeremiah's prophecy in 605 BC to the death of Onias III in c. 171 (the high priest "anointed one" deposed and "cut off" [v. 26a] by Antiochus), thus bringing us to the time of Antiochus IV. The seventieth week refers to seven years of fighting over control of the temple. The Jews led by the Maccabees ultimately rededicated the temple in c. 164 BC. During the second half of the seventieth week (167–164), Antiochus IV attempted to abolish the Jewish religion, turning the temple of Yahweh into a temple of Zeus, offering a pig on the altar. This idolatry is Daniel's abomination of desolation (cf. 1 Macc 6:7). Supporting this view is the fact that the reference to "abomination of desolation" in Dan 11:31 clearly refers to events during the time of Antiochus.

This view has several weaknesses. First, it assumes arbitrarily that the seven sevens and the sixty-two sevens overlap, both starting in 605 BC. Given that the text counts the whole period as 70

---

[22] The three common views discussed here, as well as five additional views, are evaluated by D. R. Ulrich, "The Need for More Attention to Jubilee in Daniel 9:24–27," *BBR* 26.4 (2016): 481–500.

[23] W. Porteous, *Daniel: A Commentary*, OTL (Philadelphia: Westminster, 1965), 134.

weeks, this overlap seems unlikely. If the years do not overlap, then the numbers become very imprecise. Second, this view oddly makes the "anointed prince" of v. 25 have a double meaning, both Cyrus and Antiochus IV, though the coming prince of v. 26 refers only to Antiochus. Third, the events of 164 BC hardly put an end to rebellion, sin, and iniquity, nor did they bring in everlasting righteousness contra v. 24. Fourth, although Antiochus desecrated the temple and damaged Jerusalem, contrary to v. 26b, he destroyed neither. In other words, Antiochus does not fit the wording of the prophecy.

Classical dispensationalism view. Classical dispensationalism is a view defended in modern times by J. Walvoord,[24] Leon Wood,[25] and Stephen Miller;[26] and in the nineteenth century it was popularized in a book-length treatment by Sir Robert Anderson.[27] It takes the seventy weeks of v. 24 to be "weeks of years," that is, 490 very precise years. "Your people" (v. 24) refers to the Jews (not the church). The words "to bring the rebellion to an end, to put a stop to sin, to wipe away iniquity, to bring in everlasting righteousness" (v. 24) are in principle fulfilled at the first advent, but for the Jews are fulfilled at the second advent and the establishment of the millennial kingdom. "Anoint the most holy place" (v. 24) refers to anointing the temple during the great tribulation in a yet future, rebuilt temple in Jerusalem.

Classical dispensationalism takes "decree to restore and rebuild Jerusalem" (v. 25) to refer to one of two events: (1) the decree of Artaxerxes I in 458 (Ezra 7), which causes the sixty-ninth week after 483 ordinary years to end at AD 26, about the time Jesus was baptized (assuming an AD 30 crucifixion),[28] or (2) more often, to the second decree of Artaxerxes in 445 or 444, which requires an assumption of 360 days to a year to make the sixty-nine weeks of years end at AD 33 (assuming an AD 33 crucifixion).[29] Both AD 33 and AD 30 are possible dates for Jesus' crucifixion. Only on those two years did the Passover begin on a Friday, as stated in the Gospel accounts. Thus,

---

[24] J. F. Walvoord, *Daniel: The Key to Prophetic Revelation* (Chicago: Moody, 1971), 219–37.

[25] L. Wood, *A Commentary on Daniel* (Grand Rapids: Zondervan, 1973), 243–63.

[26] S. R. Miller, *Daniel*, NAC 18 (Nashville: Broadman & Holman, 1994), 249–73.

[27] R. Anderson, *The Coming Prince* (London: Hodder and Stoughton, 1881).

[28] Wood, *Daniel*, 253.

[29] Walvoord, *Daniel*, 219–20.

Robert Anderson's theory, which dates Daniel's seventy weeks from Artaxerxes' second decree in 445 to the crucifixion in AD 32, does not seem possible.[30] Hoehner adjusts Anderson's assumptions and calculations to fit an AD 33 crucifixion.[31] The phrase "Messiah the Prince" (KJV; "an Anointed One, the ruler" CSB) refers to Christ who comes at the end of the sixty-nine weeks of years, which is either his baptism or crucifixion. The first forty-nine years (seven sevens) perhaps covers the time of Ezra/Nehemiah. "After those sixty-two weeks the Anointed One will be cut off" (v. 26) refers to Christ crucified.

"The people of the coming ruler will destroy the city and the sanctuary" (v. 26) is taken by this view to refer to the antichrist during the great tribulation. This is similar to the view of Irenaeus, which sees the antichrist as appearing in Daniel's seventieth week (*Against Heresies* 25.4).[32] Hippolytus "posits a period of time between the sixty-ninth and the seventieth weeks, a period that sees the gospel preached and that comes to an end with the events of the last week," during which the two witnesses of Rev 11:3 (whom Hippolytus takes as Elijah and Enoch) come.[33] Hippolytus is the earliest known advocate of the "great parenthesis" theory. The great parenthesis is the (now) two-millennia time gap between the sixty-ninth week (that ends at the first advent) and the seventieth week, a parenthesis that skips over the "church age." Classical dispensationalists see the seventieth week as a time when God deals again directly with ethnic Israel, Daniel's people. This is in accord with classical dispensational theology, which sharply distinguishes between God's dealings with the church and his dealings with Israel.

According to this view, "he will make a firm covenant with many for one week" (v. 27a) refers to some sort of treaty the antichrist makes with the Jews during the seventieth week. The phrase, "but in the middle of the week he will put a stop to sacrifice and offering," refers to the interference with worship in the rebuilt temple, a violation of the treaty.

---

[30] Anderson, *The Coming Prince*, 107, 112, 215–16.

[31] H. W. Hoehner, "Chronological Aspects of the Life of Christ: Part VI: Daniel's Seventy Weeks and New Testament Chronology," *BSac* 132 (1975): 47–65.

[32] See L. E. Knowles, "The Interpretation of the Seventy Weeks of Daniel in the Early Fathers," *WTJ* 7.2 (1944): 139.

[33] See ibid., 141.

In this view the seventieth week corresponds with the "great tribulation." Revelation often mentions three-and-a-half-year periods, described variously as "times, time, and half a time" (Rev 12:14, cf. Dan 7:25), "1,260 days" (Rev 11:3; 12:6), and "forty-two months" (Rev 11:2; 13:5). Note that these numbers assume 360-day years. The antichrist makes a covenant with the Jews ("many") for the week of the tribulation period, but halfway through it, after three and a half years, he violates that covenant and desolates the rebuilt temple ("the abomination of desolation"), so that sacrifices cease to be offered. "The decreed destruction is poured out on the desolator" (v. 27) refers to the antichrist being destroyed at the second advent of Jesus.

There are many problems with this approach. A minor problem is that it works on the assumption (related to Jeremiah's prophecy of a seventy-year captivity) that "weeks" are weeks of years. This is merely an assumption, not stated. The numbers could represent other time periods. More problematic is the version of the dispensational view that understands the years to be 360 days long rather than ordinary 365-and-one-fourth day years. Having 360-day years is inherently unlikely over long periods of time because of the regular and universal use of intercalculary months among Jews and Babylonians to keep the lunar and solar calendars together.

Even more problematic is making the "decree to restore and rebuild Jerusalem" (9:25) refer to either of the two decrees of Artaxerxes I. Daniel was writing about the time of Cyrus' decree that allowed exiles to go back to Palestine and rebuild both the temple and Jerusalem (Ezra 1:1–4; Isa 44:28). This decree (near the time of the prophecy of Daniel 9) seems the far more important decree to "restore and rebuild Jerusalem" than either decree of Artaxerxes I. Indeed by 520 BC many in Jerusalem lived comfortably in "paneled houses" (Hag 1:4). Thus, we would expect Daniel to start the seventy sevens from his own day, in conjunction with Cyrus' decree that effectively marks the end of Jeremiah's initial prophecy of the seventy years, rather than to start it much later during the time of Artaxerxes I—a far less significant era when Jerusalem had mostly been rebuilt.

Perhaps the most serious problem with the classic dispensational view is its awkward "parenthesis" consisting of two millennia between the sixty-ninth and the seventieth weeks. The two-millennia gap seems inconsistent with Daniel's purpose to give a chronological timetable.

Furthermore, the identity of the "prince/ruler" is in doubt. The text describes an anointed ruler, but it never clearly identifies this ruler as the Messiah. All Israel's kings were "anointed," as were priests. The text also does not clearly distinguish the first ruler from the second. They could be the same. Finally, Revelation, while it speaks of a three-and-a-half-year time of trouble, never speaks of a seven-year tribulation, which this interpretation requires for its seventieth week.

Roman view. A third interpretation sees this prophecy as fulfilled in the coming of the Messiah at the first advent and shortly thereafter during first-century-AD-Roman times. This was a view argued in the early church (though with individual variations) by Theodoret of Cyrus,[34] Africanus,[35] Clement of Alexandria,[36] and Tertullian.[37] Later it was advocated by John Calvin[38] and is defended by many non-dispensational conservative scholars in modern times.

According to E. J. Young, "seventy sevens" could refer to an indefinite period of time.[39] Since Jeremiah's seventy years (Dan

---

[34] Theodoret of Cyrus, *Commentary on Daniel*, trans R. C. Hill (Atlanta: Society of Biblical Literature, 2006), 241–61.

[35] Julius Africanus, "On the Seventy Weeks of Daniel," Extant Fragments of the Five Books of the Chronology of Julius Africanus, in *Fathers of the Third Century,* The Ante-Nicene Fathers 6, ed. A. Roberts et al., trans. S. Salmond (Buffalo: Christian Literature Company, 1886), 6134–35. Africanus is quoted extensively on this by St. Jerome (*Jerome's Commentary on Daniel*, trans. G. L. Archer [Grand Rapids: Baker, 1958], 95–98).

[36] Clement of Alexandria, "The Stromata, or Miscellanies," in *Fathers of the Second Century*, ed. A. Roberts et al., The Ante-Nicene Fathers 2 (Buffalo: Christian Literature Company, 1885), 2329. Clement's view of the seventy weeks is mentioned by St. Jerome (*Daniel*, 105) and discussed by Knowles, "Seventy Weeks of Daniel in the Early Fathers," 142–45.

[37] Tertullian, "An Answer to the Jews," in *Latin Christianity: Its Founder, Tertullian*, ed. A. Roberts, et. al., trans. S. Thelwall, The Ante-Nicene Fathers 3 (Buffalo: Christian Literature Company, 1885), 3158–60. Tertullian's view is cited by St. Jerome (*Daniel*, 106–8) and discussed by Knowles, "Seventy Weeks of Daniel in the Early Fathers," 145–49.

[38] John Calvin, *Commentary on the Book of the Prophet Daniel*, trans. T. Myers, 2 vols. (Bellingham, WA: Logos Bible Software, 2010), 2:203.

[39] E. J. Young, *The Prophecy of Daniel: A Commentary* (Grand Rapids: Eerdmans, 1949), 196.

9:2) represents a lifetime, seventy sevens might be thought of as something like seven lifetimes. Alternatively, according to J. Barton Payne, it could be precisely 490 years, beginning with Artaxerxes' decree to Ezra in 458 BC.[40] The first seven sevens in Young's approach take us generally through the time of Ezra and Nehemiah, while in Payne's interpretation the first seven weeks take us past the era of Ezra and Nehemiah specifically to 409 BC. Both Young's and Payne's approaches terminate the seventy weeks around the time of the first advent of Christ, but Payne's approach ends the sixty-two weeks at Jesus' baptism in AD 26, some 483 years (69 weeks of years) after Artaxerxes' first decree to Ezra (bearing in mind that is no year zero in the Christian calendar). The advantage of Payne's view is that it allows the seventy weeks to be precise weeks of years.

In the Roman view "your people" (v. 24) refers to the people of God, not excluding the church. These seventy weeks serve "to bring the rebellion to an end, to put a stop to sin, to wipe away iniquity, to bring in everlasting righteousness, to seal up vision and prophecy, and to anoint the most holy place." This ending of sin is consistent with the prayer of confession of sin in the first part of the chapter, indicating that sin will in a sense be done away with. These things are accomplished by Christ's death on the cross. After Christ and the completion of the new covenant, "vision and prophecy" (v. 24) become less prominent. This view often understands "most holy place" to mean "most holy one" (which is grammatically possible; see commentary at v. 24) in reference to Christ, or it sees a double application to the temple and to Christ as the new temple (see §7.4.3). Alternatively, "anointing the most holy" could refer metaphorically to the inauguration of proper worship.

Daniel 9:25–27 arguably follows a chiastic structure that provides support for this interpretation, placing the death of Christ at the center.[41]

---

[40] J. B. Payne, "The Goal of Daniel's Seventy Weeks," *JETS* 21.2 (1978): 97–115; "Daniel," in *Encyclopedia of Biblical Prophecy: The Complete Guide to Scriptural Predictions and Their Fulfillment* (New York: Harper and Row, 1973), 96–97.

[41] S. Greidanus, *Preaching Christ from Daniel: Foundations for Expository Sermons* (Grand Rapids: Eerdmans, 2012), 292.

A   Construction of Jerusalem (9:25a)
  B   Coming of the Anointed One (9:25b)
    C   Construction of Jerusalem (9:25c)
      D   Death of the Anointed One (9:26a)
    C'   Destruction of Jerusalem (9:26b)
  B'   Activities of the Anointed One (9:27a)
A' Destruction of Jerusalem (9:27b)

The "Anointed One will be cut off" after sixty-two weeks (v. 26) refers more specifically in the middle of the seventieth week (v. 27) to Christ's death on the cross where he establishes "a firm covenant" (v. 27)—namely, the new covenant. "The people of the coming ruler" (v. 26) who destroy the city refers to Titus and the Romans who destroyed Jerusalem in AD 70, though this happens outside the seventy weeks.

"Make a firm covenant with many for one week" describes the seven-year period from Jesus' baptism (perhaps AD 26) through his crucifixion three and a half years later in the middle of the seventieth week and concluding with the stoning of Stephen (c. AD 33). In the middle of this week Jesus established the new covenant through his death, which in principle and eventually in practice puts an end to "sacrifice and offering." The "one week" is a transitional period between the Mosaic covenant and the new covenant. The end of the week could be marked by the stoning of Stephen (Acts 7:58) and the flight of the church from Jerusalem. The "abomination of desolation" refers to Titus who destroyed the temple, a structure no longer required under the new covenant in view of the sacrifice of Christ. The Gospels cite Daniel's "abomination of desolation" (Matt 24:15; Mark 13:14) and interpret it as "Jerusalem surrounded by armies" (Luke 21:20), a reference to Titus's armies in AD 70. That Daniel's prophecy of desolation (9:27) is fulfilled by the Roman destruction of Jerusalem is also argued by Josephus,[42] who lived through it.

Although the Roman view is attractive, it is not without difficulties. For one, Christ's death does not immediately put an end to sin and rebellion (v. 24).[43] Another problem is that this requires an event after the seventy weeks—the destruction of Jerusalem in AD 70.

---

[42] *Antiquities* 10.11.7.

[43] G. L. Archer, "Daniel," in *The Expositor's Bible Commentary*, ed. Frank E. Gaebelein, vol. 7 (Grand Rapids: Zondervan, 1985), 7:112.

Baldwin tries to solve these problems by extending the seventieth week to the second advent, though this makes the weeks disproportionate in length.

Theodoret[44] takes Daniel's "abomination of desolation" to be Pilate's defilement of Jerusalem (and by implication its temple) by temporarily bringing into it idolatrous ensigns with images of Caesar. This produced such fervent Jewish protests that he relented and had the images removed, an event mentioned by Josephus[45] and Philo.[46] He also used money from the temple Corban offerings for public works, which provoked Jewish protesters, some of whom his soldiers killed.[47] Against Theodoret's view is that Pilate relented of displaying the idolatrous shields in Jerusalem, so ultimately neither this event nor Pilate's use of temple monies seem important enough to be the abomination of desolation.

Payne's view that starts the weeks at 458 BC suffers from the fact that Cyrus' decree is more important for rebuilding Jerusalem than Artaxerxes' decrees. Cyrus' decree also fits the context of Daniel 9 better, since both date to the same year (9:1; Ezra 1:1–4). Young's view suffers from his seventy weeks not being precise weeks of years. The expression "anoint the most holy" (v. 24) could be applied to a person rather than a place or thing, though the expression "the holy of holies" elsewhere applies to things rather than people. Applying the expression to the inauguration of God-ordained worship is possible but not the most obvious interpretation.

Three Views of Daniel 9:24–27			
	Antiochus View	**Classic Dispensational View**	**Roman View**
Beginning of seventy weeks	605 BC (Jeremiah 25)	Decree of Artaxerxes I in Nehemiah 2 (444 or 445 BC) or possibly decree of Artaxerxes I in Ezra 7 (458 BC)	Cyrus' decree in Ezra 1:1–4 and/or Daniel's prayer (538 BC) or possibly decree of Artaxerxes I in Ezra 7 (458 BC)

---

[44] Theodoret, *Commentary on Daniel*, 257.

[45] Josephus, *Antiquities* 18.55–59; *Jewish War* 2.169–174.

[46] Philo, *Embassy to Gaius*, 299–305.

[47] Josephus, *Jewish War* 2.175–177; *Antiquities* 18.60–62

Three Views of Daniel 9:24–27 (continued)			
	Antiochus View	Classic Dispensational View	Roman View
End of seven weeks	Cyrus ("the anointed prince") crowned (558 BC)	Past the era of Ezra and Nehemiah	To or past the era of Ezra and Nehemiah
End of sixty-nine weeks	Onias III ("the anointed prince") deposed and killed (c. 171 BC) Sixty-two and seven weeks overlap	Triumphal entry of Christ (30 March AD 33) or possibly Jesus' baptism (AD 26) Messiah "cut off" refers to Christ crucified, marking the end of the 62 weeks	AD 26 or whenever Jesus' baptism occurs
Seventieth week	Antiochus IV persecutes the faithful Jews and makes covenant with Hellenizing Jews (171–164 BC)	The "great tribulation" of the end times, following the "great parenthesis" of the church age	From Jesus' baptism until the stoning of Stephen (Acts 7), putting an end to the old covenant (AD 26–33 or alternatively AD 29–36)
Middle of seventieth week	Antiochus dedicates temple to Zeus (167 BC)	Antichrist makes covenant with Jews midway through great tribulation	Christ crucified to deal with the problem of sin, to bring in eternal righteousness, and establish the new covenant
End of seventieth week and beyond	Temple rededicated by Judas Maccabeus (164 BC)	Second coming of Christ to establish millennial kingdom	Stephen stoned (AD 33 or 36) and after the seventy weeks Titus desolates Jerusalem/temple (AD 70)

As the discussion above shows, none of the interpretative schemes offered are without difficulty. In my own evaluation, the Antiochus view seems the weakest since it implies failed prophecy.

The dispensational approach also seems weak, though it is interesting that some in the early church (Hippolytus) placed Daniel's seventieth week just before the second coming. The Roman view seems most attractive, though it is not without weaknesses. I lean toward the view of Young that sees the weeks as general time periods and starts the clock in the year of Daniel's prophecy at Cyrus' decree to restore Jerusalem (Isa 44:28; Ezra 1:1–4). Though the specific-year view of Payne allows for a chronologically precise fulfillment starting from Artaxerxes' decree in 458 BC, it is not really a decree to "restore and rebuild Jerusalem" (v. 25) and so is not the best starting point for the prophecy.

Bridge

Though Daniel 9:20–27 is a difficult text and no interpretation is without difficulty, it includes biblical-theological themes that apply regardless of overall interpretation. The passage is a prophecy of hope, reminding believers that God answers prayer (see §4.7). It affirms the reality of angels as mediators of God's revelation (compare Acts 7:53; Gal 3:19; Heb 2:2) and that through prayer angels can help people in their extreme weariness (9:21; cf. Luke 22:43; see §5). It affirms that God directs the course of history for his people (9:24, 25, 26, 27; see §7.1) and enables them to endure a terrible "abomination of desolation" (9:27; see §4.5), something Jesus sees happening (or happening in an analogous way again) in the future (Matt 24:15; Mark 13:14) in the destruction of Jerusalem (Luke 21:20). God's predetermined plan shows his sovereignty over human history (see §3.8). His plan ultimately deals with sin (see §4.5) and establishes righteousness (see §4.1, §4.2). Despite sin and desolation God's Jubilee purposes (comments v. 24) will win in the end.

Daniel 9:20–27 develops a broader biblical-theological theme around the concept of Sabbath that shows how God blesses and saves his faithful people (see §4.4, §4.5). Daniel's seventy sevens builds on Jubilee and Sabbatical years (see comments at 9:24) that prescribed rest, restoration, and redemption for the land, and forgiveness of debts, provision of food, and justice for the poor. Jubilee and Sabbatical years themselves build on the Sabbath day, which is associated with holiness, rest, redemption, and refreshment for people and animals (Exod 20:11; Deut 5:14–15). The Sabbath day in turn builds on the Edenic Sabbath rest following God's good creation, which is associated with blessing and holiness (Gen 2:2–3). By drawing on the Sabbatical theme, Daniel seems to be conferring to his seventy weeks concepts associated with various Sabbath celebrations. This suggests that the consummation of Daniel's seventy sevens will result in such things as rest, restoration, justice, redemption, holiness, refreshment, and blessing for both the land and God's people.[48] Hebrews 3:7–4:11 develops Sabbath and rest language along similar lines. The writer of Hebrews, like Daniel, finds in the Sabbath theme an anticipation of God's redemption, restoration, and salvation of his people.

---

[48] R. Haydon, *"Seventy Years Are Decreed": A Canonical Approach to Daniel 9:24–27*, Journal of Theological Interpretation Supplements 15 (Winona Lake, IN: Eisenbrauns, 2016), 84–85, drawing on B. Childs, *Old Testament Theology in a Canonical Context* (Philadelphia: Fortress, 1985), 70–71.

I. Court Narratives (Daniel 1–6)

II. Visions of Daniel (Daniel 7–12)
>First vision: Four beasts and son of man figure (Daniel 7)
>Second vision: Ram and male goat (Daniel 8)
>Third vision: Seventy weeks (Daniel 9)
>**Fourth vision: Kings of North/South, distress/resurrection (Daniel 10–12)**
>>**Angels in conflict (10:1–11:2a)**
>>Preview of Persian and Greek kings (11:2b–35)
>>World kingdoms ended and the righteous established (11:36–12:3)
>>Vision sealed until the end (12:4–13)

(A) Beginning of story (1:1–21)
>(B) Dream about four world kingdoms ended by the kingdom of God (2:1–49)
>>(C) Judeans faithful in the face of death (3:1–30)
>>>(D) Royal pride humbled (4:1–37)
>>>(D′) Royal pride humbled (5:1–31)
>>(C′) A Judean faithful in the face of death (6:1–28)
>(B′) Vision about four world kingdoms ended by the kingdom of God (7:1–28)
>>(E) Vision of Persian and Greek kingdoms to Antiochus (8:1–27)
>>>(F) Vision of seventy weeks (9:1–27)
>>**(E′) Vision of Persian and Greek kingdoms to Antiochus (10:1–11:35)**
>>>**Part 1: Angels in conflict (10:1–11:2a)**
>>>Part 2: Preview of Persian and Greek kings (11:2b–35)
>(B″) World kingdoms ended and the righteous established (11:36–12:3)
(A′) End of story: Vision sealed until the end (12:4–13)

[1] In the third year of King Cyrus of Persia, a message was revealed to Daniel, who was named Belteshazzar. The message was true and was about a great conflict. He understood the message and had understanding of the vision.

[2] In those days I, Daniel, was mourning for three full weeks. [3] I

didn't eat any rich food, no meat or wine entered my mouth, and I didn't put any oil on my body until the three weeks were over. ⁴On the twenty-fourth day of the first month, as I was standing on the bank of the great river, the Tigris, ⁵I looked up, and there was a man dressed in linen, with a belt of gold from Uphaz around his waist. ⁶His body was like beryl, his face like the brilliance of lightning, his eyes like flaming torches, his arms and feet like the gleam of polished bronze, and the sound of his words like the sound of a multitude.

⁷Only I, Daniel, saw the vision. The men who were with me did not see it, but a great terror fell on them, and they ran and hid. ⁸I was left alone, looking at this great vision. No strength was left in me; my face grew deathly pale, and I was powerless. ⁹I heard the words he said, and when I heard them I fell into a deep sleep, with my face to the ground.

¹⁰Suddenly, a hand touched me and set me shaking on my hands and knees. ¹¹He said to me, "Daniel, you are a man treasured by God. Understand the words that I'm saying to you. Stand on your feet, for I have now been sent to you." After he said this to me, I stood trembling.

¹²"Don't be afraid, Daniel," he said to me, "for from the first day that you purposed to understand and to humble yourself before your God, your prayers were heard. I have come because of your prayers. ¹³But the prince of the kingdom of Persia opposed me for twenty-one days. Then Michael, one of the chief princes, came to help me after I had been left there with the kings of Persia. ¹⁴Now I have come to help you understand what will happen to your people in the last days, for the vision refers to those days."

¹⁵While he was saying these words to me, I turned my face toward the ground and was speechless. ¹⁶Suddenly one with human likeness touched my lips. I opened my mouth and said to the one standing in front of me, "My lord, because of the vision, anguish overwhelms me and I am powerless. ¹⁷How can someone like me, your servant, speak with someone like you, my lord? Now I have no strength, and there is no breath in me."

¹⁸Then the one with a human appearance touched me again and strengthened me. ¹⁹He said, "Don't be afraid, you who are treasured by God. Peace to you; be very strong!"

As he spoke to me, I was strengthened and said, "Let my lord speak, for you have strengthened me."

²⁰He said, "Do you know why I've come to you? I must return at once to fight against the prince of Persia, and when I leave,

the prince of Greece will come. ²¹ However, I will tell you what is recorded in the book of truth. (No one has the courage to support me against those princes except Michael, your prince.
¹ In the first year of Darius the Mede, I stood up to strengthen and protect him.) ² Now I will tell you the truth."

Context

Daniel 10–12 concludes the book with Daniel's fourth vision. The first part of this vision is 10:1–11:2a, which serves as a prologue to a preview of history. In the second part, Daniel 11:2b–35, an angel reveals to Daniel what happens in the Persian and Greek periods (the second and third beasts of Daniel 7) when the southern kingdom of Egypt (the Ptolemies) and the northern kingdom of Syria (the Seleucids) fight for control of Palestine. This culminates in Antiochus IV Epiphanes' blasphemous reign. Daniel 11:36–45 jumps from type to antitype, from Antiochus to an evil future figure who seems to be identified with the little horn of Daniel 7. Daniel 11 ends with the demise of this eschatological figure. Then Daniel 12:1–3 envisions the resurrection of the just and the unjust at the end of the age. The last section, Daniel 12:4–13, serves as an epilogue discussing the mysterious nature of God's revelation to Daniel.

In the outline of the book, 10:1–11:35 parallels Daniel 8, which speaks of Medo-Persia and the Greek kingdoms. The prologue to Daniel's fourth vision, 10:1–11:2a, reveals something of the mysterious supernatural operations of the forces of good and evil. We see demons associated with Persia and Greece engaged in invisible battles with angels, though these heavenly struggles have visible effects in earthly history.

Daniel 10:1–11:2a can be outlined as follows. Note that the "book of truth" (v. 21) and the "message … about a great conflict" (v. 1) are the same thing:

A   Daniel to receive message about a great conflict (10:1)
    B   Man in linen comes after Daniel fasts for three weeks (10:2–6)
        C   Daniel falls into trance but roused by angel (10:7–11)
    B′   Angel comes in answer to Daniel's prayer after supernatural delay (10:12–14)

> C′   Daniel overwhelmed but strengthened by angel
>   (10:15–19)
> A′   Angel to convey the book of truth (10:20–11:2a)

10:1 The voice of the narrator/editor interrupts Daniel's autobiographical memoir, giving a heading to the whole vision of Daniel 10–12. This prophecy dates to 536 BC (see further at v. 4), Cyrus' third year, about two years after the vision of Daniel 9. There are parallel date formulae with the other four visions. The first two visions date to the first and third years of Belshazzar (7:1; 8:1), and the next two visions date to the first and third years of Darius/Cyrus (9:1; 10:1). On Belteshazzar see comments at 1:7. God's "message" (or "word" ESV) is "true" (אֱמֶת), a quality Daniel often ascribes to God's revelation (8:26; 10:1; 11:2a; see §2).

"Great conflict" could also be rendered "great war" (NIV), though the syntax of the Hebrew is awkward, so other ways of understanding צָבָא ("military service, army, war, host") cannot be ruled out (NJPS, "it was a great task to understand the prophecy"). If it denotes a great conflict or war, then it signifies all the conflicts of Daniel 10–12 (10:13; 11:2–4, 5–35), all of which culminates in an eschatological battle (11:36–12:3). "Had understanding of the vision" is better rendered "through the vision" (NJPS; cf. NET, "gained insight by a vision").

10:2–3 "Mourning" rites (v. 2) can involve fasting and imply prayer. In this case Daniel conducted a partial, vegetables-only fast for twenty-one days (cf. 10:13). This is similar to the diet he adopted in Daniel 1, though for different reasons. "Rich" (חֶמְדֹּת) in the expression "rich food" (v. 3a) refers to what is "the best, most costly, or most valued,"[1] a word used also at 9:23 (see comments). This fast excludes choice foods or delicacies, including animal flesh ("meat") and "wine." For poor people at this time, meat was a luxury item only enjoyed on special occasions. Daniel, as a government official, was not poor and could enjoy meat regularly. But as part of his dedication to God in prayer he deliberately abstained from these things. On the religious significance of fasting, see commentary at 9:3.

---

[1] "חֲמֻדוֹת (ḥămŭ·dôṯ)," in J. Swanson, *Dictionary of Biblical Languages with Semantic Domains: Aramaic and Hebrew (Old Testament)*, electronic ed. (Oak Harbor: Logos Research Systems, 1997).

Daniel while mourning also abstained from "oil" (v. 3b), probably for grooming. Oil is listed along with food and clothing as a staple commodity (Hos 2:5; Eccl 2:7–8). Grooming oil was used as a perfume (Ruth 3:3; Ps 45:7) and for maintaining the skin against the sun (Eccl 2:8). Daily anointing was commonplace in biblical times (2 Sam 12:20; Matt 6:17). To not anoint was an act of deprivation.

It is not immediately clear why Daniel was "mourning." Was he still concerned over the sins of his people and the state of Jerusalem (9:1–19)? Was he thinking about his earlier visions (Daniel 7, 8, and 9) with their traumatic predictions of persecution for his people? Was he concerned about those returning from exile with Sheshbazzar about this time (Ezra 1:5–11)? Or a combination of these?

10:4–5 The "first month" (v. 4a) in the Babylonian lunar calendar is Nisan (March/April in our calendar). Not partaking of meat or wine till the twenty-fourth day of the first month (v. 4) probably means Daniel did not participate in the Passover that occurred on the fourteenth day of the first month (Nisan).[2] As argued at 9:2, the first year of Cyrus/Darius began after the regnal year 0 on 1 Nisan 538 BC, so the first month of his third year would be 536 BC. The twenty-fourth day was 23 April 536 BC.[3]

The Tigris (v. 4b) and the Euphrates are the two "great" rivers of Mesopotamia, a geographic term derived from Greek denoting the land between these two rivers (μέσος, "between" + ποταμός, "river"). The Tigris presently lies roughly fifty miles east of Babylon, though both the Tigris and Euphrates have shifted course from time to time. The Euphrates in Cyrus' day passed through Babylon, though it now flows about ten miles west of it. This vision resembles that of Daniel 8 in the third year of Belshazzar when Daniel was on the banks of the Ulai near Susa (8:1–2).

"Linen" (v. 5a) is a simple if rough fabric made from flax.[4] Priests entering God's presence in the tabernacle wore linen (Exod 28:39, 42; Lev 6:10, 16:4), and angels in the presence of God also are described as wearing linen (Ezek 9:2–3, 11; 10:2; Dan 10:5). "Gold from Uphaz" (v. 5b) employs a relatively rare term for gold (כֶּתֶם; the common word is זָהָב). The geographic term "Uphaz" is of unknown

---

[2] A. E. Steinmann, *Daniel*, Concordia Commentary (St. Louis: Concordia, 2008), 496–97.

[3] Ibid., 482.

[4] "בַּד (*bǎḏ*)," in Swanson, *Dictionary of Biblical Languages with Semantic Domains.*

location but known for its gold (Jer 10:9). Uphaz may be an alternate term for Ophir, a location also known for its gold (1 Kings 5:28; 10:11), which is what a few Hebrew manuscripts actually read (CSB note). Ophir's location, while disputed, is likely in Arabia, though East Africa and even India are possible identifications. Yet another possibility is that Uphaz (אוּפָז) is a mistake for וּפָז, "even refined gold." Revelation portrays angels as persons in linen girded with gold (Rev 15:6) and applies similar imagery to Christ (Rev 1:13, though without the linen).

10:6 "Beryl" is a likely identification of this precious stone, though some suggest it is either "yellow jasper" or "topaz." There are three options for the man dressed in linen:

1. One suggestion is that the man is Gabriel, who has appeared previously in the book (Dan 8:16 and 9:21). His prominence "above" two other angels in 12:5–7 who make inquiries of him is consistent with this view. Against this view, however, is the fact that he is not identified by name. Given that Gabriel has already appeared by name twice, one would expect him to be named here.

2. Some Christian commentators have suggested that this figure is a theophany, a manifestation of God, or, more specifically, a pre-incarnate appearance of Jesus Christ.[5] In favor of this is the fact that the imagery of this figure resembles that of God in Ezek 1:26–28 and of Christ in Rev 1:13–16. The latter describes Christ in a robe (linen?), girded with a golden sash, having eyes like flaming fire, feet like burning bronze, and a voice like many waters. But this view is also problematic. If this figure is a theophany, how is he hindered by the prince of Persia until he receives assistance from Michael in v. 13? To salvage the theophany view, one might posit that the man in linen is God, who disappears after Daniel falls asleep. Then the theophany is replaced in v. 10 by a vision of an angel.[6] While not impossible, the transition does seem too abrupt to be likely.

---

[5] E.g., E. J. Young, *The Prophecy of Daniel* (Grand Rapids: Eerdmans, 1949), 225; J. F. Walvoord (Chicago: Moody, 1971), 243; S. R. Miller, *Daniel*, NAC 18 (Nashville: Broadman & Holman, 1994), 281–82; Steinmann, *Daniel*, 498–501.

[6] Walvoord, *Daniel*, 245; Miller, *Daniel*, 283.

Ezekiel 1:26b–28b	Daniel 10:5–6	Revelation 1:13b–16
On the throne, high above, was someone who looked like a human. From what seemed to be his waist up, **I saw a gleam like amber,** with what looked like fire enclosing it all around. From what seemed to be his waist down, I also saw what looked like fire. There was **a brilliant light all around him.** The appearance of the brilliant light all around was like that of a rainbow in a cloud on a rainy day. This was the appearance of the likeness of the Lord's glory.	I looked up, and there was a man dressed **in linen,** with a **belt of gold** from Uphaz around his waist. **His body was like beryl, his face like the brilliance of lightning,** his **eyes like flaming torches,** his arms and **feet like the gleam of polished bronze,** and the sound of his **words like the sound of a multitude.**	… one like the Son of Man, **dressed in a long robe** and with a **golden sash** wrapped around his chest. The **hair of his head was white like wool—white as snow—**and his **eyes like a fiery flame.** His **feet were like fine bronze as it is fired in a furnace,** and **his voice like the sound of cascading waters.** He had seven stars in his right hand; a sharp double-edged sword came from his mouth, and **his face was shining like the sun** at full strength.

3. The simplest and most likely view is that the man dressed in linen is an unnamed angel, different than Gabriel. Angels elsewhere appear clothed in linen (Ezek 9:2–3, 11; 10:2; Rev 15:6) and can be girded with gold (Rev 15:6). They can appear nearly as glorious as deity (see Ezek 1:7; Matt 27:2–3; Rev 10:1–3). Hence this is likely an unnamed angel.

10:7–9 "Vision" (מַרְאָה) is a less common term for prophetic revelation (see §2). It refers to something seen, in this case an "apparition."[7] Those with him, though unable to see the apparition, had a terrorizing sense of the supernatural that led them to run away and abandon Daniel. "Terror" (חֲרָדָה) is from a root meaning "to tremble" and thus refers to the manifestation of fear in the body. The Hebrew of "my face grew deathly pale" reads, "my splendor was changed to destruction/corruption." "Splendor" (הוֹד) has the sense of bright "complexion" of a vibrant person. Daniel's face turning pale echoes the Aramaic in Dan 5:6–10 and 7:28. On "deep sleep" with one's face to the ground, see comments at 8:18.

10:10–11 "Suddenly" seems too strong a rendering for Hebrew הִנֵּה. Though the particle can add a sense of vividness to the narration, it may mean little more than "then" (NRSV, NJPS) or be legitimately left untranslated (NIV). "Set me shaking" (v. 10b) is the H-stem of נוע ("shake"), so the sense seems to be that the angel "shook me onto my hands and knees" (NJPS). The Hebrew of "you are a man treasured by God" (v. 11a) reads as a vocative, "O man of treasured things," meaning that he was a treasured or precious person (on "treasured" see comments at 9:23). By implication he is "treasured by God" though God is not mentioned. "Understand" (v. 11b; H-stem of בין) seems to be an internal causative "make [yourself] understand" as at 8:5 and 9:23, though the specific sense here may be "pay attention" (NJPS, "mark my words"). "Stand on your feet" (v. 11c) reads in the Hebrew, "Stand in your place." The CSB "trembling" (v. 11d) is the H-stem participle of רעד. The CSB rendering makes for a fluent translation, but the form appears to be an internal causative meaning "making [myself] tremble." It is hard to translate that well into English.

10:12–13 On "understand" (v. 12b) see comments at v. 10. To "humble yourself" (v. 12b) or "afflict yourself" (HtD of ענה, "to be wretched") picks up on the fact that Daniel has been fasting (10:2–3). It is remarkable enough that God once again sent an angel to answer Daniel's prayer (v. 12c; cp. 9:20–27). Even more remarkable is that a supernatural being could be delayed for three weeks (v. 13a) from his appointed task. The angel was opposed by the "prince [שַׂר] of the kingdom of Persia" and was only able to arrive after a certain "Michael" (v. 13b) helped him. The name Michael (v. 13b) in Hebrew is a rhetorical question "Who is like God?" for which the answer is: Nobody! Michael is called "one of the chief princes." On "prince" [שַׂר], see comments at 8:11. Michael is elsewhere in Daniel identified as "the great prince who stands watch over your people" (12:1). He also appears in the NT as an "archangel" under whom are other angels (Jude 1:9; Rev 12:7). In the intertestamental period Michael appears as a character in 1 Enoch 20:5 and 24:5.

The prince of the kingdom of Persia (v. 13a) is associated with the "kings of Persia." Some take "kings of Persia" as a plural of majesty that means "the king [singular] of Persia" (NIV, Vulgate). The prince (שַׂר) of Persia can hardly be a human,[8] for only a supernatural being could delay an angel. He and Michael are both referred to by the same title: "prince" (in contrast to the "kings" of Persia). Since this "prince" is opposed to God's angels, he can reasonably be labeled a demon.

While William Shea wrongly takes the princes of Persia and Greece to be the human princes of Persia and Greece (Cambyses and Alexander),[9] he more plausibly takes "kings of Persia" (v. 13b) to refer to the two kings, Cyrus the emperor and Cambyses the crown prince.[10] This might imply a co-regency or refer to the fact that Cambyses became the Babylonian head of state and took the title "king of Babylon" in addition to being crown prince of Persia.[11] It appears that the demonic "prince of the kingdom of Persia" who "opposed" the angel was engaged in a spiritual battle with him over these kings. This demon sought to influence the kings of Persia to harm God's people just as another territorial demon, the "prince of Greece" (v. 20), attempted to do the same through the Greeks. While Cyrus helped the Jewish people return from exile (cf. Ezra 1:1–4), later during the time of Xerxes (Ahasuerus), Haman tried to get Xerxes to destroy the Jews (Esth 3:6). Behind such plots and the actions of Esther to save the Jewish people were battles between unseen spiritual forces, demonic and angelic. The angel was delayed because he was "left" with the kings of Persia to counter the efforts of the demonic prince of Persia, intervening on Israel's behalf. This angel, along with Michael, sought to protect God's people from the prince of Persia.

10:14 The angel left his assignment with the kings of Persia for a revelatory task, causing Daniel to "understand" (H-stem בִּין) his people's future. The Hebrew rendered "the last days" ("the latter days" KJV, ESV) reads more literally "the end of the days" (אַחֲרִית הַיָּמִים; cf.

---

[8] John Calvin identifies him as Cambyses (*Commentary on the Book of the Prophet Daniel*, trans. Thomas Myers, 2 vols. [Bellingham, WA: Logos Bible Software, 2010], 252). Tim Meadowcroft sees human, temporal princes somehow participating in heavenly battles ("Who Are the Princes of Persia and Greece [Daniel 10]? Pointers Towards the Danielic Vision of Earth and Heaven," *JSOT* 29.1 [2004]: 99–113).

[9] William H. Shea, "Wrestling with the Prince of Persia: A Study on Daniel 10," *AUSS* 21.3 (1983): 234–35.

[10] Ibid., 240–46.

[11] David E. Stevens, "Daniel 10 and the Notion of Territorial Spirits," *BSac* 157:628 (2000): 425.

the similar expression in Aramaic at 2:28). This idiom simply means "the future" (NIV) or "the days to come" (NJPS). CSB sometimes renders this expression "the future" (Num 24:14; Deut 31:29) or "the days to come" (Gen 49:1). Judging from the prophecy that follows, "the last days" here includes everything from the immediate future in the Persian period (11:3), through the Greek period (11:3–35), and even to the end-time resurrection of the just and the unjust (12:2).

10:15–16 The vision struck Daniel mute until the angel ("one with human likeness") roused him by touching his lips (v. 16a). On the over-translation "suddenly," see comment at v. 10. Daniel acknowledged the superior status of the angel by addressing him as "my lord" (v. 16c; אֲדֹנִי). "Anguish" ("pains," ESV; "pangs," NJPS) is the plural of Hebrew צִיר, a term that can refer to the physical pain of childbirth (Isa 21:3). Here psychological anguish, anxiety, or torment seems more appropriate. "Overwhelms" is the N-stem of הפך, a verb that normally means "overturned, changed." With צִיר and the preposition עַל ("upon"), it is used to indicate that a woman's labor pains "fell upon" her (1 Sam 4:19). So the sense may be that Daniel's "pains" or "anguish" overwhelmed him like a woman's birth pangs. "I am powerless" reads in the Hebrew "I retain no strength" (ESV, NRSV), meaning "I feel very weak" (NIV).

10:17–19 The Hebrew of the first part of verse 17 is awkward. It reads, "How can this servant of my lord speak with this my lord," which seems to mean, "How can I your servant speak with you my Lord." This expresses Daniel's humility, along with his sense of being faint ("no strength") and gasping for air ("no breath") in finding himself speaking with a supernatural being. Daniel had similar experiences in his other visions (7:15; 8:27).

On "touched again" (v. 18) see vv. 10, 15. "Don't be afraid" (v. 19a) repeats v. 12. "Treasured by God" repeats v. 11 (see comments there and at 9:23). "Peace to you" (v. 19b) can be taken as a friendly greeting (Gen 37:4, Darby), but expressed in conjunction with "do not be afraid," it appears to seek to inculcate "peace" as the opposite of fear (cf. Judg 6:23). "Be very strong" uses repetition for emphasis (literally, "be strong and be strong"), though some Hebrew manuscripts (supported by the Old Greek and Theodotion) read "be strong and courageous" (חֲזַק וֶאֱמָץ), which in any case is the general sense. Having been strengthened, Daniel permitted the angel to continue.

10:20 The angel did not pause to let Daniel answer his "why" question but hurried to explain that his time was limited since he needed to leave to fight the territorial demon, the prince of Persia. "Fight" (N-stem of לחם), like the word "host" in 8:10, applies the language of war to angels. The "prince of Greece" is the territorial demon that influenced the Greeks against God's people. This coming of the "prince of Greece" anticipates how Greece would succeed Persia as the new great power (11:2–3; cf. 8:5–7). Daniel's angel knew that his fight with the prince of Persia would be followed by conflicts involving Greece and the demonic forces that influenced it. The greatest threat to the Jewish people during the Persian period came from the attempted genocide during the time of Esther, though this was passed over by the prophecy that follows. The vision focuses instead on the greatest threat to the Jewish people during the Greek period: the attempt of Antiochus IV to abolish the Jewish religion (11:21–35; cf. 8:9–14, 23–26).

10:21 Verse 21 indicates that the angel's purpose is revelatory, to convey "truth" (see v. 11b below). "Recorded" (or "written") is the Qal passive participle of רשׁם, a root that occurs only here in the Hebrew Bible (it is common in Aramaic so it is probably an Aramaism). The "book of truth" (or "writing of truth," NASB; כְּתָב, "writing, document") is in part recorded in the "true" prophecy (cf. 11:2) that follows in Daniel 11–12. This surveys what will happen to Palestine and God's people in the Persian and Greek periods and beyond, showing God's foreknowledge of the future (see §3.5). Daniel 11–12 represents a portion of this larger divine plan for history (see §7) that records Israel's future in advance. Compare the scroll of destiny in Rev 5:7–9. This book of truth was possible because God determined and/or foreknew his people's future.

"Has the courage to support me" is a plausible rendering of the HtD participle of חזק ("be strong"). This text reads formally, "strengthens himself with me." Other possible understandings of this phrase include "stands strong with me" (CEB), "contends by my side" (RSV), and "is helping me" (NJPS). "Against them" (or "these" ESV) refers to the hostile spiritual forces against which they contended. Michael is "your prince." In Hebrew the pronoun "your" is plural so the sense is not merely that Michael is Daniel's prince but rather Israel's prince and protector (see further at 10:13 and 12:1).

Why Michael alone came (or had the courage to come) to this angel's aid is a mystery left unexplained.

11:1–2a CSB takes Dan 11:1–2a as a continuation of the last paragraph of chapter 10. The angel's narrative flashes back two years to the beginning of the "first year of" Persian rule. Theodotion and the Old Greek both interpret "Darius" as "Cyrus," which is the most likely identification of Daniel's Darius (see the Introduction). It was in that year that Cyrus allowed Jews to return to Judah and begin rebuilding the temple (Ezra 1:1–4). Here we learn that there was invisible, angelic influence (see §5) as he began his reign that led to his allowing the Jews to return.

The MT rendered "stood" (עָמְדִי) is a Qal infinitive construct of עמד "to stand" plus suffix "my" or else the noun עֹמֶד "location, place" plus suffix "my." Either way the text is awkward. This form should probably be corrected from עָמְדִי to the perfect עָמַדְתִּי ("I stood"), which involves adding one consonant taw (ת) or more to the participle עֹמֵד, which involves deletion of the seemingly extraneous yod (י). Despite this problem, the general sense is clear. The Hebrew of "protect" is actually a noun מָעוֹז ("fortress, refuge") that could be rendered "to strengthen and as a protection for him" (cf. LEB, NASB). Alternatively, מָעוֹז might be an Aramaism, an infinitive after the Aramaic pattern. God's revelation about the future is reliable "truth" (11:2a; אֱמֶת). See further at 8:26 and 10:1.

Bridge

Daniel 10:1–11:2a gives us further insight into prayer (see §4.7) and a fascinating glimpse into the invisible realm of angels and demons (see §5). In particular it affirms that God sometimes sends angels to assist and strengthen people in response to prayer (10:1–11) and that spiritual war rages in the heavenly realms over the direction of history. This corresponds with what Paul tells the Ephesians, "For our struggle is not against flesh and blood, but against the rulers, against the authorities, against the cosmic powers of this darkness, against evil, spiritual forces in the heavens" (Eph 6:12). "Rulers" and "authorities" (cp. Col 2:15) refer to demonic powers that can influence people and events on earth, just as the prince of Persia influenced the kings of Persia (Dan 10:13). Revelation reflects the same concept. The war between Michael and the devil (along with their angels) in heaven corresponds to the persecution of the saints on earth.

The reality of powerful, demonic forces in the unseen world working against us, and the announcement of a coming "great conflict" involving them (10:1), can frighten us. Yet this passage also offers encouragement and comfort in that God's forces are ultimately more powerful. These will work on our behalf to protect and strengthen us and to answer our prayers. The cross of Christ has disarmed the forces of darkness and given us victory (Col 2:15). A death blow to Satan's power has been provided though the blood of the Lamb, which enables us to overcome the forces of evil (Rev 12:10–11). Moreover, human destiny is controlled by God, who records it in advance in his "book of truth" (10:21) (see §3.8).

I. Court Narratives (Daniel 1–6)

II. **Visions of Daniel (Daniel 7–12)**
First vision: Four beasts and son of man figure (Daniel 7)
Second vision: Ram and male goat (Daniel 8)
Third vision: Seventy weeks (Daniel 9)
Fourth vision: Kings of North/South, distress/resurrection (Daniel 10–12)
Angels in conflict (10:1–11:2a)
Preview of Persian and Greek kings (11:2b–35)
World kingdoms ended and the righteous established (11:36–12:3)
Vision sealed until the end (12:4–13)

(A) Beginning of story (1:1–21)
  (B) Dream about four world kingdoms ended by the kingdom of God (2:1–49)
    (C) Judeans faithful in the face of death (3:1–30)
      (D) Royal pride humbled (4:1–37)
      (D') Royal pride humbled (5:1–31)
    (C') A Judean faithful in the face of death (6:1–28)
  (B') Vision about four world kingdoms ended by the kingdom of God (7:1–28)
    (E) Vision of Persian and Greek kingdoms to Antiochus (8:1–27)
      (F) Vision of seventy weeks (9:1–27)
    (E') Vision of Persian and Greek kingdoms to Antiochus (10:1–11:35)
      Part 1: Angels in conflict (10:1–11:2a)
      Part 2: Preview of Persian and Greek kings (11:2b–35)
  (B'') World kingdoms ended and the righteous established (11:36–12:3)
(A') End of story: Vision sealed until the end (12:4–13)

"Three more kings will arise in Persia, and the fourth will be far richer than the others. By the power he gains through his riches, he will stir up everyone against the kingdom of Greece. ³Then a warrior king will arise; he will rule a vast realm and do whatever he wants. ⁴But as soon as he is established, his kingdom will be broken up and divided to the four winds of heaven, but not to his descendants; it will not be the same kingdom that he ruled, because his kingdom will be uprooted and will go to others besides them.

⁵ "The king of the South will grow powerful, but one of his commanders will grow more powerful and will rule a kingdom greater than his. ⁶ After some years they will form an alliance, and the daughter of the king of the South will go to the king of the North to seal the agreement. She will not retain power, and his strength will not endure. She will be given up, together with her entourage, her father, and the one who supported her during those times. ⁷ In the place of the king of the South, one from her family will rise up, come against the army, and enter the fortress of the king of the North. He will take action against them and triumph. ⁸ He will take even their gods captive to Egypt, with their metal images and their precious articles of silver and gold. For some years he will stay away from the king of the North, ⁹ who will enter the kingdom of the king of the South and then return to his own land.

¹⁰ "His sons will mobilize for war and assemble a large number of armed forces. They will advance, sweeping through like a flood, and will again wage war as far as his fortress. ¹¹ Infuriated, the king of the South will march out to fight with the king of the North, who will raise a large army, but they will be handed over to his enemy. ¹² When the army is carried off, he will become arrogant and cause tens of thousands to fall, but he will not triumph. ¹³ The king of the North will again raise a multitude larger than the first. After some years he will advance with a great army and many supplies.

¹⁴ "In those times many will rise up against the king of the South. Violent ones among your own people will assert themselves to fulfill a vision, but they will fail. ¹⁵ Then the king of the North will come, build up a siege ramp, and capture a well-fortified city. The forces of the South will not stand; even their select troops will not be able to resist. ¹⁶ The king of the North who comes against him will do whatever he wants, and no one can oppose him. He will establish himself in the beautiful land with total destruction in his hand. ¹⁷ He will resolve to come with the force of his whole kingdom and will reach an agreement with him. He will give him a daughter in marriage to destroy it, but she will not stand with him or support him. ¹⁸ Then he will turn his attention to the coasts and islands and capture many. But a commander will put an end to his taunting; instead, he will turn his taunts against him. ¹⁹ He will turn his attention back to the fortresses of his own land, but he will stumble, fall, and be no more.

[20] "In his place one will arise who will send out a tax collector for the glory of the kingdom; but within a few days he will be broken, though not in anger or in battle.

[21] "In his place a despised person will arise; royal honors will not be given to him, but he will come during a time of peace and seize the kingdom by intrigue. [22] A flood of forces will be swept away before him; they will be broken, as well as the covenant prince. [23] After an alliance is made with him, he will act deceitfully. He will rise to power with a small nation. [24] During a time of peace, he will come into the richest parts of the province and do what his fathers and predecessors never did. He will lavish plunder, loot, and wealth on his followers, and he will make plans against fortified cities, but only for a time.

[25] "With a large army he will stir up his power and his courage against the king of the South. The king of the South will prepare for battle with an extremely large and powerful army, but he will not succeed, because plots will be made against him. [26] Those who eat his provisions will destroy him; his army will be swept away, and many will fall slain. [27] The two kings, whose hearts are bent on evil, will speak lies at the same table but to no avail, for still the end will come at the appointed time. [28] The king of the North will return to his land with great wealth, but his heart will be set against the holy covenant; he will take action, then return to his own land.

[29] "At the appointed time he will come again to the South, but this time will not be like the first. [30] Ships of Kittim will come against him, and being intimidated, he will withdraw. Then he will rage against the holy covenant and take action. On his return, he will favor those who abandon the holy covenant. [31] His forces will rise up and desecrate the temple fortress. They will abolish the regular sacrifice and set up the abomination of desolation. [32] With flattery he will corrupt those who act wickedly toward the covenant, but the people who know their God will be strong and take action. [33] Those who have insight among the people will give understanding to many, yet they will fall by the sword and flame, and be captured and plundered for a time. [34] When they fall, they will be helped by some, but many others will join them insincerely. [35] Some of those who have insight will fall so that they may be refined, purified, and cleansed until the time of the end, for it will still come at the appointed time.

Context

Daniel 11:2b–35 is the second unit of the vision that begins at 10:1 and continues through 12:13. The content parallels Daniel 8 (see outline), considering the future from Daniel's time in 536 BC through the Persian period, the conquests and breakup of the Greek kingdom, the struggles between the Ptolemies and the Seleucids of the Hellenistic period (with focus on Antiochus IV), and on until the end of the age.

Since the following discussion has a considerable amount of historical detail, it is helpful to lay out in table form an outline of the matters about which Daniel 11 prophecies.

Passage	Dates	Fulfillment of Events Prophesied
11:2	536–465 BC	Persians beyond Cyrus stir up the Greeks.
11:3–4	334–301 BC	Alexander arises and at his death his kingdom breaks up among his "successors," the *diadochoi*.
11:5	323–281 BC	Ptolemy I of Egypt helps Seleucus I become king of Syro-Babylonia, though Seleucus I ultimately wins the larger kingdom.
11:6	252–246 BC	A marriage alliance, in which Ptolemy II of Egypt gives his daughter Berenice in marriage to the Seleucid king Antiochus II, seals the end of the Second Syrian War. Bernice, her son, and Antiochus II are assassinated by Antiochus' ex-wife Laodice.
11:7–9	246–241 BC	Ptolemy III, the brother of Berenice, invades the Seleucid territory of Seleucus II to avenge Berenice's murder, bringing back from temples some items taken away from Egypt by the Persians.
11:10–12	225–217	Antiochus III initiates the Fourth Syrian War (219–217 BC) and invades Palestine with a large army but suffers defeat to Ptolemy IV at Raphia.
11:13–16	204–195 BC	Child-king Ptolemy V is attacked by Antiochus III, who begins the Fifth Syrian War (202–195 BC). When Antiochus III wins battles at Panium and Sidon against Egyptian general Scopus, the century-long Ptolemaic rule of Phoenicia-Palestine ends.

Passage	Dates	Fulfillment of Events Prophesied
11:17–19	196–187 BC	Cleopatra I, daughter of Antiochus III, marries the boy king of Egypt Ptolemy V, though she is loyal to Egypt and not Antiochus. Antiochus III invades Thrace in Europe but loses the battles of Thermopylae (191) and Magnesia (190) to Roman general Scipio Asiaticus and is forced to pay for the cost of the war and send his own son Antiochus (IV) as a hostage to Rome. Antiochus III is killed by locals while robbing a temple in Elymais.
11:20	187–175 BC	Seleucus IV sends a tax collector named Heliodorus to rob the temple in Jerusalem. Seleucus IV is not killed in battle but is assassinated by Heliodorus.
11:21–35	175–164 BC	These verses describe the rule of Antiochus IV Epiphanes who attempts to abolish the Jewish religion.
11:36–46	Disputed	The meaning of this section is disputed, whether it elaborates further on Antiochus IV, or whether it speaks of an eschatological, antichrist figure (or perhaps both at the same time).

I understand 11:36–46 to refer to what I call "Rome-and-beyond" rather than Antiochus IV, so those verses are treated in the next section of the commentary.

11:2b This verse previews the Persian period and anticipates the rise of Alexander's kingdom. The king at the time of the prophecy was Cyrus II (559–530 BC), who conquered Babylon in 539 BC and died on a campaign against northern Iranian tribes in 530 BC. Cyrus was followed by "three more" and a "fourth." First came his son Cambyses (530–522 BC), best known for his conquest of Egypt in 525 BC. The other three are probably Gaumata/Smerdis (522 BC), Darius I (521–486 BC), and Xerxes (485–465 BC). Darius (not the Darius of the book of Daniel) reconsolidated the kingdom after rebellions, took Asia Minor, and also invaded Greece. But in 490 BC Darius suffered a devastating defeat at the battle of Marathon. He made administrative reforms in which he reorganized the satrapies into twenty-two, Judah being in the Trans-Euphrates province. This made for more efficient tax collection.

"Will be far richer than the others" is better rendered "will gain far more riches than all" (NASB). The H-stem of עשׁר does not mean "become rich" (the G-stem stative meaning), but to "increase riches, gain riches." The fourth successor of Cyrus who is "richer than the others" is Xerxes (485–465 BC), the Ahasuerus of the book of Esther. This can be supported from extrabiblical sources. Xerxes campaigned against Greece from 483 to 479 BC and thus would "stir up everyone against the kingdom of Greece." A series of defeats forced him to withdraw back to Asia Minor, but he produced lasting animosity between the Greeks and Persians, which ultimately found expression in Alexander's invasion.

Xerxes was not the great leader his father was. Although he suppressed a revolt in Egypt, he failed badly in his large-scale campaign against the Greeks. His burning of Athens united the Greek city-states against him. In 480 BC he was humiliated by the battle of Thermopylae in which three hundred Spartans led by Leonidus and other Greeks held off the huge Persian army at the mountain pass. Also in 480 BC Xerxes lost the sea battle of Salamis. In 479 BC his general lost the battle of Plataea despite numeric superiority because the battle occurred in close straits where his cavalry was of no use. Herodotus paints a picture of Xerxes and all Persian monarchs that makes the harem a dominating influence on their lives (Herodotus, *Histories* 1.135.1; 3.69.6), a picture that can be compared with that of Ahasuerus/Xerxes in the book of Esther. His riches came from the empire building of his predecessors, making him the pinnacle of Persian glory and power, after which came a period of stagnation and decline in Persian history.

The identification of the fourth king as Xerxes requires finding another king between Cambyses and Darius. The likely candidate is Gaumata/Smerdis, who briefly took the throne in 522 BC by claiming to be Cambyses' brother. Before Cambyses' Egyptian campaign, Cambyses had his brother Smerdis (Bardiya in Persian sources) killed (Herodotus, *Histories* 3.30.3), though this was kept secret (Herodotus, *Histories* 3.61.1; Darius, Behistun Inscription). In 522 Cambyses had to return to Egypt to put down a rebellion. While gone, a usurper whose real name was Gaumata, a Median magician, pretended to be Bardiya and tried to seize the throne (Behistun Inscription). Cambyses died in Syria before he could come back and address this usurpation.

Darius' Behistun Rock Inscription shows Darius with his foot placed on the neck of Gaumata, the rebel leader whom he had defeated.[1] A few scholars think it really was Bardiya who rebelled and that Darius made up the story of impersonation as a coverup. Cambyses himself initially suspected that his order to kill his brother had not been carried out and that his brother was the one who seized the throne (Herodotus, *Histories* 3.62.3). Gaumata ruled only a few months in 522 BC, although he evidently was able to institute some religious and social reforms in an effort to gain popular support, including a three-year remission of taxes. There is some debate as to whether reference in Greek sources to a Smerdis is to the same or a different usurper. Our analysis assumes they are the same. There were also rebellions by Nebuchadnezzar III and IV according to Darius' Bihistun Rock Inscription, though some think there was only one rebel by this name who was made two by exaggeration to magnify Darius' feats. A certain Vahyazdata of Persia also claimed to be the real (actually dead) Bardiya, and so Media and Parthians also rebelled (Darius, Behistun Inscription).

The above interpretation is not without difficulties. Goldingay questions whether Xerxes was the richest of all Persian monarchs.[2] The fact is that all of them were fabulously wealthy. Goldingay argues instead that "four kings" is a round number that should not be pressed. By this approach Gaumata/Smerdis need not be counted among the Persian kings. Most historians do not count him as an emperor at all. Moreover, to identify the last king with Xerxes leaves an awkward gap of one hundred years between Xerxes and Darius III (335–331 BC), whom Alexander conquers. Strictly speaking, there is no Greek empire until Philip of Macedon united the Greeks at the end of the Persian period. Baldwin feels the weight of these arguments and argues that the "three" and "four" here, like the four heads on the beast earlier, do not represent an exact number but are round or poetic numbers (as the "three" and a "fourth" of Prov 30:15, 18, 21, 29).[3] That said, Xerxes is a prime candidate for a Persian king who stirred up the Greeks. Moreover, interpreting the four kings precisely is more satisfying than a general number. Thus I prefer this interpretation.

---

[1] L. K. Crocker, "Art and Architecture, Persian," in *Lexham Bible Dictionary*, ed. John D. Barry, et al. (Bellingham, WA: Lexham, 2012–2016), n.p.

[2] J. E. Goldingay, *Daniel*, WBC 30 (Dallas: Word, 1989), 294.

[3] J. G. Baldwin, *Daniel*, TOTC (Leicester: Inter-Varsity, 1978), 185.

11:3–4 These verses describe the rise of the Greek kingdom of Alexander the Great and its division among his generals, the *diadochoi* (cf. Dan 8:5–8, 21–22 describing the same thing).

Alexander conquered the entire Persian Empire from 334 to 331 BC. Many versions render "warrior king" as "mighty king," though Hebrew adjective גִּבּוֹר ("mighty") is often used substantivally of mighty men in the sense of strong warriors (Josh 10:7; 2 Sam 17:8; Jer 48:41; Joel 2:7). Here it rightly designates Alexander the Great as a heroic military king. His "vast realm" eventually included Greece, Asia Minor, Syria and the Levant, Egypt, Mesopotamia, Persia, and briefly all the way to the Indus River in India. "As soon as he is established" (כְּעָמְדוֹ) should perhaps be emended to "when he becomes strong" (כְּעָצְמוֹ), as at 8:8.

When Alexander died at age thirty-two in Babylon (323 BC), his kingdom was divided among his generals "to the four winds of heaven." Earlier this breaking up of his kingdom was represented by the four heads of the third beast (7:6) and four horns pointing in four directions that come out of the male goat (8:8, 22). For more historical details, see comments at 7:6 and 8:8. "Divided to the four winds" could mean simply that Alexander's kingdom broke apart in every direction (east, west, north, south). If "four" is something more specific, then it likely refers to the divisions of the kingdom to Ptolemy I (Egypt, 323 BC, south), Seleucus I (Middle East/Babylon, 312 BC, north and east), Cassander, son of Antipater (Greece/Macedonia, 301 BC, west), and Lysimachus (Asia Minor/Thrace, 301 BC, north and west). Starting around 306–305 BC, they began calling themselves kings rather than satraps (see below).

Hebrew אַחֲרִית ("afterpart, end") in the sense of "descendants" (v. 4b) is rare but attested elsewhere (Ps 109:13; Sirach 16:3 Hebrew). When Alexander died, he left no legitimate heir except Alexander IV, whom his wife Roxana bore him after his death. Initially the kingdom was divided up among regents purportedly for Alexander's "descendants" who consisted of his elder, illegitimate half-brother Philip Arrhidaeus and his infant son Alexander IV. But this did not last. Philip Arrhidaeus was called "deficient in intellect owing to bodily disease," perhaps related to a failed attempt to poison him by Olympias, Alexander's mother who wanted no rivals for her son Alexander (Plutarch, *Alexander* 77.5). So Philip Arrhidaeus could never rule without a coregent, and it would in principle be years before Alexander's son would be able to rule on his own. As wars among the *diadochoi* intensified, Philip Arrhidaeus was captured and executed by Alexander the Great's mother, Olympias, in 317 BC (Diodorus, *History* 19.11). By order of Cassander, Alexander's son Alexander IV was poisoned in Egypt in 311 BC at age thirteen before he could attempt to assume his father's throne (Diodorus, *History* 19.52, 105; Pausanias, *Description of Greece* 9.7.2). According to legend, when Alexander was approaching death he was asked who should succeed him. He was heard by some to say "to the strongest" or "to the best" (τῷ κρατίστῳ; Arrian, *Anabasis* 7.26). In fact it went to the most ruthless.

Fights among the *diadochoi* vying for control led to the battle of Ipsus (301 BC) in which Antigonus, one of Alexander's generals, was killed. This secured the kingdoms of Cassander and Lysimachus with the help of Seleucus I. These kings decided to give the Syrian satrapy of Antigonus to Seleucus I. However, Ptolemy I refused an order to withdraw and continued to occupy the southern part of this satrapy (Diodorus, *History* 21.5; Appian, *Syriaca* 55; Polybius, *Histories* 5.67). Thus Ptolemy controlled Palestine, though Seleucus never renounced his claim on this satrapy. So began a long-lasting struggle between the Seleucids (the king of the North) and the Ptolemies (the king of the South) over the control of Syro-Palestine.[4]

11:5 "The king of the South" is Ptolemy I Soter who ruled Egypt starting in 323 BC, taking the title king in 305 BC.[5] He reigned as sole king until 285 BC, then as coregent with his son Ptolemy II till his death in 282 BC. His "commander" (שַׂר; see comments at 8:11) who grows more powerful refers to another of Alexander's generals, Seleucus I Nicator (ruled Babylonia, 312–281 BC). Seleucus became satrap of Babylon in 321 BC while Antigonus was satrap of Phrygia, Lycia, and Pamphylia (Appian, *Syriaca* 53), but civil war among the *diadochoi* led to changing alliances. In 316 BC Antigonus turned on Seleucus so that he was forced to flee for his life from Babylon and take refuge in Egypt (Diodorus, *History* 18.73; 19.2–3, 55; Appian, *Syriaca* 53). With the help of Ptolemy I, Lysimachus, and

---

[4] D. Gera, *Judaea and Mediterranean Politics: 219 to 161 B.C.E.*, Brill Series in Jewish Studies 8 (Leiden: Brill, 1997), 4.

[5] D. J. Thompson, "Ptolemy I Soter" and "Ptolemy II Philadelphus" in *The Oxford Classical Dictionary*, 4th ed., ed. Hornblower and A. Spawforth (Oxford: Oxford University Press, 2012), 1234–35.

Cassander, Seleucus was able to defeat Antigonus' army under his son Demetrius at the battle of Gaza in 312 BC (Diodorus, *History* 19:80–81, 83; Appian, *Syriaca* 53). Then with Ptolemy's help, Seleucus continued on to Babylon where he was again made ruler in 312 BC (Diodorus, *History* 19:86, 90–91; Appian, *Syriaca* 54–55), though he only assumed the title king in 305, the same year he moved the capital to Seleucia.[6] He ruled there until 281 BC. Having consolidated his position, Seleucus proceeded to expand his kingdom to the east, conducting campaigns into Persia and as far east as India (Appian, *Syriaca* 55; Strabo, *Geography* 15.1.3; 15.2.9). CSB's rendering as a comparative ("A kingdom greater than his [kingdom]") probably[7] assumes a slightly different text than the Masoretic Text, which can be rendered "kingdom; his kingdom will be great" (cf. NASB). The CSB assumes the addition of a preposition that shows up as one additional מ (ממשלתו vs. ממשלתו). Historically, Seleucus attained a kingdom "greater than" Ptolemy I's in Egypt (Arrian, *Anabasis* 7.22.5).

11:6 "After some years" correctly renders an idiom whose Hebrew reads, "at the end of years" (ASV; cf. KJV). After the *diadochoi* there followed a period of conflicts over the control of Palestine with off and on wars between the Ptolemies of Egypt and the Seleucids. These included the First Syrian War (274–271 BC) and the Second Syrian War (c. 260–252 BC). This verse jumps to about 252 BC by describing the marriage alliance between Ptolemy II Philadelphus of Egypt (Ptolemaic king 285/282–246) and Antiochus II Theos (Seleucid king 286–246 BC), which brought to an end the Second Syrian War. Ptolemy's daughter Berenice ("the daughter of the king of the South") was married to Antiochus II as part of a peace "alliance."

---

[6] O. Mørkholm, *Early Hellenistic Coinage from the Accession of Alexander to the Peace of Apamaea (336–188 B.C.)* (Cambridge: Cambridge University Press, 1991), 77, 188.

[7] Possibly the MT text is orginal, but the text is elliptical that assumes a comparative preposition מִן without actually writing it because the word to which it would be attached already begins with the letter מ. This is analogous to what happens when the preposition בְּ is omitted before a word beginning with בְּ (most commonly בְּבֵית "in the house of," which is reduced to בֵּית; see Paul Joüon, *Grammar of Biblical Hebrew*, trans. and rev. T. Muraoka, 2 vols. [Rome: Pontificio Intituto Biblico, 1991], §133c). By that view the MT itself could be rendered as the CSB takes it as a *comparison* with an implied but elliptical, unwritten מִן.

"Seal the agreement" is an idiom occurring only here. The Hebrew reads, "to make uprightnesses [מֵישָׁרִים]." Alternatively, the phrase can be rendered, "to make equitable conditions" (Darby) or "make an equitable arrangement" (BDB),[8] or "to come to terms." The deal required Antiochus to divorce his first wife Laodice and make any male issue from Berenice heir to the throne.[9] But Berenice "will not retain power" (literally, "strength of arm") and "her father" [literally, "the one bearing her"] would not have "strength ... endure." By another vocalization of זרעו as זַרְעוֹ (zar'o) rather than זְרֹעוֹ (zero'o), it can be rendered "his offspring [seed] will not endure" (NRSV, Theodotion). In other words, the advantages Ptolemy sought through this agreement that made his daughter queen of his rival's kingdom failed, because "she [Berenice] will be given up." This is all fulfilled when Laodice, Antiochus' divorced wife, unhappy with how she had been treated and operating in exile until 246 BC, had Berenice and her infant son assassinated, her ex-husband Antiochus poisoned, and Laodice's own son Seleucus II proclaimed king (Appian, *Syriaca* 65).

The meaning of the rest of this verse is not as clear. "Her entourage" is an H-stem participle of בוא ("come, enter"), which on the surface means "those that brought her" (NASB). Whether this refers her "entourage" (CSB), "her attendants" (ESV), or even the advisers/officials responsible for promoting and/or completing the deal is unclear. Nothing is known historically about what happened to Berenice's entourage/attendants. Perhaps they were destroyed with their mistress. Those officials that brought her from Egypt or who promoted the deal failed to accomplish their purposes. The identity of "the one who supported [literally, "strengthened"] her" is probably Antiochus II, who also was poisoned.

"Her father" in the Masoretic Text is literally a participle with a suffix, "and he who begat her" (KJV), though the Masoretic consonants and vowels have both been questioned. The Hebrew Bible was originally written without most vowels. Vowels were added by the Masoretes in the Christian era. If והילדה, vocalized by the Masoretes as וְהַיֹּלְדָהּ (wehayyoledah) meaning "and he who begat

---

[8] "מֵישָׁר," BDB 449.2.

[9] St. Jerome, *Jerome's Commentary on Daniel*, trans. G. L. Archer (Grand Rapids: Baker, 1958), 121–22.

her," were vocalized instead as וְהַיַלְדָּה (*wehayyalda*), it would mean, "and the girl/young woman" (so Theodotion, ἡ νεᾶνις), probably referring to Berenice herself. The NRSV gives another possibility: "her child" (presumably a reference to Berenice's son), deleting the first ה as scribal error (וילדה instead of והילדה) and revocalizing as וְיַלְדָּה (*weyaldah*). Though plausible, the NRSV rendering is less likely since it is a speculative, conjectural emendation. Theodotion provides a reasonable interpretation of the MT consonants, but its reference to Berenice as "the young woman" seems redundant with what appears earlier in the verse. Thus the MT interpretation, in the end, is probably correct.

11:7–9 These verses initially describe events from 246–241 BC, the Third Syrian War. The Egyptian king Ptolemy III Euergetes (ruled 246–222 BC), the brother of the assassinated Berenice, invaded the Seleucid territory of Seleucus II Callinicus Pogon (ruled c. 246–225 BC) to avenge Berenice's murder. According to Appian he succeeded in killing Laodice, who had poisoned his sister and advanced as far as Babylon (*Syriaca* 65). A marble throne inscription of Aduli, known from a copy made by Cosmas Indicopleustes, a sixth-century Greek monk-traveler, indicates that Ptolemy III

> made himself master of all the country on this side of the Euphrates, and of Cilicia and Pamphylia and Ionia, and the Hellespont and Thrace, and of all the forces in the provinces, and of the Indian elephants, and had also made subject to his authority all the monarchs who ruled in these parts, he crossed the Euphrates river, and when he had subdued Mesopotamia and Babylonia and Susiana and Persis and Media, and all the rest of the country as far as Bactriana, and had collected all the spoils of the temples which had been taken away from Egypt by the Persians, he conveyed them to that country along with the other treasures, and sent back his troops by canals which had been dug.[10]

---

[10] Cosmas Indicopleustes, *Christian Topography*, trans. and notes, J. W. McCrindle (London: Hakluyt Society, 1897), 57–59.

The Aduli Inscription is a work of propaganda subject to exaggeration. But it is no doubt correct in indicating that Ptolemy III Euergetes marched into Babylonia and for a time took control of it.[11]

Jerome (probably based on Porphyry) indicates Ptolemy III "carried off as booty forty thousand talents of silver, and also precious vessels and images of the gods to the amount of two and a half thousand. Among them were the same images which Cambyses had brought to Persia at the time when he conquered Egypt." This return of images was why he received the title "Euergetes" meaning "Benefactor."[12] A cuneiform tablet in the British Museum (BM 34428) labeled the "Ptolemy III Chronicle" seems to confirm that Ptolemy Euergetes campaigned in Babylonia.[13] The "fortress of the king of the North" is its capital Seleucia. According to Polybius (*Histories* 5.58), Seleucia was made an Egyptian garrison by Ptolemy III Euergetes, who took it when he invaded Syria to revenge the murder of Berenice.

"For some years he will stay away from the king of the North" refers to Ptolemy III, who did not press his advantage in Babylonia but withdrew to Egypt to deal with troubles there. Nonetheless, the peace of 241 BC that ended the Third Syrian War was on favorable terms for Egypt that allowed him to maintain much of his Syrian gains.[14] In the next decade Ptolemy did not personally campaign against Seleucus II, who maintained himself in Asia Minor. "Will enter the kingdom of the king of the South and then return to his own land" refers to some time after Ptolemy returned to Egypt, when Seleucus II regained some of his territory in northern Syria that had been taken by Ptolemy III.

11:10–12 The story now shifts to "his sons" (v. 10a), that is, the sons of Seleucus II, namely Seleucus III Ceraunus (c. 243–223 BC) and Antiochus III Megas ("the Great") (223–187 BC). They were like Assyria that previously invaded and saturated Judah (Isa 8:7–8). They too swept through militarily like an irresistible flooding river to

---

[11] G. Hölbl, *A History of the Ptolemaic Empire* (New York: Routledge, 2001), 49.

[12] Jerome, *Daniel*, 123.

[13] BM 34428 was published preliminarily online (http://www.livius.org/cg-cm/chronicles/bchp-ptolemy_iii/bchp_ptolemy_iii_01.html), though the initial print publication is in preparation by R. J. (Bert) van der Spek of the Free University of Amsterdam.

[14] Hölbl, *A History of the Ptolemaic Empire*, 50.

Judah's peril. This allusion to Isaiah suggests that the flooding invasions of vv. 10, 22, and 40 were simply part of a larger ongoing pattern of periodic but temporary threats against God's people.[15]

The main source for these events is the history of Polybius. The first three Syrian Wars record no battles south of Damascus.[16] But that changed. According to Jerome, during the reign of Ptolemy IV Philopater (c. 240–204) both "sons" of Seleucus II, Seleucus III and Antiochus III, attempted to regain Syrian territory lost to the Ptolemies, though the older son, Seleucus III, was assassinated before making much progress.[17] Around 221 BC, not long after taking the throne, Antiochus III attempted to invade Syria and Phoenicia (then called Coele-Syria), though he was turned back by its governor Theodotus.[18] Two years later Antiochus initiated the Fourth Syrian War (219–217 BC). This constituted the most serious attempt by the Seleucids to attack Phoenicia-Palestine, which had been in Egyptian-Ptolemaic hands since 301 BC. This time Antiochus IV was aided by Theodotus, governor of Phoenicia-Syria. Theodotus handed over Tyre and Ptolemais to Antiochus, joined forces with him, and later even attempted personally to assassinate Ptolemy IV at the battle of Raphia (Polybius, *Histories* 4.37; 5.61, 81; 3 Macc 1:2–3). Antiochus III moved into Palestine and besieged Dor (which refused to surrender), took a fortress on Mt. Tabor, and invaded Samaria.[19] The Seleucids had "a large number of armed forces" (v. 10b) and a "large army" (v. 11b). Antiochus IV, according to Polybius, had "62,000 infantry, 6,000 cavalry, and 102 elephants." But Ptolemy IV, the "king of the South" (v. 11a), mobilized his own forces, going from a phalanx army of 25,000 Greeks with other supporting troops to the point where he "set out from Alexandria with 70,000 infantry, 5,000 cavalry, and 73 elephants" (Polybius, *Histories* 5.65, 79).

"He will become arrogant and cause tens of thousands to fall" (v. 12) was fulfilled in 217 BC when these two armies met in battle. Antiochus III suffered defeat by Ptolemy IV at Raphia near Gaza,

---

[15] G. B. Lester, *Daniel Evokes Isaiah: Allusive Characterization of Foreign Rule in the Hebrew-Aramaic Book of Daniel*, LHBOTS 606 (London: Bloombury T&T Clark, 2015), 62–65.

[16] Gera, *Judaea and Mediterranean Politics*, 9.

[17] Jerome, *Daniel*, 123–24.

[18] Gera, *Judaea and Mediterranean Politics*, 10.

[19] Ibid., 11.

not far from the Egyptian border ("as far as his fortress") in far southwest Palestine. Polybius in part attributes Antiochus' defeat to his presumptuous "youthful inexperience" that led him to advance one flank only to become vulnerable on another flank (Polybius, *Histories* 5.85). Antiochus III's actions caused "tens of thousands to fall." "Tens of thousands" (רִבֹּאוֹת) is not a precise number but here means "immense numbers." At the battle of Raphia alone Ptolemy killed "large numbers," while his losses were much less (Polybius, *Histories* 5.86). "He will not triumph" (v. 12c). Antiochus' loss at Raphia forced him to return home and negotiate a peace that ceded Syro-Palestine back to Ptolemy (Polybius, *Histories* 5.87).

11:13-16 In the years that followed, the Seleucid kingdom grew stronger while the Egyptian kingdom grew weaker. The native Egyptians "rise up against" (v. 14) the Greek Ptolemies. They created a separate kingdom in Upper Egypt shortly before the death of Ptolemy IV Philopater in 204 BC.[20] Immediately after his death, Philopater's wife Queen Arsonoe and other members of the royal family were assassinated by the powerful officials Sosibius and Agathocles. They then crowned Philopater's son, the child Ptolemy V Epiphanes (204-181 BC), as king with themselves as his regents (Polybius, *Histories* 15.25), though neither survived long after seizing power. It is not certain whether Sosibius died by natural or unnatural causes. But Agathocles died as a result of riots in Alexandria, killed by his own soldiers who mercifully kept the mob from doing far worse to him (Polybius, *Histories* 15.33).

To Egypt's north Antiochus III Megas ("the Great"), assisted by Philip V of Macedon with whom he made a secret alliance, "rise[s] up against" Egypt (Polybius, *Histories* 3.2). Antiochus and Philip evidently agreed to seize and divide Ptolemaic territories, with Aegean and Anatolian possessions going to Philip and Syro-Palestine going to Antiochus III (Livy, *History of Rome* 31.14.5). Thus in 202 BC Philip took the Ptolemaic island of Samos[21] while Antiochus III began the Fifth Syrian War (202-195 BC) against Ptolemy V.

Verse 14 is the first mention of Daniel's own Jewish people in this chapter ("Violent ones among your own people"), reminding us that it is the effect of these events on God's people that makes

---

[20] Ibid., 20.
[21] Ibid., 22-23.

them important. Antiochus III again invaded Palestine with a large army. He besieged and took Gaza in 201 BC, a city that held out for a long while because of its exceptional loyalty to Ptolemy (Polybius, *Histories* 16.22). The Egyptians counter-attacked in 200 BC under their general Scopus the Aetolian who succeeded in re-capturing Jerusalem (Josephus, *Antiquities* 12.135). This is perhaps when v. 14 ("Violent ones among your own people will assert themselves to fulfill a vision, but they will fail") was fulfilled. "Fail" is literally "stumble" (NABRE; root כשל; cp. vv. 19, 33, 35, and 41).

"Violent ones" is from a noun פָּרִיץ that can refer to vicious animals (Isa 35:9) and blood-shedding people (Ezek 18:10). It means to tear down or make a breech in a wall. This may be a case of synecdoche in which "violent ones, ones who tear down" means the "lawless" (NRSV; *HALOT*[22]), just as English "cutthroat" means "a murderer" who need not cut throats. Nothing is known about this "vision" of which Daniel speaks, but v. 14 may refer to the defeat of the pro-Seleucid Jewish faction in Jerusalem by Scopus.[23] Jerome (probably based on Porphyry) records that to punish the Jews, Scopus "took the aristocrats of Ptolemy's party [of Judea] back to Egypt with him."[24] This statement probably refers not to Ptolemy V king of Egypt but to Ptolemy son of Thraseas, the last Ptolemaic governor of Syria and Phoenicia who joined forces with Antiochus III.[25]

In 200 Scopus lost the battle of Panium (at modern Banias) at the source of the Jordan River near Caesarea Philippi where Antiochus III destroyed a great part of Scopus' army (Josephus, *Antiquities* 12.132). This battle allowed Antiochus III to take control of Judea and Samaria (Polybius, *Histories* 16.39; 28.1), "the beautiful land" (v. 16; cf. 8:9; 11:41). Israel is "beautiful" to God because it is the land promised by his covenant (see §4.3). Ultimately Scopus was forced to surrender at the "well-fortified" city of Sidon after a besiegement in 198 BC.[26] This marked the end of Ptolemaic rule in Judea.

11:17–19 "An agreement with him … daughter in marriage to destroy it" (v. 17ab) alludes to the peace that came in 195 BC in conjunction with a marriage alliance proposal in which Cleopatra I,

---

[22] "פָּרִיץ," *HALOT* 3:968.
[23] Ibid., 28.
[24] Jerome, *Daniel*, 126.
[25] Gera, *Judaea and Mediterranean Politics*, 29.
[26] Jerome, *Daniel*, 126.

daughter of Antiochus III, married the boy king of Egypt Ptolemy V (Diodorus, *History* 28.12). This marriage was consummated in 194/3 BC (Livy, *History of Rome* 35.13.4) when Ptolemy V Epiphanes was about sixteen. Antiochus III hoped eventually to use this marriage, alliance to "destroy" the Ptolemaic rule by bringing Egypt under Seleucid rule. "She will not stand with him" (v. 17c) refers to Cleopatra, who despite her Seleucid origins remained loyal to her husband and Egypt. She even ruled alone as queen-regent for her son Ptolemy VI Philometor for a short time after her husband's death in 181 BC, thwarting her father's plans of uniting a rule of north and south under her son Ptolemy VI who in fact did not favor Syria.

The "coasts and islands" (v. 18a) or "coastlands" (ESV, NIV) is אִיִּים, which refers here to Asia Minor and its islands to which Antiochus turned his attention. In 196 BC Antiochus III fought in the Aegean and Thrace. Thrace was located in what is today the southeastern regions of Bulgaria and northwestern modern Greece in Europe. Antiochus III attempted to regain territories once belonging to Seleucus I, which the Seleucids still claimed. Antiochus' concentration of troops in Europe brought him into direct conflict with the Romans who had forced Philip V of Macedon into vassal status. Rome then insisted that Greek cities in Asia Minor once subject to Ptolemy or Philip remain free, that he not carry off prizes of war obtained by Rome, and that Antiochus and his fleet stay out of Europe (Polybius, *Histories* 18.47, 50; Livy, *History of Rome* 33.34.2; 33.39.4–7). Antiochus III insisted that the Romans had no right to interfere in Asia, that he was only reclaiming lands that had belonged to the Seleucids in times past, and that the marriage alliance with Ptolemy V had already dealt with the issue of former Ptolemaic possessions in Asia (Polybius, *Histories* 18.51; Diodorus, *History* 28.12; Appian, *Syriaca* 3).[27]

Antiochus III ignored the Roman warning and in 192 BC cooperated with Aetolians against Thrace and the Peloponnesians. The Romans joined with their Greek allies and defeated Antiochus at the battle of Thermopylae in 191 BC, forcing Antiochus to retreat to Asia Minor.

"But a commander will put an end to his taunting" (v. 18b) found fulfillment in 190–189 BC when Antiochus fought with the

---

[27] Gera, *Judaea and Mediterranean Politics*, 81–82.

Romans in Asia Minor. He was defeated by the Roman general Scipio Asiaticus in the battle of Magnesia (Appian, *Syriaca* 28–36). This general, the "commander" of v. 18, dictated the terms of peace in the Treaty of Apamea in 188 BC. This forced Antiochus III to cede his elephants and his navy, hand over Hannibal the Carthaginian who had taken refuge with him, pay the expenses of the war, turn over some of his territory (Lydia, Media, India) to Eumenes II of Pergamum, and deliver up twenty select hostages, including his son Antiochus (later Antiochus IV Epiphanes) (Appian, *Syriaca* 38–39; Polybius, *Histories* 21.17; Diodorus, *History* 29.10; 1 Macc 8:8). "Taunting" can also be rendered "scorn" (NASB) or "insolence" (ESV, NRSV). Antiochus III's "taunting/insolence" met with disaster.

"He will turn his attention back to the fortresses of his own land, but he will stumble, fall, and be no more" (v. 19) refers to the death of Antiochus III in 187 BC when he accused his subjects in Elymais (ancient Elam, modern southwest Iran) of rebellion. As punishment and to raise money for war enmities, he tried to rob the temple of Bel there, but its inhabitants rose up in pious rage and killed him, an act interpreted by Diodorus as divine retribution (Diodorus, *History* 28:3; 29.15).

11:20 This verse describes the uneventful rule of Seleucus IV Philopator (187–175 BC) who spent his reign paying off his father's war debts levied by the Treaty of Apamea. According to 2 Macc 3:7–40, Seleucus IV sent a "tax collector" (fulfilling 11:20a) named Heliodorus to rob the temple in Jerusalem, but Heliodorus saw two angels who beat him senseless and left him near death. The priest Onias III prayed for him and he recovered. Heliodorus ultimately returned emptyhanded. Subsequently, Apollonius son of Menestheus governor of Coele-Syria and Phoenicia accused Onias III of plotting against the government and other wrongdoing. Although historians usually reject the miracle story, Heliodorus is a known historical figure, and this account of his attempting to obtain temple treasures fits the historical context in which Seleucus IV needed funds to pay his father's war debts. So the essence of the story is probably true.[28] Seleucus IV died, "not in anger or in battle" (v. 20b), but was assassinated in a plot engineered by that same finance minister, Heliodorus (Appian, *Syriaca* 45).

---

[28] Ibid., 106–7.

11:21 Daniel 11:21–35 describes the greatest enemy of the Jewish people and threat to their religion during the intertestamental period: Antiochus IV Epiphanes (175–164 BC). Daniel already prophesied about Antiochus in 8:9–14, 23–26 (see further comments there). Antiochus IV Epiphanes, son of Antiochus III, was "despised" (or "despicable" NASB; "contemptible" ESV; N-stem בזה, "despise"). His title "Epiphanes" means either "illustrious"[29] or, more likely, "manifest [appearing of a god]." The latter interpretation makes his title a blasphemous claim to demigod status. His critics behind his back called him "Epimanes," meaning "madman" (Polybius, *Histories* 26.1).

According to classical historians, Antiochus Epiphanes was an utterly unpredictable personality. At one moment he appeared to be a capable, energetic administrator, a shrewd tactician, and a man of great generosity. At another moment he became fiercely tyrannical and unstable, a "madman" (Polybius, *Histories* 28:18; Diodorus, *History* 30:18; Livy, *History of Rome* 41.19.8–9). The latter characteristic is seen in his harsh treatment of the Jews.[30]

"Royal honors" reads in the Hebrew "the honor [הוֹד] of kingship," in which הוֹד (used of facial countenance in 10:8) combines the ideas of splendor, honor, majesty, and authority. The passive "will not be given" is expressed in the original by an indefinite plural active: "they will not give" (NKJV). Heliodorus' attempt to seize the throne by assassinating Seleucus IV (see above) was not successful, but Antiochus IV faced obstacles in his path to the throne. There were two legitimate heirs ahead of him: his nephew Demetrius I and Demetrius' younger brother, also named Antiochus. The latter was too young to rule. Demetrius was next in line to rule, but Antiochus' brother Seleucus IV sent his son Demetrius I to Rome in 175 BC to serve as a substitute hostage in place of Antiochus, who had already spent twelve years there. When Seleucus IV was assassinated, Antiochus ruled as regent for and co-king with his nephew for five years (for details see comments at 8:23) because Demetrius was still held hostage by Rome.[31] But when a certain official named Andronicus killed the young nephew (Diodorus, *History* 30.7.2),

---

[29] F. L. Cross and E.A. Livingstone, eds., *The Oxford Dictionary of the Christian Church* (New York: Oxford University Press, 2005), 79.

[30] J. Whitehorne, "Antiochus IV," *ABD* 1:270.

[31] Gera, *Judaea and Mediterranean Politics*, 115.

perhaps at Antiochus' direction, Antiochus IV claimed the throne solely himself.

"During a time of peace" is בְּשַׁלְוָה from בְּ ("in, during") and שַׁלְוָה ("ease, rest, tranquility, security"). This expression is used here as well as at 8:25 (also of Antiochus IV). Perhaps the sense is "without warning" (ESV; CSB), "when they feel secure" (NIV), "when they don't expect it" (GW; Old Greek, ἐξάπινα), or even "in deceit/treachery, unscrupulously" (Theodotion, δόλῳ).

The details of Antiochus' rise to power are obscure, but it undoubtedly involved political "intrigue" (חֲלַקְלַקּוֹת), a term that sometimes has to do with "smoothness/slipperiness" (Jer 23:12; Ps 35:6) and metaphorically can denote "flattery" (Prov 6:24), "insincerity" (Dan 11:34), or "hypocrisy" (*HALOT*).[32] This is consistent with his character trait of "deceit" (8:25; 11:23). One element of intrigue has to do with Antiochus' marriage to Laodice. This was probably the same Laodice who was the wife of Antiochus' assassinated brother Seleucus IV and the mother of his nephew Antiochus, whom Antiochus IV then adopted as his own "son" (as a Babylonian inscription calls the young Antiochus). If this reconstruction is correct, the marriage to Laodice and adoption of her son was a scheme by Antiochus IV to strengthen his own claim to legitimacy.[33]

Other intrigues are probable, though the historical facts are fuzzy. Is it coincidence that Antiochus did not return to the court of his brother but stayed a couple of years in Athens instead (Appian, *Syriaca* 45)? Is it coincidence that a couple of years after Antiochus IV was released from Rome that his brother Seleucus IV was assassinated? Did Rome have something to do with this? Antiochus IV came to the throne with the help of King Eumenes II of Pergamum and Eumenes' brother Attalus (Appian, *Syriaca* 45). According to an Athenian decree, Eumenes and his brothers accompanied Antiochus in his journey from Athens to the border of his own land, provided him with money and troops, and put a diadem on his head.[34] Were promises made by Antiochus to win such support? Antiochus IV initially served as regent, along with their mother, for his two nephews. Did Antiochus IV have something to do with the murder of

---

[32] "חֲלַקְלַק," *HALOT* 1:324
[33] Ibid., 116.
[34] Ibid., 113.

his nephew Antiochus so he could claim the throne outright? The possible intrigues are many.

11:22 The Hebrew of "a flood of forces" reads "the forces of the flood" (NJPS), perhaps in the sense of an "overwhelming army" (NIV), echoing Isa 8:7–8 (see comments at v. 10). Alternatively, without changing any consonants, the vowels of "the flood" could be emended from הַשֶּׁטֶף to an N-stem verb הִשָּׁטֵף, "he will flood away [for himself]," and render the phrase, "forces he will flood away" (cf. CEV).

King Ptolemy VI Philometor of Egypt was Antiochus IV's nephew, the son of his sister Cleopatra I who married into Egyptian royalty (see above). Philometor was under the regency first of his mother and after her death under two courtiers, a eunuch named Eulaeus and a Syrian named Lenaeus (Diodorus, *History* 30.15–16; Polybius, *Histories* 28.21). Egypt under its regents considered an invasion of the portion of Coele-Syria taken from Egypt by Antiochus III (Diodorus, *History* 30.16; Polybius, *Histories* 28.1; Livy, *History of Rome* 42.29.7), but Antiochus IV in 170–69 BC anticipated this and attacked first, routing Egypt's army and plundering Egypt (Livy, *History of Rome* 42.29.5; 1 Macc 1:16–19). As his army was being "swept away," Ptolemy VI was urged by his regents to flee to Samothrace in the Aegean, though it does not appear that he went (Polybius 28.21; Diodorus, *History* 30.17).

"Prince" (נָגִיד) in the phrase "covenant prince" can apply to a variety of leaders, including kings (1 Sam 10:1; Ps 76:13; Ezek 28:1), military commanders (1 Chr 13:1), court officials (1 Chr 26:24; 2 Chr 19:11), and priestly temple officials, perhaps the leader of the temple guard or possibly the high priest (Jer 20:1; Neh 11:11). The identity of the "covenant prince" (or "covenant leader" NJPS) of v. 22 is disputed. Three proposals are Onias III, Antiochus the son of Seleucus III, and Ptolemy VI.

1. Onias III. Some commentators identify this "covenant prince" with Onias III, the high priest in Jerusalem and chief representative of God's "covenant" with Israel at the beginning of Antiochus IV's reign. Onias was considered a godly, law-observing priest by the writer of 2 Maccabees (2 Macc 3:1), though he was removed from office at Antiochus Epiphanes' accession in 175 BC because of his alleged pro-Egyptian sympathies. Onias was replaced by his brother Jason, a Hellenizing priest who had bribed Antiochus IV for the office. Thus Jason was considered an impious, law-ignoring, illegitimate priest (2 Macc 4:7–17; cf. 1 Macc 1:10–15). In 172 BC Jason was replaced by Menelaus, who made a higher bid for the appointment. Menelaus had Onias III killed c. 171 (2 Macc 4:30–38).

2. Antiochus, son of Seleucus IV. Another strong possibility for the "covenant prince" is Seleucus IV's son also named Antiochus. The "covenant" in this view is the agreement adopted by Antiochus IV to serve as regent for his nephew until he came of age. This nephew of Antiochus IV was assassinated by Andronicus, one of Antiochus' officials, who was executed for this crime (Diodorus, *History* 30.7.2). But the assassination order may have come from Antiochus IV.

3. Ptolemy VI Philometor. The "covenant" could refer to Antiochus' covenant with Ptolemy VI, king of Egypt. The eunuch Eulaeus wanted Ptolemy VI to gather his treasures and flee to Samothrace (Polybius, *Histories* 28.21; see above). Egyptian documents suggest Philometor was reduced to co-ruler with his brother Ptolemy VIII Euergetes and his sister Cleopatra II even before Antiochus IV invaded.[35] Antiochus captured Memphis (modern Cairo) in the First Egyptian Campaign and besieged Alexandria (Livy, *History of Rome* 44.19.8; Josephus, *Antiquities* 12.243). Philometor left Alexandria, reached an agreement ("covenant") with Antiochus IV in 169 BC, and joined his camp. This probably involved renouncing all Egyptian claims on Palestine, Phoenicia, and Syria. Antiochus, in turn, agreed to help his nephew Philometor regain sole ownership of his throne, deposing his brother and sister (Livy, *History of Rome* 44.19.8–12; 45.11.1–2).[36] This is the "covenant" for which Ptolemy VI is the "prince."

Since the first part of the verse refers to Egypt, it is attractive to see the last part doing the same. However, this view makes the next verses awkward, jumping back and forth in person and time. Hence the first two views seem more likely than the third.

11:23 The identities of "alliance" and "small nation" are uncertain. Antiochus' deceit (מִרְמָה) was already mentioned in 8:25 (see comments there) and his possible "intrigues" are cataloged in the commentary at v. 21. One possibility is that the deceitful alliance here is one made with King Eumenes II of Pergamum whose nation,

---

[35] Ibid., 124–25.
[36] Ibid., 136–37.

though smaller than the Seleucid Empire, helped Antiochus IV come to power (see comments at v. 21).

11:24 Verse 24 describes Antiochus IV's nefarious character. But a couple of exegetical cruxes complicate the interpretation. The phrase "during a time of peace" (בְּשַׁלְוָה), also used in v. 21 and 8:25, has been variously rendered: "without warning" (ESV; CSB note), "when they feel secure" (NIV), "with ease" (Goldingay), "when they don't expect it" (GW; Old Greek, ἐξάπινα), or even "in deceit/treachery, unscrupulously" (Theodotion, δόλῳ). Another difficulty is the phrase "into the richest parts [of the province]" (בְמִשְׁמַנֵּי), which could instead be rendered "with choice warriors" or "the richest men" of the province. The term מִשְׁמָן can mean "place of fatness" in the sense of "richest parts," or of people, the "richest men" (ESV margin), but the term is also used of stout, well-fed men or warriors (Ps 78:31; Isa 10:16 [ESV]).

If "into the richest parts of [the province]" is the correct rendering of בְמִשְׁמַנֵּי, the verse may refer to Antiochus IV's actions within his own country. According to 1 Macc 3:27–31, at the time of the Maccabean revolt Antiochus paid his army's wages a year in advance. But this made him short on funds, so he withdrew to Persia to get money. Polybius states that in terms of honors paid to the gods he far surpassed his predecessors (Polybius, *Histories* 26.1.10–11). Whereas it was common for Seleucid rulers to plunder other lands, Antiochus IV plundered his own country and redistributed to dignitaries, gods, or his cronies. But God in his sovereignty (see §3.8; §7.3) limits this, "only for a time"—that is, till the end of his reign.[37]

Alternatively, v. 24 may refer to Antiochus IV's plundering of Egypt after his first invasion of it (1 Macc 1:18–19), an act unprecedented by previous Seleucid kings. In that case, "only for a time" would mean he pilaged until Rome forced him to abandon his Egyptian campaigns (see below).

11:25–27 "Courage" (v. 25a) is לֵבָב, a word usually rendered "heart" (ESV; CSB in v. 27). The CSB rendering makes sense in this context and is probably correct. If, instead, לֵבָב means "mind," it would represent his schemes or strategies against Egypt ("the king of the South").

---

[37] L. Wood, *A Commentary on Daniel* (Grand Rapids: Zondervan, 1973), 296.

As already noted, Antiochus IV's First Egyptian Campaign in 169 BC led him to ally himself with his nephew Ptolemy VI Philometor and attempt to restore Ptolemy VI's rule after Philometor was reduced to co-ruler with his brother Ptolemy VIII Euergetes and his sister Cleopatra II. But neither man achieved his goal. Antiochus IV captured Memphis (modern Cairo) and besieged Alexandria, but he did "not succeed" in capturing all of Egypt because of "plots" against him (v. 25c).

Antiochus IV justified his invasion on the guise of restoring Philometor to the throne, but his promises were meant to disguise that he really hoped to control Egypt through his nephew and make him a puppet ruler. Philometer received from Antiochus his "provisions" (פַּתְבַּג) of food (v. 26), a Persian loanword used of the royal provisions given to Daniel and his friends (Dan 1:5, 8, 13, 15–16). Yet they both spoke "lies at the same table" (v. 27). Philometer deduced Antiochus' duplicity and for his part double-crossed Antiochus by secretly negotiating an agreement with his brother and sister. According to the deal, Philometor would return to the throne, though he did "not succeed" in regaining sole rulership. He was made senior member of the triumvirate, thus eliminating Antiochus IV's legal basis for invading (Livy, *History of Rome* 45.11.2–7). Philometor thanked Antiochus for his help and asked him to return home. But Antiochus IV, angry over being tricked, purposed to fight against both Philometor and Euergetes unless the region around the Egyptian city of Pelusium and the island of Cyprus were ceded to him by Egypt (Livy, *History of Rome* 45.11.8–10).

Yet Antiochus also did "not succeed." In the fall of 169 BC, having lost his "legitimate" cause of restoring Ptolemy VI to his throne, Rome pressured Antiochus IV to leave Egypt alone, break his besiegement of Alexandria, and withdraw (Josephus, *Antiquities* 12.243–246; Polybius, *Histories* 29.25).[38] Antiochus then attempted to repair his relationship with Rome by sending emissaries (Polybius, *Histories* 28.22), hoping soon to renew his Egyptian activities without Roman interference. All of this came at the "appointed time"

---

[38] Gera, *Judaea and Mediterranean Politics*, 142–43. I follow Gera's view that Josephus, *Antiquities* 12.243–246, refers to a warning from Rome in conjunction with Antiochus' first invasion, not the warning by C. Pompillius Laenas that stops his second invasion.

(v. 27c) (מוֹעֵד) or a fixed time, a term that also occurs in 8:19; 11:29, 35. It implies the sovereign working of God (see §3.8, §7.3).

11:28 Antiochus IV's first campaign to Egypt in 169 BC ended in a frustrating withdrawal, though he did return home with "great wealth" (v. 28a)—that is, considerable plunder (1 Macc 1:18–19). As he passed through Judea he addressed a problem that turned him "against the holy covenant" (v. 28b). Antiochus previously sold the high priesthood to Jason (2 Macc 4:7–10, 23), deposing Jason's bother and rightful high priest Onias III. Three years later Antiochus replaced Jason as high priest with Menelaus, who outbid Jason (2 Macc 4:24–25). In c. 171 BC the previous high priest, Onias III, was assassinated (2 Macc 4:36–44). This produced conditions ripe for unrest.

Gera argues that 2 Macc 5:1 refers not to Antiochus' second invasion of Egypt but to his second "approach" to Egypt (δευτέραν ἔφοδον), that is, to his security measures taken after his failed plan of using Ptolemy VI as his puppet. If Gera is correct, then it was in 169 BC during Antiochus' First Egyptian Campaign that Jason initiated an uprising to regain his high priesthood and depose Menelaus (2 Macc 5:5–6).[39] Conservative Jews probably supported this since Menelaus was a Benjaminite and not of priestly descent (2 Macc 3:4; 4:23), whereas Jason was brother of the rightful priest Onias III (2 Macc 4:7). Note, however, that Old Latin and Armenian manuscripts of 2 Macc 3:4 read "Balgea" rather than "Benjamin." This reading permits an alternative view, supported by the Mishnah (Sukkah 5.8), that Menelaus was of the non-Zadokite priestly line of Bilga (1 Chr 24:14), though not in the line of succession for the high priesthood.[40]

When Antiochus passed through Palestine on his way from Egypt, he put down the Jason-inspired revolt, slaughtering many. As further punishment he took booty from the temple, including the table for the bread of the Presence, the cups for drink offerings, the bowls, the golden censers, the curtain, the crowns, and the gold decoration on the front of the temple (1 Macc 1:20–23; 2 Macc 5:15–20). This constituted an attack on the "holy covenant." Subsequently he left Judea for "his own land" with even more plunder (1 Macc 1:24; 2 Macc 5:21).

---

[39] Gera, *Judaea and Mediterranean Politics*, 156.
[40] M. Hengel, *Judaism and Hellenism*, 2 vol. (Philadelphia: Fortress, 1974), 1:279.

11:29-31 "Appointed time" (v. 29) is also used in v. 27. It refers to the time fixed by God in his sovereignty (see §3.8, §7.3). Antiochus IV came again (v. 29) in 168 BC to renew his campaign against Egypt ("the South") and its co-rulers, Ptolemy VI Philometor, Ptolemy VIII Euergetes, and Cleopatra II. But "this time" turned out differently than the first campaign (v. 29). Antiochus started by attacking Cyprus, then a subject of Egypt, and initiated the Second Egyptian Campaign in Egypt proper. He took most of Egypt including Memphis. But Egypt further strengthened ties to Rome. Ptolemy VIII and Cleopatra appeared in pitiful condition before the Roman Senate seeking military support against Antiochus, and also sought support from the Greeks (Livy, *History of Rome* 44.19.5–7; Polybius, *Histories* 28.19–20).

As a result, a Roman fleet, the "Ships of the Kittim" (v. 30a; literally "Kittim ships," echoing the obscure Num 24:24) intervened. Hebrew כִּתִּים denotes the descendants of Javan (Gen 10:4). They settled in Cyprus, whose city Citium may be the basis of this term (Josephus, *Antiquities* 1.6.1). However, as Cyprus became increasingly influenced by the Greeks, Kittim by synecdoche expanded to include the Greeks (1 Macc 1:1) and other maritime powers. Here it includes Egypt's (and Cyprus') ally Rome (Old Greek, Ῥωμαῖος, "Roman"). Cyprus, Greece, and Rome all became allies against Antiochus IV. This fleet led by Gaius Popilius Laenas intervened to stop Antiochus' war against the Egyptian triumvirate in Alexandria (Polybius, *Histories* 29.2; Livy, *History of Rome* 45.12.1–3). Popilius met with Ptolemy VI and then with Antiochus IV. He demanded that the latter read a decree from the Roman Senate, declaring that whichever party did not cease hostilities would no longer be considered a friend of Rome, with an implied threat of war (Livy, *History of Rome* 44.19.13–14).

Rome's anger with Antiochus was compounded by the fact that he violated the Treaty of Apamea (see comments at vv. 17–20) that his father Antiochus III had signed.[41] Popilius, taking a stick, drew a circle in the sand around Antiochus and demanded that he decide whether he would comply with Rome's decree before stepping out of it! Having been hostage in Rome and seen firsthand its military might, Antiochus was "intimidated" (N-stem כאה could

---

[41] Gera, *Judaea and Mediterranean Politics*, 156.

be rendered, "cowered with fear"; cf. ESV) and subsequently "withdrew" (v. 30a; or had to "turn back [שׁוב]," NIV). He had no desire for confrontation with Rome and abandoned his Egyptian campaign (Livy, *History of Rome* 45.12.4–8; Polybius, *Histories* 29:27; Diodorus 31:2; Justin, *Historiarum* 34.3; Appian, *Syriaca* 66). Unlike before, this time he did not return with much plunder. This effectively marked Rome's replacement of the Greeks as the greatest power of the Mediterranean world.

This humiliation put Antiochus IV into a foul mood that led him to "rage against the holy covenant" (v. 30b). After his failed second invasion of Egypt, Antiochus put down another rebellion in Jerusalem, perhaps again incited by Jason. Enraged by the rejection of his appointee to the high priesthood and generally irritated by his Jewish subjects, Antiochus took drastic action. He attempted to abolish the Jewish religion and force the Jews to adopt Greek religion instead. In particular, Antiochus acted to "desecrate the temple fortress" (v. 31a; or "the sanctuary fortress," NASB, NKJV; הַמִּקְדָּשׁ הַמָּעוֹז), turning it into a temple of Zeus. He commanded Israel to build altars to idols in the temple sanctuary, allowed prostitution in the temple precincts, abolished the Sabbath and sacred festivals, and demanded that Greek religious festivals be adopted instead (1 Macc 1:41–50; 2 Macc 6:1–11). He forbade the "regular sacrifice" (see comments at 8:11) to the Lord (v. 31b; cf. Dan 8:11; 12:11) as well as other Jewish offerings (1 Macc 1:45).

In contrast Antiochus was happy to "favor those who abandon the holy covenant" (v. 30c). The expression rendered "favor" (Qal of בִּין + עַל; also in v. 37) is an unusual nuance of a verb that usually means "to understand." Other suggestions are "pay attention/heed to" (ESV, NRSV) and "show regard for" (NASB; CSB at v. 37). Many Jews became Hellenists, that is, Jews speaking Greek and following Greek customs. Some went so far as to abandon Jewish religious customs completely, removing the marks of circumcision from their flesh and establishing "gymnasiums," which observant Jews considered shameful. Gymnasiums were educational facilities where boys were instructed in the (sometimes idolatrous) values of Hellenism and where athletic actives were conducted in the nude (1 Macc 1:11–15). The high priest Jason, a Hellenist, won Antiochus' support for the priesthood both by bribes and by encouraging the establishment of a gymnasium in Judah to teach youth the Greek way of life

(2 Macc 4:9–12). Jason influenced not only laymen but also priests to participate in the gymnasium, to the neglect of their priestly duties and in violation of the Mosaic law (2 Macc 4:13–17).

On "abomination of desolation" (v. 31c), see comments at 9:27. Antiochus IV's abomination or sacrilege was epitomized by the idolatry introduced to the temple and his offering of pigs and other unclean animals on a pagan altar placed atop the temple's altar (1 Macc 1:47, 59; 6:7; Josephus, *Antiquities* 12.253). He made continuing to practice Judaism punishable by death (1 Macc 1:49). Children who were circumcised were killed, along with their families (1 Macc 1:60–61; 2 Macc 6:10).

11:32–35 "With flattery" (v. 32a) is literally with "smooth things" (חֲלַקּוֹת), a word cognate with "intrigue" in v. 21 and "insincerity" in v. 34. Here it implies "falsehoods." The verb "he will corrupt" (H-stem חנף) is not certain in meaning and may instead mean "flatter," as in Rabbinic Hebrew,[42] or perhaps "seduce" (ESV, NRSV). The expression "those who act wickedly" (H-stem participle רשע; v. 32a) can also be an internal causative, "those making themselves guilty concerning,"[43] in contrast with the righteous who know God. Many of the upper classes of the Jews did not oppose Hellenization. A significant number remained pro-Hellenistic even after the Maccabees came to power. They willingly adopted Greek religious values and forsook their distinctive, separatist form of Judaism.

To "know ... God" (v. 32b) is to have a relationship with God according to his covenant (see §4.3). "Know" (ידע) can refer to sexual intimacy between husband and wife (Gen 4:1), and knowing God is similarly a personal relationship. Knowing God results in right behavior toward others (Jer 22:15–16). Lack of knowledge of God results in wickedness and oppression of others (Hos 4:1–2). Those "who know their God" in v. 32 refers to pious Jews led by the Maccabees in resisting Antiochus IV's attempt to abolish Judaism. Mattathias, an aged priest with five sons (1 Macc 2:1–4), opposed Antiochus' introduction of pagan Greek religious practices into his village of Modein. Mattathias killed the first Jew who approached the altar to sacrifice and the royal official who presided (1 Macc

---

[42] "חָנַף," in M. Jastrow, *A Dictionary of the Targumim, the Talmud Babli and Jerushalmi, and the Midrashic Literature* (1886–1903; repr., Brooklyn: P. Shalom, 1967), 484.

[43] "רשע," *HALOT* 4:1295.

2:24–25). Thus began the Maccabean Revolt. Three of Mattathias' sons (Judas, Jonathan, Simon) would successively be key leaders in Judah's drive for independence. This family, among others, would "be strong and take action" and "give understanding" (vv. 32c, 33b) to other Jews. They were "those who have insight" (v. 33a; H-stem participle שׂכל), a characteristic shared with Daniel (Dan 1:17; 5:11) and the suffering servant (Isa 52:13). "Those who have insight" will flourish in the resurrection (Dan 12:3).

Certain pious Jews at the time of Antiochus IV "die [literally "stumble"; see comment at v. 14] by the sword and by the flame" (v. 33b). Some Jews let themselves be massacred rather than violate the Sabbath when the Seleucids attacked them (1 Macc 2:29–38). The Maccabees for practical reasons did fight on the Sabbath (1 Macc 2:39–41). Some were captured and plundered (1 Macc 1:32; 5:11–13), though this was limited by God in his sovereign plan for history (see §3.8, §7), lasting only "for a time" (v. 33; literally "days").

Judas Maccabeus' military campaign repeatedly defeated larger Syrian armies with his smaller Jewish forces. He made alliances with those who "helped" him (v. 34a), including the Romans who were supporting Ptolemy VI against Antiochus IV (1 Macc 8:17–21), though some joined "insincerely" (v. 34b). With Judas' help the temple was cleansed and rededicated to the Lord on the twenty-fifth day of Kislev (December) in 164 BC, an event subsequently celebrated by the feast of Hanukkah.

These events allowed the Jewish people to be "refined, purified, and cleansed" (v. 35a) by restraining the process of Hellenization that was undermining the Jewish faith. As a result of the Maccabean Revolt, and subsequent challenges to the Jewish people, the Jews as a whole became more faithful to their covenant with God. The expression "the time of the end" (v. 35b) was previously used of the future time of judgment at the time of Antiochus IV (8:17, 19). But here it seems to extend to the fixed eschatological time of judgment (see §7.4), as at 11:40. See further comments at 8:17 and 11:36–46 below.

Bridge

This passage reveals to Daniel what will occur in "the last days" (10:14) from Daniel's perspective, though it is ancient history from today's perspective. This unit constitutes some of the most remarkable fulfillment of prophecy in the Bible. It predicts in detail events from the Persian period (11:3) and the Greek period (11:3–35) and demonstrates God's foreknowledge of the future (see §3.5). This theological interpretation requires rejection of the critical view that considers Daniel's prophecies to be history in the guise of prophecy (see §1). The traceable fulfillments laid out in the commentary show the supernatural nature of biblical prophecy and the truth of God's revelation (11:2; see §2). Though the Macedonian-Greek kingdoms were powerful and at times their rulers did whatever they wanted (11:3, 16), they too experienced frustration and failure, showing the fleeting nature of conquest (see §7.3). Human endeavors quickly fall into futility (Eccl 1:1–2, 14).

God works on behalf of his people throughout history and will eventually bring all present troubles to an end (see §7.3). Violence against God's people will periodically sweep through like a flooding river that seems irresistible (11:10, 22; cf. Isa 8:7–8), but God has established an "appointed time" for coming events (11:27, 29, 35) and limits evil to only "for a time" (11:24, 33). Though God is in control, there will still be travails and distress for God's people (see §4.5). "You will have suffering in this world" (John 15:33). "It is necessary to go through many hardships to enter the kingdom of God" (Acts 14:22). Christians are to expect persecution (John 15:18–21; 16:1–4; 1 Thess 3:3). Daniel learned that God's people would face great hostility. But God's people can be comforted and encouraged that God remains in control (see §3.8) and has a plan for history (see §7.3). He will see his people through various trials as history moves toward the coming kingdom of God (see §7.4.3). Thus God's people must remain faithful and holy (see §4.1) as those "who know their God" (11:32). Allowing persecution is part of God's plan to purify God's people (11:35; see §4.1, §4.8). God holds such in high esteem and will reward them (see §4.4). The ultimate reward awaits the resurrection of the dead (cf. 12:2–3; see §7.4.4).

I. Court Narratives (Daniel 1–6)

II. Visions of Daniel (Daniel 7–12)
First vision: Four beasts and son of man figure (Daniel 7)
Second vision: Ram and male goat (Daniel 8)
Third vision: Seventy weeks (Daniel 9)
Fourth vision: Kings of North/South, distress/resurrection (Daniel 10–12)
Angels in conflict (10:1–11:2a)
Preview of Persian and Greek kings (11:2b–35)
World kingdoms ended and the righteous established (11:36–12:3)
Vision sealed until the end (12:4–13)

(A) Beginning of story (1:1–21)
  (B) Dream about four world kingdoms ended by the kingdom of God (2:1–49)
    (C) Judeans faithful in the face of death (3:1–30)
      (D) Royal pride humbled (4:1–37)
      (D′) Royal pride humbled (5:1–31)
    (C′) A Judean faithful in the face of death (6:1–28)
  (B′) Vision about four world kingdoms ended by the kingdom of God (7:1–28)
    (E) Vision of Persian and Greek kingdoms to Antiochus (8:1–27)
      (F) Vision of seventy weeks (9:1–27)
    (E′) Vision of Persian and Greek kingdoms to Antiochus (10:1–11:35)
(B″) World kingdoms ended and the righteous established (11:36–12:3)
(A′) End of story: Vision sealed until the end (12:4–13)

[36] "Then the king will do whatever he wants. He will exalt and magnify himself above every god, and he will say outrageous things against the God of gods. He will be successful until the time of wrath is completed, because what has been decreed will be accomplished. [37] He will not show regard for the gods of his fathers, the god desired by women, or for any other god, because he will magnify himself above all. [38] Instead, he will honor a god of fortresses—a god his fathers did not know—with gold, silver, precious stones, and riches.

³⁹ He will deal with the strongest fortresses with the help of a foreign god. He will greatly honor those who acknowledge him, making them rulers over many and distributing land as a reward.

⁴⁰ "At the time of the end, the king of the South will engage him in battle, but the king of the North will storm against him with chariots, horsemen, and many ships. He will invade countries and sweep through them like a flood. ⁴¹ He will also invade the beautiful land, and many will fall. But these will escape from his power: Edom, Moab, and the prominent people of the Ammonites. ⁴² He will extend his power against the countries, and not even the land of Egypt will escape. ⁴³ He will get control over the hidden treasures of gold and silver and over all the riches of Egypt. The Libyans and Cushites will also be in submission. ⁴⁴ But reports from the east and the north will terrify him, and he will go out with great fury to annihilate and completely destroy many. ⁴⁵ He will pitch his royal tents between the sea and the beautiful holy mountain, but he will meet his end with no one to help him.

¹ At that time
Michael, the great prince
who stands watch over your people, will rise up.
There will be a time of distress
such as never has occurred
since nations came into being until that time.
But at that time all your people
who are found written in the book will escape.
² Many who sleep in the dust
of the earth will awake,
some to eternal life,
and some to disgrace and eternal contempt.
³ Those who have insight will shine
like the bright expanse of the heavens,
and those who lead many to righteousness,
like the stars forever and ever.

Context

Daniel 11:36–12:3 continues Daniel's fourth vision that encompasses 10:1–12:13. This third part of the fourth vision parallels the fourth beast with its little horn and the establishment of God's kingdom as described in Daniel 7 (see outline).

The meaning of 11:36–46 is disputed. Critical scholars hold that it elaborates further on Antiochus IV, though the prophecy fails, showing that the author has gone from history in the guise of prophecy to genuine prediction, which, as it turns out, he is not very good at. Conservative and traditional scholars usually hold that this passage speaks of an eschatological antichrist figure, so the prophecy is yet to be fulfilled. Occasionally it is argued that it refers both to Antiochus and antichrist at the same time.[1]

In favor of the Antiochus IV view is the fact that there is no obvious break between vv. 21–35 and vv. 36–46. Thus "the king" in vv. 36–39 could be a further elaboration on Antiochus IV and his wicked character—which no subsequent Seleucid king exhibited. But critical scholars say the prophecy fails because it predicts that Antiochus starts a third campaign against Egypt (vv. 40–43), which historically never happened (much less that Libya and Cush ever submitted to him). It also predicts that Antiochus would die in Judea "between the sea and the beautiful holy mountain" (v. 45), whereas according to Roman historians (Polybius, *Histories* 31.11; Appian, *Syriaca* 66) he died in Tabae in Elymais (Elam, modern southwest Iran) of a wasting disease after having robbed or attempted to rob a temple, possibly the same temple robbed by his father (see comments at 11:19). He never returned to Judea or Egypt after 167 BC. Mangano, a conservative scholar holding to the Antiochus IV view, does not see failed prophecy here. Mangano thinks that these verses recapitulate and speak again of Antiochus' first invasion of Egypt to summarize his character rather than predicting a third invasion of Egypt. He also thinks v. 45 only means that Antiochus pitches his tent in Judea, not that he dies there.[2] Lucas, another conservative, sees the language as hyperbole as befitting Antiochus' hubris and that the text only means to convey that, like other rulers who give way to arrogance, Antiochus has an untimely end.[3]

Against this view is the theological objection that the critical view makes Daniel's prophecy of "truth" (11:2) into a lie. Furthermore, the

[1] J. G. Baldwin, *Daniel*, TOTC (Leicester: Inter-Varsity, 1978), 199–201.

[2] M. Mangano, *Esther & Daniel*, College Press NIV Commentary (Joplin, MO: College Press, 2001), 300–301.

[3] E. C. Lucas, *Daniel*, Apollos Old Testament Commentary (Downers Grove: InterVarsity, 2002), 293.

description of the king of vv. 37–38 does not fit Antiochus IV.[4] The text says the king "will not show regard for the gods [CSB note, "God"] of his fathers," but in fact Antiochus showed plenty of regard to Zeus, Jupiter, Apollo, and other gods. He exalted both Zeus and Apollo on the reverse side of his coinage.[5] Polybius writes that in Antiochus' "public sacrifices and the honors paid to the gods, he surpassed all his predecessors on the throne" (*Histories* 26:1). Various ancient sources speak of Antiochus building temples and honoring gods at various places (Strabo, *Geography* 9.1.17; Pausanius, *Description of Greece* 5.12.4; Ammianus Marcellinus, *Rerum Gestarum* 22.13.1; Livy, *History of Rome* 41.20.9). He established games at Daphne that involved a procession of images of "every god or demigod or hero accepted by mankind" (Polybius, *Histories* 31.3). Among the Jews he promoted the festival of Dionysus (2 Macc 6:7–8), the god of wine. His deification of himself (the title "Epiphanes") is not a denial of his ancestral, Greek gods. Some take "the god longed for by women" (11:37; see comments below) to refer to Tammuz/Adonis (Ezek 8:14), but there is no evidence that Antiochus IV suppressed the worship of any god whatsoever except Yahweh. The writer of Daniel 11 was remarkably accurate historically up until this point. For him to fail here seems unlikely. More likely Daniel is speaking of someone else.

A case can be made that Dan 11:36–46 describes neither Antiochus IV nor first-century BC Roman dealings in Palestine.[6] Rather, it describes a future figure, the antichrist. Verse 35 states that Daniel's people would be purified "until the time of the end"; therefore, it is reasonable to expect the next discussion to bring us to "the time of the end." With 11:36–46 we have arrived "at the time of the end" (v. 40). Moreover 11:36–44 is closely connected with 12:1–3, which predicts an unprecedented great distress and a clearly eschatological event, the resurrection of the just and unjust "at that time" (12:1). Thus 12:1–3 seems to place 11:36–44 in an eschatological context, making 11:36–12:3 as a unit parallel with Daniel 7 and

[4] M. Mercer, "The Benefactions of Antiochus IV Epiphanes and Dan 11:37–38: An Exegetical Note," *Master's Seminary Journal* 12.1 (Spring 2001): 89–93.

[5] O. Mørkholm, "The Monetary System in the Seleucid Empire after 187 B.C.," in *Ancient Coins of the Graeco-Roman World*, ed. W. Heckel and R. Sullivan (Waterloo, Ontario: Wilfrid Laurier University Press, 1984), 99.

[6] Contra J. T. Parry, "Desolation of the Temple and Messianic Enthronement in Daniel 11:36–12:3," *JETS* 54.3 (2011) 485–526.

Daniel 2 in which the kingdoms of the world are displaced by the kingdom of God (see outline).

This fits the pattern of the four kingdoms of Daniel. We have argued earlier that the four kingdoms of Daniel 2 and 7 are Babylon, Medo-Persia, Greece, and Rome-and-beyond. Here we argue that "the king" of verse 36 may be from the fourth kingdom of Rome-and-beyond (not the Greeks), a view also held by Calvin.[7] Hence there is consistent transition in Daniel 10–12 as found elsewhere in Daniel from Medo-Persia to Greece to Rome-and-beyond to the kingdom of God (see chart). Earlier the Persians "stir up" the Greeks, leading to the rise of the "warrior king" Alexander (11:3–4). So here Antiochus IV stirs up the Romans, leading to "the king" of v. 36. The transition from Greece to Rome as the great power occurs historically when the "ships of the Kittim" (Rome) led by Popilius put an end to Antiochus IV's expansionist ambitions in Egypt (see comments at 11:29–31). Thus mention of Rome next makes historical and literary sense, following the earlier pattern from Persia to Greece to Rome.[8]

The Four Kingdoms in Daniel 2, 7, 8, 10–12				
Daniel 2	**Daniel 7**	**Daniel 8**	**Daniel 10–12**	**Identification**
Gold	Lion			Babylon
Silver	Bear	Ram	10:13, 20a; 11:2	Medo-Persia
Bronze	Leopard	Male goat	10:20b; 11:3–35	Greek kingdoms
Iron and clay	Beast		11:36–45	Rome-and-beyond
Mountain	Coming of the Son of Man		12:1–3	God's kingdom

This line of interpretation also finds support in the NT. Paul sees in Dan 11:36–45 a description of the future "man of lawlessness" rather than Antiochus IV Epiphanes (see chart). The antichrist interpretation of 11:36–45 makes the passage a continuation of the description of the antichrist in Daniel 7. The description of the "little horn" antichrist in Daniel 7 is followed by the description of the

---

[7] J. Calvin, *Commentary on the Book of the Prophet Daniel*, trans. T. Myers, 2 vols. (Bellingham, WA: Logos Bible Software, 2010), 2:338–39.

[8] A. Steinmann, "Is the Antichrist in Daniel 11?" *BSac* 162.646 (2005): 201.

"little horn" Epiphanes in Daniel 8. So the description of Epiphanes in 11:21–35 is followed by the description of the antichrist in 11:36–45. The logic is to show how Epiphanes is a prototype and foreshadowing of the end-time antichrist.

Paul's "Man of Lawlessness" (2 Thessalonians 2)	Daniel's "King of the North" (Daniel 11)
"the man doomed to destruction" (2 Thess 2:3)	"He will meet his end" (Dan 11:45; cp. 7:11) "He will be successful until the time of wrath is completed" (Dan 11:36)
"He opposes and exalts himself above every so-called god or object of worship" (2 Thess 2:4)	"He will exalt and magnify himself above every god, and he will say outrageous things against the God of gods" (Dan 11:36) "He will not show regard for the gods of his fathers ... or for any other god ... he will magnify himself above all [gods]" (Dan 11:37)
"proclaiming that he himself is God" (2 Thess 2:4)	"He will exalt and magnify himself above every god" (Dan 11:36) "He will magnify himself above all [gods]" (Dan 11:37)

Daniel 11:36–12:3 can be outlined as follows:

I. Battles at time of the end (11:36–45)
    Character of "the king" (vv. 36–39)
    Battles involving kings of North and South (vv. 40–43)
    The king meets his end in Israel (vv. 44–45)

II. Eschatological redemption of God's people (12:1–3)
    Michael and the great distress (v. 1)
    Resurrection of the just and unjust (vv. 2–3)

11:36 As with Persia (8:4) and Antiochus III (11:16), so this king (the antichrist, see §7.4.1) will "do whatever he wants"—that is, have his way militarily. Antiochus IV had the title "Epiphanes" ("manifest [appearing of a god]"), a blasphemous claim to deity or near divine greatness ("even against the Prince of the heavenly army," 8:11). This king in v. 36 will be worse than Antiochus Epiphanes. He does not merely claim a semi-divine status, but superiority to all gods (v. 36b).

Daniel's God is "the God of gods" (v. 36c), a title that to non-Jews could mean "greatest of the gods" (Dan 2:47), but to Jews meant "the most divine One" or "the God without peer."

Against the true God, this king will "say outrageous things" (v. 36c), an N-stem participle from פלא ("be wonderful, astounding"). This root refers predominately to unusual acts of God beyond human capacities which awaken the astonishment of people. But at 8:24 it refers to Antiochus IV's "terrible/astounding" destruction. Here this king speaks "astonishing things" (ESV), "horrendous things" (NRSV), or "awful things" (NJPS) that shock the pious. Like Antiochus this king will be successful (v. 36d; cf. Dan 8:12, 24–25) in what he does but this will last only until divine "wrath" (זַעַם; cf. 8:19) is expressed and "what has been decreed" (N-stem participle חרץ; see comments at 9:25, 26) by God occurs (cf. 9:27). The phrases "[time of] wrath is completed" (כָּלָה זַעַם) and "what has been decreed" (נֶחֱרָצָה) echo Isa 10:23–25, "[my] wrath will be spent" (כָּלָה זַעַם) and "[destruction] that was decreed" (נֶחֱרָצָה).[9] Isaiah and Daniel use these thoughts to encourage Judah not to fear their enemies since God will limit the hostility to his people. All of this speaks of the predetermined plan and sovereignty of God over history (see §7).

11:37 Unlike Antiochus IV, this king lacks respect for deity, regarding himself as superior to any god. On "show regard for" (Qal of בִין + עַל; v. 37a), see comment at v. 30, where the same idiom is rendered "favor" (CSB). Hebrew אֱלֹהִים can mean either "God" or "gods," so אֱלֹהֵי אֲבֹתָיו in v. 37a can be rendered either "gods of his fathers" (Theodotion, Old Greek) or "God of his fathers" (KJV, Vulgate). Elsewhere this expression always refers to Yahweh (Exod 3:16; 2 Kgs 21:22; 2 Chr 21:10; 28:25; 33:12; though cp. Josh 24:14–15). Those who accept the singular meaning of אֱלֹהִים here sometimes argue that the antichrist must be Jewish (of the circumcision), a view held by some church fathers (e.g., Irenaeus, *Against Heresies* 5.30; Hippolytus, *On Christ and Antichrist* 6). Even if the meaning were singular ("God/god of his fathers"), this would not preclude the antichrist being a gentile. This אֱלֹהִים could be his family's patron "god" or even Israel's "God" previously worshiped by his gentile

---

[9] G. B. Lester, *Daniel Evokes Isaiah: Allusive Characterization of Foreign Rule in the Hebrew-Aramaic Book of Daniel*, LHBOTS 606 (London: Bloombury T&T Clark, 2015), 65–66.

(Christian?) ancestors. But since the kings in Daniel 11 are elsewhere non-Israelite, the plural rendering "gods" makes good sense contextually. That this king is Jewish seems unlikely.

The meaning of "the god desired by women," literally "desire of women" (cf. KJV), is ambiguous. The form of חֶמְדָּה ("desire") was translated "[their] precious articles" at v. 8 and is cognate with חֲמֻדוֹת, rendered "riches" in v. 38. Thus this root often pertains to what is treasured, precious, or desirable. The Hebrew lacks "the god." It might refer to a god especially desired by or precious to women, as was Tammuz/Adonis in Ezekiel's day (Ezek 8:14–15). This fits the context immediately before and after, which refers to deities. Archer[10] takes this as referring to this king's disregard for what women want, suggesting that he is abusive of them, a misogynist, or too self-absorbed to care for others. Or perhaps he does not care for "womanly affection" or has no "desire for women" (GW) because he is a homosexual. Miller[11] sees in the expression a reference to the Messiah, whom Jewish women longed to bear. Understanding the syntax differently, it could mean, "He will not show regard for the gods of his fathers but instead [adversative *waw*, parallel with the adversative *waw* in v. 38] [he will show regard] for the lust of women" (cp. Douay-Rheims). This would suggest one of his real "gods" is his sexual conquest of women. The ambiguity precludes nailing down the meaning.

11:38–39 Though he has no use for God or gods, this king does pay homage to and devote enormous wealth ("gold, silver, precious stones, and riches") to "a god of fortresses" (v. 38), that is, to military might. That this is not a "god" known by his ancestors may be a matter of hyperbole since worshiping military power is not uncommon in human history, but to do so to the exclusion of ordinary religion is not common. Military power is the "foreign god" ("strange god," KJV) of v. 39, strange in this case because it is not really a god. He will use his power and associated wealth to buy ("honor") friends, giving them land or territory to win their support. Honor (כָּבוֹד) includes money (NRSV, "make more wealthy") as well as respect. CSB renders כָּבוֹד as "wealth" at Gen 31:1 and "abundance" in Nah 2:9.

---

[10] G. L. Archer, "Daniel," in *The Expositor's Bible Commentary*, ed. Frank E. Gaebelein, vol. 7 (Grand Rapids: Zondervan, 1985), 144.

[11] S. R. Miller, *Daniel*, NAC 18 (Nashville: Broadman & Holman, 1994), 306.

11:40 The expression "the time of the end" is used at 8:17 and 19 for the future judgment at the time of Antiochus IV (see comments at 8:17). Its meaning here is clarified by 12:1–3, where "at that time" refers to an unprecedented great distress (12:1) when the resurrection of the just and unjust occurs (12:2). This context places this "time of the end" in the eschatological future from our perspective (see §7.4). Pierce, who applies 11:36–39 to Antiochus IV, sees a transition to the eschatological end here.[12] This king will sweep through militarily like a flood, just as the king of the North does in 11:10, echoing the language of Isa 8:7–8 concerning Assyria's invasion of Judah.

Who are the king of the South and the king of the North in v. 40 in relation to the king in v. 36? There are two plausible options. One is a "two-king" interpretation that identifies the king of the North with the king of vv. 36–39. This makes vv. 36–45 consistent with the conflicts between the kings of the South and the North in vv. 5–35. If the two-king view is correct, the king of the North must be the antichrist figure.

The other view is the "three-king" interpretation. In this case the king of the South and the king of the North are distinct from the king of vv. 36–39, against whom they both fight. This view associates "the king" with the fourth beast of Daniel, namely Rome-and-beyond. Rome showed itself the dominant power in v. 30 when the ships of Kittim (= Rome) halted the ambitions of Antiochus IV, so a transition to Roman dominance makes sense in the immediate context. An advantage of the three-king hypothesis is that it allows one more readily to identify the king here with the little horn figure of Daniel 7. If instead the king of the North is the same as "the king" of v. 36, then this king likely occupies territory once belonging to the Seleucids (Syria, Asia Minor, Babylonia), making a connection with the Rome-and-beyond "antichrist" figure from the fourth beast of Daniel 7 more problematic.

11:41–43 The "beautiful land" (v. 41) is Israel (see comments at v. 16; 8:9) where this wicked king causes many to fall (literally, "stumble"; N-stem כשל). "Many" is probably better rendered "tens of thousands" (ESV, NRSV, Symmachus), a change that involves vocalizing the Masoretic consonants רבות as רִבּוֹת ("tens of thousands")

---

[12] R. W. Pierce, *Daniel*, Teach the Text (Grand Rapids: Baker, 2015), 187.

rather than the MT vocalization of רַבּוֹת ("many"). He will bypass Edom, Moab, and most of Ammon, lands in modern-day Jordan east of Israel. The "prominent people of the Ammonites" is sometimes taken as a reference to Ammon's leader or leaders but is better rendered "main part of the sons of Ammon" (ESV; cf. HALOT[13]) as a geographic reference rather than to its leaders. A few translations follow the Syriac rendering, "remnant [of the Ammonites]" (NEB), which implies an original reading of שְׁאֵרִית ("remnant") instead of רֵאשִׁית ("what is first, best"), a change involving metathesis of ר and שׁ, though other ancient versions do not support this change.

This king conquers Egypt and its environs, which he will plunder (vv. 42–43a). Libya and Cush (v. 43c) were sometimes allies of Egypt in OT times (2 Chr 12:3; 16:8; Nah 3:9). "In submission" (v. 43c) is literally "at his steps" (CSB note), suggesting Libya and Cush will be trampled by this wicked king.

11:44–45 Certain "reports" (v. 44a) lead this king to withdraw his army from the vicinities of Egypt. Compare this report from the "east" and "north" to the rumor that caused Sennacherib of Assyria to withdraw from Israel (Isa 37:7). The king will end up in the land of Israel between the Mediterranean ("the sea") and Mount Zion in Jerusalem ("the beautiful holy mountain"; cf. Dan 9:16, 20), where he apparently meets his fate (unlike Antiochus IV, who dies in Persia). Compare Dan 7:11 and 22 with Rev 16:12–16 and 19:11–21, where Revelation's antichrist figure ("the beast") gathers the kings of the east (among others) to the battle of Armageddon (in the vicinity of Megiddo in Israel) and is defeated by Christ and cast into the lake of fire.

12:1 The climax of the vision of Daniel 10–12 is 12:1–3, which depicts the end of world kingdoms and the establishment of everlasting righteousness with the resurrection of the just and the unjust (vv. 1–3). It is in continuity with 11:38–45 but transitions from Rome-and-beyond to the kingdom of God. CSB and NET format this section as poetry, and verse 3 gives evidence of poetic parallelism, but the case for seeing vv. 1–2 as poetry is weak.

The angelic narrator introduced in Daniel 10 now returns to the theme of angels (see §5). The angel Michael is mentioned at 10:13 and 21 where he is called a "chief prince" and "your [= Israel's] prince."

---

13 "רֵאשִׁית," HALOT 3:1170.

He helped the angelic visitor escape from the prince of Persia and engaged in spiritual warfare with the prince of Persia and the prince of Greece. He is called the "great prince" because he is superior in rank to other angels (Jude 1:9 calls him an "archangel"). As Israel's prince he stands guard over Daniel's people.

Michael, as patron of God's people, takes his stand in preparation for action because of a "distress" or tribulation that will affect them. Hebrew צָרָה is a term used to denote a variety of distressing circumstances (Gen 42:21; 2 Chr 15:6; 20:9; Neh 9:27; Jer 4:31; 6:24; Jonah 2:3). This distress in v. 1 echoes Jeremiah's language concerning the "time of trouble [צָרָה] for Jacob"—"there will be no other like it" (Jer 30:7). Jeremiah refers to the Babylonian exile. This distress will likewise be unprecedented, the worst such distress in human history. The phrase "since nations came into being" might rather mean "since the nation [Israel] came into being" (NJPS; NABRE). The NT seems to expand on v. 1 (see Matt 24:21–22; Mark 13:19–20; Rev 7:14), placing its fulfillment in the eschatological future in God's plan for history (see §7.4.2). This distress is presumably caused by "the king" or antichrist of 11:36–45 who makes war on the saints (7:21). Under Michael's watchful care at least a remnant of Daniel's people will escape, those "found written in the book," describing those who will receive a favorable judgment from God. The book is similar to the books of 7:10 used to condemn the fourth beast and the book of truth in 10:21 that records human destiny. Several texts in Daniel (7:25b; 12:7, 11–12) suggest that the length of this distress is three and one-half years.

12:2 The OT occasionally speaks of an afterlife (see §7.4.4), but 12:2 is the first text that unambiguously affirms the general resurrection of the dead. "Many" (רַבִּים) appears to have the more inclusive meaning of "all" or "everybody" (as at Ps 109:30; Prov 19:6; Isa 53:11–12; Dan 9:27).[14] "Those who sleep" refers to the dead (cp. Matt 27:52; John 11:11–14; Acts 7:60). "Dust of the earth" (literally "land/ ground of dust"; cp. LEB, NET, "dusty ground") alludes to Gen 3:19, which speaks of the decomposition of dead bodies: "For you are dust, and you will return to dust."

"Awake" and "dust" may also allude to the resurrection of Isa 26:19: "Your dead will live; their bodies will rise. Awake and sing,

---

[14] "רַב," *HALOT* 3:1171; cp. T. Hartmann, "רַב," in *TLOT*, 1197–98.

you who dwell in the dust!" The righteous gain the reward of eternal life, and the wicked are condemned to shame and eternal contempt (cp. Matt 25:46; John 5:28–29). The word translated "shame" (חֶרְפָּה) is in the plural and can also be rendered "reproaches" (NJPS) or as a plural of abstraction "reproach" (NABRE). The word translated "contempt" (דֵּרָאוֹן) is only used once elsewhere in the Hebrew Bible—in the context of the new heavens and new earth in Isa 66:24. That verse, to which Daniel probably alludes,[15] speaks of the "abhorrence," "horror," or "loathing" that the righteous will have for those who rebel against God, concerning whom "the worm will not die and the fire will not be quenched." Mark 9:47–48 applies this language to hell. The general meaning is partly derived from the Arabic cognate verb *dara³a* ("repel, to ward off danger"), suggesting דֵּרָאוֹן has to do with repulsiveness, and from the Old Greek and Theodotion, which render it with αἰσχύνη ("shame").

12:3 "Those who have insight" (H-stem participle שׂכל) is used similarly in 11:33 and 35 for the godly who would convey spiritual insight during the Maccabean revolt. Being insightful/wise is also a characteristic of Daniel (1:17; 5:11) and evokes the suffering servant (Isa 52:13), who causes the "many" to be declared righteous (Isa 53:11) and with whom the "many" are implicitly associated.[16] These wise are among the godly who flourish after the resurrection of the just (v. 2).

To "shine" or "be radiant" (NJPS) like the bright sky employs a rare verb and cognate noun (H-stem זהר and זֹהַר). The only other occurrence of the noun in the Hebrew Bible is Ezek 8:2, where it denotes the glow of the glory of God. In later Aramaic its cognate can mean the moon, a meaning Lucas adopts, making "luminary of the expanse" (= the moon) in parallel with the stars.[17] Here the sense may be that they will convey spiritual insight (11:33, 35) and reflect the glory of God (cp. Moses in Exod 34:29). "Those who have insight" is a synonym for "those who lead many to righteousness." "Like the stars" may reflect the use of stars for navigation purposes. Just as the North Star can help someone know the right direction to go, so the wise direct many in a godward direction. The stars, which

---

[15] Lester, *Daniel Evokes Isaiah*, 99–101.
[16] Ibid., 97–99.
[17] Lucas, *Daniel*, 263.

last from generation to generation, also convey a sense of eternity. Having received "eternal life" (v. 2), the wise can continue to shine and flourish "forever and ever."

Bridge

Like the little horn of Daniel 7, the king of 11:36–45 refers to the antichrist (see §7.4.1). Even if it were a description of Antiochus IV, Paul sees in this figure a prototype of the "man of lawlessness" (antichrist) who was to come (2 Thess 2:3–4; see table above). Either way this suggests that the antichrist will be a blasphemous, atheistic, military-political leader who will meet his fate without achieving his machinations against God's people. His actions will lead to an unprecedented "time of distress" (12:1; see §7.4.2) to which Jesus refers (Matt 24:21; cp. Rev 7:14), an eschatological event in conjunction with his second coming (Matt 24:30–31; cp. Dan 7:13–14). This is consistent with the general theme of suffering that God allows his people to endure (see §4.5). Revelation 16:12–16 and 19:11–21 indicate that "the beast" (antichrist and his kingdom) will gather the kings of the east (among others) to the battle of Armageddon (in the vicinity of Megiddo in Israel). But he will be defeated by Christ and cast into the lake of fire (cp. Dan 7:11, 22).

God's people should be encouraged and comforted by knowledge of his ultimate victory. However, the wicked are warned of God's coming judgment and the need to repent. God shows his presence with his suffering people by employing supernatural angelic forces (cp. 10:13, 21 and Rev 12:7) to watch over and defend them (those "written in the book") so that they will escape death (12:1; Matt 24:22; see §5, §4.5). Suffering in the present age is nothing in comparison with the glorious rewards Christians will receive (Rom 8:18). All of us experience sufferings of our own (John 16:33) and encounter various antichrists who precede the final one (1 John 2:18). We can be encouraged that God supernaturally watches over us in times of trouble and that the faithful will be resurrected and rewarded at the final judgment.

Ultimately there are only two humanities, the just and the unjust, the saved and the lost. The righteous dead will be resurrected and rewarded with eternal life, shinning and flourishing like stars (see §7.4.4). The unrighteous dead will also be raised, but they will experience eternal contempt as their punishment (12:2–3). The themes of resurrection and final judgment occur repeatedly in the NT. Those who trust in the resurrected Christ will themselves be resurrected, and he will preside over the final judgment on the Father's behalf (Matt 25:31–46; 2 Cor 5:10; 2 Thess 1:8–10; 20:11–15).

I. Court Narratives (Daniel 1–6)

II. Visions of Daniel (Daniel 7–12)
First vision: Four beasts and son of man figure (Daniel 7)
Second vision: Ram and male goat (Daniel 8)
Third vision: Seventy weeks (Daniel 9)
Fourth vision: Kings of North/South, distress/resurrection (Daniel 10–12)
Angels in conflict (10:1–11:2a)
Preview of Persian and Greek kings (11:2b–35)
World kingdoms ended and the righteous established (11:36–12:3)
Vision sealed until the end (12:4–13)

(A) Beginning of story (1:1–21)
  (B) Dream about four world kingdoms ended by the kingdom of God (2:1–49)
    (C) Judeans faithful in the face of death (3:1–30)
      (D) Royal pride humbled (4:1–37)
      (D′) Royal pride humbled (5:1–31)
    (C′) A Judean faithful in the face of death (6:1–28)
  (B′) Vision about four world kingdoms ended by the kingdom of God (7:1–28)
    (E) Vision of Persian and Greek kingdoms to Antiochus (8:1–27)
      (F) Vision of seventy weeks (9:1–27)
    (E′) Vision of Persian and Greek kingdoms to Antiochus (10:1–11:35)
  (B″)World kingdoms ended and the righteous established (11:36–12:3)
(A′) End of story: Vision sealed until the end (12:4–13)

⁴ "But you, Daniel, keep these words secret and seal the book until the time of the end. Many will roam about, and knowledge will increase."

⁵ Then I, Daniel, looked, and two others were standing there, one on this bank of the river and one on the other. ⁶ One of them said to the man dressed in linen, who was above the water of the river, "How long until the end of these wondrous things?" ⁷ Then I heard the man dressed in linen, who was above the water of the

river. He raised both his hands toward heaven and swore by him who lives eternally that it would be for a time, times, and half a time. When the power of the holy people is shattered, all these things will be completed.

⁸ I heard but did not understand. So I asked, "My lord, what will be the outcome of these things?"

⁹ He said, "Go on your way, Daniel, for the words are secret and sealed until the time of the end. ¹⁰ Many will be purified, cleansed, and refined, but the wicked will act wickedly; none of the wicked will understand, but those who have insight will understand. ¹¹ From the time the daily sacrifice is abolished and the abomination of desolation is set up, there will be 1,290 days. ¹² Happy is the one who waits for and reaches 1,335 days. ¹³ But as for you, go on your way to the end; you will rest, and then you will stand to receive your allotted inheritance at the end of the days."

Context

This is the last segment of Daniel's final vision (10:1–12:13). In our chiastic outline (see above), 12:4–13 parallels the introductory chapter of Daniel and forms the book's conclusion. Daniel 12:4–13 alludes to the elimination of regular sacrifice and the abomination of desolation mentioned previously in the book, and it ends with obscure remarks about chronology (1,290 days and 1,335 days) while reflecting on the mysteries of apocalyptic-prophetic revelation. While the command to "seal the book" applies in the immediate context to the vision of Daniel 11–12, it also makes a fitting conclusion to the book as a whole.[1] Daniel 12:4–13 can be outlined as follows:

A Seal book till the end (12:4)
  B Question One: How long till the end? (12:5–6)
  Answer: Time, times, half a time (12:7)
  B′ Question Two: What is the outcome of these things? (12:8)
  Answer 1: Details sealed till time of end (12:9)

---

[1] E. C. Lucas, *Daniel*, Apollos Old Testament Commentary (Downers Grove: InterVarsity, 2002), 296.

Answer 2: But many will be purified, the insightful
will understand, and those who reach 1,335 days will
be happy (12:10–11)
A′   Daniel to go on his destiny till the end (12:12–13)

12:4 Three times Daniel is told to keep secret (סתם) his vision
(8:26; 12:4, 9), on which see comments at 8:26. This is clarified by
"seal [the book]," using חתם, a verb that can mean "to seal [a document with a seal]." Since this vision of Daniel 10–12, like the one
at 8:26, was subsequently published in the book of Daniel without
a seal, the prophecy is not literally kept secret. Perhaps the sense
of this command is that Daniel himself should not inquire of the
angel about the exact details of the meaning of the vision of Daniel
10–12, which will only become clear in the future fulfillment
(12:9). He is to seal it in a book in the sense of preserving it until
"the time of the end" for the future generations who at that time
might better grasp the meaning. For Daniel the "time of the end"
includes events in the distant future from his perspective, both the
time of Antiochus IV (8:17, 19) and also the eschatological future
(11:40; cf. 12:1–2). Revelation 22:10 picks up on Daniel's words
by affirming the opposite: "Don't seal the prophetic words of this
book, because the time is near." Revelation speaks of the breaking of the seals of the book of destiny (Rev 5:2–5), suggesting that
"John's prophecy contains the fulfillment of the latter-days prophecies of Daniel."[2]

This revelation for future believers seems in contrast with those
"roaming about" or who "range far and wide" (NJPS). The D-stem
(polel) of שוט ("rove") multiplies the action to "rove hither and yon"
or similar. Theodotion renders as "until many are taught," which may
imply a different *Vorlage*. Among these "knowledge will increase,"
though not truth from divine revelation (cp. Amos 8:12). The Old
Greek says, "until many rage violently and the earth is filled with
injustice," a reading implying a Hebrew text containing הרעה ("evil")
instead of הדעת ("knowledge"). This alternative reading is adopted
by some versions (NRSV; NABRE; NEB, "punishment").

---

[2] G. K. Beale and S. M. McDonough, "Revelation," in *Commentary on the New
Testament Use of the Old Testament*, ed. G. K. Beal and D. A. Carson (Grand Rapids:
Baker, 2007), 1101.

12:5–7 Daniel saw two more angels besides the one in linen (10:5) who had been addressing him, one on each side of the river. This description of angels forms an inclusio with the beginning of the vision of Daniel 10–12, serving to draw the vision (and the book) to a close. The word for "river" (יְאֹר) usually refers to the Nile and its canals, though it can be a synonym for Hebrew נָהָר, "river" (cf. Isa 33:21). Here it refers to the Tigris, where Daniel received the vision (Dan 10:4).

For "one of them said" (v. 6a), the Vulgate and some Old Greek manuscripts read instead "I said." This implies a Hebrew text that lacks one letter (*yod*) as compared with the MT (ואמר versus ויאמר), a reading adopted by some versions (RSV, DRA, NEB). The "man dressed in linen" (v. 6a) is the angel who has been speaking to Daniel all along (10:5). On "linen" and the man's identity, see commentary at 10:4–6. The linen-clad angel seems superior in rank to the "two others" in that he is "above" them (v. 6b) and they make inquiries of him. "How long until the end?" (v. 6c) echoes the question of 8:13. "These wondrous things" (פְּלָאוֹת), or more literally "the wonders" (LEB), employs the root פלא ("be wonderful, astounding") that refers predominately to unusual acts of God (beyond human capacity) that awaken the astonishment of people. It could refer to the eschatological wonderous resurrection of 12:2–3. On the other hand, the N-stem participle is used at 8:24 of Antiochus IV's "terrible/astounding" destruction and at 11:36 of the "outrageous" (CSB) or "horrendous" (NRSV) things said by the king (antichrist). So here at 12:6c the cognate noun could mean "these appalling things" (NABRE) or "these awful things" (NJPS) and might be a double allusion to 8:24 (Antiochus IV, the type) and 11:36 (antichrist, the antitype).

Raising "both hands toward heaven" (v. 7b), literally "his right and his left" (CSB note), as opposed to raising one hand, adds focus on God whose abode is in heaven. He is the one who controls these events (see §3.8) and the one from whom the angel has received his message. Swearing an oath (v. 7b) makes a commitment in God's name, often using the formula "as the Lord lives" (e.g., Judg 8:19; Ruth 3:13; 1 Sam 14:45) or a formula like "may the Lord do such and such to me if I do not do X" (see 1 Kgs 2:23). God is described as "him who lives eternally" (literally, "the living one of eternity"; see §3.3), and thus eternally able to bring about these predictions. An oath makes a promise more solemn and underscores the seriousness of the person making the oath. By swearing in God's name, the angel, who is God's messenger, is emphatically affirming the validity of his prophecy based on the trustworthiness of God (see §2).

"Time, times, and half a time" (v. 7c) gives the Hebrew equivalent of the Aramaic of 7:25, which describes the three-and-one-half-year persecution of the saints by the little horn (antichrist), to which v. 1 also alludes. This is the time when "the power [literally, "hand"] of the holy people is shattered" (v. 7c), bringing us to the climax of the prophecies of Daniel. Immediately after this, the son of man figure appears with the clouds, and the kingdom goes to the holy ones, that is, the holy people (7:13–14, 18). That said, it is not impossible that this refers to an analogous period of persecution under Antiochus (see 8:14 where 2,300 evenings and mornings could mean 1,150 days, a bit more than three years).

12:8–12 As with the first two visions, Daniel does not fully grasp the meaning of this revelation (cf. 7:15–16; 8:15, 27). When he inquires of the angel (v. 8b), he is told again that the words are "secret and sealed" (v. 9; comments at v. 4 above), only to be more fully grasped at "the time of the end"—the three and one-half years of v. 7 and 7:25 (see comment at v. 7 above). It is preserved for the godly in the future who will experience the events predicted. The statement about many being "purified, cleansed, and refined" (v. 10a) reaffirms for the end times what 11:35 says regarding the time of Antiochus IV. "Purified, cleansed, and refined" (יִתְבָּרֲרוּ וְיִתְלַבְּנוּ וְיִצָּרְפוּ) uses the same roots though a different stem as "that they may be refined, purified, and cleansed" (לִצְרוֹף בָּהֶם וּלְבָרֵר וְלַלְבֵּן) in 11:35, to which it alludes. "Those who have insight will understand" (v. 10b) echoes 11:33, where the godly wise with "insight" at the time of Antiochus IV will "give understanding." These future godly wise in 12:10b in "the time of the end" will be able to understand Daniel's vision more than Daniel himself. Revelation 22:11 echoes Dan 12:10: "Let the unrighteous go on in unrighteousness; let the filthy go on being made filthy; let the righteous go on in righteousness; and let the holy go on being made holy." Those who ignore God's revelation, the "wicked," naturally will not understand.

On "daily sacrifice" (v. 11), a word previously rendered "regular sacrifice" (8:11, 12, 13; 11:31), see comments at 8:11. On "abomination of desolation" see comments at 9:27 and 11:31. "Happy" (v. 12) or "blessed" (ESV, NIV) is אַשְׁרֵי, a plural construct noun that refers to the bliss or good fortune of the person who (in this case) waits and reaches 1,335 days.

The text of vv. 11–12 is a cryptic riddle. Which "abomination of desolation" is in mind? Is it the one at the time of Antiochus IV who puts an end to legitimate "regular sacrifice" (8:11–13; 11:31)? Is it the (possibly) different abomination of desolation in 9:27 (see commentary and excursus there)? Is it from our perspective an eschatological event or a past event? If it is eschatological, does the statement about regular offerings being abolished imply a rebuilt future temple, or is this only symbolic for sacrilege of true worship? What exactly is the 1,290 days? How does it differ from the "time, times, and half a time" of v. 7, if at all? If this and Revelation 12 both are eschatological, what distinction is there between Daniel's 1,290 days and Revelation's 1,260 days (Rev 12:6)? What does the interval between the 1,290 days and the 1,335 days in Daniel 12 signify? The fact that a blessing or happiness is attached to the 1,335 number (v. 12) suggests that to reach that number is to have passed beyond the time of trial.

Answers to these questions are speculative. Here are some of the proposed interpretations, but none commend themselves as indisputably correct.

- If the abomination of desolation here is when Antiochus IV ends sacrifice, it could depict events at the end of the period of Antiochus' persecution of the Jews. Mangano[3] takes the 1,290 days to be the three-and-one-half-year persecution of the Jews (1,290 days) culminating in the rededication of the temple. Mangano goes on to take the forty-five-day gap to be that between the rededication of the temple and Antiochus IV's death. However we lack historical data to prove that this is the timing of those two events. By one chronology, the temple was dedicated in December 164 BC and Antiochus died about the same time in late 164,[4] which does not leave room for the forty-five days.

- Critical scholars regularly identify the abomination of desolation with Antiochus IV and often (e.g., Hartman and

---

[3] M. Mangano, *Esther & Daniel*, College Press NIV Commentary (Joplin, MO: College Press, 2001), 306.

[4] J. Whitehorne, "Antiochus (Person)," *ABD* 1:271.

Di Lella [5]) see these as successive corrections to the author's failed prophecies about Antiochus' defiling of the temple. But, even if one were to accept this view of Scripture, one would still have expected the author to remove the failed prophecies with each revision of his work—not leave his mistakes for all to see.

- Some take the numbers as symbolic. For example, Steinmann takes each temporal description—"time, times, and half a time," 1,290 days, and 1,335 days—as symbolic time periods that conclude with the second coming of Christ. These start from the birth of Christ, from Antiochus IV, and from the beginning of the vision in Daniel 10, respectively.[6] Against such an approach is that any symbolism is at best obscure. Steinmann's particular symbolic view must, with little basis, take these "days" as much longer time periods but not particularly proportional periods.

- Premillennialists usually take the abomination of desolation here as eschatological. Walvoord,[7] a pretribulational premillennialist, sees the 1,260 days as marking the second advent (Rev 11:3; 12:6), followed by a period of divine judgments (Matt 25:31–46) and the regathering of Israel (Ezek 20:34–38), followed by the start of the millennium at 1,335 days (Dan 12:12). Gundry,[8] a posttribulational premillennialist, takes the seventy-five days between the 1,260 days and the 1,335 days as a transitional period between the second advent (when the resurrection of the just of Dan 12:2 takes place) and the beginning of the millennium, during which time many Jews (mortals) convert (cf. Zech 12:10–13:1). Rosenthal,[9] a "pre-wrath" premillennialist, takes the view that the second advent occurs at the end of the 1,260 days (Rev 11:3; 12:6),

---

[5] L. F. Hartman and A. A. Di Lella, *The Book of Daniel*, AB 23 (New Haven, CT: Yale University Press, 2008), 276.

[6] A. E. Steinmann, *Daniel*, Concordia Commentary (St. Louis: Concordia, 2008), 575–77.

[7] J. F. Walvoord, *Daniel: The Key to Prophetic Revelation* (Chicago: Moody, 1971), 295–96.

[8] R. H. Gundry, *The Church and the Tribulation* (Grand Rapids: Zondervan, 1977), 164.

[9] M. Rosenthal, *The Pre-Wrath Rapture of the Church* (Nashville: Thomas Nelson, 1990), 275–76.

the battle of Armageddon occurs at 1,290 days (Dan 12:11), and the millennium begins at 1,335 days (Dan 12:12). During the thirty days after the tribulation, between 1,260 and 1,290 days, there will be thirty days of mourning (cf. Zech 12:10–14). After Armageddon there will be an additional forty-five days to cleanse the hypothesized, rebuilt millennial temple. He also points to Hanukkah being seventy-five days after Yom Kippur.

Whatever the interpretation of the 1,290 days and the 1,335 days, the text encourages the faithful during this and similar times of persecution to endure to the end. Those who do will be "blessed."

12:13 The words "to the end" imply Daniel's death. The Old Greek and Theodotion lack "to the end." But even without it the phrase "you will rest" implies Daniel's death. "Then you will stand to receive your allotted inheritance" alludes to v. 12, meaning that Daniel will be rewarded when he arises at the resurrection.

Just as this vision is sealed for Daniel, so it remains in part sealed to readers today. Clearly our "knowledge" has "increased" (12:4), since we have historical data that Daniel lacked about the Persian and Greek kingdoms (11:2–35). Nevertheless, we too must remain content not to have certainty about the exact fulfillment of (at least) the eschatological parts. Even for us, the book remains sealed and obscure until the fulfillment at "the time of the end." Yet it remains important for giving us a glimpse of what God has in store for his people.

Bridge

This final section of Daniel reminds us that, when it comes to God's revelation (see §2), we often walk by faith and not by sight (2 Cor 5:7). Even though we know that God will bring history to a predetermined end (12:4, 6, 9, 13; see §7.4) and that his prophetic word is reliable (12:7; see §2), much remains "secret" and "sealed" (12:4, 9) for us, as it was for Daniel. The questions, "How long until the end?" (12:6; cf. 8:13; Rev 6:10) and "What will be the outcome of these things?" (12:8), reflect our natural curiosity. But Daniel received no further revelation. Similarly, when the disciples asked about the timing of future events, Jesus told them, "It is not for you to know times or periods that the Father has set by his own authority" (Acts 1:7).

Much of Daniel's prophecy remained sealed to the prophet himself (12:9), who often was baffled by his own visions (7:15; 8:15, 27). Naturally, much is sealed to us too. Only at the time of fulfillment will some of the righteous who "have insight" be able to understand (12:10; cf. Rev 13:18; 17:9). We gladly receive all that is clearly revealed to us in Scripture about God's plans for history. These truths affect how we live now, allowing us to be "purified, cleansed, and refined" (Dan 12:10a; see §4.1; cf. Rev 22:11b), while the wicked continue to "act wickedly" (Dan 12:10b; cf. Rev 22:11a). But some of our questions about God's plans for history will remain known only by him; thus Moses' words apply to us: "The hidden things belong to the Lord our God, but the revealed things belong to us and our children forever, so that we may follow all the words of this law" (Deut 29:29). What we do not understand is less important than living in accordance with what we do understand. As we await the end of days in hope and faith, we too will be "happy/blessed" (cf. Dan 12:12).

BIBLICAL AND
THEOLOGICAL THEMES

§1 Theological Implications of Introductory Matters

Daniel is one of the most disputed books in the Hebrew Bible (see Introduction). To most theological conservatives, the book of Daniel gives historically reliable accounts of Daniel and his friends and contains genuine, detailed, and remarkably fulfilled prophecies. To critical scholars it is a work of fiction with many historical errors and prophecies that are only "fulfilled" after the fact—that is, written after the events they supposedly foretell.

Some argue that it matters little theologically whether the book of Daniel is history or fiction. The story of the Good Samaritan (Luke 10:25–37) remains true theologically and morally regardless of whether there really was a "good Samaritan." So, some say, the theological and moral message of Daniel likewise remains true regardless of whether the events actually happened.

But the book of Daniel is not a parable. Its genre appears to be historical narrative (Daniel 1–6) and autobiography (7–12), both of which contain predictive prophecy. In my view, a rejection of the historicity and genuine predictive nature of Daniel's prophecies undermines the book's theology. As James Hamilton puts it,

> There is a massive difference between the theological meaning of a wish-fantasy and that of a historically reliable account of God miraculously preserving someone alive in a fiery furnace. Dismissing a false fable as irrelevant to my conduct reflects my view of the theological meaning and

value of fairy tales. Risking my life because I believe the stories result from convictions about theological meaning that cannot be separated from historicity. ...

If some Maccabean-era author is making fraudulent claims, if these are fictional deliverances and not future predictions but recitals of what has already happened presented *as though* being predicted by Daniel, then there is no real proof that Yahweh can either deliver from death or predict the future. This means there is no proof that he is any better than the false gods who can neither reveal the future nor deliver their worshippers, which is exactly what the book of Daniel claims Yahweh can do. ...

The whole theological meaning of the book depends upon Yahweh's ability to deliver his people and declare the future before it takes place. If he cannot do these things, no one should "stand firm and take action" and risk his life for Yahweh (Dan. 11:32).[1]

If God saved Daniel and his friends from death, this provides proof of and confidence for believers that God can save them. But if Daniel is fictional, the book proves nothing. Moreover, if Daniel is a fictional character who did not write about the abomination of desolation (9:27; 11:31; 12:11), it implies that Jesus misspoke when he asserted that Daniel "spoke of" it (Matt 24:15), a conclusion with negative christological implications. If Daniel's prophecies are real, they are among the most detailed fulfilled predictions in the Bible, demonstrating that God has foreknowledge of the future and the ability to shape future things. It also illustrates the supernatural character of biblical prophecy.

Conversely, if the prophecies are *vaticinium ex eventu* (prophecy after the fact), as critical scholars argue, Daniel's theology of God's foreknowledge of the future (see §3.5) and his affirmation that God moves history toward predetermined goals (see §7) are seriously undermined if not completely gutted. God and his prophets become no better than the pagan diviners and their gods whom the book ridicules for their inability to explain revelation. If, as most critical

---

[1] J. M. Hamilton Jr., *With the Clouds of Heaven: The Book of Daniel in Biblical Theology*, New Studies in Biblical Theology 32 (Nottingham, England: Apollos, 2014), 31–32.

scholars believe, the prophecy about the one like a son of man (7:13–14) is really about Israel or an angel, then this undermines the authority of the NT, which interprets it as a prophecy about Jesus Christ. If Daniel's predictions about the end of Antiochus IV's life failed along with his timing on the appearance of the kingdom of God, the book would be an unreliable guide in matters divine and leave us with no basis for accepting any other of its theological claims—such as the resurrection of the dead (12:2). Thus, rejecting the critical view of the book is essential to preserving its theological and practical value.[2]

§2 Revelation of God

God reveals himself in various ways: through nature (Ps 19:1; Rom 1:19–20), through mighty works in history like the Passover and exodus from Egypt, and through the incarnation in Jesus Christ. He reveals himself in dreams and visions. And he reveals himself in a foundational way though Scripture conveyed by apostles and prophets (Eph 2:20; 2 Pet 3:2). The book of Daniel contributes to our understanding of God as a "revealer of mysteries" (Dan 2:47).

Prophets play a prominent role in conveying God's revelation. Though the book of Daniel never calls Daniel a prophet, his revelations from God and prophet-type activities (e.g., calling on Nebuchadnezzar to repent, 4:27) allow the NT to call him one (Matt 24:15). The Bible warns of false prophets who wrongly claim to convey supernatural revelation (Deut 13:1–3; 18:20–22; Jer 14:14; Matt 7:15; 2 Pet 2:1). Since false gods have no real existence, all "prophets" who prophesy in their name are considered false. The book of Daniel shows that not all claims of supernatural revelation are true. In Dan 2:8–12 Nebuchadnezzar concludes rightly that his diviner wise men are largely frauds. Diviners repeatedly prove useless to explain God's dream-revelations (2:2–11; 4:6–7; 5:7–8), developing a theme also found in the Joseph story (Gen 41:8, 16, 24–25) that only someone with the Spirit of God can reveal such mysteries (Gen 41:38; Dan 2:27–28; 4:8–9). Exposing false "miracle workers" or prophets does not justify rejection of all things supernatural. Such a conclusion goes from one extreme to another. Daniel proves himself a true conveyer of God's revelation in contrast with Nebuchadnezzar's

---

[2] This paragraph draws on A. E. Steinmann, *Daniel*, Concordia Commentary (Saint Louis: Concordia, 2008), 18–19.

fraudulent diviners (Daniel 2). The book reveals that the true God reveals himself and his ways to his prophets.

Daniel's God can and does reveal truth to people (2:22, "He reveals the deep and hidden things"). God, as the "revealer of mysteries," can indicate what will happen in the future:

> But there is a God in heaven who reveals mysteries, and he has let King Nebuchadnezzar know what will happen in the last days. ... Thoughts came to your mind about what will happen in the future. The revealer of mysteries has let you know what will happen. As for me, this mystery has been revealed to me, not because I have more wisdom than anyone living, but in order that the interpretation might be made known to the king. (2:28–30)

The purpose of revelation is so that "the living will know" things about God (4:17), sometimes warning people to change their ways to avoid catastrophe (4:26) and sometimes explaining why the catastrophe must inevitably come (5:22–25).

God conveys revelation through dreams (Daniel 2, 4) and visions (2:19; 7:2; 8:1; 9:23; 10:1), the two terms often being interchangeable (2:28; 4:2; 7:1). The revelation involves the recipient being asleep or in a trance (8:18; 10:8–9). Such revelatory experiences sometimes terrified Daniel, either by their ominous content or by the numinous experience itself (2:1; 4:5; 5:6; 7:15, 28; 8:17, 27; 10:7–8, 12, 19).

Various Aramaic terms elaborate on the nature of God's revelation.[3] God reveals (גלה) secrets, hidden things, and wisdom (2:19, 22, 29–30, 47). He shows/tells (D- and H-stem of חוה) what no diviner can (2:11; 2:27; 5:7, 12, 15). He makes known (H-stem ידע) what will happen in the future and interprets mysteries (2:28–30, 45; 5:8, 15–17). He causes prophets to "see" (חזה) visions that others cannot (7:1, 2, 15; cf. 10:7). God's revelation allows prophets like Daniel to give "interpretation" (פְּשַׁר) of mysterious dreams and visions (2:30; 4:24; 5:12–17). Daniel receives revelation in the form of the "law [דָּת] of his God," devotion to which no doubt contributed to his being a man of integrity (6:4–5). While Aramaic (and Persian loanword) דָּת might mean little more than religion or religious practice, Ezra is

---

[3] D. R. Davis, *The Message of Daniel: His Kingdom Cannot Fail*, The Bible Speaks Today (Downers Grove: InterVarsity, 2013), 41, 72.

called an "expert in the דָּת of the God of the heavens" (Ezra 7:12, 21), and in the Hebrew portion of Ezra he is called a scribe skilled in the תּוֹרָה ("law") of Moses and the תּוֹרָה of Yahweh (Ezra 7:6, 10). Thus in Dan 6:5, Aramaic דָּת ("law") is probably the equivalent of Hebrew תּוֹרָה ("law, instruction"), referring to the written revelation of God through his prophet Moses.

In the Hebrew portion of Daniel, some of God's revelation can be found "written in the law [תּוֹרָה] of Moses" (9:13). God's revelation is described as a message or word (דָּבָר) from God that is revealed (N-term of גלה; cp. Aramaic גלה above) (8:26; 10:1). Daniel also "sees" (ראה) visions (חָזוֹן, 8:1–2, 13, 15, 17, 26; מַרְאֶה, 8:15–16, 26–27; 9:23; 10:1) and vision-apparitions (מַרְאָה) (10:7–8, 16). Through angels God caused him to understand (H-stem of בין) the vision (8:16; 10:14) and "make known" to him (H-stem of ידע; הוֹדִיעַ = Aramaic הוֹדַע) what will happen (8:19 ESV). Daniel also "understood" (Qal of בין) the ways of God and his will by reading prophetic books like Jeremiah (9:2), whose divine revelations were recorded. God by his angel Gabriel gave understanding (H-stem of בין) by giving Daniel insight (H-stem of שׂכל) in understanding (בִּינָה) as part of the prophecy of the seventy weeks (9:22) or by giving him understanding (בִּינָה) by means of a vision (10:1).

In paganism idols served as signs of divine presence and were thought to convey revelation.[4] But pagan diviners themselves sometimes considered the gods too remote to disclose much (2:11). Daniel showed the black arts of diviners to be futile in revealing divine mysteries that God freely revealed to him (2:4–11, 27–28; 4:6–7; 5:8). This demonstrated the superiority of Daniel's God who can genuinely reveal truth through his prophets (2:19).

The book of Daniel may affirm that Daniel prophesied by God's Spirit. At least Nebuchadnezzar and Belshazzar recognized that Daniel spoke from a divine spirit: "the spirit of the holy gods" (4:8–9, 18; 5:14), something not unconnected with Daniel's "extraordinary spirit" (5:12; 6:3). This "spirit of the holy gods" may mean that "the divine Holy Spirit" was in him (*The Message*; see discussion at 4:8). But even if it is correctly rendered "spirit of the holy gods," Nebuchadnezzar's statement is close to the truth: biblical theology

---

[4] J. H. Walton, *Ancient Near Eastern Thought and the Old Testament: Introducing the Conceptual World of the Hebrew Bible* (Grand Rapids: Baker Academic, 2006), 116–18.

affirms that prophets like Daniel speak from God's Holy Spirit (2 Pet 1:20–21; cf. Gen 41:38; Num 11:25–26; 1 Sam 10:6; Neh 5:30; Joel 2:28; Zech 7:12; Acts 1:16).

Daniel 9 exhibits a considerable degree of intertextuality, alluding to earlier written Scriptures (see the following chart). Daniel affirms the reliability and authority of the law of Moses by acknowledging that the curses of that law for covenant disobedience (Leviticus 26; Deuteronomy 28) had come upon his people (Dan 9:11–13; cf. 6:5). He read "the books," referring to the Scriptures, including Jeremiah (Dan 9:2; cp. Jer 25:11; 29:10). As a result, he had confidence to pray for the restoration of his people based on Jeremiah's prophecy of a seventy-year captivity and exhortation to seek God from exile (Dan 9:1–19; cp. Jer 29:10–14). Clearly Daniel expected God's prophecies through Moses and Jeremiah to be ful-filled (9:2, 12). Elsewhere Daniel may draw on Jeremiah's imagery to describe Nebuchadnezzar (Dan 4:20–22; cp. Jer 27:5–7), and he also frequently evoked passages in Isaiah.[5]

Intertextuality in Daniel 9	
Dan 9:2	Jeremiah's "seventy years" (Jer 25:11; 29:10)
Dan 9:3	Daniel obeyed Jeremiah's call to pray and "seek/search for" (בקש) God for restoration from exile (Jer 29:12–14)
Dan 9:4	"keeps his gracious covenant" (Deut 7:9; 1 Kgs 8:23)
Dan 9:5	"sinned, done wrong, acted wickedly" (1 Kgs 8:47)
Dan 9:6	"[God's] servants the prophets" (Jer 44:4–5); kings and leaders disobeyed God (Jer 37:2; 44:21)
Dan 9:10	Disaster for ignoring God's word through his "servants the proph-ets" (Jer 7:25–26; 25:3–7; 29:19; 32:23; 35:15; 44:2–6)
Dan 9:11, 13	Curses "written" in the law of Moses (Lev 26:14–39; Deut 28:15–68)
Dan 9:12	"Nothing like what has been done to Jerusalem has ever been done" (Ezek 5:9)
Dan 9:13	"turning" (שוב) (e.g., Jer 3:12, 14; 4:1; 5:3; 8:5; 15:19)
Dan 9:14	"kept … in mind" (שקד) or "kept watch [over the disaster]" (NRSV) (Jer 1:12, 14; 31:28; 44:27)

---

[5] See G. Brooke Lester, *Daniel Evokes Isaiah: Allusive Characterization of Foreign Rule in the Hebrew-Aramaic Book of Daniel*, LHBOTS 606 (London: Bloombury T&T Clark, 2015).

Intertextuality in Daniel 9 (continued)	
Dan 9:15	"brought your people out of Egypt with a strong hand" (e.g., Exod 13:9; Deut 5:15)
Dan 9:16	"anger and wrath" (אַף, חֵמָה) against Jerusalem (Jer 32:31); "holy mountain" (Jer 31:23; cf. e.g., Joel 3:17; Pss 2:6; 3:4)
Dan 9:24	"seventy" weeks (Jer 25:11; 29:10; cp. Dan 9:2)

God also speaks through "miracles/signs and wonders" that show that he is great and mighty (4:2–3; 6:27). The miracle in the fiery furnace proves to Nebuchadnezzar that the God of Shadrach, Meshach, and Abednego is superior to his gods ("For there is no other god who is able to deliver like this," 3:29). This leads the king to threaten severe punishment for anyone who defames God (3:28–29). The miracle of saving Daniel from the lions reveals to Darius God's power and willingness to save (see §3.7, §4.5), which leads to a similar proclamation to show reverence to Daniel's God (6:25–27). Miracles typically are not used alone to reveal God but in conjuction with prophetic revelation to explain the meaning. Daniel's prophetic message helped Nebuchadnezzar understand the significance of the miracles he experiences in his madness and recovery (4:19–27).

In some cases God revealed to Daniel what he would do before Daniel passed it on to others (Dan 7:16–28; 10:4–6; 12:8–10).[6] But Daniel often did not initially understand the visions, needing angelic help to interpret them (7:15–16; 8:15; 9:22–23). In contrast with earlier prophets who were the sole mediators of divine revelation, in late prophetic and biblical apocalyptic writings angels often appear to present or interpret visions to prophets.[7] Thus, the prophet became the mediator of the (angelic) mediator. This motif of interpretative angel may serve a polemical function to repudiate divination as a means of revealing the future (cf. Deut 18:9–14).[8] The reason for this change is a matter of speculation. One suggestion is that God

---

[6] D. Stuart, "The Old Testament Prophets' Self Understanding of Their Prophecy," *Themelios* 6.1 (September 1980): 13.

[7] Ezek 40:1–3, 45; 41:22; 42:13; 47:3, 6; Zech 1:9, 14, 18–19; 2:1–4; 4:1–7; 5:2, 5, 10; 6:4–5; Dan 8:13–16; 9:21–22; 10:10–14; 12:7–9; Rev 1:1; 7:13–14; 10:1–10; 17:1, 7; 18:1–3; 19:9; 22:8–11.

[8] See D. P. Melvin, *The Interpreting Angel Motif in Prophetic and Apocalyptic Literature* (Minneapolis: Fortress, 2013), esp. 1–5, 159–72.

distanced himself from people in conjunction with his departure from his temple (cf. Ezekiel 7–11; cp. §3.4).[9] The NT indicates that even earlier revelation, namely the Mosaic law, was mediated by angels (Acts 7:53; Gal 3:19).

The book of Daniel emphasizes repeatedly that all genuine revelation from God, including predictive prophecy, is true, reliable, trustworthy, and certain (2:45; 8:26; 9:13; 10:1, 21; 11:2). "The great God has told the king what will happen in the future. The dream is certain, and its interpretation reliable" (Dan 2:45). Unlike false prophets who change their message depending on how they are paid (cf. Mic 3:5), a true prophet conveys God's revelation without modification (Dan 5:17). The trustworthiness of revelation depends on the faithfulness of God whose works are true (4:37). Daniel expected prophetic revelation and warning to come true "just as it is written" (9:13), including Jeremiah's prophecy of a seventy-year Babylonian desolation of Jerusalem (9:2). However, he probably assumed that God would mercifully shorten prophesied judgments in response to prayer. God's revelation is true in that it accurately predicts what will happen in the future (2:45; 8:26; 10:1; 11:2). Taken at face value, Daniel 8 and 11 preview Persian and Greek history with some of the most detailed, fulfilled predictive prophecies of the entire Bible, demonstrating the supernatural nature and reliability of prophetic predictions. Since God's predictions of judgment are reliable, they must be heeded (9:6, 10–11).

Revelation is truth progressively grasped over time. Some prophetic truths are mysterious and will remain hidden and sealed till the time of the end (12:4, 9, 13), when some with "insight" will understand them (12:10). Until then God's people must "go on [our] way" (12:9) and remain satisfied with only a partial understanding of God's future plans (cf. Matt 24:36; Acts 1:7).

§3 God

The name Michael (Dan 10:13; 12:1) in Hebrew means, "Who is like God?" and "Mishael" (1:6–7) means, "Who is what God is?" Such rhetorical questions demonstrate that God is incomparable.

---

[9] D. P. Melvin, "Revelation," *Lexham Bible Dictionary*, ed. John D. Barry et al. (Bellingham, WA: Lexham Press, 2012–2015).

This section will explore the description of God in the book of Daniel, his character and attributes.

§3.1 God Exists, unlike Pagan Gods

The famous Shema affirms that God "is one" (Deut 6:4), which means that he alone is God and there is no God beside him (Mark 12:32). To Daniel and his friends, only their God could be worshiped (3:12, 28c). In a sense it did not matter to a Jew whether or not other gods existed. Even if other gods theoretically might exist, for them only Yahweh was to be worshiped.

When Nebuchadnezzar called Daniel's God the "God of gods" (Dan 2:47), he probably meant that he is "the greatest of the gods" within a polytheistic worldview. But the expression is also used by Daniel and other Israelites (Dan 11:36; cp. Deut 10:17; Ps 136:2) to mean "the most divine One" or "the God without peer." God is unique. Daniel's God, unlike Babylonian idols, actually exists. The Bible from its first verse assumes the existence of God (Gen 1:1). It considers the denial of God's existence foolish (Ps 14:1). On the other hand, the Bible prohibits the worship of other gods (Exod 20:3) who do not exist (Deut 4:35; Isa 44:6) and are thus powerless to save (Jer 11:12). Antecedent passages like Isa 44:12–20 and 46:6–7 underscore that these gods have no existence beyond their physical images.

The inability of Babylonian diviners or their gods to explain divine mysteries (2:2–11; 4:6–7; 5:7–8) derides paganism and its non-existent gods (see §2). Daniel intentionally mocked idolatry by conveying the grotesque dimensions of Nebuchadnezzar's idol-statue (3:1) and by emphasizing the various materials of their idols—"gold and silver, bronze, iron, wood, and stone" (5:4). Shadrach, Meshach, and Abednego raised the theoretical possibility that their God might not exist: "If the God we serve exists, then he can rescue us from the furnace of blazing fire" (3:17a). They did not doubt God's existence, as the next verse (3:18) shows, but they made a hypothetical argument to defend their refusal to serve Babylonian gods. Later Daniel denied that "gods made of silver and gold, bronze, iron, wood, and stone" have any existence, for they "do not see or hear or understand" (5:23). The appearance of the fourth man in the furnace who "looks like a son of the gods" (3:25) affirms that the God of the three men really exists, whether that fourth figure represents an angel or a theophany (see §6.5). Consequently, Nebuchadnezzar immediately acknowledged the existence of the Jewish God and his unsurpassed ability to save, praised him, and prohibited slandering him (3:28–29). Darius, after Daniel was delivered from the lions, declared Daniel's God "the living God" (6:26), which for Darius affirmed God's eternality but which to Jewish ears contrasted with dead idols (Lev 26:30; Jer 10:9–10; Acts 14:15).

Michael Segal[10] challenges the view that the whole book of Daniel denies the existence of any god except Yahweh. Segal argues instead that Daniel 7 at least reflects a polytheistic worldview. Segal compares the son of man figure with passages that in his view draw on Canaanite mythology, such as Yahweh flying on the clouds (e.g., Pss 68:5 MT; 104:3 MT; Isa 19:1 MT). In Canaanite mythology Baal appears as the "Cloud Rider." This leads Segal to conclude that the son of man figure is not a symbol of Israel nor an angel nor the Messiah, but Yahweh. Segal takes Dan 7:27 to say not that the kingdom is given to "the people, the holy ones of the Most High" (which takes "holy ones" as Israel), nor to "the people of the holy ones of the Most High" (in reference to holy angels), but to "the people of the most high Holy One," in which both "Holy One" (קַדִּישֵׁי) and "most high" (עֶלְיוֹנִין) are plurals of majesty in reference to Yahweh—that is, the son of man figure. Thus Segal concludes that the vision of Daniel 7 has two divine figures: Yahweh as represented by the son of man and the divine Ancient of Days. Segal attributes this to a polytheistic backdrop of the original vision that assumes the existence of a deity who is above Yahweh.

While Segal's interpretation has some insights, his conclusion about polytheism in Daniel 7 should be rejected. It is unlikely that the final editor of the book of Daniel would have knowingly allowed in the book a unit that contradicts the monotheism of the rest of the book. Moreover, while Segal rightly argues for the divinity of the son of man figure and of the Ancient of Days, this need not imply polytheism. The NT sees Jesus the Son of God as the Son of Man figure (see §6.1) which implies the Ancient of Days is God the Father. NT theology affirms the divinity of Jesus (e.g., John 1:1) and of the Father, seeing them as distinguishable persons, while at the same time affirming that God is one (Jas 2:19) within a Trinitarian

---

[10] M. Segal, *Dreams, Riddles, and Visions: Textual, Contextual, and Intertextual Approaches to the Book of Daniel*, BZAW 455 (Berlin: De Gruyter, 2016), 132–54.

framework. While there is no polytheism here, Daniel 7 does suggest complexities in the nature of God only understandable on the basis of NT revelation.

§3.2 Names and Titles of God

Parts of the book of Daniel include various attributes and descriptive titles for God that speak of his essence and acts. While sprinkled throughout the book, these ideas are especially concentrated in Daniel's prayers (2:20–23; 9:4–19), in Daniel's vision of God (7:9–10, 13–14), and in the responses of Nebuchadnezzar and Darius to God's miracles (2:47; 3:28–29; 4:1–3, 34–37; 6:25–27).

Apart from its use in the names Hananiah (meaning, "Yahweh is gracious") and Azariah (meaning, "Yahweh helps"), God's personal name Yahweh occurs only in Daniel's prayer of repentance (9:2, 4, 8, 10, 13–14, 20). Yahweh most likely means, "he is," in the sense that he both exists and is a present help in time of need (cf. Exod 3:12–15). "Lord" (אֲדֹנָי, ʾadonay), or literally, "my Lord" (CEB), occurs at 1:2; 9:3, 4, 7, 9, 17. It designates God as one with whom a worshiper can have a personal relationship ("*my* Lord") and one to whom his people are to submit as servants or subjects and give their allegiance. The Masoretes regularly substituted this word for the divine name Yahweh in an attempt to avoid taking the name Yahweh in vain (Exod 20:7). They regularly left the consonants of Yahweh (*YHWH*, יהוה) but added the vowels for אֲדֹנָי to indicate that the latter word was to be read instead of Yahweh. Substituting ʾadonay for Yahweh became customary some time after the Babylonian exile, and the practice is reflected in the LXX, which usually translates Yahweh with Greek κύριος "Lord." Daniel already reflects the postexilic custom of using ʾadonay as a designation for God, interchangeable with and increasingly in place of Yahweh. The Aramaic portion of Daniel refers to God as "Lord [מָרֵא] of kings" (2:47), designating God as superior to earthly sovereigns.

In the Hebrew portion of Daniel God is usually designated using the common word אֱלֹהִים (ʾelohim) and in the Aramaic portion using the term אֱלָהּ (ʾelah). Twice he is designated using the term אֵל ("great and awe-inspiring God," 9:4a; "God of gods," 11:36). Daniel's own name in Hebrew means, "God [אֵל] is (my) judge" or similar. God shows his character as judge in 7:9–14, where the Ancient of Days judges the fourth beast and the little horn, and in 12:2–3, where

God rewards some with eternal life and bright glory but punishes others with shame and eternal contempt.

Various other designations for God occur in Daniel. God is the "revealer of mysteries" (2:47)—that is, a source of revelation of concealed matters (see §2). God is the "Most High God" (Dan 3:26; 4:2, 17; 5:18, 21; 7:18, 22, 25, 27), a title going back to Genesis (Gen 4:18–22), which indicates that the true God is exalted and transcendent above all, even other so-called "gods" (Ps 97:9), with authority over all the earth (Ps 47:2). Daniel's God is also called the "God of the heavens" (2:18–19, 37, 44). Like the similar titles "King of the heavens" (4:37) and "Lord of the heavens" (5:23), it emphasizes his existence beyond this world, his superiority over the world, and his power to control the world and its kingdoms (Dan 2:37; 44). God's chariot throne is portrayed as being in the clouds (7:9, 13). From his abode beyond this world God looks down, cares for us, and answers our prayers. His "army of heaven" (4:35; or possibly his "strength of heaven") expresses his dominion over the earth. God is the "the Prince of the heavenly army" or "Prince of the host" (שַׂר־הַצָּבָא; 8:11). This refers to God as a commander-warrior, just as the similar expression "commander of the LORD's army" (שַׂר־צְבָא־יְהוָה) does in Josh 5:14. Specifically, God is commander of the heavenly, angelic army. He is also called the "Prince of princes," or better the "commander of commanders" (8:25)—that is, the greatest of all commanders to whom other commanders ought to submit.

§3.3 God Is Living, Immortal, Eternal

Like the rest of the Bible (e.g., Ps 90:2; Deut 33:27; Isa 40:28; Rev 22:13), Daniel portrays God as living eternally. He is portrayed with white hair like an old man and called the "Ancient of Days" (Dan 7:9), a term that hints at his eternality. Nebuchadnezzar came to recognize that Daniel's God is "[he] who lives forever" (4:34). Accordingly, this God is to be praised forever and ever (2:20). He was there for ancient ancestors like Abraham, Isaac, and Jacob as "God of my fathers" (2:23), just as he remains with us. His kingdom is eternal (4:3b, 34b). King Darius rightly affirmed that Daniel's God is "the living God" (6:20). Darius may have echoed a title Daniel and other Jews gave to God (e.g., Deut 5:26; Josh 3:10; 1 Sam 17:26, 36; Ps 42:2), which contrasted the true God with dead idols (Jer 10:9–10). For Darius the expression "living God" may mean instead, "undying, immortal": "For he is the living God, and he endures forever" (6:26a). At the end of the book God is described as he "who lives eternally" (12:7b, the Hebrew equivalent of Aramaic at 4:34).

§3.4 God Is Transcendent

What Babylon's wise men say about their gods—that their "dwelling is not with mortals" (2:11)—truly applies to Daniel's God, who is the "God of the heavens" (2:18, 19, 37, 44), the "king of the heavens" (4:37), and the "Lord of the heavens" (5:23). He abides in heaven (2:28), metaphorically far above his creatures, and is independent from them. God's transcendence is seen in his appearing on his heavenly chariot throne above the earthly realms (represented by the beasts). He predetermines the judgment of future kingdoms and kings, directing that their kingship be given to the son of man and the holy ones in the kingdom of God (7:9–10, 13–14, 22). Conveying the heavenly kingdom to the "holy ones" (God's people) indicates that elements of God's transcendence over humanity one day will be conveyed also to them.[11]

Another indication of God's transcendence in Daniel is the employment of angelic intermediaries. In answering Daniel's prayers and conveying the interpretation of revelations given to him, God did not speak directly but rather mediated his response through angels (7:16; 8:16–17; 9:21–23; 10:10–11, 24; 12:5–8; cf. Heb 2:2). In opposing territorial demons and protecting his people, God did use Michael and an unnamed angel (10:12–13; 12:1). However, Lucas warns against overemphasizing : "While [the active role of angels in the historical process] could be taken to imply a distancing of God from human history, it is more likely that it is simply a more nuanced way of speaking of God's involvement in history than that used by the Hebrew prophets."[12] Perhaps it is best to say that that employment of angelic intermediaries preserves a theology of God's transcendence while simultaneously affirming a balancing of transcendence with God's immanence and involvement in the world (see §4).

---

[11] A. LaCocque, *The Book of Daniel* (Louisville: John Knox, 1979; repr., Eugene, OR: Wipf and Stock, 2015), 128.

[12] E. C. Lucas, "Daniel," *New Dictionary of Biblical Theology*, ed. T. D. Alexander and B. S. Rosner (Downers Grove: InterVarsity, 2000), 234–35.

God saved Shadrach, Meshach, and Abednego from the furnace and Daniel from the lions by his angel (3:28; 6:22). If this means an ordinary angel, then this is consistent with God's acting transcendently through intermediaries. Even if "angel" at 3:28 and/or 6:22 means "the angel of Yahweh" in the sense of a theophany (see discussion in commentary), by appearing in the form of his "angel" God was still a step removed from appearing in his essence, thus reflecting his transcendence. Another hint of God's transcendence is the author's reluctance to refer to God by his personal name Yahweh (see §3.2).

§3.5 God Is Wise, Omniscient, and Foreknows the Future

Daniel's God is wise, even "powerfully wise" or "wisely powerful" (2:20, taking "wisdom and power" as a hendiadys), and enlightened ("light dwells with him," 2:22). He shows his wisdom and knowledge by giving wise people further wisdom and knowledge (1:17; 2:21, 23), specifically by revealing truth (2:22). God "reveals mysteries" (2:28). His wisdom and foreknowledge is unmatched by human wise men or practitioners of occult arts (2:27). That God alone reveals secrets and gives wisdom echos a biblical-theological theme found also in Isaiah (Isa 42:9; 45:19, 21).[13]

Pagan gods were supposed to be wise. Various Akkadian hymns extol the wisdom of the gods. They speak of Enlil as the "knowing counselor, wise, of broad intelligence" and speak of Ea as "the wise, whose counsel is supreme." Thorth is called "wise among the Ennead" and Ninazu is one "who gathers wisdom to himself." Ishtar is said to be "wise in understanding and perception."[14] But the book of Daniel shows the futility of the wisdom of pagan gods and their diviner spokespeople. The diviners could not tell the king what he had dreamed, and though the gods may know, they are too remote for even diviners to consult (2:10–11). There was thus a stark contrast between the wisdom of the diviners and their gods and the wisdom of Israel's God and his spokesman Daniel (2:27–28).

Daniel's God is not merely wise. He is all-knowing. He knows what is in the darkness, demonstrating his omniscience by revealing

---

[13] Lester, *Daniel Evokes Isaiah*, 33.
[14] Walton, *Ancient Near Eastern Thought and the Old Testament*, 108.

unfathomable and hidden ideas (2:22), specifically by revealing the secret of Nebuchadnezzar's dream (2:23, 47).

God demonstrates his foreknowledge, which allows him to reveal future events. Daniel made this explicit before he told Nebuchadnezzar the meaning of the king's dream (Dan 2:27–28). Daniel had no power to reveal anything, but "there is a God in heaven who reveals mysteries, and he has let King Nebuchadnezzar know what will happen in the last days." Because God knows the future, he can reveal in considerable detail (see the commentary) the coming of future kings/kingdoms and their actions (Daniel 2, 7, 8, 11). This includes his ability to reveal what will happen at the end of the age. He foresees that the "little horn" antichrist will rise to power (7:8, 24–25; see §7.4.1), God's people will endure a never-to-be-surpassed distress (7:21; 12:1; see §7.4.2), sovereignty will be turned over to the son of man and the saints (7:13–14, 18, 22, 27; see §7.4.3), and the dead will be raised, judged, and rewarded or punished (12:2; see §7.4.4).

§3.6 God Is Morally Good (Holy, Righteous, Merciful, and Gracious)

The book of Daniel, like the rest of the Bible (e.g., Pss 73:1; 107:1; 145:9), affirms that God is good. This goodness is seen in his holiness, righteousness, mercy, compassion, and grace.

God and his realm are holy. It was not typical of Mesopotamian religion to speak of its gods as holy (comments at 4:8). But Nebuchadnezzar spoke of Daniel having the "spirit of the holy gods" (or the "divine Holy Spirit" [*The Message*] or "a holy spirit of God") (4:8). Speaking of Daniel's divine spirit as "holy" may reflect the influence of Daniel's theology on the king. Israel emphasized the holiness of God, who is morally and ritually set apart and who in turn calls on his people to be holy (cf. Lev 11:44–45). Those dedicated to God, both angels (4:17) and people (7:18, 21–27; 8:24), are called "holy ones." The fire-throne scene of 7:9–10, though it does not use the word holy, portrays God's holiness.[15]

The theological themes of desecration and restoration of God's holy temple occur several times in Daniel (1:2; 5:2; 8:11–14; 9:26–27; 11:31; 12:11). As God's symbolic dwelling place—and copy of God's holy, heavenly sanctuary (cf. 7:9–14; Isa 6:1; Heb 8:5)—the temple

---

[15] W. Vogel, *The Cultic Motif in the Book of Daniel* (New York: Peter Lang, 2009), 197.

was where Daniel directed his prayers (6:10) and that for which Daniel prayed for restoration (9:17). God's sanctuary-dwelling (מִקְדָּשׁ, 8:11) is a holy place (from root קדשׁ, "be holy"), and its objects were to be treated as holy, deriving their holiness from God's holiness. This is why Belshazzar's defilement of the temple utensils (Daniel 5) was considered so reprehensible and why when God's sanctuary was defiled it needed to be restored or cleansed (8:13–14).[16] To destroy what or who is holy (הַקֹּדֶשׁ) is a sacrilege (9:26, see comments there). The mountain imagery of 2:34–35, 44–45 also employs holy-temple imagery (cf. Isa 2:1–4) for the future rule of God at the end of the age.[17]

God is also righteous. Righteousness stands for moral norms that reflect God's character. God's righteousness is seen in his just laws (6:5; cf. 7:25 and commentary; see §4.2), even if they require his people to disobey the laws of the nation where they live (see Daniel 1, 3, 6). His snow-white clothing symbolizes his absolute moral purity (7:9). An effect of God's righteousness is that sin angers God so that he expresses wrath or anger (אַף, חֵמָה) against his people for their sins (9:16; see §4.2). By implication the "wrath" (זַעַם) against Antiochus IV (8:19) and against "the king" (11:36) was also divine wrath against their sins. God showed his righteousness by punishing Israel with disaster for their sins (9:14). Nebuchadnezzar rightly recognized that "all [God's] works are true and his ways just" (4:37). "Just" is the Aramaic term for "justice" (דִּין), and "true" more literally reads "truth" (Aramaic קְשֹׁט), a noun that can include the notions of justice and privilege.[18] Positively, God's righteousness means he keeps his covenant promises (9:4). Negatively, his righteousness results in the curses in the law of Moses being carried out to punish his people for disobeying his commands (9:11–14; see §4.3).

Righteousness in a person requires more than justice. God's righteousness and holiness are balanced by his compassion, grace, and forgiveness (9:9). Part of God's righteousness is that he shows mercy (9:16; see commentary there). The meaning of the name Hananiah (1:6) affirms, "Yahweh is gracious." Daniel prays to God, confident that he is merciful (Aramaic 2:18) (רַחֲמִין). Daniel also uses

---

[16] Ibid., 196.

[17] G. Goswell, "The Temple Theme in the Book of Daniel," *JETS* 55.3 (2012): 515–16.

[18] "קשׁט," in *HALOT* 5:1974.

the Hebrew cognate, רַחֲמִים, "mercy, compassion" (1:9; 9:9, 18), to indicate that God's compassion leads him to forgive despite Israel's lack of merit. God's "righteous acts" include his mercy (9:16; see comments there). Though God punishes the king with madness, he shows mercy to proud Nebuchadnezzar by restoring him to power upon his repentance in a process that humanizes—and perhaps converts—him (4:34–37; 7:4). God keeps his "gracious covenant" with his people (9:4), an expression that uses the Hebrew חֶסֶד, which includes within its semantic range such notions as love, grace, mercy, faithfulness, kindness, and loyalty, or acts thereof. In 1:9 God shows חֶסֶד to Daniel in the sense of favor. More broadly, God's grace is seen in Daniel's expecting him to preserve a remnant of his people through exile, return them to the land promised to Abraham, and restore his holy city Jerusalem (9:16–19). On the sacrificial system that allows God graciously to forgive sinners, see §4.5.

§3.7 God Is Infinitely Great

The book of Daniel also affirms that God is infinitely great (see also Pss 139:7–9; 145:3, 6; Isa 40:26; 66:1; Jer 10:6). God's overwhelming glory is reflected by his glorious appearance in Daniel's vision (Daniel 7). There he wears dazzling white clothing, has white hair, rides a glorious chariot throne ablaze with fiery wheels, with a river of fire flowing from his presence (7:9). All of this shows that the glory of his kingship surpasses that of all other kings and provokes the proper fear that the great king and judge deserves.

The incomparable greatness of God is affirmed by the rhetorical question in the Hebrew personal names Mishael (1:6), meaning "Who is what God is?" and Michael (10:13), meaning "Who is like God?" Daniel also describes God as "great and awe-inspiring" (9:4), an expression that may be a hendiadys meaning simultaneously "greatly awe-inspiring" and "awe-inspiringly great."

God's greatness is seen in his fixing epochs and ages for great powers, including establishing and deposing kings at will (2:21; 4:25). Great kings and great kingdoms may seem invincible, but they ultimately come and go. God in his power will establish a kingdom that will crush all the great kingdoms and itself will never fail (2:44). All of humanity combined are like nothing in comparison to God and unable to thwart God's will (4:35). God shows his power by performing miracles throughout the world, both in heaven and on earth

(6:27). He is unsurpassed in his power to save (3:29b). God showed his omnipotence by saving Shadrach, Meshach, and Abednego from the middle of a fiery furnace so that not a hair of their heads was singed (3:17, 26–29) and by saving Daniel from the lions (6:20–22). God's power is seen in his ability to take away Nebuchadnezzar's sanity and then to restore it (4:34–36; 7:4b). His power is also seen in his ability to preserve his people. He effortlessly judges and destroys the little horn (7:11). A lesson for God's people is that though fierce nations may dominate them (Daniel 2, 7, 8, 11), including eschatological enemies like the little horn (Daniel 7), God in his power will preserve his people though every trial and ultimately deliver to them the kingdom of God.

God in Daniel is the supreme king over all others: the "King of the heavens" (4:37) and the "Lord of kings" (2:47), superior even to emperors such as Nebuchadnezzar who was himself regarded as the "king of kings" (2:37). His is an eternal kingdom (4:3b, 34b), and he is the real "ruler over human kingdoms" (4:17).

§3.8 God Is Sovereign over the Affairs of Men

Before the exile, Israel affirmed and celebrated in worship the kingship of God and his sovereignty over the nations (Exod 15:18; Pss 22:28; 47:8; 93:1; 96:10; 103:19; Isa 52:7). This theme continues in the NT (1 Tim 6:15; Titus 1:17; Rev 15:3). Daniel elaborates on this theme in great detail.

By outward appearances, great human kingdoms and kings are sovereign. The book of Daniel begins at a time when Judah had been taken over first by Egypt in 609 and then by Babylon in 605. Shortly after this, Daniel and his friends went into exile (Dan 1:1–4). This is "a time when it seemed to all the world that [Yahweh's] cause was lost and that the gods of the heathen had triumphed."[19] In this historical context, Daniel reaffirms the sovereignty of God despite outward appearances.

Daniel shows the superiority of the kingship of God as compared with human sovereigns who are themselves subject to God (2:47) and whose decrees can be supernaturally reversed by God (3:28, 6:20–21). Human kings can be unreasonable and cruel (2:5;

---

[19] G. L. Archer, "Daniel" in *The Expositor's Bible Commentary*, vol. 7, ed. Frank E. Gaebelein (Grand Rapids: Zondervan, 1985), 8.

3:6); arrogant, insolent, and proud (4:30, 37; 5:22–23; 8:23); beastly (7:3–7; 8:1–8); fooled by advisers to issue unjust decrees (6:6–8); subject to infirmities like madness (4:4–33); lose composure and even bodily control (5:6); and can be in constant war (Dan 11:2–45). In contrast, God is good (see §3.6), his kingdom is human rather than beastly (7:13), his laws and judgments are just (9:11–14), and the establishment of his kingdom ends warfare among beastly human kingdoms (Daniel 2, 7). God's kingship is eternal, whereas human kingdoms come and go (6:26; 7:14, 27). God's sovereignty also implies a suprahuman ability to direct world events, whereas human kings often fall victim to world events (Daniel 11).

Daniel maintains that God has something to do with everything that happens in this world. Some have argued that the sovereignty of God is the main theological theme of the book of Daniel.[20] Whether or not it is the main theme, it is certainly one of the most important. For example, according to 1:2, "the Lord handed King Jehoiakim of Judah over to [Nebuchadnezzar]." Daniel does not say that Nebuchadnezzar politically and militarily dominated Jehoiakim, the way a secular historian would put it, but expresses a prophetic view of history that affirms God's sovereignty. The prophets who wrote the historical books of the Bible often use this kind of language to assert God's sovereignty in history (e.g., Josh 11:8; Judg 1:4; 13:1; 2 Chr 24:24). That God's temple was plundered would have raised questions in the mind of Jews as to whether God was really sovereign,[21] though in fact God as an expression of his sovereignty was himself responsible for allowing the sanctuary to be destroyed (9:16; cf. Lam 2:7). God warned his people that if they turned away from him and his covenant, he would allow Israel to be driven from the land (Deut 28:64–66). About the time that Daniel was deported, Jeremiah reaffirmed this threat and in accord with it announced a seventy-year Babylonian captivity (Jer 25:5–11). This prophetic view of history sees beyond the historical event to the root theological causes. This is a remarkable statement. Why would God allow the treasures of the temple, symbolic dwelling place of God, to be taken to a pagan

---

[20] E.g., S. R. Miller, *Daniel*, NAC 18 (Nashville: Broadman & Holman, 1994), 50; T. Longman, *Daniel*, NIVAC (Grand Rapids: Zondervan, 1999), 20; E. Carpenter, "Daniel," in *Cornerstone Biblical Commentary: Ezekiel & Daniel*, vol. 9, ed. Philip W. Comfort (Carol Stream, IL: Tyndale House, 2010), 9306–9.

[21] Goswell, "The Temple Theme in the Book of Daniel," 514.

temple? One answer is to show that God is in control. Great powers can be used as pawns in the hand of God to accomplish his purposes. Similarly, it is not simply that Daniel was so likable that Ashpenaz wanted to help him. Rather, "God had granted Daniel kindness and compassion from the chief eunuch" (Dan 1:9). Favorable circumstances, intellect, and academic success are gifts from God. God gave these four young men knowledge and understanding in every kind of literature and wisdom (1:17; cp. Jas 1:17; 1 Cor 4:7). That Daniel, unlike the diviners, was allowed extra time implies God's providential protection (2:8–9, 16). The dream of Daniel 2 and the vision of Daniel 7 show that God is sovereign over history and has a plan for its culmination in the establishment of the kingdom of God (see §7.1).

God in his sovereignty answers prayer (2:23). He saves and preserves his people (1:15; 3:28; 6:22, 27). God is in control of the nations and holds their fates in the balances. He establishes and deposes kings (2:21; 4:25; 5:26). Proud Nebuchadnezzar needed to learn that "the Most High is ruler over human kingdoms" (4:17, 25, 32) and that ultimately "Heaven rules" (4:26). Specifically, God granted Nebuchadnezzar his authority to rule, his military might, and his glory (2:37; 5:18). He granted Persia the privilege of replacing Babylon (5:28). Though it is ambiguous, 9:1 may imply that Darius was "made king" by God (see commentary).

The narrative of Belshazzar's sacrilegious abuse of temple utensils in Daniel 5 and of Darius' decree in Daniel 6 subvert the claimed sovereignty of human kings in order to exalt the sovereignty of the true God.[22] Absolute monarchs like Belshazzar can be under the "influence" or "command" (טְעֵם) of wine (5:2), showing them less absolute than they suppose. The power of a king is only possible through the help of his administration, including scribes to inform him and others to extend and apply his power. In 5:8–9 Belshazzar (who may have been illiterate) lacked the ability to read the mysterious handwriting on the wall, and his vast bureaucracy of scribes and diviner-advisers were unable to read and interpret the inscription. Only the divine king through his prophetic spokesman Daniel was able to reveal the meaning of his own writing. This portrays the

---

[22] D. C. Polaski, "Mene, Mene, Tekel, Parsin: Writing and Resistance in Daniel 5 and 6," *JBL* 123 (2004): 649–69.

divine king and his administration (Daniel) as superior to Belshazzar and his administration, as well as to his gods whom Belshazzar has been profusely praising (5:4). Having exalted himself against the Lord of heaven, and his gods over the true God, Belshazzar and his court were humbled by the superior sovereignty of God, including (assuming the "hand" is that of an angel) his angelic "scribe" who wrote the message and his prophetic administrator Daniel who provided the interpretation. All this occured because Belshazzar failed to acknowledge the truly sovereign one who held Belshazzar's fate in his hands (5:23).

In Daniel 6 Darius expressed his supposed absolute sovereignty by issuing an immutable decree, though ironically the story shows that this human king's sovereignty is limited by the fact that Darius was manipulated by his administrators into issuing it (6:6–9). Moreover, when it had undesirable effects—the condemnation of Daniel—Darius was trapped by his own decree, which couldn't be revoked, and was helpless to save Daniel (6:13–18). God, on the other hand, showed his sovereignty by reversing Darius' irrevocable decree, closing the mouths of the lions (6:22) so that the will of God triumphed over human decrees.

Various narratives end with a king acknowledging the superior kingship of Daniel's God (Nebuchadnezzar at 2:47; 3:28–29; 4:34–35, 37; Darius at 6:26–27). Pagan theology also attributes providence and sovereignty to their gods. It was announced at the time of Nebuchadnezzar's father Nabopolassar that "the god Bel [= Marduk], in the assembly of the gods has (given) the ruling power to Nabopolassar."[23] But Daniel's God is the true sovereign. He can give authority to whomever he wishes, including the lowliest of men (4:17; 5:18–19, 21c). Conversely, especially if a king becomes arrogant, God can drive him away from men in madness (4:21; 5:20–21b) or end his kingdom (5:26). God can overturn the machinations of wicked administrators and cause their plots against the righteous to fall on their own heads (6:24). And God can restore a mad king to sanity and authority when he acknowledges God's superior sovereignty (4:31–32, 36; 5:21c).

---

[23] D. J. Wiseman, *Nebuchadnezzar and Babylon* (London: Oxford University Press, 1983), 20.

Daniel 7:5–6 does not mention God explicitly, but it implies divine permission for nations to act. Concerning the bear (symbolizing Persia) in Daniel's vision, "It was told [literally, "They say to it"], 'Get up! Gorge yourself on flesh' " (7:5). The indefinite plural "they" expresses the passive and implies divine permission as the ultimate agent, perhaps through angels. Thus, God grants a nation permission to devour peoples ("flesh") through conquest. The leopard (symbolizing Greece) "was given dominion" (7:6). Again, the agent of the passive verb is God who can grant a nation dominion. God's sovereignty is symbolized in the vision by his being seated on a heavenly, fiery chariot-throne (7:9). This same God predetermines the "time" when kingdoms will cease and when the kingdom of God will be fully established (7:12, 22). Even the most formidable human king like the little horn is powerless to alter these times once God decrees them (7:25c by one interpretation; see commentary).

God establishes set times for future events. He determines an "appointed time" (מוֹעֵד) or "the time fixed for the end"[24] regarding Babylon's invasion of Judah (Hab 2:3), the Greek kingdom (Dan 8:19), Antiochus IV (11:27, 29, 35), and a "time of wrath" for "the king" (11:36). Antiochus IV's other wicked actions are allowed only "for a time" (11:24, 33).

Daniel 9 indicates that God expresses his sovereignty by sending Israel into exile for seventy years (9:2). Daniel prayed to God on the assumption that, just as God sovereignly carried out the Mosaic curse for disobedience (9:12–14), he can also forgive, bless, and restore Israel from its desolations upon their repentance (9:18–19). In the prophecy of the seventy weeks God showed his sovereignty by decreeing or determining desolations (9:26). God's sovereignty also showed a sovereign purpose in using suffering and persecution to mold and perfect his people: "Some of those who have insight will fall so that they may be refined, purified, and cleansed until the time of the end" (11:35).

God is not only sovereign on earth, he is also sovereign in heaven, being the "Prince of the heavenly army" (8:11)—that is, the commander of the angelic armies. In both realms God "does what he wants with the army of heaven and the inhabitants of the earth. There is no one who can block his hand or say to him, 'What have

---

[24] "מוֹעֵד," *HALOT*, 558.

you done?' " (4:35). In his sovereignty God sends angelic messengers to reveal his will and do his bidding (3:28; 4:17; 6:22; 7:16; 8:16; 9:21–23; 10:10–12; 12:1).

Although God is the supreme sovereign, his sovereignty falls short of a strict determinism that excludes all freewill and resistance by his creatures. Rulers are said to do whatever they want at times (5:19; 8:4; 11:3, 16, 36) even if this is contrary to God's moral will. In the account of the dream portending Nebuchadnezzar's madness, Daniel advised the king that the disaster might be averted if he chose to change his behavior: "Separate yourself from your sins by doing what is right, and from your injustices by showing mercy to the needy. Perhaps there will be an extension of your prosperity" (4:27). His sanity would return when Nebuchadnezzar acknowledged "that the Most High is ruler over human kingdoms" (4:25, 32), which appears to be an act of freewill. The Greek king Antiochus IV stands against God, the "Prince of princes" (8:25), and rages against God's holy covenant (11:30). On the positive side, "those who have insight" can choose to influence others for good (11:33). See §7.1 for more on God's sovereignty versus human freedom in history.

Although God's power and sovereignty are absolute, he often chooses to work though angelic intermediaries who are finite in power (see §5). God's will through his angelic representatives is successfully resisted for a time by the forces of darkness, such as the demonic princes of Persia and Greece. God's angelic representatives (e.g., Michael) must struggle and fight in a cosmic battle (10:13, 20–21) with these forces despite God's overall sovereignty. This angelic/demonic struggle suggests, as Baldwin states, that "there is a measure of contingency in human history, even though the final outcome is certain."[25] Yet God's absolute sovereignty does express itself above these struggles by his predetermining history in his "book of truth" (10:21). Among things predetermined are the comings and goings of the four kingdoms (Daniel 2 and 7). History would lead to the persecution of God's people by the Greek king Antiochus IV (8:24–25; 11:33) and by the little horn antichrist (7:21). But the son of man figure will come to destroy and take over sovereignty from the little horn (7:11–14) in conjunction with the establishment of the kingdom of God for God's people (2:44; 7:26–27). Beyond all

---

[25] J. G. Baldwin, *Daniel*, TOTC (Leicester: Inter-Varsity, 1978), 181.

earthly persecutions of God's people will be the resurrection of the just and the unjust when the wicked will suffer eternal shame while the righteous will shine in glory (12:2–3). In these cases, as with the fall of the antichrist, God's sovereignty is determinative: "what has been decreed [by God] will be accomplished" (11:36).

§4 God Relates to People

While in some ways God shows himself transcendent (see §3.4), in other ways he is a relational God who is present and responds personally to his creatures, communicates with them (see §2), and expects them to respond personally to him. As Goswell puts it, the book promotes "a species of kingdom ethics, with loyalty to God as King the virtue repeatedly on display in the actions of the protagonists,"[26] as opposed to giving first loyalty to transient, human kingdoms. According to Daniel faithful believers are "people who know their God" (11:32). It is also possible for pagan kings like Nebuchadnezzar to know that God is "God of gods, Lord of kings, and a revealer of mysteries" (2:47) and that he miraculously is "able to deliver" (3:29). God is "ruler over human kingdoms" (4:17), is eternal and omnipotent (4:34–35), is "true" and "just," and "is able to humble those who walk in pride" (4:37). Over time Nebuchadnezzar came to know about God increasingly well and may have come to know him personally. Thus the book of Daniel, like much of the Bible, balances the concept of God's transcendence with his immanence and knowability.

§4.1 God Demands Goodness and Holiness

God is morally good (see §3.6) and he expects his human creatures to reflect something of his goodness. Thus he told Nebuchadnezzar through Daniel to do what is right and show mercy to the needy (4:27). Daniel spoke for God in telling Belshazzar he ought to have shown goodness by humbling himself and honoring the true God who gave him life (5:22–23). God uses travails in life and history to purify his people morally (11:35; 12:10). He expects goodness from gentiles as well as from Israel, which explains why he holds the nations accountable for their sins (see §4.2).

---

[26] G. Goswell, "The Ethics of the Book of Daniel," *ResQ* 57:3 (2015): 142.

God expects even more from his own people. He requires them not only to be good, but to be a "holy people" (Dan 8:24; 12:7)—that is, set apart from the gentiles morally and spiritually as his people who share his holiness (see §3.2). God's people are to act as members of a holy covenant (11:28, 30), which established God's holy city of Jerusalem (9:24) and its temple on Mount Zion (9:16, 20; 11:45). The term for God's people in Daniel 7 is "holy ones" or "saints" (ESV) (7:18, 21–22, 25, 27), a description that may influence NT language referring to ordinary Christians as "saints" or "holy ones" (e.g., Rom 1:7; 1 Cor 1:2; Eph 1:1). This desire to maintain holiness appears to be behind Daniel's refusal to eat the king's food (Daniel 1). The cultic food laws of Leviticus 11 and Deuteronomy 14 were intended to keep Israel holy and distinct from gentiles (Lev 11:44–45; Deut 14:21). Daniel determined to follow these holiness rules in response to Babylon's pressuring him to assimilate to pagan ways. Daniel and his friends also sought to maintain their distinctive Jewish holiness in exile by avoiding idolatry (Daniel 3), praying regularly (Dan 6:10, 13), and not hiding their faith (Daniel 3, 6; see §4.7). They demonstrated competence (6:3), integrity (6:4, 22), courage and faith (3:16–18, 28; 6:10a), and religious devotion (6:10b, 13). They are exemplary models of godliness whose stories are meant to inspire God's people to imitate them.

The holiness of God's people was maintained through special times of sacrifice (9:21) and by giving attention to prophetic books and the law of Moses (9:2, 11, 13). By one interpretation (see commentary for another view) the little horn antichrist seeks to attack the commitment of God's people by changing "religious festivals and laws" (7:25 CSB) that contributed to Israel's holiness. This biblical-theological theme of the holiness of God's people goes back to the beginning of God's covenant with Israel in which he described them as a holy nation (Exod 19:6) and a holy people (Deut 7:6; 14:2) who were called to holiness (Exod 22:31) in order to reflect the holiness of God (Lev 11; 20:26). Christians are similarly called to holiness (1 Pet 1:15–16; 2:9; 2 Pet 3:11), even if holiness under the new covenant is applied differently (e.g., food laws of holiness are abolished, Mark 7:14).

§4.2 God Is a Lawgiver and Judge Who Holds People Accountable for Sins

The idea of God as lawgiver and judge begins in Genesis 1–3 with the command to be fruitful and multiply, the prohibition against eating of the tree of knowledge, and the expulsion of Adam and Eve from Eden for violating that "law." The Mosaic law (the Ten Commandments and other laws) underscores this biblical-theological theme. Though there is a change of law under the new covenant—specifically the OT ceremonial and civil laws do not apply directly today—God still holds people accountable for his moral law as "lawgiver and judge" (Jas 4:12).

Daniel recognized this truth. His own name means "God is (my) judge" or something similar. The narratives of Daniel 1, 3, and 6 show how Daniel and his friends sought to obey God's laws in a foreign land: laws about food, avoiding idolatry, and the need to pray and worship. The description of God as "just" (4:37; literally "his ways are justice," דִּין) and who sits for "justice" (7:10 ESV; דִּין) uses a noun from the same root as Daniel's name. His role as judge appears explicitly at 7:9–14 and 7:21–22 where he issues a judgment for his people and against the little horn and the fourth beast. As judge God is to be feared. He can terrify puny, weak people and even great kings when he chooses (4:2; 5:6). He assesses them in accord with the scales of his justice, and if they are found wanting he can punish them (5:25–28; see commentary). As chief judge God sits on his chariot-throne above all others and renders judgment on behalf of his people and against the wicked like the little horn (7:9, 22). That God is to be feared as judge is symbolized by Daniel's vision of a judgment scene in which blazing fire surrounds God's chariot-throne and a river of fire flows before him (7:9–10). In judgment he burns the fourth beast and its wicked little horn in fire (7:11). Even non-Israelite kings like Nebuchadnezzar and Belshazzar are answerable to God for sins like pride, though when Nebuchadnezzar repented by acknowledging the superior kingship of God, God mixed judgment with mercy (see also §3.6) and restored Nebuchadnezzar's sanity and rule (4:32, 34, 36). Belshazzar failed to do this and died (5:22, 30). Ultimately at the last judgment God will determine the eternal destiny of the resurrected dead (12:2).

God judges people for their sins. David recognized that he was a sinner from birth (Ps 51:5; cf. Rom 3:21), humanity is morally and spiritually corrupt (Pss 14:2–3; 53:2–3; cf. Rom 3:12), and God judges people for what they do (Pss 7:8; 58:11; cf. Isa 3:13; Jer 11:20). Daniel likewise assumes that people have a propensity to sin and that God stands as judge, holding them accountable for their moral failures and vindicating the righteous. A psychological effect of sin is shame (בֹּשֶׁת; 9:7–8). Nebuchadnezzar is shamed by God when he is driven to madness in which he acts like a beast (4:33).

The NT defines sin as breaking God's law (1 John 3:4), as does Daniel (Dan 9:11) who also describes sin as not heeding God's word through his prophets (Dan 9:6, 10). Many different terms and descriptions for sin are used in Daniel's prayer of confession (Daniel 9). These are piled up for emphasis to show the enormity of sin before God and to indicate how sin brings divine curse and punishment.[27] Some terms for sin in Daniel follow:

- To sin (9:5; 8, 11, 15) (חטא). This has to do with missing the mark of God's standards or deviating from God's norms.
- To do wrong (9:5) (עוה) and the noun "iniquities" (plural עָוֹן) (9:13). These have to do with acting in a twisted, perverse, or crooked way in contrast with following straight or upright moral standards. The Aramaic cognate noun עֲוָיָה is used in the plural of "injustices" toward the poor in parallel with sins (4:27).
- To be guilty/wicked (G-stem 9:15) (רשׁע), to act wickedly (H-stem 9:5) (רשׁע). To be wicked is the most important antonym in the OT to being righteous (צדק).[28]
- Rebellion, transgression, crime (8:12, 13; 9:24) (פֶּשַׁע) and the cognate participle "rebels" (8:23). The root פשׁע can refer to rebellion against authority (2 Kgs 8:20–22) but more basically denotes criminal acts like defrauding someone, theft, slave trading, atrocities of war, and perverting justice by accepting bribes (Gen 31:36; Exod 22:9; Prov 28:24; Amos 1:6, 13; 2:6). In Dan 8:12–13, 23 פשׁע is probably used in reference to Antiochus IV's rebellion against God and his sins against God's people. The seventy weeks bring all פֶּשַׁע to an end (9:24).

---

[27] J. E. Rosscup, "Prayer Relating to Prophecy in Daniel 9," *Master's Seminary Journal* 3.1 (1992): 58–62.

[28] C. van Leeuwen, "רשׁע rš', " *TLOT*, 1262.

- Pride (Aramaic 4:37) (גֵּוָה) and insolence (Hebrew עַז־פָּנִים, literally "strong of face"; see commentary) (8:23). Nebuchadnezzar showed an arrogant presumption and idolatrous self-worship by glorying in his accomplishments (4:30) while not acknowledging God's role in making them possible. Antiochus Epiphanes went beyond pride to insolence in his hostility toward the true God (8:23–25). Arrogance leads people to act presumptuously/impiously (H-stem זיד) (5:20).
- Deceit (8:25) (מִרְמָה) is used of Antiochus IV. מִרְמָה regularly refers to betrayal, fraud, deceit, or treachery carried out by various parties against another party,[29] including such things as dishonest scales (Prov 11:1), misleading and deceptive responses (Gen 34:13), dishonest words/lips (Ps 17:1), swearing falsely (Ps 24:4), false witness (Prov 12:17), and plotting evil (Prov 12:20).
- To rebel (מרד) (9:5, 9). As a "sin," מרד refers to defying the authority of God.
- To turn aside from or disobey God's commandments or instructions (סור) (9:5, 11, 14). This can mean idolatry or apostasy (Exod 32:8; Deut 9:12; 11:16) and is in effect turning away from God (Ezek 6:9).
- Disloyalty, treachery, sacrilege (מָעַל) against God (9:7; see comments there). Compare also the use of "anything offensive" (שֵׁלָה) in the probable sense of "blasphemy, sacrilege, insult" at 3:29 (comments there). The word "abomination" (שִׁקּוּצִים) in "abomination of desolation" (9:27; 11:31; 12:11) probably implies sacrilege (see comments at 9:27).

In Daniel various sins are described. Nebuchadnezzar's threats of excessive punishments show him a cruel tyrant (2:5; 3:6). Envy and murderous acts show up in self-serving Babylonian administrative officials who maliciously accused Shadrach, Meshach, and Abednego out of jealousy for their positions and hatred of their Judaism (Dan 3:8–12). Envious Persian administrative officials plotted to change laws so that they could use Daniel's religious practices to get him killed and take his high office (Dan 6:4–5).

---

[29] E. Carpenter and M. A. Grisanti, "רָמָה," *NIDOTTE* 3:1122–24.

A practical consequence of Israel's sin is God's curse for covenant disobedience as warned in the law (9:11–12). Sin makes God angry and inclined to punish the sinner (9:16). Similarly, for wicked kings like Antiochus IV and the king of 11:36, God has decreed a time of wrath (9:19; 11:36). The proper response of the sinner to sin is to confess it as Daniel did (9:4–19), seeking to appease or soften God's anger (9:13a; D-stem חלה), accompanied with turning away from it or repenting of it (9:13b; שוב).

Nebuchadnezzar displayed the sin of arrogance in thinking that God could not deliver Shadrach, Meshach, and Abednego from his power (3:15b). His pride is also revealed in Daniel 4 when he strutted about self-absorbed, conceited, and presumptuous. In response God humbled him (4:37; 5:20–21). In this case God used Daniel to confront Nebuchadnezzar with his personal sin, specifically his callous disregard for the poor (4:27). Prophets often call out sins in the Bible (2 Sam 12:1–9; Isa 5:8, 11, 19, 20; Jer 5:7–9), hinting that Daniel should be regarded as a prophet. In a vision given to Nebuchadnezzar, a magnificent tree representing the king and his rule was cut down, but it survived in the stump. After Daniel interpreted the dream, God did not carry out the decree immediately, perhaps giving the king time to repent (cf. 2 Pet 3:9). Eventually Nebuchadnezzar's pride was cut down by a madness in which he acted like a beast—eating grass like cattle. He remained mad until he acknowledged the superior sovereignty of God. At the end of seven periods of time (seven years?) his sanity returned to him. In Dan 7:4 Nebuchadnezzar's humiliation and loss of authority is symbolized by a vision of a lion whose wings are torn off. But his restoration is portrayed by a human mind being given to this beast. Nebuchadnezzar, duly humbled, acknowledged that no one can stop or even rightly question God's judgments (4:35). Nebuchadnezzar himself gave the moral of this story: "Now I, Nebuchadnezzar, praise, exalt, and glorify the King of the heavens, because all his works are true and his ways are just. He is able to humble those who walk in pride" (4:37). While God punishes human pride, he is also willing to restore those who repent, as he did for Nebuchadnezzar, who was made greater than before his madness (4:36, "even more greatness came to me").

Daniel 5 is another story of God's humbling human pride and punishing insolence. Previously Nebuchadnezzar recognized that sacrilege against God was wrong and issued an edict prohibiting it

(Dan 3:29; see commentary), but in Daniel 5 Belshazzar committed the sin of sacrilege against cultic objects. Belshazzar used the holy Jewish temple utensils brought from Jerusalem by Nebuchadnezzar (1:2) in a banquet that included drunkenness and licentious behavior toward the women present. He committed further sacrilege by defiling those utensils with idolatry: he and his guests "praised their gods made of gold and silver, bronze, iron, wood, and stone" (5:1–4). Then a mysterious hand appeared and wrote on the wall a message of judgment on Belshazzar and his kingdom. Belshazzar is more culpable than Nebuchadnezzar because Belshazzar should have learned from his predecessor's pride and resulting humiliation, yet he failed to do so. Instead he arrogantly exalted himself against God and did not give him his due honor (5:22–23). Unlike Nebuchadnezzar he did not repent. Belshazzar, who boasted in false gods and defiled the holy utensils, was humiliated even while alive, scared to the point of wetting his pants (5:6; see commentary). Then by God's edict he was killed and replaced (5:30–31).

In Daniel 6 God held accountable the treacherous officials who duped Darius into issuing an edict that demanded people for a month to pray only to the king. Their ultimate goal was to have pious Daniel thrown to the lions. In an act of poetic justice, God providentially had the officials thrown to the lions as punishment instead.

In Daniel 7, conquering and empire-building nations are likened to evil, predatory animals—a lion, a leopard, a bear, and an indescribably horrible animal—devouring other nations, trampling and crushing them (Dan 7:4–7, 19, 23). The first beast representing Babylon and Nebuchadnezzar was humbled, and its power was removed by God, symbolized by the removing of its wings. However, in view of his acknowledgment of God (see Daniel 4), it was restored and given a human mind (7:4). The fourth beast and its little horn displayed the evils of arrogance, blasphemous boasting, and severe persecution of "the holy ones" (7:8, 11, 20–21, 25). But unlike Nebuchadnezzar, this beast did not repent. Threfore the beast (a kingdom) and its horn (leader) stand judged and condemned to destruction by the divine court (7:9–14, 22, 26).

The little horn of Daniel 8 (Antiochus IV) and his troops were guilty of acts of rebellion or transgression or crimes (Dan 8:12–13, 23; see פֶּשַׁע above). This included the audacious claim to be a heavenly being (evidently deifying himself with the title Epiphanes,

"Manifestation [of deity]"), arrogantly trampling down and killing God's holy people, and wreaking destruction. He also committed cultic offenses against God's holiness: the sacrilege of making the temple sanctuary desolate, putting an end to the legitimate sacrifices (by turning it into a temple of Zeus), and opposing the true God (8:10–13, 23–25). This little horn was broken, "not by human hands" but by an act of God (8:25; see commentary).

Daniel's prayer in Daniel 9 affirms that God is "awe-inspiring" (9:4b; נוֹרָא), an N-stem participle from a root (ירא) meaning to "be afraid." Formally נוֹרָא would mean someone/something "feared" or "fearsome." Fear of God in the Bible is not usually meant to produce terror in his people (see commentary for details) but a respect that results in obedience, trust, and worship. But if God's people disobey, they should fear that as judge he may punish them. It is like the fear or respect a subject should show to a great king (Ps 47:3).

God sent Israel into exile because of their sins. Though God is faithful (9:4), God's people (with whom Daniel identifies) sinned in every imaginable way and degree: "We have sinned, done wrong, acted wickedly, rebelled, and turned away from your commands and ordinances. We have not listened to your servants the prophets, who spoke in your name to our kings, leaders, fathers, and all the people of the land" (9:5–6). The exile was the "promised curse" that God warned Israel would be the consequence of covenant violations: "The promised curse written in the law of Moses, the servant of God, has been poured out on us because we have sinned against him" (9:11b). God in the Mosaic law swore that he would bless Israel if they obeyed the covenant (Deut 28:9, 11; cf. Lev 26:3–12), but he correspondingly warned of various curses if they disobeyed, culminating in expulsion from the land (Deut 28:15–68, esp. vv. 63–64; Lev 26:14–33, especially v. 33). Daniel affirmed that this was exactly what had caused the exile. Note that though Daniel included himself in this confession of sin ("we"), in fact he was not one of the faithless Jews who brought God's wrath on his people. It was an inevitable result of God's covenantal punishments for sin that the innocent, like Daniel, suffered along with the guilty.

Daniel perhaps hoped for an end to sin and judgment after Jeremiah's seventy years, but the answer he received to his prayer was that sin would only be fully atoned for and ended after seventy weeks (of years) (Dan 9:24–27).[30] On the positive side, this indicates that God indeed planned to deal with the problem of human sin through an atonement involving the death of the Messiah (see §6.3), analogous to the OT sacrificial system, an atonement that would allow sins to be forgiven.

In Daniel 11:12 the arrogance of the king of the North (Antiochus III in context) led to his defeat (at Raphia, see commentary on this and the following). Daniel 11:14 speaks of "violent ones among your people" (בְּנֵי פָּרִיצֵי עַמְּךָ) that can be taken as "ones who tear down" or perhaps "lawless ones" (NRSV; HALOT[31]) among the Jews at the time of Antiochus III. This appears to be a pejorative term, though the historical reference of who these Jews were and what they did is uncertain. In 11:18 Antiochus III is guilty of "taunting," a term that can also be rendered "scorn" (NASB) or "insolence" (ESV, NRSV), and this offense appropriately ended in disaster when the Roman general Scipio Asiaticus defeated him at the battle of Magnesia in 189. Antiochus IV sinned by raging against the "holy covenant" by attempting to end the Jewish sacrificial system and Judaism itself while supporting unfaithful, Hellenistic Jews who violated their covenant with God and abandoned their faith (11:28–32). The king in 11:36–39 (antichrist or Antiochus IV) sinned by exalting himself above all gods, including the one true God.

By nature God is opposed to and angered by sin, which is why Daniel called upon Nebuchadnezzar to separate from his sins (Aramaic חֲטָי) and injustices (or "iniquities"; Aramaic עֲוָיָה) and do what is right by showing mercy to the poor (4:27). This could have averted the decree of the watchers from coming into effect. Later when Nebuchadnezzar acknowledged God's sovereignty as an act of repentance, God restored him to his throne (4:32–37). Admitting one's guilt, confessing one's sins, and turning away from them can avert or lessen God's punishment, which is why Daniel confessed the sins of his people and prayed for God's forgiveness (9:9, 13, 16–19).

Ultimately God holds everyone accountable at the last judgment (see §7.4.4) when the wicked will be condemned to "disgrace and eternal contempt" (12:2). "Disgrace" (חֶרְפָּה) can also be translated "reproaches" (NJPS) or "shame" (ESV). "Contempt" (דְּרָאוֹן) can

---

[30] R. W. Pierce, Daniel, Teach the Text (Grand Rapids: Baker, 2015), 162.
[31] "פָּרִיץ," in HALOT 3:968.

be translated as "abhorrence," "horror," "loathing," or "repulsiveness." God and the righteous will show contempt/loathing for these rebels at the end of the age, as they experience what the NT calls hell. The righteous, however, will be granted eternal life and glory (12:2–3).

§4.3 *God Keeps Covenant Promises and Threats*

Covenant is a major biblical-theological theme. God made covenants with Noah (Gen 9:9–17), Abraham (Gen 15:18), Moses (Exod 19:5; 24:7–8), and David (2 Sam 7:11b–16; 2 Chr 7:17–22; Ps 89:3–4) in which each successive covenant is incorporated into Israel's covenant pattern. Jeremiah 31:31–34 anticipates a new covenant that the NT sees fulfilled in the covenant established by Jesus Christ (Luke 22:20; Heb 8:8–12).

Daniel speaks of God's covenant with Israel (Dan 9:4; 11:28, 30, 32) established with the "fathers" or patriarchs (2:23). In Dan 9:4 he uses covenant-related vocabulary also found in Deut 7:9–12: "keeps" (שָׁמַר), "covenant" (בְּרִית), "grace, faithful love" (חֶסֶד), and "commands" (מִצְוָה).[32]

A covenant establishes and regulates a relationship between parties. In an often-repeated covenant formula, God affirms Israel as "my people" and himself as "your God" (Exod 6:7; Lev 26:12; Ps 50:7; Jer 7:23; 30:22; Ezek 26:28; 37:27). Thus, God and his people belong to each other. Daniel refers to God as "*my* God" (Dan 6:22; 9:4, 18–20), and Daniel's people can call him "*our* God" (9:9–10, 13–15, 17), as Christians under the new covenant also do. Correspondingly, Israel can be called "*your* [God's] people" (9:15–16, 19), and Jerusalem with its temple "*your* city," "*your* holy mountain," or "*your* sanctuary" (9:16–17, 19). Jerusalem is holy (9:24) because of its temple mount, which symbolizes Israel's covenant relationship with God. He set Israel apart from the nations (Exod 19:5–6) and dwells among his people in the temple (Exod 15:17; 1 Kgs 8:12–13).

Jerusalem and the people of Israel are called by God's name (Dan 9:18–19) in that they belong to God by covenant. God's people are said to be holy ones (7:18–27)—that is, people set apart to the Lord within the covenant and who are to live moral lives. Those in right covenant relationship with God are said to be "people who know their God" (11:32), a reference in context to pious Jews led

---

[32] Steinmann, *Daniel*, 436.

by the Maccabees who sought to remain faithful to God and resist Antiochus IV's attempt to abolish Judaism. This is similar to statements elsewhere where knowledge of God results in right behavior and avoidance of sin (cf. Jer 22:15–16; Hos 4:1–2). The root "know" (ידע) within the marriage covenant can refer to sexual intimacy between husband and wife (Gen 4:1). Within God's covenant with his people, to know God arguably refers by analogy to spiritual intimacy with him.

God keeps his covenant promises and threats. The presence of Daniel and his friends of royal descent in exile (Dan 1:3–4) is a fulfillment of God's threats to Israel if they disobeyed his covenant commands (Lev 26:32–33; Deut 4:27–28; 28:64) and a fulfillment of Isaiah's prophecy that some of Hezekiah's descendants would be taken into exile (Isa 39:7). Yet those very threats also contain promises of restoration beyond exile once the nation repents (Lev 26:40–45; Deut 4:29–31; 30:2–3). Daniel 1–6 unfolds a theme of "the trustworthiness of God, even in the remote and difficult circumstances of exile."[33]

The covenant includes stipulations or obligations, namely laws and commands, that those in the covenant are obligated to keep. Daniel scrupulously attempted to follow the "law of his God" (6:5), including food laws (Daniel 1) and the obligation to pray (6:10), even when this put him out of compliance with the human laws of the Medes and Persians (6:8). Similarly, his Jewish colleagues were careful not to violate the prohibition of idolatry (3:18; cf. Exod 20:4–6; Lev 26:1). Israel as a whole, however, was not faithful in keeping God's covenant laws (Dan 9:5, 11). Some at the time of Antiochus IV abandoned the covenant and acted wickedly toward it (11:30, 32).

Covenants involve promises as well as curses. God maintains his covenant and its promises with those who love him and keep his commandments (9:4; cf. Deut 7:9). Part of that covenant is God's promise of land, descendants, and blessing (Gen 12:1–3). Israel is the "beautiful land" (Dan 8:9; 11:16, 41) because it is the inheritance promised by God's covenant (Exod 6:4, 8; Josh 1:6). On the other hand, Israel's covenant contains a sworn curse and warning of disaster for disobedience (Dan 9:11–14). Daniel and his people experienced that curse when God expelled them from the land of

---

[33] W. Sibley Towner, *Daniel*, Interpretation (Atlanta, GA: John Knox, 1984), 27.

promise by the Babylonian exile. The element of the covenant promising David's seed an eternal kingdom (2 Sam 7:11b–16; 2 Chr 13:5) finds fulfillment in the eschatological promises that the eternal kingdom of God will be given to the messianic son of man (7:13–14; see §6.1). Daniel expected God to keep his gracious covenant promise of limiting the Babylonian captivity to seventy years as Jeremiah had predicted (9:2, 4; cf. Jer 25:11–12; 29:10).

Since God has a covenant relationship with his people, he treats them with mercy rather than strict law (see also §3.6). By strict law God had every right to abandon and curse his people and even permanently nullify the covenant because of Israel's violations of it (9:11). But his relationship with them is a "gracious covenant" (9:4; cf. commentary on this nuance of חֶסֶד) that does not operate strictly on the basis of law. God showed special mercy to his people in consideration of his relationship that he established when he saved them from Egypt (9:15). By covenant, God's name or reputation is associated with both Jerusalem and Israel (9:19c). If he failed to act on his people's behalf, it would sully his reputation. On this basis Daniel asked God for compassion and forgiveness (9:9) and that he turn away his wrath despite their sins (9:16), reasonably expecting that God might show compassion on his desolate sanctuary "for the Lord's sake" (v. 17c)—that is, to maintain his own reputation. If our interpretation of Dan 9:24–27 is correct, Messiah in the process of atoning for sin established a new covenant between people and God (9:27a; cf. Isa 42:6; 49:8; 55:3; Jer 31:31–34; Ezek 37:25–26).

Although God has a special covenant relationship with his people, he is not unsympathetic toward gentiles. Daniel's concern for the well-being of Nebuchadnezzar (4:19) reflects God's concern, as seen in his willingness to restore the king upon his repentance (4:34–37). The book of Daniel positively portrays the praise that Nebuchadnezzar and Darius gave to God (2:47; 3:28; 4:34, 37; 6:25–27), suggesting that God accepted non-Israelite worshipers who, in some covenant-like sense, could also belong to him.

In a broader sense, all the predictive prophecies in Daniel are part of his covenant promises given to his people. As God is one who faithfully keeps his promises, we can expect these prophecies to come true (see §2). The commentary has attempted to trace the fulfillments of the prophecies about kings in Daniel's own day (Daniel 4–5; see §7.2) and about Babylon, Persia, Greece, Rome, and the first coming of Messiah beyond Daniel's day (Daniel 2; 7; 8; 9:24–27; 11; see §7.3). We can equally expect predictive prophecies about events yet future (antichrist, the great tribulation, the second advent, the resurrection of the just and the unjust, and the establishment of the kingdom of God) to come true as well (see §7.4).

§4.4 God Blesses Faithful People

Blessing is a common biblical theme, starting with creation (Gen 1:28), and is part of the patriarchal promise both for Abraham's descendants and all the nations (Gen 12:2–3)—a blessing ultimately fulfilled in Christ and the gospel (Gal 3:8). The law promises blessing in proper worship (Exod 20:24) and blessings generally for obeying God's commands (Lev 26:3–13; Deut 28:1–14). The NT also promises blessings for those who mourn and strive for self-control, righteousness, mercy, and purity (Matt 5:4–9). Those who obey Christ's commands and the word of God (John 13:17; Luke 11:28), who have faith like Abraham (Gal 3:9), and who read and keep John's prophecy (Rev 1:3; 22:7) are blessed. God blesses those who endure trials and persecution and those who do good works (Matt 5:10–11; Jas 1:12, 25; 1 Pet 3:14; 4:14). Even in death the faithful are blessed since their works follow them beyond this life (Rev 14:13). In the NT blessings are funneled through Christ (Eph 1:3).

Blessing for the faithful is an important theme in Daniel. God granted Daniel favor and compassion (1:8). He gave Daniel and his three friends aptitude, success in learning, and wisdom (1:17, 20; 5:11, 14). The court narratives (Daniel 1–6) have sometimes even been classified as wisdom literature, giving examples of godly wisdom to be imitated.[34] Daniel exhibits a practical wisdom that enables him to navigate through difficult situations and avoid catastrophe (1:8–16; 2:14, 16). Wisdom belongs to God, and wisdom is a blessing that can be given to people through revelation (2:20–21, 23; 9:22; 10:14). This wisdom goes beyond what human wisdom can supply (2:27–28, 30; 4:6–7, 18). The godly who learn from God are described as "those who have insight" (11:33, 35; 12:3, 12).

God blesses some people, even non-Israelites, with sovereignty, greatness, glory, and majesty (2:37; 5:18, 21). By granting rulers sovereignty, God can bless their subjects with safety and abundance.

---

[34] Longman, *Daniel*, 58, 89.

This is seen when Nebuchadnezzar was symbolized by a tree where birds and animals found shelter (4:11–12; cf. Rom 13:1–7). God blessed Daniel with an extraordinary spirit (5:12; 6:3), probably a reference to his human spirit enhanced by God's Holy Spirit (4:8–9 [see comments], 18; 5:11, 14). God renders judgment against the little horn and delivers the blessing of the kingdom of God to his holy people (7:22, 27–28) who share in the kingdom given to the messianic son of man figure (7:13–14).

Several times Daniel is said to be "treasured" or a man of "treasures" (חֲמוּדֹת 9:23; 10:11, 19 and comments there)—that is, like all faithful servants of God, Daniel was precious and beloved by him. This too is a blessing from God.

God blessed Shadrach, Meshach, Abednego, and Daniel for their faithfulness in the face of persecution, and he prospered them (3:30; 6:28). He promised to bless his people after a time of trouble with the end of rebellion and sin, atonement for iniquity, and the establishment of everlasting righteousness (9:24). He will bless his people through a time of great distress by helping them escape through the assistance of their patron angel Michael (12:1). God will bless even his martyred or deceased people at the resurrection of the just by raising them from the dead, granting them eternal life, and giving them glory (12:2–3), a promised blessing specifically applied to Daniel (12:13). Finally, a cryptic blessing or happiness is pronounced on those who reach forty-five days past the 1,290 days following the abolition of regular sacrifice, though the precise meaning of this promised blessing is sealed till the end (12:11–12).

§4.5 God Allows Suffering But Often Saves

God sometimes allows his people to suffer and be tested by horrific trials—from the oppression of Israel by Pharaoh, to the oppression of Israel in the book of Judges, to the persecution of prophets like Elijah (1 Kgs 18:3–4; 19:1–2), Uriah (Jer 26:20–23), and Jeremiah (Jer 37:15; 38:6). This theme also occurs in the NT with the martyrdoms of John the Baptist, Stephen, and James (Mark 6:21–29; Acts 7:58–60; 12:1–2), and the persecution and ultimate execution of Paul (Acts 14:19; 2 Tim 3:11; 4:6–8). Jesus Christ is the supreme example. He subjected himself to persecution and execution, obeying the Father unto death (Phil 2:8). Christians are appointed for persecutions (Mark 13:9; 1 Thess 3:3; 2 Tim 3:12), and persecutions will continue into the eschatological future (Rev 6:9–11; 12:13). Yet in many cases God intervenes to save his people who are suffering persecution. He acts to save his people even when they suffer because of their own sin, a premise that forms the basis for Daniel's prayer in Daniel 9.

In Daniel the theme of persecution is prominent. The "fourth man" in the fiery furnace (3:24–27) illustrates and perhaps alludes to the principle stated in Isa 43:2: "I will be with you when you pass through the waters, and when you pass through the rivers, they will not overwhelm you. You will not be scorched when you walk through the fire, and the flame will not burn you." God is present with his people when they pass through trials.

God first demonstrated his salvation in Daniel 1. Daniel and his young friends found themselves in a situation where they were expected to act against their conscience by eating food contrary to Jewish law or else face severe consequences. The severity of the punishment for disobedience is indicated by the chief official's concern that failure to feed them the royal provisions could cost him his head (1:10; see commentary). But Daniel faithfully sought a vegetable diet despite the risks. He trusted God to protect him if he remained faithful. In this instance, God did not save Daniel and his friends by miraculous means but by the wisdom he provided. Daniel prudently exercised this wisdom by asking the guard to test them with a vegetable diet instead of the royal provisions (1:11–15), and God providentially gave Daniel favor with those supervising them (1:9, 11–14). By wisely appealing to authority rather than simply defying orders, Daniel maintained his conscience and avoided punishment. His wisdom and the resulting salvation came from God.

In Daniel 2 God rescued Daniel and his three friends from the decree to kill all the wise men of Babylon by revealing to Daniel the secret of Nebuchadnezzar's dream (2:17–19). Though the text does not say so explicitly, God seems to have providentially moved Nebuchadnezzar to grant Daniel time to learn the dream's meaning—time the king did not grant his magicians (2:8–9, 16).

In the story of Nebuchadnezzar's statue and the fiery furnace of Daniel 3, Shadrach, Meshach, and Abednego are sentenced to death for not practicing idolatry. They affirmed God's ability to save: "If the God we serve exists, then he can rescue us from the furnace of blazing fire, and he can rescue us from the power of you, the king" (3:17;

see commentary). There was no certainty that God *would* in fact save them (3:18a), but the young men were resolute that he *could* save. After the miraculous deliverance, Nebuchadnezzar praised God because, "He sent his angel and rescued his servants who trusted in him. ... There is no other god who is able to deliver like this" (3:28–29).

Daniel 4 illustrates a biblical-theological pattern of divine judgment followed by human repentance and then divine redemption, a theme found throughout Scripture. An essential element of repentance is a commitment to do what is right, which is why Daniel advised the king: "Separate yourself from your sins by doing what is right, and from your injustices by showing mercy to the needy. Perhaps there will be an extension of your prosperity" (4:27). Repentance would not automatically save the king, but it was a necessary prerequisite. God saved Nebuchadnezzar from his insanity after he looked to heaven, praised God, and acknowledged that God ruled over men (4:25–26, 34–37).

God also demonstrated his ability to save in the account of Daniel and the lions' pit. With no animus against Daniel, King Darius was tricked by his administrators into passing an irrevocable decree that condemned Daniel. Darius prayed indirectly for Daniel's salvation, "May your God, whom you continually serve, rescue you!" (6:16). The next day the king inquired, "Has your God, whom you continually serve, been able to rescue you from the lions?" (6:20). To this Daniel responded, "My God sent his angel and shut the lions' mouths; and they haven't harmed me, for I was found innocent before him. And also before you, Your Majesty, I have not done harm" (6:22). Daniel's response suggests that God is more likely to rescue those who pray to him and who are found morally innocent (cf. Jas 5:16). The narrator adds that Daniel was unharmed because "he trusted in his God" (6:23). Those who lack faith in God and who suffer for their own bad behavior are less likely to be rescued by God. Compare NT teaching concerning salvation by faith (John 3:16; Acts 16:31; Rom 1:16; Eph 2:8).

The suffering of God's people is related to his allowing us to participate with him in a cosmic struggle.[35] Daniel 7–8 hints at this cosmic struggle. Daniel 10 and 12 describe it more explicitly. The

---

[35] Pierce, *Daniel*, 125.

struggle involves God's holy people and angels (see §5) who fight against angelic and human powers that oppose God and his kingdom, though salvation and victory are ultimately handed over to the people of God (7:11, 21–22). When Antiochus fights against God's Jewish people and abolishes legitimate sacrifice in the temple, he simultaneously is fighting against the angelic "army" and its leader, "the Prince of the heavenly army"—God himself (8:10–12). It is comforting for God's people to know that we do not fight evil alone. God and his supernatural forces fight alongside us.

Daniel 9 is another example of judgment, repentance, and redemption. Israel's exile was a judgment for their sins. For God to save them from punishment required their repentance (9:13) and God's merciful forgiveness despite their lack of merit (9:19). He saved them out of his compassion (9:9, 18), to fulfill his promises (9:2), and for his own glory (9:17–19).

Forgiveness of sin comes through atoning sacrifice (cf. Lev 3:20, 26, 31, 35) that appeases God's righteous anger against sin, thereby facilitating forgiveness (cf. Rom 3:23–26). In the OT cultic system, sacrifice typically involved unblemished animals (Lev 1:3; 4:3, 23), something to which Daniel and his friends are implicitly compared (Dan 1:4). The association of sacrifice with forgiveness of sin and salvation adds importance to the detail that Gabriel came "about the time of the evening offering" (9:21) to answer Daniel's prayer requesting Israel's forgiveness. It also explains why the abolition of "sacrifice and offering" and the daily "regular sacrifice" (הַתָּמִיד) by Antiochus IV (and possibly the antichrist) is so terrible (8:11–13; 11:31; 12:11). Gabriel spoke of God's plan "to put a stop to sin, to atone for iniquity" (9:24), using language of the sacrificial system, a plan in which "the Anointed One [or "the Messiah"] will be cut off" (9:26) in a sacrificial-type death (cf. Isa 53:8, 10; see further under §6.3). In accord with the Jubilee/Sabbatical Year pattern of the seventy weeks, this would accomplish a Jubilee of Jubilees restoration for God's people that conveys to them rest, restoration, justice, redemption, holiness, refreshment, and blessing (see commentary at the Bridge for Daniel 9:20–27; cf. Isa 61:1), a "rest" of salvation that Joshua's rest from enemies only foreshadowed (Heb 4:1–11).

In Daniel 10:10 God illustrates how he supports, revives, and strengthens his people by helping Daniel recover from his weak condition. God's angel touched him and raised him up, probably in the sense that he "shook me onto my hands and knees" (NJPS). God through his angel revived Daniel from his renewed speechless stupor by twice touching his lips, strengthening him and allowing him again to speak (10:15–16, 18). The angel described how God uses his angels to help and protect God's people by fighting against demonic forces (10:20–21).

Jews abandoning their covenant with God (11:30) did the expedient thing in the days of Antiochus IV, but those who know their God (some of whom die for their commitment) are commended (11:32–33). God will save his people, all those "written in" God's "book," from the unprecedented time of tribulation at the end of time. Even those who have died can anticipate "eternal life" through the resurrection (12:1–2).

§4.6 God Is to Be Respected and Worshiped

Part of God's covenant with Israel involved his people worshiping him for who he is and for what he had done. This is exactly what many of the psalms do (see Psalms 8, 100, 103, 104, 111, 112, 113, 116, 117, 146, 147, 148, 149, 150). Examples of such worship are found throughout the Bible (e.g., Exodus 15; Philippians 2; Revelation 4–5).

Daniel praised and worshiped God (2:19–23; 6:10; 9:4–19, 20–21). The book of Daniel also portrays in a positive way pagan kings praising and paying homage to Daniel's God, specifically Nebuchadnezzar (2:47; 3:28; 4:2–3, 34–37) and Darius (6:26–27). These acts of worship include praise for the nature and acts of God, and can involve the posture of kneeling (6:10) or falling facedown (8:17–18; cf. 3:5–6, 10–11, 15 where falling down precedes worship of Nebuchadnezzar's statue).

There are different terms for worship in Daniel:

- "Praise, bless" (Aramaic/Hebrew בְּרַךְ) means to make a pronouncement or bestowal of good. When Aaron blessed Israel he prayed for them, asking for good things for them from God (Num 6:23–26). When God blesses us, he bestows the goodness he pronounces on us, including such things as material blessings or wealth (Gen 24:35). But when people bless God, they "praise" him, proclaiming good things about him (Dan 2:20–23). In Daniel God is blessed for revealing mysteries

(2:19), for saving people from death (3:28), and for healing a mental illness (4:34).

- "Praise" (D-stem Aramaic/Hebrew שבח) can be rendered "honor," "laud," "praise," or "commend." God is praised for such things as his granting wisdom (2:23), his eternal dominion (4:34), his true and just ways (4:34), and his humbling of the proud (4:37).

- "Glorify" (Hebrew/Aramaic הדר) means to "glorify, honor, adorn" (4:34, 37). It is related to the noun הָדָר that is used of the splendor/majesty/grandeur of kings and nature.[36] To ascribe splendor and majesty to the king who has an eternal dominion is only appropriate. God should be glorified because he holds our life breath and course of life in his hands (Dan 5:23). In Daniel הדר reinforces other words for praise.

- "Exalt" (polel of Aramaic רום, "be high") means more literally, "to proclaim the highness of." In Daniel it is used to reinforce other words for praise (4:37).

- "Praise/give thanks" (H-stem ידה) is used in 2:23 and 6:10 in prayers of worship. The former specifically expresses gratitude for answered prayer, while the latter appears to be a more general act of praise.

- "Serve" (Aramaic פלח, Hebrew עבד). Like Hebrew עבד, Aramaic פלח can mean to worship or venerate, as can the Akkadian cognate palāḫu ("fear, respect, venerate"). Other gods must not be served by faithful believers (3:12, 14, 18), but the true God is to be served (3:17, 28; 6:16, 20). The fact that the "one like a son of man" messianic figure (7:13–14, 27) is "served" by all peoples and nations suggests that he is divine. Nebuchadnezzar called Shadrach, Meshach, and Abednego "servants of the Most High God" (3:26), and Darius called Daniel "servant of the living God" (6:20), whom Daniel "serves" continually (6:16). This implies that Daniel and his friends are God's worshipers. Daniel spoke of himself as God's "servant" in the sense of worshiper and follower (9:17).

- "Tremble and fear" (Aramaic זוע and דחל). Darius demanded that people "tremble in fear" before Daniel's God (6:26) as an expression of worship or homage. This language is reminiscent

---

[36] G. Wehmeier, "הָדָר hādār," in TLOT 1:353–54.

of the concept of fear of the Lord in the wisdom books. People should fear or show reverence for God (Ps 33:8) because it causes one to turn away from evil (Prov 8:13; Job 1:8; 28:28) and obey God's commandments (Gen 22:9–12).

God accepts and is worthy of worship because of who he is (see §3) and what he does. Daniel worshiped and praised God for revealing the secret of Nebuchadnezzar's dream (2:19–20, 23). Nebuchadnezzar praised God for the same thing (2:47), for saving Shadrach, Meshach, and Abednego from the furnace (3:28), and for restoring his sanity and humbling him (4:34, 37). Darius praised God for delivering Daniel from the lions (6:25–27). The book of Daniel describes with some approval Nebuchadnezzar's call to all peoples that they not speak ill of the God of Daniel's friends (3:29). Later the book indicates that one day all peoples will worship the divine son of man (7:14; see §6.1).

Daniel worshiped God "continually" (6:16). He was unwilling to cease praying for a month until Darius' decree had expired, though he was threatened with death (6:6–9). "Continually" may also mean "with duration" in the sense that he worshiped God for a lifetime. Daniel's example shows that God is worthy of worship no matter how severe the consequences.[37]

Improper worship includes idolatry (Daniel 3), Nebuchadnezzar's "worship" of Daniel (2:46), and the honoring of "a god of fortresses"—that is, military might (11:38–39). Belshazzar's worship of lifeless idols and failure to glorify the true God offends God (5:22–23) and illustrates Rom 1:21–23.[38]

The English word "worship" is derived from an Old English word that had to do with acknowledging worthiness. True worship goes beyond words to actions that acknowledge God's worth. Such actions in Daniel include Daniel's refusal to eat the king's food in order to obey the Jewish food laws (Daniel 1), Shadrach's, Meshach's, and Abednego's refusal to bow to Nebuchadnezzar's image (Daniel 3), and Daniel's prayer despite a royal prohibition (Daniel 6). Each of these actions acknowledge God's worth and so constitute worship.

---

[37] Pierce, *Daniel*, 113.
[38] Davis, *Daniel*, 79.

§4.7 God Receives and Answers Prayers

Prayer is ubiquitous throughout the Bible. Daniel showed by his example the importance of prayer as a continual and vital element in a worshiper's life. He prayed three times a day, kneeling and facing Jerusalem. He considered the practice so vital that he made himself subject to death rather than cease to pray (6:10–16). Thus, by refusing to hide the fact that he prayed, Daniel used prayer as a witness about God to others. Regular prayer is a moral and spiritual duty.

In Daniel's prayer of confession and petition on behalf of the Jewish people (9:1–19), he showed his earnestness by accompanying it with fasting, sackcloth, and ashes (9:3; cf. 6:18). A fast with prayer could be partial rather than total (10:2–3). Daniel based his prayer on God's covenant promises, his antecedent acts of salvation, his reputation, and his merciful character (9:4, 9, 15–16, 18–19). Daniel's friends, according to one of several possible interpretations, uttered a quick, indirect prayer: "Let him deliver us" (3:17 NRSV). Darius did the same for Daniel: "May your God, whom you serve continually, rescue you!" (6:16). Because Daniel was innocent before God (6:22) and "treasured by God" (9:23), God was inclined to hear his prayer (cf. Jas 5:16).

There are many terms used for or about prayer in Daniel, several of which overlap with terms for worship (see §4.6).

- "Seek, petition" (Aramaic בְּעָא). To pray is to seek or petition God (6:7, 11). It involves making a request, such as asking for mercy (2:18) or asking him to reveal a mystery (2:23).
- "Bless" or "get down on knees" (Aramaic G-stem participle of ברך). "Got down on his knees" (6:10c) uses בְּרֵךְ ("knee"), a homonym of "he praised, blessed" (D-stem of ברך) and in this context hints at a double entendre ("he blessed/kneeling on his knees").
- "Pray" (D-stem of Aramaic צלא). In 6:10 צלה may imply a posture of leaning or bending, but certainly includes the idea of "beseeching" and "imploring," as in praying "for the life of the king and his sons" (Ezra 6:10). This is also true of the Akkadian cognate *tsallu*. Thus Daniel was in direct violation of the king's interdict.

- "Praise/give thanks" (H stem of ידה) and "confess" (HtD of ידה). The former is used in 2:23 and 6:10 in prayers of worship. The latter is used in a prayer of confession of sin (9:4).
- "Imploring" (HtD of Aramaic חנן, "show grace, favor"). This term used in 6:11 has to do with making "supplication" (KJV; NJPS) or "seeking mercy before" (NRSV). It is cognate with Hebrew חֵן ("grace, favor"), with the HtD verb meaning to seek such.
- "Petitions" (תַּחֲנוּנִין). This term is used in 9:3. It is related to the root חנן ("show grace, favor") and so seems to connote a "pleading for grace/favor/mercy."
- "Pray" and "prayer" (noun, תְּפִלָּה; verb HtD of פלל) are broad terms for prayer. The etymology of the verb "to pray" (9:4) and the related noun "prayer" (9:3) is disputed, but traditionally they have been taken to refer to seeking a favorable judgment/assessment for oneself. Prayer is a way to "seek" God (9:3). Outside of Daniel, "prayer" refers to intercessions for others or to making requests for favor, protection, or help. In 9:1–19 it expresses remorse and confession of sin.

The book of Daniel includes various kinds of prayers: prayers of petition, as when Daniel prays to discover the mystery of Nebuchadnezzar's dream (2:17–18); prayers of praise and worship, sometimes in response to answered petitions (2:20–23); and prayers of intercession and confession (9:1–19). Daniel prayed that God would help his people on the basis of his promises (9:2). He also prayed for him to act "for the Lord's sake" or "for your own sake" (9:17, 19) since God's honor and reputation are tied to the condition of his people called by his name.

God in Daniel responded to the prayers of his people, often through angelic intermediaries (see §5). In 2:17–19 God answered the prayer of Daniel and his friends. Their banding together in prayer suggests "the effectiveness of prayer may be heightened when believers unite in common supplication."[39] In contrast, Nebuchadnezzar's diviners did not pray for their gods to deliver them from Nebuchadnezzar's threats (2:4–11) since they assumed their gods "whose dwelling is not with mortals" (v. 11) were too distant

---

[39] Archer, "Daniel," 43.

and uncaring to address their predicament.[40] Daniel 9:20–27 constitutes God's response through Gabriel to Daniel's prayer in 9:4–19, a prayer hoping for the end of the seventy-year exile. The answer was bittersweet since it involved a prediction of future suffering for God's people. God sometimes answers prayer even before worshipers finish calling on him (9:20–21; cf. Isa 65:24). Answers to prayer are not always what the petitioner wants or expects. Daniel also fasted and prayed over the course of three weeks (10:2) and received another angelic answer (10:12).

Prayer in some cases may be implied. Hebrews 11:33–34 alludes to Daniel who "by faith ... shut the mouths of lions" (cf. Dan 6:22) and to Shadrach, Meshach, and Abednego who by faith "quenched the raging of fire" (cf. Dan 3:24–27). Almost certainly this faith expressed itself through petitionary prayer for deliverance. Scripture affirms the importance and efficacy of prayer and God's willingness to answer.

§4.8 God Expects People to Be Faithful Even If It Risks Their Lives

Christians are commended for being willing to suffer unjustly for the faith (1 Thess 2:1–3:10; 1 Pet 2:19–21) and are commanded to "be faithful to the point of death," with the crown of life promised as a reward for doing so (Rev 2:10).

The narratives of Daniel 1–6 give examples of men willing to do that. Daniel and his three friends courageously maintain their covenant identity, despite an oppressive pagan environment, and are willing to suffer unjustly because of their faithfulness to God. The book of Daniel uses them as role models to encourage God's people to remain faithful even when they find themselves in environments hostile to their faith. Intertwined in these stories is a fundamental question: To which kingdom do we give our first loyalty, the kingdoms of the earth or the kingdom of God?

This theme begins in Daniel 1. Daniel purposed not to defile himself with the king's food (1:8), showing the kind of moral resolve necessary for faithful living, for being "in the world" but not "of the world" (John 17:11, 14–16). Everything from the education they received, the pagan names they were given, and the food they were served pressured Daniel and his friends to assimilate to Babylonian

---

[40] Pierce, *Daniel*, 31.

pagan values, with the prospect of rich rewards for fully cooperating. But Daniel refused. Instead, at risk of his career and possibly even his life, he resolved not to defile himself with the royal food and wine (1:8). The book of Daniel clearly sees Daniel's refusal as exemplary. God's people should remain faithful to God and the laws he has given his people even in environs that discourage it, trusting God to reward them for their faithfulness.

Daniel was not blindly obstinate. He was willing to accept the Babylonian education and study their literature. He even accepted appointment as an administrator over Babylon's idolatrous wise men/diviners (2:48) and served in an otherwise corrupt pagan government (6:4), all the while conducting himself honorably among gentiles despite their treacherous accusations against him (6:13; cp. 1 Pet 2:12). But Daniel refused to adopt the Babylonian lifestyle. In doing so he became a model for God's people to resist and to remain faithful to God despite cultural pressures to do otherwise.

In Daniel 2 Daniel is a model of prayer and worship (2:16–23), and he showed courage by requesting an audience with the king threatening to kill him (2:24). In Daniel 3 Nebuchadnezzar made a proclamation that everyone must worship his golden statue. Whether the statue represented the king, Marduk, or another Babylonian god, it symbolized the deified state.[41] The demand that people worship it in effect asked them to give allegiance to the state that only properly belongs to God (cp. Exod 20:3–5; Deut 6:13; Matt 4:9–10). Shadrach, Meshach, and Abednego, while they affirmed that God could save them, were prepared to die rather than betray him with idolatry (Dan 3:17–18). By this story the book of Daniel calls on God's people to stand together against idolatry in every form. Hebrews 11:34 commends Shadrach, Meshach, and Abednego as heroes of faith (similarly 1 Macc 2:49). Where loyalty to the kingdom of God conflicts with loyalty to the kings of this world, God's people are to choose him (cp. Acts 5:29).

In Daniel 4–5 Daniel courageously delivered revelations from God that he knew Nebuchadnezzar and Belshazzar would not like (4:19–27; 5:17–24), rebuking their sins (4:27; 5:22–23) even though doing so made him liable to royal anger and retaliation. Daniel's empathy and concern for Nebuchadnezzar is also commendable

---

[41] J. E. Goldingay, *Daniel*, WBC 30 (Dallas: Word, 1998), 73.

(4:19b). In Daniel 6 Daniel refused to break God's law (6:5) that expected his people to pray only to him, despite Darius' law (6:8, 12, 15) forbidding prayer to anyone but the king for thirty days. Daniel's competence (6:3), integrity (6:4, 22), courage (6:10a), and religious devotion (6:10b, 13) despite threats to his life were exemplary, which is why the writer of Hebrews also alludes to Daniel as a model of faith (Heb 11:33).

The visions of Daniel (Daniel 7–12) also instruct God's people to remain faithful to God even if this puts their lives at risk from coming world powers. Daniel 7 describes God's people as "holy ones," those who are morally and spiritually set apart to God. As such they put their lives at risk of persecution and death. The "little horn" of the fourth beast, taken in the commentary as a reference to the antichrist, severely persecutes and kills God's holy people (7:21, 25). And yet the holy ones are encouraged to persevere by the promise that the little horn will be judged and the kingdom will ultimately be given to the son of man figure and the holy ones (7:13–14, 18, 22, 26–27).

Daniel 8:23–26 anticipates the years 167–164 BC when Antiochus IV Epiphanes, the Seleucid Syrian king of Greek cultural heritage, overtly sought to Hellenize Palestine and abolish the practice of Judaism. Daniel 8 describes Antiochus IV as a little horn who would defile the temple and abolish its daily offerings. He would seek to destroy the holy people and stand against God, but the holy people are encouraged to be faithful by the knowledge that this little horn in due time (2,300 evenings and mornings) will himself be shattered by an act of God and the sanctuary will be restored (8:13, 24–25).

Though the interpretation of the prophecy of the seventy weeks is disputed, it is clear that God's people will face "difficult times" (9:25). In broad terms God's people are forewarned that, in the words of Acts 14:22, "It is necessary to go through many hardships to enter the kingdom of God" (Acts 14:22). God's people should prepare themselves for such times so they can persevere in faith.

Daniel 10, part of Daniel's fourth vision, also promotes faithfulness among God's people. Though evil spiritual forces are at work in the world—e.g., demonic territorial princes of Persia and Greece (10:13, 20)—even more powerful forces fight on behalf of God's people (10:10–13, 19–20). The NT elaborates on this warfare that involves "Michael and his angels" (Rev 12:7; cf. Jude 9). Paul, who may have had Daniel 10 in mind, calls the dark spiritual powers "rulers" and "authorities" against whom believers struggle (Eph 6:12). Nonetheless, God's people can be encouraged that good angels can strengthen and help them (Ps 91:11–12; Luke 22:43; Heb 1:14). See more on angels at §5.

Daniel 11 warns God's people of troubles from conflicts between great powers that will affect them but encourages God's people to be faithful despite this. The text speaks of especially terrible times during the days of Antiochus IV (introduced in Daniel 8), who would "rage against the holy covenant" (11:30b)—that is, the Jewish religion. Antiochus IV encouraged apostasy and favored Hellenistic Jews who abandoned their faith (11:30c, 32a), but the prophecy speaks admiringly of "the people who know their God" and who "have insight" even though some "will fall by sword and flame, and be captured and plundered for a time" and otherwise be defeated (11:32b–34a). Antiochus IV's persecution has the positive effect that God's people will "be refined, purified, and cleansed" (11:35a), halting the processes of Hellenization undermining the Jewish faith. The chapter goes on to warn of a king, taken by the commentary as the antichrist, who will invade the "beautiful land" of Israel, cause many to fall, and "will go out with great fury to annihilate and completely destroy many" (11:41a, 44b; cf. 7:21, 25), but God's people are encouraged by the knowledge that he too will "meet his end with no one to help him" (11:45; cp. 7:11, 22, 26).

God's people are encouraged to remain faithful, yet they are not promised exemption from suffering and death. Indeed, at the very end of the age there will be a distress worse than any that God's people have ever experienced before or ever will thereafter (12:1). And yet they are exhorted to faithfulness because they have the hope of resurrection to eternal life, whereas the unfaithful will suffer resurrection to eternal contempt (12:2). "Those who have insight," a term for the godly wise who "lead many to righteousness," will eternally flourish after the resurrection of the just, shining like Moses did (Exod 34:29) reflecting the glory of God (12:3).

§5 Angels

Like other parts of the Bible, Daniel affirms the reality of another sphere of existence beyond the realm of human beings and the visible world. This world is inhabited by supernatural beings known commonly as angels. God has a heavenly council that consists of a "host" or "army" or "divine assembly" of angels (1 Kgs 22:19–23; Ps 82:1; Isa 6:1–4; Jer 23:18, 22) who do his bidding and among whom God acts as judge (Ps 82:1). God is the "Lord of Armies [צְבָאוֹת]" (1 Sam 1:3) in that he is the leader of the heavenly armies (Ps 103:20–21; cf. Dan 8:11). So angels constitute "God's [military] camp" (Gen 32:1–2). These beings worship God (Ps 29:1), who is incomparably greater than they (Exod 15:11; Ps 89:6–7). An interpreting angel who conveys revelation and insight is a common motif in symbolic prophetic and apocalyptic visions in Daniel (7–12), Ezekiel (40–48), Zechariah (1–6), and Revelation (see §2).

The two angels named in Daniel are Gabriel and Michael (Dan 8:13; 10:21). They are the only named angels in the Bible (the Catholic Bible adds Raphael; see Tobit 12:15). Daniel affirms that angels play a role in saving God's people (3:28; 6:22), carrying out God's commands (4:13–17), strengthening people (9:21; 10:9–11), and conveying revelation (5:5 [if the hand is an angel's]; 7:16; 8:16; 9:21–22; 10:10–14). Gabriel and Michael appear again in the NT many centuries later (Luke 1:19, 26; Jude 9; Rev 12:7), implying that their lives are indefinitely long. Angels are nonetheless finite beings who occupy time and space, so they can be hindered and delayed by supernatural opposition (10:12–13). Regarding the latter, Daniel also affirms the existence of demons who work against the purposes of God. The demons in Daniel are given titles: the prince of Persia and the prince of Greece (10:20).

God sent his "angel" to save Shadrach, Meshach, and Abednego from the fiery furnace and to save Daniel from the lions (Dan 3:28; 6:22). Though both of these instances may refer to ordinary angels, it is possible that either or both refer to the angel of the Lord—God manifested in visible form. See the commentary at 3:24–25 for a discussion.

In Nebuchadnezzar's vision of the great tree, he sees a supernatural creature called a "watcher" and a "holy one" (4:13, 17, 23). "Watcher" is the Aramaic noun עִיר from a root (Hebrew עוּר) meaning "to be awake" and thus refers to "a wakeful one" (see commentary at 4:13). Watchers come down from heaven (4:13, 23), the abode of God. This suggests they remain ever vigilant in performing their duties. They are called "holy ones" because angels are separated to God for divine service (though it is disputed, the "holy ones/saints" in 7:18, 21–27 are probably not angels). The angel of the tree vision showed angelic might by speaking loudly and barking out orders under God's authority to cut down Nebuchadnezzar and his kingship, reducing the king to madness (4:13–17, 20–27). The word of a watcher is authoritative and constitutes a "decree" (4:17) so that his orders come to pass (4:31–34). If "army of heaven" is the right rendering (see commentary), it refers to God's angelic host through which God "does what he wants," an expression of his dominion (4:35).

Myriads of, presumably, angels appear before the throne of God in heaven, some of whom escort the son of man figure to the Ancient of Days (7:10, 13). In 7:15 angels appeared to Daniel, one of whom helped him interpret his vision (7:16). Subsequently Gabriel interpreted Daniel's dreams (8:16; 9:21–22). (For the unlikely view that the "son of man" figure in Dan 7:13–14 is an angel, see §6.1 and the excursus in Daniel 7.)

God is the "Prince [or Commander] of the heavenly army" (8:11) in that he is the supreme leader of the angelic host/army. Daniel 8:10 hints at the idea of spiritual warfare in heaven corresponding to events on earth. On earth Antiochus IV, having exalted himself to heaven, makes "some of the host fall." What happens in the heavenly realm corresponds with what happens in the earthly realm: Antiochus persecutes God's people on earth who will one day shine like stars (12:3) in parallel with events in heaven. Compare the similar case in Rev 12:7–12 where Michael's heavenly war with Satan and his angels corresponds with the persecution of the saints on earth. Daniel 8 portrays a conversation between two "holy ones" (angels) and Gabriel who helped Daniel interpret the vision of the ram and the male goat (8:13–16).

Modern portrayals of angels often depict them as cute or harmless beings, but Daniel was gripped with fear when Gabriel approached him (8:17). Gabriel's name indicates his greatness. In Hebrew it probably means "man [גְּבַר] of God," though others propose that it means "strength of God"[42] or "God is my mighty one."[43] Since the root גבר relates to being strong, there is probably

---

[42] R. J. Bauckham, "Gabriel," in *New Bible Dictionary*, 3rd ed., ed. D. R. W. Wood (Leicester: Inter-Varsity Press, 1996), 389.

[43] R. B. Vinson, "Gabriel," in *The New Interpreter's Dictionary of the Bible*, ed. Katharine Doob Sakenfeld (Nashville: Abingdon Press, 2006–2009), 501.

a connotation of might in his name. He conveys God's revelation to Daniel ("Gabriel, explain the vision to this man," 8:16).

Daniel 9 and 10 indicate that God can send angels to assist and strengthen his servants in answer to prayer. Following the prayer of confession (9:1–19), God sent Gabriel to support Daniel "in his extreme weariness" (9:21; cp. Luke 22:43). The man dressed in linen who responded to Daniel's fasting and prayer strengthened and revived the prophet who fainted at his appearance (10:10–11, 18–19). The appearance of an angel can cause terror and lead a person to be powerless, dumbfounded, and trembling (10:7–11, 15–17).

It seems likely that the "man dressed in linen" (10:5–6) is an angelic being rather than a theophany (see commentary and §6.4). It is, as Archer says, "probably the most-detailed description in Scripture of the appearance of an angel."[44] Like the angel of Ezek 9:2, this angel was clothed in linen in the manner of Israelite priests (Exod 28:42; 1 Sam 22:18; Ezek 44:17), perhaps because, like priests, he enters the presence of God. His belt of gold is consistent with this idea. As one approached the Most Holy Place in the tabernacle/temple, items became more precious and covered with gold: the incense altar, the table of showbread, the lamp stand, the ark of the covenant (Exod 25:10–11, 23–30, 31; 30:1–5). The high priestly breast piece had chains and rings of gold (Exod 28:22–28). This "man's" person is god-like, with a glorious body like a precious stone, shining arms and leg like polished bronze, a face flashing bright like lightning, penetrating eyes that burn like torches, and a thunderous voice like the roar of a crowd (10:6). Daniel acknowledged the superiority of this angel to himself by addressing him as "my lord" and indicating his unworthiness to speak to such a one (10:16–17).

Daniel 10:1–21 also elaborates on guardian angels, territorial demons, and spiritual warfare. Daniel would have known about spiritual warfare from the stories of Joshua, David, and Elisha. In these stories God's invisible host helps Israel behind the scenes when they face overwhelming odds (Josh 5:13–15; 2 Sam 5:22–25; 2 Kgs 6:16–17). This theme also occurs in the NT (Rev 12:7–12). The battles of God's people on earth are not without the involvement of heaven. Lucas generalizes this:

---

[44] Archer, "Daniel," 123.

History is not merely the outworking of human decisions and actions, though these play an important part in it. Nations, and other entities which embody power, are more than purely human and earthly. There is a suprahuman, spiritual realm that "meshes" in some way with the human, earthly realm. Because of this, conflicts on earth have their counterpart in heavenly conflicts. However, it is important to note that Daniel does not fall into a simple dualism. The Most High God is not matched by some equally powerful opponent. The opposition comes only at the level of the "princes" of the nations. God remains the supreme sovereign in heaven and on earth. [45]

Whereas God could in his sovereignty impose his will in the spiritual realm, he grants to demonic forces, just as he has to humans, the freedom to rebel against him and temporarily obstruct his purposes. This teaching is not unique to Daniel. Jesus often cast out demons (Mark 1:34; 6:13; Luke 4:41, etc.). The NT calls these beings unclean or evil spirits (Matt 10:1; 12:43; Luke 7:21; 8:2; 11:26; Acts 5:16; 19:12, 15–16; Rev 16:13). Perhaps drawing on Daniel, Paul tells Christians that we strugle not merely against "flesh and blood" but against "evil, spiritual forces," which he calls "rulers" and "powers" (Eph 6:12), over whom Christ has triumphed in the cross (Col 1:15). The battle between the satanic forces and the angelic forces will continue in this age (Rev 12:9). They will only be fully defeated when they are cast by Christ into hell (Matt 25:41; Rev 20:10).

The prince of Persia is a territorial demon who for twenty-one days hindered an angel from coming to Daniel in answer to prayer. Opposite of the prince of Persia was the chief prince Michael who helped the angel to reach Daniel (10:13, 21). The warfare between angels and demons is called a "great conflict" (10:1) and a "fight" (N-stem of 10:20) (לחם) of supernatural forces making war in the spiritual realms. Opposed to the angel and Michael were the prince of Persia and the prince of Greece (10:12–13, 20–21), who evidently sought to influence their respective nations to harm God's people. The outcome of these unseen spiritual battles affects human affairs on earth. An angel helped and protected Darius the Mede (=

---

[45] Lucas, "Daniel," 235.

Cyrus?) in his first year (11:1), an act presumably related to influencing Cyrus to let Jews return from exile (Ezra 1:1–4). The battles with the prince of Persia affected events among Persian monarchs (11:2), and the battle against the prince of Greece affected how the Greeks treated God's people (11:3–20). All this culminated in Antiochus IV's attempts to abolish Judaism (11:21–35). The invisible battle continued until a great, final conflict that takes the story to the time of the resurrection (11:36–12:3). At that time Michael will continue to watch over God's people, though this will not prevent an unprecedented time of distress (12:1).

The description of Michael indicates that Daniel understood angels to have ranks. Michael is "one of the chief princes" (10:13), implying that not all angels have that rank. He is "your [Israel's] prince" (10:21), "the great prince who stands watch over [Daniel's] people" (12:1). In the same chapter the man dressed in linen seems to be higher in rank than two other angels who make inquiries of him (12:5–7). Just as there are territorial demons (of Persia and Greece) who work against God's people, so the angel Michael watches over Israel.

Daniel's teaching about angels and demons has a practical application. Leupold expresses this well:

> There are powerful forces of evil at work in and through the nations and their rulers to defeat and to overthrow the people of God. This may alarm and cause terror when one considers how powerful these demon potentates are. On the other hand, there are still more powerful agents of good at work who, by harmonious cooperation, will prevail over their wicked opponents. So the cause of the kingdom is in good hands, and its success is assured.[46]

§6 Messiah

The OT promises an ideal human royal figure from the tribe of Judah (Gen 49:10) and the line of David (Isa 9:6–7; 11:1–10; Jer 23:5–6; cf. 2 Sam 7:12–16) originating from David's hometown of Bethlehem (Mic 5:2), whom prophets sometimes simply labeled as

---

[46] H. C. Leupold, *Exposition of Daniel* (Grand Rapids: Baker, 1949), 459–60.

"David" (Jer 30:9; Ezek 34:23–24; 37:24–25; Hos 3:5). These promises are fulfilled in Jesus Christ. Traditional Christian interpretation identifies several passages in the book of Daniel as referring to this same messianic figure. The most important and probable of these is the description of the son of man in Dan 7:13–14. Other descriptions that likely refer to the Messiah are the "stone" at 2:34–35, 45 and the anointed prince in 9:24–27. Additional possible references to the Messiah include the fourth man in the furnace (3:25), the angel who saved Daniel (6:22), the man dressed in linen (10:5–6), and the prince of the heavenly army (8:11, 25).

§6.1 *"One like a son of man" (Dan 7:13–14)*

Although some take the son of man in 7:13–14 as either Israel or an angel, the most likely view is that it refers to the Messiah (see Excursus: "Who Is the 'One Like a Son of Man' in Dan 7:13–14?"). The NT applies the imagery of the son of man coming with power and glory on the clouds of heaven to Jesus, presumably with regard to the second coming (Matt 24:30; 26:64; Mark 13:26; 14:62; Luke 21:27; Rev 1:7).[47] Although the background to Jesus' title "son of man" is complex and widely debated, the use of this expression in Dan 7:13–14 appears to be a major source of Jesus' usage. Though the expression "son of man" is intentionally ambiguous (it could mean no more than "human being"), Jesus probably used the title as a self-designation to indicate that his messiahship was to be explained by reference to the son of man in Daniel 7.[48] Thus he likely identified himself with that figure.

James Hamilton sees a biblical-theological pattern between the son of man imagery of Daniel 7 and that of Ps 8:4. In the latter, David speaks of God placing all rule under the "son of man" (בֶּן־אָדָם). Psalm 8:4 is about mankind, but Heb 2:5–9 sees Ps 8:4 as only completely

---

[47] The view that Mark 13:46 and 14:62 refer to Jesus' parousia is rejected by R. T. France, *The Gospel of Mark: A Commentary on the Greek Text*, New International Greek Testament Commentary (Grand Rapids: Eerdmans, 2002), 342–43, 500–503, 530–37; 610–13, and N. T. Wright, *Jesus and the Victory of God*, Christian Origins and the Question of God, vol. 2 (London: SPCK, 1996), 341, 360–67, 510–19, 632, but is convincingly defended by E. Adams, "The Coming of the Son of Man in Mark's Gospel," *Tyndale Bulletin* 56.1 (2005): 39–61.

[48] R. N. Longnecker, " 'Son of Man' as a Self-Designation of Jesus," *JETS* 12.3 (1969): 149–58.

fulfilled in the man Jesus. The pattern through which Daniel filters his dream, according to Hamilton, is between the first Adam and the second Adam, the "son of man." The first Adam was made in God's image and likeness and in principle was given dominion over the beasts while the dominion of the snake was curtailed (Gen 1:26–28; 3:14–15; Ps 8:6–8). But in Daniel 7 the beasts, like the snake, sought to usurp the dominion given to man, as if the seed of the serpent rather than the seed of the woman should rule. The "son of man" (בַּר אֱנָשׁ) is in a father-son relationship with the Ancient of Days (see below) and is, therefore, in the image of the Ancient of Days (cp. Gen 5:3). In accordance with the pattern of the dominion of man (Adam) over the beasts, the son of man (Adam) ultimately receives dominion over beastly kingdoms (Dan 7:13–14).[49]

That the son of man figure in Daniel 7 is a king is seen by his kingly description, which includes authority to rule, glory, a kingdom, and dominion (v. 14), all of which he receives from "the Ancient of Days." But in Daniel's context the one like a son of man is not only a king, he is also divine, like the Ancient of Days. His abode is in heaven. He has "god-like" functions, being worshiped/served by all nations (7:14a). Daniel uses Aramaic פלח, a term frequently used of worshiping gods (3:12, 14, 17–18, 28; 6:16, 21). Moreover, the son of man is an eternal being, ruling over an everlasting dominion (7:14b; cf. 2 Sam 7:13–14), which echoes God's eternal kingship (Ps 145:13; Dan 6:26).

A good case can be made that the son figure sits on a throne besides the Ancient of Days and with him renders heavenly judgment on behalf of God's holy people (see commentary at 7:9, 22). Daniel draws on the imagery of enthronement in Psalm 2 where the Davidic king is called God's son and is promised a worldwide kingdom (Ps 2:7–9) just as the "son" receives a worldwide kingdom from the Ancient of Days father figure (Dan 7:14). He also draws from Ps 110:1 where David's "Lord" sits at the right hand of God as the son of man sits on a throne in a coronation ceremony as he receives worldwide kingship (Dan 7:9). The NT picks up on this imagery from Daniel and Psalm 110, describing Christ as seated at God's right hand (e.g., Mark 14:62, see below). His worldwide dominion

---

[49] Hamilton, *With the Clouds of Heaven*, 90–91, 93.

picks up on language used elsewhere of God's universal kingship (Ps 103:19).

The one like a son of man is to be worshiped by all races, nations, and languages (7:14). Goldingay[50] notes the contrast: in Daniel 3 all races, nations, and languages were to bow down to the statue (3:7) that represents the deified state, but now all races, nations, and languages are called upon to worship the one like a son of man (7:14).

The figure is "like" a son of man, that is, like a human. Similarly God in theophanies appears "like a man" (Ezek 1:26–28). The word "like" does not deny that he is human, for Daniel 7 is making a comparative contrast between the son of man figure and the beast-like kings/kingdoms that come before. But there is a hint in this language that he is more than human. This supports the Christian doctrine that Christ is both God and man. His elevated role before the Ancient of Days sets him apart from angelic heavenly beings. Indeed this "son" appears before a white-haired father figure in the Ancient of Days, suggesting the two have a father-son relationship, as is said of Davidic kings in 2 Sam 7:14 and Ps 2:7. The son of man appears on the clouds, and elsewhere in the Hebrew Bible God appears on the clouds (Isa 19:1; Nah 1:3; Pss 18:10; 97:2; 104:3). In the OT angels never do. Likewise, ancient Near Eastern gods appear in the clouds. To portray the son of man on the clouds is to portray him as divine.

The divine-Messiah view of Dan 7:13–14 finds intertextual support. In Psalm 110 David's messianic "Lord" (cf. Matt 22:41–45) sits enthroned at the right hand of Yahweh's (heavenly) throne in a father-son type imagery (cf. Ps 2:7), just as the "son" appears, and is probably "enthroned" (see commentary at Dan 7:9), with the Ancient of Days as a father-figure in heaven. In Psalm 110 the enemies of David's "Lord" are subdued, and he is given a worldwide kingdom just as the little horn is subdued and the son of man receives a worldwide kingdom in Daniel 7. Perhaps Daniel's vision is intentionally drawing on imagery from Psalm 110 to identify its son of man with the Davidic Messiah and, conversely, to suggest that the Davidic Messiah is more than a man (cp. Isa 9:6–7 which describes the Messiah as "Mighty God, Eternal Father" who has an eternal reign).

Though this son of man (the Son) is divine like the Ancient of Days (the Father), he is functionally subordinate to him as seen by

---

[50] Goldingay, *Daniel*, 159.

the son of man's being escorted before the throne of the Ancient of Days and granted from him glory and authority to rule (Dan 7:13–14). The doctrine of the functional subordination of the Son to the Father is also seen in the NT. The Son and the Father are equal in essence as God (John 1:1, 18; Phil 2:5–6; Col 1:15; Heb 1:3), but the Son is subordinate in role in that he obeys, submits to, and is exalted by the Father (John 5:19, 30; 12:49; 15:10; Acts 5:31; 1 Cor 15:28; Phil 2:9; Rev 2:26). Daniel's description may imply that this subordination is eternal, continuing throughout the son of man's everlasting dominion under the authority of the Ancient of Days.[51]

§6.2 The Stone Cut without Hands (Dan 2:34–35, 45)

The traditional Christian view, a view that also appears in the rabbinic literature,[52] is that the "stone" that "broke off without a hand touching it" is a reference to the Messiah. The alternative view is that the stone represents the kingdom of God without reference to the Messiah.

A reasonable case can be made for the messianic interpretation of the stone in Daniel 2 from the parallel vision of Daniel 7. In Daniel 2 "king" and "kingdom" are used interchangeably. The head of gold is Nebuchadnezzar the king (2:38), but the other materials are called kingdoms (2:39–40). The first kingdom (Babylon) is thus represented by its king. The same is true of the four kingdoms of Daniel 7 where the four beasts are called four kings (7:17) but are also kingdoms (7:23). It can be freely acknowledged that the stone represents the kingdom of God, but a kingdom implies, and is represented by, a king. In Daniel 7 the royal figure associated with the crushing of the fourth kingdom is the one like a son of man, a figure that is messianic and divine (see §6.1, excursus in Daniel 7). If the "stone" is a symbol of both Messiah and his kingdom, the parallel between Daniel 2 and

---

[51] The doctrine of the subordination of the Son has in recent years become tied with the question of the subordination of women in Christian doctrine. Against the idea of the eternal subordination of the Son is K. Giles, *The Trinity and Subordinationism: The Doctrine of God and the Contemporary Gender Debate* (Downers Grove: InterVarsity, 2002); while essays both for and against the eternal subordination of the Son are found in D. W. Jowers and H. W. House, eds., *The New Evangelical Subordinationism?: Perspectives on the Equality of God the Father and God the Son* (Eugene, OR: Pickwick, 2012).

[52] See J. Jeremias, "λίθος, λίθινος," *TDNT* 4.272–73.

Daniel 7 would be even stronger. In his work *Treatise on Christ and Antichrist*, Hippolytus makes this connection between the stone of Dan 2:34, 45 and the son of man in Dan 7:13–14:

> After a little space the stone [Dan 2:34, 45] will come from heaven which smites the image and breaks it in pieces, and subverts all the kingdoms, and gives the kingdom to the saints of the Most High. This is the stone which becomes a great mountain, and fills the whole earth, of which Daniel says: "I saw in the night visions, and behold one like the Son of man came with the clouds of heaven, and came to the Ancient of Days, and was brought near before Him. And there was given Him dominion, and glory, and a kingdom; and all peoples, tribes, and languages shall serve Him: and His dominion is an everlasting dominion, which shall not pass away, and His kingdom shall not be destroyed" [Dan 7:13–14].[53]

Another argument in favor of the stone being Christ comes from the NT, which uses "stone" as a symbol of Jesus Christ (Matt 21:42; Mark 12:10; Luke 20:17–18; Rom 9:32–33; Acts 4:11; 1 Pet 2:6–8). Luke 20:17–18 states,

> But he looked at them and said, "Then what is the meaning of this Scripture:
>
> > The stone that the builders rejected
> > has become the cornerstone?
>
> Everyone who falls on that stone will be broken to pieces, but on whomever it falls, it will shatter him."

Jesus is quoting Ps 118:22 ("The stone that the builders rejected"), alluding to Isa 8:14–15 ("a stone to stumble over"), and alluding to the stone that pulverizes the kingdoms of the world in Dan 2:34–35. This allusion suggests that Jesus identified himself as Daniel's "stone"

---

[53] Hippolytus of Rome, "Treatise on Christ and Antichrist," in *Fathers of the Third Century: Hippolytus, Cyprian, Novatian, Appendix*, ed. A. Roberts, J. Donaldson, and A. C. Coxe, trans. S. D. F. Salmond, The Ante-Nicene Fathers 5 (Buffalo, NY: Christian Literature Company, 1886), 5209.

that pulverizes, just as he also identified himself with Daniel's son of man figure. Dempster sees an intentional parallel between the small stone that destroys the giant statue (Dan 2:34–35, 45) and David's small stone that felled the giant Goliath,[54] further supporting the view that Daniel's stone is a Davidic stone representing Messiah.

Theodoret argues that the metaphor of a stone cut from a rock alludes to Messiah's human ancestry. The rock was the patriarchs in the case of Israel (Isa 51:1, "Look to the rock from which you were cut"), but the stone here as Messiah is cut from the line of David and his kingdom.[55] That this stone was cut "without a hand" (Dan 2:34, 45) implies its supernatural origin. This is consistent with a messianic interpretation: the Messiah has a supernatural origin through his virgin birth (virginal conception) without assistance of the hands of a human father.[56] For a complementary view of this stone relating to the temple and Messiah, see §7.4.3 below.

§6.3 "The Anointed One will be cut off" (Dan 9:24–27)

Another passage referring to the Messiah is 9:24–27, the prophecy of the seventy weeks (or weeks of years). According to the "Roman view" interpretation of this passage adopted here (see commentary for this and other views), Daniel's seventy weeks looks forward to the work of "an Anointed One, the ruler" (v. 25) who will appear after sixty-nine weeks. The angel came in answer to Daniel's confession of sin (9:1–23) to explain how God would ultimately deal with the problem of sin. The prophecy is fulfilled in the coming of Messiah at his first advent. The passage builds on Daniel 2 and Daniel 7, adding depth to the messianic son of man figure of Dan 7:13–14 and details about the turbulent process that leads to the final establishment of the kingdom of God under the one who puts an end to sin and brings in everlasting righteousness (9:24).[57]

---

[54] Stephen G. Dempster, *Dominion and Dynasty: A Biblical Theology of the Hebrew Bible*, New Studies in Biblical Theology 15 (Downers Grove: InterVarsity, 2003), 214.

[55] Theodoret, *Daniel*, 53.

[56] St. Jerome, *Jerome's Commentary on Daniel*, trans. Gleason L. Archer (Grand Rapids: Baker, 1958), 32; Theodoret of Cyrus, *Commentary on Daniel*, trans., introduction, and notes by R. C. Hill (Atlanta: Society of Biblical Literature, 2006), 51, 53; Hippolytus, "Treatise on Christ and Antichrist," 5209.

[57] Hamilton, *With the Clouds of Heaven*, 117–22.

These seventy weeks serve "to bring the rebellion to an end, to put a stop to sin, to wipe away iniquity, to bring in everlasting righteousness, to seal up vision and prophecy, and to anoint the most holy place" (9:24), all things that can be related to Jesus Christ. This ending of sin is connected to the prayer of confession of sin in the first part of the chapter. Sin will be done away with and made forgivable by the atoning death of Messiah just as Isa 53:5–6 and 11 predicted, a passage to which Daniel may be alluding.[58] These things are inaugurated by Christ's death on the cross, which deals with the problem of sin in a way analogous to atoning OT animal sacrifices (see Leviticus 1; 4–5). After Christ, and the completion of the new covenant, "vision and prophecy" (v. 24) become less prominent.

The anointing of "the most holy place" (9:24c) could instead refer to the anointing of "the most holy one" (see commentary), that is, Christ whose anointing corresponds with his baptism, though the expression "anoint the most holy" elsewhere applies to things rather than people. James Hamilton takes it to mean "appoint the most holy place" but relates this to Christ through a biblical-theological understanding of the Messiah. There was no temple in Daniel's day. To Hamilton, "anoint the most holy" is about a future anointed place (the "temple") being destroyed in conjunction with the anointed man (the Messiah) being cut off.[59] Theologically, the death of Christ "put a stop to sacrifice and offering" (9:27a) in that the sacrificial system of the temple became theologically irrelevant. Historically, Titus of Rome in what can be called an "abomination of desolation" militarily destroyed the temple in AD 70 (9:27b; Matt 24:15; Mark 13:14; cp. Luke 21:20).

Daniel's connection between Messiah's work and the temple's destruction fits into a larger biblical-theological pattern that connects messianic kings with the temple and sees the Messiah as ultimately supplanting the temple. A descendant of David was prophesied to build God's house and establish the kingdom forever (2 Sam 7:13). Solomon initially fulfilled this role by building and dedicating God's temple (1 Kings 8). Later Zerubbabel who is of Davidic, messianic descent played a similar role (Hag 1:14). Ezekiel depicts a future, visionary temple (Ezekiel 40–48) in conjunction with Israel's coming

---

[58] Ibid., 118.
[59] Ibid., 117, 119.

to be under "David" the Messiah (Ezek 37:24–25) following an eschatological battle with Gog of Magog (Ezekiel 37–38).

The connection between Messiah and the temple continues in the Gospels, though now the idea of Messiah supplanting the temple comes to the fore. Jesus, whose zeal for God's house would consume him (John 2:17), speaks of building a new temple after the temple would be destroyed (Matt 26:61, "I can destroy the temple of God and rebuild it in three days"; John 2:19, "Destroy this temple, and I will raise it up in three days"). This "temple" that Jesus promised to build denotes "the temple of his body" (John 2:21)—Jesus' own resurrected body. In Revelation John arguably combines what the Gospels say about the temple and Jesus with Ezekiel's temple. By drawing imagery from Ezekiel (e.g., Rev 21:3 and Ezek 37:27; Rev 21:13 and Ezek 48:30–34; Rev 21:15 and Ezek 40:3; Rev 22:1 and Ezek 47:1–2), and placing the new heavens and earth after an eschatological battle involving Gog and Magog (Rev 20:7–10; cp. Ezekiel 38–39), John places Ezekiel's visionary temple in the new heavens and earth (Revelation 21–22). But there will be no temple building in the new heavens and earth, for God Almighty and the Lamb (Jesus Christ) serve as its temple (Rev 21:22). In other words, the symbolic presence of God among his people represented by the temple was ultimately to be supplanted by Jesus and the Father who constitute the real, visible presence of God among his people. This biblical-theological pattern that associates Messiah with the temple and then has the Messiah supplant the temple in his own person fits with Daniel's vision of the anointed temple being destroyed in conjunction with the work of the Messiah.

"He will make a firm covenant" (9:27a) during that one week (NJPS; see commentary) refers to Messiah's establishing the new covenant (Jer 31:31–34) that Jesus established at the Last Supper ("This is my blood of the covenant, which is poured out for many for the forgiveness of sins," Matt 26:27–28).

A criticism of this view is that it is problematic to say that the first coming of Christ "put a stop to sin." Baldwin tries to solve this by extending the seventieth week to the second advent, though this makes the weeks disproportionate in length. If taken this way, both the first coming and the second coming could be regarded as in view. At the first coming Christ inaugurated the process of ending sin, making atonement available, righteousness everlasting, and prophecy unnecessary—and replacing the to-be-destroyed temple with something better (Dan 9:24). But that process is only completed at the second advent.

The classical dispensational interpretation of this passage also sees mention of the death of Christ in the Anointed One being cut off in v. 24 but then sees the seventieth week as jumping to the end times and the antichrist who is the coming prince. (See the commentary for the reasons for rejecting this view.) It seems simpler to see the following chronological sequence: Daniel 8 takes us to the time of Antiochus IV, 9:24–27 to the time of the first advent and its immediate aftermath, and 11:36–12:3 to the time of antichrist and the resurrection—events associated with the second advent. In this sequence, 9:24–27 does not yet refer to antichrist.

In sum, the most likely view of Dan 9:24–27 is that God though the angel Gabriel reveals to Daniel how sin is to be brought to an end (9:24). This occurs in conjunction with the Messiah being "cut off" (cf. Isa 53:8), the inauguration of a most holy temple (see further at §7.4.3), and the establishment of a covenant (9:24, 26)—the new covenant (Jer 31:31; Luke 22:20) made possible by the sacrificial death of Jesus Christ for the sin of the world. The events of Daniel's seventieth week end the need for sacrifice and offering (9:27) and vision and prophecy (9:24), perhaps because Christ's death is the final sacrifice and ultimate revelation from God. It also brings in the age of eternal righteousness (9:24)—that is, the righteousness of the age to come.

§6.4 The Man Dressed in Linen (Dan 10:5–6)

A disputed passage is that of the man dressed in linen in 10:5–6. Some take this person to be a theophany on the basis of the god-like description and the similarities with God in Ezek 1:26–28 and Jesus Christ in Rev 1:13–16. Christian commentators often suggest that this figure is more specifically a pre-incarnate appearance of Jesus Christ. See the commentary at 10:5–6 for the reasons for rejecting the messianic view of this man and affirming that he is an angel.

§6.5 The Fourth Man in the Furnace and the Angel in the Lion's Den (Dan 3:25, 28; 6:22)

Nebuchadnezzar is amazed to see a fourth person in the furnace after the three Jewish men had been thrown in (Dan 3:24–27). Nebuchadnezzar describes this man as "like a son of the gods" and concludes that God "sent his angel and rescued his servants" (3:25, 28). Some see this figure as an ordinary angel. Others see him as God in the form of the angel of Yahweh. Some who see this figure as God take it more specifically as a reference to the preincarnate Christ. The same question occurs at 6:22 where God sent his angel to save Daniel from the lions. See commentary on 3:24–25 and 6:22 for discussion of this possible but uncertain messianic interpretation.

There might still be an indirect reference to Christ, however, even if an ordinary angel is the reference. Jerome suggests that though the fourth man is an angel, there is typology in which the angel foreshadows Christ as Savior "who descended into the furnace of hell, in which the souls of both sinners and of the righteous were imprisoned, in order that He might without suffering any scorching by fire or injury to His person deliver those who were held imprisoned by chains of death."[60]

§6.6 "The Prince" (Dan 8:11, 25)

Some traditional commentators take the "Prince of the heavenly army" and the "Prince of princes" in Dan 8:11, 25 as not merely God but specifically as the Second Person of the Trinity. This seems appropriate to Steinman because "the preincarnate Christ fits the context of the temple and sacrifice."[61] Given Daniel's frequent allusions to Isaiah, the term "Prince" (שַׂר) may evoke its messianic use in Isa 9:6, which would identify this figure as the divine Messiah. Unfortunately, there is no clear way of distinguishing the persons of the godhead in a passage such as this.

§7 Theology of History

The United States has been a great world power. How long will it last? Many other great nations have come and gone. The Sumerians, the Egyptians, the Hittites, the Assyrians, the Babylonians, and the Persians all were flourishing civilizations. The Roman Empire was once great not only in size but in duration, lasting hundreds of years longer than the United States has existed. But it too came to an end.

Some argue that history is an endless, repetitive cycle. Some think history is simply a series of meaningless events. Towner argues

---

[60] Jerome, *Daniel*, 44.
[61] Steinmann, *Daniel*, 403.

that Daniel also takes the view that history, other than God's deterministic acts in it, is meaningless.[62] But is history really without purpose and direction, an infinite chain or cycle of pointless events? Or
does history have purpose and a goal?

According to Daniel, God does have a plan for history, a plan in
which human history follows certain patterns that ultimately mesh
with God's saving purposes, making human history part of salvation
history. The book of Daniel affirms that God is in control of human
history and destiny, including the fate of great nations. This gives
history meaning. Lucas writes that according to Daniel,

> [H]istory does have a purpose, and therefore a meaning. It
> is to establish a holy people (12:7). This gives history a mor-
> al meaning. It matters whether one acts wisely or wickedly.
> This meaning may not be apparent in the midst of all the
> ambiguities of history. It becomes apparent only in the light
> of what happens at the end. ... What awaits us at the end ...
> gives the motivation to persevere and remain faithful even
> in the face of death. But there is also the understanding
> needed to live appropriately within a particular historical
> situation. ... The pattern of the self-pleasing king who, in
> his pride, overreaches himself and so precipitates his own
> downfall acts as a warning to those tempted to throw in
> their lot with such kings when they seem to be prospering.[63]

Daniel 2, 7–8, and 10–12 show a pattern to history in which
wicked powers exercise beastly dominion in accord with mankind's rebellion against God's righteous dominion. All four beasts
in Daniel 7 follow this pattern. The first beast (Babylon) under
Nebuchadnezzar plundered the temple and promoted idolatry, and
under Belshazzar it profaned sacred temple items (1:2; 3:1–6; 5:3–4).
This fits into a broader biblical-theological theme of the arrogant
greatness of Babylon (4:30) as a place opposed to God, a theme that
begins with the tower of Babel (= Babylon; Gen 11:1–9), which, like
the tree representing proud and great Nebuchadnezzar, extended
into the sky (Gen 11:4; Dan 4:11, 20). Babel was arguably ruled by

---

[62] Towner, *Daniel*, 175.

[63] E. C. Lucas, *Daniel*, Apollos Old Testament Commentary (Downers Grove:
InterVarsity, 2002), 301.

the similarly powerful and proud king Nimrod (Gen 10:8–11). This continued with the neo-Babylonian king contemporary with Daniel who in arrogant pride wanted to ascend to heaven and be like God (Isa 14:13–14). The biblical-theological theme of Babylon is elaborated upon by the prophets who speak of its downfall as a judgment (Isa 13:19–23; 14:22–23; 47:1; Jer 25:12–14; 27:7; 50:1–51:64). The NT uses Babylon as a metaphor for Rome, which similarly opposed God (1 Pet 5:13), and as the label for the immoral capital of the beast that is destined for destruction by God's wrath in the last days (Rev 14:8; 16:19; 17:5; 18:2–24).

The other gentile powers in Daniel are also beastly—from Medo-Persia, which issued an unjust decree to kill pious Daniel (6:6–15), to the Greek King Antiochus IV Epiphanes and his abomination of desolation (11:31), to the fourth beast's little horn who wars against God's people (7:21, 25). This pattern will continue until the kingdom of God and the one like a son of man arrive to establish a righteous dominion that displaces the kingdoms of this world (Daniel 2, 7). The book of Daniel teaches that arrogant, wicked rulers will act only until their "appointed time" ends (11:27, 35) and God's justice and kingdom prevails.

§7.1 God in History: Determinism versus Freedom

Daniel's elaborate theology of history affirms that the future is predetermined and/or foreknown by God, so that it can be recorded in advance in God's "book of truth" (10:21). Keil states, " 'The Scripture of truth' is the book in which God has designated beforehand, according to truth, the history of the world as it shall certainly be unfolded."[64] God in the book of Daniel reveals the future of what will happen to his people until the end of the age.

Daniel's theology of history begins with the nature of God, something described in some detail (see §3). According to Daniel, from "Nebuchadnezzar's kingdom to God's final kingdom, God is in control, setting up and taking down kings to accomplish his perfect

---

[64] C. F. Keil and Franz Delitzsch, *Commentary on the Old Testament*, vol. 9 (Peabody, MA: Hendrickson, 1996), 775.

will."[65] Dunnett describes well the central role of God in the OT's theology of history:

> What God intends, what he has in mind, what he purposes and plans, what he pleases—these together give the basis for a theology of history. God stands in the center of history as One who acts. He has a goal in what he does. Nothing can thwart his plan. His purpose is consistently related to what he does in the world.[66]

The book of Daniel affirms that God not only foreknows history, but in his sovereignty he influences and directs history toward a predetermined goal. It is the common view of the OT that God sovereignly works in all human affairs to accomplish his purposes. Certain future events such as the coming of the son of man, the coming and judgment of the fourth beast with its evil little horn, the resurrection and judgment of the just and the unjust, and the deliverance of the kingdom of God to the holy ones and the son of man have been predetermined by God.

Some scholars wrongly assert that whereas the Hebrew prophets have a more open view of man's role in history, Daniel (like other apocalyptic books) is strictly deterministic in which God intrudes into history to reassert his control.[67] Evidence of the more open view of the prophets includes Jer 18:7–10, which states in principle that God's threats and promises can be changed by human behavior. This actually occurs in Jonah, where Nineveh's repentance nullifies an unconditional-sounding announcement of judgment (Jonah 3:4, 10; cf. Zeph 2:4). Thus, even when the prophets make prophecies of judgment that sound unconditional, there may be an unstated possibility that God will relent if people respond to the prophetic message.

---

[65] Kenneth Boa and William Kruidenier, *Romans*, HNTC 6 (Nashville: Broadman & Holman, 2000), 392.

[66] Walter M. Dunnett, s.v. "Purpose," in *Evangelical Dictionary of Biblical Theology*, electronic version (ed. Walter A. Elwell; Grand Rapids: Baker, 1996).

[67] D. S. Russell, *The Method and Message of Jewish Apocalyptic* (Old Testament Library; Philadelphia: Westminster, 1964), 230–34; "Eschatology," *Eerdmans Bible Dictionary*, ed. Allen C. Myers (Grand Rapids: Eerdmans, 1987), 347.

But is Daniel actually different than other prophets? While it is true that Daniel sometimes uses deterministic language (Dan 4:35, "He does what he wants. ... There is no one who can block his hand or say to him, 'What have you done?' ") and certain events have been unconditionally predetermined, the sharp distinction between the determinism of Daniel and the more open view of the prophets is exaggerated. Lucas rightly argues that Daniel's so-called determinism is not so different from that of other prophets:

> Clearly the framework of history seems fixed in the dream of chapter 2 and the vision of chapter 7. The long survey of history in chapter 11 deals with specific events in the reigns of specific rulers, and the statement "for what is determined shall be done" (11:36) seems quite deterministic. However, the equally deterministic language of 4:17 is followed by Daniel's plea to Nebuchadnezzar in 4:27 which implies that this is a warning of something which need not happen if the king responds rightly. Also, the long prayer of repentance in chapter 9 assumes that human response to God can affect the course of history. Goldingay seems to strike the right balance when he says, "Daniel assumes that human beings make real decisions which do shape history, yet that human decision–making does not necessarily have the last word in history. Daniel affirms the sovereignty of God in history, sometimes working via the process of human decision-making, sometimes working despite it."[68]

God's control over the nations in history is complex, as seen by the different ways nations relate to God's people. God gave Judah into the hands of Nebuchadnezzar (1:2) and justly used him to punish Israel violently for covenant violations (9:7–14). Nebuchadnezzar in Daniel 4 and Darius in Daniel 6 are portrayed sympathetically as kings who can freely repent and act decently. On the other hand, kings who act contrary to God's will can be excessively cruel (Daniel 3), proud (Daniel 4), and sacrilegious (Daniel 5). They can

---

[68] E. C. Lucas, "Daniel," *New Dictionary of Biblical Theology,* ed. T. D. Alexander and B. S. Rosner (Downers Grove: InterVarsity, 2000), 234, citing J. E. Goldingay, *Daniel,* Word Biblical Themes (Dallas: Word, 1989), 24.

defy God's moral law by enacting immoral laws (Daniel 6) and unjustly persecute God's people (Dan 7:21; 8:24–25; 11:30–35). In the broad sweep of history the nations seem to move toward ever increasing rebellion against God (Daniel 7; 8; 11), culminating with Antiochus IV Epiphanes in the second century BC and the antichrist of the endtimes whom Epiphanes foreshadows. Yet even here God can override unjust acts of kings, punish their pride, and make the kingdom of God ultimately triumph, so that God's sovereign control over history prevails.

§7.2 God in Israel's Past and Present

Daniel's theology of history begins in the second verse of the book where it affirms the same kind of prophetic view of history seen in the historical books of the OT: "The Lord handed Jehoiakim king of Judah over to him [Nebuchadnezzar], along with some of the vessels from the house of God" (Dan 1:2a). The historical books repeatedly speak of God handing over people in battles (Josh 10:32; Judg 1:4; 1 Sam 24:10; 2 Chr 24:24) the way Daniel does. So do the prophets. Isaiah calls Assyria the "rod of God's anger" whom God sent to punish Israel, even though Assyria's own goal was merely to destroy (Isa 10:5–7). In terms of promise and fulfillment, Daniel's statement in 1:2 of the prophetic view of history corresponds closely to the covenant warning that disobedience would lead to exile (Lev 26:32–33; Deut 28:64), Isaiah's prophecy that Hezekiah's treasures and descendants would someday be taken to Babylon (Isa 39:6–7), and Jeremiah's prophecy that the temple vessels would be taken to Babylon until the Lord restored them (Jer 27:21–22).

Secular historians would not characterize it this way. They would say that Babylon was militarily stronger and took advantage of circumstances to rob the Jewish temple in Jerusalem. Nor would the Babylonians themselves characterize it that way. They might attribute their victories to their god Marduk who prevailed over Judah's God. But Daniel, like the prophetic authors of the historical books of the Bible, takes a prophetic view of history that sees the working of God in history and behind human historical outcomes.

Daniel 2:21 states this in principle: "He [God] changes the times and seasons; he removes kings and establishes kings." "Times and seasons" probably here means "epochs and eras" (Moffatt Bible). God's control of the times is underscored by the causative verbs in which God "changes"/"causes to change" (H-stem of שנה) epochs and eras, "removes"/"causes to go away" (H-stem of עדה) kings, and "establishes"/"causes to stand" (H-stem of קום) kings. God exerts control over history and fixes periods of times for certain nations and kings to dominate, as seen in Nebuchadnezzar's dream in Daniel 2. Why God chooses to remove kings, the timing of when he so chooses, and how this fits into a broader salvation history are mysteries not always revealed.

Daniel 2:37–38 applies this specifically to Nebuchadnezzar's reign: "Your Majesty, you are king of kings. The God of the heavens has given you sovereignty, power, strength, and glory. Wherever people live—or wild animals, or birds of the sky—he has handed them over to you and made you ruler over them all." Nebuchadnezzar's kingship is something God has "given" him, and "handed over" to him (cf. also Dan 5:18). In other words, Nebuchadnezzar gained the rule and all the fruit of kingship by divine permission. Nebuchadnezzar is the "king of kings," but the "God of the heavens" is supreme over him, as Nebuchadnezzar later acknowledges (2:47). For God intervenes in the affairs of men and sovereignly directs history itself.

Daniel 4:17 repeats the principle of God's direction of history in terms of Nebuchadnezzar's own reign, though this time the discussion includes the involvement of the angelic watchers and God's holding human rulers accountable for sins:

> This word is by decree of the watchers,
> and the decision is by command from the holy ones.
> This is so that the living will know
> that the Most High is ruler
> over human kingdoms.
> He gives it to anyone he wants
> and sets the lowliest of men over it.

This verse restates the idea that God is "ruler over human kingdoms." It adds that God expresses that sovereignty by decrees mediated though angelic watchers who pass on his commands and implement his verdicts. That God can remove and establish kings is illustrated in Nebuchadnezzar whose kingship God temporarily removes as a punishment for his pride (4:37; 5:20). The verdict from God is given by a watcher from heaven who announces the king's imminent period of madness (4:31–32). These events are also portrayed in visionary symbolism in Dan 7:4 when the first beast of the vision (the lion) stands for Babylon and its king Nebuchadnezzar. The passive verbs first allude to God as agent giving Nebuchadnezzer over to madness ("its wings were torn off") and then his restoration that humanizes him and restores his sanity ("It was lifted up from the ground, set on its feet like a man, and given a human mind"). All this shows God's sovereignty over human kings.

This is not to say that human history is absolutely determined or that human volition plays no role in history (see §3.8; §7.1). Daniel indicates that Nebuchadnezzar could have averted the predicted catastrophe if he had changed his behavior: "Separate yourself from your sins by doing what is right, and from your injustices by showing mercy to the needy. Perhaps there will be an extension of your prosperity" (4:27). Similarly, Belshazzar's bad behavior led to the message of judgment written on the wall because Belshazzar had learned nothing from Nebuchadnezzar's experience and failed to humble himself (5:22–24). Instead, Daniel told him, "you have exalted yourself against the Lord of the heavens" by desecration of the temple vessels and idolatry, and "you have not glorified the God who holds your life-breath in his hand and who controls the whole course of your life. Therefore, he sent the hand" (5:23–24a). These verses balance God's sovereignty and human responsibility. On the one hand, "God … controls the whole course of your life," including the power of life and death. On the other hand, had Belshazzar not behaved so badly, the disaster could have been avoided.

The miracle stories of Daniel 3 and 6 do not make explicit statements about theology of history, but they do illustrate how God intervenes in history to annul the decrees of monarchs on behalf of his people. Nebuchadnezzar did not believe any god could save Shadrach, Meshach, and Abednego from his royal sentence of fiery death in a furnace (3:15). Darius' decree, which inadvertently sentenced Daniel to death by lions, was like all Medo-Persian decrees supposedly "irrevocable" (6:8, 15). But in both cases God intervened in history to save Daniel and his friends from seemingly immutable royal edicts of death (3:25–27; 6:22).

Daniel's prayer of confession of sin (9:4–19) speaks of God's actions from Israel's past to Daniel's present. The background is God's choice of Abraham and promise to him that his descendants would become numerous and inherit the land of Canaan (Gen 12:1–3). This promise was later formalized as a covenant (Gen 15:17–21) and repeated to Isaac and Jacob (Gen 26:2–5; 28:13–15). In fulfillment of that promise God brought the Israelites out of Egypt (Dan 9:15) and returned them to Canaan, and at Mt. Sinai he established a gracious covenant with the whole nation (Dan 9:4; cf. Exod 24:7–8). That covenant came with blessings for obedience and curses for disobedience (Dan 9:11; Leviticus 26; Deuteronomy 28). Israel's present suffering is a result of God's punishment of their past sins: "Because of our sins and the iniquities of our fathers, Jerusalem and your people have become an object of ridicule to all those around us" (9:16b). In saying this Daniel sees in history promise/threat fulfillment from Leviticus 26 and Deuteronomy 28 (see commentary at 9:1–19) that brings about Israel's expulsion from the land.

Leviticus 26 in particular has a pattern of sevens:[69] there God would discipline Israel seven times for their sins (Lev 26:18, 21, 23, 28) and the land would make up missing its seventh-year Sabbatical Years by lying desolate for many years (Lev 26:34–35, 43). This pattern of sevens is taken up by Jeremiah, who predicts a seventy-year Babylonian captivity (Jer 25:11–12; 29:10). Daniel meditated on Jeremiah's prophecy (Dan 9:2). The Chronicler sees Jeremiah's seventy-year captivity as fulfilling the warning from Leviticus 26 of enforcing Sabbath rests for the land (2 Chr 36:21). Moreover, this pattern of seven does not end with seventy years, since God has a plan that involves seventy sevens (of years) beyond the fulfillment of Jeremiah's prophecy (9:24).

Since Israel disobeyed, the covenant curses came upon them, resulting in unprecedented disaster on Jerusalem (9:12–14) and exile for God's people (9:7) just as God warned through Moses (Lev 26:32–33; Deut 28:64). God brings the disaster on his covenant people. Since God has a plan for the restoration of his people consistent with his covenant promises (the land, blessing) when they repent and confess their sin (Lev 26:40–45; Deut 4:27–31; 30:1–10), Daniel looked to God for restoration in fulfillment of these promises. Thus Daniel confessed his people's sins and begged God for forgiveness and grace so that they could return to the land of promise and rebuild Jerusalem (9:16–19). Here again Daniel's theology of history

---

[69] Hamilton, *With the Clouds of Heaven*, 43–44.

is not purely deterministic since there is a balance between God's sovereignty and human responsibility. Bad behavior brings on punishment and exile, while repentance can bring on God's restoration. According to Ezra, around the time of Daniel's prayer (first year of Cyrus [Ezra 1:1] = first year of Darius [Dan 9:1]) God influenced Cyrus to allow Jews to return to Judah and rebuild the temple (Ezra 1:1–5). It appears that Daniel's prayer of confession helped change history.

The importance of that first year of Cyrus shows up again in 11:1 where the unnamed angel said, "In the first year of Darius the Mede, I stood up to strengthen and protect him." The previous chapter describes how events on earth correspond with events in heaven where there is an invisible spiritual battle involving good angels who struggle with the demonic prince of Persia. Daniel 11:1 flashes back two years to the beginning of the "first year of" Persian rule. It was in that year that Cyrus (= Darius the Mede) allowed Jews to return to Judah and begin rebuilding the temple (Ezra 1:1–4). Behind this critical event in Jewish history there is invisible, angelic (and hence divine) influence.

§7.3 God in Israel's History before the Arrival of the Heavenly Son of Man

According to the book of Daniel, God knows the future of kings and kingdoms in advance (see §3.5). Great powers from Babylon in Daniel's day to the coming of God's kingdom at the end of history will come and go in accord with the plan of God. God reveals the future to Daniel "to help you understand what will happen to your people in the last days" (10:14). The term "last days" here simply means "the future" (NIV) or "the days to come" (NJPS). In context, these "last days" include everything from the immediate future in the Persian period (11:3), though the Greek period (11:3–35), and even to the end-time resurrection of the just and the unjust (12:2). In these "last days" there will be times of hostility toward God's people, especially at the time of the Seleucid king Antiochus IV. But God remains in control and will see his people through various trials as history moves toward the coming kingdom of God.

God's preview of history begins in Daniel 2 and the mysterious dream given by God to Nebuchadnezzar and interpreted by Daniel. The dream starts with Nebuchadnezzar, the "head of gold" (2:38), and continues through three subsequent kingdoms represented by different materials (arms of silver, thighs of bronze, legs of iron), each of which appears before the coming of the kingdom of God. The visions here and in Daniel 7 are a way of saying that though the future is mysterious, it is known by God. This commentary takes the second kingdom as Medo-Persia, the third as Greece, and the fourth as Rome-and-beyond (see Introduction). During the first-year reign of Cyrus king of Persia, Jews were allowed by the king to return from exile (Ezra 1:1–4). Some who returned at that time may have supposed that the full establishment of the kingdom of God was imminent. But this passage makes clear that many great kings and kingdoms would come and go before the kingdom of God would appear in its fullness. Similarly wrong conclusions about the kingdom of God might be deduced on the basis of Jeremiah's prophecy of the seventy years (Jer 25:11–12; 29:10), on which Daniel meditated in that same first year of Darius/Cyrus (Dan 9:2). Jews reading Jeremiah's prophecy might wrongly deduce that this seventy-year Babylonian period would be immediately followed by the inauguration of the kingdom of God. But God informed Daniel through the angel Gabriel that this was not the case. There would be a period of no less than seventy times seven periods that would occur subsequent to Jeremiah's period of seventy years before "everlasting righteousness" would be established (9:24).

Daniel 5 elaborates on the prediction in Daniel 2 that the kingdom of Nebuchadnezzar would be displaced by a different kingdom. Daniel 5 predicts that Babylon would fall to the Medes and Persians (5:28), a prophecy that begins to be fulfilled that very night with Belshazzar's death (5:30). Daniel's theology of history is brought out in 5:26–28 when he announces, "God has numbered the days of your kingdom and brought it to an end ... you have been weighed in the balance and found deficient ... your kingdom has been divided and given to the Medes and Persians." The first statement explicitly refers to God who numbers the days of kingdoms and ends them. The passive verbs ("weighed," "divided," "given") show God to be the agent of these actions. God "weighs" kings and kingdoms in his role as judge who determines when and how they are "deficient" and the length of time they are allowed to rule. In most cases, why God allows kings to rise or fall remains a mystery known only by him. But in this particular case the cryptic and miraculous handwriting on the wall as interpreted by Daniel revealed that Belshazzar had been "found deficient" or "stumbled" (5:25–28) for (among other reasons) his arrogant and blasphemous use of the sacred temple vessels in a drinking party while worshiping other gods (5:22–24). Had he repented and confessed his sin, there might have been a prolongation of his rule. Since he did not, God determined immediately to divide his kingdom and give his authority to Darius (5:31).

The vision of Daniel 7 elaborates on the theme of the four kingdoms described in Daniel 2. It describes Nebuchadnezzar's past rule (represented by a lion), his period of madness (symbolized by the lion's wings being torn off), and his restoration to sanity ("given a human mind"). All of these actions were controlled by God and his angelic watchers (7:4; see Daniel 4). The bear (Medo-Persia) was given permission, presumably from God, to devour other nations symbolized by three ribs in its mouth: "It was told, 'Get up! Gorge yourself on flesh'" (7:5). Likewise the leopard (Greece) was under divine control, since it "was given dominion" (7:6) by God. The fourth beast (Rome-and-beyond) was not initially said to be under divine control, though it is ultimately judged and brought to an end by God and the son of man figure (7:7–14).

The vision of the ram and the male goat in Daniel concentrates on the future of the second and third of Daniel's four kingdoms, namely the kingdoms of Medo-Persia and Greece, culminating in the horrible reign of Antiochus IV. At first glance the ram appears to do whatever it wants with no reference to divine permission (8:4). Historically, Persia's doing whatever it wanted is hyperbole since Persia was thwarted in its plans to take Carthage in North Africa, and Ethiopia or Nubia (modern Sudan) south of Egypt (see commentary). Nonetheless, Medo-Persia was remarkably successful in quickly building its empire. But what on the surface appears to be purely acts of human volition must be read in the light of 7:5, which indicates Persia is given heavenly permission to conquer (see above). Thus humans act within parameters established by God. The vision goes on to predict that the Persian kingdom would be bought to an end by the male goat with a conspicuous horn (8:5–8), fulfilled by Alexander the Great (cf. 8:21), who rapidly conquered the Persian empire from 334–331 BC. This shows how God allowed powerful empires to be humbled and defeated. The vision also foresees the breakup of Alexander's kingdom among his generals after his death (8:8, 22).

The vision of Daniel 8 (and 11:21–35) culminates with and focuses on the Greek rule of Antiochus IV. In Daniel 8 he is described as a "little horn" who persecutes God's people and abolishes the morning and evening sacrifices in the temple (8:10–14, 25–26). Human volition is demonstrated in that he "acted arrogantly" (8:11) and "will exalt himself" (8:25). Both of these are H-stem of גדל, which probably means he caused himself to be regarded as great by "talking big," declaring himself great by boasting. His adoption of the presumptuous and blasphemous title Epiphanes ("Manifestation [of a god]") is an example of this and reflects a deep-seated insecurity. He magnified himself against "the Prince of the heavenly army" and "the Prince of princes" (8:11, 25)—that is, God (see §3.2).

James Hamilton sees biblical-theological parallels between this language concerning Antiochus and the language about the king of Babylon in Isa 14:12–15. There the king in pride rivals God ("I will ascend to the heavens; I will set up my throne above the stars of God"). Therefore as a representative of the serpent of Eden, he promotes god-like independence from God (Gen 3:4–5) in opposition to the messianic king who is the human representation of Yahweh on earth (Isa 7:14; 9:6; cf. Ps 45:6). Likewise the ruler of Tyre in Ezek 28:1–19 claims god-like greatness ("I am a god; I sit in the seat of gods in the heart of the sea," 28:2), his royal splendor is compared with Eden's ("You were in Eden, the garden of God," 28:13), and his kingship is likened to the serpent, the cherub in Eden ("You were an anointed guardian cherub," 28:14). In both cases god-like but serpent-inspired heavenly pretensions are brought to earth (Isa 14:12, 15; Ezek 28:6–10, 16–17). Paul also uses this kind of language of his "lawless one," antichrist, whom Antiochus IV foreshadows (2 Thess 2:9, "The coming of the lawless one is based on Satan's working"). Daniel's vision of Antiochus IV should be read through such imagery.[70]

In attacking God's people and claiming the blasphemous title Epiphanes, Antiochus IV stood against God. But divine sovereignty is demonstrated in 8:19, which speaks of "the appointed time of the end" (מוֹעֵד קֵץ)—that is, a time fixed by God in his sovereign control over history. His desolation of the sanctuary is limited to 2,300 evenings and mornings (8:14), and his other nefarious acts are only "for

---

[70] Hamilton, *With the Clouds of Heaven*, 96–97.

a time" (11:24, 33). In poetic justice, God deposed him. Antiochus IV falls "not by human hands" (v. 25c), that is, "not by human power" (NIV), but by a divine act. Specifically, according to the most probable reconstruction of the events, Antiochus IV died by disease after trying to plunder a temple of the goddess Nanea in Persia (1 Macc 6:1–13; 2 Macc 9:1–28; Appian, *Syriaca* 66; Polybius, *Histories* 31.11; Josephus, *Antiquities* 12.9.357–360). Jewish writers (Josephus, *Antiquities* 12.9.358; 2 Macc 1:17; 9:18) saw Antiochus' death as an act of God, a punishment for his plundering of Jerusalem's temple (among other crimes). Some non-Jews also attributed Antiochus' death to divine retribution, though in their case mostly for his plundering of the temple of Nanea in Persia (Polybius, *Histories* 31.11). According to Daniel, God not only foreknew these events—insisting that the "the vision of the evenings and the mornings that has been told is true" (8:26)—but also intervened and played an active role in history, bringing to a fitting end one of the worst persecutors of God's people.

Daniel 9:24–27 is a prophecy concerning Israel's future given in response to Daniel's prayer of confession based on his meditation on Jeremiah's prophecy of a seventy-year Babylonian captivity (9:1–19). Daniel's prophecy covers not just seventy years but seventy weeks of years (v. 24) that will involve trouble: "rebellion," "sin," "iniquity" (v. 24); "difficult times" (v. 25); destruction of "the city" of Jerusalem and its "sanctuary," "war," "desolations" (v. 26); and "abomination of desolation" through a "desolator" (v. 27). Yet God has a plan for Daniel's people and the holy city of Jerusalem that ends sin, atones for iniquity, and brings in everlasting righteousness (9:24). This plan involves an "Anointed One," the Messiah. On the messianic theological implications of this passage see §6.3. God has decreed certain desolations (9:26) and has decreed destruction (9:27). Thus, in general this passage indicates that God actively foresees and decrees for his people both troubles and salvation through the Messiah. God has predetermined the course of history in which the death of Messiah plays a central role. Though Titus's destruction happens outside the seventy weeks, it contributes to a broader theme in Daniel by being "an installation in the pattern of fourth kingdom activity"[71] that will involve further abominations. It also confirms what Jesus says about

---

[71] Hamilton, *With the Clouds of Heaven*, 132.

wars continuing between the first advent and the "end" (Matt 24:6, 15; Mark 13:7, 14; Luke 21:9, 24).

The final vision of Daniel 10–12 purports to preview for Daniel "what will happen to your people in the last days" (10:14), in which "last days" includes everything from the Persian period (11:2) to the resurrection of the just and the unjust at the end of the age (12:2). It begins with a description of a supernatural battle between God's angels (the unnamed angel and Michael) and the demonic prince of Persia, which affects what happens among Persian monarchs (10:13; cf. 11:1–2). This anticipates their future battle with the demonic prince of Greece, which affects what happens among the Greeks (10:20; cf. 11:3–35). The invisible battle with earthly consequences for God's people will continue until a great, final conflict that takes the story to the time of the resurrection (11:36–12:3). At that time Michael will continue to watch over God's people, though this will not prevent an unprecedented time of distress (12:1). The description of supernatural angel-demon conflicts is a way of showing how God works behind the scenes to shape and direct history toward his predetermined ends.

Daniel 11:2–35 gives some of the most remarkably fulfilled, detailed predictive prophecies in all of Scripture, showing that God foreknows the future in great detail. For a concise summary of what God demonstrably foreknows historically in Daniel 11, see §3.5. In the description of various kings and kingdoms in Daniel 11, both the positive and negative features are emphasized. They arise (11:2–3, 7, 14, 21–22), become rich and powerful (11:2, 5, 24, 28), have large armies (11:10–11, 13, 25), and are for a while triumphant (11:7, 10, 15, 18) to do whatever they wish (11:3, 16). But then they fail due to arrogance (11:12) or plots (11:25–26). They experience frustration and futility. Their kingdoms break up (11:4), their alliances and invasions fail (11:6, 9), their armies are handed over to enemies or carried off (11:11–12), they fail to stand (11:14–15), their machinations prove futile (11:17–18), they stumble and fall (11:19), they are shattered (11:20), or other forces confront and intimidate them (11:30). All of this shows the fleeting glory of conquest[72] in contrast with the abiding glory of the kingdom of God.

---

[72] Baldwin, *Daniel*, 189.

God's sovereign direction of history is evident in the expression "appointed time" (11:27, 29, 35; cf. 8:19). Similarly, Antiochus IV's actions against the Jewish people were limited to a "time" (11:33). In other words, certain events are fixed in time or limited in time by God and destined to occur at the precise time and way God foresees, allows, and/or directs to happen. Illustrative but not exhaustive examples of these "appointed times" include Antiochus IV's invasions of Egypt and his subsequent failed attempt to abolish Judaism (11:25–27, 29–31). One purpose of these horrible times is so God's people "may be refined, purified, and cleansed" (11:35a). God's refining process will continue throughout history "until the time of the end, for it will still come at the appointed time" (11:35b)—that is, until the appointed eschatological time at the end of the age fixed by God.

Human kings may think themselves in control of events, and even God's people may at times put too much stock in political actions, but God is in ultimate control of history and overrides the actions of human kings as he chooses. This encourages God's people when oppressed, for they know that God's sovereignty will ultimately prevail.

§7.4 *The End of the Earthly Kingdoms (Eschatology)*

Daniel indicates that history is moving toward an end (2:44; 8:17, 19; 9:26; 11:35, 40; 12:4, 6, 9, 13). Stagg perceptively observes, "Eschatology is a theology of history, the view that history under God is moving toward a goal (*eschaton*)."[73] According to the book of Daniel, God's plan for history ultimately results in great earthly powers being displaced by the kingdom of God. In Nebuchadnezzar's dream a "stone" cut without human hands smashes the statue representing four great kingdoms of the world. The stone pulverizes them and grows into a great mountain (2:34–35). This stands for the kingdom of God (and probably its human king, the Messiah; see §6.2) which will replace the kings and kingdoms of this world. This kingdom will be eternal, never to be destroyed or displaced (2:44–45), for unlike the kingdoms of the world, God's kingdom is an eternal kingdom that will never be destroyed (4:3, 34; 6:26; 7:14, 18, 27).

---

[73] F. Stagg, "Eschatology: A Baptist Perspective," *Review and Expositor* 79.2 (1982): 379.

Sinful human nations that deify themselves are "beasts" in God's sight and destined to be judged, destroyed, and displaced by the kingdom of God (Daniel 2, 7). The authority of the little horn antichrist figure will be transferred instead to the son of man figure, the Messiah (7:13–14). Like animals, these powers are fierce and predatory (7:3–7), but God's eternal kingdom will prevail over the fiercest of them (7:26–27).

As Goldingay writes,

> Daniel 3–6 has portrayed [world empires] inclined to make themselves into God; they are thus also inclined to put mortal pressure on those who are committed to God (chaps. 3; 6), but are themselves on the way to catastrophe (chaps. 4; 5). These motifs are taken up and taken further in chap. 7. The tension between the human and the bestial that appeared in chaps. 4 [Nebuchadnezzar's madness makes a beast out of him] and 6 [Daniel given to the beasts, lions] becomes a key motif: bestiality is now turned on God himself (Barr), but he puts an end to the reign of the beast and gives authority to a humanlike figure (Lacocque).[74]

§7.4.1 The Antichrist

Part of God's plan for salvation history revealed in Daniel involves an evil "little horn" (7:8) who will be active just before the appearance of the son of man figure and the establishment of the kingdom of God. This little horn makes war on the holy ones. Though critical scholars identify this "little horn" as Antiochus IV Epiphanes, who is indeed called a "little horn" (8:9), in the light of the NT and internal considerations within Daniel, he appears instead to be what John calls the "antichrist" (1 John 2:18) and what Paul calls "the man of lawlessness" (2 Thess 2:3–4). This little horn and his fourth kingdom are related to the beast of the book of Revelation, which picks up on the imagery of Daniel 7 (Rev 13:1–10). (See the

---

[74] Goldingay, *Daniel*, 158. Goldingay is citing J. Barr, "Daniel," *Peake's Commentary on the Bible*, ed. M. Black and H. H. Rowley (London/New York: Nelson, 1962), 597–98, and A. Lacocque, *The Book of Daniel*, trans. D. Pellauer (London/Atlanta: SPCK/Knox, 1979), 14, 145–48.

excursus, "Who is the 'Little Horn' of Daniel 7?" in chapter 7 of the commentary.)

Daniel 7 reveals the following about the "little horn" antichrist.

1. The antichrist arises from Daniel's fourth kingdom, a beast with ten horns, which will appear at the end of the age in conjunction with the appearance of Christ ("one like a son of man," 7:11–13). It will be "different" from the earlier three kingdoms in the sense of being fiercer and more brutal (7:7, 23). This commentary argues that this fourth beast represents "Rome-and-beyond." John describes this "beast" as having characteristics of the three earlier beasts: a leopard's body, a bear's feet, and a lion's mouth (Rev 13:2; cf. Dan 7:4–6). This may be John's interpretation of Daniel's statement that the first three beasts had an extension of life for a period of time (Dan 7:12) since their characteristics, especially their predatory and violent ones, live on in the fourth beast.

2. The antichrist is a braggart, "speaking arrogantly" (Dan 7:8). Revelation 13:5 echoes this language concerning the beast: "A mouth was given to him to speak boasts and blasphemies."

3. The antichrist will depose other political leaders (7:24). The fourth beast has "ten horns" (as does "the beast" in Rev 13:1) that represent ten kings (7:7, 20, 24). This might mean there are a series of rulers (dictators?), but since the little horn antichrist puts down three of them, it seems more likely that this kingdom is a coalition government of multiple states. These kings "fall" before him, which may mean they are defeated militarily.

4. Fourth, the antichrist will oppose God and persecute God's people. The little horn speaks ill of God (7:25a) and wages war against the "holy ones" (7:21; cf. Rev 13:7), oppressing or persecuting them (7:25b). This will come to an end when God and the son of man judge the beast and its little horn in favor of the holy ones and save them with the assistance of the angel Michael (7:9–14, 22, 26–27; 12:1). This war is probably what 12:1 refers to as an unprecedented and never-to-be-surpassed time of distress. Antichrist persecutes the holy ones for "time, times, and half a time," that is, for three-and-one-half years (7:25d; cf. Rev 13:5, "forty-two months"). He also seeks to change "religious festivals [literally 'times'] and laws [or 'decree']" (7:25c), that is, the legally established dates for religious activities. The word "law" could be a reference to Jewish law (as in 6:5; Ezra 7:12). Thus this "changing times and laws" would be part of

the persecution of God's people. Perhaps more likely, though, is that he thinks he can change "times and laws/decree" in that he presumes he can overcome the times established by God's decree for removing kings (Dan 2:21), and specifically God's judgment against him (7:26) that will bring his "time" to an end (7:11, 22).

5. The antichrist and his kingdom will come to a complete and abrupt end by God's judicial decree and the appearance of the son of man figure (Jesus Christ). The beast to which the little horn is attached is killed and burned with fire (7:11), which Rev 19:19–21 interprets as being thrown into the lake of fire (hell). This comes as a result of God (the Ancient of Days) making a judgment against that beast and its little horn (7:9, 22, 26), with Christ (the son of man) co-seated in judgment with him (see commentary at 7:9).

6. The authority of the little horn and all previous kingdoms will be taken away and transferred to the son of man figure—that is, to Christ (7:13–14, 27b) and to his people, the "holy ones" (7:18, 22, 27a; see §7.4.3).

7. The antichrist will be egocentric, blasphemous, and atheistic. He will consider himself greater than any of the gods (11:36b, 37c) and speak against the true "God of gods" (11:36c). In fact, he pays no attention to his ancestral God/gods (11:37a), something untrue of Antiochus IV. Rather his "gods" are his military power and material possessions: fortresses on which he spends his money like an offering to a god (11:38). Military might is the "foreign god" that helps him take strong fortresses (11:39a).

8. The antichrist will use rewards to manipulate people: "He will greatly honor those who acknowledge him, making them rulers ... distributing land as a reward" (11:39b).

9. The antichrist will be both a political and a military leader. He will succeed for a while militarily (11:36a). He invades and plunders the king of the South (Egypt), along with Egypt's allies Libya and Cush (11:40a, 43). Although this is debated, according to the three-king hypothesis mentioned in the commentary, the antichrist is from "Rome-and-beyond" and is distinct from the king of the North (originally Syria/Babylonia), in which case the antichrist also fights against the king of the North (11:40b). Even if he is the same as the king of the North, rumors from the east affect his military actions and lead him to leave Egypt and relocate to Palestine between Mount Zion/Jerusalem and the Mediterranean Sea (11:44–45a).

10. The antichrist meets his fate in Palestine. The antichrist will only be successful until the time of the end decreed by God (11:36d). It is while he pitches his royal tent in Palestine that he will "meet his end with no one to help him" (11:45b). Compare 7:11, 22, and 26, where the divine court led by the son of man brings an end to the little horn's dominion (cp. also Rev 19:11–20).

The prototype of this eschatological, evil figure is Antiochus IV Epiphanes, of whom Daniel prophesies in Daniel 8 and 11. They are distinct but also remarkably similar (see the above-mentioned excursus in chapter 7 and the commentary at 11:36–45). Both are described as a "little horn" (7:9; 8:9). This in addition to other similarities explains why the discussion of antichrist (Daniel 7) can flow into a discussion of Antiochus IV (Daniel 8), and a discussion of Antiochus IV (11:21–35) can flow directly into a discussion of the antichrist (11:36–45). Antiochus IV Epiphanes foreshadows the antichrist typologically. Thus a study of Antiochus' character in Daniel (8:9–12, 23–25; 11:21–35) provides insight into what the antichrist might be like. Antiochus was full of arrogance, insolence, intrigues, deceit, and cunning (8:23, 25; 11:21, 23). He used money to reward his followers (11:24), was bent on evil (11:27), sought to destroy the people of God, rewarded religious apostates (8:24; 11:28, 30, 32–33), exalted himself to equality with and opposed God (8:10–11, 25), sought to abolish proper worship of the true God and to promote false worship (8:13–14, 26; 11:31), and died by an act of God (8:25). These characteristics are similar to those of the antichrist listed above. So we can understand the antichrist by looking back to Antiochus.

§7.4.2 The Great Distress

Daniel 12:1 anticipates a time of great distress (צָרָה), the end of time traditionally labeled "the great tribulation." This will be the worst time of trouble in human history, a "time of distress such as never has occurred since nations came into being until that time." This will be even worse than the previously unprecedented trouble/distress (צָרָה) for Jacob/Israel at the time of the Babylonian exile (Jer 30:7) and the trouble at the time of Antiochus IV Epiphanes. The description of this time of trouble occurs in conjunction with a discussion of the antichrist (11:36–45), whose kingdom in an earlier passage is said to trample and pulverize the whole earth (7:23) and who wages war against the holy ones (7:21). This suggests that the great distress coincides with the world domination and persecution of God's people under the antichrist.

Jesus affirms that Christians can generally expect to experience "tribulation" in this life (Matt 24:9; John 16:33). Such times of distress only end at Christ's second coming (Matt 24:29–31). Jesus speaks of an eschatological tribulation that appears identical to Dan 12:1, a great distress "that hasn't taken place from the beginning of the world until now and never will again" (Matt 24:21). Those days will be limited for the sake of the elect who otherwise would not survive (Matt 24:22; Mark 13:19–20). Revelation 7:14 (as well as the other sufferings under the antichrist) may also refer to the same event, assuming a futurist (or preterist-futurist) view of that book (see §7.4.1).

Under the protective, watchful care of Israel's guardian angel, "the great prince Michael," at least some of Daniel's people ("all your people who are found written in the book") will escape (Dan 12:1a, c). Conversely the fourth beast's actions, recorded in books (7:10), will not escape judgment. The nature of this "book" in Dan 12:1c is not explained, though it would seem to record what Jesus calls "the elect" (Matt 21:22; Mark 13:20)—that is, those chosen by God among the godly destined to survive this time of trouble. Compare the "book of life" in Revelation. Those who worship the beast (antichrist and his kingdom) are not written in the book of life (Rev 13:8; 17:8), and those not written in the book of life are thrown into the lake of fire (Rev 20:15).

The length of this tribulation or distress is roughly three-and-one-half years (Daniel 7:25b; 12:7, 11–12; Rev 11:3; 12:6; 13:5). Dispensationalists make this eschatological time of distress seven years because they identify this tribulation with Daniel's seventieth week in 9:24–27. However, if Daniel's seventieth week has come and gone by this point (see the commentary), then there is no basis for making the tribulation seven years. Revelation, like Daniel, speaks of a three-and-one-half-years time of trouble (Rev 12:14; 13:5), but never refers to a seven-year period.

§7.4.3 The Kingdom of God and the One like a Son of Man

God is a great king (see §3.8), and by virtue of his creation of the world (Genesis 1) he has the right to rule over it (1 Chr 29:11–12). The book of Daniel expands on this. It teaches that God will establish a worldwide "kingdom that will never be destroyed," that will "crush" all earthly kingdoms and "bring them to an end, but will itself endure forever" (Dan 2:44), and that will "fill the whole earth" (2:35). The NT similarly affirms that God's eschatological plan for history is for all the kingdoms of the world to be displaced by the kingdom of God (1 Cor 15:24; Rev 11:15).

New Testament teaching has a degree of nuance about the eschatological kingdom of God, which has already come in a special way in the person of Jesus who inaugurated it at his first advent (see Matt 4:17; 12:28; Luke 17:20–22)—note that this happened during the Roman Empire "in the days of those kings" (Dan 2:44), not during the time of the Greek Empire. However, the kingdom will not be consummated until his second coming (Matt 6:10; Mark 13:24–26 [echoing Dan 7:13–14]; Luke 19:11). This NT teaching in no small part derives from Daniel. God even now is king, sovereign over the affairs of men (Dan 4:17, 25). But there is a future aspect to God's rule (as seen in Daniel 2, 7, and 12) in which his kingdom will displace the kingdoms of the world under the son of man figure, the Messiah (Dan 2:31–35, 44–45; 7:13–14; cf. 1 Cor 15:24).

In Daniel 2 the kingdom of God is represented by a stone made without hands that becomes a great mountain (2:34–35, 45). I have argued that the stone cut without hands represents the messianic son of man figure as well as his kingdom (see §6.2). Beale and Steinmann have a different yet complementary biblical-theological understanding, connecting the stone that becomes a mountain both with Christ and with the end-time Mount Zion temple.[75] The temple is God's "holy mountain" (Pss 2:6; 43:3), and in pre-Daniel prophecy the "mountain of the LORD's house" is established in the "last days" and is "raised above the hills" (Isa 2:1–4; Mic 4:1–5). This is parallel with the stone becoming a great mountain in Daniel 2. Temple imagery is also placed in an eschatological setting in Ezek 40:2 and Rev 21:10. In the latter text, the kingdoms of the world (especially the beast; see §7.4.1) have been destroyed and God begins to reign fully (Rev 11:15; 19:6). Temple imagery is connected to the kingdom of God. The temple mount is seen as the place from which God reigns

---

[75] G. K. Beale, *The Temple and the Church's Mission: A Biblical Theology of the Dwelling Place of God*, NSBT 17 (Downers Grove: InterVarsity, 2004), 145–48; Steinmann, *Daniel*, 142.

enthroned above the cherubim (Pss 80:1; 99:1). Jesus refers to the destruction of the "temple made with human hands" and building "another not made by hands" (Mark 14:58). This probably alludes to the "stone ... without a hand" (Dan 2:34, 45), though Jesus' "temple" not made by hands refers to his own body to be resurrected in three days (Matt 26:61; John 2:19–21). Jesus is like the temple in that his person is the place where God dwells or tabernacles (John 1:14; Col 1:19), and yet he is greater than the temple (Matt 12:6). The NT incorporates believers into God's temple founded on Christ (1 Cor 3:16–17; Eph 2:19–22; 1 Pet 2:4–9; Rev 3:12). In the new heavens and earth there will be no sanctuary, but God and Christ will be its sanctuary (Rev 21:22). Thus this temple imagery of a stone "not made by hands" that becomes a great mountain can be associated with the Messiah and his kingdom. As previously discussed, the destruction of the anointed most holy place (temple) and the cutting off of the Anointed One (Messiah) in Dan 9:24–27 follows this same biblical-theological pattern that culminates in the Messiah displacing the earthly temple (see §6.3).

Daniel's fourth kingdom, with its little horn antichrist (Dan 7:7–8) and persecution of God's people (7:21), will be destroyed in conjunction with the appearing of "one like a son of man" in the clouds of heaven (7:9–14) who thus takes a central role in God's plan for history. The NT applies that language to the second coming of Jesus (Matt 24:30; 26:64; Mark 13:26; 14:62; Luke 21:27; Rev 1:7; see further in §6.1). The royal son of man figure arguably sits in judgment alongside the Ancient of Days (see commentary at 7:9) and receives the eternal kingdom (7:9–10, 13–14; cf. Matt 25:31–46; 2 Cor 5:10). The kingdom of God is also said to go to God's people, the holy ones who ultimately inherit it (7:18). This is consistent with Isaiah's statements about the nations one day serving God's people Israel (Isa 14:1–2; 49:22–23; 60:10–12). The NT also refers to Christ receiving authority to rule from the Father, subduing all his enemies, and returning the kingdom to the Father (1 Cor 15:23–28). It also speaks of believers sharing in Christ's reign (Matt 19:28; 25:34; 1 Cor 6:3; 2 Tim 2:12; Rev 5:10).

§7.4.4 Resurrection

The OT rarely speaks of an afterlife. First Samuel 28 describes Saul's use of a medium to consult with the dead prophet Samuel.

Second Kings 2:11 recounts Elijah going to heaven in a whirlwind. Isaiah 14:9–11 speaks of the dead as if they still have some shadowy existence after death. Several psalms hint at an afterlife (Pss 16:10–11; 17:15; 49:15; 73:24). A couple of texts speak of individuals resuscitated from death in conjunction with Elisha (2 Kgs 4:35; 13:21), and a few texts either use the idea of resurrection metaphorically for national revival or hint at a general resurrection (Job 19:25–26; Isa 26:19; 66:22–24; Ezek 37:1–14; Hos 6:2). But Dan 12:2–3 is the first text in the OT that clearly and unambiguously affirms the doctrine of the general resurrection of the dead and by implication a last judgment.

Daniel 12:2 uses "sleep" as a metaphor for death (similarly John 11:11–13; 1 Cor 11:30; 15:18; 1 Thess 4:13–15), implying that at the resurrection the dead will awaken. "All" (for "many" meaning "all," see commentary) who sleep in death will awake and come back to life. The text specifically refers to the resurrection of the just and the unjust, with the righteous gaining the reward of eternal life, while the wicked are condemned to shame and eternal contempt (cf. Matt 25:46; John 5:28–29), what the NT calls hell. Thus Daniel affirms a resurrection and last judgment, doctrines on which the NT elaborates (Matt 25:31–46; 2 Cor 5:10; Heb 9:27; 1 Pet 4:5; Rev 20:11–15).

Among those who gain eternal life are "those who have insight" and "those who lead many to righteousness" who will shine like the bright sky, reflecting the glory of God (Dan 12:3). Since they have eternal life they can shine and flourish like the stars "forever and ever" (12:3). Jesus picks up Daniel's language in the parable of the wheat and the weeds about the last judgment. There the unjust experience fire, weeping, and gnashing of teeth while the righteous "will shine like the sun" (Matt 13:42–43). Paul elaborates on the resurrection body of the just, calling it incorruptible and immortal (1 Cor 15:51–54). God treats the righteous differently than the unrighteous, indicating that human responsibility is a factor in the results of history within the predetermined plan of God.

Daniel plays a role in the Bible's development of the teachings about hell. The book describes the condemnation of the wicked at the last judgment—awakening to "eternal contempt" as opposed to "eternal life" (12:2). This probably draws on Isaiah's description of the wicked in an eschatological passage related to the new heavens and earth (Isa 65:17; 66:22; cp. Rev 21:1). Isaiah speaks of the wicked as being where "their worm will never die, their fire will never go out" (Isa 66:24), a passage taken by Jesus as a description of hell (Mark 9:48). Isaiah says of these wicked that they will be a "horror" (דֵרָאוֹן) to all mankind. This rare word has to do with repulsiveness or abhorance (see commentary at 12:2). In Isa 66:24 the wicked and their fate inspire דֵרָאוֹן in others. The word is used in only one other place in the Hebrew Bible: Dan 12:2. There the wicked will be the object of דֵרָאוֹן in the sense of "contempt" or repulsion (דְרָאוֹן עוֹלָם "eternal contempt," CSB)—that is, repulsion and separation from God. The NT elaborates on both Isaiah and Daniel by describing hell as a place of eternal fire (Matt 18:8; 25:41; Jude 7), eternal destruction with separation from God's presence (2 Thess 1:9), eternal torment (Rev 14:11; 20:10), a second death (Rev 2:11; 20:14), and eternal punishment (Matt 25:46).

Daniel 12:2 presents a challenge for those holding to premillennialism. According to that eschatological scheme, most of the "just" are resurrected before the millennium of Revelation 20, but all the unjust are resurrected a thousand years later. However, Dan 12:2 (as well as Matt 25:46 and John 5:28–29) describe the two resurrections as if they occur at the same time. Thus amillennialists and postmillennialists cite these verses in support of their eschatology and against premillennialism. Premillennialists see Dan 12:2 as an example of a split reference in Bible prophecy in which events that are chronologically far apart are spoken of together, as when the first and second comings of Christ are spoken of together (e.g., Isa 9:6–7; Joel 2:28–32). Accordingly, they argue that since Revelation 20 clearly teaches the idea of a millennium, there must be a thousand-year gap between these two resurrections: the resurrection of the just primarily occurring at the second coming of Jesus before the millennium (1 Thess 4:14–17; Rev 20:4–5) and the resurrection of the unjust and just mortals who lived during the millennium after the millennium (Rev 20:11–15), even though this is not stated elsewhere.

Daniel 12:1–2 presents an additional problem for dispensational premillennialists. Dispensationalists usually hold that the resurrection of the just occurs primarily before the great tribulation (equated with Daniel's seventieth week in 9:24–27), in conjunction with the rapture of the church to meet the Lord in the air (1 Thess 4:16–17). But a case can be made that Dan 12:1–2 implies a different sequence. Here the resurrection of the just (12:2) follows the great tribulation

(12:1). In 1 Thess 4:16–17 the voice of the archangel (presumably Michael, the only archangel named in the Bible) precedes the resurrection of "the dead in Christ" and the "rapture," while in Daniel 12:1–2 Michael intervenes before the resurrection of the just. Both passages refer to the dead as sleepers, hinting that Paul may have Daniel in mind as he writes. Thus Paul may be placing the resurrection of the dead in Christ and the rapture of believers still alive at the second coming after the great tribulation too (cp. Matt 24:29–31 which Paul also echoes and which likewise seems to place a "rapture" after the great tribulation). On the other hand, Dan 12:1–2 may not be in strict chronological sequence, so this is not a conclusive argument against pretribulationalism.

§7.5 *Purpose of Daniel's Theology of History*

Daniel's theology of history constitutes a theodicy that addresses a number of fundamental questions: Who is in control of history? Why does evil exist now? When will evil come to an end?[76] Daniel answers these. God is ultimately in charge of history. Evil is a result of human sin, including the sins of Israel, which God allows for now. Evil will wax and wane in the predetermined plan of God through the rise and fall of many empires. God will chasten his people for their sins, and yet he will see them through terrible times of trouble. Eventually he will restore the fortunes of his sinful people in accord with his covenant promises. God will make atonement for his people's sins, and the heavenly court will judge the earthly nations for their evil. In the end God will direct history to deliver his kingdom to both his people and the messianic son of man. Evil will only come to a full end with the arrival of the kingdom of God to displace the kingdoms of the world, at which time there will be a resurrection of the just and the unjust to receive their due rewards and punishments. For God's people in exile experiencing a sometimes hostile, foreign environment, this message brings encouragement and hope. Wicked, pagan nations and kings that dominate God's people already stand judged by God. He will faithfully keep his covenant promises

---

[76] P. Niskanen, *The Human and the Divine in History: Herodotus and the Book of Daniel*, JSOTSup 396 (London: T&T Clark, 2004), 89; D. J. Harrington "The Ideology of Rule in Daniel 7–12," *SBL 1999 Seminar Papers* 38 (1999): 540–51.

given to his people and ultimately bless them by bringing them into the fullness of his kingdom.[77]

This confidence in the ultimate victory of the kingdom of God in turn is meant to help the faithful throughout history to stand firm and resist even at times when evil seems overwhelmingly powerful and irresistible. God is active in shaping history, and his people are to live in the light of his plan for history. History, according to Daniel, is neither an endless cycle nor a series of meaningless events. Rather, history moves toward a predefined goal. Arguably, the main object of this theology of history is "to teach the crushed and afflicted to place unshaken confidence in God."[78] No matter how bad our situation, God will see his people through and reward the just with resurrection and glory (12:1–3).

---

[77] Niskanen, *Human and the Divine in History*, 90.

[78] F. W. Farrar, "The Book of Daniel," in *The Expositor's Bible*, ed. W. Robertson Nicoll (Hartford, CT: S.S. Scranton Co., 1903), 4:4371.

SELECT BIBLIOGRAPHY

Adams, Edward. "The Coming of the Son of Man in Mark's Gospel." *Tyndale Bulletin* 56.1 (2005): 39–61.

Ammianus Marcellinus. *Rerum Gestarum* (English). 2 vols. Edited by John C. Rolfe. Perseus Digital Library. Medford, MA: Harvard University Press, 1935–1940.

Appian. *The Foreign Wars.* Edited by Horace White. Perseus Digital Library. Medford, MA: Macmillan, 1899.

Archer, Gleason L., Jr. "The Aramaic of the 'Genesis Apocryphon' Compared with the Aramaic of Daniel." Pages 160–69 in *New Perspectives on the Old Testament.* Edited by J. Barton Payne. Waco: Word, 1970.

———. "Daniel." Pages 1–157 in vol. 7 of *The Expositor's Bible Commentary.* Edited by Frank E. Gaebelein. Grand Rapids: Zondervan, 1985.

———. "The Hebrew of Daniel Compared with the Qumran Sectarian Documents." Pages 470–81 in *The Law and the Prophets: Old Testament Studies Prepared in Honor of Oswald Thompson Allis.* Edited by John H. Skilton, Milton C. Fisher, and Leslie W. Sloat. Nutley, NJ: Presbyterian & Reformed, 1974.

———. "Modern Rationalism and the Book of Daniel." *BSac* 136:542 (April–June 1979): 129–47.

———. *Survey of Old Testament Introduction.* 3rd edition. Chicago: Moody, 1994.

Arrian. *The Anabasis of Alexander.* Translated by E. J. Chinnoch. London: Hodder and Stoughton, 1884.

———. *Flavii Arriani Anabasis Alexandri.* Edited by A. G. Roos. Perseus Digital Library. Leipzig: B. G. Teubneri, 1907.

Baldwin, Joyce G. *Daniel.* Tyndale Old Testament Commentaries. Leicester: Inter-Varsity, 1978.

———. "Is There Pseudonymity in the Old Testament?" *Themelios* 4.1 (1978): 6–12.

Barry, John D., et al., eds. *Lexham Bible Dictionary*. Bellingham, WA: Lexham Press, 2012–2016.

Barstad, Hans M. "After the 'Myth of the Empty Land': Major Challenges in the Study of Neo-Babylonian Judah." Pages 3–20 in *Judah and the Judeans in the Neo-Babylonian Period*. Ed. Oded Lipschitz and Joseph Blenkinsopp. Winona Lake, IN: Eisenbrauns, 2003.

Barthélemy, Dominique, et al. *Preliminary and Interim Report on the Hebrew Old Testament Text Project*. Volume 5. Prophetical Books II: Ezekiel, Daniel, Twelve Minor Prophets. New York: United Bible Societies, 1980.

Bartlett, J. R. *The First and Second Book of Maccabees*. Cambridge Bible Commentaries on the Apocrypha. Cambridge: Cambridge University, 1973.

Baukal, Charles E., Jr. "The Fiery Furnace." *Bibliotheca Sacra* 171 (April–June 2014): 148–71.

Beale, G. K. *The Temple and the Church's Mission: A Biblical Theology of the Dwelling Place of God*. New Studies in Biblical Theology 17. Downers Grove: InterVarsity, 2004.

Beale, G. K., and D. A. Carson, eds. *Commentary on the New Testament Use of the Old Testament*. Grand Rapids: Baker, 2007.

Beasley-Murray, George. "A Conservative Thinks Again about Daniel." *Baptist Quarterly* 12 (1948): 341–46, 366–71.

Beaulieu, Paul-Alain. "The Babylonian Background of the Motif of the Fiery Furnace in Daniel 3." *Journal of Biblical Literature* 128.2 (2009): 273–90.

———. "Nebuchadnezzar's Babylon as World Capital." *Journal of the Canadian Society for Mesopotamian Studies* 3 (2008): 5–12.

———. "A New Inscription of Nebuchadnezzar II Commemorating the Restoration of Emaḫ in Babylon." *Iraq* 59 (1997): 93–96.

———. *The Reign of Nabonidus, King of Babylon, 556–539 B.C.* Yale Near Eastern Researches 10. New Haven, CT: Yale, 1989.

Beckwith, Roger T. "Early Traces of the Book of Daniel." *Tyndale Bulletin* 53.1 (2002): 75–82.

———. *The Old Testament Canon of the New Testament Church*. Grand Rapids: Eerdmans, 1985.

Boa, Kenneth, and William Kruidenier. *Romans*. Holman New Testament Commentary 6. Nashville: Broadman & Holman, 2000.

Botterweck, G. J., et al. *Theological Dictionary of the Old Testament*. 15 vols. Grand Rapids: Eerdmans, 1974–2006.

Brand, Chad, et al., eds. *Holman Illustrated Bible Dictionary*. Nashville: Holman Bible Publishers, 2003.

Brewer, David Instone. "*MENE, MENE, TEQEL UPARSIN*: Daniel 5:28 in Cuneiform." *Tyndale Bulletin* 42.2 (Nov 1991): 310–16.

Briant, Pierre. *From Cyrus to Alexander: A History of the Persian Empire.* Translated by Peter T. Daniels. Winona Lake, IN: Eisenbrauns, 2002.

Brown, F., S. R. Driver, and C. A. Briggs. *Enhanced Brown-Driver-Briggs Hebrew and English Lexicon.* Electronic edition. Oxford: Clarendon Press, 1907.

Calvin, John. *Commentary on the Book of the Prophet Daniel.* Translated by Thomas Myers. 2 vols. Bellingham, WA: Logos Bible Software, 2010.

Carpenter, Eugene. "Daniel." Pages 9315–470 in vol. 9 of *Cornerstone Biblical Commentary.* Edited by Philip W. Comfort. Carol Stream, IL: Tyndale House, 2010.

Carter, Elizabeth, and Matthew Stolper. *Elam: Surveys of Political History and Archaeology.* Berkeley: University of California Press, 1984.

Chicago Assyrian Dictionary of the Oriental Institute of the University of Chicago. 21 vols. Chicago: University of Chicago, 1956–2010.

Christensen, Duane L. "Josephus and the Twenty-Two-Book Canon of Sacred Scripture." *Journal of the Evangelical Theological Society* 29 (1986): 37–46.

Colless, Brian E. "Cyrus the Persian as Darius the Mede in the Book of Daniel." *Journal for the Study of the Old Testament* 56 (1992): 113–26.

Collins, John J. "The Court-Tales in Daniel and the Development of Apocalyptic." *Journal of Biblical Literature* 94 (1975): 218–20.

–––. *Daniel.* Hermenia. Minneapolis: Fortress, 1993.

Cook, Edward M. "In the Plain of the Wall (Dan 3:1)." *Journal of Biblical Literature* 108.1 (Spring 1989): 115–16.

Cosmas Indicopleustes. *Christian Topography.* Translation and notes by J. W. McCrindle. London: Hakluyt Society, 1897.

Cowley, A. *Aramaic Papyri of the Fifth Century B.C.* 1923. Reprint, Osnabrück: Otto Zeller, 1967.

Coxon, Peter W. "Ashpenaz (Person)." In *Anchor Bible Dictionary* (New York: Doubleday, 1992), 1.490–91.

Crocker, Lacy K. S.v. "Art and Architecture, Persian." *Lexham Bible Dictionary.* Edited by John D. Barry et al. Bellingham, WA: Lexham Press, 2012–2015.

Cross, F. L., and Elizabeth A. Livingstone, eds. *The Oxford Dictionary of the Christian Church.* New York: Oxford University Press, 2005.

Dalley, Stephanie. *The Mystery of the Hanging Garden of Babylon: An Elusive World Wonder Traced.* Oxford: Oxford University Press, 2013.

Dandamaev, M. A. *A Political History of the Achaemenid Empire.* Leiden: Brill, 1997.

Danker, Frederick W., Walter Bauer, William F. Arndt, and F. Wilbur Gingrich. *Greek-English Lexicon of the New Testament and Other Early Christian Literature.* 3rd ed. Chicago: University of Chicago Press, 2000.

Davis, Dale Ralph. *The Message of Daniel: His Kingdom Cannot Fail.* The Bible Speaks Today. Downers Grove: InterVarsity, 2013.

Dempster, Stephen G. *Dominion and Dynasty: A Biblical Theology of the Hebrew Bible.* New Studies in Biblical Theology 15. Downers Grove: InterVarsity, 2003.

Diodorus Siculus. *Diodorus of Sicily in Twelve Volumes with an English Translation.* Translated by C. H. Oldfather, et al. Loeb Classical Library. Cambridge, MA: Harvard University Press, 1933–1967.

Dougherty, Raymond Philip. *Nabonidus and Belshazzar.* Yale Oriental Series Researches 15. New Haven, CT: Yale University Press, 1929.

Driver, S. R. *The Book of Daniel with Introduction and Notes.* The Cambridge Bible for Schools and Colleges. Cambridge: Cambridge University Press, 1900.

Dunnett, Walter M. "Purpose." In *Evangelical Dictionary of Biblical Theology.* Edited by Walter A. Elwell. Electronic version. Grand Rapids: Baker, 1996.

Elwell, Walter, and Barry J. Beitzel, eds. *Baker Encyclopedia of the Bible.* Grand Rapids: Baker, 1988.

Farrar, Frederick W. "The Book of Daniel." Pages 4361–432 in vol. 4 of *The Expositor's Bible: Jeremiah to Mark.* Edited by W. Robertson Nicoll. Expositor's Bible. Hartford, CT: S.S. Scranton Co., 1903.

France, R. T. *The Gospel of Mark: A Commentary on the Greek Text.* New International Greek Testament Commentary. Grand Rapids: Eerdmans, 2002.

Freedman, D. N., ed. *Anchor Bible Dictionary.* 6 vols. New York: Doubleday, 1992.

Frye, Richard Nelson. *The History of Ancient Iran.* Part III. Vol. 7. Handbuch der Alterlumswissenschaft. München, Germany: C. H. Beck, 1984.

Gaston, Thomas E. *Historical Issues in the Book of Daniel.* Oxford: Taanathshilo, 2009.

Gera, Dov. *Judaea and Mediterranean Politics: 219 to 161 B.C.E.* Brill Series in Jewish Studies 8. Leiden: Brill, 1997.

Gesenius, F. *Gesenius' Hebrew Grammar.* Edited by E. Kautzsch. Translated by A. E. Cowley. 2nd ed. Oxford: Oxford University Press, 1910.

Giles, Kevin. *The Trinity & Subordinationism: The Doctrine of God and the Contemporary Gender Debate.* Downers Grove: InterVarsity, 2002.

Ginsburg, H. L. "The Composition of the Book of Daniel." *Vetus Testamentum* 4 (1954): 246–75.

Glueck, Nelson. *Ḥesed in the Bible.* Translated by A. Gottschalk. Cincinnati: Hebrew Union College Press, 1967.

Goldingay, John E. *Daniel.* Word Biblical Commentary 30. Dallas: Word: 1989.

———. *Daniel.* Word Biblical Themes. Dallas: Word, 1989.

———. "Daniel in the Context of Old Testament Theology." Pages 639–60 in *The Book of Daniel Composition and Reception.* Vol. 2. Supplements to Vetus Testamentum 83. Edited by John Collins and Peter Flint. Leiden: Brill, 2001.

Goswell, Greg. "The Ethics of the Book of Daniel." *Restoration Quarterly* 57:3 (2015): 129–42.

———. "The Temple Theme in the Book of Daniel." *Journal of the Evangelical Theological Society* 55/3 (2012): 509–20.

Grabbe, Lester L. "Another Look at the *Gestalt* of Darius the Mede." *Catholic Biblical Quarterly* 50 (1988): 198–213.

Grayson, A. K. *Babylonian Historical-Literary Texts.* Toronto: University of Toronto, 1975.

Greidanus, Sidney. *Preaching Christ from Daniel: Foundations for Expository Sermons.* Grand Rapids: Eerdmans, 2012.

Gundry, Robert H. *The Church and the Tribulation.* Grand Rapids: Zondervan, 1977.

Gurney, R. "The Four Kingdoms of Daniel 2 and 7." *Themelios* 2 (1977): 39–45.

———. *God in Control: An Exposition of the Prophecies of Daniel.* Worthing, England: Henry E. Walter, 1980.

Hallo, William W., and K. Lawson Younger. *Context of Scripture.* 3 vols. Leiden: Brill, 1997–2002.

Hamilton, James M. *With the Clouds of Heaven: The Book of Daniel in Biblical Theology.* New Studies in Biblical Theology 32. Nottingham, England: Apollos, 2014.

Harrington, Daniel J. "The Ideology of Rule in Daniel 7–12." *SBL 1999 Seminar Papers* 38 (1999): 540–51.

Harris, R. Laird, et al., eds. *Theological Wordbook of the Old Testament.* Chicago: Moody 1999.

Hartman, Louis F., and Alexander A. Di Lella. *The Book of Daniel.* Anchor Bible 23. New Haven, CT: Yale University Press, 2008.

Hassler, Mark A. "The Identity of the Little Horn in Daniel 8: Antiochus IV Epiphanes, Rome, or the Antichrist?" *Master's Seminary Journal* 27.1 (Spring 2016): 33–44.

Haydon, Ron. *"Seventy Years Are Decreed": A Canonical Approach to Daniel 9:24–27.* Journal of Theological Interpretation Supplement 15. Winona Lake, IN: Eisenbrauns, 2016.

Hayes, John. *An Introduction to Old Testament Study.* Nashville: Abingdon, 1979.

Hengel, Martin. *Judaism and Hellenism.* 2 vols. Philadelphia: Fortress, 1974.

Herodotus. *Herodotus, with an English Translation by A. D. Godley.* Perseus Digital Library. Edited by A. D. Godley. Medford, MA: Harvard University Press, 1920.

Hesiod. *Works and Days.* In *The Homeric Hymns and Homerica with an English Translation by Hugh G. Evelyn-White.* Cambridge, MA: Harvard University Press; London: William Heinemann, 1914.

Hill, Andrew E. "Daniel." Pages 19–212 in vol. 8 of *The Expositor's Bible Commentary.* Edited by Tremper Longman and David E. Garland. Grand Rapids: Zondervan, 2008.

---, and John H. Walton. *A Survey of the Old Testament.* 2nd edition. Grand Rapids: Zondervan, 2000.

Hinson, David Francis. *Theology of the Old Testament.* SPCK International Study Guide 15. London: SPCK, 2001.

Hippolytus of Rome. "Treatise on Christ and Antichrist." In *Fathers of the Third Century: Hippolytus, Cyprian, Novatian, Appendix.* Edited by Alexander Roberts, James Donaldson, and A. Cleveland Coxe. Translated by S. D. F. Salmond. Vol. 5. The Ante-Nicene Fathers. Buffalo, NY: Christian Literature Company, 1886.

Hoehner, Harold W. "Chronological Aspects of the Life of Christ: Part VI: Daniel's Seventy Weeks and New Testament Chronology." *Bibliotheca Sacra* 132 (1975): 47–65.

Hölbl, Günther. *A History of the Ptolemaic Empire.* New York: Routledge, 2001.

Holm, Tawny L. "The Fiery Furnace in the Book of Daniel and the Ancient Near East." *Journal of the American Oriental Society* 128.1 (Jan/Mar 2008): 85–104.

Hornblower, Simon, and Antony Spawforth, eds. *The Oxford Classical Dictionary.* 4th ed. Oxford: Oxford University Press, 2012.

Ignatius of Antioch. "The Epistle of Ignatius to the Magnesians." *The Apostolic Fathers with Justin Martyr and Irenaeus,* vol. 1. Edited by Alexander Roberts et al. The Ante-Nicene Fathers. Buffalo, NY: Christian Literature Company, 1885.

Jackson, S. M., ed. *New Schaff-Herzog Encyclopedia of Religious Knowledge.* New York: Funk & Wagnalls, 1908–1914.

Jastrow, Marcus. *A Dictionary of the Targumim, the Talmud Babli and Yerushalmi, and the Midrashic Literature.* London: Luzac & Co.; New York: G. P. Putnam's Sons, 1903.

Jenni, E., and C. Westermann, eds. *Theological Lexicon of the Old Testament.* Translated by M. E. Biddle. 3 vols. Peabody, MA: Hendrickson, 1997.

Jerome, St. *Jerome's Commentary on Daniel.* Translated by Gleason L. Archer. Grand Rapids: Baker, 1958.

Jerusalmi, Isaac. *The Aramaic Sections of Ezra and Daniel: A Philological Commentary.* Cincinnati: Hebrew Union College-Jewish Institute of Religion, 1982.

The Jewish Encyclopedia (1906). S.v. "Daniel." http://www.jewishencyclopedia.com/.

Josephus, Flavius. *The Life; Against Apion.* Complete Works of Josephus, vol. I. Loeb Classical Library 186. Translated by H. St. J. Thackeray. Cambridge, MA: Harvard University Press, 1926.

———. *The Works of Josephus: Complete and Unabridged.* Translated by William Whiston. Peabody MA: Hendrickson, 1987.

Joüon, Paul. *Grammar of Biblical Hebrew.* Translated and revised by T. Muraoka. 2 volumes. *Subsidia Biblica* 14/1–2. Rome: Pontificio Intituto Biblico, 1991.

Jowers, Dennis W., and H. Wayne House, eds. *The New Evangelical Subordinationism?: Perspectives on the Equality of God the Father and God the Son.* Eugene, OR: Pickwick, 2012.

Justin (Marcus Junianus Justinus). *Epitome of the Philippic History of Pompeius Trogus.* Translation and notes by John Selby Watson. London: Henry G. Bohn, 1853.

Kaufman, Stephen A., ed.. *Comprehensive Aramaic Lexicon, Targum Lexicon.* Cincinnati: Hebrew Union College Press, 2004.

Keil, Carl F., and Franz Delitzsch. *Commentary on the Old Testament.* Peabody, MA: Hendrickson, 1996.

Kent, Roland G. *Old Persian: Grammar, Text, Lexicon.* 2nd ed. New Haven, CT: American Oriental Society, 1953.

Kitchen, K. A. "The Aramaic of Daniel." Pages 31–79 in *Notes on Some Problems in the Book of Daniel.* Edited by D. J. Wiseman, et al. London: Tyndale, 1965.

———. *On the Reliability of the Old Testament.* Grand Rapids: Eerdmans, 2003.

Kittel, Gerhard, and Gerhard Friedrich, eds. *Theological Dictionary of the New Testament.* Abridged ed. Grand Rapids: Eerdmans, 1985.

Knowles, Louis E. "The Interpretation of the Seventy Weeks of Daniel in the Early Fathers." *Westminster Theological Journal* 7.2 (1944): 135–60.

Koehler, L., W. Baumgartner, and J. J. Stamm. *The Hebrew and Aramaic Lexicon of the Old Testament.* Translated and edited under the supervision of M. E. J. Richardson. 4 vols. Leiden: Brill, 1994–1999.

Koldewey, Robert. *The Excavations at Babylon.* Translated by Agnes S. Johns. London: McMillan, 1914.

LaCocque, André. *The Book of Daniel.* Louisville: John Knox, 1979. Reprint, Eugene, OR: Wipf and Stock, 2015.

Ladd, George E. "Why Not Prophetic Apocalyptic?" *Journal of Biblical Literature* 76 (1957): 192–200.

LaSor, William S., David A. Hubbard, and Frederic W. Bush. *Old Testament Survey.* Grand Rapids: Eerdmans, 1982.

Law, George. *Identification of Darius the Mede.* Pfafftown, NC: Ready Scribe Press, 2010.

Lawson, Jack N. *The Concept of Fate in Ancient Mesopotamia of the First Millennium: Towards an Understanding of "Shimtu."* Orientalia Biblica et Christiana 7. Weisbaden: Harrassowitz, 1994.

Lefebvre, Michael. *Collections, Codes, and Torah: The Re-characterization of Israel's Written Law.* Library of Hebrew Bible/Old Testament Studies 451. London: Bloomsbury T&T Clark, 2008.

Leiman, Sid Z. *The Canonization of Hebrew Scriptures: The Talmudic and Midrashic Evidence.* Hamden, CT: Archon, 1976.

Lessing, R. Reed, and Andrew E. Steinmann. *Prepare the Way of the Lord: An Introduction to the Old Testament.* St. Louis: Concordia, 2014.

Lester, G. Brooke. *Daniel Evokes Isaiah: Allusive Characterization of Foreign Rule in the Hebrew-Aramaic Book of Daniel.* Library of Hebrew Bible/Old Testament Studies 606. London: Bloomsbury T&T Clark, 2015.

Leupold, H. C. *Exposition of Daniel.* Grand Rapids: Baker, 1949.

Liddell, Henry George, and Robert Scott. *A Greek-English Lexicon.* Revised and augmented by Henry Stuart Jones. Oxford: Clarendon, 1968.

Liverani, Mario. *The Ancient Near East: History, Society and Economy.* Translated by Soraia Tabatabai. New York: Routledge, 2013.

Livy. *History of Rome.* Edited by Canon Roberts. Perseus Digital Library. Medford, MA: E. P. Dutton, 1912.

Longman, Tremper. *Daniel.* The NIV Application Commentary. Grand Rapids: Zondervan, 1999.

———, and Raymond Dillard. *An Introduction to the Old Testament.* 2nd edition. Grand Rapids: Zondervan, 2006.

Longnecker, Richard N. " 'Son of Man' as a Self-Designation of Jesus." *Journal of the Evangelical Theological Society* 12.3 (1969): 149–58.

Lowery, Daniel DeWitt. S.v. "Anatolia." *Lexham Bible Dictionary.* Edited by John D. Barry et al. Bellingham, WA: Lexham, 2012–2015.

Lucas, Ernest C. *Daniel.* Apollos Old Testament Commentary. Downers Grove: InterVarsity, 2002.

———. "Daniel." Pages 232–36 in *New Dictionary of Biblical Theology.* Edited by T. Desmond Alexander and Brian S. Rosner. Downers Grove: InterVarsity Press, 2000.

———. "Daniel: Book of." Pages 110–23 in *Dictionary of the Old Testament: Prophets.* Edited by Mark J. Boda and Gordon J. McConville. Downers Grove: IVP Academic, 2012.

Lust, Johan, Erik Eynikel, and Katrin Hauspie. *A Greek-English Lexicon of the Septuagint.* Rev. ed. Stuttgart: Deutsche Bibelgesellschaft, 2003.

MacDonald, William Graham. "Christology and the 'Angel of the Lord.' " Pages 324–35 in *Current Issues in Biblical and Patristic Interpretation.* Feststchrift Merrill Tenney. Edited by Gerald Harthone. Grand Rapids: Eerdmans, 1975.

Makujina, John. "Dismemberment in Dan 2:5 and 3:29 as an Old Persian Idiom, 'To Be Made into Parts,' " *Journal of the American Oriental Society* 119.2 (April–July 1999): 309–12.

Mangano, Mark. *Esther & Daniel.* College Press NIV Commentary. Joplin, MO: College Press, 2001.

Martin, B. A. "Daniel 2:46 and the Hellenistic World." *ZAW* 85.1 (1973): 80–93.

Marzahn, Joachim, and Benjamin Sass. *Aramaic and Figural Stamp Impressions on Bricks of the Sixth Century B.C. from Babylon.* Drawings by Noga Z'evi. Wissenschaftliche Veroffentlichungen der Deutschen Orient-Gesellschaft 127. Weisbaden: Harrassowitz, 2010.

McComiskey, T. E. "The Seventy 'Weeks' of Daniel against the Background of Ancient Near Eastern Literature." *Westminster Theological Journal* 47 (1985): 18–25.

McIntosh, Jane R. *Ancient Mesopotamia: New Perspectives.* Santa Barbara, CA: ABC-CLIO, 2005.

McLain, Charles E. "Daniel's Prayer in Chapter 9." *Detroit Baptist Seminary Journal* 9 (2004): 265–301.

McLay, R. Timothy. "Sousanna: To the Reader." Pages 986–87 in *A New Translation of the Septuagint.* Edited by Albert Pietersma and Benjamin G. Wright. New York: Oxford University Press, 2007.

Melvin, David P. *The Interpreting Angel Motif in Prophetic and Apocalyptic Literature.* Minneapolis: Fortress, 2013.

———. S.v. "Revelation." *Lexham Bible Dictionary.* Edited by John D. Barry et al. Bellingham, WA: Lexham Press, 2012–2015.

Mercer, Mark. "The Benefactions of Antiochus IV Epiphanes and Dan 11:37–38: An Exegetical Note." *Master's Seminary Journal* 12.1 (Spring 2001): 89–93.

Milgrom, Jacob. *Leviticus.* Anchor Bible 3, 3A, 3B. 3 vols. New York: Doubleday, 1991–2000.

Millard, Alan R. "Daniel 1–6 and History." *Evangelical Quarterly* 49.2 (1977): 67–73.

———. "Daniel in Babylon: An Accurate Record." Pages 263–80 in *Do Historical Matters Matter to Faith?* Edited by James K. Hoffmeier and Dennis Magary. Wheaton: Crossway, 2012.

———. "Incense—the Ancient Room Freshener: The Exegesis of Daniel 2:46." Pages 111–22 in *On Stone and Scroll: Essays in Honor of Graham Ivor Davies*. Edited by James K. Aitken, et al. Beihefte zur Zeitschrift für die alttestamentliche Wissenschaft 420. Berlin: de Gruyter, 2011.

———, and Pierre Bordreuil. "A Statue from Syria with Assyrian and Aramaic Inscriptions." *Biblical Archaeologist* 45 (1982): 135–41.

Miller, Stephen R. *Daniel*. New American Commentary 18. Nashville: Broadman & Holman, 1994.

Mitchell, T. C. "Achaemenid History and the Book of Daniel." Pages 68–78 in *Mesopotamia and Iran in the Persian Period: Conquest and Imperialism 539–331 BC*. Edited by John Curtis. London: British Museum, 1997.

———, and R. Joyce. "The Musical Instruments in Nebuchadnezzar's Orchestra." Pages 19–27 in *Notes on Some Problems in the Book of Daniel*. Edited by D. J. Wiseman. London: Tyndale, 1965.

Montgomery, J. A. *Daniel*. International Critical Commentary. Edinburgh: T&T Clark, 1927.

Mørkholm, Otto. *Early Hellenistic Coinage from the Accession of Alexander to the Peace of Apamaea (336–188 B.C.)*. Cambridge: Cambridge University Press, 1991.

———. "The Monetary System in the Seleucid Empire after 187 B.C." Pages 93–114 in *Ancient Coins of the Graeco-Roman World*. Edited Waldemar Heckel and Richard Sullivan. Waterloo, Ontario: Wilfrid Laurier University Press, 1984.

Myers, Allen C., ed. *Eerdmans Bible Dictionary*. Grand Rapids: Eerdmans, 1987.

Negev, Avraham, ed. *The Archaeological Encyclopedia of the Holy Land*. New York: Prentice Hall, 1990.

Neusner, Jacob. *The Babylonian Talmud: A Translation and Commentary*. Peabody, MA: Hendrickson, 2011.

Newsom, Carol A. *Daniel*. Old Testament Library. Louisville: Westminster John Knox, 2014.

Niskanen, Paul. *The Human and the Divine in History: Herodotus and the Book of Daniel*. Journal for the Study of the Old Testament Supplements 396. London: T&T Clark, 2004.

Olmstead, A. T. *History of the Persian Empire*. Chicago: University of Chicago Press, 1948.

Oppenheim, A. Leo. *Ancient Mesopotamia*. Revised by Erica Reiner. Chicago: University of Chicago Press, 1964.

———. *The Interpretation of Dreams in the Ancient Near East with a Translation of an Assyrian Dream Book*. Transactions of the American Philosophical Society 46.3. Philadelphia: American Philosophical Society, 1956.

Origen. "A Letter from Origen to Africanus." Translated Frederick Crombie. *Fathers of the Third Century: Tertullian, Part Fourth; Minucius Felix; Commodian; Origen, Parts First and Second.* Edited by Alexander Roberts, et al. The Ante-Nicene Fathers 4. Buffalo, NY: Christian Literature Company, 1885.

Parry, Jason Thomas. "Desolation of the Temple and Messianic Enthronement in Daniel 11:36–12:3." *Journal of the Evangelical Theological Society* 54.3 (2011): 485–526.

Patterson, Richard D. "Daniel in the Critics' Court." *Journal of the Evangelical Theological Society* (1993): 444–54.

Paul, Shalom M. "Daniel 3:29—A Case Study of 'Neglected' Blasphemy." *Journal of Near Eastern Studies* 42.4 (1983): 291–94.

Pausanias. *Description of Greece with an English Translation.* Edited by W. H. S. Jones and H. A. Ormerod. 4 vols. Perseus Digital Library. Medford, MA: Harvard University Press, 1918.

Payne, J. Barton. *Encyclopedia of Biblical Prophecy: The Complete Guide to Scriptural Predictions and Their Fulfillment.* New York: Harper and Row, 1973.

———. "The Goal of Daniel's Seventy Weeks." *Journal of the Evangelical Theological Society* 21.2 (1978): 97–115.

Pierce, Roland W. *Daniel.* Teach the Text. Grand Rapids: Baker, 2015.

Pietersma, Albert, and Benjamin G. Wright, eds. *A New Translation of the Septuagint.* New York: Oxford University Press, 2007.

Plutarch. *Alexander (English).* Plutarch's Lives. Perseus Digital Library. Edited by Bernadotte Perrin. Medford, MA: Harvard University Press, 1919.

Polaski, Donald C. "Mene, Mene, Tekel, Parsin: Writing and Resistance in Daniel 5 and 6." *Journal of Biblical Literature* 123 (2004): 649–69.

Polybius. *Histories.* Perseus Digital Library. Medford, MA: Macmillan, 1889.

Porteous, W. *Daniel: A Commentary.* Old Testament Library. Philadelphia: Westminster, 1965.

Pritchard, James Bennett, ed. *The Ancient Near Eastern Texts Relating to the Old Testament.* 3rd ed. with supplement. Princeton: Princeton University Press, 1969.

Romerowski, S. "Que signifie le mot *ḥesed*?" *Vetus Testamentum* 40 (1990): 89–103.

Rooker, M. F. "Theophany." Pages 863–64 in *Dictionary of the Old Testament: Pentateuch.* Edited by T. Desmond Alexander and David Baker. Downers Grove: InterVarsity, 2003.

Rosenthal, Franz. *A Grammar of Biblical Aramaic.* Wiesbaden: Harrassowitz, 1974.

Rosenthal, Marvin. *The Pre-Wrath Rapture of the Church.* Nashville: Thomas Nelson, 1990.

Rosscup, James E. "Prayer Relating to Prophecy in Daniel 9." *Master's Seminary Journal* 3.1 (1992): 46–71.

Rowley, H. H. *The Servant of the Lord and Other Essays on the Old Testament.* 2nd ed. London: Oxford, 1965. Pages 249–80.

———. "The Unity of the Book of Daniel." *Hebrew Union College Annual* 23 (1950): 233–73.

Russell, D. S. *Daniel.* Daily Study Bible. Louisville, KY: Westminster John Knox, 1981.

———. *The Method and Message of Jewish Apocalyptic.* Old Testament Library. Philadelphia: Westminster, 1964.

———. *Prophecy and the Apocalyptic Dream.* Peabody, MA: Hendrickson, 1994.

Ryle, H. E. *The Canon of the Old Testament.* 2nd ed. London: Macmillan, 1909.

Saggs, H. W. F. *The Greatness That Was Babylon.* Rev. ed. London: Sidgwick & Jackson, 1988.

———. *The Might That Was Assyria.* London: Sidgwick & Jackson, 1984.

Sakenfeld, Katherine D. "Love (OT)." In *Anchor Bible Dictionary* (New York: Doubleday, 1992), 4:377–81.

———. *The Meaning of Ḥesed in the Hebrew Bible: A New Inquiry.* Missoula, MT: Scholars, 1978.

———, ed. *The New Interpreter's Dictionary of the Bible.* 5 vols. Nashville: Abingdon, 2006–2009.

Scheetz, Daniel. "Daniel's Position in the Tanach." *Old Testament Essays* 23.1 (2010): 178–93.

Schmitt, Rüdiger. "Personal Names, Iranian III. Achaemenid Period." Encyclopedia Iranica, online edition. Updated July 20, 2005. http://www.iranicaonline.org/articles/personal-names-iranian-iii-achaemenid.

Schürer, Emil. *The History of the Jewish People in the Age of Jesus Christ.* Vol. 3.2. Revised and edited by Geza Vermes, et al. Edinburgh: T&T Clark, 1986.

Segal, Michael. *Dreams, Riddles, and Visions: Textual, Contextual, and Intertextual Approaches to the Book of Daniel.* Beihefte zur Zeitschrift für die alttestamentliche Wissenschaft 455. Berlin: de Gruyter, 2016.

Shea, William. "Bel(te)shazzar meets Belshazzar." *Andrews University Seminary Studies* 26.1 (1988): 67–81.

———. "Darius the Mede: An Update." *Andrews University Seminary Studies* 20.3 (1982): 229–47.

———. "Darius the Mede in His Persian-Babylonian Setting." *Andrews University Seminary Studies* 29.3 (1991): 235–57.

———. "Nabonidus, Belshazzar and the Book of Daniel." *Andrews University Seminary Studies* 20.2 (1982): 133–49.

———. "Wrestling with the Prince of Persia: A Study on Daniel 10." *Andrews University Seminary Studies* 21.3 (1983): 225–50.

Shepherd, Michael B. "Daniel 7:13 and the New Testament Son of Man." *Westminster Theological Journal* 68.1 (2006): 98–111.

Smith, James E. *The Major Prophets*. Old Testament Survey Series. Joplin, MO: College Press, 1992.

Smith, J. Payne, ed. *A Compendious Syriac Dictionary*. Oxford: Clarendon, 1903.

Snell, D. C. "Why Is There Aramaic in the Bible?" *Journal for the Study of the Old Testament* 18 (1980): 83–100.

Spero, Shubert. "Turning to Jerusalem in Prayer." *Jewish Bible Quarterly* 31.1 (2003): 97–100.

Spieckermann, H. "God's Steadfast Love: Towards a New Conception of Old Testament Theology." *Biblica* 81 (2000): 305–27.

Sprinkle, Joe M. *Biblical Law and Its Relevance*. Langdon, MD: University Press of America, 2006.

———. *'The Book of the Covenant': A Literary Approach*. Journal for the Study of the Old Testament Supplements 174. Sheffield: JSOT Press, 1994.

———. *Leviticus and Numbers*. Teach the Text. Grand Rapids: Baker, 2015.

Stagg, Frank. "Eschatology: A Baptist Perspective." *Review and Expositor* 79.2 (1982): 379–94.

Steinmann, Andrew E. *Daniel*. Concordia Commentary. St. Louis, MO: Concordia, 2008.

———. "Is the Antichrist in Daniel 11?" *Bibliotheca Sacra* 162.646 (2005): 195–209.

Stevens, David E. "Daniel 10 and the Notion of Territorial Spirits." *Bibliotheca Sacra* 157:628 (2000): 410–31.

Stuart, Douglas. "The Old Testament Prophets' Self Understanding of Their Prophecy." *Themelios* 6.1 (September 1980): 9–17.

Swanson, James. *Dictionary of Biblical Languages with Semantic Domains: Aramaic and Hebrew (Old Testament)*. Electronic ed. Oak Harbor: Logos Research Systems, 1997.

Theodoret of Cyrus. *Commentary on Daniel*. Writing from the Greco-Roman World. Translation, introduction, and notes by Robert C. Hill. Atlanta: Society of Biblical Literature, 2006.

Thiele, Edwin R. *The Mysterious Numbers of the Hebrew Kings*. Grand Rapids: Zondervan, 1983.

Toorn, Karel van der. "Scholars at the Oriental Court: The Figure of Daniel against Its Mesopotamian Background." Pages 37–54 in vol. 1 of *The Book of Daniel: Composition and Reception*. Edited by J. J. Collins and P. W. Flint. Supplements to Vetus Testamentum 83. Leiden: Brill, 2001.

Towner, W. Sibley. *Daniel*. Interpretation. Atlanta: John Knox, 1984.

Ulrich, Dean R. *The Antiochene Crisis and Jubilee Theology in Daniel's Seventy Sevens*. Old Testament Studies 66. Leiden: Brill, 2015.

———. "The Need for More Attention to Jubilee in Daniel 9:24–27." *Bulletin for Biblical Research* 26.4 (2016): 481–500.

Vanderhooft, David. "Dura." Page 167 in vol. 2 of *The New Interpreter's Dictionary of the Bible*. Edited by K. D. Sakenfield. 5 vols. Nashville: Abingdon, 2006–2009.

VanGemeren, W., ed. *New International Dictionary of Old Testament Theology and Exegesis*. 5 vols. Grand Rapids: Zondervan, 1997.

Vermes, Geza. *The Dead Sea Scrolls in English*. Revised and extended 4th ed. Sheffield: Sheffield Academic Press, 1995.

Vogel, Winfried. *The Cultic Motif in the Book of Daniel*. New York: Peter Lang, 2009.

von Sodon, W. *Akkadisches Handwörterbuch*. Weisbaden: Harrassowitz, 1965.

Wade, Loron. " 'Son of Man' Comes to the Judgment in Daniel 7:13." *Journal of the Adventist Theological Society* 11 (2000): 277–81.

Walbank, F. W., A. E. Astin, M. W. Frederiksen, and R. M. Ogilvie, eds. *The Hellenistic World*. Vol. 7, Part 1 of *Cambridge Ancient History*. 19 vols. London: Cambridge University Press, 1984.

Waltke, Bruce. "Antiochus IV Epiphanes." In vol. 1 of *International Standard Bible Encyclopedia*. 4 vols. Edited by Geoffrey W. Bromiley. Grand Rapids: Eerdmans, 1975.

———. "The Date of the Book of Daniel." *Bibliotheca Sacra* 133.532 (1976): 319–29.

———, and M. O'Connor. *An Introduction to Biblical Hebrew Syntax*. Winona Lake, IN: Eisenbrauns, 1990.

Walton, John H. *Ancient Near Eastern Thought and the Old Testament: Introducing the Conceptual World of the Hebrew Bible*. Grand Rapids: Baker Academic, 2006.

———. "The Decree of Darius the Mede in Daniel 6." *Journal of the Evangelical Theological Society* 31 (1988): 279–86.

———. "The Four Kingdoms of Daniel." *Journal of the Evangelical Theological Society* 29 (1986): 25–36.

Walvoord, John F. *Daniel: The Key to Prophetic Revelation*. Chicago: Moody, 1971.

Wenham, Gordon J. "Daniel: The Basic Issues." *Themelios* 2.2 (1977): 49–52.

Whitcomb, John C. *Darius the Mede*. Grand Rapids: Eerdmans, 1959.

Wilson, E. Jan. *"Holiness" and "Purity" in Mesopotamia*. Alter Orient und Altes Testament. Veröffentlichungen zur Kultur und Geschichte des Alten Orients und des Alten Testament 237. Neukirchen-Vluyn: Neukirchener Verlag, 1994.

Wilson, Gerald H. "The Prayer of Daniel 9: Reflection on Jeremiah 29." *Journal for the Study of the Old Testament* 48 (1990): 91–99.

Wiseman, Donald J. "Dura." Page 284 in *New Bible Dictionary*, edited by D. R. W. Wood and I. Howard Marshall. Downers Grove: InterVarsity, 1996.

———. *Nebuchadrezzar and Babylon.* Oxford: Oxford University Press, 1985.

———. "Some Historical Problems in the Book of Daniel." Pages 9–18 in *Notes on Some Problems in the Book of Daniel.* Edited by D. J. Wiseman. London: Tyndale, 1965.

Witherington, Ben, III. *What's in the Word: Rethinking the Socio-Rhetorical Character of the New Testament.* Waco, TX: Baylor University Press, 2009.

Wolters, Al. "The Riddle of the Scales in Daniel 5." *Hebrew Union College Annual* 62 (1991): 155–77.

———. "Untying the King's Knots: Physiology and Wordplay in Daniel 5." *Journal of Biblical Literature* 110:1 (Spring 1991): 117–22.

Wood, D. R. W., and I. Howard Marshall, eds. *New Bible Dictionary.* Downers Grove: InterVarsity, 1996.

Wood, Leon. *A Commentary on Daniel.* Grand Rapids: Zondervan, 1973.

Wright, N. T. *The New Testament and the People of God.* Christian Origins and the Question of God, vol. 1. London: Society for Promoting Christian Knowledge, 1992.

———. *Jesus and the Victory of God.* Christian Origins and the Question of God, vol. 2. London: Society for Promoting Christian Knowledge, 1996.

Xenophon. *Xenophon in Seven Volumes.* Translated by Walter Miller. London: William Heinemann, 1914.

Yamauchi, Edwin M. "The Greek Words in Daniel." Pages 170–200 in *New Perspectives on the Old Testament.* Edited by J. Barton Payne. Waco: Word, 1970.

———. *Persia and the Bible.* Grand Rapids: Baker, 1990.

Zehnder, Marcus. "Why the Danielic 'Son of Man' Is a Divine Being." *Bulletin for Biblical Research* 24.3 (2014): 331–47.

Zobel, H. -J. "חֶסֶד Ḥesed." Pages 44–64 in vol. 5 of *Theological Dictionary of the Old Testament.* Edited by G. J. Botterweck et al. 15 vols. Grand Rapids: Eerdmans, 1974–2006.

SCRIPTURE INDEX

DANIEL